T0189209

IFIP Advances in Information and Communication Technology 438

IFIP – The International Federation for Information Processing

IFIP was founded in 1960 under the auspices of UNESCO, following the First World Computer Congress held in Paris the previous year. An umbrella organization for societies working in information processing, IFIP's aim is two-fold: to support information processing within its member countries and to encourage technology transfer to developing nations. As its mission statement clearly states,

> IFIP's mission is to be the leading, truly international, apolitical organization which encourages and assists in the development, exploitation and application of information technology for the benefit of all people.

IFIP is a non-profitmaking organization, run almost solely by 2500 volunteers. It operates through a number of technical committees, which organize events and publications. IFIP's events range from an international congress to local seminars, but the most important are:

- The IFIP World Computer Congress, held every second year;
- Open conferences;
- Working conferences.

The flagship event is the IFIP World Computer Congress, at which both invited and contributed papers are presented. Contributed papers are rigorously refereed and the rejection rate is high.

As with the Congress, participation in the open conferences is open to all and papers may be invited or submitted. Again, submitted papers are stringently refereed.

The working conferences are structured differently. They are usually run by a working group and attendance is small and by invitation only. Their purpose is to create an atmosphere conducive to innovation and development. Refereeing is also rigorous and papers are subjected to extensive group discussion.

Publications arising from IFIP events vary. The papers presented at the IFIP World Computer Congress and at open conferences are published as conference proceedings, while the results of the working conferences are often published as collections of selected and edited papers

Any national society whose primary activity is about information processing may apply to become a full member of IFIP, although full membership is restricted to one society per country. Full members are entitled to vote at the annual General Assembly, National societies preferring a less committed involvement may apply for associate or corresponding membership. Associate members enjoy the same benefits as full members, but without voting rights. Corresponding members are not represented in IFIP bodies. Affiliated membership is open to non-national societies, and individual and honorary membership schemes are also offered.

Bernard Grabot   Bruno Vallespir   Samuel Gomes
Abdelaziz Bouras   Dimitris Kiritsis (Eds.)

Advances in Production Management Systems

Innovative and
Knowledge-Based Production Management
in a Global-Local World

IFIP WG 5.7 International Conference, APMS 2014
Ajaccio, France, September 20-24, 2014
Proceedings, Part I

 Springer

Volume Editors

Bernard Grabot
LGP ENIT, Tarbes, France
E-mail: bernard.grabot@enit.fr

Bruno Vallespir
Université de Bordeaux, IMS, Talence, France
E-mail: bruno.vallespir@ims-bordeaux.fr

Samuel Gomes
Université de Technologie de Belfort-Montbéliard, M3M, Belfort, France
E-mail: samuel.gomes@utbm.fr

Abdelaziz Bouras
Qatar University, College of Engineering, ictQatar, Doha, Qatar
E-mail: abdelaziz.bouras@qu.edu.qa

Dimitris Kiritsis
EPFL/STI-IGM-LICP, Lausanne, Switzerland
E-mail: dimitris.kiritsis@epfl.ch

ISSN 1868-4238   ISSN 1868-422X (electronic)
ISBN 978-3-662-52602-6   ISBN 978-3-662-44739-0 (eBook)
DOI 10.1007/978-3-662-44739-0
Springer Heidelberg New York Dordrecht London

Typesetting: Camera-ready by author, data conversion by Scientific Publishing Services, Chennai, India

Printed on acid-free paper

Springer is part of Springer Science+Business Media (www.springer.com)

Preface

For the last decades, APMS has been a major event and the official conference of the IFIP Working Group 5.7 on Advances in Production Management Systems, bringing together leading experts from academia, research, and industry. Starting with the first conference in Helsinki in 1990, the conference has become a successful annual event that has been hosted in various parts of the world including Washington (USA, 2005), Wroclaw (Poland, 2006), Linköping (Sweden, 2007), Espoo (Finland, 2008), Bordeaux (France, 2009), Cernobbio (Italy, 2010), Stavanger (Norway, 2011), Rhodos (Greece, 2012), and State College (PA, USA, 2013).

By returning to Europe, APMS 2014 took place in Ajaccio (Corsica, France). This issue was organized in a collaborative way, as its organization was supported by four French universities and engineers schools: ENIT-INPT / University of Toulouse, the University of Bordeaux, the University of Lyon and the University of Technology of Belfort-Montbéliard.

The topics of APMS are similar to those of the IFIP WG 5.7. They concern all the facets of the systems of production of goods and services. For its 2014 issue, APMS selects the "Innovative and knowledge-based production management in a global-local world" theme, focusing on innovation, knowledge, and the apparent opposition between globalization of the economy and local production. 233 papers were accepted, based on blind peer-review. They were written and proposed by more than 600 authors and co-authors coming from 28 countries. The main review criteria were the paper quality and contributions to science and industrial practice. Accepted papers of registered participants are included in this volume. According to the new standard of APMS conference, full papers have been submitted and reviewed from the outset, allowing for the final proceedings to be available at the time of the conference.

Through an open call for special sessions and papers, APMS 2014 sought contributions in cutting-edge research, as well as insightful advances in industrial practice. The intent of the special sessions is to raise visibility on topics of focused interest in a particular scientific or applications area. This year, 21 special sessions were planned. They were consistent with the theme of the conference and focused on key areas of simulation, design, service, process improvement, sustainability, human & organizational aspects, agility and flexibility, maintenance, future and smart manufacturing, ontology, co-evolution of production and society, lean production, factories lifecycle, experience, knowledge & competence, and optimization.

Following the tradition of past APMS conferences, the 7th APMS Doctoral Workshop offered Ph.D. students the opportunity to present, discuss, receive feedback, and exchange comments and views on their doctoral research in an inspiring academic community of fellow Ph.D. students, experienced researchers, and professors from the IFIP WG 5.7 community.

Three awards were distributed during APMS 2014:

- Burbidge Award for best paper,
- Burbidge Award for best presentation,
- Doctoral Workshop Award.

The Scientific Committee, consisting of 78 researchers, most of them being active members of the IFIP WG 5.7, played a key role in reviewing the papers in a timely manner and providing constructive feedback to authors, allowing them to revise their manuscripts for the final draft.

Papers in these three volumes are grouped thematically as follows:

Volume 1:

- **Part I: Knowledge Discovery and Sharing**: Knowledge management, creative enterprise, quality management, design tools, system engineering, PLM, ontology, decision support system, collaboration maturity, Business Intelligence, enterprise 2.0, etc.
- **Part II: Knowledge-Based Planning and Scheduling**: Scheduling, optimization, production planning and control, assembly line balancing, decoupling points, inventory management, supply chain management, multi-echelon supply chain, analytic hierarchy process, enterprise resource planning, decision support systems, problem solving, vehicle routing, physical internet, etc.

Volume 2:

- **Part III: Knowledge-Based Sustainability**: Cleaner production, green IT, energy, energy-efficiency, risk management, disturbance management, resilience, end of life, reverse logistics, creative industry, eco-factory, environmental innovation, solidarity economy, social responsibility, glocalization, etc.
- **Part IV: Knowledge-Based Services**: Service production, service engineering, service governance, healthcare, public transportation, customer satisfaction, after sales, smart manufacturing, etc.

Volume 3:

- **Part V: Knowledge-Based Performance Improvement**: Performance measurement system, evaluation, quality, in-service inspection, inspection programs, lean, visual management, standardization, simulation, analysis techniques, value stream mapping, maturity models, benchmarking, change management, human behavior modeling, community of practice, etc.

- **Part VI: Case Studies**: sectors (petroleum industry, aeronautic industry, agribusiness, automobile, semiconductors), tools (ERP, TQM, six sigma, enterprise modeling, simulation), concepts (supply chain, globalization), etc.

We hope that these volumes will be of interest to a wide range of researchers and practitioners.

August 2014

Bernard Grabot
Bruno Vallespir
Samuel Gomes
Abdelaziz Bouras
Dimitris Kiritsis

Organization

General Chair

Bernard Grabot   ENIT-INPT/University of Toulouse, France

Doctoral Workshop Committee

Chair
Abdelaziz Bouras   University of Lyon, France & Qatar University,
                                  Qatar

Organizing Committee

Chair
Samuel Gomes   University of Technology of
                                  Belfort - Montbéliard, France

Members
Cédrick Béler   University of Toulouse, France
Abdelaziz Bouras   Qatar University, Qatar; Université Lumiere
                                  Lyon 2, France
Laurent Geneste   University of Toulouse, France
Raymond Houé   University of Toulouse, France
Daniel Noyes   University of Toulouse, France
Bruno Vallespir   University of Bordeaux, France

Organization

R-Events

Conference Secretariat

Catherine Eberstein   University of Technology of
                                  Belfort-Montbéliard, France
Cécile De Barros   Marie Robert, ENIT-LGP, INP, University of
                                  Toulouse, France

Sponsors

IFIP WG 5.7 Advances in Production Management Systems
IODE: Research Federation on Distributed Organizations Engineering
GdR MACS: CNRS Research Group on Modelling and Analysis of Complex Systems
IRTES: Research Institute on Transports, Energy and Society
Mairie d'Ajaccio

Special Sessions

Discrete event simulation for distributed production systems
    Paul-Antoine Bisgambiglia   University of Corsica, France

The practitioner's view on "Innovative and Knowledge-Based Production Management in a Global-Local World"
    Gregor von Cieminski   ZF Friedrichshafen AG, Germany

Integrated design in collaborative engineering
    Claude Baron   LAAS CNRS, France

Service manufacturing systems
    Toshiya Kaihara   Kobe University, Japan

Process improvement programmes for sustainability
    Jose Arturo Garza-Reyes   University of Derby, UK

Sustainable initiatives in developing countries
    Irenilza de Alencar Nääs   Paulista University, Brazil

Human and organizational aspects of planning and scheduling
    Ralph Riedel   TU Chemnitz, Germany

Agility and flexibility in manufacturing operations
    D. Jentsch   TU Chemnitz, Germany

Asset and maintenance management for competitive and sustainable manufacturing
    Marco Garetti   Politecnico di Milano, Italy

Manufacturing of the future
    R.S.Wadhwa   Høgskole i Gjøvik, Norway

Smart manufacturing system architecture
    Hyunbo Cho   Postech University, Republic of Korea

Production capacity pooling vs. traditional inventory pooling in an additive manufacturing scenario
    Jan Holmström   Aalto University, Finland

Ontology based engineering
    Soumaya El Kadiri   EPFL, Switzerland

Co-evolving production and society in a global-local world
    Paola Fantini   Politecnico di Milano, Italy

Lean in high variety, low volume production
    Erlend Alfnes   Norwegian University of Science and
                                   Technology, Norway
Lean system development
    Elise Vareilles   École des Mines d'Albi, France

Managing factories lifecyle in a global-local world
    Claudio Palasciano   Politecnico di Milano, Italy

Experience, knowledge and competence management for production systems
    Laurent Geneste   INP-ENIT, France

IFIP WG5-7 research workshop
    Hermann Lödding   Hamburg University of Technology,
                                   Germany

Optimization models for global supply chain management
    Ramzi Hammami   ESC Rennes School of Business, France

Product Service System information system
    Thècle Alix   University of Bordeaux, France

International Scientific Committee

Bruno Vallespir (Chair)	University of Bordeaux, France
Erlend Alfnes	NTNU Valgrinda, Norway
Eiji Arai	Osaka University, Japan
Frédérique Biennier	INSA de Lyon, France
Umit S. Bititci	University of Stratchlyde, UK
Abdelaziz Bouras	Qatar University, Qatar; Université Lumière Lyon 2, France
Luis Manuel Camarinha-Matos	Universidade Nova de Lisboa, Portugal
Sergio Cavalieri	University of Bergamo, Italy
Stephen Childe	University of Exeter, UK

Byoung-Kyu Choi	KAIST, Republic of Korea
Gregor von Cieminski	ZF Friedrichshafen AG, Germany
Indra Djodikusumo	Institute of Technology Bandung (ITB), Indonesia
Alexandre Dolgui	École Nationale Supérieure des Mines de Saint-Etienne, France
Slavko Dolinšek	University of Ljubljana, Slovenia
Guy Doumeingts	Interop Vlab, France
Heidi Carin Dreyer	Norwegian University of Technology and Science-NTNU, Norway
Eero Eloranta	Helsinki University of Technology, Finland
Christos Emmanouilidis	ATHENA, Greece
Peter Falster	Technical University of Denmark, Denmark
Jan Frick	Stavanger University, Norway
Susumu Fujii	Kobe University, Japan
Marco Garetti	Politecnico Di Milano, Italy
Samuel Gomes	Belfort-Montbéliard University of Technology, France
Bernard Grabot	University of Toulouse, France
Robert W. Grubbström	Linköping Institute of Technology, Sweden
Gerhard Gudergan	Aachen University of Technology, Germany
Gideon Halevi	Hal Tech LTD, Israel
Bernd Hamacher	University of Bremen, Germany
Hironori Hibino	Tokyo University of Science, Japan
Hans-Henrik Hvolby	Aalborg University, Denmark
Ichiro Inoue	Kyoto Sangyo University, Japan
Harinder Jagdev	National University of Ireland, Ireland
John Johansen	Aalborg University, Denmark
Toshiya Kaihara	Kobe University, Japan
Dimitris Kiritsis	EPFL, Switzerland
Tomasz Koch	Wroclaw University of Technology, Poland
Ashok K. Kochhar	Aston University, UK
Andrew Kusiak	University of Iowa, USA
Lenka Landryova	Technical University of Ostrava, Czech Republic
Jan-Peter Lechner	First Global Liaison, Germany
Ming K. Lim	University of Derby, UK
Hermann Lödding	Hamburg University of Technology, Germany
Vidosav D. Majstorovich	University of Belgrade, Serbia
Kepa Mendibil	University of Strathclyde, UK
Kai Mertins	Knowledge Raven Management GmbH, Germany
Hajime Mizuyama	Aoyama Gakuin University, Japan

Table of Contents – Part I

Knowledge Discovery and Sharing

Knowledge-Based Planning and Scheduling

Knowledge Discovery and Sharing

Aligning Supply Chain Strategy with Product Life Cycle Stages

João Gilberto Mendes dos Reis, Sivanilza Teixeira Machado,
Pedro Luiz de Oliveira Costa Neto, and Irenilza de Alencar Nääs

Paulista University, Postgraduate Studies Program in Production Engineering
Dr. Bacelar 1212, 04026-002 São Paulo, Brazil
betomendesreis@msn.com.br,
sivateixeira@yahoo.com.br,
politeleia@uol.com.br,
irenilza@gmail.com

Abstract. Product Life Cycle (PLC) has been used to analyze the behavior of a product during its time of production. The success of enterprises depends on its capacity of aligning Supply Chain Strategy (SCS) with PLC. The purpose of this work was to develop a model to align the right SCS with PLC stage. This research shows three case studies and results provides that different companies used diverse approaches on managing life cycle of its products. However, they were successful in reaching competitive advantage due to correct alignment between SCS with PLC.

Keywords: Agile Supply Chain, Responsive Supply Chain, Flexible Supply Chain, Lean Supply Chain.

1 Introduction

The results of a company are connected directly to the adopted strategy. An enterprise may aspire total quality of its products, but if it uses an aggressive cost reduction strategy, may not achieve the desired result. In fact, it is fundamental to an organization to align market, production and business strategy to reach its goals.

First of all, strategies of enterprise must be established considering the Product Life Cycle (PLC) [1] and its correct alignment with strategy of Supply Chain Management [2]. Nowadays, we consider that SCM has four strategy approaches: lean, flexible, responsive and agile [3]. These strategies are known as an evolution of manufacturing strategy thinking. For this reason, when a company applies a manufacture strategy, this strategy extends all along the supply chain.

This paper aims to analyze the relevance of aligning Supply Chain Strategy (SCS) with Product Life Cycle and the consequences for the companies.

B. Grabot et al. (Eds.): APMS 2014, Part I, IFIP AICT 438, pp. 3–10, 2014.

2   Theoretical Background

2.1   Supply Chain Strategies

In order to understand the Supply Chain Management Strategies, four approaches were defined [2]:

Lean Supply Chain (LSC) focus on major productivity with cost reduction, through the elimination of wastes [4].

Flexible Supply Chain (FSC) flexible behavior of system. Involves equipments, workforce and transportation network. The main types of flexibility are represented by the flexibilization of the production systems [5].

Responsive Supply Chain (RSC) corresponds the capacity of response to market needs, considering time and cost. [6].

Agile Supply Chain (ASC) involves the capacity of introducing new products to supply new markets. Agility is the capability of a company to structure the business process in order to answer the new clients' requirements and wishes [7].

Each one of these strategies needs to align with demand and supply characteristics. And it is considered whether the product is innovative or functional [2], [3] and [8].

2.2   Product Life Cycle

PLC may be defined as the process of existence of a product since its idea and development until its recycling [1]. In this process, the product passes through different stages, such as demand analysis, conception, manufacturing, test, execution, evaluation, maintenance and discard [9]. PLC deals with the evolution of a chain product, that may occur in two ways: a) the creation of a new product in the market, and b) referring to mature products that there are already in the market [1]. The PLC function shows four clear stages: introduction, growth, maturity and decline [10].

3   Methodology

This article includes the proposition of a model aiming to explain the relation between PLC and SCS and the performance of case studies to check the pertinence of the model in real industrial conditions. To do so, this study was conducted based on these steps:

1. A literature review regarding the concepts of PLC and SCS;
2. Development of model based in Literature Review, using authors such as [1], [2], [8], [9], [10] and [11];
3. Three case studies were realized using public data, annual management reports of companies, interviews and informations published in the last 30 years;
4. Discussion of the cases considering the data collected and the model proposed.

4 Developing a Model to Align Supply Chain Strategy and Product Life Cycle

To develop a model that represents SCS with PLC, the authors analyzed different contributions in the theme [1], [2], [8], [9], [10] and [11], resulting the model shown in Figure 1.

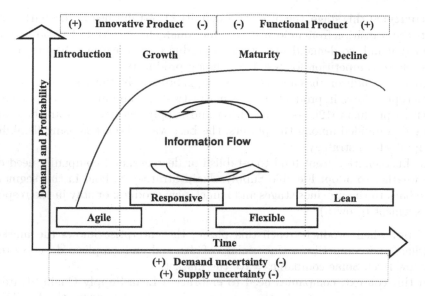

Fig. 1. Proposed Model

To explain Figure 1, it is necessary to study PLC through its four stages:

Introduction: represents launching the product in the market. The product is considered innovative, with high profit margins and no competitors. According to different studies, a product needs to comply with some criteria, to be considered innovative [2], [3] and [8]. However, in this scenario, there is high demand uncertainty, because it is not know how consumers react to new products. On the introduction stage a high supply uncertainty occurs due to the difficulty in finding suppliers.

In addition, the more applicable SCS in this context is Agile Supply Chain [2] and [8].

Growth: in this stage, on similar products are put in the market and consumers begin to have options. Competitors develop copies of the product at lower prices, reducing profit margin. However, supply uncertainty starts to reduce, because new suppliers arise. Now the chain perspective is responsiveness, which means to attend clients requirements faster. On the other hand, the enterprise needs to reduce manufacturing and distribution costs. This stage allows new opportunities to reach competitive advantage [12].

On Growths phase, for a short time period, companies that adopt agile supply chain or responsive supply chain strategies may compete. However, the enterprise that launches a product must decide if it should change its strategy to responsiveness, or maintain agility and production of that item. In doing so, it does not no represent that PLC product is over, because the company may license the product for manufacturing to other enterprises in different countries. Meanwhile, there are companies that keep manufacturing similar products.

Maturity: at this stage, the product is definitively established in the market and starts the transition from innovative to functional. Organizations have knowledge about demand, so demand uncertainty is reduced, whereas supply uncertainty rises due to competition for resources among producers.

Another condition that affects companies is brought by the costumers, who do not accept failures in products on the maturity stage, and also do not pay more for these products [12]. As competition and supply uncertainties are high and demand is divided among the players, the best way to react is using flexibility in supply chain strategy.

In this scenario, profit tend to establish or decrease, and companies need decide weather to adopt Flexible Supply Chain Strategy to hold in this segment; come back to the previuos stages and launch new producs; or stay in the responsive segment (growth).

Decline: when products reach this phase, the enterprise knows the market, suppliers and competitors. Uncertainty of demand and suppliers decrease to a very low level. Some companies leave the market.

In this context, companies need to embrace a Lean Supply Chain Strategy. They must reduce wastes in the supply chain nodes, to ensure the feasibility of selling the products [13]. Of course, much has been discussed about lean manufacturing after the work of Womack and Jones [13] and the relationship between agility and lean approach [4], but in this research the focus is put on the relation between the decline stage and lean supply chain strategy.

5 Case Studies

The alignment between PLC and SCS is an opportunity for enterprises to obtain success in their markets. To illustrate this, three case studies are presented, related to the model proposed in this paper.

5.1 FIAT

The Italian Automobile Factory Torino (FIAT) arrived in Brazil in the 70's. After a difficult period, with a lot of questions about quality of its products, the enterprise became the biggest company in selling vehicles for the last twenty years in Brazil.

A reason for this success was the launching of a small vehicle called Uno (one). It was showed for the first time in 1983 and started to be produced in Brazil in

1984. The innovative car got immediate success. Until 1988 the firm sold three millions of these cars in the world [14].

In Brazil, the car spreads in the streets and its production increases with the rise of the so called 'popular cars', in the beginning of the 90's. This kind of vehicle consisted of compact cars without some safety items and comfortable equipments, but with an attractive price. Brazilian government established the price of the popular car in 7.350 american dollars [15]. This was interesting for the people and for the producers, since Brazilian currency had parity with the dollar from 1994 to 1999.

Afterwards, the Brazilian scenario of vehicle production changed and popular cars received many versions with different prices. Actually, a car considered popular, without air conditioning and electric power steering costs 10.200 dollars [16].

In the 90's, the opening of the market by the Brazilian government, caused an invasion of many companies. Firms like Renault, Honda and Hyundai changed the national market and became a concern to the four local automobile factories previously installed in the country, Volkswagen, Fiat, Ford and General Motors. So, Fiat was forced to launch new models, while maintaining its major success. For that, the company changed the name Uno to Mille, readjusting the car in the market. The name represents an analogy with the engine that had a cylinder capacity to 1.000 cubic metric centimeters.

Some years ago, Fiat introduced a vehicle called 'New Uno', but it was a totally new product with new lines and another concept. However, the Mille was produced until 2013, when, with legislation change in Brazil, its production became unfeasible. The problem was the impossibility of including airbag systems and ABS brake in the project, an obligation for vehicles produced in Brazil since 2014.

When we analyzed Fiat SCS linked to PLC, the model connects perfectly with the case Fiat Uno/Mille. When Fiat launched Uno in Brazilian market, the vehicle changed the paradigm of car production, creating one of the products with longest longevity of the country. This allowed to the company an immense return of investment along thirty years of production.

The Uno's success made competitors enter in the segment with models like Gol (Volkswagen), Chevette (General Motors) and Escort (Ford). As a result, Fiat needed to adequate itself to answer new market challenges and establish a Responsive Supply Chain strategy. To do this, the company launched many different products, such as the sedan Premio, Station wagon Elba, and sporting models of Uno. The increase of consumption in Brazil, motivated by economic stability, made the Brazilian market very attractive and concurrent. This fact also made the company change its strategy to a Flexible Supply Chain, as a reaction to a scenario of maturity for the product and segment. In doing so, Fiat assembly lines became more flexible to produce different kind of products. Suppliers oriented their stocks and production to supply Fiat according to factory programmation.

In the XXI century, the major objective of the firm was to make Mille the cheapest car in the country, so the company needed to reduce costs and wastes. With this aim, Fiat applied the Lean Supply Chain strategy, with the purpose to maintain the product competitive in the market.

5.2   Apple

Apple is a company known around the globe and its founder, Steve Jobs, is the image of tireless search for better results and a shining mind capable of creating innovations constantly, characteristics that built a very profitable company even after Jobs' death. Innovative products have a natural uncertainty of demand and supply, due to the uncertain supplier capacity to respond to all the requirements of the new products.

Authors argue that innovative products have a short PLC [10], [14]. However, when we analyze for instance, the longevity of battery radios, it may be seen that this is not an absolute truth. What happens is that some products, even when its inventor loses interest in production, are still produced by many other firms, and although this is a way of survive, these producers are not entitled to ask for patents.

An enterprise in constant innovation process has its image connected to this performance and, in doing so, maintains high profitability margins. In this case, we can infer that Apple used an opposite strategy than Fiat. The company kept itself in an innovative way and established an Agile Supply Chain Strategy. For example, the IPAD [17], the tablet of 10 inch launched in 2010, may be considered a reference Very quickly it became a successful innovation by Apple. So this market called attention of enterprises like Samsung, that launchedan concurrent tablet called Galaxy to dispute in this new market. The evolution of products in PLC context required Apple to decide between applying an Agile Supply Chain Strategy or change its strategy to Responsive Supply Chain. The decision is clearly known; the company opted to continue with innovation of its products and maintain an Agile Supply Chain Strategy.

In 2011, Apple launched IPAD II and started the PLC of a new product. Despite the exterior similarity of the products, in conception they are really completely different. The demand for these new tablets did not prevent its previous generation's demand. In fact, there are a lot of people in the world that want to be inserted in a technologicalogic market, but have not money enough to pay for the products. For this reason, some enterprises keep on producing items of ancient generation and extend its PLC to the following stages using Flexible and Lean Supply Chain Strategies. Many Chinese companies are acting in this segment. Meanwhile, Apple continues its process of creating and innovating. The IPAD is now in the fifth version.

5.3   Intel

The North American company Intel was founded in 1960. This company embraced a hybrid strategy between Fiat and Apple. The firm was the first bigger processors manufacturing in the world and is not the only one, because it did not establish patents for its products in the 286, 386 and 486 versions. These processors were copied by other companies using reverse engineering.

In 1993 Intel launched the Pentium Processor, which started a new era of processors, adding value to the brand and changing competition scenario [18]. The product followed the same PLC of IPAD in Apple, however in a slower way. The company adopted an Agile Supply Chain Strategy, and although it continued to create innovative products, it realized that it could establish different strategies to processors.

The company understood that its products were really good for a significant part of world population. Many people use computer for simple things, such as to send an email, type a text or make a calculation, and they do not need a modern processor. With this idea in mind, the company perceived that it could launch a new processor, while maintaining the old one.

Different from the Apple case, competition in manufacturing processors is very limited, only two players respond to major demand around the world. So when Intel launched Pentium II in 1997 [18], it decided to keep two lines of products with the same main name. However, this was not good for its business image, because Intel was a technology and innovative company. The image of an innovative company is not in agreement with the dichotomy high technologies and old product altogether, because consumers see this as a second category product, an item not 'so good enough'. So, in 1998 Intel launched a new generation of processors, the ‚Celeron'.

Indeed, Celeron line was a Pentium I in a new format with some modifications. The negative image of using a second line product was substituted by the pleasant image of an economic and efficient processor. In doing so, the company was able to prolong PLC cycle and apply different supply chain strategies without harming the brand. So, Intel could adopt the Agile Supply Chain Strategy to new products of Pentium line and a different Responsive Strategy to the Celeron line.

The strategy reduced risks of stolen technology, and as a result, Intel is nowadays the major processors producer of the world and continues with innovation processes in many other types of processors and brands.

6 Conclusion

This paper deals with the alignment between SCS and PLC. A model was proposed and discussed in practice, through three case studies with different kind of enterprises. Our analysis indicates that these firms used different approaches to the strategies and alignments with good results. However, it may be considered that, in all cases, the profitability of the companies was related with adequate alignment between SCS and PLC.

Despite of the results presented in this paper, new studies in other companies shall be conducted to better validate the model. So, the next steps of this research is to analyze other companies using the proposed model.

This is an interesting and very present discussion, which does not finish with the examples here presented. The authors remain in the research of the problems referent to supply chain aspects, and will be glad there are other persons interested in interacting with them on these issues.

References

1. Tang, X., Yun, H.: Data model for quality in product lifecycle. Computers in Industry 59, 167–179 (2008)
2. dos Reis, J.G.M., de Oliveira Costa Neto, P.L.: Method for quality appraisal in supply networks. In: Emmanouilidis, C., Taisch, M., Kiritsis, D. (eds.) Advances in Production Management Systems, Part II. IFIP Advances in Information and Communication Technology, vol. 398, pp. 519–526. Springer, Heidelberg (2013)
3. Lee, H.L.: Aligning supply chain strategies with product uncertainties. California Management Review 44(3), 105–119 (2002)
4. Stratton, R., Warburton, R.D.H.: The strategic integration of agile and lean supply. Supply Chain Management 85(2), 183–198 (2003)
5. Sanchez, A.M., Perez, M.P.: Supply chain flexibility and firm performance: A conceptual model and empirical study in the automotive industry. International Journal of Operations & Production Management 25(7), 681–700 (2005)
6. Gunasekaran, A., Lai, K.: Responsive supply chain: A competitive strategy in a networked economy. Special Issue on Logistics: New Perspectives and Challenges 36(4), 549–564 (2008)
7. Pandey, V., Garg, S.: Analysis of interaction among the enablers of agility in supply chain. Journal of Advances in Management Research 6(1), 99–114 (2009)
8. Fisher, M.: What is the right supply chain for your product? Harvard Business Review 75(2) (1997)
9. Xiao, S., Xudong, C., Li, Z., Guanghong, G.: Modeling framework for product lifecycle information. Modeling and Simulation for Complex System Development 18(8), 1080–1091 (2010)
10. Kotler, P., Armstrong, G.: Principles of Marketing, 12th edn. PrenticeHalll (February 2007)
11. Mahapatra, S.K., Das, A., Narasimhan, R.: A contingent theory of supplier management initiatives: Effects of competitive intensity and product life cycle. Journal of Operations Management 30(5), 406–422 (2012)
12. Christopher, M.: Logistica e o gerenciamento da cadeia de suprimentos, 3rd edn. Cengage Learning, Sao Paulo (2011)
13. Womack, J., Jones, D., Roos, D.: The Machine That Changed the World: The Story of Lean Production. Harper Perennial (1991)
14. Car and Driver, http://caranddriverbrasil.uol.com.br
15. Carplace, http://carplace.virgula.uol.com.br
16. Auto Esporte, http://revistaautoesporte.globo.com
17. Apple, http://www.apple.com
18. Intel, http://www.intel.com

An Overview of Design Tools Applied in Civil Construction Area at Brazilian Southeast Region

Samuel Dereste dos Santos[1,2], Oduvaldo Vendrametto[1], and Miguel León González[2]

[1] Paulista University-UNIP, Dr. Bacelar St. 1212, São Paulo, Brazil
samuel_dereste@yahoo.com.br,
{oduvaldov,miguel.leon}@uol.com.br
[2] Cruzeiro do Sul University-UNICSUL, Dr. Ussiel Cirillo Ave. 225, São Paulo, Brazil

Abstract. The construction area in Brazil have different challenges to become more productive, efficient and sustainability. The objective is analyze the profile of projects offices at Brazil´s southeast region to determine the design tools used for project development and their characteristics in civil construction area. The strategy was a technical review about this issue in periodic papers and a survey, applied online, for project experts. The results shows that CAD – Computer Aided Design – tools still have more presence and BIM – Building Information Modeling – software is gaining space inside offices, but still have problems that need be resolved. Besides, inside the context, BIM tools have qualities aligned with actual demands that put it in evidence to resolve historical problems at civil construction context.

Keywords: CAD, BIM, Brazilian Southeast productivity, sustainability.

1   Introduction

The civil construction industry in Brazil is one of the most important in the country under different aspects. The huge territorial extension combined with the poor infrastructure requires the direct application of the civil area resources. However, when compared to the other industry sectors, is still considered delayed because of the particularities of organization, work division, productive process and product characteristics.

The informatics tools have gained great importance in this scenario. As a direct replacement of the clipboard and handmade draws, the CAD tools - Computer Aided Design - mean a revolution in the design process, making it more productive and effective. Moreover, CAD-Based solutions favor the exchange of tools among the professionals what cover various technological areas such as aeronautics, mechanics and construction. However, the CAD model, specifically for buildings, presents bottlenecks which are difficult to overcome, and thus, the BIM tools - Building Information Modeling - emerge as an option to this problem.

BIM technology has appeared with a different concept. While CAD technology is based on vector information, BIM is based on parametric objects. In this case, it allows the designer to define a series of objects that make the process more interactive

B. Grabot et al. (Eds.): APMS 2014, Part I, IFIP AICT 438, pp. 11–18, 2014.

and rich, solving several problems before construction. Furthermore, BIM architecture uses the same file under different disciplines, such as facilities, structure, masonry, foundations, etc. As a result, the higher compatibility among the files improves significantly the project process. This technology has been deployed worldwide in order to adjust its parameters According to [1,2], the implementation of BIM systems requires the adjustment of variables that need to be carefully studied to obtain a better project performance.

In Brazil, BIM technology has been also gaining greater visibility. The Brazilian Army has applied such technology to improve the military projects. Moreover, the Foundation for the Education Development of Sao Paulo State – FDE - has been developing a database to make all its projects using BIM solutions. In addition, builders and developers are increasingly investing on the technology, seeking the benefit of the integration of the construction process and post-construction [3].

Despite the benefits, it is difficult to estimate the technology acceptation degree in the Brazilian building industry. In order to answer this question, the goal of this paper is to analyze the profile of the project offices in Brazilian Southeast, trying to find how kind of technology they are using and its features. The strategy to develop this work is based on a technical review focused on periodical papers as well as a survey that was applied online to experts in projects of the southeast region of Brazil.

2   Technical Review

2.1   The Production of Projects and Their Importance – A National and International Context

The concepts of project management and project production are very important and need be carefully studied. In general, many different professionals are involved in the production of buildings, and each one is responsible for a specific part of the process. The production of projects in Brazil is quite different when compared to other countries.

Current construction projects are becoming even more complex and requiring more labor time, especially as the amount of project data and active project participant increase [4,5]. Besides, both projects and management can be defined in a number of ways, but a reasonable view would be that projects are the creation or the extension of assets, and management is the conduct of controlling this activity. Project management can then be seen as the controlled direction of the use of resources in order to achieve this creative process [6].

The construction engineering process presents three stages: planning, design and execution [4]. Each stage is equally important, and carelessness during any stage can cause budget overruns, improper design and construction, and work delays. If the routine planned procedures can be simulated using a reliable data, construction costs can be reasonably estimated, thus providing feedback that can help to control the annual budget, increasing the resource allocation efficiency.

The concepts of [4,5] shows that the organization of the process is aligned to this different actors, that completes the idea of [6], whose definitions are the bases of the controlling process. All this concepts are linked to effective tools, and informatics tools can be one answer for these questions.

Besides, the importance of the project in the building conception process is very important to avoid errors and minimize the costs and failures. In Brazil, some entrepreneurs understand that the project is a mere expense in the production system, and most of the projects start without all the projects finished [7,8]. According to [8], a largest investment in the project (in all steps) (fig. 1) could reduce the non-provided costs and also can aggregate more quality to the final product. Moreover, it permits a better financial management with reduction of the payments (non-provided mainly) during the process.

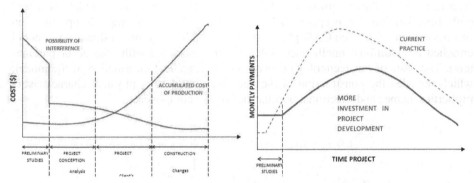

Fig. 1. Investment in Projects [8]   **Fig. 2.** Costs and Monthly Payments [8]

2.2   Informatics Tools Used in the Project Development

To define the most common tools used in the development of projects in the civil construction, it is necessary to study the importance of CAD and BIM tools for the project of buildings.

2.2.1   CAD Tools

Early applications of computers to assist the stages of engineering began in 1950, when the Massachusetts Institute of Technology (MIT) started the discussion about Computer Aided Design – technology. CAD systems of that generation were limited to the description of two-dimensional geometric entities, creating and manipulating drawings in monochrome graphics terminals. Right now [9], CAD systems present several advantages:

— Ability to send and receive drawings electronically;
— Better management of drawings and information;
— Accuracy in sizing;
— Faster recovery, modification and update of drawings

During the 60s and 80s, the use of CAD systems was limited to large companies, such as aerospace and automotive due to the high costs, involving software, hardware and qualification level of the operators However, at the end of 90s, with the development of the Windows Operating System, there was a migration of the companies to use Windows-Based tools. As a result, the costs reduced as well as the necessity of the highly skilled users [9].

For the project offices in Brazil, with the popularization of computers was responsible to the gradual migration of manual design processes (clipboard) to the computer and with the advent of the internet, the process became even more streamlined and integrated when compared to the previous stage. This fact has made the *.DWG interface the most popular of all CAD tools into nowadays [9].

2.2.2   BIM Tools

According to [1] the definitions of BIM are broad and do not have a widely accepted definition. The initial concepts of BIM date back to the first attempts of optimization of information within the CAD platforms (fig. 3). This is a three-dimensional model enriched by additional intelligence (information associated with graphic or parameters). The basis of this technology consists of the graphical information of the model, which includes the construction of the geometric model, its physical characteristic, properties, names and functional peculiarities of the components.

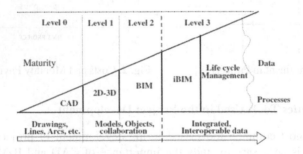

Fig. 3. Costs and Monthly Payments [10]

BIM systems are adequate to support the simulation of a construction project in a virtual environment, with the advantage of using software, which means to perform several steps in advance of the construction process, allowing the necessary adjustments before the real work. The assembly instructions can be associated with BIM components. So the visual context of the specific location on the 3D model can assist the communication of such instructions.

The BIM tools involves modeling of information surrounding the production of a building by creating a digital model that integrates all the interfaces that make up a building, covering the entire life cycle of the building, which starts in the project, involves the implementation, use, rehabilitation and demolition.

According to [10], BIM systems have been gradually applied in the worldwide panorama of AEC – Architecture, Engineering and Construction- industries. However, there is no uniformity in the use of the tool. The low demand for BIM customers also becomes a major obstacle to the widespread use of the tool in Canada, with an absorption of 30%. Besides that, in the United States, the AEC market has a greater use of the tool (50%) viewing the adoption of BIM as an excellent return on investment.

3   Case Study

In order to estimate a degree about the acceptation level of CAD and BIM software in the Brazilian Southeast Context, a survey was applied using a Survey Server (www.surveymonkey.com) to understand the particularities of the design process.

3.1   Sampling

Twenty-three companies in the Southeast Region of São Paulo were interviewed, being formed by medium and large companies. The profile of the companies (fig. 4) shows that 20% are involved with Residential Building Construction, 42.5% with Commercial Building Construction, 16% with Infrastructural Projects of Roadwork and 22.5% with Infrastructural Projects in general. 40% of the respondents were small/individuals companies and 35% big ones (fig. 5).

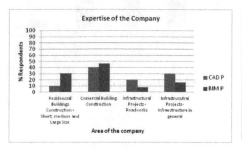

Fig. 4. Expertise of the Company   **Fig. 5.** Size of the Company

3.2   Time Spent on Project Development

Analyzing the time spent on project development (fig. 6), is possible to see that BIM tools require more time in the project (52%) when compared with CAD tools (40%). This can be explained by the necessity that the BIM user needs to develop the projects. The project routine in CAD tools permit the omission of several information that cannot be omitted in BIM tools.

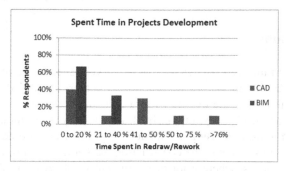

Fig. 6. Spent time in Projects Development

3.3   Labor Productivity Coefficients

To know the efficiency of the tools, the labor hour of each solution was compared as presented in fig. 7. This analysis shows that the users of BIM tools spent 50% more time in the development of the project due to the time needed to define all instances. The 4 most cited BIM software in the Brazil Southeast are Revit Architecture®, Revit Structure® and Revit MEP®, from Autodesk Corporation, with 27.5%, 25% and 25%, respectively. Vector Works is used only for 2.5 % of the users. Other specific software solutions were cited by 19% (fig. 8).

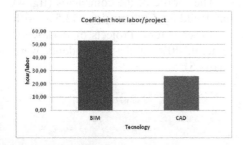 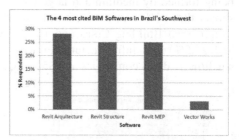

Fig. 7. Labor/project   Fig. 8. The most cited software

4   Discussion

The CAD and BIM tools have particularities that need to be analyzed before comparing both solutions. Nowadays, in Brazil, the construction market is familiarized with the routines and specifications of CAD tools, and the most part of the actors uses this technology proficiently. This characteristic can explain the differences between them.

In the project process, the customer needs different degrees of information, and at this point, CAD tools are more efficient because it needs less information to generate the final product. For BIM tools, is necessary to insert/define more information from the beginning of the project, what requires more time. On the other hand, for the next steps, BIM tools also require less information to continue the development of the projects, what could compensate this time lost at the beginning of the process.

5   Conclusions

Design processes in the civil construction area are very specific because they present some particularities that makes it different from another areas. CAD tools were the first tool applied in large-scale that transformed the project processes, while the BIM tools are considered the CAD evolution. In Brazil the offices are initiating the implementation of BIM tools, increasing the spent time of the users in order to use the tool in the correct way. Besides that, the construction market in Brazil is accustomed with less information projects, where a lot of details are resolved later. This practice increases the price of the products and, in a competitive market, is difficult to take gain.

The construction market in Brazil has grown in the past seven years and the challenge for the growing continuity is to become more efficient with a better quality product. To achieve this issue, is necessary to use more effective tools with the possibility to manage different variables and parameters. BIM tools present such characteristics and they permit the Brazilian offices to improve their projects.

Acknowledgment. The authors would like to thank CAPES (Coordenação de aperfeiçoamento de pessoal de nível superior) and Paulista University (UNIP) for the financial support to develop this work.

References

1. Migilinskas, D., Popov, V., Juocevicius, V., Ustinovichius, L.: The Bene-fits, Obstacles and Problems of Practical Bim Implementation. In: 11th International Conference on Modern Building Materials, Structures and Techniques, MBMST 2013. Science Verse (2013), http://dx.doi.org/10.1016/j.proeng.2013.04.097 (acessed on: March 2014)
2. Meireles, A.R.: Estratégia para uma integração avançada do BIM no processo construtivo in 3º Seminário BIM - Sinduscon (March 24, 2013), http://www.sindusconsp.com.br/envios/2013/eventos/bim/Apresenta%C3%A7%C3%A3o_AntonioMeireles.pdf (accessed on March 2014)
3. Song, S., Yang, J., Kim, N.: Development of a BIM-based structural framework optimization and simulation system for building construction. Computers in Industry 63, 895–912 (2012), http://dx.doi.org/10.1016/j.compind.2012.08.013 (accessed on March 2014)
4. Chou, J.S.: Cost simulation in an item-based project involving construction engineering and management. Internacional Jornal of Project Management (2014), http://dx.doi.org/10.1016/j.ijproman.2010.07.010 (accessed on March 2014)
5. Wu, I.C., Hsieh, S.H.: A framework for facilitating multi-dimensional information integration, management and visualization in engineering projects. Internacional Jornal of Project Management, Published Online http://dx.doi.org/10.1016/j.ijproman.2010.07.010 (accessed on March 2014)
6. Campbell, J., Project management and the civil engineer. Internacional Jornal of Project Management, Published Online http://dx.doi.org/10.1016/0263-7863(85)90056-0 (acessed on March 2014)
7. Franco, L.S.: Aplicação de diretrizes de racionalização construtiva para evolução tecnológica dos processos construtivos em alvenaria estrutural não armada. Tese de Doutorado em Engenharia Civil – Escola Politécnica da Universidade de São Paulo (1992)
8. Peralta, A.C.: Um modelo do processo de projeto de edificações, baseado na engenharia simultânea, em empresas construtoras incorporadoras de pequeno porte. Master Dissertation in Production Engineering. Universidade Federal de Santa Catarina, Published Online https://repositorio.ufsc.br/bitstream/handle/123456789/.../188665.pdf (accessed on March 2014)

18   S.D. dos Santos, O. Vendrametto, and M.L. González

9. Souza, A.F., Coelho, R.T.: Tecnologia CAD/CAM - Definições e estado da arte visan-do auxiliar sua implantação em um ambiente fabril. In: XXIII Encontro Nacional de Engenharia de Produção – ENEGEP, Published Online (October 24, 2003) http://www.abepro.org.br/biblioteca/ENEGEP2003_TR0504_0920.pdf (accessed on: March 2014)
10. Porwal, A., Hewage, K.N.: Building Information Modeling (BIM) partnering framework for public construction projects. In: Automation in Construction, (31), pp. 203–214, Published online http://dx.doi.org/10.1016/j.autcon.2012.12.004 (accessed on: March 2014)

A Framework for Improving the Sharing of Manufacturing Knowledge through Micro-Blogging

Richard David Evans[1], James Xiaoyu Gao[1], Oladele Owodunni[1], Satya Shah[1], Sara Mahdikhah[2], Mourad Messaadia[2], and David Baudry[2]

[1] University of Greenwich, Chatham Maritime, Kent, United Kingdom
{R.D.Evans,J.Gao,O.O.Owodunni,S.Shah}@gre.ac.uk
[2] CESI/IRISE, Rouen, France
{smahdikhah,mmessaadia,dbaudry}@cesi.fr

Abstract. The purpose of this paper is to report on an industrial investigation, conducted within a leading power generation manufacturer, to better understand the organisational processes and challenges present in relation to the management and sharing of knowledge during product manufacturing. Findings reveal that the organisation is failing to fully benefit from web 2.0 technologies and particularly micro-blogging. Details of the investigation results are presented and a conceptual framework is proposed to demonstrate how organisations may enhance the sharing of explicit manufacturing knowledge using micro-blogging tools.

Keywords: Employee Collaboration, Enterprise 2.0, Knowledge Management, Manufacturing Management, Micro-Blogging.

1   Introduction

In a globally integrated enterprise environment, engineering and manufacturing organisations are increasingly required to develop flexible and responsive work processes to ensure their survival. Previous practices concentrating upon product cost, quality and time to market are no longer sufficient to maintain competitive advantage. The focus is progressively turning towards innovation with clearly differentiated product offerings being the result. Against this background, effective employee knowledge sharing is paramount and remains a significant challenge for both Small to Medium sized Enterprises (SMEs) and large multi-national organisations. The management and effective sharing of knowledge is recognised [1] as crucial for the survival of global manufacturing organisations. Research [2] suggests that, by sharing explicit employee and organisational knowledge already captured, companies are able to become more productive, enhance corporate performance and are more likely to survive than those that fail to discover hidden organisational knowledge.

The term Micro-Blogging falls under the technology umbrella of "Web 2.0", a term first coined by Tim O'Reilly [3] in 2004 to define the next stage in the development of the World Wide Web; O'Reilly identified that modern websites were providing users with a more interactive experience and enabled them to become

B. Grabot et al. (Eds.): APMS 2014, Part I, IFIP AICT 438, pp. 19–26, 2014.
© IFIP International Federation for Information Processing 2014

responsible for the generation of their own content. More importantly, Web 2.0 offered the potential for greater collaboration and knowledge sharing; in this regard, micro-blogging may be defined as the posting of short character-limited messages (usually 140 characters), images or videos online and is different from traditional forms of blogs, which are often lengthy and published less frequently [4]. By employing Web 2.0 technologies, enterprises are able to connect people to people and people to information more effectively; they can facilitate connectivity, sharing and collaboration across boundaries, capture a wide range of views and information that is typically informal or highly dispersed and help colleagues locate previously unknown experts [5]. More specifically, employees are able to identify and share organisational resources more easily via a less formal communication channel; this inturn provides for greater interactivity and collaboration in the workplace. Current published research into the use of Web 2.0 technologies in enterprises has primarily focussed on the use of individual technologies, such as Wikis [6], and social networking sites [7]. However, there is limited research into how each of these tools may be used in a manufacturing setting to share explicit employee and organisational knowledge.

The purpose of this paper is to report on the findings of an exploratory industrial investigation conducted within a leading power generation manufacturer to understand the current challenges and opportunities in relation to the sharing and management of explicit knowledge. A conceptual framework is presented in Figure 1 to demonstrate how manufacturing organisations might make greater use of micro-blogging tools to improve the sharing of explicit knowledge in their operations.

2   The Importance of Employee Knowledge Sharing within Manufacturing Organisations

In today's commercial environment, where manufacturing organisations are continually striving to achieve and maintain competitive advantage, successful employee knowledge sharing is fundamental to corporate success. According to Shin, Holden and Schmidt [8], knowledge management can be sub-divided into four categories – knowledge capture, knowledge management, knowledge sharing and knowledge application – while knowledge can be found in two forms – explicit and tacit; for the purpose of this article, the sharing of explicit knowledge is explored. Effective knowledge sharing in the workplace is observed to enhance employee learning, which inturn increases the agility of a company and improves the quality of products designed and manufactured [9]. O'Dell and Grayson [10] add that the knowledge sharing process involves getting the collected knowledge to the right people at the correct time in order to improve business functionality. Manufacturing organisations must, therefore, improve methods of capturing and sharing employee knowledge, while minimising barriers created by the use of different languages, the varying levels of technological competence of employees and, indeed, the potential unwillingness of individuals to share in the workplace.

3   Adoption of Micro-Blogging within Business

Along with other Web 2.0-based technologies, micro-blogging is increasingly being used in our social lives and amongst the academic research community to share and disseminate information. However, this is not perceived to be the case in industry where there appears to be a lack of recognition of the potential on offer to enhance knowledge sharing. Micro-blogging has been identified [11] as a particularly useful tool to facilitate employee collaboration and knowledge sharing and its specific benefits include: an ability to inform others easily and rapidly of current activities; a facility to provide colleagues with current work schedules, product availability, feedback and other explicit information in a timely manner; an accessible channel for the marketing and promotion of products/services and solicitation of customer feedback; the facilitation of communication with third parties, including potential customers and suppliers; and the potential to direct colleagues to informative content by re-posting.

The activity of knowledge sharing faces numerous barriers typically relating to either social factors or the technology adopted or a combination of both. Businesses often cannot identify what is known within their organisations and, consequently, best practices, expertise and knowledge and skills cannot easily be applied and transferred. Successful knowledge sharing within an organisation requires openness and a willingness to share between two parties. Trust inter alia is a key issue with regard to sharing knowledge with colleagues. Dyer and Singh [12] acknowledged that knowledge sharing could generate relational incomes for both parties, although Simatupang and Sridharan [13] stated that more often than not, companies do not like to share their private information completely.

4   Industrial Investigation

An Industrial Investigation was conducted within a leading power generation manufacturing company in the UK between October 2013 and March 2014 and, for the purpose of this report, the organisation is referred to as 'the Company'. The aim of the investigation was to gain an understanding of the Company's current practices and challenges in relation to knowledge management and sharing. The methodology used during the investigation was informal audio-recorded face to face interviews lasting between 60 and 90 minutes. In total, 17 employees were selected for interview and participants included the Plant Manager, Maintenance Engineers and Assembly Line Operatives. Interviews were conducted on an individual basis by a panel consisting of two PhD students and one post-doctoral research fellow. The interviewers followed a standardised questionnaire, which asked participants a variety of open-ended and closed questions to identify the knowledge management methods, practices and tools employed within the Company; the findings relating to these questions are now summarised.

4.1   Analysis of Responses to the Question: How Do Employees Currently Identify Best Practice Knowledge for Specific Manufacturing Problems?

Employees explained that for every manufacturing project, a set of work instructions are produced detailing relevant knowledge in relation to the design, manufacture and assembly process for a complete product. This explicit knowledge is stored on an internal database, which is the first point of reference for operators working on the Assembly line. The database is accessible directly from the shop floor using touch screen monitors and product designers and change engineers can modify product documentation remotely. It was reported that the company promotes a "who you know" culture, whereby employees are encouraged to ask colleagues to share knowledge and, if that colleague does not have the required knowledge, ask if they can suggest someone who does. If it is not possible to find required knowledge internally, employees are encouraged to use external resources, such as commercial search engines. There is no system in place for the storage, identification and retrieval of explicit knowledge of employees. Currently, information is captured in word document format when users are completing work processes, although no further action is taken to convert it into explicit knowledge. Finally, if someone experiences a problem, they are encouraged to visit Team Room, an intranet accessible by colleagues working within the same project group, and ask questions via an instant messaging tool.

4.2   Analysis of Responses to the Questions: How Does the Organisation Currently Store Best Practice Knowledge?

Employees confirmed that best practice knowledge is typically stored in spreadsheets and then made available via the EASE touch-screen system. Knowledge is occasionally input into 'Team Room', although this is not considered a standard practice. It is recommended by the corporate IT department that employees store all manufacturing documentation on a shared server or on the internal intranet, but this does not always happen and often information is stored locally on personal hard-drives. During the NPD process, the company aims to capture lessons learnt during projects at the product closure stage. This activity informs colleagues of issues which arose during manufacture, testing and execution and is stored for future reference. After product delivery, however, there is no requirement to update this information (e.g. when a product is repaired in the field) and in-service experiences are not added to the lessons learnt document. It was stated that the company is currently seeking to adopt paperless working and a new system called EASE has recently been introduced, which offers a Touch-screen workstation for assembly line operatives. The system stores all product development project documentation, from work instructions to training manuals and all critical product characteristics. The company also operates a system called "QSI", where all training materials are stored; this is an electronic system controlled through revision changes and approval processes and allows for the preparation of operator instructions when new products are introduced.

4.3   Analysis of Responses to the Questions: How Do You Currently Share Best Practice Knowledge with Dispersed and Co-located Colleagues?

It was confirmed that the Company does not currently have a standardised method for sharing knowledge relating to best practices, although employees commented that they try to make their knowledge as easy as possible to understand; to this end, they aim to remove from documentation any unnecessary technical jargon for stakeholders who do not have a technical background. It was revealed by interviewees that they usually use e-mail as their preferred communication tool when sharing knowledge. An internal intranet facility, called Team Rooms, exists to support project work and it is the responsibility of functional team leaders to ensure effective communication between team members.

4.4   Analysis of Responses to the Questions: What Knowledge Management Tools Are Currently Used within the Company? How Frequently Are These Tools Used?

With regard to the use of specific knowledge management tools employed within the organisation, none were identified. For the recording of maintenance issues, a T-card system is employed where users note down in paper format any problems or issues being experienced with manufacturing and assembly equipment. Interviewees reported that the company relies heavily on e-mail and corporate management are trying to encourage employees to collaborate more pro-actively and, thereby, share greater knowledge through informal communication. It was confirmed that the Company provides an instant messaging system for informal communication and a corporate intranet is available to transmit company-wide information. It was pointed out that project groups are also able to create and manage their own intranet sites for communication purposes, although no micro-blogging functionality is available to facilitate business processes.

5   The Proposed Conceptual Framework for Improved Knowledge Sharing

Based on the findings of the industrial investigation, which conclude that no formal business process exists within the Company for the sharing of explicit manufacturing knowledge, a conceptual framework, displayed in Figure 1, is proposed to illustrate a new method for enhancing knowledge sharing and collaboration within organisations through the deployment of micro-blogging. The process demonstrates how an engineer or operative may search for explicit manufacturing knowledge by searching for specific keywords and phrases on public activity feeds, which may be accessed through an internal or external micro-blogging tool.

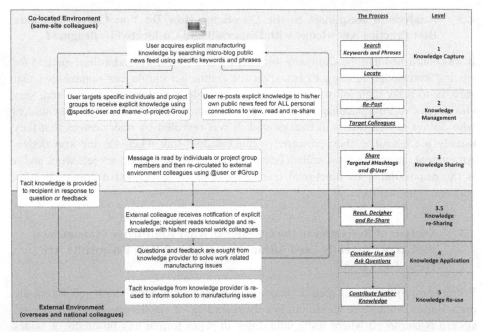

Fig. 1. Conceptual Framework to improve the Sharing of Explicit Manufacturing Knowledge through Micro-Blogging

In Figure 1, in the column headed 'The Process', guidance is given on what actions users should take at each level of the knowledge management process in order to improve the sharing of explicit manufacturing knowledge, through the use of micro-blogging tools. Further explanation of this process is now provided in Table 1.

Table 1. Business Process for improving the sharing of explicit manufacturing knowledge

Level	User...
Knowledge Capture	Searches and locates explicit manufacturing knowledge employing targeted keywords and phrases.
Knowledge Management	Targets internal colleagues who would benefit from receipt of explicit manufacturing knowledge. Re-posts knowledge to his/her own personal news feed so that others can search and locate knowledge.
Knowledge Sharing	Shares manufacturing knowledge with targeted colleagues and project groups using specified #Hashtag or @user functionality.
Knowledge re-Sharing	Reads and deciphers knowledge and shares with targeted colleagues and project groups using specified #Hashtag or @user functionality.
Knowledge Application	Considers supplied knowledge and applies to business needs, where appropriate. Posts questions and gives feedback to knowledge provider.
Knowledge Re-Use	Provides tacit or further explicit knowledge in response to knowledge recipients' questions or feedback. Re-uses knowledge received to improve business processes and re-distributes to project group members.

6   Conclusions and Further Work

The industrial investigation confirmed that the Company does not currently have any formalised method for sharing explicit employee knowledge. Some tools and procedures exist to facilitate knowledge exchange, but the organisation lacks a standardised process for the capture, management and sharing of explicit knowledge. Given the relatively flat organisational structure and a corporate culture of "who you know", employees are expected to seek out knowledge from identifiable colleagues. This is frequently completed on an oral face-to-face basis while written documentation is shared. However, it may be concluded that the Company is failing to embrace social technologies to facilitate employee collaboration and enhance knowledge sharing; furthermore, the investigation highlighted how web 2.0 technologies, such as micro-blogging, may offer significant benefits to the Company and allow employees to collaborate and share knowledge more effectively, while moving towards paperless operations. Utilising the findings of the industrial investigation, it has been possible to develop a conceptual framework for the improvement of sharing of explicit knowledge in extended manufacturing organisations. The framework has been developed to address specific issues highlighted during the investigation, but further work is recommended to identify how bespoke web 2.0-based technologies may be employed to enhance knowledge sharing in other industrial sectors and functional areas.

Micro-blogging in particular is able to help both SMEs and larger organisations improve knowledge management practices. The introduction of micro-blogging can provide employees with real-time access to explicit knowledge and allow them to raise questions and queries with knowledge producers. Employees are able to access knowledge through ubiquitous computing devices, such as smart phones and tablets, and this is possible from most locations around the globe. Micro-blogging facilitates and encourages communication through less formal and potentially more inclusive channels, with individuals employing established communication practices used in their social lives. It is important to recognise, however, that micro-blogging cannot overcome all barriers to knowledge sharing which may be present within organisations, both large and small. Within SMEs, the barriers may appear less evident than in large organisations as colleagues may often hold meetings to share knowledge more easily, but difficulties still exist. Knowledge silos may exist which restrict the sharing of knowledge, but these may be minimised if knowledge is made available via a micro-blogging tool accessible throughout the organisation. Language barriers can also occur in large multi-national companies, but these may be overcome through the use of an integrated translation mechanism. The adoption of the proposed knowledge sharing framework, based on micro-blogging functionality, which is discussed in this paper, offers significant potential to enhance knowledge sharing within manufacturing organisations.

Acknowledgements. This paper is based on work funded by the European Program INTERREG IVA France-Channel-UK under the project "Building an Expertise Network for an Efficient Innovation and Training System (BENEFITS)". The authors would like to thank all at the collaborating company for their support with this project and their input to the Industrial Investigation.

References

1. Argote, L., Beckman, S.L., Epple, D.: The persistence and transfer of learning in industrial settings. Journal of Management Science 36(2), 140–154 (1990)
2. Beckman, T.: A Methodology For Knowledge Management. In: International Association of Science and Technology for Development AI and Soft Computing Conference, Banff, Canada, 27 July-1 August (1997)
3. O'Reilly, T.: What Is Web 2.0: Design Patterns and Business Models for the Next Generation of Software. Journal of Communications and Strategies 65, 17–37 (2007)
4. Kwak, H., Lee, C., Park, H., Moon, S.: What is twitter, a social network or a news media? In: Proceedings of the 19th International Conference on World Wide Web, Raleigh, USA, pp. 591–600 (2010)
5. Lee, I.: Trends in E-Business, E-Services, and E-Commerce: Impact of Technology on Goods, Services, and Business Transactions. Western Illinois University. IGI Global, USA (2013)
6. Leino, J., Tanhua-Piiroinen, E., Sommers-Piiroinen, J.: Learning with social technologies: Workplace learner experiences of wiki and blog and perceptions of PLE. In: Ley, T., Ruohonen, M., Laanpere, M., Tatnall, A. (eds.) OST 2012. IFIP Advances in Information and Communication Technology, vol. 395, pp. 59–68. Springer, Heidelberg (2013)
7. Novielli, N., Marczak, S.: Social Network Analysis for Global Software Engineering: Exploring Developer Relationships from a Fine-Grained Perspective. In: IEEE 8th International Conference on Global Software Engineering Workshops, Bari, Italy, pp. 47–48 (August 2013)
8. Shin, M., Holden, T., Schmidt, R.A.: From knowledge theory to management practice: Towards an integrated approach. Journal of Information Processing and Management 37(2), 335–355 (2001)
9. Riege, A.: Three-dozen knowledge-sharing barriers managers must consider. Journal of Knowledge Management 9(3), 18–35 (2005)
10. O'Dell, I., Grayson, C.J.: If only we know what we know. Free Press, New York (1998)
11. Evans, R.D.: An Enterprise 2.0 Groupware and Framework to facilitate Collaboration and Knowledge Sharing in Dispersed Teams during the Product Development Process within the Aerospace and Defence Industry. BAE Systems & University of Greenwich, Rochester (2013)
12. Dyer, J.H., Singh, H.: The Relational View: Cooperative Strategy and Sources of Interorganizational Competitive Advantage. Academy of Management Review 23(4), 660–679 (1998)
13. Simatupang, T., Sridharan, R.: The Collaborative Supply Chain. International Journal of Logistics Management 13(1), 15–30 (2002)

How to Recognize a Creative SME?

Cynthia Lavoie and Georges Abdulnour

Industrial Engineering, Université du Québec à Trois-Rivières, Canada
{lavoic,georges.abdulnour}@uqtr.ca

Abstract. In the actual knowledge-based economy, intangible assets are crucial. Those assets cannot be created without the creativity of the employees. Despite the phenomenal amount of works published on creativity, only a few are related to Small and Medium Enterprises (SME). Furthermore, a literature review made evident that a proper definition of what is a creative SME does not exist, even though it is important for practitioners, researchers and professionals in this domain. A definition of a creative SME needs to include external characteristics, ones that are easy to recognize from an observer's point of view. This research is thus trying to answer the following question: "How can we recognize a creative SME?" By using a Delphi with a group of experts, the researchers obtained a list of characteristics to recognize a creative SME. A case-study based research on internal factors that affect creative SME characteristics will follow.

Keywords: Creative enterprise, Creativity, SME, Small and Medium Size enterprise.

1 Introduction

The human capital is a transforming driver of enterprises and is an integral part of their competitive advantage to build on. This capital must be created based on the creativity of the members of an organization.

Despite the incredible amount of literature written about creativity[1] by professionals and academics, the researchers in the domain of creativity concentrated their work on large organizations. However, Small and Medium Enterprises (SME), like large organizations, are looking for more assets to be successful in building a competitive advantage based more and more on knowledge and obviously on creativity and innovation (Raymond, Abdul-Nour, & Jacob, 2003).

Some authors have addressed the issue of creativity in SME, but a clear distinction between a creative and a non-creative SME does not exist. Following this statement, the question that is addressed in the present research is: "What is a creative SME and how can we recognize it?" The answer to this question is important for researchers and practitioners in the field because researchers need dependant variables to study creativity, either in SMEs or in large organizations. For practitioners, it will be useful to know what to aim for as they put in place practices to increase creativity in their enterprises.

---

[1] More than 30 000 publications found in Scopus Database, on July 2nd, 2014.

B. Grabot et al. (Eds.): APMS 2014, Part I, IFIP AICT 438, pp. 27–33, 2014.

A literature review done by the authors on the subject revealed that, even for large organizations, researchers do not agree on a way to distinguish a creative enterprise from a non-creative one. Furthermore, according to what we know, of the few researchers that have tried to define a creative enterprise, none of them addressed the case of the SME. The term, "creative enterprise" is often used to distinguish cultural, high-tech or marketing firms and enterprises, but without presenting a concrete definition or specific characteristics.

The main objective of this paper is to get a list of external characteristics that will be used to recognize a creative SME. To fill up this objective, the collaboration of experts was requested. Following this, the results obtained will serve as an input for the next step, which consists in selecting a sample of creative SME to be included in a case study. The case study will allow to study different factors of the SME creativity.

In the following sections a literature review, the methodology, the results obtained, a discussion and a conclusion will be presented.

2   Literature Review

2.1   Definitions of Creativity

Definition of creativity has evolved in many areas: psychology, sociology, education, management, etc. In this particular research, the concept of creativity is studied in the context of organizations. Batey and Furnham (2006) classified the definitions of creativity in four categories (Batey & Furnham, 2006) : 1) New and useful. The definitions in this category include two characteristics: the product must be new and useful or adapted to reality; 2) Observable product. Here, the emphasis is put on the product obtained with creativity, which must be of quality and creative according to the evaluation of external observers; 3) Part of a process. Here, the creativity is seen as a part of a process, a problem resolution, an innovation or a mental process; 4) A set of components. In this last category, creativity is seen as a set of interrelated components. According to Mumford (2003), it seems that it exists a certain agreement around the following definition in the context of organization (Mumford, 2003): Creativity consists of the production of new and useful ideas in a domain. Those ideas has to be qualified as such by observers who are familiar with the domain (T. Amabile, Contti, Coon, Lazenby, & Herron, 1996).

Since the present work tries to study SME and their organizational context, a definition of a creative SME enterprise is required. In this context, definitions of organizational creativity have to be taken into account. Organizational creativity is defined as the creation of a new, valuable and useful product, service, idea, procedure or process, by individuals who work together in a complex social system (Moneta, Amabile, Schatzel, & Kramer, 2010; Woodman, Sawyer, & Griffin, 1993). Creativity can also refer to the employees that use a diversified spectra of competencies, abilities, knowledge, views and experiments to generate new ideas for decision making, problem resolution and effective execution of tasks (Cheung & Wong, 2011).

Those definitions are clear and useful for some kind of researches, but as the present research seeks to answer the question "How to recognize a creative enterprise?" it is difficult to do so without some precisions on the external characteristics of a creative enterprise.

2.2   Impacts of Creativity

A creative enterprise will be influenced by organizational creativity, even though real impacts of creativity are not well documented. A review of impacts of creativity is therefore useful.

According to Amabile (1982), the creative performance of an enterprise can be measured in an external manner by the products or the accomplishments that can be observed as: "A product or response is creative to the extent that appropriate observers independently agree it is creative. Appropriate observers are those familiar with the domain in which the product was created or the response articulated. Thus, creativity can be regarded as the quality of products or responses judged to be creative by appropriate observers, and it can also be regarded as the process by which something so judged is produced" (T. M. Amabile, 1982).

Furthermore, Pitta (2009) underlines that "The enterprises that cannot bring creativity and innovation in their daily tasks find that their failures are related to their weakness in establishing an appropriate culture and climate which value new ideas and this will decrease profits"(Pitta, 2009). It means that an increase of creativity plays a role in the financial success of enterprises. For Heunks (1998), this financial success is related to creativity only if innovation is present (Heunks, 1998).

Actually, creativity is, for some researchers, considered as a component of innovation (Wright, Lewis, Skaggs, & Howell, 2011) or as part of the innovation process (Westwood & Low, 2003). Innovation comes from creativity and then creativity is considered as "pre-innovation." Consequently, creativity leads to innovation (Burbiel, 2009).Considering that, a brief review of the impacts and measures of innovation can be taken into account to measure or recognize a creative enterprise.

2.3   Impacts and Measures of Innovation

Aas and Pedersen (2010) suggest that management literature on innovation measures is a heterogeneous set of knowledge. Particularly, they highlight the work of Tidd (2001), who suggests two classes of performance measurements: "(1) accounting and financial performance measures, and (2) market performance measures." Tidd et al. (2001) suggest that the impact of innovation is threefold, resulting in: (1) financial benefits, (2) increased customer value, and (3) strategic success (Tidd, 2001).

On the other hand, Milway, Azer and al. (2011), propose to measure innovation and the value it creates with the gross domestic product (GDP) per capita (Milway et al., 2011). According to the Organization for Economic Co-operation and Development (OECD), innovation is a permanent process in continuous movement, which makes it difficult to measure. The OECD suggests some measurements that can be used such as: the impacts on the net sales, the impacts of the innovation process on costs and employment and the impacts of innovations on productivity (OCDE, 2005).

It is true that this offers some avenues on how to measure the impacts of creativity, however exploring the measures used in the literature on creativity is crucial in order to build a list of characteristics that allows to recognize a creative organization.

2.4 Creativity Organizational Measurements

In the literature, the measurement of creativity on the organizational level is conducted by measuring some aspects of the organizational climate that are known to have an impact on creativity. KEYS, a tool conceived by Professor Amabile, is a tool commonly used to measure the stimulants and the obstacles of creativity in a work environment based on empirical researches and theories related to the creativity in organizations. It uses 78 items; 66 describing the work environment and 12 validating the performance at work evaluated according to creativity and productivity (T. Amabile et al., 1996).

The performance criteria presented in the KEYS can be used to measure organizational creativity in an "organization or a creative unit where a high creativity is needed and where people think they produce creative work." This measurement is a self-evaluation and consists of the following items: 1- My department is innovator; 2- My department is creative; 3- Globally, my actual work environment helps me to develop my own creativity; 4- A lot of creativity is needed in my day-to-day work; 5- Globally, my actual work environment helps me to develop my work group creativity; 6- I think I am really creative in my work. This tool can be used in a department, a division or a small organization, as long as the individuals in the group perceive the same work environment, because the perceived work environment makes a difference on the creativity level of the organization (T. Amabile et al., 1996).

To conclude, the characteristics provided in the literature are not specific and concrete to recognize creative SMEs among the other SMEs. In the following section, the methodology used to close the gap of the researches regarding SME creativity is presented.

3   Methodology and Discussion

Following the literature review, the Delphi Method was used to elaborate a list of external characteristics of a creative SME. Then, the results obtained will serve as an input for the next step, which consists in selecting a sample of creative SME to be included in a case study. The case study will allow to test the effects of some factors on SME creativity.

The Delphi method was invented by Dalkey (1969) of the RAND Corporation, in the 1960s. This method aims at refining the judgment of group members using questionnaires. Three elements are important in the Delphi Method: anonymous responses, iteration and controlled feedbacks, and statistical group responses. "These features are designed to minimize the biasing effects of the dominant individuals, irrelevant communications and of group pressure toward conformity"(Dalkey, 1969). In this study, all three features were respected. To ensure that, open questions were asked to make sure every expert had a chance to express his/her opinion. Two iterations were done in order to obtain a consensus among the experts.

Emails and web-based software (SurveyMonkey.com) were used to collect the data. On the first round, an email, including a brief introduction, a presentation of the researchers and the project and a link to the survey, was sent. On the second round, only a brief introduction and the link to the survey were sent. The details about the survey are presented in a following section, while a description of the respondents is presented in the next section.

3.1   The Respondents

Criteria. The experts were chosen according to a list of criteria, developed by the researchers and evaluated in the first part of the survey. The different criteria included: expertise in defining creativity, knowledge on tools, techniques and success factors related to creativity, SME field experience and finally researcher on SME. The expert group had to include at least: 1 researcher in SME, 1 practitioner in SME, 1 researcher in creativity and 1 practitioner in creativity.

Evaluation. Seventeen experts were asked to answer the survey. Ten of them accepted to fill up the survey. Among this group of experts, nine out of ten who answered were kept according to the conformity of the answers. From those nine people, three were creativity experts, three were experts in creativity tools and techniques, two were experts in success factors of creativity, three were field SME practitioners and five were SME researchers. As for the group composition, three were researchers in SME, two were practitioners in SME, one was practitioner in creativity and three were researchers in creativity.

In the second round, ten people answered the revised and updated questionnaire. From those ten respondents, nine were the same that answered in the first round and one was a new respondent.

Experts' Qualification. According to their evaluation, eight out of nine people had at least one criteria evaluated as "expert in this domain" or "high knowledge of this domain". Furthermore, some of them had more than one criteria evaluated as "expert in this domain". The global results show that, in average, 22% of the participants consider having a high knowledge of the domain, and 34% think they are experts in these domains, for a total of 56%.

3.2   External Characteristics

First Round. In the first round of the Delphi, the question asked on the external characteristics to the experts has to be answered on a 6-point scale basis.

Twenty external characteristics, based on the literature review, were given and the experts had to answer whether they believed those characteristics were appropriate to differentiate a creative enterprise from a non-creative one or not. For example, points like the "number of ideas implemented or commercialized in a time period" and the "originality of the ideas, according to a group of experts" were included.

Seven characteristics were chosen by the experts as characteristics being impacted by creativity in a SME:

- Turnover rate of ways to do things
- Impact of the innovations on a targeted market
- Impact of the innovations on the society
- Offer of distinctive products or services (not available at competitors)
- Number of ideas implemented or commercialized by period of time
- Ability to attract and retain key employees
- Percentage (%) of growth by year (net sales) in comparison to the market

Second Round. The purpose of the second round was to prioritize the list of external characteristics. The experts were then asked to prioritize the seven external characteristics that obtained the best score in the first iteration. The results show that the top characteristics to consider in recognizing a creative enterprise are: 1) Offer of distinctive products or services (not available at competitors); 2) Turnover rate of ways to do things, 3) Impact of the innovations on the targeted market.

4   Implications and Conclusion

Furthermore, the external characteristics will be useful for researchers in this research. Following this results, a case-study research will be conducted in order to study the detailed internal success factors or characteristics that will create a creative SME, recognized and measured with the external characteristics obtained in this part of the research. To select those cases to study, those external characteristics have to be detailed in an objective way to concretely qualify the enterprises. The following table show how each external characteristic has been transcribed in concrete measures by the authors to select the SMEs.

Table 1. Objective measures of external characteristics

External characteristic	Objective measure
1) Offer of distinctive products or services (not available at competitors)	The products or processes of the enterprise must include at least one characteristic not available in their competitive market.
2) Turnover rate of ways to do things	The enterprise must have a process to improve its way to do things as a R&D department, suggestion system or continuous improvement system. The enterprise must have review at least a process or product in the last year.
3) Impact of the innovations on the targeted market	The increase of market share related to an innovation has to be positive.

Even if creativity is a subject well studied in the literature, describing the external characteristics is an emerging, if not a new, research area to be investigated. Knowing the external characteristics of a creative enterprise, especially a SME, will lead enterprises to aim for those results as implementing practices to create a creative enterprise and will facilitate the work of researchers as they will know which dependant variables to use for their research.

References

Amabile, T., Contti, R., Coon, H., Lazenby, J., Herron, M.: Assessing the work environment for creativity. Academy of Management Journal 39(5), 1154–1184 (1996)

Amabile, T.M.: Social psychology of creativity: A consensual assessment technique. Journal of Personality and Social Psychology 43(5), 997–1013 (1982), doi: 10.1037//0022-3514.43.5.997

Batey, M., Furnham, A.: Creativity, intelligence, and personality: A critical review of the scattered literature. Genetic, Social, and General Psychology Monographs 132(4), 355–429 (2006), doi:10.3200/mono.132.4.355-430

Burbiel, J.: Creativity in research and development environments: A practical review. International Journal of Business Science and Applied Management 4(2), 35–51 (2009)

Cheung, M.F.Y., Wong, C.S.: Transformational leadership, leader support, and employee creativity. Leadership and Organization Development Journal 32(7), 656–672 (2011), doi:10.1108/01437731111169988

Dalkey, N.C.: The Delphi Method: An Experimental Study of Group Opinion (1969),
    http://www.rand.org/pubs/research_memoranda/RM5888 (retrieved)

Heunks, F.J.: Innovation, Creativity and Success. Small Business Economics 10, 263–272 (1998)

Milway, J., Azer, T., Chan, K., Kidwai, A., Martin, L., Meyer, A., Mohsenzadeh, S.: Canada's innovation imperative: REPORT ON CANADA 2011: Institute for Competitiveness & Prosperity (2011)

Moneta, G.B., Amabile, T.M., Schatzel, E.A., Kramer, S.J.: Multirater assessment of creative contributions to team projects in organizations. European Journal of Work and Organizational Psychology 19(2), 150–176 (2010), doi:10.1080/13594320902815312

Mumford, M.D.: Where Have We Been, Where Are We Going? Taking Stock in Creativity Research. Creativity Research Journal 15(2-3), 107–120 (2003)

OCDE, La mesure des activités scientifiques et technologiques; Manuel d'Oslo: Principes Directeurs Pour Le Recueil Et L'Interprétation Des Données sur L'Innovation, Paris (2005)

Pitta, D.A.: Creating a culture of innovation at Portugal Telecom. The Journal of Product and Brand Management 18(6), 448–451 (2009),
    http://dx.doi.org/10.1108/10610420910989767

Raymond, L., Abdul-Nour, G., Jacob, R.: L'entreprise-réseau: Dix ans d'expérience de la Chaire Bombardier Produits récréatifs. Les Presses de l'Université du Québec, Quebec (2003)

Tidd, J.: Innovation management in context: environment, organization and performance. International Journal of Management Reviews 3(3), 169–183 (2001), doi:10.1111/1468-2370.00062

Westwood, R., Low, D.R.: The multicultural muse: Culture, creativity and innovation. International Journal of Cross Cultural Management 3(2), 235–259 (2003),
    doi:10.1177/14705958030032006

Woodman, R.W., Sawyer, J.E., Griffin, R.W.: Toward a theory of organizational creativity. Academy of Management. The Academy of Management Review 18(2), 293 (1993)

Wright, G., Lewis, T., Skaggs, P., Howell, B.: Creativity and innovation: A comparative analysis of definitions and assessment measures, Vancouver, BC (2011)

Manufacturing *Reporting* Knowledge Representation: A Case Study at *STMicroelectronics*

Manel Brichni[1,2,3], Sophie Dupuy-Chessa[2], Lilia Gzara[1], and Corinne Jeannet[3]

[1] Univ. Grenoble Alpes, G-SCOP, F-38000 Grenoble, France
CNRS, G-SCOP, F-38000 Grenoble, France
{manel.brichni,lilia.gzara}@g-scop.grenoble-inp.fr
[2] Laboratoire d'Informatique de Grenoble
sophie.dupuy@imag.fr
[3] STMicroelectronics
corinne.jeannet@st.com

Abstract. This paper addresses the problem of manufacturing *Reporting* knowledge representation in manufacturing companies. An approach to characterize these knowledge is proposed. The solution is applied to the *Reporting* process at *STMicroelectronics* for capitalizing knowledge in the *Wiki* of the company and responding to users' needs. In such an approach, the user participates throughout the knowledge representation definition process, even in choosing knowledge characteristics to represent it. For that aim, three dimensions are taken into consideration: the know *What*, the know *Why* and the know *How*.

1 Introduction

The rapid growth of companies and their business needs, the departure of employees, the complexity of new technologies and the rapid proliferation of information, are reasons why companies seek to capitalize their expert knowledge. In the *Reporting* team at *STMicroelectronics*, the number of created reports is highly growing, while knowledge about their creation is lost. Consequently, this requires to capture and to capitalize knowledge about their creation in order to help not only users to understand the purpose of the report but also engineers to analyze the way it was created, in less time. Among other solutions, *STMicroelectronics* has opted for the use of a *Wiki* to capitalize its expert knowledge, called *Stiki*. In a previous publication [4], an evaluation of *Stiki* use for knowledge sharing was performed. One of the evaluation findings concerns the importance of pages structuring in *Wiki*. This helps readers searching for knowledge, but also contributors capitalizing their work, in an appropriate and effective way. However, this depends on the way knowledge is represented. Our aim, therefore, is to propose a way to represent knowledge while including its different aspects. In this paper, the definition of knowledge characteristics is proposed to integrate those required by users in the capitalization tool and to

B. Grabot et al. (Eds.): APMS 2014, Part I, IFIP AICT 438, pp. 34–41, 2014.

promote their reuse and exploitation. The proposed solution is applied to the *Reporting* process at *STMicroelectronics* that encounters capitalization issues. Before presenting the proposed solution for knowledge characteristics representation (section 3), we present, firstly, related work and background (section 2). We end this paper with a conclusion and some perspectives (section 4).

2 Background and Related Work

This section describes related work in knowledge representation and motivates the need for a new solution. The capitalization process involves knowledge capture, representation, storage, sharing and reuse [1, 12, 15]. Many approaches have discussed the capitalization issue [9, 13]. For example, the CommonKads approach is based on the construction of a collection of models, where, each one captures specific aspects of knowledge [1, 15]. Even tough our goal is not to develop expert systems, we can retain from it the construction of a collection of models in order to capture different aspects of knowledge (The UML models for example). The AKM (Active Knowledge Modeling) [8] is an other approach supporting the knowledge capitalization. Being able to support collaborative work and participative learning in managing knowledge will decide of its quality. That is why, in addition to using different and complementary models to represent knowledge, our approach should support the user participation through the whole process. Among steps described in the knowledge capitalization process, in this paper, we focus on the representation problem [2, 6], as discussed in the following.

Knowledge presents three different and complementary characteristics: *What*, *Why* and *How*. Each one describes knowledge in a different level and should be modeled in an appropriate way. First, the *What* corresponds to the conceptual level of knowledge. It represents manipulated objects and their relationships. Second, the *Why* is described in the behavioral level of knowledge which involves an understanding of principles behind processes. Finally, the *How* addresses the level of the knowledge configuration and integration in systems as well as *How* it could be used by different types of users. We note that these characteristics are generalized so that they could include other ones (when, who, etc.). We note that these three different characteristics are related through sharing common concepts, mainly manipulated *Reporting* objects.

Know-*What*: According to the author's thesis, [5] considers that the know-*What* concept treats procedural aspects of knowledge, while [12] describes the know-*What* as a set of concepts, knowledge and experience. In both cases, it concerns describing what knowledge to be considered throughout the execution of a task. In the literature, the *What* model is represented in different ways: Symbolic models [3] or a UML diagram based on classes and associations [14]. In fact, our aim is to describe effectively and simply the manipulated objects and their relationships during the *Reporting* processes at *STMicroelectronics* while involving different types of users (experts or simple users). That is why during our representation process, complex solutions like [3] are not favorite, but we retain the simplicity and efficiency of proposals like [14], while involving users throughout the capitalization process, even in defining knowledge characteristics.

Know-*Why*: Generally, the reasons for design decisions, can change throughout the designing business process and context, which could make them easily lost. Usually, a system is defined in terms of specifications to describe the way it works, but it does not include a description of *Why* it is designed the way it is, which forms the basis for a causal ambiguity. In the literature, the *Why* model is represented in different ways: Expert systems could be a solution, but mainly in problem resolving, which is not our goal, or design rationale notations [5] such as QOC (Questions, Options, Criteria) or DRL (Decision Representation Language) [7]. As our goal is to provide users with a comprehensible way to represent the know *Why*, design rationale could be adapted to our case study.

Know-*How*: it can represent both knowledge spaces (types, accesses, configurations, etc.) and business processes. Generally, it is neglected compared to the know *What* and *Why*. Our solution is based on a user centred approach requiring, therefore, accessible languages and solutions. For this purpose the IRTV solution (Information-Roles-Tasks-Views) [11] deals, among other objectives, with platform configurations, delivery, extension and improvement. Technical consultants build this model to design and implement systems, to define *how* knowledge is stored, roles access control is enforced, tasks should be executed, views are presented in workplaces, etc. In this paper, we will study how this methodology could cover our know *How* representation. As we have seen in the previous section, studies in the literature do not define (ie with the same names) and represent knowledge aspects similarly (know *What*, *Why* and *How*). In the following, we present our proposal for defining knowledge characteristics that we will apply it later to the *Reporting* activity at *STMicroelectronics*.

3 Our Proposal for Knowledge Representation: A Case Study on Manufacturing *Reporting* Process

Our approach consists in exploring current uses, users' expectations and needs, in co-designing with them a new solution and in validating it by applying it on real problems. Because of the lack of space, we do not detail these steps. To create a report, the *Reporting* engineer at *STMicroelectronics* has to define his/her objectives, to access to data, to select his/her data, to define his/her objects (indicators, dimensions, etc.), to create the report, share and capitalize it and to exploit it. Throughout the process, many objects interact via their relationships which are of different natures. The main ones are the "Indicators" or "Dimensions", where, a *dimension* is an analysis parameter that carries the analysis in a query and an *indicator* provides numerical information used to quantify a dimension object. Generally, it is the calculation result on data from databases, for example, the evolution of the turnover of different product lines within an organization. In this case, "the turnover" represents the indicator that is calculated according to the dimensions "years" and "product lines". In the following, we describe each characteristic representation (*What*, *Why* and *How*).

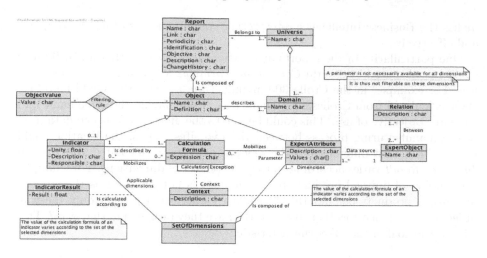

Fig. 1. Know *What* representation through *Reporting* process

The Know *What* Representation. By describing the know *What* related to the *Reporting* activity, we aim at representing manipulated objects through the process and their relationships. Such a model will not only facilitate the comprehension of objects interaction but also will guide the way knowledge should be simply and effectively capitalized and shared. In the business intelligence domain, the relationship between *Indicators* and *Dimensions* is represented with a cube, where edges of the cube are made of dimensions and the content of the cube cell corresponds to the value of the indicator according to the combination of the selected dimensions. [10] demonstrated how the cube presentation can be modeled using UML to be more easily perceived by designers and programmers. In our work, we are interested in the meta level of the cube, i.e, not the cube but its concepts. We propose in the following our representation of the know *What* with a UML model applied to the *Reporting* process. Since in the *Reporting* process, engineers and users manipulate expert objects of different nature, we choose therefore to represent our know *What* by a class diagram (figure 1).

As depicted in figure 1, a **report** belongs to a *Universe* and one or more *Domains* in order to classify them according to their content description. It is composed of **objects** that can be **indicators** measuring a production activity (for example, the number of products successfully achieved) or an **expert attribute** representing an **expert object**. For example, a report describing the number of achieved products per technology, is composed of an **indicator** measuring the **"number of products"**, as well as **the expert attribute** **"technology group"** representing **the expert object "technology"**. In this case, the *"technology group"* is the dimension representing analysis parameter that carries the analysis of the report. In the *Business Intelligence* domain, depending on the objective of the report, the engineer has the possibility to filter objects (data, indicators, dimensions) in order to restrict results and target specific knowledge (about a specific type of products, for example). That what makes the Business Intelligence interpreting voluminous data friendly, properly and effectively.

One particularity of the reports at *STMicroelectronics*, is that an **indicator** could be calculated by several *Calculation Formulas* according to its *Context* of use. For example, in the Crolles300 manufacture, an indicator could be differently calculated from Crolles200 manufacture, while having the same name and the same objective of use. This could be due to the difference between data used in the manufacturing process between the two sites. Thus, the location could be a *Context* that differentiates the way an indicator is calculated. Besides, an *Indicator Result* varies according to the selected set of dimensions. For example, the number of finished products per technology is not the same as the number of finished products per month. The UML model could present only the way objects are designed together, but not *Why* are they designed in that way? This will be the goal of the *Why* characteristic.

The Know *Why* Representation. Our aim is to represent the behavioral aspect of knowledge in order to effectively capitalize explanations about decisions that were made while performing tasks. Therefore, keeping track of the know-*Why* will provide help to users and designers to resolve problems and to explore more design options. Relying on knowledge described in the conceptual level through objects interaction in the *Reporting* process, we particularly consider, *Why* creating a report? *Why* is an indicator differently created? *Why* choosing a formula instead of another to calculate an indicator? *Why* an indicator could not be calculated or associated to a specific dimension? etc. As in our work, we aim at studying the various directions explored during the *Reporting* process, identified alternatives or why certain options have been made (for the calculation of indicators for example). Therefore, we decided to study the QOC model, present our vision of a possible solution, as well as discuss how we could represent it to deal with the know *What*, previously described. It is composed of *questions* about certain design *options* which represents alternative solutions and *criteria* to explicitly justify the options' selection. The model presented in figure 2 is based on the QOC model (Questions-Options-Criteria). Based on the know *What* model described above (figure 1), the principles behind the use of manipulated objects through the *Reporting* process are detailed.

This example (figure 2) treats the *indicator* object and the principles behind its use. We will study in the future if this model could be applied or adapted to treat other objects of the *What* model. The **indicator WIP** (Work In Progress), which is an object of the know *What* model, calculates the number of lots being processed in the clean room at *STMicroelectronics*. It could be calculated by more than one **formula** according to its **context** of use. Therefore, one of the most important questions asked when selecting an indicator is "*Why* is the **WIP** indicator calculated in that way?". Such an indicator is one of the most used for creating reports. It is important to understand its behavior. In fact, the first part of the QOC model used in figure 2, treats the *Question* part that corresponds to the Indicator **WIP**. *Options* presents its second part. In our context of use, options provide different formulas calculating the same indicator.

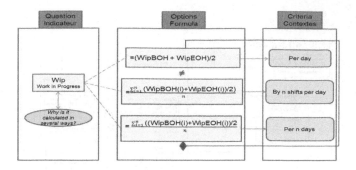

Fig. 2. Know *Why* representation with the QOC model

For example the indicator **WIP** could be calculated by either **Formula 1, 2** or
3. For each one, *Criteria* explain its selection. In our case, contexts of selection
of formulas correspond to the *Criteria* in the QOC model. For example, if the
user is in the **Context 3** when he/she wants to calculate the **WIP**, then he will
select the **Formulas 3** to calculate it. The particularity of this example is that
logically, the obtained result of an indicator should be the same whatever the
formulas, when considering the same conditions and goal. For example, in both
calculation formulas 1 and 2 of the *WIP*, the objective is to calculate the number
of achieved lots at the end of the day. However, the results of both formulas are
different. Besides, while studying some existing indicators, we realized that the
existence of different calculation formulas is due to the selection of the indicators'
names. This is the case of **WIP** indicator where even having the same name,
the formulas 1 and 2 are actually used to calculate different types of indicator.
It could generate a misunderstanding problems between users. To this end, in
the future, we will study how the QOC Model could be adapted to deal with
such a problem. Using the QOC model facilitates the formulas selection and
understanding, depending on their context of use, but understanding *How* each
formula was created and integrated in the production system, is considered as a
technical knowledge. Such knowledge is not necessarily capitalized and risks to
be lost. This will be the goal of the *How* model.

The Know *How* Representation. As we have discussed above, the know *How*
treats the knowledge integration and configuration in systems. Capitalizing such
knowledge in industrial contexts is a crucial step since the technology evolves and
important configuration process could be easily lost. Keeping track of technical
details facilitates engineers' work and saves time. The IRTV (Information-Roles-
Tasks-Views) methodology deals with platform configuration, delivery, extension
and improvement [11]. In figure 3, the IRTV solution is applied to describe the
know *How* related to the use of a report (the WIP Status Report) that actually
represents an expert object of the know *What* model, as follows:

Information: considers knowledge required for the users to create, to manage or to use a report and knowledge produced by them (inputs and outputs).

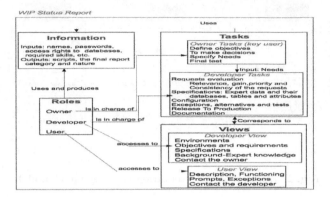

Fig. 3. *How* modeling using the IRTV methodology (the WIP Status Report)

This is not what we described in the *What* model, but, technical knowledge required by an IT member. For example, to create a report, inputs are passwords, access rights, etc. Outputs are scripts or the final report category and nature.

Roles: represents different users who are confronted with the use of a report (Owner, developer and simple user).

Tasks: each role is in charge of specific tasks. For example, as depicted in figure 3, a developer is in charge of evaluating requests of users (the owner role in the Figure, for example) in terms of relevance, priority, gain, etc. He/she needs also to detail data technical specifications (databases, tables, attributes and how to extract them). In addition to documenting these technical knowledge, he/she is in charge of specifying exceptions, alternatives and tests. If needed, he/she has to contact the owner since he is in charge of the request.

Views: Each role accesses to a specific view. As depicted in figure 3, a developer performing technical tasks needs to have a technical view which is different from the view needed by a simple user. He/she needs to have a clearer view about the environment he/she should work on (platforms, tools, etc.), as well as requirements and specification definition, etc.

These knowledge need to be capitalized and shared with other users, particularly between the same category, for an eventual reuse in an effective way.

4   Conclusion

Applied to the *Reporting* process at *STMicroelectronics*, three complementary characteristics know *What*, *Why* and *How* were defined and represented. Our short-term goal is, first, to study how the QOC Model can be adapted to deal with the confusion problem in the know *Why* representation, as well as if it could be applied to other objects of the *What* model or if it has to be completed with other methods. Second, the representation of the know *How* will be improved in order to involve both process modeling and control mechanism. Finally, the relationship between knowledge representation and its sharing and reuse in *Stiki* will be studied. The idea consists in providing, automatically through proposed models, *Stiki* templates for objects, where each one treats all knowledge characteristics, according to the concerned models. In the long term, we aim at studying the semantic aspect of knowledge representation, as well as knowledge reuse and evolution as other stages of our capitalization process, through which, we will discuss how capitalized knowledge could be reused in an effective way by users. Eventually, we will discuss how new users can search for information while learning existing vocabulary. At *STMicroelectronics*, such an approach for knowledge capitalization could be generalized to other contexts.

References

1. Bera, P.: Knowledge requirements analysis: A case study. PhD thesis, The University of British Columbia (2002)
2. Blaise, J.C., Lhoste, P., Ciccotelli, J.: Formalisation of normative knowledge for safe design. Safety Science, 241–261 (2003)
3. Bombardier, V., Lhoste, P., Mazaud, C.: Expert knowledge modeling and expert knowledge integration for defect identification by fuzzy linguistic rules. traitement du signal 21 (2004)
4. Brichni, M., Dupuy, S., Gzara, L., Mandran, N., Rozier, D.: A wiki for knowledge sharing: A user-centered evaluation approach. Unpublished
5. Frey, A.G.: Quality of Human-Computer Interaction: Self-Explanatory User Interfaces by Model-Driven Engineering. PhD thesis, Laboratoire d'Informatique de Grenoble (2013)
6. Horkoff, J., Borgida, A., Mylopoulos, J., Barone, D., Jiang, L., Yu, E., Amyot, D.: Making data meaningful: The business intelligence model and its formal semantics in description logics. In: ODBASE, pp. 700–717 (2012)
7. Lee, J., Lai, K.Y.: Whats in design rationale? Human-Computer Interaction, 251–280 (1991)
8. Lillehagen, F., Krogstie, J.: Active knowledge modeling of enterprises. ACM Computing classification (2008)
9. Malvache, P., Prieur, P.: Mastering corporate experience with the rex method. ISMICK 93 (1993)
10. Maniatis, A.S.: Olap presentation modeling with uml and xml. In: Proceedings of the 1st Balkan Conference in Informatics (2003)
11. Marthinusen, I.: The active knowledge modeling approach-to configurable product and process design. Master's thesis, Norwegian university of science and technology (2011)
12. Mathieu, S.: Knowledge management appliqué à la rénovation d'une unit de production de produits biologiques. PhD thesis, Faculté de pharmacie de Grenoble (2012)
13. Matta, N., Ermine, J.L., Aubertin, G., Yves Trivin, J.: How to capitalize knowledge with the mask method? In: IJCAI Workshop, pp. 1–13 (2001)
14. Page, M., Gensel, J., Capponi, C., Bruley, C., Genoud, P., Ziebelin, D.: Representation de connaissances au moyen de classes et d'associations. LMO (2000)
15. Schreiber, G.: Knowledge enineering and management. MIT Press (2000)

Data Quality in Materials Science: A Quality Management Manual Approach

Thorsten Wuest, Jakub Mak-Dadanski, and Klaus-Dieter Thoben

BIBA - Bremer Institut für Produktion und Logistik an der
Universität Bremen, Bremen, Germany
{wue,dad,tho}@biba.uni-bremen.de

Abstract. Experimental research data in the materials science domain is often insufficiently described with regard to metadata and frequently displays an incoherent form of documentation. These circumstances often hinder current and future researchers significantly in reuse and comprehension of data. To support researchers during the archiving and provision of materials science research data (incl. supplementing material), a Quality Management Manual (QMM) approach as an established QM tool is proposed in this paper. Quality-assurance of experimental research data and the perpetuation of good scientific practice in provision and archiving research data are examined before the QMM approach is applied in a case study. The preliminary results indicate that QMM allows to provide practitioners basic guidelines which support integrity, availability and reusability of experimental research data in materials science for subsequent reuse.

Keywords: data quality, experimental research data, materials science, QM.

1 Introduction

Research data plays a central role in the scientific process and is the basis of scientific knowledge creation. However, without adequate documentation and corresponding metadata, research data cannot be understood and managed [1]. Neatly stored research data (incl. metadata) allows researchers to e.g., test their hypotheses, evaluate experimental results and disseminate the findings in a cohesive way that furthers the state of the art. Thus, a coherent and long-term archiving of research data supports the scientific process. Additionally, the quality assurance of research data can be considered to be essential for the competitiveness of the research location [2].

The focus of this work has been placed on the development of Quality Management Manual (QMM) guidelines, which are intended to support researchers during the archiving and provision of materials science research data and to complement the quality manuals of research institutes with the research data aspect. The usage of the above mentioned guidelines is supposed to ensure the quality-assurance of research data and simultaneously perpetuate the terms of good scientific practice in archiving of the created research data.

B. Grabot et al. (Eds.): APMS 2014, Part I, IFIP AICT 438, pp. 42–49, 2014.

Research data generally represent the result of experiments and/or observations. These experiments and observations often consist of informal workflows, which may frequently exhibit differences. The so obtained data is often insufficiently described by researchers with regard to its metadata and displays an incoherent form of documentation. This condition hinders the current and future researchers significantly in the reuse and comprehension of the data [3], which in turn affects the scientific knowledge creation progress.

Following, the fundamentals of data quality as well as materials science research data will be succinctly addressed. On this basis, a framework for the model of quality assurance of materials science data will be created and presented in the following section. Thereafter, an exemplary guideline for documentation of materials science research data will be constructed. In the following discussion and limitations section, the developed solution is critically discussed. Furthermore, potential challenges concerning the implementation of quality assurance measures are illustrated. In the final section, the results are summarized and a short outlook on future work is presented.

2 State of the Art

In this section, a short overview of the basic terms and the current state of the art of Quality Management (QM) in the domain of research data management are presented. First, existing guidelines, in this case based on a German foundation, regarding the handling of research data are illustrated before the topic of research data in material science is highlighted in more detail. The last subsection is looking into data quality measures for research data.

2.1 Existing Guidelines of Research Data Management

The German Research Foundation (DFG) serves as the self-governing organization of science in Germany. On the basis of the association's issued recommendations for safeguarding good scientific practice [4] and recommendations for the secure storage and delivery of digital primary research data [5] a substantive framework for quality assurance of research data has been created. The recommendations state that securing and storing of primary (research) data should be guided by the rules of good scientific practice, as these form the basis of the scientific value chain. Research data should be kept for at least ten years in the institution where they originated. This is useful for efficiency reasons, since it allows the researchers to access the results of previous experiments or observations without having to repeat them. This takes also the often expensive (money and time efforts) creation processes into consideration. Additionally, the long storage time serves the preservation of evidence in the event the published results are ever doubted. Because each discipline is different when it comes to the needs and challenges in the area of research data handling, each domain should develop its own subject-specific approach to safeguarding research data [5]. The handling and storage of data should take place within (internationally) recognized and established standards. All information required for repeated use of the research data should be included and stored [5]. Each research institution should, therefore, place clear rules for the storage of primary data and data carriers [4].

2.2   Research Data in Materials Science

For each scientific discipline research data are the result of an individual scientific value chain. Materials science is no exception. Research and development of materials are the main tasks in the field of materials science [6]. Experiments and tests examine the properties of materials under different conditions. The number of different test methods and the necessary testing machines make data gathering and data analysis partially demanding, since although the older machines are considered good and reliable, they often are not compatible with the latest software. Due to the high research worker turnaround of universities, it is particularly important to collect the relevant metadata and store it in a comprehensive way. Metadata provides the research data with context and describes the contents by means of controlled vocabulary [7]. It involves, in case of e.g. material delivery, information on the name of supplier, place of manufacture, chemical composition and possible prior heat treatment of the material.

2.3   Data Quality Measures for Research Data

The DIN EN ISO 8402 standard defines quality as "the totality of characteristics of an entity that bear on its ability to satisfy stated and implied needs" [8]. According to a survey by K. C. Tan et al., many companies define quality, as the fulfillment or surpassing of customer-specific product requirements [9]. It is generally accepted that the degree with which customer requirements are fulfilled represent the most decisive quality criterion [8]. However research data, unlike a physical product, is not produced in accordance to the quality specifications of a client, but in a particular framework of the scientific research question. The performing of experiments, the evaluation and analysis of generated data are an essential part of scientific research [10]. The subsequent use of the research data defines the framework of requirements for the quality of the research data. An important requirement for the quality of research data is to enable its use outside of the original research question, which originally led to the creation of the research data. To say with certainty how a research data set was generated, all input variables have to be known. The quality of scientific research data can therefore be measured by the extent to which anyone who wants to continue to work with these data objects may comprehend the circumstances of the data generation and the information gained from the data.

3   Background for the Development of a QMM Framework for Experimental Research Data

In this section, the background of the developed QM method is described before it is applied in the next section. First, a case study which frames the application is introduced before the QM procedure of choice, QMM, is elaborated in more detail.

3.1   Case Description

The scope of the conducted case study is limited to the Department of Structural Mechanics of the *"Foundation Institute of Materials Science"* in Bremen, Germany (IWT). The mechanical experiments carried out in 2011/2012 were subjected to an analysis (according to test type and frequency). 47% of these experiments formed the tensile test. It was thus chosen for the creation of the requirements for the research data. On the basis of the evaluated test figures, and with the aid of expert interviews with scientific staff of the IWT, a picture of the state of data-handling in IWT has been created.

The projects are financed from public funds, or performed within an industrial partnership. The project defines many input variables for a series of experiments. The sample dimensions are therefore project-dependant. The tensile test testing machine generates tension values, which, through software interfaces, are evaluated to first characteristic values and converted to an Excel data set. The researcher analyzes the data on his or her workstation, PC or laptop, where the copies of the converted Excel data sets and framework data are also individually stored. Information on the chemical material composition, sample size, heat treatment conditions and surface characteristics are required for a complete analysis of the sample. However, since the data are located at different places and with different researchers, it is very difficult to access the original research data and metadata among older (> 6-8 years) publications.

3.2   QMM and Procedural Instructions

A QMM is the central document of every QM system (QMS). It describes the quality policy and it's scope, and regulates the responsibilities and powers of quality assurance measures [11]. The function of the manual is that of a reference book [12]. All necessary contents of a QMM are generally defined in ISO 9001:2008 [13].

The transparency, the ability that a third party can understand and comprehend the processes and procedures in an organization is a central point of each QMS. One can transfer this perspective on to the quality of research data. Information and data necessary for repeated testing are the minimum requirements considering the quality of research data. A viable solution would be to pass all input parameters that can be captured and measured with a plausible effort (in terms of efficiency). Every relevant input parameter, which has not been passed on, reduces the reproducibility of the research data and thus reduces the data quality. According to ISO 9001:2008 clause 4.2.3 Control of Documents and 4.2.4 Control of Records [13], procedural instructions can be used as in-house regulations for implementation of quality requirements for research data. They can be used to establish clear structures of information transmission [14] and thus support linkage of relevant research data documents.

4   Exemplary Application of QMM

In this section the case study with an exemplary application of the previously described QMM method is presented. First, the scope of the method application within the case is detailed before the specifications are elaborated briefly. Subsequently, an exemplary reference sheet illustrates the application in practice.

4.1   Scope of Method Application and Specification

The procedural instructions regulate certain cross-divisional process flows [14]. In the presented case, these are designed to ensure the processes of archiving and provision of materials science research data are based on clear criteria and contribute to quality assurance of the research data. An exemplary procedural instruction has been created, designed to support the documentation workflow of tensile tests for testing metallic materials (as illustrated in Figure 1).

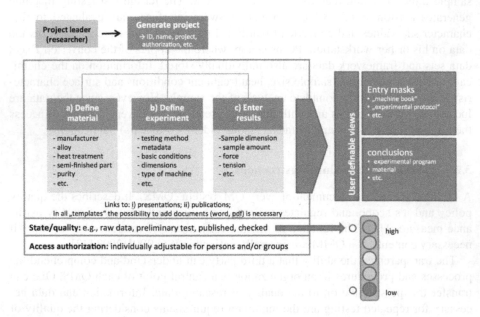

Fig. 1. Illustration of data model from user perspective

Research data management needs to include monitoring of the entire process of scientific work. This can be achieved through description of the necessary steps into the procedural instructions. Necessary for a completeness of a data set are (among many other factors) project description, the affected actors (e.g. researcher and technician), their tasks, and responsibilities along the process chain, material and experiment description. The in Figure 1 illustrated data model presents, as such, all the essential data required for a quality assured materials science data set. The researcher defines the framework of the experiment and the accompanying metadata. The technician performs the experiment, and forwards the results to the researcher. The traffic lights in Figure 1 indicate the 'completeness' of the data set and its quality.

The aim of procedural instructions in the QMM would be to define the scope and system boundaries of research data generation, as well as ensuring a link between all relevant input variables (e.g. sample size) and metadata (e.g. project number, material composition, heat treatment) necessary to recreate the test results, or at least to repeat critical processes. Following points of a procedural instruction could be determined and adapted [11; 14]: Objective of the instruction; Scope; Terminology; Description; References to documents; ID-Key; Responsibilities; Contact person for the process.

4.2   Exemplary Reference Sheet of a Procedural Instruction

Figure 2 (based on: [14; 15]) illustrates the structure of an exemplary reference sheet of a procedural instruction designed for documentation of the tensile testing of metallic materials. The top header of the pattern sheet contains general document information. The second header contains the version, the title of the instruction, and page numbers. The main area includes the previously identified elements of the instruction. The bottom line of the sheet contains information on the person responsible for the publication of the document, date of publication, information on the person who approved the document and the date of approval.

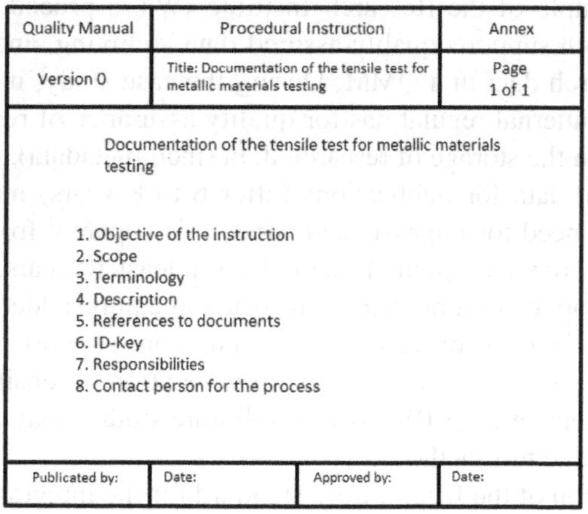

Quality Manual	Procedural Instruction	Annex
Version 0	Title: Documentation of the tensile test for metallic materials testing	Page 1 of 1

Documentation of the tensile test for metallic materials testing

1. Objective of the instruction
2. Scope
3. Terminology
4. Description
5. References to documents
6. ID-Key
7. Responsibilities
8. Contact person for the process

Publicated by:	Date:	Approved by:	Date:

Fig. 2. QM, procedural instruction reference sheet

5   Discussion and Limitations

Compliance with the above described exemplary procedural instruction can contribute to the quality assurance of the research data, as laid down by the DFG recommendations. A quality assurance representative would be responsible for the implementation of the procedural instructions into the documentation of the quality system, management and distribution among the affected employees. In terms of the continuous improvement of processes and workflows in the QMS, the procedural instructions should be continuously maintained and developed. This could be done by systematic routine internal auditing, according to the ISO 19011:2011 guidelines.

To ensure the success of the procedural instructions, it is essential that the affected employees recognize and use them regularly. Employee participation is indispensable and the basis of the continuous improvement process [16]. Therefore it is important to convey to the employees the positive effects of a complete documentation, the procedural instructions, and the benefits of process transparency on the quality of the research data [17]. By knowing where research data and documents can be found, unnecessary duplication of effort can be avoided and access to information is improved [18]. The procedural instructions and included regulations, should be checked regularly and developed simultaneously with the affected employees. It is necessary to always remain critical, while examining existing processes and workflows [17].

6   Conclusion and Outlook

Missing format requirements lead to inadequate description of the research data with metadata. This condition complicates the re-use of research data and thus reduces their quality. The quality of research data results from the ability to use the data under conditions different from the original scientific question. Only when this condition is reached in the documentation of the data, is the research data ready for sustainable use. Using the example of the Research Institute IWT a procedural instruction has been identified, which supports quality-assured data archiving, and -provision of materials science research data in a QMM. During the case study, it was found that the employees have no internal regulations for quality assurance of research data. Due to the inconsistencies in the storage of research data (incl. metadata), the retrievability of the original research data for publications (after 6 to 8 years) may be considerably hindered. There is a need for improvement, since it is apparent from the DFG recommendations that research data should be stored for at least 10 years.

The presented template of a procedural instruction can be added to the annex of an existing QMM and, in form of an in-house regulation, support it. The solution described here has been specially tailored to data generation of tensile testing in department of structural mechanics of IWT Bremen. Future studies may address the transfer to further processes and test methods.

The implementation of the Dublin Core standard for the integration of the metadata in the project documentation and a solution for potential national and free provision of research data, in terms of Open Access principles, would further benefit the documentation and quality of the research data. The creation of a documented process for updating the procedural instruction is another open issue. The procedural instructions should be maintained and further developed, within the terms of continuous improvement of processes and workflows of a QM system, e.g. through systematic routine internal auditing, according to the ISO 19011:2011 guidelines.

Acknowledgement. This work was funded by the "Deutsche Forschungsgemeinschaft" via the project "InfoSys". The authors would like to extend their gratitude to project partners and funding party for their generous support.

References

1. Enke, H., Fiedler, N., Fischer, T., Gnadt, T., Ketzan, E., Ludwig, J., Rathmann, T.: Leitfaden zum Forschungsdaten-Management, WissGrid Deliverable 2.3.1, Version 0.6, WissGrid (2011)
2. Winkler-Nees, S.: Der Umgang mit Forschungsdaten in Wissenschaft und Lehre. DFG, Bad Honnef (2010)
3. Neuroth, H., Oßwald, A., Scheffel, R., Strathmann, S.: nestor Handbuch: Eine kleine Enzyklopädie der digitalen Langzeitarchivierung, M. Jehn (Hrsg.). Verlag Werner Hülsbusch, Boizenburg (2009)
4. DFG: Vorschläge zur Sicherung guter wissenschaftlicher Praxis: Empfehlungen der Kommission 'Selbstkontrolle in der Wissenschaft, Deutsche Forschungsgemeinschaft, Weinheim, Wiley-VCH (1998)
5. DFG: Empfehlungen zur gesicherten Aufbewahrung und Bereitstellung digitaler Forschungsprimärdaten, Deutsche Forschungsgemeinschaft, Bonn (2009)
6. Acatech: Materialwissenschaft und Werkstofftechnik in Deutschland, Empfehlungen zur Profilierung, Lehre und Forschung, acatech – Deutsche Akademie der Technikwissenschaften, Fraunhofer IRB Verlag, Stuttgart (2008)
7. Severiens, T., Hilf, E.R.: nestor: Langzeitarchivierung von Rohdaten", nestor Materialien 6, nestor - Kompetenznetzwerk Langzeitarchivierung und Langzeitverfügbarkeit Digitaler Ressourcen für Deutschland (2006)
8. Spur, G., Stöferle, T.: Handbuch der Fertigungstechnik, Band 6 Fabrikbetrieb. Carl Hanser Verlag, München (1994)
9. Tan, K.C., Kannan, V.R., Handfield, R.B., Ghosh, S.: Quality, manufacturing strategy, and global competition: An empirical analysis. Benchmarking: An International Journal 7(3), 174–182 (2000)
10. Blumbergs, I., Kleinhofs, M., Chatys, R.: Experimental Research Data Series Quality Analysis, XIX Intl. Scientific-Technical Conference, pp. 96–98 (2011)
11. Linß, G.: Qualitätsmanagement für Ingenieure: mit Handbuch Qualitäts-management, 2. Auflage, Carl Hanser, München Wien (2005)
12. Rothery, B.: Der Leitfaden zu ISO 9000; mit QM-Musterhandbuch und Erläuterungen, Carl Hanser Verlag, München (1994)
13. DIN EN ISO 9001:2008: Quality management systems – Requirements (2008)
14. Schmidt, S.: Das QM-Handbuch: Qualitätsmanagement für die ambulante Pflege, 2. Auflage. Springer, Heidelberg (2010)
15. Glaap, W.: ISO 9000 leichtgemacht: Praktische Hinweise und Hilfen zur Entwicklung und Einführung von QS-Systemen. Carl Hanser, München (1993)
16. Torre, P.G., Adenso-Díaz, B., González, B.A.: Empirical evidence about managerial issues of ISO certification. The TQM Magazine 13(5), 355–360 (2001)
17. Petzoldt, J., Schorcht, H., Haaßengier, C.: "Qualitätsmanagement für Lehre und Forschung: Erfahrungen der Technischen Universität Ilmenau. Beiträge zur Hochschulforschung 30.1, 74–93 (2008)
18. Jones, S., Ball, A., Ekmekcioglu, C.: The Data Audit Framework: A First Step in Data Management Challenge. The International Journal of Digital Curation 3(2), 112–120 (2008)

Setting the International Logistics Strategy: Empirical Investigation of Its Evolutionary Stages

Gino Marchet, Marco Melacini, Sara Perotti, and Elena Tappia[*]

Department of Management, Economics and Industrial Engineering,
Politecnico di Milano, Milano, Italy
{gino.marchet,marco.melacini,sara.perotti,
elena.tappia}@polimi.it

Abstract. A company may face the international challenge by tackling several issues, such as international sales and marketing, international sourcing, and foreign direct investments (FDI). The academic literature firstly focused on the reasons behind company internationalisation and then adopted the above-mentioned issues related to the international challenge as perspectives in the investigation of the company internationalisation process. However, the literature review showed that the internationalisation process from a logistics perspective has not been fully investigated so far. Specifically, the relationship between company internationalisation choices and international logistics strategies has not adequately taken into account. This paper represents a first attempt to fill this gap by studying the relationship between the evolutionary stages of the company internationalisation and the key variables defining its international logistics strategy by providing empirical-based evidence.

Keywords: Sales Internationalisation, Logistics Strategy, Case Studies.

1   Introduction

A company may face the international challenge by tackling several issues such as international sales and marketing, international sourcing, and foreign direct investments (FDI). The academic literature firstly focused on the explanations of the reasons behind company internationalisation (e.g. [1]) and then used the above-mentioned issues related to the international challenge as the perspectives to study the company internationalisation process. Previous contributions widely agree that the growth in the international trade implies that supply chains become more international and complex ([2]) and that logistics play a key role in such context ([3,4]).

However, our analysis of the literature showed that the internationalisation process from a logistics perspective has not been fully investigated so far. Specifically, the relationship between company internationalisation choices (e.g. export via independent agents and creation of sales subsidiary) and international logistics strategies has not been in-depth examined. The different internationalisation choices

---

[*] Corresponding author.

B. Grabot et al. (Eds.): APMS 2014, Part I, IFIP AICT 438, pp. 50–58, 2014.

of a company have been widely studied in the literature (e.g. [5]), whereas the international logistics strategies have been examined by focusing only on specific topics, such as global supply chain planning centralisation (e.g. [6]), logistics strategies for entering new markets (e.g. [4]), and global supply strategies (e.g. [7]).

The above-mentioned issues represent a gap in the extant literature, as in company experience the international logistics strategy evolves and its evolution seems to be related to the stage in the company internationalisation process. This paper represents a first attempt to fill this gap by studying the relationship between the key variables defining the company international logistics strategies and internationalisation process by providing empirical-based evidence.

The remainder of the paper is organised as follows. The next section summarises the theoretical background. Afterwards, the research framework and methodology are reported, and findings are discussed. Finally, conclusions and limitations are drawn.

2   Literature Review

Coherently with the aim of this paper, the theoretical background is hereinafter discussed according to the two different issues involved, i.e. the company internationalisation process, and the company international logistics strategy.

2.1   Internationalisation Process

The entry modes into foreign markets can be classified into two main types, i.e. equity or non-equity. In the first case, the company acquires an existing local company or makes a green-field investment and has to decide whether partially or wholly own the local enterprise. In the second case, the company exports via agents and/or licensing. In the literature, the choice of the entry mode and the factors that impact on this decision has received a considerable attention and different theories have been developed to explain the reasons behind company internationalisation, such as the internalisation theory ([8]), the transaction cost theory ([1]), and the eclectic paradigm ([9]).

As far as the internationalisation process is concerned, the Uppsala model represents the most interesting contribution, especially considering the purpose of this study. Proposed by [5] and supported by several empirical studies (e.g. [10,11,12]), it is a behavioural and dynamic model that considers the internationalisation process as a sequence of incremental decisions. According to this model, all stages in the internationalisation process can be explained using the concepts of "State" and "Change" aspects. The "State Aspects" refer to the foreign market knowledge and commitment. The "Change Aspects" allowing to move along the stages of the internationalisation process lies in the commitment decisions that can strengthen the position in the foreign market and the learning from the experience of the current business activities. The Change and State Aspects affect each other, so that a stronger position in the market and better performance lead to a higher level of commitment and market knowledge. According to the Uppsala model and other contributions (e.g. [13]), four progressive stages can be selected by a company to sell products in foreign markets over time: no regular export activities, export via independent agents, creation of sales subsidiary, and production establishments.

2.2   International Logistics Strategy

The concept of "international logistics strategy" is widely used in the literature, but a detailed description of its related variables has not been developed so far. For the purpose of this study, we try to summarise as follows the main decisions involved in the definition of the company international logistics strategy that may be affected by the internationalisation choices.

The primary decision involved in the definition of the company international logistics strategies concerns the global supply chain network design that has a significant impact on the logistics performance (e.g. [14,15]). The design of the global supply chain networks refers to the number, location and capacities of warehouses and manufacturing plants, or the material flow through the logistics network (e.g. [16,17]).

Another key issue defining the international logistics strategy refers to the centralisation level in the global supply chain planning ([18]). Although planning is more critical to handle in case of inter-organisational supply chains, it represents a critical challenge also in internal supply chains ([19]). Moreover, it is particularly demanding for companies selling their products in different foreign markets when considering the planning of demand, inventory and transport ([18,20,21]). Previous contributions (e.g. [18]) also showed a strong correlation between the levels of internationalisation and centralisation of the supply chain planning process: the higher the internationalisation of production and procurement processes, the stronger the need for centralising the planning due to the increase of logistics complexity.

Also the planning of transport activities is part of the international logistics strategy and it is strictly connected with the company internationalisation choices, as they may be characterised by different pressures on lead times. The transport mode has been considered in numerous studies. For example, [22] and [23] considered three global transport service categories: airfreight, less than container load (LCL) shipping, and full container load (FCL) shipping. A more recent study by [17] evaluated different international logistics strategies mainly in terms of logistics network configuration and transport mode.

Finally, also the Incoterms (International Commercial Terms) contribute to describe the international logistics strategy, as they represent an indicator for the level of control on logistics flows. According to [24], a strategic advantage can be gained by a company willing to facilitate the sale of its products by assisting the importer in the shipment. Therefore, it can be assumed that the company interest in being involved in the shipment planning depends on the internationalisation choice.

3   Research Framework and Questions

The literature review showed that both the company internationalisation process and the related motivations have been widely studied. The stages along which a company may increase its international expansion can be considered well-defined, as well as the description of the dynamics for moving along the stages. At this regard, the Uppsala model seems to be the most consolidated. The key aspects explaining the evolution of the internationalisation process are the company commitment and learning over time, mostly related to the sales growth. Additionally, the evolution of the international logistics strategy, especially its relationship with the internationalisation process, has not been investigated so far. Specifically, there is no clear definition of the variables involved and, although a number of specific aspects have been addressed, they were studied separately from each other and independently from the internationalisation process. The literature review led us to develop the following research questions (also reported in Figure 1):

RQ1: *What are the main variables involved in the definition of the company international logistics strategy that are related to their internationalisation choices? How are they related to the internationalisation choices?*

RQ2: *Is there a model for describing the evolution of the company international logistics strategy during the internationalisation process? Is the volume of the international sales the key variable of such model?*

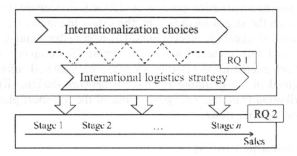

Fig. 1. Research framework

4   Methodology

In order to empirically investigate the designed research framework, the development of a series of case studies was considered as the most suitable methodology. In fact, the objective of the present research is to in-depth investigate *how* the variables involved in the definition of the international logistics strategy are affected by the company internationalisation choices ([25]). The companies included in the sample are big national or multi-national companies with plants concentrated in Europe. Additionally they export their finished goods in countries belonging to other continents with a make-to-stock production system. A deeper overview of the sample features is provided in Table 1. In line with the aim of the paper, the units of the analysis are represented by the single export areas of a company, so that multiple case studies were performed. Additionally, we used retrospective multiple case studies to collect longitudinal data on the evolution of the international logistics strategy during the different internationalisation stages that companies have experienced. Case studies were performed through semi-structured interviews with Logistics and Supply Chain Directors. General information about the company and the context in which it operates were also collected using secondary sources.

Table 1. Summary of the characteristics of the four companies of the sample

Company	Business sector	Annual group sales	Value to weight ratio	Unit of analysis
A	Baby, health & beauty care	1.5 billion €	Medium	A1: South America A2: Asia-Pacific area A3: Russia
B	Porcelain stoneware	0.5 billion €	Low-medium	B1: North America B2: Israele
C	Medical technology	1.1 billion €	Medium	C1: Asia-Pacific area C2: Russia
D	Sanitary technology	1.8 billion €	Low-medium	D1: Pacific area D2: South America

As far as the internationalisation process evolution is concerned, we defined three levels, based also on the stages identified by the extant literature: (i) early stage, i.e. export via independent agents or distributors, (ii) intermediate stage, i.e. export via sales subsidiary, and (iii) advanced stage, i.e. export via company own stores. To assess the company international logistics strategy, we gathered information on the variables highlighted in the literature review: (i) network design, (ii) centralisation level in the distribution planning, (iii) governance of the transport planning, and (iv) level of control on logistics flows.

5   Discussion and Findings

5.1   Variables Defining the Company International Logistics Strategy

Network Design. All companies have confirmed that the decisions on the supply chain network design are much related to the internationalisation choices. According to the information collected through the case studies, the types of decisions mainly refer to the selection among direct shipment, 1-echelon networks and 2-echelon networks. In fact, a company can sell its products without having local distribution centres (as in the B2 case in which there are monthly shipments to distributors) or, on the contrary, it can be decided whether it is necessary to have stocks near its point of sales based for instance on the lead-time constraints (as in the C1 case). The adoption of a 2-echelon network has been observed in case of logistics networks delivering products in different countries of the same continental area (as in the A1 case).

Centralisation Level in the Distribution Planning. In line with the extant literature, the level of distribution planning centralisation is a key aspect to manage when defining the logistics strategy of global supply chains. The following aspects are those mainly involved in such process with reference to each export area: sale forecasts, inventory management, service level to the customers, and transport planning.

The distribution planning can be decentralised (as in the B1 case), i.e. only some decisions made by the subsidiaries are shared with the headquarter (e.g. the maximum stock levels and service levels that have to be provided by the logistics service providers), or centralised (as in the A1 case), i.e. the subsidiaries are not autonomous. Besides, as for example in the company C case, the distribution planning can be coordinated, i.e. the company develops the sale forecasts together with the independent agents but is not involved in managing the logistics process as it does not have an own network in the export area.

Governance of the Transport Planning. In line with the literature, the transport planning is a variable of the international logistics strategy and the related decision process varies according to the company internationalisation choices. When a company exports via independent agents, the governance of the transport planning is "low" as the transport organisation depends only on the lead times and order quantities required by the customers (e.g. in the D2 case). Instead, when a company exports via sales subsidiary and its logistics network is more complex (e.g. a local warehouse delivers goods to the sales subsidiary), the governance of the transport planning is "high" (e.g. in the C1 case). In this case, the company has to manage the delivery of goods to the warehouse and has the possibility to optimise the transport activity (e.g. use of sea instead of air freight or use of FCL service).

Level of Control on Logistics Flows. According to the information collected through case studies, the Incoterms can be viewed as an indicator of the level of company control on the logistics and transport process to the foreign market and strictly related with the internationalisation choices, although quite disregarded by past literature on the logistics process in global supply chains. The case study analysis shows that companies exporting via independent agents (e.g. D2 case) or subsidiaries (e.g. C1 case) select Incoterms E and F. In fact, in this case the company sells its products to the agents and it not interested in managing the transport and logistics process. Instead, a company that a company selling its products via company own stores manages the distribution process and uses Incoterms C and D (e.g. A1 case).

Three international logistics strategies have been identified based on the values assumed by each variable and the correlation among them (Table 2): (i) International sale, (ii) International outpost, and (iii) International network.

Table 2. International logistics strategies from the case studies

		International logistics strategies		
		International sale	International outpost	International network
Dimension of the international logistics strategy	Network design	Not significant	1-echelon network	2-echelon network
	Centralisation level in the distribution planning	Coordinated	Decentralised	Centralised
	Governance of the transport planning	Not significant	Medium	High
	Level of control on logistics flows	Low	Medium	High

5.2   Evolution of the Company International Logistics Strategy during the Internationalisation Process

The case study analysis provides evidence supporting the relationship between the company international logistics strategy and its internationalisation choices. As shown in Table 3, the *International sale* strategy is more likely to be selected by companies in the early stage of the internationalisation process evolution, the *International outpost* by companies in the intermediate stage, and the *International network* by companies in the advanced stage. Additionally, for a given export area the evolution of the international logistics strategy incrementally evolves together with the internationalisation process as the sales and the learning in the foreign market growth.

Table 3. Alignment between internationalisation process and international logistics strategies

International logistics strategies	International network	A1		
	International outpost	A1; A2; A3; B1; C1; D2		
	International sale	A2; A3; B1; B2; C1; C2; D1; D2		
		Early stage	Intermediate stage	Advanced stage
		Internationalisation process stages		

When a company is in the early stage of the internationalisation process, its export volume is typically low as well as its market knowledge. As a consequence, it operates in a foreign market with a low level of control on the logistics and transport process, which is a key feature of the *International sale* strategy. According to the case study analysis, at this stage, the choice of exporting via independent agents (as in the D2 case) or distributors (as in the D1 case) allows the company to not have own resources, and therefore sunk costs, that are implied instead when it has subsidiaries or store networks. Additionally, the benefits related to have no local warehouses and to overcome complexities (e.g. to face the local regulations and to collaborate with local logistics providers) have been cited by companies of the sample as other benefits of selecting the *International sale* strategy in the early stage of the internationalisation process. Such approach for entering a new market has been adopted in all cases except for the A1 case in which the company opened a subsidiary when starting to sell its products in the new market.

Looking at the sample, companies A, B and C developed their logistics strategy from the *International sale* to the *International outpost* when they started to export via sales subsidiary (i.e. the intermediate stage of their internationalisation process) in South America, North America and Asia-Pacific, respectively. They report the increasing in sales and market experience as enabling factors to develop the second stage of the internationalisation process and the international logistics strategy. The transition to this second stage can occur through the acquisition of the local distributor by the company (as in the A3 case). At this stage, the companies let the subsidiaries work autonomously in developing the sale forecasts, defining the order quantities (i.e. decentralised planning), and also managing the transport and logistics process (i.e. adoption of Incoterms E or F). The local logistics network is composed of one distribution centre (i.e. 1-echelon network) that receives FCLs.

In the examined sample, no companies have already developed the *International network* strategy. Only company A is evaluating the adoption of such approach in South America where the advanced stage of the internationalisation process has been reached by selling its products via own stores. It intends to build a 2-echelon logistics network composed of a central distribution centre for the entire export area and other regional depots in each country belonging to the area. This approach seems to imply a more centralised planning and control on the transport process.

It should be noted that a company has not necessarily to go through all the stages. For instance, a company can directly go to the intermediate stage by adopting the *International outpost* as logistics strategy without exporting via independent agents or distributors before this settlement (as in the A1 case).

6   Conclusion

This paper explores the relationship between company international logistics strategy and its internationalisation process through case study methodology. Findings suggest that companies progressively develop their international logistics strategy based on the stage of their internationalisation process. Three international logistics strategies have been identified, that diverge in terms of network design, level of centralisation in the distribution planning, governance of the transport planning, and level of control on logistics flows. The *International sale* strategy is more likely to be chosen by companies in the early stage, the *International outpost* by those in the intermediate stage, whereas the *International network* by those in the advanced stage. Although interesting, the conclusions drawn require further effort to be more generalised. Other case studies are recommended with the aim of i) verifying whether the variables considered are comprehensive and consistent, and ii) further exploring the variables driving the evolution of the logistics strategy. Finally, additional effort should be devoted to the development of a normative model supporting companies in aligning the international logistics strategy with their plans in term of internationalisation.

References

1. Hennart, J.-F.: A Theory of Multinational Enterprise. University of Michigan Press, Ann Arbor (1982)
2. Monczka, M., Trent, J.: Achieving Excellence in Global Sourcing. Sloan Manage Rev. 47(1), 24–32 (2006)
3. Peterson, K.J., Frayer, D.J., Scannel, T.V.: An Empirical Investigation of Global Sourcing Strategy Effectiveness. J of Supply Chain Manage 36(2), 29–38 (2000)
4. Straube, F., Ma, S., Bohn, M.: Internationalisation of Logistics Systems – How Chinese and German Companies Enter New Markets. Springer, Heidelberg (2008)

5. Johanson, J., Vahlne, J.E.: The Internationalisation Process of the Company – A Model of Knowledge Development and Increasing Foreign Market Commitments. J. Int. Business Stud. 8(1), 305–322 (1977)

6. Jonsson, P., Rudberg, M., Holmberg, S.: Centralised Supply Chain Planning at IKEA. Supply Chain Manage Int. J. 18(3), 337–350 (2013)

7. Loppacher, J.S., Cagliano, R., Spina, G.: Key Factors in Global Supply Headquarters-subsidiary Control Systems. J. Manuf. Technol. Manage. 21(7), 794–817 (2010)

8. Buckley, P.J., Casson, M.: The Future of the Multinational Enterprise. Holmes & Meier, New York (1976)

9. Dunning, J.H.: Toward an Eclectic Theory of International Production: Some Empirical Tests. J. Int. Business Stud. 11(1), 9–31 (1980)

10. Barkema, H.G., Bell, H.J., Pennings, J.M.: Foreign Entry, Cultural Barriers, and Learning. Strategic Manage J. 17(2), 151–166 (1996)

11. Bello, D.C., Barksdale, H.C.: Exporting at Industrial Trade Shows. Ind. Market Manag 15(3), 197–206 (1986)

12. Luo, Y., Peng, M.: Learning to Compete in a Transition Economy: Experience, Environment and Performance. J. Int. Business Stud. 30(2), 269–295 (1999)

13. Johanson, J., Wiedersheim-Paul, F.: The Internationalization of the Company: Four Swedish Cases. J. Man. Studies 12(3), 305–322 (1975)

14. Sezen, B.: Relative Effect of Design, Integration and Information Sharing on Supply Chain Performance. Supply Chain Manage. Int. J. 13(3), 233–240 (2008)

15. Pero, M., Rossi, T., Noé, C., Sianesi, A.: An Exploratory Study of the Relation Between Supply Chain Topological Features and Supply Chain Performance. Int. J. Prod. Econ. 123(2), 266–278 (2010)

16. Chopra, S., Meindl, P.: Supply Chain Management: Strategy, Planning and Operations. Prentice Hall, Upper Saddle River (2004)

17. Creazza, A., Dallari, F., Melacini, M.: Evaluating Logistics Network Configurations for a Global Supply Chain. Supply Chain Manage Int. J. 15(2), 154–164 (2010)

18. Melacini, M., Creazza, A., Perotti, S.: Analysis of Supply Chain Planning Centralisation for Multinational Companies. Int. J. Logistics Systems Manage 9(4), 478–500 (2011)

19. Forget, P., D'Amours, S., Frayret, J.M.: Multi-behavior Agent Model for Planning in Supply Chains: An Application to the Lumber Industry. Robot Cim-Int. Manuf. 24(5), 664–679 (2008)

20. Pirttila, T., Niemi, P.: Generic Organizational Choices for Logistics in Decentralized Organizations: Implications for inventory management. Int. J. Prod. Econ. 45(3), 195–202 (1996)

21. Rudberg, M., West, B.M.: Global Operations Strategy: Coordinating Manufacturing Networks. Omega: Int. J. Manag. Sci. 36(1), 91–106 (2008)

22. Zeng, Z.: Global Sourcing: Process and Design for Efficient Management. Supply Chain Manage Int. J. 8(4), 367–379 (2003)

23. Colicchia, C., Dallari, F., Melacini, M.: Increasing supply chain resilience in a global sourcing context. Prod Plan Control 21(7), 680–694 (2010)

24. David, P.A., Stewart, R.D.: International Logistics: the Management of International Trade Operations. Cengage Learning (2010)

25. Eisenhardt, K.M.: Building Theories from Case Study Research. Acad. Manage Rev. 14(4), 532–550 (1989)

Exploitation of a Semantic Platform
to Store and Reuse PLM Knowledge

Giulia Bruno[1], Dario Antonelli[1], Roman Korf[2],
Joachim Lentes[3], and Nikolas Zimmermann[4]

[1] Politecnico di Torino, Corso Duca degli Abruzzi 24, 10129 Torino, Italy
[2] USU Software AG, Karlstrasse 52, 76137 Karlsruhe, Germany
[3] Fraunhofer Institute for Industrial Engineering IAO, Nobelstr. 12, Stuttgart, Germany
[4] University of Stuttgart IAT, Nobelstr. 12, Stuttgart, Germany

Abstract. Products generate a large amount of information during their life-cycles. Small and medium enterprises are often not structured enough to enable the efficient management of such amount of information. Several tools of product lifecycle management have been developed in the last years to address this issue, but they are rarely exploited by companies, especially SMEs. The aim of our work is to present a semantic platform to integrate data along the whole product lifecycle to allow semantic search and knowledge reuse. The integration of data is realized with a reference PLM ontology, containing the main concepts and relations to describe a PLM. This ontology has a modular structure, so that it can be easily extended to describe concrete product lifecycles. An example of a real application of the semantic platform in an industrial case is reported.

Keywords: PLM, knowledge management, semantic model, ontology, UML.

1   Introduction

The process from the idea for a new product over its development and production to the market is typically fragmented across different functional units, but requires input and activities from experts from a variety of disciplines using different methods and tools. This leads to a high coordination effort to synergize work and information transfer, to sub-optimal decisions, and unused knowledge as well as experiences. The resulting waste in engineering processes results in an unnecessary extension of time-to-market and time-to-production of new products and to a loss of competitiveness of companies. To tackle the resulting challenges for engineering in manufacturing companies, the amePLM (advanced platform for manufacturing engineering and PLM) project is based on an ontology that serves as an interoperable model and integrating element for an open engineering system. Furthermore, the usage of an ontology-based approach advances the information provision in activities during product creation.

An essential advantage of the application of ontologies in product development is knowledge sharing. Bradfield and Gao determined three main problem categories for knowledge sharing in the new product development (NPD) process of a manufacturing

B. Grabot et al. (Eds.): APMS 2014, Part I, IFIP AICT 438, pp. 59–66, 2014.

company: inappropriate information about the knowledge in the NPD process, multi-lingualism as well as multidisciplinary, and insufficient information provision to users [1]. By means of an ontology-based approach, knowledge sharing in NPD may be facilitated. Lutters et al. work to apply information management based on an ontological approach on design and engineering processes under special consideration of manufacturing, i.e. process planning and cost estimation [2]. Young et al. showed the benefits of applying ontologies to support knowledge sharing in PLM with a focus on manufacturing processes [3]. By using a product ontology as pivotal element, Panetto et al introduced an approach to support interoperability in Product Data Management (PDM) [4]. Matsokis and Kiritsis developed an ontology of concepts and rules to support PLM, emphasizing the product and its role in closed-loop PLM [5]. Raza et al. tested an approach building up on existing work by usage of ontologies for knowledge management [6]. Furthermore the ongoing work of Fiorentini et al. using ontologies to model the engineering data of nuclear power plants to leverage interoperability with external information systems shows the potential of an ontological approach [7]. So, the principal applicability of ontology-based approaches to PLM as in the platform amePLM (cf. [8]) has been shown, but there still is a potential for improvement in automated information provision in PLM to reduce manual efforts for information management and retrieval.

The rest of the paper is organized as follows. Section 2 describes the semantic platform for PLM knowledge structuring and reusing, while Section 3 reports the structure of the PLM ontology at the basis of the platform. Section 4 shows how the developed semantic platform can be used for semantic search and information reuse. Finally, Section 5 draws conclusions and states future works.

2   Advanced Platform for Manufacturing Engineering and PLM

The architecture of the amePLM platform is shown in Fig. 1. It functions as a middleware by allowing the integration of information as well as it provides interfaces for several engineering modules and applications.

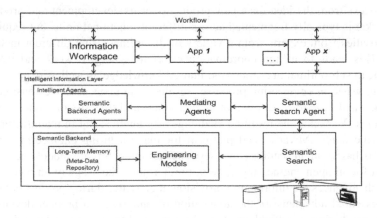

Fig. 1. Architecture of the semantic platform

The platform is based on the semantic web framework Apache Jena [9]. The technology decision for Apache Jena is based on an original review of semantic web technology [10]. It is open source, provides a wide range of APIs to manipulate and reason with RDF and OWL ontologies and allows querying and manipulating ontologies using SPARQL 1.1 [11].

Based on the engineering models (i.e., the PLM ontology, cf. section 3), the knowledge is structured and concrete relationships between knowledge artifacts within the PLC are established. The semantic search provides access to arbitrary information sources of the PLC like databases, document management systems, CAx systems and documents on file systems. The knowledge is indexed based on the PLM ontology which directly integrates indexed knowledge artifacts into the knowledge base. An intelligent agent layer allows applications and other engineering modules to access knowledge using a single access point. The workflow orchestrates the services and knowledge access along the PLC. An example to illustrate the interaction of graphical user interface (GUI), i.e. the 3D-workspace, the working memory, the agent-based platform and the semantic backend is provided in Fig. 2.

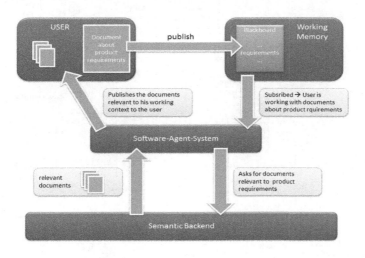

Fig. 2. Context-based user support

In the simplified example, the user is working in a document concerning requirements of a specific product (e.g. with id "4711"). The related user input and the name of the document as well as the used software module are published to the blackboard of the working memory. By reasoning, the memory can determine that the user's current work is concerned with product requirements of product 4711. This finding enables the consequence to support the user with related information. So, a related request is sent to the semantic backend that in turn delivers information about product requirements and about product 4711 (if available). The information or documents provided by the backend to the respective software agent can then be supplied to the user, preferably in a non-obtrusive manner, e.g. in a background window of his virtual working desktop.

3   PLM Ontology

The PLM ontology at the basis of the semantic platform is shown in Figure 2, according to the UML class diagram formalism.

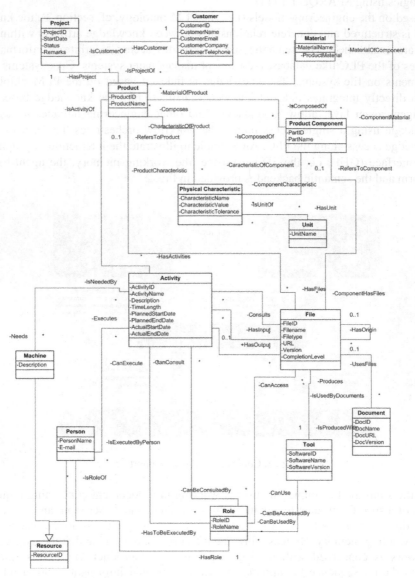

Fig. 3. UML class diagram of the PLM ontology

The three core concepts are the product (i.e., whatever it is produced by a company which serves a need or satisfies a want), the activity (i.e., an action executed during the product lifecycle for a specific product that can be univocally be identified), and the file (i.e., an electronic information stored as a single object in the file system). A product is associated with all the activities of its lifecycle and with all the files containing information about it. There are several kinds of associations between an activity and a file, due to the different kind of usage of the file done by the activity. An activity can (i) consult a file, if it is simply read, (ii) have a file as input, if it is used and modified by the activity, and (iii) produce a new file as output.

The product class is linked to the project class because a product is developed during a project. The project class is associated with the customer class to store the involvements of customers in projects. A product is also associated to the product component class, because each product can be made of several components. Both the product and the product component are associated to the material class and to the physical characteristic class, to store their material and their characteristics of interest.

To keep trace of the people involved in the activities, the person class, which is a specialization of the resource class, is represented, which includes personal data and contacts. The other specialization of the resource class is the machine class, which represents the machines used in each activity. To each person is also assigned a role. For each activity, it is known the roles that have to execute it and the roles that are allowed to consult it. For each file the software tool exploited to produce it and the roles that can access it are known. Files or groups of files can be used to create documents. Additional information on the PLM ontology can be found in [12,13].

4   Knowledge Exploring by Using the Semantic Platform

The following section describes the access of knowledge within the semantic platform along the product lifecycle (PLC). In this example the PLC starts with a customer request for quotation where a customer specifies the requirements on the product enquiry. The responsible needs to get an overview on the details of capabilities of the company based on past projects with similar requirements to assess the feasibility.

A RFQ will result in creating a new customer project for the product 4711. The SPARLQ update statement for the RFQ populating the PLM ontology is the following:

```
PREFIX amePLM: <http://www.amePLM.org/PLM#>
PREFIX p4711: <http://www.my-company.com/amePLM/4711#>
PREFIX rdf: <http://www.w3.org/1999/02/22-rdf-syntax-ns#>
INSERT {
     # Creating/retrieving the customer instance
     p4711:thisCustomer rdf:type amePLM:Customer.

     # Creating the new product instance for product 4711
     p4711:Product4711 rdf:type amePLM:Product.

     # Creating a new project instance
     p4711:thisProject rdf:type amePLM:Project;
```

```
# Linking project instance with customer
amePLM:HasCustomer p4711:thisCustomer;

# Linking product and project
amePLM:isProjectOf p4711:Product4711.

# Adding some product characteristics coming from the RFQ form
# Characteristics are product dependent.
# Here we use the example length.
p4711:thisPhysicalCharacteristicLen rdf:type amePLM:Length.

# Creating unit for length; could also be retrieved by variable
p4711:thisMMUnit rdf:type amePLM:Unit.

# Creating instance for length 100
p4711:thisLenValue rdf:type amePLM:Value;
        amePLM:value 100.

# Setting the value
p4711:thisPhysicalCharacteristicLen
        amePLM:HasUnit p4711:thisMMUnit;
        amePLM:CharacteristicValue p4711:thisLenValue;

# Setting the characteristic for the product
p4711:Product4711 amePLM:ProductCharacteristic
        p4711:thisPhysicalCharacteristicLen.          }
```

Integrating the information into the knowledge structure now allows us to asses this information and to compare it with requirements of previous projects. For the comparison we currently use a naïve approach by comparing the RFQ features of the current enquiry with the once of previous projects.

```
PREFIX amePLM: <http://www.amePLM.org/PLM#>
PREFIX rdf: <http://www.w3.org/1999/02/22-rdf-syntax-ns#>
PREFIX xsd: <http://www.w3.org/2001/XMLSchema#>
SELECT *
WHERE {
    # Find any project...
    ?project rdf:type amePLM:Project.

    # ...of products...
    ?project amePLM:IsProjectOf ?product .

    # ...with length...
    ?length rdf:type amePLM:Length.
```

```
?product amePLM:ProductCharacteristic ?length.

# ...of characteristic value...
?valueInst rdf:type amePLM:Value.
?valueInst amePLM:value ?value.

# ... with average deviation of 10%...
# Here we put in the concrete value 100 to reduce query length.
# Usually an agent would query the value of the current project
# 4711 and use it for the query to retrieve similar projects.
Filter (xsd:integer(?length) > 100*0.9)
Filter (xsd:integer(?length) < 100*1.1)                    }
```

Once the similar projects have been collected, their information gathered along the PLC is to be assessed. The following simplified query retrieves the documents containing information about a previous project with product 4710:

```
PREFIX amePLM: <http://www.amePLM.org/PLM#>
PREFIX rdf: <http://www.w3.org/1999/02/22-rdf-syntax-ns#>
SELECT *
WHERE {
    # Find any project...
    ?project rdf:type amePLM:Project;
            # ...of products...
            amePLM:IsProjectOf p4710:Product4710 .

    # ...with product files...
    p4710:Product4710 amePLM:HasFile ?file.

    # ...and some details if they exist in the knowledge base.
    OPTIONAL {?file amePLM:Filename ?fileName.}
    OPTIONAL {?file amePLM:Filetype ?fileType.}
    OPTIONAL {?file amePLM:URL ?fileURL.}                    }
```

This short set of over-simplified queries has the purpose of giving a brief overview on how the amePLM approach explores knowledge stored in the amePLM platform and how to apply simple heuristics using software agents.

5   Conclusions

In this paper we have described a semantic platform to structure the PLC knowledge of companies. The current version of this platform has been successfully applied in an industrial use-case and proven to be a feasible approach. It provides basic functionality necessary to support information needs within the PLC and it already integrates workflow, information workspace and other engineering modules with the information layer. However, it still needs improvements for extensibility and adoptability. One of the improvements will be the simplification of the integration of engineering modules (e.g. applications for CAx or simulation) and knowledge sources (e.g. product data management, customer feedback or failure statistics). Future works will also consider the integration of a semantic search engine into the platform.

Acknowledgments. The research presented in this paper is supported by the EU-FP7 research project on Advanced Platform for Manufacturing Engineering and Product Lifecycle Management (amePLM, contract number 285171).

References

1. Bradfield, D.J., Gao, J.X.: A methodology to facilitate knowledge sharing in the new product development process. International Journal of Production Research 45, 1489–1504 (2007)
2. Lutters, E., Brinke, E.T., Streppel, T., Kals, H.: Information management and design & engineering processes. International Journal of Production Research 38, 4429–4444 (2000)
3. Young, R.I.M., Gunendran, A.G., Cutting-Decelle, A.F., Gruninger, M.: Manufacturing knowledge sharing in PLM: a progression towards the use of heavy weight ontologies. International Journal of Production Research 45, 1505–1519 (2007)
4. Panetto, H., Dassisti, M., Tursi, A.: ONTO-PDM: Product-driven ONTOlogy for Product Data Management interoperability within manufacturing process environment. Journal Advanced Engineering Informatics 26, 334–348 (2012)
5. Matsokis, A., Kiritsis, D.: An ontology-based approach for Product Lifecycle Management. Computers in Industry 61, 787–797 (2010)
6. Raza, M.B., Kirkham, T., Harrison, R., Reul, Q.: Improving Manufacturing Efficiency at Ford Using Product Centred Knowledge, Digital Information Management. In: ICDIM 2009(2009)
7. Fiorentini, X., Paviot, T., Fortineau, V., Goblet, J.-L., Lamouri, S.: Modeling nuclear power plants engineering data using ISO 15926. In: Proceedings of 2013 Industrial Engineering and Systems Management, IESM (2013)
8. Lentes, J., Eckstein, H., Zimmermann, N.: A platform for information and decision support in engineering. In: 22nd International Conference on Production Research (2013)
9. https://jena.apache.org/
10. Fielding, R.T., Taylor, R.N.: Principled Design of the Modern Web Architecture. ACM Transactions on Internet Technology 2, 115–150 (2002)
11. http://www.w3.org/TR/sparql11-query/
12. Antonelli, D., Bruno, G., Schwichtenberg, A., Villa, A.: Full exploitation of Product Lifecycle Management by integrating static and dynamic viewpoints. In: IFIP Advances in Information and Communication Technology, vol. 398 (part 2), pp. 176–183 (2013)
13. Bruno, G., Villa, A.: The exploitation of an ontology-based model of PLM from a SME point of view. In: IFAC Proceedings Volumes (IFAC-PapersOnline), pp. 1447–1452 (2013)

Detect and Correct Abnormal Values in Uncertain Environment: Application to Demand Forecast

Éric Villeneuve, Cédrick Béler, and Laurent Geneste

Laboratoire Génie de Production (LGP), INPT-ENIT,
Université de Toulouse, Tarbes, France

Abstract This article presents the first results of a study which deals with the detection and the correction of abnormal values in data series intended to forecast demand. This work fits in the broader context of performance management for proximity retailers. Indeed, when this kind of point of sales (POS) is studied, sales volumes are often too small to be effectively exploited by statistical processing methods. It is therefore useful to consolidate the information with expertise and additional knowledge resulting from similar POS. It is also relevant to take into account the inherent uncertainty of such information. The proposal of this paper is a methodological contribution which uses consolidated knowledge to detect and correct abnormal values and to improve the quality of data used to implement forecast methods.

Keywords: Possibility theory, Combination rules, Similarity measures, Forecast.

1 Context of the Study

The sector of proximity retail of so-called "high tech" products is currently undergoing a major transformation. Indeed, the increasing competition with online sales and supermarkets offers a significant challenge for the retailers. French telecommunications vendors are a good example of these changes. The introduction on the French market of a new stakeholder with a very aggressive marketing policy based mainly on online sales pushed long-established operators to revise their offers. These operators have responded by shifting their activity to online sale and therefore have increased the pressure on retailers which were previously their privileged partners. The main consequence of this market changes for retailers is a significant decrease in their incomes. The need for better demand forecasting is essential to ensure the survival of their points of sales (POS).

1.1 Demand Forecast

Conventional forecast methods [1,2] produce suitable results but improving the forecast accuracy is a difficult challenge. To achieve this goal, it is necessary

B. Grabot et al. (Eds.): APMS 2014, Part I, IFIP AICT 438, pp. 67–75, 2014.

to take account of many parameters, such as competition, commercial and hazard management or POS typology. In addition, for retailers who want control more precisely their activity (sale forecast of a particular product by a particular seller or in a particular POS), the amount of available data is often insufficient to obtain reliable statistics. This work is a follow-up of previous studies that have begun to offer a forecast methodology adapted to these activities when the amount of data is insufficient [3]. The proposed methodology is based on similarity measures and human expertise to consolidate data and compensate them for the lack of statistical data. The goal is to use data from other POS to inject knowledge into the model. This knowledge must be corrected to take account of the differences between POS. The correction can be done by considering similarity measures used to compare POS contexts according to criteria defined by experts. Subsequently, this consolidated knowledge allow to build a complete solution for decision support system designed to control POS commercial activity.

1.2 Abnormal Values

One of the challenges of this work lies in the selection and the formatting of the data used to produce a forecast. The main difficulty to format the data concerns the correction of abnormal values that affect the quality of the forecast. These abnormal values are the result of exceptional events (whether they have positive or negative outcomes) that disrupt the traditional sale process of a POS. For example, the release of a product which was long-awaited by the public will cause a temporary increase of sales for a given period that will not be repeated on a regular basis. This increase can disrupt all the future forecasts. It is therefore necessary to identify and correct these abnormal values to obtain better forecasts.

The method studied here aims to automate the detection and the correction of abnormal values. To achieve this goal, several time series are available. They represent the sales of different POS of a retailer. Each time series is characterized by its context which is used to compare the studied series to the results of other POS using a similarity measure. Then, each new value of the series is tested to identify abnormal value. Finally, abnormal values are corrected using similar time series adapted to the context of the studied series. To avoid expert overload, the expert is only engaged in the description of the context of each point of sale and in the choice of indicators used to forecast demand. This article focuses only on the mechanisms related to formalize knowledge from multiple POS and to merge this knowledge to detect and correct abnormal values.

1.3 Issues Addressed

The study of mechanisms to detect and correct abnormal values in a time series generates several issues:

(a) How to formalize the time series to deal with the lack of data?
(b) How to take into account contextual differences between data series, i.e. the similarity level between the studied series and other series in the model?

(c) How to merge information of different POS time series?

(d) How to identify abnormal values according to resulting merged information?

(e) How to correct abnormal values by taking into account the information from different POS and similarity measures between contexts?

This article will therefore seek to answer these issues. The next part will detail the proposal. Then, the methodology will be illustrated on a case study and the results will be discussed. Finally, a conclusion with prospects will be presented.

2 Proposal

The methodology developed to address the issues mentioned above, consists in a five steps process described in figure 1.

Fig. 1. The proposed methodology

The first two steps of this process are not detailed in this article where the choice was made to focuses on the last three steps. The first step aims at formatting the data to be able to compare information sources. The second step enables to compare the contexts of each source to obtain similarity measures [4] to be used as confidence indicators during the combination step.

2.1 Knowledge Formalization

The main problem identified for knowledge formalization lies in taking into account the uncertainty related to the lack of data. The choice was made to use possibility theory to address this issue. This section introduces the formalism and how it was used to meet identified requirements.

Possibility Theory: The problem of incompleteness of information (lack of data) is widely discussed in the literature related to the more general notion of imperfect information. According to [5], incompleteness is an aspect of knowledge uncertainty. Uncertainty is defined as the fact that the information source is unable to distinguish the veracity of an information. It therefore measures a degree of conformity of information to reality. It is possible to distinguish two kinds of uncertainty. The random uncertainty is induced by the variability of an entity in a population and is the result of random experiments. The epistemic uncertainty is due to lack of knowledge and therefore is related to the notion of incompleteness. Taking into account incompleteness requires the use of a representation formalism taking into account the epistemic uncertainty. Probability theory is the most widespread representation formalism of uncertainty but it does not allow to unambiguously represent the epistemic nature of the information [6]. Therefore, possibility theory was chosen. By extending the fuzzy set theory [7], Zadeh [8] and Dubois and Prade [9] introduced the possibility theory to represent imprecise but also uncertain knowledge. In this theory, from a possibility distribution, $\pi(A)$, it is possible to construct the possibility(Π) and the necessity (N) measures thanks to the following relations:

$$N(A) = 1 - \max_{x \notin A} \pi(x) \text{ and } \Pi(A) = \max_{x \in A} \pi(x) \tag{1}$$

$$\max \pi(x) = 1 \tag{2}$$

It is therefore possible to characterize the uncertainty of an event, not with a value as in the context of probability theory, but with two values representing the possibility and necessity of the event. Figure 2a illustrates the principle of this theory to represent the information "*I am sure that the parameter is in [1, 5] (Support), but the values of [2, 3] (Kernel) seem the most likely*".

Building of Possibility Distributions: The objective is to associate possibility distribution for each value representing the studied period. For example, to detect or correct an abnormal value related to the first quarter of the current year, a possibility distribution is created for each value representing the first quarter of the past years stored in the data history of the studied source but also for all the other information sources.

To build a possibility distribution, the confidence interval of the data set which contains the values corresponding to the studied period in previous years for each information source is calculated. The confidence interval, CI_i, for each source, i, of the data series which contains the values of n last years, $X_i = \{x_{i1}, x_{i2}, \ldots, x_{in}\}$, with a confidence level, $1 - \alpha$, can be determined by the following formula [10]:

$$CI_i = \left[\overline{x_i} - t_{1-\frac{\alpha}{2}}(n-1) \times \frac{\sigma(X_i)}{\sqrt{n}}, \ \overline{x_i} + t_{1-\frac{\alpha}{2}}(n-1) \times \frac{\sigma(X_i)}{\sqrt{n}} \right] \tag{3}$$

with $\overline{x_i}$, the mean of the values of X_i, $t_{1-\frac{\alpha}{2}}(n-1)$, the fractile of the Student law at the level $1 - \frac{\alpha}{2}$ with $n-1$ freedom degrees, and $\sigma(X_i)$, the standard deviation of the sample.

Then a triangular possibility distribution is associated for each data series value by selecting as support, the confidence interval of the source, and as kernel, the concerned value (Figure 2b). The result is composed of n distributions by source.

2.2 Knowledge Combination

After the knowledge formalization step, it is necessary to combine different sources to obtain a global information gathering all the available knowledge. Two levels of fusion should be made. The first level concerns the fusion of all information about one source taking into account the context evolution of this source throughout years (using similarity measures) resulting in a combined

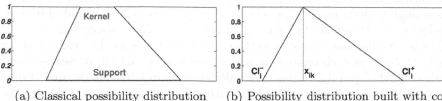

(a) Classical possibility distribution   (b) Possibility distribution built with confidence interval

Fig. 2. Possibility distributions

possibility distribution for each source. The second level relates to the fusion of these combined possibility distributions by taking into account the contextual differences between sources (using similarity measures). The result of this two successive fusion is a global possibility distribution which synthesize the entire knowledge about the problem.

The literature identifies many combination rules applicable to the possibility theory. The majority of these merging operators are based on t-norms and t-conorms, generalizing respectively the intersection and union in the context of fuzzy set theory [11]. The t-norm combination rules are difficult to use because they produce results difficult to interpret due to a very high sensitivity to changes in initial possibility distributions [12]. The t-conorm fusion rules are also difficult to use, particularly for decision-making problems because of the too uncertain results they provide [12]. Therefore, adaptive rules of combination have been developed to obtain results more adapted to the reality of the studied problems.

Among the existing adaptive rules, the Dubois and Prade rules [13,14] or the Deveughele rule [15] are quite common but the Delmotte rules [16,12] were chosen because they allow to explicitly take into account the confidence in information sources. This notion of confidence incorporates the similarity between information sources during the combination. The more the context of a source is similar to the context studied, the more the source is considered reliable (with a high confidence).

In this article, only the first rule of Delmotte [16] is presented. The use of the rule developed in [12] is a prospect of this work. The first rule of Delmotte [16] requires the use of a reliability $t_i \in [0,1]$ associated with each source i. The combination between sources is done with the following formula:

$$\pi_0^*(x) = \left(1 - \prod_{i=1}^{n}(1-t_i)\right) \times \left(1 - \prod_{i=1}^{n} t_i\right) \times \max_{i=1}^{n}(t_i \times \pi_i(x)) + \prod_{i=1}^{n} t_i \times \min_{i=1}^{n}(t_i \times \pi_i(x)) \quad (4)$$

This combination behaves as a conjunction when all sources are reliable and as a disjunction of the most reliable sources when no source is completely reliable. The resulting distributions have to be normalize to respect the constraint (2).

2.3   Decision-Making

The studied problem generates two kind of decision. The first decision is about determining whether a value is abnormal or not by using the possibility distribution which represents the fusion of all opinions from the different sources. It is enough to determine the possibility level of the tested value and, if its level is below a user threshold, the value is therefore considered abnormal.

The second decision is related to the correction of an abnormal value and is a classic problem of decision-making under uncertainty. Indeed, decision-making in the context of possibility theory usually consists in removing the uncertainty of a possibility distribution to end up with a unique and precise value for the studied variable. This is exactly the purpose of the correction value which aims to obtain a precise value, by using a possibility distribution representing the combined opinion of all information sources. This corrected value will be used to make the forecast. There are several "defuzzification" methods for such purpose [17]. One of the most common, Mean Of Maximum (MOM) method, has been used in this study and consists in choosing the mean value of the set of maximum possibility level values.

3   Application to a Case Study

To illustrate the proposal, a realistic case study has been built. The studied retailer has four POS and has a history of quarterly sales for each POS during the last three years. The objective is to consolidate the data of the POS n°1 using data from other POS to check if the value of the year 4 first quarter is abnormal and, if necessary, correct it.

Data Formatting: To facilitate the comparison between POS, the expert chose to work with seasonal coefficients (SC) (ratio of sale volume in the period divided by the mean sale volume for the year). This choice allows to easily compare POS with similar seasonal variations. To test the first quarter SC of the year 4, all the first quarter SC in database are selected (Table 1).

Context Comparison: The Contextual Similarity measures (CS) between the studied POS and the other POS are made by using different attributes of their contexts. For example, differences in POS locations (downtown, commercial area, ...) influence the evolution of sale volume and therefore must be taken into account in the similarity measures between POS.

Also using an Annual Similarity (AS) allows to reduce the influence of older data coming from previous years to deal with the fact that the older the data are, the less relevant they are. Table 1 summarizes the information on the similarity measures (elicited by experts).

Knowledge Formalization: Formalization starts with the calculation of the confidence interval for each POS using the equation 3. In a conservative approach, the confidence levels of the interval can be set to 99% ($\alpha = 1\%$). For example, the confidence interval of POS n°3 is [0.1666, 1.3263]. Then the triangular possibility distributions are built using these confidence intervals. Figure 3 shows the three possibility distributions (corresponding to three years of data set) for the POS n°3.

Table 1. Initial seasonal coefficients and similarity measures

| | POS n°1 | | POS n°2 | | POS n°3 | | POS n°4 | |
| | $CS_1 = 1$ | | $CS_2 = 0.95$ | | $CS_3 = 0.6$ | | $CS_4 = 0.7$ | |
	AS	SC	AS	SC	AS	SC	AS	SC
Year 1	0.8	0.5116	0.8	0.4812	0.8	0.6565	0.8	0.3526
Year 2	0.9	0.5227	0.9	0.4907	0.9	0.7268	0.9	0.3636
Year 3	1	0.5322	1	0.4963	1	0.8560	1	0.4000

Knowledge Combination: Possibility distributions must be combined to obtain a global information. The first combination is done at the POS level. The first Delmotte rule of combination (equation 4) uses AS (considered as confidence levels) to achieve combination. The result is then normalized. The figure 3 shows the result of this combination for the POS n°3.

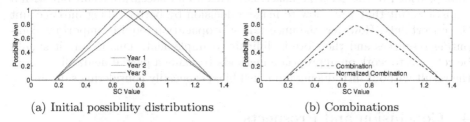

(a) Initial possibility distributions   (b) Combinations

Fig. 3. Possibility distributions of POS n°3

Once each POS has a combined possibility distribution, it is necessary to combine opinions of different POS by taking now into account CS. These are, in the same manner as AS, considered as reliabilities in Delmotte rule. The result of this combination is also normalized. The figure 4 shows the result of the global combination for the case study.

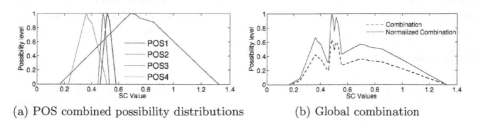

(a) POS combined possibility distributions   (b) Global combination

Fig. 4. Global combination for the case study

74   É. Villeneuve, C. Béler, and L. Geneste

Decision-Making: As described above, there are two levels of decision-making. The first is to determine whether a value is abnormal or not based on a threshold set by the user. In the above example, if the threshold is set at 0.7, the value must be in the interval [0.4707, 05407] to be validated. The second level is to determine the most appropriate value to correct an abnormal value. Given that there is only one maximum, the MOM method allows to chose this value for the correction. The value in this example will be corrected to 0.4840.

Discussion: These results raise several issues, including the choice of the combination rule. Tests were conducted with other combination rules but none takes naturally into account the source confidence. In addition, the adaptive behavior of the Delmotte rule is an advantage for the treatment of complex and varied problems as studied here. The other issue is related to the defuzzification method. The choice of the MOM method is questionable and requires further work. Ideally, the result should not be subjected to defuzzification and uncertainty should be fully propagated to the final result (i.e. the forecast result). This choice would retain all the information and improve the quality of the results provided to the decision maker, not with a more accurate result but with a realistic result that will allow to make a decision by better taking into account the uncertainty. However, the uncertainty propagation requires important computing resources and therefore is difficult to implement. This is why it should be relevant to work on appropriate methods to make a partial defuzzification of the result without introducing too much bias, especially considering side effects.

4 Conclusion and Prospects

This article describes a method to detect abnormal values in data used in demand forecast. This method also allows to correct these abnormal values by consolidating the initial data. This consolidation is done by using data from similar data sources together with human expertise (for the contextual analysis of the sources and the model parameterization). The implementation of a case study have illustrated the feasibility of this method. A prospect of this work is the replacement of the first version of the Delmotte combination rule by its improved version [12] to enhance the fusion accuracy. However, this rule requires the setting of two additional parameters to adjust the combination sensitivity. A test campaign must be conducted to optimize the parameter adjustments. The next step is to apply the improved method to real data from business partners.

References

1. Bourbonnais, R., Usunier, J.C.: Prévision des ventes. Economica, Paris (2007)
2. Box, G.E.P., Jenkins, G.M., Reinsel, G.C.: Time Series Analysis: Forecasting and Control. Wiley (2008)
3. Malo, A., Villeneuve, E., Geneste, L., Martinez, O.: Consolidation des données statistiques par expertise et similarité pour la prévision des ventes. In: 10éme Congrés International Pluridisciplinaire en Qualité et Sûreté de Fonctionnement: QUALITA 2013, Compiégne, France (2013)

4. Bisson, G.: Why and how to define a similarity measure for object based representation systems. In: 2nd International Conference on Building and Sharing Very Large-Scale Knowledge Bases (1995)
5. Dubois, D., Prade, H.: Formal representation of uncertainty. In: Decision-Making Process, Wiley, UK (2009)
6. Denoeux, T.: Introduction to belief functions. In: First BFTA Spring School on Belief Functions, Autrans, France (2011)
7. Zadeh, L.A.: Fuzzy sets. Information and Control (1965)
8. Zadeh, L.A.: Fuzzy sets as a basis for a theory of possibility. Fuzzy Sets and Systems (1978)
9. Dubois, D., Prade, H.: Possibility theory. In: Wiley Encyclopedia of Electrical and Electronics Engineering, John Wiley and Sons, Inc. (2001)
10. Kendall, M.G., Stuart, A.: The Advanced Theory of Statistics, Vol.1: Distribution Theory. Griffin and Co. (1943)
11. Weber, S.: A general concept of fuzzy connectives, negations and implications based on t-norms and t-conorms. Fuzzy Sets and Systems (1983)
12. Delmotte, F.: Detection of defective sources in the setting of possibility theory. Fuzzy Sets and Systems (2007)
13. Dubois, D., Prade, H.: Adaptive combination rules for possibility distributions. In: 2nd European Congress on Intelligent Technics and Soft Computing (1994)
14. Dubois, D., Prade, H.: La fusion d'informations imprécises. Traitement du Signal (1994)
15. Deveughele, S., Debuisson, B.: The influence of a conflict index in the frame of the adaptive combination. In: CESA 1996 IMACS Multiconference: Computational Engineering in Systems Applications (1996)
16. Delmotte, F., Borne, P.: Modeling of reliability with possibility theory. IEEE Transactions on Systems, Man and Cybernetics, Part A: Systems and Humans (1998)
17. Runkler, T.: Selection of appropriate defuzzification methods using application specific properties. Transactions on Fuzzy Systems (1997)

Paraconsistent Method of Prospective Scenarios (PMPS)

Nélio Fernando dos Reis[1], Cristina Corrêa de Oliveira[1],
Liliam Sayuri Sakamoto[1], André Gomes de Lira[1], and Jair Minoro Abe[1,2]

[1] Paulista University-UNIP, Graduate Program in Production Engineering,
Dr. Bacelar St. 1212, São Paulo, Brazil
[2] Institute for Advanced Studies – University of São Paulo
{Nelio Fernando dos Reis,neliojundiai}@ig.com.br

Abstract. This work presents the Paraconsistent Method of Prospective Scenarios (PMPS) in order to support organizations in their strategic planning, being a useful tool, as it serves a noble task. The method is based on non-classical logic, called the Paraconsistent Annotated Evidential Logic Eτ (Logic Eτ), this logic is excelling in the fields of research and it's main characteristics are set by the thought of experts, generating input parameters and been consolidated by the collective way that translates into mathematical terms. Logic Eτ is not trivial and has the capacity to manipulate imprecise and conflicting information.

Keywords: Prospective Scenarios, Paraconsistent Annotated Evidential Logic Eτ, Method.

1   Introduction

This study aims to present the paraconsistent method of prospective scenarios, proposing a new way of constructing based on non-classical logic with technical and operational criteria, in such way that future studies can take the contradictions into consideration and can be not only reliable but also operationally efficient.

This method presents numerical output generated by the model, so that they are easily understood by the decision makers. It shows results of strategic topics between truth and falsehood, answering the following question: is it possible to develop future prospectives scenarios with conflicting and paracomplete data?

The paraconsistent method was developed with Paraconsistent Annotated Evidential Logic Eτ (Logic Eτ). The main advantages of using the Logic Eτ are due to the fact of the input parameters are set by the structure of the thinking of experts, consolidating a collective logic translated into mathematical terms.

2   Literature Review

Throughout history many philosophers incited debates about the future. The medieval philosopher Augustine of Hippo who lived between 354-430, also known as St. Augustine, approached the so-called "problem of time", he considered it

B. Grabot et al. (Eds.): APMS 2014, Part I, IFIP AICT 438, pp. 76–84, 2014.

impossible to forecast the future [1]. The nature link between past, present and future, according to Kant, makes the story to be deterministic [2]. Hegel states that "man's immediate action can contain something beyond what is in the will and consciousness of the author" [3] and also that "reason rules the world, and, therefore, the universal history is also a rational process" [3]. Philosophy, therefore, does not give us a definitive answer about the future.

Help companies make decisions in the present with eyes on the future is the large role of prospective scenarios. The reflection on how future situations can impact the production management is a way to prepare for the future.

Godet says that currently "the Futurists have exaggerated scenarios and poorly built projects" [4]. Ringland argues that prospective scenarios have two key roles in supporting the organizations strategy in an uncertain environment, "mental models and serve as a methodology to allow exploration of the future" [5].

Scenarios should represent a set of internally consistent pictures of futures and nature states based on logic and rationality [6]. Scenario construction may be used to valuable functions in companies. "Scenarios refer to narratives of possible futures that might arise beyond the control of the company" [7].

To Schoemaker, scenarios should reflect a wide range of viewpoints from inside and outside the organization, so that, together they represent a broad spectrum of future possibilities. Milestad, Svenfelt and Dreborg assert that "the central element of scenarios is the focus on conditions beyond the control of the main actors" [8].

For Ramirez and Wilkinson prospective scenarios have value greater than a mathematical matrix. The challenge of the purpose and use of scenarios is often overlooked when choosing method of scenarios construction: "Given the diversity of the different thought traditions and methods of scenarios construction, the potential for methodological confusion and misunderstanding is considerable" [9].

We observe, therefore, that the subject conquer room and meaning in academic and professional circles, especially when it comes to the future of organizations. The emphasis on the matter is due to environmental instability and the issue of competitiveness.

The first logician to build a system of paraconsistent propositional calculus, between 1948 and 1949, was the Polish Stanislaw Jaskowski (1906-1965), following the suggestion of Łukasiewicz [10]. He called his system of Discussive logic (or Discursive).

But who is acknowledged as the inventor of Paraconsistent Logic is the Brazilian Newton Carneiro Affonso da Costa [11]. This is due, mostly, to the independent manner in which, since 1958, developed the ideas that led to the construction of several paraconsistent systems, not only in propositional level but also at the level of predicates (with and without equality).

A logical (or calculation) is called paraconsistent if it can be the underlying logic of paraconsistent theories (inconsistent but non-trivial) [11]. Therefore, in paraconsistent theories exist A formulas such that, from A and ¬A, does not follow any formula B, in other words, there is always a B formula from a set of all sentences such that B is not theorem of the theory. The Paraconsistent Annotated Logic allows handle subjective real-world data in precise data with numeric outputs [12]. One of its advantages is to perform the translation of natural language (linguistic terms) used in daily communications in mathematical expressions. This is achieved through the properties of the lattice of annotations. According to Da Silva Filho and Abe [13], benefits in the development of paraconsistent systems are: how quickly the system construction is carried out in relation to those based on "fuzzy" (common or Boolean) logic models and to make no longer necessary the knowledge or development of a mathematical model.

According to De Carvalho and Abe say that logics Eτ associates to each proposition p, a pair (μ,λ), representing by the Greek letters mi (μ) e $lambda$ (λ), representing by the following way: $p_{(\mu;\lambda)}$. μ and λ varies in the real closed interval [0, 1]. The pair $(\mu; \lambda)$ belongs to the Cartesian product [0, 1] x [0, 1]. Intuitively, μ represents the degree of favorable evidence expressed in p, and μ, the degree of contrary evidence (or degree of disbelief) expressed by p. The pair (μ,λ) is called annotation constant. The logic Eτ atomic propositions are the type $p_{(\mu;\lambda)}$ [14].

One can interpret the pair as follows [19]:

(0; 0) indicates the total absence of favorable evidence or maximum contrary evidence to p (it translates a logical state called paracompleteness);

(1; 0) means, extreme point of favorable evidence and no contrary evidence to p (it translates a logical condition called truth);

(0; 1) represents no favorable evidence and maximum contrary evidence to p (it translates a logical condition called falsehood);

(1; 1) means, simultaneously, maximum favorable evidence and maximum contrary evidence to p (it translates a logical condition called inconsistency);

De Carvalho and Abe [14] claim that "all the constants annotations $(\mu; \lambda)$ can be represented in Cartesian coordinate system by the unit square [0, 1] x [0, 1], called Unit square in the Cartesian plane (USCP) ".

As a result of the foregoing, it appears that the perfectly defined line (PDL) and a perfectly indefinite line (PIL) divides the USCP into four regions, as shown in the figure below.

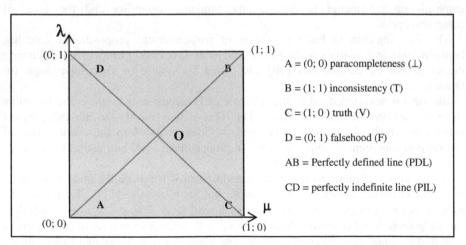

Fig. 1. USCP divided in four regions by lines PDL AND PIL (Source: DE CARVALHO and ABE, 2011)

Some initial considerations are required due to the generic use of language, not being separated the concepts of straight line AB, line AB, or segment AB; or line segment AB "connects" to the points A and B; when it "crosses" from point A to point B; or "on" the line BC. Will also be used expressions like "almost true", "maximum truth", "maximum falsehood", etc.

Note that the line segment CD "connects" to points C and D in the figure above, in which there are situations of perfect definition (truth or falsity). Therefore, the segment CD is called a perfectly definite line (PDL). The equation is $\mu + \lambda - 1 = 0$ [14].

De Carvalho and Abe [14] says it is very reasonable to define the contradiction degree of an annotation $(\mu; \lambda)$ as: $G_{contr} = \mu + \lambda - 1$, called perfectly indefinite line (PIL) the line AB of USCP. The equation of line AB is $\mu - \lambda = 0$. Defining this way the degree of certainty (H_{cert}) of an annotation $(\mu; \lambda)$ as $H_{cert} = \mu - \lambda$

It is thus a model of atomic propositions easily understood, without being trivial. Recently, Jair Minoro Abe and other researchers have developed applications for Logic Eτ, highlighting the viability analysis [15] and decision making [16].

In the pioneering work of De Carvalho *et al* [17] makes comparisons with inductive logic by using the statistical method and also with the Fuzzy Logic stating that: "by fixing the same value for the level of demand, the fuzzy decision gets stronger than paraconsistent" [11]. The use of Annotated Paraconsistent Logic, however, is practical and without need of complex math calculations [18].

3   Methodology

This study methodology used techniques and processes on a systematic way to objectively achieve the knowledge of the proposed subject. Research empirically applied, after literature review, with exploratory purpose. The phases of the methodological process used in this study were as follows:

1) Issue formulation:

- How to develop prospective scenarios working with contradictory data?
   2) Hypothesis formulation:
- To use logic that does not exclude contradiction in prospective scenarios.

3) Literature review:

- Theoretical background of prospective scenarios and Logic Eτ;

4) Data gathering:

- Specialists systems, invited randomly, six (06) of which have volunteered and were divided into three groups:

   - A: 02 (two) economists;
   - B: 02 (two) executives;
   - C: 02 (two) professors.

- extensive direct observation through measure of specialists opinion.

These specialists identified 50 (fifty) Future Facts Carriers, which are actual facts existing at present and will continue to impact our environment in the future.

After identifying these facts, brainstorming sessions were conducted to identify three (03) strategic topics to trial. After identifying the topics was built the strategic proposition which is a hypothesis of future occurrences of events identified based on a strategic issue. The proposition is for setting strategic goals, organizing a Delphi survey and identify future alternatives. The topics and propositions are presented in the board below.

Board 1. Topics and Strategic Propositions

Factors	Strategic Topics	Strategic Proposition
F1	Public Finances	Reduction of indebtedness as a proportion of GDP, so that the net public debt stays below 30% of GDP by 2022.
F2	Higher Education	Expansion of Higher Education System, to include, by 2012, about 40% of the population, aged 18 to 24.
F3	Brazilian Exportation	Increase in exports, so that Brazil will respond, in 2022, for about 2% of the world's exports value.

This phase of prospective analysis was made in two (02) Delphi rounds that sought to: identify the sure of the topic occurrence the consultation was conducted by a form via e-mail - in two rounds. The major difference between them is that, in the second round, was informed the answer's results of each question in the first round, giving the answerer an opportunity to revise their earlier answers, if he so wished.

The query was organized in three (03) strategic topics, and for each one there was a brief ambiance about the subject and a proposition about the future (p): "the issue occurs in 2022".

4   Application

Regarding the factors must be reason that they are independent of each other. Therefore, we attempted to assign degrees of favorable evidence (μ) and contrary evidence (λ) according to the specialists, as below.

Table 1. Database of specialist's evidences

FACTORS	GROUP A				GROUP B				GROUP C			
	Specialist 1 (E1)		Specialist 2 (E2)		Specialist 3 (E3)		Specialist 4 (E4)		Specialist 5 (E5)		Specialist 6 (E6)	
	μ_1	λ_1	μ_2	λ_2	μ_3	λ_3	μ_4	λ_4	μ_5	λ_5	μ_6	λ_6
F1	1,0	0,0	0,5	0,3	0,0	1,0	0,2	0,7	0,3	0,6	0,6	0,3
F2	0,1	1,0	0,1	0,7	0,3	0,7	0,2	0,8	1,0	0,0	0,9	0,1
F3	0,5	0,6	0,6	0,3	0,3	0,3	0,2	0,1	1,0	0,0	0,0	0,0

Based on the database of the specialist's evidence (Table 1), we can extract the opinions of specialists about the prospective scenarios. They are shown in Table 2 using OR and AND rules.

4.1   Maximization (OR) and Minimization (AND) Rules

The next step was to apply the rule of maximizing (OR) and minimization (AND) from Logic $E\tau$ to the opinions of specialists for each one of the strategic topics. the rule of maximizing the intra-group favorable evidence is applied so that the connective (OR) is used in the favorable evidence and the connective (AND) in contrary evidence within each group, and the rule of minimizing favorable evidence between the groups is applied using the connective (AND) for favorable evidence and the connective (OR) for contrary evidence for the results obtained at both groups (betwen groups), clustered according to table 2, in other words:

[(Specialist1) OR (Specialist 2)] AND [(Specialist 3) OR (Specialist 4)] AND [(Specialist 5) OR (Specialist 6)]

4.2   Results Analyses

We analyze these final results, after applying the rules of maximization and minimization, by the device para-analyzer. Therefore, it is necessary to plot it in USCP, in which, to have more accuracy in conclusion, was adopted as the limits of truth and falsehood the lines determined by degree of certainty $H_{cert} = 0,6$ and as limits of paracomplete and indeterminacy, the lines determined by the degree of contradictions $G_{cont} = -0,6$. Thus, there is a scenario of evidence favorable or contrary the certainty of occurrence of topic, if there is a module degree of certainty equal to or greater than 0,6.

In short, the division criterion is:

a) Hcert $\geq 0,6 \rightarrow$ Truth (V), the topic happens;
b) Hcert $\leq -0,6 \rightarrow$ Falsehood (F), the topic does not happen;
c) $-0,6 <$ Hcert $< 0,6 \rightarrow$ Area between Truth and Falsehood.

The database was treated with OR and AND connectives and the results of the three topics are shown in the table below.

Table 2. Resulting evidence degrees by application of the OR and AND rules

Factors	Group A		Group B		Group C		Betwen Groups		Strategics topics: 03 (three)		
									Requirement levels: $\geq 0,600$		
									Conclusion		
	μ_{OR}	λ_{AND}	μ_{OR}	λ_{AND}	μ_{OR}	λ_{AND}	μ_{AND}	λ_{OR}	H_{cert}	G_{contr}	Decision
F1	1,0	0,0	0,2	0,7	0,6	0,3	0,2	0,7	-0,5	-0,1	almost (F), tending to ⊥
F2	0,1	0,7	0,3	0,7	1,0	0,0	0,1	0,7	-0,6	-0,2	(F) doesn't happen
F3	0,6	0,3	0,3	0,1	1,0	0,0	0,3	0,3	0,0	-0,4	almost (⊥), tending to V

Observing the degrees of favorable and contrary evidence resulting from the application of the rules of maximization (OR) and minimization (AND) the opinions of specialists in the study of future, we note that the degree of certainty (H_{cert}) of F1 (public finances) and F3 (Brazilian exportations) are below 0,6 as established in the criteria for certainty of occurrence. For example, though the specialist 1 of F1 and the specialist 5 of F3 assigned evidence ($\mu_{1,0}$; $\lambda_{0,0}$) which is a statement of (V) truth, namely, certainty of occurrence, when taking into account other evidences of other specialists, the result is neither (V) truth nor (F) falsehood of occurrence's certainty of the strategic topic for 2022. However, it can be said in which region of certainty they are, as shown in the figure below. The F1 topic are plotted in ($\mu_{0,2}$; $\lambda_{0,7}$) at area OHTI= Almost (F) falsehood, tending to ($\perp$) paracompleteness and the F3 topic are plotted in ($\mu_{0,3}$; $\lambda_{0,3}$) at area OEMK= Almost ($\perp$) paracomplete, tending to (V) truth. F2 (higher education) has its collective evidence in the region (F) falsehood, that is, the proposition of the strategic topic will not occur in 2022, as shown below.

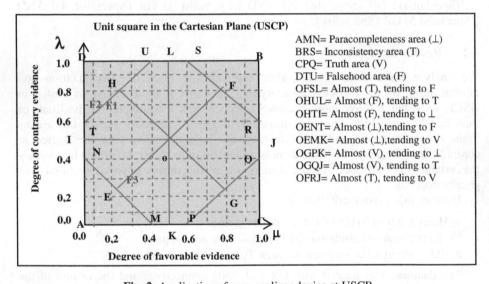

Fig. 2. Application of para-analizer device at USCP

If there is need of a more stringent criteria for decision making, for a more reliable, safer decision, it is necessary to increase the requirement level by approaching the lines PQ and TU from C and D points, respectively, also may be used a larger number of specialists, or even to consider the evidence assigned depending on the weight of each specialist.

So, the development of prospective scenarios with the Paraconsistent Annotated Evidential Logic Eτ allows to determine possible data inconsistencies and verify to what extent they are acceptable or not in decision rules.

5   Final Considerations

A major advantage of this method is its great versatility. The specialists may suffer influence, but in general it is not the same for everyone. Certainly, in a moment of depression, the specialist tends to disbelieve the future and more than believing and the opposite can happen as well in moments of euphoria or joy, but hardly all specialists will be experiencing the same emotions. Finally, virtually all problems where uncertainty, ambiguity or the natural language of human being is relevant are favorable situations for the method application. This method has many advantages, among which we reaffirm briefly: versatility, precision, reliability and trustworthiness, and allows dealing with contradictory data.

References

1. Agostinho, S.: Confissões. Martin Claret, p. 15 (2002)
2. Hegel, G.W.F.: Filosofia da História. UNB, Brasília (1995)
3. Kant, I.: Textos seletos, pp. 37–38. Editora Vozes, Petrópolis (1985)
4. Godet, M.: Future memories. International Journal of Technological Forecasting & Social Change, 1458 (2010)
5. Ringland, G.: The role of scenarios in strategic foresight. International Journal of Technological Forecasting & Social Change, 1493 (2010)
6. Vacik, E., Zahradnícková, L.: Scenarios as a Strong Support for Strategic Planning. In: 24th DAAAM. International Symposium on Intelligent Manufacturing and Automation (2013), International Journal of Elsevier Procedia Engineering, p. 667. Elsevier, Sciencedirect (2014)
7. Schoemaker, P.J.H., Day, G.S., Snyder, S.A.: Integrating organizational networks, weak signals, strategic radars and scenario planning. International Journal of Technological Forecasting & Social Change, 817 (2013)
8. Milestad, R., Svenfelt, A., Dregorg, K.H.: Developing integrated explorative and normative scenarios: The case of future land use in a climate-neutral Sweden. International Journal of Futures, 61 (2014)
9. Ramirez, R., Wilkinson, A.: Rethinking the 2 × 2 scenario method: Grid or frames? International Journal of Technological Forecasting & Social Change, 260 (2014)
10. Łukasiewicz, J.: On the principle of contradiction in Aristotle. Review of Metaphysics XXIV, pp. 485–509 (1971)
11. Abe, J.M., et al.: Lógica Paraconsistente Anotada Evidencial E, pp. 38–39. Comunnicar, Santos (2011)
12. Reis, N.F.: Construção de Cenários através da Lógica Paraconsistente Anotada Evidencial E. 121 p. Dissertation (MSc) - Universidade Paulista, São Paulo (2007)
13. Da Silva Filho, J.I., Abe, J.M.: Paraconsistent analyzer module. International Journal of Computing Anticipatory Systems 9 (2001) ISSN 1373-5411, ISBN 2-9600262-1-7, 346-352
14. De Carvalho, F.R., Abe, J.M.: Tomadas de decisão com ferramentas da lógica paraconsistente anotada. São Paulo. Blucher, pp. 37–47 (2011)
15. De Carvalho, F.R., Brunstein, I., Abe, J.M.: Paraconsistent annotated logic in analysis of viability: in approach to product launching. In: Dubois, D.M. (ed.), vol. 718, pp. 282–291. Springer – Physics & Astronomy (2004) ISBN 0-7354-0198, ISSN 0094-243X
16. De Carvalho, F.R., Brunstein, I., Abe, J.M.: Decision Making based on Paraconsistent Annotated Logic, pp. 55–62. IOS Press (2005)

17. De Carvalho, F.R., Brunstein, I., Abe, J.M.: Decision making Based on Paraconsistent annotated Logic and Statistical Method: a Comparison. In: Dubois, D.M. (ed.), vol. 1.051, pp. 195–208. Springer – Physics & Astronomy (2008) ISBN 978-0-7354-0579, ISSN 0094-243X
18. Reis, N.F., Abe, J.M.: Cenários Empresariais: a construção lógica de futuros possíveis nas empresas. São Paulo. Editora Paco Editorial, p. 32 (2012)
19. Dill, R.P., Da Costa Jr., N., Santos, A.A.P.: Corporate Profitability Analysis: A Novel Application for Paraconsistent Logic. Applied Mathematical Sciences 8 (2014)

Considerations on a Lifecycle Model
for Cyber-Physical System Platforms

Klaus-Dieter Thoben[1], Jens Pöppelbuß[2], Stefan Wellsandt[1],
Michael Teucke[1], and Dirk Werthmann[1]

[1] BIBA – Bremer Institut für Produktion und Logistik, Hochschulring 20,
28359 Bremen, Germany
and
University of Bremen, Germany
{tho,wel,tck,wdi}@biba.uni-bremen.de
[2] Industrial Services Group, University of Bremen,
Wilhelm-Herbst-Str. 5, 28359 Bremen, Germany
jepo@is.uni-bremen.de

Abstract. Cyber-physical system platforms are information infrastructures connecting different cyber-physical systems and other information systems. This infrastructure is the base for realizing the "Industrie 4.0" paradigm aiming for collaborative industrial processes involving smart objects and smart factories. In inter-organizational value networks, a cyber-physical system platform becomes a shared resource that has to be managed cooperatively along its lifecycle. This paper looks at cyber-physical system platforms from a lifecycle perspective. It describes the complexity of networks of cyber-physical systems and cyber-physical system platforms within value networks and the resulting restrictions influencing their various lifecycles. A selection of different lifecycle models from literature is reviewed to extract aspects that provide a promising basis for the development of a specific lifecycle model of cyber-physical system platforms.

Keywords: Shared Resources, Industrie 4.0, Lifecycle Management, Shared Information Systems, Cyber-physical System Platform.

1 Introduction and Problem Statement

The concept of "Industrie 4.0" has been developed as a strategic agenda for the future development of the German manufacturing industry in the Internet-driven age. Industrie 4.0 assumes that industrial processes, services and applications will be based on so called cyber-physical systems (CPS). These CPS are embedded systems integrated into physical/mechanical systems. Sensors and actuators as well as hardware and software are part of them. For interaction with human beings, CPS can be endowed with human-machine interfaces. By using an integrated communication infrastructure, they can also interact with other systems [1]. Instances of such CPS may comprise smart machines, storage systems and production facilities that autonomously

B. Grabot et al. (Eds.): APMS 2014, Part I, IFIP AICT 438, pp. 85–92, 2014.

exchange information, trigger actions and control each other independently. A characteristic property of CPS is their vertical integration into business processes and networked manufacturing systems within factories and enterprises and their horizontal connections to CPS in other value networks to manage them in real time [2]. As such, CPS platforms can be considered a specific kind of shared resources [4] that are cooperatively managed by two or more independent companies to improve inter-organizational processes within a value network. CPS platforms have been defined to act as federated, inter-organizational information systems [3] exchanging information between different CPS. The ongoing evolution of such technologies will increasingly allow implementing the already proclaimed Internet of Things.

Some research projects have already implemented parts of CPS platforms as prototypes. For example, Fraunhofer's Virtual Fort Knox project uses a CPS platform offering IT-based services and applications for the machine tool industry, based on a Software as a Service (SaaS) concept [5]. Another relevant research project in context of CPS platforms, called RFID-based Automotive Network (RAN), has developed and implemented concepts based on Electronic Product Code Information Services (EPCIS) specifications [6] for improving automotive value networks [7]. Some further related work is performed in a European context. This includes e.g. the research project FITMAN [8] within the Future Internet initiative [9], the EFFRA research association [9] within the Factories of the PPP Future initiative [10] and the recently established Industrial Internet Consortium (IIC) [11].

In addition to technical issues, the use of CPS in value networks also raises many economic, legal, and ethical issues, including, e.g., costs of introduction and operation, legal guarantee of proper operation of these systems, or their impacts on the workforce. Value networks are evolving continuously over their entire life-span, as new partners become part of the particular value chain, while former member companies leave. Main reasons for the mentioned continuous modification of value networks are dynamic influences of markets, products, technologies and processes [12]. Due to the dynamic nature of value networks, related CPS platforms are subject to ongoing change.

Frequent changes and complexity of the platforms challenge their management significantly. One driver of this challenge is the fact that hardware, software, services, applications and the network itself evolve along individual yet connected lifecycles. To our knowledge, the underlying lifecycle models for information exchange infrastructures in value networks (i.e.,CPS platforms) have not been investigated yet.

This paper aims to point out the importance of lifecycle models for the management of CPS within the Industrie 4.0 paradigm, particularly in relation to value networks. Its main argument is that lifecycle models are a viable approach to deal with this challenging complexity of CPS operating in dynamic enterprise networks. The main argument is derived from a review of different lifecycle models.

The paper's content is organized as follows. Section 2 describes the relation between CPS and value networks and points out requirements for efficient management of all elements of CPS platforms over the entire life span of such platforms. In section 3, existing lifecycle models are examined. We derive suitable components from them, which can be used to create a holistic lifecycle concept for CPS platforms as shared resources in industrial value networks. Finally, some directions for future research are outlined in order to guide the development of a lifecycle model for CPS platforms.

2   Lifecycle Perspective on CPS Platforms

Different elements are needed to realize the Industrie 4.0 paradigm in industrial value networks. Each value network typically consists of a number of companies as supply chain partners. To improve the processes within the value network, many CPS will be needed, operating at the involved companies to generate necessary information or trigger actions. In order to coordinate processes within the whole value network, one or more CPS platforms will connect different CPS with each other or with additional software systems as well as human beings through user interfaces. Moreover, CPS platforms can act as platforms for running services. This means CPS platforms and CPS are connected by information and communication technology for interacting with each other, as illustrated in Fig. 1. Furthermore, most companies are participating in more than one value network. This means that their CPS platforms and CPS have to connect to CPS platforms and CPS being part of other value networks. This increases the complexity of CPS platforms and CPS as well.

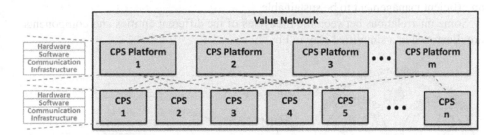

CPS: Cyber-physical systems

Fig. 1. Value network in context of Industrie 4.0 [2]

Obviously a high variety of different CPS platforms and CPS will be necessary to address all individual needs present in various value networks. In consequence, CPS platforms and CPS consist of a high variety of hardware, software, communication infrastructure and other components. To cope with the resulting complexity, inter-organizational CPS platforms, which are used for connecting different CPS and other CPS platforms, need to be based on a common reference architecture.

Regarding the fact that CPS platforms are shared resources, the management of those CPS platforms has to consider the interests of all the involved partners. That means the whole functionality of the CPS platform, based on the hardware, software and communication technology, need to consider these interests.

These interests have to be taken into account during the whole lifecycle of the different hardware, software, communication infrastructure and other components. Moreover the lifecycle of the dynamically changing value network itself has to be considered. From a more generalized perspective the different lifecycles have to be synchronized to achieve high performance processes within the whole value network under respect of the interests of the involved partners.

In the following specific characteristics of CPS platforms from a lifecycle perspective were investigated. The "lifecycle" concept can be found in different domains, such as manufacturing, information systems, service engineering or marketing. A key proposition of the concept is that a certain object (e.g., product, software and service) and its related states are described through a sequence of activities or situations. The beginning of the sequence is characterized by the creation of the object or its integration into a network of objects, while the end typically concerns its destruction. In between these two extremes, the lifecycle typically covers a dedicated activity representing an object's operational time.

Adopting a lifecycle perspective on shared CPS platforms, it is obvious that the lifecycles of the platforms may differ from that of the value network. Furthermore, the different components making up a CPS platform may have lifecycles that again differ from each other – the lifecycles of hardware components, for instance, may differ from those of system software components, and of services. In addition, different instances of components can have individual lifecycles that are running asynchronously. This implies that a large number of different, but interrelated lifecycles requires an efficient management to be sustainable.

Some interrelations between the lifecycles of the different entities and components are illustrated in a simplified way in Fig. 2.

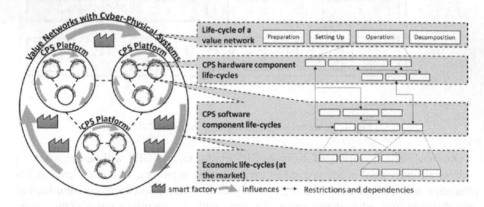

Fig. 2. Relations between lifecycles of different CPS platform components

We therefore see the following requirements to be fulfilled by a lifecycle model for CPS platforms in value networks:

-   The value network lifecycle should adequately describe the development of the value network structure over time. Existing partners within a network might terminate existing relations between them and create new relations instead. In addition, new partners might be included into the value network, while previous partners leave the network, resulting in an overall expansion or contraction of the value network. A lifecycle model has to take into account the *changing network structure*.

- Development of the hardware and software components and their dynamic relation should be adequately covered as well. New hardware components may be needed within the life of a CPS platform, thus existing hardware will be replaced by new or updated *hardware components*.
- Software may be updated, because improved or new software becomes available or because new hardware components may need new or reconfigured software.
- The technical lifecycles of components (e.g., hardware) are not independent of their respective economic lifecycles (i.e., the market situation). Thus, in addition to the technical perspective, a *market perspective* on the lifecycles of CPS platforms is required.
- Since value networks can employ thousands of individual CPS that must be produced (e.g., rare resources), operated (e.g., energy), maintained (e.g., spare parts) and disposed (e.g., waste), the environmental impact of these systems needs to be concerned. For this reason, an ecologic or *sustainability perspective* on the lifecycle should be taken into account.

To sum it up, a lifecycle model concerning CPS platforms in value networks should include technical, market and environmental perspectives for hardware, software and services both at type and instance level, as well as a perspective on the dynamic aspects of enterprise networks employing the platforms and CPS.

3   Review of Lifecycle Models

In this section, different lifecycle models are introduced covering a range of aspects that can be relevant for the management of CPS platforms in value networks. Domains utilizing the lifecycle concept defined their own characteristic lifecycle models to describe objects of interest in light of domain-specific problems. For this reason, there can be numerous models in each domain. Furthermore, among the domains very different models evolved. The differences typically concern the covered activities and situations of the model, as well as different emphasis on flows of information, material and energy. One of the application fields for lifecycle models is the domain of product lifecycle management (PLM). This domain is particularly rich in diverse perspectives on lifecycles. Table 1 provides a non-comprehensive selection of different lifecycle models. These models are selected because they provide a large spectrum of different aspects of lifecycles that should be taken into account when managing CPS platforms in value networks. Model A argues the lifecycle from a perspective of environmental impacts. A focus of this model is on three different scenarios that can be selected to discard the product, i.e., reuse, remanufacturing and recycling [13]. Model B is introduced to argue the suitability of item-level based product information handling to support PLM strategies [14]. Model C extends earlier work of Kiritsis and focuses on the information and knowledge flows among different lifecycle activities [15]. Model D is different from the other models in so far as it proposes three types of activity classes, i.e. engineering, operation and support [16]. Because of the three activity classes labeled as "chains", there is a similarity of the concept with Porter's traditional value chain concept characterizing an organization's activities [17].

Table 1. Selected examples of different lifecycle models

Id	Domain	Activities (the → symbol represents the sequential order of different activities)
A	PLM (Environmental Impact) [13]	Raw material extraction → Primary industry → Manufacturing → Use → Product discard (Reuse, Remanufacturing, Recycling) → Treatment and final disposal
B	PLM (Information Management) [14]	**Beginning of Life:** Product design → Manufacturing (design) → Logistics → Distribution **Middle of Life:** Use → Maintenance/Service **End of Life:** Re-use → Recycling → Remanufactured → Disposal
C	PLM (Information Management) [15]	**Beginning of Life:** Conceptualization → Definition → Realization **Middle of Life:** Use → Service → Maintenance **End of Life:** Reuse of products with refurbishing → Reuse of components with disassembly and refurbishing → Material reclamation without disassembly → Material reclamation with disassembly → Disposal with incineration → Disposal without incineration
D	PLM (Maintenance) [16]	**Engineering Chain:** Product design → Process planning → Factory planning **Operation Chain:** Production planning → Production scheduling → Production control **Support Activities Chain:** Marketing → Procurement → Sales → Distribution → After Sales → Quality → Maintenance
E	IT-Systems Development [18]	Stakeholder requirements definition → System requirements analysis → System architectural design → Implementation → System integration → System qualification testing → Software installation → Software acceptance support Software operation → Software maintenance → Software disposal
F	Marketing [19]	Market development → Growth → Maturity → Decline
G	Enterprise Networks [20]	Preparation → Setting Up → Operation → Decomposition

Model E is taken from the ISO/IEC 12207 standard and is a complex framework to describe individual software lifecycles in detail [18]. The complete framework consists of more than 40 activities but only the technical processes are covered in this paper. Model F concerns a widely accepted marketing perspective, where four phases are introduced describing a certain characteristic of revenue development [19]. Model G addresses the dynamic assembly and decomposition of enterprise networks through the lifecycle concept [20].

In summary, each of the selected models covers a certain aspect relevant to the management of CPS platforms in value networks. The required perspectives argued in section 2 are covered by the models, though the models do not provide a comprehensive view and must be revised according to the actual value network's requirements. One of the key challenges concerns the identification of relations among the models (e.g., sustainability and information perspectives), due to their differences in content.

4   Conclusion and Outlook

The paper is meant to be a position paper providing an overview of relations between CPS platforms as shared resources in value networks from a lifecycle oriented perspective. It argues that the complexity of the system poses challenges to current management approaches. It is argued that a driver of the complexity is related to the heterogeneous and typically asynchronous lifecycles of the system elements. In order to provide grounds for efficient management approaches of CPS platforms in value networks, important lifecycle perspectives are described. The paper closes with a selection of examples for lifecycle models that cover the relevant lifecycle perspectives.

While the provided selection of lifecycle models is a first step to create efficient management approaches for CPS platforms, further validation is necessary and questions from different perspectives still have to be answered. These questions concern many research domains, such as system interoperability, drivers and barriers of information exchange, employee acceptance of large scale CPS infrastructures, IT-security in dynamic enterprise networks, flexibility and standardization decisions for CPS-Platforms, and disposal of large scale CPS infrastructures or parts of it. A specific point of interest for future work is the refinement of existing lifecycle models, to establish a diversified collection of relevant activities and situations. Further research should investigate the relations between the different lifecycle models. This could be done through the identification of activities and situations that significantly influence each other across the different models. The relations between activities and situations from different models can be used to tailor management processes for specific value networks. A complementary research topic concerns quantification of the network's complexity problem. Real CPS platforms and real use cases could serve as valuable sources to gain quantifiable arguments for revised management approaches of CPS platforms within value networks.

References

1. Broy, M.: Cyber-Physical Systems: Wissenschaftliche Herausforderungen bei der Entwicklung. In: Broy, M. (ed.) Cyber-Physical Systems: Innovation Durch Software-Intensive Eingebettete Systeme, pp. 17–31. Springer, Heidelberg (2010)
2. Kagermann, H., Wahlster, W., Helbig, J. (eds.): Umsetzungsempfehlungen für das Zukunftsprojekt Industrie 4.0: Abschlussbericht des Arbeitskreises Industrie 4.0. acatech – National Academy of Science and Engineering, Munich (2013)

3. Pöppelbuß, J., Teucke, M., Werthmann, D., Freitag, M.: Managing the Life Cycle of IT-Based Inter-firm Resources in Production and Logistics Networks. In: Kotzab, H., Thoben, K.D., Pannek, J. (eds.) Proceedings of the Fourth International Conference, LDIC 2014. Springer, Heidelberg (in print, 2014)

4. Schönberger, J., Kopfer, H., Kotzab, H.: A micro- and macro-economic view on shared resources in logistics. In: Kotzab, H., Thoben, K.-D., Pannek, J. (eds.) Proceedings of the Fourth International Conference, LDIC 2014 (Lecture Notes in Logistics), Bremen, Germany, Springer, Heidelberg (in print 2014)

5. Diemer, J.: Sichere Industrie 4.0-Plattform auf Basis von Community-Clouds. In: Bauernhansl, T., ten Hompel, M., Vogel-Heuser, B. (eds.) Industrie 4.0 in Produktion, Automatisierung und Logistik: Anwendung, Technologien und Migration, Springer, Vieweg (2014)

6. EPCglobal Inc. EPC Information Services (EPCIS) Version 1.0.1 Specification, http://www.gs1.org/gsmp/kc/epcglobal/epcis/epcis_1_0_1-standard-20070921.pdf

7. Lepratti, R., Lamparter, S., Schröder, R.: Transparenz in globalen Lieferketten der Automobilindustrie: Ansätze zur Logistik- und Produktionsoptimierung. Publicis Publishing, Erlangen (in print 2014)

8. Future Internet Technologies for MANufacturing industries (FITMAN): http://www.fitman-fi.eu/, http://www.fitman-fi.eu/

9. The European Factories of the Future Research Association (EFFRA), http://www.effra.eu/

10. Factories of the Future, http://ec.europa.eu/research/industrial_technologies/factories-of-the-future_en.html

11. The Industrial Internet Consortium: A Nonprofit Partnership Of Industry, Government And Academia, http://www.iiconsortium.org/about-us.htm

12. Hülsmann, M., Windt, K.: Changing Paradigms in Logistics – Understanding the Shift from Conventional Control to Autonomous Cooperation and Control. In: Hülsmann, M., Windt, K. (eds.) Understanding Autonomous Cooperation & Control: The Impact of Autonomy on Management, Information, Communication, and Material Flow, pp. 1–16. Springer, Heidelberg (2007)

13. Pigosso, D.C., Zanette, E.T., Filho, A.G., Ometto, A.R., Rozenfeld, H.: Ecodesign methods focused on remanufacturing. J. Clean. Prod. 18(1), 21–31 (2010)

14. Ranasinghe, D.C., Harrison, M., Främling, K., McFarlane, D.: Enabling through life product-instance management: Solutions and challenges. J. Netw. Comput. Appl. 34(3), 1015–1031 (2011)

15. Kiritsis, D.: Closed-loop PLM for intelligent products in the era of the Internet of things. Comput. Aided Des. 43(5), 479–501 (2011)

16. Kovacs, G., Kopacsi, S., Haidegger, G., Michelini, R.: Ambient intelligence in product lifecycle management. Eng. Appl. Artif. Intell. 19(8), 953–965 (2006)

17. Porter, M.E.: Competitive Advantage: Creating and Sustaining Superior Performance. Simon and Schuster, New York (2008)

18. ISO/IEC/IEEE: Standard for Systems and Software Engineering: Software Life Cycle Processes, IEEE STD 12207-2008, pp. 1–138. Geneva, New Jersey (2008)

19. Levitt, T.: Exploit the Product Life Cycle, http://hbr.org/1965/11/exploit-the-product-lifecycle/ar/1

20. Thoben, K.-D., Jagdev, H.S.: Typological issues in enterprise networks. Prod. Plan. Control 12(5), 421–436 (2001)

An Interactive Approach for the Post-processing in a KDD Process

Paula Andrea Potes Ruiz, Bernard Kamsu-Foguem, and Bernard Grabot

Laboratoire Génie de Production / INP-ENIT - Université de Toulouse
47, Avenue d'Azereix, BP 1629, F-65016 Tarbes Cedex – France
{paula.potesruiz,bernard.kamsu-foguem,bernard.grabot}@enit.fr

Abstract. Association rule mining is a technique widely used in the field of data mining, which consists in discovering relationships and/or correlations between the attributes of a database. However, the method brings known problems among which the fact that a large number of association rules may be extracted, not all of them being relevant or interesting for the domain expert. In that context, we propose a practical, interactive and helpful guided approach to visualize, evaluate and compare the extracted rules following a step by step methodology, taking into account the interaction between the industrial domain expert and the data mining expert.

Keywords: Knowledge Discovery from Databases, Association Rules Mining, Post-processing phase, Interactivity, Decision Support System.

1   Introduction

Advances in information and storage technology have promoted the interest of companies for research works like Knowledge Discovery from Databases (KDD). Particularly, the generalization of the ERP (Enterprise Resource Planning) in industrial environments, make available a large amount of information. Hence, data mining techniques can be used to process this information and extract new knowledge, potentially useful to support decision-making. Nevertheless, this extraction should include a post-processing phase assessing the usefulness and reliability of the results, before their validation [1]. We propose in this paper an interactive approach for this post-processing phase, controlled by an industrial domain expert and a data mining expert.

2   Knowledge Discovery from Databases (KDD)

The knowledge extraction approaches have developed new intelligent tools, more efficient than traditional data analysis methods for discovering new knowledge in an industrial context. Knowledge Discovery from Databases is defined as a "*non-trivial process of identifying valid, novel, potentially useful and ultimately understandable patterns in data*" [2], in order to create a significant competitive advantage in companies. Given the great potential of the available data as a source of new knowledge [3],

B. Grabot et al. (Eds.): APMS 2014, Part I, IFIP AICT 438, pp. 93–100, 2014.

KDD has become essential in many industrial fields, including product and process design, materials planning, quality control, scheduling, maintenance, customer relationship management, etc.

The general process involves three main phases: pre-processing, data mining, and post-processing.

2.1   Pre-processing Phase

This phase requires a special attention in order to have reliable data before applying the extraction algorithms, guaranteeing therefore the quality of the results generated. Data cleaning, data discretization, data reduction or data transformation techniques can be used in that purpose.

2.2   Data Mining Phase

Data mining consists in applying data analysis and discovery algorithms to find hidden knowledge (relations or patterns) in large volumes of information [3, 4]. Our focus is on the association rules mining approach [5] to discover relationships between a set of attributes (or items) in a database. The obtained relationships are based on the co-occurrence of attributes [6] showing correlation, but not a cause.

An association rule is formally defined as a relationship between two itemsets through relations of the form "If X, then Y", denoted as $(X \rightarrow Y)$, where $X, Y \in I$ and $X \cap Y = \emptyset$. X is usually called hypothesis and Y conclusion, i.e. the presence of X allows to conclude on the presence of Y. Two classical measures are usually related to assess the discovered association rules: support and confidence. The support of a rule is the proportion of transactions in a database that contain both X and Y, and the confidence indicates the proportion of transactions containing Y among those containing X.

$$Support(X \rightarrow Y) = P(X \cap Y) \tag{1}$$

$$Confidence(X \rightarrow Y) = P(Y|X) = \frac{Suport(X \rightarrow Y)}{Suport(X)} \tag{2}$$

2.3   Post-processing Phase

The last phase of the process is the analysis and interpretation of discovered information. Over the years, many efforts have focused on improving algorithmic performance (in terms of execution time and memory consumption) but this phase has been surprisingly neglected. The post-processing of the results is nevertheless becoming increasingly important in companies, in order to find and validate the most interesting rules for each specific problem.

We present in more details in the next sections an original approach aiming at an easier interpretation and comparison of the obtained rules, their interest being decided with the assistance of an industrial domain expert to ensure the relevance of the extraction process in a given company.

3   An Interactive Post-processing Phase in the KDD

Four notions characterize the interest of extracted models [7]: validity, novelty, use-fulness and comprehension by the user. The models should validate the analysed data set and to some extent, new data sets; bring new knowledge to the user; be useful to support decision making, and be understandable by the decision maker. We focus especially here on the usefulness and comprehension by the user, within an interactive approach, underlining the indispensable role of the human in the process [8].

3.1   Interaction between the Industrial Domain Expert and a Data Mining Expert

In practice, it is difficult to find a data mining expert (DM expert) who is also an ex-pert in the industrial domain considered. We address in this section the importance of the collaboration between the experts in the process, to guarantee the quality of results and to make the knowledge extraction process more relevant for the enterprise.

The industrial domain expert (ID expert) is notably the person who knows the field and is responsible for decision-making. In contrast, the DM expert develops and man-ages the data mining techniques that will obviously support decision. In that context, we want to involve the ID expert in the interpretation and evaluation of the results obtained by the DM expert, and then in the validation of the elements of interest of these results. Interaction in the post-processing phase is a means for sharing knowl-edge [9]. Inspired by the work of Wang and Wang [9], we suggest a model that articu-lates the knowledge between these two experts (Fig. 1).

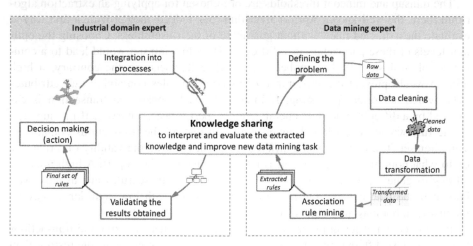

Fig. 1. Knowledge sharing between the ID expert and DM expert

The KDD cycle related to the DM expert (right path in Fig. 1) concerns firstly a phase of exchange between experts, to define the initial problem. The pre-processing phase (data cleaning and data transformation) and data mining phase (association rule mining) are then carried out. Finally, the post-processing phase is considered to interpret and evaluate the results obtained with the assistance of an ID expert. This phase, which is in our opinion of specific interest, is necessary to filter extracted rules. We consider that it should not be automated. On the other hand, the ID expert centered cycle (left path in Fig. 1) concerns the post-processing of results derived from the data mining phase, then a validation according to the needs and/or expectation of the domain, a decision making and an integration in the industrial field for improving existing processes. Finally, a positive and/or negative feedback outcome of this cycle must be carried out to the DM expert to enhance the new data mining tasks, during a new knowledge extraction cycle.

3.2   Interpreting and Evaluating Extracted Knowledge

We suggest three ways to evaluate the association rules, inspired from a classification presented by Geng and Hamilton [10]: *i)* an "objective evaluation" (based on the support and confidence), *ii)* a "semantic evaluation" (based on the domain knowledge), and *iii)* a "subjective evaluation" (based on the goals and beliefs of the domain expert).

Objective evaluation is a traditional knowledge evaluation performed during the association rules mining. Although other statistical measures have been proposed in the literature, an objective rule evaluation is often done by determining the rules that have a support and a confidence superior or equal to user-defined thresholds. So, we focus here on the interpretation of *minsup* and *minconf* thresholds, and of the support and confidence of the obtained rules.

The minsup and minconf thresholds are pre-chosen for applying an extraction algorithm (here, the well-known Apriori algorithm [5]). Indeed, they provide a first way to evaluate the extracted rules, without guarantee of their usefulness. Choosing the optimal levels of these parameters is a difficult task: a low minsup would lead to a combinatorial explosion of the number of candidate itemsets; on the contrary, a high minsup would prevent the appearance of association rules containing rare attributes [11], which are often interesting. If minsup=0, each considered transaction is expressed by a different rule (no generalization is performed), otherwise if minsup=1, a single rule would be generated under condition that all the transactions contain the same itemset. The minconf has a different interest: it shows the validity of a rule, i.e. up to what point the conclusion part is related to the hypothesis part. A high minconf allows to generate very robust rules, but in practice, these rules are usually well known by domain experts. On the opposite, the rules with low confidence may be inconsistent, but may also express unusual but interesting situations.

In practice, an efficient processing of the attributes characterizing the transactions requires to test different thresholds, since rare rules are often more interesting than frequent ones.

In that context, many studies on association rules evaluation are limited to determine the interest of a rule from a statistical point of view, resulting in a lot of inconsistent rules, or just uninteresting ones from the point of view of the expert user.

We describe here an attempt to complete the classic rules evaluation in order to improve the quality of the results, in terms of quantity and quality. As a complement to "objective measures" (support-confidence), we suggest a semantic and subjective evaluation to create new and more relevant knowledge for the industrial domain expert user.

Semantic evaluation facilitates the evaluation of the interest of a rule according to the domain knowledge. In this regard, we propose to use the following step-by-step approach (illustrated in section 4) as a methodology to interpret and understand the extracted rules: *i)* analyse "elementary" rules (involving only two attributes), *ii)* express each analysed attribute by a question, *iii)* express the problem addressed by each rule by combining the questions, *iv)* interpret the support and confidence of rules, *v)* analyse the potential use of each rule for improving the industrial processes, *vi)* check whether the reverse rule is, or should be, present. Indeed, analysing the rules (present but also absent), given their support and confidence, allows to identify inconsistencies in the databases (i.e. typing errors, data entry errors or anomalies in the definition of the attributes), *vii)* analyse more complex rules by comparison with the elementary ones through three logical operations, denoted here as *extension* (of hypothesis or conclusion part of rules), *permutation* (of attributes between hypothesis and conclusion part of rules) and *junction* (of the hypothesis or conclusion part of rules), and then using the same steps described above, *viii)* represent an overall structure of the extracted rules (indicating the relationship between the identified rules), thereby facilitating understanding and a visual exploration of the mined rule set by users, *ix)* formalise a "metarule" to generalize a rule-set and provide a new abstraction level grouping the rules. We intend to summarize the mined rule set from a general to a specific level (graphical model). Thus, rules of an upper level provide a general overview of the knowledge (i.e. elementary rules) whereas rules of a lower level are more specific.

Subjective evaluation is related to looking for specific types of rules according to the user expectations (ID expert). Structuring the rules indeed facilitates a visual exploration and assists the expert in this validation step.

In our KDD process, the target knowledge is not predetermined during the application of the extraction algorithm, unlike others techniques constraining the number of items and/or determining what items are in the hypothesis or conclusion part. However, an ID expert user in a given situation has usually an idea on the type of rule that he/she expects, in relation with the decisions he/she has to make.

Mining algorithms like Apriori [5] allow to identify different types of rules, including rules that might be expected, but others that may be completely unexpected by the user. Unexpected rules can be also of high interest, providing new knowledge to the user.

In the literature, different techniques are suggested to perform the subjective evaluation of extracted rules. A study of several techniques based on knowledge/user expectations has been detailed by Marinica [7]. Several formalisms may be used to represent knowledge for filtering rules: templates, beliefs, meta-rules, queries, taxonomies and ontologies for instance. It is commonly accepted that a visual representation of association rules facilitates the interaction with the user and may for instance help to model a query (user expectation), allowing to filter the identified rules. A query Q relates to a rule skeleton, describing the a priori structure of the rules of interest for the user. A query/answering mechanism will look for "response" rules to sort a final set of potentially interesting rules.

More formally, let X be a set of extracted rules and Q a user query. Regarding the structure of the extracted rules, Liu et al. [12] suggests to distinguish four sets of potentially interesting rules:

- Conforming rules: an extracted rule $X_i \in X$ conforms with the user query Q if both hypothesis and conclusion parts of X_i are consistent with respect to Q.
- Unexpected conclusion rules: a discovered rule $X_i \in X$ has an unexpected conclusion with respect to Q if the hypothesis of X_i is consistent with Q, but not the conclusion part. Unexpected conclusion rules may be inconsistent with the existing knowledge.
- Unexpected hypothesis rules: a discovered rule $X_i \in X$ has an unexpected hypothesis with respect to Q if the conclusion of X_i is consistent with Q, but not the hypothesis part. Unexpected hypothesis rules can show other hypothesis that can lead to the same result or conclusion.
- Both-side unexpected rules: a discovered rule $X_i \in X$ is both-side unexpected with respect to Q if both the hypothesis and conclusion part of the rule X_i are not consistent with Q.

4   Application Example

We consider here a real set of reports on maintenance operations performed on equipment of production processes in a large company of the aeronautical sector. An Excel© sheet with 5955 maintenance reports extracted from the SAP ERP Production Maintenance module is our starting point, containing several attributes (date, order work number, frequency, nature, priority, equipment, model, analytical section...).

A first discussion with the maintenance expert allowed us to better understand these attributes in the context. Then, the KDD cycle was carried out: the data preparation, the application of the Apriori algorithm, and the post-processing phase considering the industrial domain expert in the interpretation and validation of results. Extracted knowledge was discussed with the domain expert by presenting him the first partial results of the KDD process. This steps allowed to improve the extraction process (for example, by not taking into account attributes of questionable interest).

For filtering the extracted rules, we have firstly empirically chosen minsup=20% and minconf=90%, leading to the extraction of 38 frequent itemsets and 16 rules. Among the results obtained, we can consider the first 6 rules established by the algorithm as "elementary". Let us now analyse in more details the meaning of some rules, taking into account the support, confidence and the absence of reverse rules.

- *Rule 1:* Frequency=Semi-annual → Nature=Preventive   sup=0.21 conf=1.0
  Question answered: link between "how often" and "what kind of intervention".
  Interpretation: 21% of the interventions are preventive and performed every 6 months. Every intervention that has a semi-annual frequency concerns a preventive intervention (conf=1.0). However, preventive interventions may have other frequencies (since the reverse rule is absent).
- *Rule 2.* Production=0001 → Type of equipment=XXX   sup=0.23 conf=0.97
  Question answered: link between "what site" and "what type of equipment".
  Interpretation: 23% of the interventions concern the type of equipment XXX on the production site 0001. 97% of the maintenance activities on this production site correspond to this type of equipment.
- *Rule 5.* Model=Booths → Production=0002   sup=0.35 conf=1.0
  Question answered: link between "what model" and "on which site".
  Interpretation: 35% of the interventions correspond to the booths on the production site 0002. In fact, all operations on the booths are made on this site (conf = 1.0).

The other rules have also been analysed and may be considered as variants of those six basic ones by means of the three logical operations (extension, permutation and junction). Therefore, we provided to the ID expert a model generalizing the extracted rules set (Fig. 2), specifying the logic relation between the elementary rules (upper part in Fig. 2) and more complex rules. For instance, R9 is an extension of R4 (new items have been added to the hypothesis part of R9), R9 is a permutation of R10 (some items of the rules R9 and R10 have been permuted), R10 is a junction between the rules R5 and R6 (combining the hypothesis parts of R5 and R6) and R10 is also a permutation of R8.

Finally, the domain expert may make queries on this structure in order to filter the different results, which may help to effectively guide human decision making related to processes, or simply suggest how to better structure the database. In the proposed approach, the role played by the domain expert and the quality of the input data are decisive; both affect the quality of the extracted knowledge.

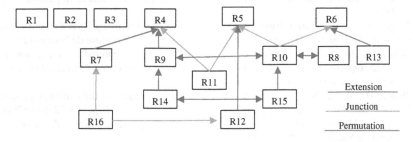

Fig. 2. Identification of the relationships between the elementary and complex rules

5   Conclusion

The interactive approach proposed for post-processing extracted association rules takes into account some efforts already reported in the literature; however, its main novelty is on the semantic interpretation and subjective evaluation of the extracted knowledge, according to several factors: support, confidence, presence and absence of expected rules, reverse rules, relationship between the extracted rules set and the frequent itemsets, and finally the interaction between the ID expert and the DM expert. The main focus is here on including considerations (positive and/or negative feedback) of the ID expert in order to improve the new knowledge extraction process in consistence with the application context. Indeed, it is essential to understand what the user is looking for in order to be able to define the problem and apply relevant data mining techniques. Other applications are in progress in the pharmaceutical and aeronautical domains, using more complex databases with more cases and attributes for improving and optimizing the interpretation and evaluation of extracted knowledge during the post-processing phase in the KDD process.

References

[1] Giudici, P.: Applied data mining: Statistical methods for business and industry. Wiley (2003)
[2] Fayyad, U.M., Piatetsky-Shapiro, G., Smyth, P., Uthurusamy, R.: Advances in knowledge discovery and data mining. MIT Press (1996)
[3] Harding, J.A., Shahbaz, M., Shahbaz, S., Kusiak, A.: Data mining in manufacturing: A review. Journal of Manufacturing Science and Engineering - Transactions of the ASME 128, 969–976 (2006)
[4] Köksal, G., Batmaz, I., Testik, M.C.: A review of data mining applications for quality improvement in manufacturing industry. Expert Systems with Applications 38(10), 13448–13467 (2011)
[5] Agrawal, R., Srikant, R.: Fast algorithms for mining association rules in large databases. In: Proceedings of the 20th International Conference on Very Large Data Bases, VLDB 1994, 1215th edn., pp. 487–499. Morgan Kaufmann Publishers Inc (1994)
[6] Choudhary, A.K., Harding, J.A., Tiwari, M.K.: Data mining in manufacturing: a review based on the kind of knowledge. Journal of Intelligent Manufacturing 20(5), 501–521 (2009)
[7] Marinica, C.: Association Rule Interactive Post-processing using Rule Schemas and Ontolo-gies-ARIPSO. PhD thesis, Ecole polytechnique de l'Université de Nantes (2010)
[8] Ben Ayed, M., Ltifi, H., Kolski, C., Alimi, A.M.: A user-centered approach for the design and implementation of KDD-based DSS: A case study in the healthcare domain. Decision Support Systems 50(1), 64–78 (2010)
[9] Wang, H., Wang, S.: A knowledge management approach to data mining process for business intelligence. Industrial Management & Data Systems 108(5), 622–634 (2008)
[10] Geng, L., Hamilton, H.J.: Interestingness measures for data mining: A survey. ACM Computing Surveys 38(3), Article 9 (2006)
[11] Baesens, B., Viaene, S., Vanthienen, J.: Post-processing of association rules. DTEW Research Report 0020, pp. 1–18 (2000)
[12] Liu, B., Hsu, W., Wang, K., Chen, S.: Visually Aided Exploration of Interesting Association Rules. In: Zhong, N., Zhou, L. (eds.) PAKDD 1999. LNCS (LNAI), vol. 1574, pp. 380–389. Springer, Heidelberg (1999)

Evaluation of Existing Work System Models with Particular Consideration of Demographic Change

Uwe Dombrowski, Anne Reimer, and Christoph Riechel

Institute of Advanced Industrial Management,
Technische Universität Braunschweig, Braunschweig, Germany
{u.dombrowski,anne.reimer,c.riechel}@tu-bs.de

Abstract. Ergonomics and the focus on human resources are widely accepted solutions to improve the performance of enterprises. Especially the influence of demographic change raises the relevance of such approaches. In the past years, different approaches were developed to realize those scientific solutions more efficiently. But which of those scientific approaches offers the optimal solution for enterprises in a turbulent market? To answer this question, this paper shows a state of the art review of different approaches of work systems. The main goal is to clarify the differences between the approaches and illustrate the academic void.

Keywords: Work System, ergonomics, demographic change.

1 Introduction

How will work systems change in the future and which influence factors have to be considered? To answer this question, it is necessary to clarify how the enterprise environment will change in the next years. On this knowledge base, the company's framework can be defined and different models of work systems are analyzed.

However, research institutes took care of this topic. In a variety of studies, different megatrends were identified. Megatrends are characterized by prominent features of global politico-economic changes. It can be defined as a pattern of changes that will profoundly impress the future of producing enterprises. [1] If the results of the studies are summarized, the following five trends can be identified. [1, 2, 3, 4]

(1) *Individualization and flexibility* is the first megatrend. It describes the fact that the customer needs for individualization affects the product development and growing variety of product variants. A direct result of this development is a compression of information. This increases the complexity in the whole value chain. [1, 2, 3, 4, 5]

The (2) *globalization* as a further megatrend describes the expansion of the industrialization in the threshold countries. New markets and new customers need to be identified. Especially the influence of the BRIC countries (Brazil, Russia, India and China) and the Next Eleven (Bangladesh, Egypt, Indonesia, Iran, Mexico, Nigeria, Pakistan, the Philippines, Turkey, South Korea and Vietnam) increase influence factors which need to be taken into account. This results in a higher product variety for most of the enterprises. [1, 2, 3, 4]

B. Grabot et al. (Eds.): APMS 2014, Part I, IFIP AICT 438, pp. 101–108, 2014.

Besides the globalization, the megatrend (3) technology and innovation influences the products as well as the production process and the organization. With regard to product life cycles of e.g. mobile phones that is less than one year, the influence of technological innovation on the product life cycles has already enforced. Every new product requires also new processes and with it the recognition in shorter planning cycles. [1, 2, 3, 4]

The megatrend (4) climate change and resource scarcity outlines the change of the climate on earth and the impact on finite resources. Companies which make sustainable use of energy, water and other natural resources will achieve a competitive advantage, but also take a risk by not recognizing this megatrend. [1, 2, 3, 4]

The named megatrends affect a work system in the way that demands on the employee increase. Especially complexity increase, technological advances and growing flexibility in the production process are leading to a higher sphere of competence. However, the greatest impact on work systems has the fifth megatrend. [6]

The fifth megatrend describes the (5) demographic change of the society. The demographic change sets challenges to the enterprises performance and global competitiveness. [7] Especially in Europe, many companies are facing this problem. [8] For the future, other countries with high industrialization have to take the consequences of demographic change into account. On the one hand, the consequences are about manpower and the guarantee having enough working age employees on the shop floor to realize a highly efficient production process. On the other hand, the challenge is about knowledge creation and lifelong learning to secure the process of innovation and productiveness of national economies. [1, 2, 3, 4]

By summarizing all the effects caused by the megatrends, it can be stated that a high impact on enterprises is expected or already has to be taken into account. In particular, the demographic change is already a challenge for the European enterprises. [9] To face those challenges, it is necessary to continuously improve and develop the methods and tools, which support the planning and operating teams within the companies. An essential requirement for this development or improving process is the definition of a state of the art work systems which takes all upcoming challenges into account.

2   Work Systems in Germany

The selection of the presented work system definitions was based on an extensive national and international research. On basis of the established research results and science based evaluation, an expert team selected the following work system definitions. These definitions represent the current national state of research.

The MTM (method time measurement) association defines the work system as a socio-technical system which is described by certain variables. The variables of this descriptive model include a task (describes the purpose of the work system), the resources which are person and work medium, input and output, the procedure (spatiotemporal interaction of the resources in the input-output transformation) and the environment. Micro work systems represent single-users, the macro-work systems teams, manufacturing cells, etc. [10]

The REFA Association characterizes a work system as an operational unit in which a person (or several) uses resources, material and information to fulfill the work under certain conditions. Work systems are the physical building units of any organization and operational processes and a core component of the process-oriented work organization. [11]

The German Institute for Standardization (DIN) defines in its DIN EN ISO 6385 standard a work system as a system which includes the interaction of one or more users with the work equipment to fulfill the function of the system within the working space and the working environment under the conditions prescribed by the work tasks. [12]

Schlick et al. characterize a work system by the elements working person(s), work assignment, work task, input, output, tools, work items and environmental influences. All those elements are interconnected and any change in the system will affect all elements.[13]

This brief introduction of work system models shall just give an overview on the various models. For the future, it is important to lay a focus on the introduced mega-trends in the work system models. Therefore, it is necessary to establish a framework in which the work system models and the impact of megatrends are assessed. For this, the four introduced work system models are used and an evaluation is conducted on the requirements of the megatrends. The choice of the evaluation characteristics is described in the next section.

3   Methodology

As shown in the previous section, there are already models which describe work systems. In order to evaluate those models with focus on the requirements caused by megatrends, it is necessary to define characteristics of a work system. Since there is no common consent on how a framework for work systems is defined, two possible approaches are introduced. The choice was made on the basis of the influence of the introduced megatrends. Especially the consideration of the demographic change as a key influence was crucial for the choice of the approaches.

The first approach is developed by Dul et al., presenting the findings of the Future of Ergonomics Committee, which was established by the International Ergonomics Association (IEA) in 2010. [14] The aim of the paper was not to provide an operational plan for human factors/ergonomics (HFE), but to give an overview on the current status in HFE. [14] Fundamental characteristics were derived from the definition of HFE and HFE specialists by the IEA, which are the following:

"Ergonomics (and human factors) is the scientific discipline concerned with the understanding of the interactions among humans and other elements of a system, and the profession that applies theoretical principles, data and methods to design in order to optimize well-being and performance." [15]

"Practitioners of ergonomics, ergonomists, contribute to the planning, design implementation, evaluation, redesign and continuous improvement of tasks, jobs, products, technologies, processes, organisations, environments and systems in order to make them compatible with the needs, abilities and limitations of people." [15]

The identified fundamentals are that HFE is a *systems approach* and that it is *design driven*. In addition, HFE focuses on *two related outcomes*, which are performance and well-being. [14] The characteristics are explained in the next paragraphs.

Seeing HFE as a *systems approach*, it is important to define the term 'system'. Generally, a system is defined as a set of interacting and interdependent components that form an integrated whole. As shown in the previous section, HFE systems consist of humans and their environment designed to focus on relevant aspects, e.g. cognitive or environmental factors, in order to create a holistic and human-centered work system. [16] The holistic view includes various level of the system, specifically for HFE the micro, meso and macro-level. Thus, a broader view is taken to the discipline and, consequently, bringing together the various levels and the human-centered system.

Related to the system approach and the improvement of the outcomes is the characteristic that HFE is *design driven*. HFE is always connected to the process design and can be applied at all stages of the process, although those stages do not necessarily appear in a certain order. However, what all stages have in common is the design planning which is brought into the process by HFE specialists.

The third characteristic is the focus on the *outcomes* performance and well-being. Those two outcomes are interdepending which can result in trade-offs in achieving the anticipated goals. [17] Hence, it is essential that a HFE specialist is involved in the process planning and to balance the two outcomes by finding an optimal solution.

A more detailed approach was introduced by Wilson who established a framework for key characteristics of systems HFE. [18] He identified six features which are the following: *Systems focus (a), Context (b), Interactions (c), Holism (d), Emergence (e) and Embedding (f)*. Those features are explained and described in the next paragraphs.

Systems focus (a) is similar to the described systems approach of the first framework approach. The focus lies on the design of a system where humans interact with their environment. The design can either be of the interactions with or within the system or of the system itself.

Context (b) is considered important to HFE, because human performance and behavior is dependent on the setting or rather environment. Nowadays, context is given in a complex social or socio-technical system. Consequently, context is part of a system and it is necessary to identify relevant elements for further analysis or development.

Interaction (c) between different elements of the system is the key characteristic of HFE. Therefore, the goal is not to design components but interactions between different system elements like a person-team-organization or person-device-person interaction. Additionally, interaction is strongly connected to system complexity which effects HFE analysis and understanding.

Holism (d) is another significant characteristic to HFE since various viewpoints are combined to get an appropriate overview on the situation. Consequently, the possibility is given that human characteristics like social or physical features are analyzed and then interactions with different system elements are designed and optimized.

Emergence (e) has to be part of the fundamentals of HFE because it describes the uncertainty of human behavior. [19] In this context, effects can occur which are not considered in the design process, e.g. people find solutions for disadvantageous designs or even create new exploitabilities which were not considered in advance.

Embedding (f) as a key characteristic describes the integration of HFE in the overall system. Essential for ergonomics is the participatory character meaning the integration of all key stakeholder and experts of the system. Yet, the organization has to decide on how to implement ergonomics in its present organization.

Comparing the two introduced approaches, the second approach is advantageous to evaluate the existing work system models due to the range of characteristics. The disadvantage of the first approach from Dul et al. is its general character and its intention to give a current status on HFE. [14] There are only three general fundamentals identified which give a first overview on important features of work systems. However, those features are not efficient for evaluation. Therefore, the second approach from Wilson provides a further range of fundamentals and allows a more detailed evaluation of the working system models.

The four introduced work systems of the previous section and the identified characteristics of Wilson are now combined to form a framework for the evaluation. A matrix is spanned with the working systems in a row and the necessary features of Wilson in the columns. The matrix is shown in figure 2.

	Systems focus (a)	Context (b)	Interactions (c)	Holism (d)	Emergence (e)	Embedding (f)
MTM	●	◑	●	◑	○	◑
REFA	◑	●	●	●	○	●
DIN EN ISO 6385	◑	◑	●	◑	○	◑
Schlick et al.	●	◑	●	●	○	◑

● Fully covered   ◑ Partially covered   ○ Not covered

Fig. 1. Evaluation matrix for different work system models

Within a research assistant team of the group factory planning and ergonomics , the different degrees of coverage were identified and will be explained in the following section. For this evaluation, all features are weighed equally as the focus lies on the comparison of the different work systems. The coverage degrees are divided into three categories which are full, partial and no coverage of the particular feature. In detail, it explains the matching degree between the feature definition and the definitions made in the work system models.

4   Results

The results of the evaluation are shown in figure 2. For each model, a coverage degree of the feature is assessed which will be explained in this section.

Obviously, there are two features which have the same coverage in all models. On the one hand, in every model the feature *interaction* is fully covered. This can be derived from the fact that all models have the focus on humans and the existing environment. In this environment, the person interacts with different things and turns the input, e.g. raw materials, into an output, e.g. products, by using tools. [10, 11, 12, 13] Besides the person-device-interaction, all models describe an interaction on an organizational level, e.g. between teams. On the other hand, all models do not cover the feature *emergence*. This is due to the fact that no possibility of other usage of the designed process is considered and no possibility of a continuous improvement process is included in a work system. One potential to cover the feature *emergence* can be a knowledge feedback as an input of the process.

The other features vary in the degree of coverage in the different models. *System focus* is only covered fully by the models of MTM and Schlick. The reason is that both models consider, in addition to the micro level, the macro level as well. MTM includes the macro-level in its definition of work systems whereas Schlick includes the macro-level in the extended model of a work system. [10, 13] REFA and DIN do not fully consider systems focus since those two models do partially include macro-levels of systems. REFA uses its work system by definition to describe the work. [11] It is not referred to the macro-level as it is in MTM or Schlick. More apparent is it in the definition in the DIN norm. There is no reference to the macro-level. [12]

Holism is fully covered by two models as well. Here, REFA and Schlick integrate this feature, by definition, the best. Those two models use different viewpoints in their work systems, for instance emotional or physical, to evaluate the system. Therefore, a holistic overview of the system can be derived. In comparison, MTM and DIN do consider the feature partly, but not in depth as the other two models.

The features *context* and *embedding* are the most heterogeneous features. For the feature *embedding*, only REFA covers it fully. This is due to the definition of REFA that the work system is integrated in the overall organization. The other models do not refer to it explicitly and therefore only cover it partially. *Context* is only fully covered by REFA as well. It is related to the feature *embedding* and the integration in the organization. With this, it is possible to evaluate the influences of the environment on a human. The other models do only partially cover the feature *embedding* and, consequently, it cannot give a complete overview as in the REFA model.

It is shown that the REFA work system model covers four out of six features and receives the best results in this evaluation. In comparison, the models of MTM and Schlick cover only three or respectively two features fully. The DIN norm only covers one feature fully. This result is due to the fact of the inherent character of a norm and its general application for any case. However, there is no model which covers all features. Especially the changing environment caused by megatrends and its impacts on the work system are not described. In addition, no integration of possible emergence and continuous improvement processes are given. As a consequence, work system models are changed from a static to a dynamic model by implementing a feedback cycle. This can be advantageous as early changes in a process can be done with little effort and cost. [20]

5   Conclusion

The requirements on work systems are changing due to the identified megatrends. These five megatrends have a big impact not only on the company itself but on the employee and the work system as well. Especially the demographic change will become important because people will get older and work longer in their lives. Hence, it is important to examine and evaluate work systems. There are just few models which consider a work system. Those depicted models do all have a different structure and vary in their definitions. Thus, a framework has to be defined in order to evaluate the existing models. Two possibilities were given and examined whereas the approach by Wilson showed to be the best choice for an evaluation framework. The features of the framework were evaluated for the models by an expert team. It was shown that no model can cover all the features to a full extent. As a result, none of those models do consider all aspects which will become important for the future. Thus, we are developing a work system model which is able to include all features of the framework and cover those to a full extent. The model will be introduced in further publications.

References

[1] Choudhury, M.A.: Global megatrends and the community. World Futures: Journal of General Evolution 53(3), 229–252 (1999)
[2] Hughes, D.: Demographic Changes and Megatrends. Foundation for Re-search Science and Technology New Zealand, FRST (1999)
[3] Tikkanen, T.: Innovative Capability and Productivity: What has Demographic Change to do with it? In: Jeschke, S., Isenhardt, I., Hees, F., Trantow, S. (eds.) Enabling Innovation, pp. 249–266. Springer, Heidelberg (2011)
[4] WDA Forum, Univerity of St. Gallen, Megatrend, Global Demographic Change: Tackling Business and Society Challenges in 2030 and beyond. St. Gallen (2011)
[5] Dombrowski, U., Ernst, S., Riechel, C.: Methodenframework der Fabrik-planung (MeFa). Wt Werkstattstechnik Online 104(4) (2014)
[6] Bruhn, M., Blockus, M.-O.: Komplexität bei Dienstleistungen. In: Töpfer, A., Hünerberg, R. (eds.) Gabler Research: Forum Marketing, Ganzheitliche Unternehmensführung in dyna-mischen Märkten: Festschrift für Univ.-Prof., 1st edn., pp. 27–47. Gabler, Wiesbaden (2009)
[7] Dombrowski, U., Evers, M., Riechel, C.: Demografiefeste Arbeitssystem-gestaltung: Am Beispiel eines adaptiven Arbeitsplatzes. ZwF Zeitschrift für wirtschaftlichen Fabrikbetrieb 108(9), 674–677 (2013)
[8] Tivig, T., Frosch, K., Kühntopf, S.: Mapping Regional Demographic Change and Region-al Demographic Location Risk in Europe. Rostock Center for the Study of Demographic Change, Series on Sustainability and CSR 2 (2008)

[9] Dombrowski, U., Hellmich, E.-M., Evers, M.: Arbeitswissenschaft in Deutschland: Bedeutung, Entwicklung und zukünftige Herausforderungen. Industrial Engineering (3), 30–33 (2012)

[10] Bokranz, R., Landau, K.: Produktivitätsmanagement von Arbeitssystemen: MTM-Handbuch. Schäffer-Poeschel, Stuttgart (2006)

[11] Hammer, W.: Wörterbuch der Arbeitswissenschaft: Begriffe und Definitionen, 1st edn. Hanser, München (1997)

[12] Grundsätze der Ergonomie für die Gestaltung von Arbeitssystemen, DIN EN ISO 6385 (2004)

[13] Schlick, C.: Arbeitswissenschaft, 3rd edn. Springer, Heidelberg (2010)

[14] Dul, J., Bruder, R., Buckle, P., Carayon, P., Falzon, P., Marras, W., Wilson, J.R., van der Doelen, B.: A strategy for human factors/ ergonomics: developing the discipline ad profession. Ergonomics, 377–395 (2012)

[15] The Discipline, I.E.A.: of Ergonomics, http://www.iea.cc/whats/index.html

[16] Karwowski, W.: The discipline of Human Factors and Ergonomics. In: Salvendy, G. (ed.) Hand-Book of Human Factors and Ergonomics, 4th edn., pp. 3–33. John Wiley & Sons, Hoboken (2012)

[17] Neumann, W.P., Dul, J.: Human factors: spanning the gap between OM and HRM. International Journal of Operations & Production Management 30(9), 923–950 (2010)

[18] Wilson, J.R.: Fundamentals of systems ergonomics/ human factors. Applied Ergonomics 45, 5–13 (2014)

[19] Grote, G.: Adding a strategic edge to human factors/ergonomics: Principles for the management of uncertainty as cornerstones for system design. Applied Ergonomics 45(1), 33–39 (2014)

[20] Hauser, J.R., Clausing, D.: The house of quality. Harvard Business School, Pub. Division, Boston (1988)

From Model Based Systems Engineering to Model Based System Realization: Role and Relevance of IVTV Plan

Vincent Chapurlat[1] and Eric Bonjour[2]

[1] Ecole des Mines d'Alès - LGI2P - Parc Scientifique G. Besse, 30035 Nîmes Cedex 1
Vincent.Chapurlat@mines-ales.fr
[2] ENSGSI - 8 rue Bastien Lepage BP647, 54010 Nancy Cedex
Eric.Bonjour@u-lorraine.fr

Abstract. The IVTV Plan (Integration, Verification, Transition and Validation of the system before its Qualification) is developed and validated during the design stage. It details all the activities, resources, requirements, means, etc. requested during the realization stage so it is the hyphen between these two crucial stages in system life cycle. It is today necessary to help companies to better transfer detailed design models towards realization for many reasons discussed in this paper. Mainly, IVTV plan remains difficult to be exploited. This article proposes a first step towards a Model-Based Realization Plan, that is, a metamodel that represents the links between models that comes from Model-Based System Engineering and information required in the IVTV plan.

Keywords: System Engineering, System Design, System Realization, Integration, Verification, Transition, Validation, Plan, meta model.

1   Introduction

Systems Engineering (SE) [1][2][3][4][5] is an engineering approach covering the whole life cycle of a system as schematized in Figure 1 and considered as a model based approach [6] *e.g.* requirements, functional, physical, operational scenarios, or configuration models.

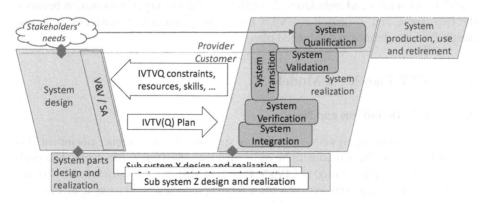

Fig. 1. From Design to Realization, IVTV plan role and position

B. Grabot et al. (Eds.): APMS 2014, Part I, IFIP AICT 438, pp. 109–116, 2014.

The IVTV Plan (Integration, Verification, Transition, and Validation prior to the Qualification of the system not considered here) is developed and validated during the design stage. It details all the IVTV activities, resources, requirements, means, etc. requested for the realization stage of a system as expected by all stakeholders. So, this plan operates belt transmission between teams, activities and processes concerning system design and system realization. It gathers the information necessary 1) to describe the subsystems and components that must be integrated, 2) how to proceed to assemble these elements to get the 'right' system and to converge step by step and in confidence towards the 'right' then the 'good' system, and 3) predict and anticipate risks and shortcomings inherent in achieving integration e.g. by defining and evaluating possible alternatives. In the mind as in the practices of design and realization team members, this plan is still often present in the form of documents generally prepared from templates facilitating, writing as reading and interpreting the plan. In this case there is no real continuum of models from the upstream design activities and IVTV activities. Causes of this rupture are multiple. First the type and nature of the expected product (single exemplar, for a small or medium to large series, software-intensive system, technical / socio-technical, etc.), the culture and practices of the company in charge of all or part of the realization (on site or in factory), etc. can be of course considered. Second design models are built by using various Design Specific Modelling Languages (DSML). These ones are generally defined by meta models highlighting at least SE core concepts and relations e.g. requirement, function, component and interface [7]. However, concepts and relations requested for the elaboration of IVTV plan are generally insufficiently detailed and linked with these SE core concepts [8][9][10]. Third, some of design models, even if they have to be adapted or transformed prior to any use, can be useful for facilitating work and assuming the relation between design and realization stages e.g. allowing integration team members to share test bench results having to be associated to a given set of requirements defined by design team members. Last, it should also be noted the significant lack of tools to use wisely the models mentioned above, or adapt / change without loss or effort or undue delays so that they become truly useful and usable. This paper aims to propose an IVTV Plan meta model to link more closely design and realization activities by 1) irrigating the latter with models issued from the former, eventually by using model transformation rules and techniques, 2) facilitating the sharing of information between the two stages, and 3) supporting IVTV project preparation and management dependently from the defined and validated plan.

2   IVTV Plan Meta Model

2.1   IVTV Definitions and Needs

Processes promoted by Systems Engineering standards [1] or reference document [11] give details about the activities to be done all along the system life-cycle. The position, the role and the relevance of IVTV Plan (detailed in [3]) is discussed below for facilitating the interactions between these main processes as illustrated in Figure 2 and then for reaching the proposed objectives.

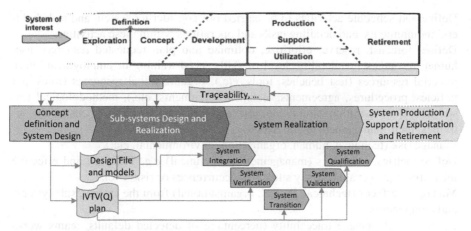

Fig. 2. System life-cycle and SE processes: IVTV plan position

We adopt the following definitions:

- **Integration:** [1] define integration process as *a process that combines system elements (implemented elements) to form complete or partial system configurations in order to create a product specified in the system requirements*. Its purpose is to prepare the system of interest (SOI) for final validation and transition either for use or for production. Integration consists of progressively taking delivery from implemented elements (*i.e.* components and sus-systems of the SOI), assembling theses ones as architected during design, and to check correctness of static and dynamic aspects of interfaces between them.

- **Verification:** [1] defines the verification as the *confirmation, through the provision of objective evidence, that specified (system) requirements have been fulfilled*. The verification process aims to ensure the system has been built correctly and ready to be validated with an acceptable level of risk.

- **Transition:** [3] defines transition process as the process *putting into operation the verified system with its useful enabling systems to demonstrate its ability to provide operational services expected by stakeholders*.

- **Validation:** [1] defines the validation as the *confirmation, through the provision of objective evidence, that the stakeholders' requirements for a specific intended use or application have been fulfilled*. The validation process aims to ensure *the system satisfies the customer and user needs as stated and agreed* [11] and ready to be qualified or exploited.

Various needs have to be taken into consideration when performing IVTV processes. Let us first mention needs common to all processes:

- Define a global IVTV strategy as soon as possible during design phase considering IVTV constraints from teams, and subsequent possible alternatives of associated plans (verification, validation, integration and transition),

- Define and schedule activities to be carried out considering system and stakeholders' requirements, and detailing tasks and operations within these activities,
- Define, forecast, reserve, prioritize, optimize and plan requested resources use: human resources (availability, level of skills, need training or employment, etc.), material resources (test benches, tools, etc.), organizational resources (rules and policies, procedures, agreements, technical documents, etc.), methodological (inspection, demonstration, simulation, test) and software resources to ensure the activities, their management and logistics,
- Manage risk (technical, human, organisation, environmental, etc.),
- Define metrics, indicators (management as technical) *e.g.* TRL/IRL and effective measures *e.g.* to evaluate risky situations occurrences or risk level,
- Manage interfaces (technical, logical, organisational) from the system, sub systems and components,
- Organise and manage traceability (percentage of detected defaults, teams workload, anomalies, requested modifications or evolutions of the product, etc.), return of experiment and of data reference models,
- Estimate costs of each activity taking into account various metrics *e.g.* related to the set of requirements,
- Manage requirements, constraints (normative, reference, linked to the contract with customer, etc.),
- Set up configurations of the target product under test and of its environment (reference configuration, configurations reachable, dysfunction configurations, etc.),
- Manage contributors and enabling systems IVTV along with target product IVTV,
- Dispose of tools supporting plan model building, checking, assessing in order to reach a consensus between team members against proposed plan, alternatives, etc.

More specifically, integration requires 1) to assume that delivered components are a) delivered in time or can be emulated by other and equivalent components in case of delay, and b) to respect the requirements in particular in terms of interfaces, and 2) to evaluate step by step the behaviour of the resulting assembly by applying various techniques. Verification requires 1) to apply verification techniques (test, audit, etc.), tools (simulators, emulators, test bench, etc.) or methodologies relevant for justifying and demonstrating requirements (functional as non-functional) defined in design phase are fulfilled, and 2) to trace the verification results even incomplete. Transition requires 1) to have available the operational environment *i.e.* validated enabling systems, associated documents and procedures, 2) to be able to put final users in training situations, and 3) to provide solutions in response to specific expectations from the customer. Finally validation requires 1) to have and to be able to use all deliverables, facts, tooled environments, etc. coming from previous activities (integration, verification and transition) and 2) to dispose of a validation environment corresponding as much as possible to the operational environment in which the future system has to work providing services and evolving.

Information (requirements, activities schedule, means, skills, resources, etc.) requested to cover these needs are defined in design stage gathered in the IVTV plan defined too during this stage. However, this plan is elaborated as a (set of) document(s) more or less easy to write, to understand in time and to interpret without ambiguities and sometimes huge efforts. The IVTV Plan Meta Model (IVTV PMM) presented below formalizes, merges and makes available in a coherent manner various concepts and relations requested and handled by the four concerned domains: design (SE core concepts), project management, risk management and IVTV (extensible to Qualification) concepts.

2.2 IVTV PMM

This meta model is conform to EMF notation and the Ecore metamodel[1]. The core SE concepts retained here are the function, component, interface, requirement and operational scenario (or use case) represented in Figure 3.

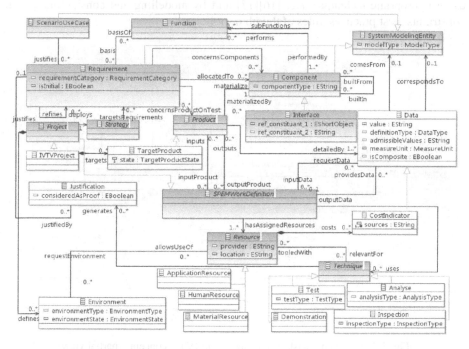

Fig. 3. Merging core SE, project management and IVTV concepts (partial view)

In a second way, the SPEM standard [12] proposed by OMG is used to describe project, process, activity, resource and other concepts and relations related to project management domain. A risk model inspired from [13] is used for covering risks management domain (technical, financial as managerial). Last, IVTV concepts and relations are defined taking into account the needs listed before *e.g.* IVTV strategy, product, technique, result, or report as schematized briefly in Figure 4.

---

[1] Eclipse Modeling Framework, available online at:
http://www.eclipse.org/modeling/emf/

Once merged, the result is a set of 77 concepts fully interoperable with various existing SE, project and risks management principles and even tools. It is then permit to progress step by step, in confidence during design stage and taking into account in a common approach design maturity level, project feasibility and risk evidence when performing the next activities:

- To define the IVTV strategy and the various alternatives of IVTV plans, preparation, determination and scheduling of activities, retained resources, needed enabling systems to design and realize, risk level and possible impacts and vulnerability of such plans or resources, etc. Teams' members can then share and dispose of all expected data, information and knowledge about system of interest, project, resources profiles and availability, etc. [14][15].

To check consistency and conformity but also relevance of the modelled plans by using appropriate techniques *e.g.* [16][17] and by modelling and considering global constraints, best practices, rules of thumb or policies.

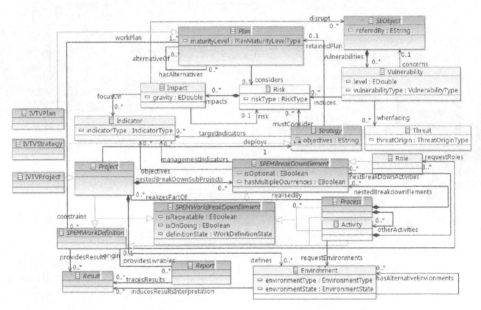

Fig. 4. Merging core Risk management and IVTV concepts (partial view)

- To simulate and to assess IVTV plans alternatives in order to compare them, then to optimise and facilitate validation of the final IVTV plan to be performed.
- To manage execution of this plan and to share in time information resulting from IVTV activities without ambiguities or doubts because reported directly in design system models.

3   Conclusion and Perspectives

The IVTV PMM presented in the previous part forms the basis of a new DSML for Systems Engineering assuming a part of the expected continuum of models between design and realization stages. It is possible to talk about Model Based Realization System principles. For this, at least another contribution is now expected.

Indeed, it is necessary to conceptualize and develop (with a great attention to DSML interoperability problematic *i.e.* to be and stay conform and compliant in order to become able to check the consistency of resulting models at least) a tooled approach supporting design model transformation in order to extract from these models specific business models used for supporting or facilitating realization as it is proposed for instance [18] in the case of transforming SysML models [19] in MODELICA [20]. This is one of the related works currently under development.

Acknowledgements. The authors wish to thank the members of the Working Group IVVQ of the Technical Committee Safety, Security and Validation of Systems (SV2S) of Association Française d'Ingénierie Système (AFIS) for the various opportunities to discuss advices and ways of working.

References

1. ISO/IEC 2008, IEEE Standards 15288.2008 – Systems Engineering – System Life Cycle Processes, 2nd edn (February 2008)
2. INCOSE, System Engineering (SE) Handbook Working Group, System Engineering Handbook, A Guide For System Life Cycle Processes And Activities Version 3.2.1, INCOSE TP 2003 002 03.2 (2011)
3. DCIS, Découvrir et comprendre l'Ingénierie Système, Collection AFIS sous la direction de Serge Fiorèse, Jean-Pierre Meinadier, CEPADUES Editions, Avril (in French 2012) ISBN: 97802036493.005.6
4. Blanchard, B.S., Fabrycky, W.J.: Systems Engineering and Analysis, 5th edn. Prentice-Hall International series in Industrial and Systems Engineering. Prentice-Hall, Englewood Cliffs (2011)
5. Faisandier, A.: Systems Architecture and Design. Sinergy'Com, Belberaud (2012)
6. INCOSE, Survey of Model-Based Systems Engineering (MBSE) Methodologies, Model Based Systems Engineering (MBSE) Initiative from International Council on Systems Engineering (INCOSE) (10 June 2008)
7. CORE V6.0, Vitech corporation (2010),
   http://www.vitechcorp.com/products/index.html
8. Braspenning, N.C., van de Mortel-Fronczak, J.M., Rooda, J.E.: A Model-based Integration and Testing Method to Reduce System Development Effort. Electronic Notes in Theoretical Computer Science 164(4), 13–28 (2006)
9. Luna, S., Lopes, A., See, Y., Tao, H., Zapata, F., Pineda, R.: Integration, Verification, Validation, Test, and Evaluation (IVVT&E) Framework for System of Systems (SoS). Procedia Computer Science 20, 298–305 (2013)
10. van Ruijven, L.C.: Ontology for Systems Engineering. Procedia Computer Science 16, 383–392 (2013)

11. BKCASE Project, System Engineering Book of Knowledge, SEBoK v1.2 (2013), http://www.sebokwiki.org/ (last visit 2013-04)
12. OMG, Software & Systems Process Engineering Meta-Model Specification, V2.0 (2008)
13. MADS MOSAR, Gestion des risques: Méthode MADS-MOSAR II Manuel de mise en oeuvre, Pierre Périlhon (2007) (in French)
14. Forsberg, K., Mooz, H., Cotterman, H.: Visualizing Project Management. In: Hoboken, N.J. (ed.), 3rd edn., J. Wiley & Sons (2005)
15. Project Management Institute, A Guide to the Project Management Body of Knowledge (PMBOK® Guide), 5th edn (2013) ISBN13: 9781935589679
16. Combemale, B., Cregut, X., Garoche, P.-L., Thirioux, X., Vernadat, F.: A Property-Driven Approach to Formal Verification of Process Models. In: Enterprise Information Systems, vol. 12, pp. 286–300. Springer, Heidelberg (2009)
17. Chapurlat, V.: UPSL-SE: A model verification framework for Systems Engineering. Comput. Ind. 64(5), 581–597 (2013)
18. Schamai, W., Fritzson, P., Paredis, C., Po, A.: Towards Unified System Modeling and Simulation with ModelicaML: Modeling of Executable Behavior Using Graphical Notations. In: Proceedings 7th Modelica Conference, Como, Italy, September 20-22 (2009)
19. System Modelling Language SysML (2010), http://www.sysml.org/
20. MODELICA - A Unified Object-Oriented Language for Physical Systems Modeling Language Specification Version 3.2 (see) (March 24, 2010), http://www.modelica.org/

Knowledge Discovery in Collaborative Design Projects

Xinghang Dai[1], Nada Matta[1], and Guillaume Ducellier[2]

[1] Tech-cico, University of Technology of Troyes, France
{xinghang.dai,nada.matta}@utt.fr
[2] LASMIS, University of Technology of Troyes, France
{guillaume.ducellier}@utt.fr

Abstract. Design projects have evolved to be collaborative, concurrent and multi-disciplinary. Due to these changes, knowledge management for design projects faces new challenges, in order to represent all the elements in a collaborative design project, it is necessary to consider not only decision-making process, but also its context and interaction with other elements.

Keywords: Knowledge representation, design project management, classification, project memory.

1   Introduction

Design is a collaborative activity, in which several actors with different skills and backgrounds work together to reach a given goal. Design project team is a short-lived organization. Moreover, projects can be done by several companies; actors can belong to different countries (i.e. in big companies). Knowledge is commonly defined by data and information used by an actor in a specific context [1]. Knowledge management aims at enhancing organizational learning in a company based on knowledge produced. It is defined as a cycle of transformation from tacit to explicit knowledge in a company [2]. This type of organizational learning will be based on "knowing how" and "knowing when" [3].

In this paper, we try to face the problem of learning from design project experience. Project memory will be defined at the beginning, and then a knowledge discovery method by classification according to different views of project memory is introduced to extract deep knowledge.

2   Background

In design industry, computer-based data process has facilitated information exchange in the whole organization [4], which gives birth to concurrent design. Apart from organizational changes, design teams become multi-disciplinary. Learning from experience can be difficult due to ambiguous interpretation caused by these two elements. We propose a project memory structure to represent collaborative elements in design projects. A project memory describes, "the history of a project and the experience gained during realization of a project" [1]. It must consider mainly project organization,

B. Grabot et al. (Eds.): APMS 2014, Part I, IFIP AICT 438, pp. 117–123, 2014.

reference frames (rules, methods, laws...) used in the various stages of the project, realization of the project, decision-making process.

We need to identify recurrent project events in order to identify routines and strategies related to event context. Strategies can be developed when human, repeating an action in similar context, identify a routine that can be applied to similar situations [7]. We propose in this work to classify collaborative design project traces in order to identify routines and problem solving strategies that help for learning.

3   Knowledge Discovery by Classification

3.1   Knowledge Discovery by Classification

Low-level data in project memory should be mapped into other forms that might be more compact, more abstract, or more useful [8]. A semantic graph enables knowledge engineers to communicate with domain experts in a comprehensive way [9]. Ontology is a description of shared concepts [10]. In our representation, a semantic network is proposed. Ontological hierarchy of concepts is employed for classification. Classification can be defined as the process in which ideas and objects are recognized, differentiated, and understood, classification algorithms are used in biology, documentation, etc. [11]. Knowledge classification is the process in which knowledge is recognized and reasoned.

3.2   Knowledge Classification Views of Project Memory

The goal of project memory is to enhance learning from expertise and past experience [12]. Current representation approaches emphasize on information structuring. The problem is that human can only learn from others by matching to one's own experience, we have to come up with classification models suited within specific context [13]. The traditional knowledge engineering methods ignore completely or partially the mutual influence between context and solution [1], and they show little about the influence of organization. More effort has been done recently to model project memory, we note especially DyPKM. It is a traceability approach developed specifically for project memory[14]. Unfortunately, it is good at knowledge capturing but proposes no solution for knowledge rule extraction. Our method will aim at these problem and classify knowledge in three steps.

Firstly, in order to classify knowledge from different context for different learning intentions, the general semantic network of project memory is decomposed into 4 sub-networks:

- Decision-making process: this part represents the core activity of design project, which helps designers to learn from negotiation and decision-making experience.
- Project organization makes decision: this part represents interaction between organization and decision, which provides an organizational view of decision-making.
- Project organization realizes project: this part represents arrangement of task and project team organization, which focuses learning on project management.

- Decision-making and project realization: this part represents the mutual influence between decision and project realization, which reveals part of work environment and background.

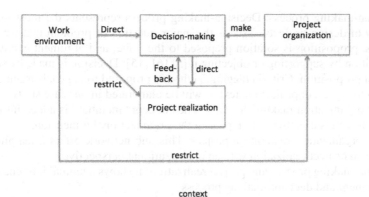

context

Fig. 1. Project memory structure

Secondly, in each sub-network, important concepts are highlighted, and ontological class hierarchy is constructed for classification. Thirdly, machine-learning technique is employed to generate rules between concepts or even networks.

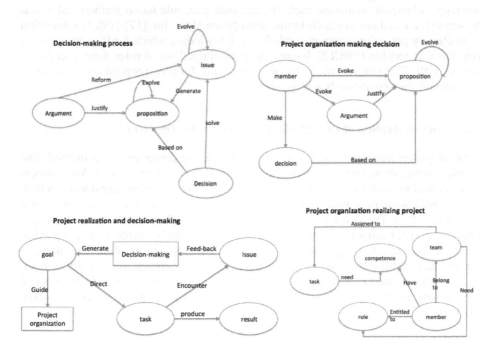

Fig. 2. Sub-networks of project memory

4   Knowledge Discovery in Project Memory

4.1   Sub-network Structure and Class Trees

1. Decision-making process: Decision-making process represents the most important activity of design projects. Issue is the major question or problem that we need to address, proposition is solution proposed to the issue, and argument evaluates the proposition by supporting or objecting it [5] [6] [15]; Decision is made by selecting the best proposition. Criteria tagging method is proposed to tag each argument with criteria to represent project context, it will be elaborated in our case study.
2. Project organization making decision: The concept "member" is added into the decision-making sub-network to represent the organizational dimension.
3. Project organization realizing a project: This sub-network offers a learning perspective on project realization with an organizational perspective.
4. Decision-making process and project realization: It shows a mutual influence of task arrangement and decision-making process.

4.2   Knowledge Discovery in Each Sub-network or between Sub-networks

In order to generate rules that represent interrelations between concepts or sub-networks, machine-learning techniques are considered. One of the most mature and widely used algorithms is classification [16]. An evaluation of major machine learning techniques (statistical methods, decision tree, rule based method and neural network) is carried out in search for the appropriate algorithm [17]-[19]. Our intention is to classify project memory into rule-based knowledge, which leads us to choose a rule-based algorithm ITRULE. It can induce an optimal set of rules from a set of examples [20]. The general rule is taken to be in the form of proposition rules, i.e. if condition A then condition B with probability p.

4.3   Demonstration of Project Memory Knowledge Discovery

An example on mechanic design project is illustrated to demonstrate our method. The problem is that the wishbone suspension breaks during test. A decision-making process was initiated in search for a solution. Two propositions were made, arguments on both propositions were presented, and finally one of the propositions was accepted as a decision (Fig. 3). The example is classified into our network in Fig. 4. Decision-making process is traced using memory meetings tools [12]. Project members are assigned to this task. We introduce a predicate member (r,c), where r is role of member and c is competence that member possesses. We have four members: member1 (project manager&designer, mechanical design), member2 (manufacture technician, mechanical fabrication), member3 (designer, electronic engineering), member4 (market analyst, marketing).

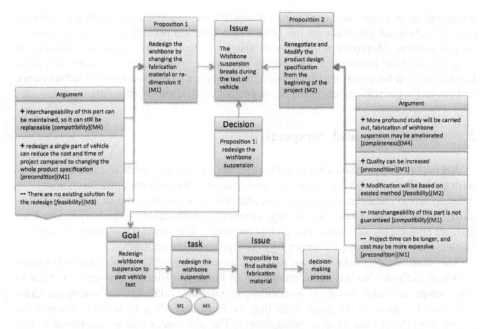

Fig. 3. Structure of the decision-making process "wishbone suspension breaks"

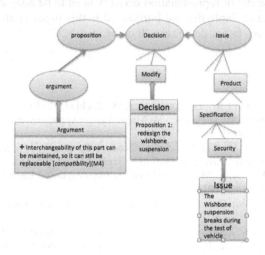

Fig. 4. Classification on issue "wishbone suspension breaks"

From this case we can see that interchangeability of wishbone suspension and project cost are crucial for the decision. However, supposing in another situation where the two elements are not strong enough, the result could be different. Hypothetically, more similar situations occur in a project memory, rules can be generated by the classification of similar graphs. A possible form of rule which can be put in ITRULE as: if issue {security, wishbone suspension breaks}, then decision {modify, redesign the wishbone suspension} and argument {compatibility; precondition} with a possibility of p. This type of graph shows the reason of a solution related to a specific issue in project context. Moreover, solutions can also be influenced by organizational context of a project, for instance: actor's skills, enterprise policy, etc. So more complete knowledge can be discovered by classification between decision-making sub-network and project organization sub-network, or project realization sub-network.

5   Conclusion and Perspective

In this paper, we presented a knowledge discovery method in order to enhance learning in organizations. At the beginning, we demonstrated the concept "project memory" in order to introduce a representation structure that is adapted to the new trend of concurrent engineering. Then, a knowledge-oriented classification method is proposed. At last, we showed the sub-networks, and a case study. We showed a technique to extract knowledge rules in project memory by classifying similar routines.

The semantic networks that we gave are based on the traditional knowledge management methods, but we make a connection between different elements in order to give design activities a context with an organizational collaborative dimension. Classification is based on the class trees that we built according to general research on engineering design and project management. The class trees that we proposed in this paper are, what we believe, the most balanced and useful form. In order to apply the classifier, class hierarchy or representation network need to be adapted to a domain.

As we can see the example that we introduced in this paper is an instance demonstration, future test on a larger database will be needed.

References

1. Matta, N., Ribière, M., Corby, O., Lewkowicz, M., Zacklad, M.: Project Memory in Design, Industrial Knowledge Management - A Micro Level Approach. SPRINGER-VERLAG: RAJKUMAR ROY (2000)
2. Nonaka, I., Takeuchi, H.: The knowledge-Creating Company: How Japanese Companies Create the Dynamics of Innovation. Oxford University Press (1995)
3. Easterby-Smith, M., Lyles, M.A.: Handbook of Organizational Learning and Knowledge Management. Wiley.com (2011)
4. Gerhard, P., Beitz, W.: Engineering Design: a Systematic Approach. Springer, London (1996)
5. Buckingham Shum, S.: Representing Hard-to-Formalise, Contextualised, Multidisciplinary, Organisational Knowledge. In: Proceedings of AAI Spring Symposium on Artificial Intelligence in Knowledge Management, pp. 9–16 (1997),
   http://ksi.cpsc.ucalgary.ca/AIKM97/AIKM97Proc.htm
6. Conklin, J.E., Begeman, M.L.: IBIS: A Hypertext Tool for exploratory Policy Discussion. ACM Transactions on Office Informations Systems 6, 303–331 (1998)
7. Richard, J.F.: Les activités mentales, Comprendre, raisonner, trouver des solutions. Armand Colin, Paris (1990)
8. Fayyad, U., Piatetsky-Shapiro, G., Smyth, P.: From data mining to knowledge discovery in databases. AI magazine 17(3), 37 (1996)

9. Sowa, J.: Knowledge representation: logical, philosophical, and computational foundations. Brooks/Cole, Pacific Grove (2000)
10. Gruber, T.: Toward principles for the design of ontologies used for knowledge sharing? International Journal of Human-Computer Studies 43(5), 907–928 (1995)
11. Cohen, H., Lefebvre, C. (eds.): Handbook of categorization in cognitive science, vol. 4(9.1). Elsevier, Amsterdam (2005)
12. Matta, N., Ducellier, G.: An approach to keep track of project knowledge in design. In: Proceeding IC3K/KMIS, 5th International Conference on Knowledge Management and Information Sharing, Vilamoura Algarve, Portugal, September 19-22 (2013)
13. Mai, J.: Classification in context: relativity, reality, and representation. Knowledge Organization 31(1), 39–48 (2004)
14. Bekhti, S., Matta, N.: Project memory: An approach of modelling and reusing the context and the design rationale. Proceedings of IJCAI 3 (2003)
15. Moran, T.P., Carroll, J.M. (eds.): Design rationale: concepts, techniques, and use, Routledge, US (1996)
16. Domingos, P.: A few useful things to know about machine learning. Communications of the ACM 55(10), 78–87 (2012)
17. Michie, D., Spiegelhalter, D.J., Taylor, C.: Machine learning, neural and statistical classification (1994)
18. Dietterich, T.G.: Machine-learning research. AI magazine 18(4), 97 (1997)
19. King, R.D., Cao, F.,, S.: Statlog: comparison of classification algorithms on large real-world problems. Applied Artificial Intelligence an International Journal 9(3), 289–333 (1995)
20. Smyth, P., Goodman, R.M.: An information theoretic approach to rule induction from databases. IEEE Transactions knowledge and Data Engineering 4(4), 301–316 (1992)

Efficiency of Informatics Tools to Project Development in Project-Based Learning Activities for Collaborative Engineering

Samuel Dereste dos Santos[1,2], Oduvaldo Vendrametto[1],
Miguel León González[2], and Mário Mollo Neto[1]

[1] Paulista University-UNIP, Dr. Bacelar St. 1212, Sao Paulo, Brazil
samuel_dereste@yahoo.com.br,
{oduvaldov,miguel.leon}@uol.com.br,
mariomollo@gmail.com
[2] Cruzeiro do Sul University-UNICSUL, Dr. Ussiel Cirillo Ave. 225, Sao Paulo, Brazil

Abstract. Informatics tools are very important for project development in the civil engineering area. CAD – Computer Aided Design - tools are freely used in different project routines, but BIM – Building Information Modeling are gaining space to allow the development of objects with a larger number of parameters and permit a collaborative engineering. Besides, the PBL - Project Based Learning – tools can be effective for teaching, allowing students to combine prior knowledge and aggregates skills in a collaborative model in engineering area. The objective of the paper is analyzing software applications in a PBL activity focusing the results of CAD and BIM tools utilization in project development. The methodology adopted was a technical review and a case study of 21 PBL projects developed by students of a civil engineering graduation course. The results shows that PBL is a good strategy for project development, and BIM tools are more efficient when compared with CAD tools.

Keywords: Project Based Learning, Building Information Modeling, Computer Aided Design, collaborative engineering.

1 Introduction

The use of computer tools in an undergraduate course in civil engineering aims to develop projects in software available in the market, establishing a bridge between what is taught in the university with is developed in the professional life. Specifically about tools for project developing, in a first moment as a direct replacement of the clipboard and handmade draws , the CAD tools - computer aided design - meant a revolution in the design process, making it more productive and enabling the exchange and use of information quite effectively, covering various technology areas such as aeronautics, mechanics and construction.

Besides CAD tools, the BIM – Building Information Modeling - was developed, specifically for the project of buildings, and have another concept. The CAD technology is based on vector information and BIM in parametric objects. It allows to the

B. Grabot et al. (Eds.): APMS 2014, Part I, IFIP AICT 438, pp. 124–131, 2014.

designer to define a series of objects that make the process more interactive and rich, allowing it to resolve several problems prior to construction. Furthermore, its architecture allows the same file under different disciplines, such as facilities, structure, masonry, foundations, etc. The production of the project information is simultaneously and significantly decreases the work for project´s compatibilization.

The formation process of a civil engineer consists of a basic curriculum, like Physics, Chemistry and Calculus, to give the basic reasoning and elementary tools for the continuity of the course. In the specific curriculum, the objective is to give the knowledge necessary for the professional life. One challenge in this context is aligning with the new challenges and consequences of globalization, like a humanist, critical and reflexive formation, enabling the development new technologies and contributions to attend the society demands.

One strategic tool that can be applied to aggregate competences in graduation courses are Project Based Learning – PBL - activities. This methodology focuses in project development and has the objective of simulating the real life. In the PBL, the center of the learning process is the student, whose role is to find information and aggregate knowledge, which is a paradigm shift.

The objective is to analyze software application in a PBL activity – inside a civil engineering graduation course - focusing the results of CAD and BIM tools utilization. The methodology was a technical review about informatics tools and Project Based Learning, besides a case study of 20 project developed by students in a PBL activity, whose results was ranged to be analyzed in the context.

2   Technical Review

2.1   Informatics Tools Used in the Development of Projects

To define the most common tools used in the development of projects in civil construction, it is necessary to study the importance of CAD and BIM tools in the context.

2.1.1   CAD Tools

The first applications of computers to assist the stages of engineering began in 1950, when the Massachusetts Institute of Technology – MIT - started the discussion about CAD - Computer Aided Design - technology. The CAD systems of this generation were limited to the description of two-dimensional vector geometrics entities for creating and manipulating drawings. The CAD tools denoted the transfer of manual draws to an electronic platform, with the advantages like electronically sent and received drawings, better management of the information, best currency in size and fast drawing modification.

At the end of the 90s, with the development of the Windows Operating System, there was a migration of the companies for Windows tools. This fact reduced the cost of hardware / software and the need for highly skilled users, popularizing the tool. [1]. The DWG interface is one of the most popular interface in civil construction planning offices, but the difficulties with files communication made the development of another software and formats to become the project process more efficient. One of these interfaces are BIM – Building Information Modeling – tools.

2.1.2 BIM Tools

The first concepts of BIM dates to the first attempts of data optimization at CAD platforms. This is a three-dimensional model enriched by additional intelligence (parameters). The basis of this technology consists of the graphical information, which includes the geometric model construction, its physical characteristic, properties, names and functional peculiarities of its components [2].

BIM systems are adequate to support the simulation of a construction project in a virtual environment, with the advantage of using software to perform several steps of the construction process, allowing it to make the necessary adjustments. The assembly instructions can be associated with BIM components, so the visual context of the specific location on the 3D (three dimension) model can assist with the communication of instructions [1].

The BIM tools involves information modeling surrounding the production of a building by a digital model that integrates all the interfaces, covering the entire life cycle of the building, which starts in the project, involves the implementation, use, rehabilitation and demolition [3].

2.2 Project Based Learning - PBL

Project Based Learning – PBL - is defined as a competence-based education that integrates knowledge, skills and values. The models integrating project-based learning have their scientific basis in generating learning processes in which students are not passive recipients of knowledge. Following the trends in psychology of knowledge, project-based learning is grounded in the belief that humans construct new knowledge over a base of what we already know and of what we have experienced, which we make available through active participation and interaction with others [4].

The development of the PBL was originated in 1900, when John Dewey (1859-1952) presented the "learning by doing", valuing the capacity of students by thinking relative knowledge to solve real problems in projects, developing the emotional, intellectual and physical aspects. [5]

The PBL has been a major focus of discussion, as not only an active learning approach, but also how to develop alternative curriculum and adopting innovative practices in engineering education. Requires a teacher to reflect on the teaching activity and change their traditional stance of content specialist for coach learning, and that students assume greater responsibility of their own learning, with the understanding that the knowledge gained from your personal effort lasts longer than that obtained only by third-party information [4,5].

The main features of this methodology are that the student is the center of the process, the work is developed in tutorial groups, it is characterized by being an active, cooperative, integrated and interdisciplinary process oriented student learning. For a good learning process in this methodology, is necessary to be aware of what the student knows and what he needs to learn and motivate the search for relevant information, stimulate the student's ability to learn to learn to work in teams, to hear other opinions, inducing him to take an active and responsible role for their learning and help students achieve the project objectives, which are: learn how to make an analytical and thorough examination of a problem, identify learning objectives, seek relevant information and learn to work in groups [4,5].

The learning projects favor the relationship of various contents making it easier for students to build their knowledge with the integration of different disciplinary knowledge in an interdisciplinary philosophy, seeking to pursue a meaningful learning. A study case about this methodology will be studied in the sequence.

3   Case Study

The case study is about an exercise developed by 21 groups in a civil engineering graduation course on 6th semester. The conceptual bases for development were a PBL methodology in the development of a Residence and a Residential Building. Into this moment of the course, the students had disciplines about Topography, Construction Technology, Construction Materials, Technical Drawings and Architecture and Urbanism. In the last two, they studied CAD and BIM tools specifically.

To the development of the activities, there was proposed a scope, with these characteristics (Table 1).

Table 1. Scope of the activity

Residence		Residential Building	
Building Sit	10 x 25 meters	Building Sit	50 x 25 meters
1st floor	-Living Room -Lavabo -Dining Room -Kitchen -Laundry -Maid Room -Maid Bathroom	Common area	-Entrance / Lobby -Hall -Elevators / Escalators -Party's Room -Technical Room -Collective Bathroom -Pool -Changing Room
2nd Floor	-TV room -2 dormitory -1 suite -Collective Bathroom	Apartment	-2 dormitory -Living Room -Kitchen -Laundry -Common Area
Technical Area	Roof	Technical Area	Roof

3.1   Work Groups and Orientation

These activities were supervised and oriented by 3 professors of design and project area. The groups were divided in 4 or 5 students, who have a scale of orientation with the professors.

3.2   Software Adoption

The students had, prior this activity, the disciplines of Technical Drawing and Architecture and Urbanism whose objective was introduce and practice CAD and BIM tools. The groups should choose between CAD or BIM tools by themselves to develop the activities. The professors would give support in both cases.

3.3   Activity Development

To develop the activities, 6 groups adopted BIM technologies, and 15 adopted CAD technologies. The groups, based on the scope, started the activities. Every group had weekly an orientation of 1 hour during 12 weeks. The tutors gave support of what was being developed and the prosecution. On the 13rd and 14rd week, they presented the projects to expose the results.

3.4   Activity Results

Each group presented the work to the professors, defending and discussing their ideas. Fig. 1 and Fig. 2 are examples of some works that were developed. All teams developed the proposed activities.

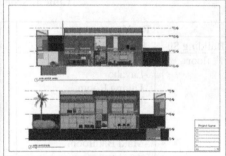

Fig. 1. Perspective   **Fig. 2.** Humanized Sections

The PBL model permitted to some students to learn some topics and change knowledge between colleagues, becoming the process very rich. Both tools permitted the analysis of all project instances (structure, masonry, electricity and hydraulics) with a good precision. Besides, the teams who adopted BIM solutions had more efficient projects representation than the teams that used CAD tools, what could inflict that the software could interfere in the process of project development. To investigate this fact, there was made, by the professors of the activity, a criteria analysis to understand this fact.

3.5   Software Analysis Criteria

To establish a criterion, all the results were scored on a Likert Scale from 1 to 5, being 1 the worst quality and 5 the best quality. There was calculated a Standard Deviation (%) for each product. It was analyzed the Graphic Representation - technical details of the execution of technical drawings norm in the construction area; Humanized Presentation - humanization of drawings for submission of the initial idea to the client, which is very important in professional life; Notations - sizes of text, dimensions, directions and projections for the proper understanding of technical drawing.

3.6   Results of Software Analysis Criteria

The result of the analysis of each project was rated in Table 2, with the respective evaluation of Graphic Representation, Humanized Presentation and Notation for BIM Teams and CAD Teams.

Table 2. Score Evaluation of the Products developed by groups

| | | Number of Groups = 6 | | Number of Groups = 15 | |
| | | BIM Teams | | CAD Teams | |
		Plans	Sections and Facades	Plans	Sections and Facades
Graphic Representation	Building	4.500	4.500	3.375	3.467
	Residence	4.667	4.667	3.813	3.313
Humanized Presentation	Building	4.500	4.667	3.733	3.533
	Residence	4.500	4.667	3.800	3.600
Notations	Building	4.167	4.333	3.467	3.267
	Residence	4.500	4.667	3.800	3.400
	Media	4.472	4.583	3.665	3.430
	Standart Deviation (%)	3.7	3.0	5.3	3.7

The Fig. 3 shows the score evaluation by technology to demonstrate the difference between each product at different technologies. The Fig. 4 shows the Score Evaluation by Product, to show the impact of the technology above each product. All the results of table 1 were analyzed in a Pearson correlation whose results are shown at table 3.

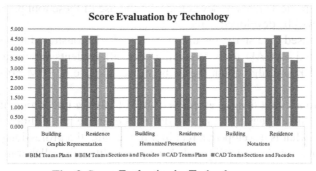

Fig. 3. Score Evaluation by Technology

Table 3. Pearson Correlation in Data Series Analyzed

Pearson Correlation in Data Series Analysed		
Object	Tecnology	Pearson
Plans	CAD	0.57
	BIM	
Sections and Facades	CAD	0.54
	BIM	

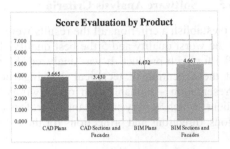

Fig. 4. Score Evaluation by Product

4   Discussion

The analysis of the data in Table 1 and Fig. 3 demonstrate that the development of a project with BIM tools is more efficient than CAD tools. The first tool had a score of 4.5 while the second had an average score of 3.5. This data demonstrates that, for a group of users with the same prior-knowledge, the utilization of BIM enhances the quality of the final product.

Analyzing the scenario set out in Fig. 4, it's possible to discern that, specifically for sections and elevations design, the use of BIM generates an increase of approximately 35 % on the final quality of the products developed. It can be explained by the parametric software interface that allows changing the 2D/ 3D interface, allowing the realization of more efficient work by the user.

Students have great difficulty in implementing sections and facades. The use of BIM make this process more didactic and efficient, allowing the project adjusting to solve the problems presented while the execution of sections and facades.

5   Conclusions

The challenges to the use of PBL tools in an undergraduate course are many. Not all students have the same level of knowledge, which significantly interferes with the quality of the projects that are developed. But the use of these tool permits the simulation of what will be developed in the working life.

In the proposed case study, the use of BIM tools demonstrated to be more efficient when compared to CAD tools. Assuming that all students involved possessed the same level of knowledge about the tools in use, the use of BIM proves to be more efficient.

Taking into account that the essences of BIM tools are integration, its use in an undergraduate course opens up a range of different exercise possibilities, allowing better simulation of what is developed in real life. In real life, the professional will deal with different professionals, and BIM tools have possibilities of collaborative engineering, which puts the tool in evidence for market evolution. The Data Set analyzed showed a >0.50 Pearson Correlation (moderate correlation) which validates the data analyzed in this case.

Acknowledgment. The authors would like to thank CAPES (Coordenação de Aperfeiçoamento de pessoal de nível Superior) and the Paulista University (UNIP) for the financial support to develop this work.

References

1. Souza, A.F., Coelho, R.T.: Tecnologia CAD/CAM - Definições e estado da arte visando auxiliar sua implantação em um ambiente fabril in XXIII Encontro Nacional de Engenharia de Produção – ENEGEP (October 24, 2003),
   http://www.abepro.org.br/biblioteca/ENEGEP2003_TR0504_0920.pdf (accessed on: March 2014)
2. Migilinskas, D., Popov, V., Juocevicius, V., Ustinovichius, L.: The Benefits, Obstacles and Problems of Practical Bim Implementation. In: 11th International Conference on Modern Building Materials, Structures and Techniques, MBMST 2013, Science Verse (2013),
   http://dx.doi.org/10.1016/j.proeng.2013.04.097 (acessed on: March 2014)
3. Porwal, A., Hewage, K.N.: Building Information Modeling (BIM) partnering framework for public construction projects. Automation in Construction 31, 203–214 (2014),
   http://dx.doi.org/10.1016/j.autcon.2012.12.004 (accessed on: March 2014)
4. Ríoz, I., Cazorla, A., Díaz-Puente, J.M., Yagüe, J.L.: Project–based learning in engineering higher education: two decades of teaching competences in real environments. Procedia Social and Behavioral Sciences 2 (2014),
   http://dx.doi.org/10.1016/j.sbspro.2010.03.202 (acessed on March 2014)
5. Masson, T.J., Miranda, L.F., Munhoz, J.R., Castanheira, A.M.P.: Metodologia de Ensino: Project-Based Learning. COBENGE – XL Congresso Brasileiro de Ensino de Engenharia (2012),
   http://www.abenge.org.br/revista/index.php/abenge/article/download/101/81 (acessed on March, 2014)

How Information Systems Assist the Management of the Supply Chain in an Emerging Country Like Brazil

Marcelo T. Okano, Fernando A.S. Marins, and Oduvaldo Vendrametto

Abstract. IT has an important role in the performance of companies, provides a flow of information that makes the supply chain become more robust and resilient, without compromising efficiency. Most companies are applying IT systems, mainly in Supply Chain Management (Supply Chain Management - SCM) to enhance their performance in competitive global markets. The research is important because it will provide a study of what are the IT systems used to manage the supply chain and likely future trends. To achieve the objective of this work was carried out a survey with consultants and professionals in IT and supply chain who work in large companies. To collect the data needed for analysis, we used the exploratory research of a qualitative nature. Thus, we can conclude that the use of IT in the supply chain directly impacts in the areas of planning, manufacturing suppliers, customers and delivery.

Keywords: IT, SCM, information systems.

1   Introduction

Rapid technological change and the need for information are always available to customers and suppliers, practically, is mandatory that all companies involved in any supply chain, use the Information Technology (IT).

Companies seek to adapt to this scenario focusing on performance, seeking to improve the level of service and reduce costs in an attempt to differentiate and increase the perceived value of their customers [1].

IT has an important role in the performance of companies, provides a flow of information that makes the supply chain become more robust and resilient, without compromising efficiency. Most companies are applying IT systems, mainly in Supply Chain Management (Supply Chain Management - SCM) to enhance their performance in competitive global markets [2].

According Prajogo & Olhager [3] IT can assist the SCM in the following aspects. First, it allows companies to increase the volume and complexity of information that needs to be communicated with its trading partners. Secondly, it allows companies to provide real-time information in the supply chain, including inventory levels, delivery status, and production planning and scheduling which enable companies to manage and control their supply chain activities. Third, it also facilitates the alignment of forecasting and scheduling operations between enterprises and suppliers.

The research is important because it will provide a study of what are the IT systems used to manage the supply chain and likely future trends.

B. Grabot et al. (Eds.): APMS 2014, Part I, IFIP AICT 438, pp. 132–141, 2014.

2   Literature Review

SCM has always been a challenge for information integration. The idea is to allow everyone involved in the flow of goods can make decisions based on the latest information and better than all others, both upstream and its downstream. The company manages its supply chain better get your product from point of origin to point of consumption in the shortest amount of time with the lowest cost [4].

According to Patterson et al. [5] a variety of factors can affect the decision of an organization to adopt and implement a technology that provides supply chain. The authors classify them into five broad categories: individual, related to task characteristics related to innovation, organizational and environmental. The authors also suggest that these factors may be important to different degrees, depending on the context or technology.

Information systems (IS) are combinations of technologies and people's activities using that technology to support operations, management, and decision-making [6].

IS provide many different solutions for almost all areas of business, the SCM uses some. Patterson et al. [5], point 18 IT systems applied to SCM. Table 1 shows the description and associated applications of various software, hardware and management systems.

Table 1. IT systems applied to SCM

Technology	Description
Legacy Systems	Legacy Systems are mainframe-based systems that operate at the operational level in only one stage. They are constructed as independent blocks, which hinders their communication with other systems. Systems were first used in SCM.
Barcode	Technology for the allocation of computer readable codes on items, boxes and containers. Employed to improve the data transmission speed and precision of the information. It is used in managing inventory, warehouses, supermarkets and so on.
CAD	Allows the realization of industrial designs on the computer screen that can be stored, manipulated and updated electronically.
BI	Set of applications that organizes and structures the transaction data of an organization, facilitating the analysis in order to benefit the operations and decision support.
EDI	It is the electronic transfer of data between business partners. The data is structured according to standards agreed in advance between the parties. Divided into two categories: traditional EDI, using services of value-added network, and WebEDI with access forms online (Internet).
Fleet tracking	Can be based on satellite transmission or by cell phone for tracking and monitoring of vehicles, being applied to control performance and safe transport. The data generated by this system feeding the TMS and WMS.

Table 1. (*continued*)

AQC	Responsible for monitoring the processes of quality assurance, inspection, specifications and calibration of measuring instruments.
MES	Planning systems that aim to optimize and synchronize their use. Supports the exchange of information between production planning and control of the production process through the monitoring and tracking of raw materials, equipment, personnel, instruction and production facilities.
TMS	Responsible for controlling the transport of loads, determining the modal, freight consolidation managing and coordinating the efforts of transport.
WMS	Optimizes operating activities (material flow) and administrative (information flow) in the process of storage, tracking and controlling the movement of inventory in the warehouse. Its use is restricted to operational decisions, such as: definition of collection routes, addressing products, etc..
CRM	Tool to unify customer information and create a single, centralized interactions and anticipating customer needs. It also provides control of promotional activities and their impact on demand as well as the control of activities of product warranty.
PDM	Manages information related to products, serving as an integration tool that connects different areas of product development.
RF	Facilitates communication, providing essential information on the status of the products. Support tool that automates and improves the management of operations, eliminating human error.
SCP	Assists in the planning, execution and measurement of processes, including modules for demand forecasting, inventory planning and distribution.
DFS	Uses mathematical methods that manipulate historical data and external data to forecast demand for products and services. In general, integrated systems, such as ERP and SCP.
WIS	Facilitates internal and external processes of enterprises, integrating enterprise information systems. In SCM, the WIS more presents are e-procurement and e-market place, which are systems of process automation corporate purchases.
B2B	Electronic marketplaces where suppliers and buyers interact to conduct transactions. It is an e-business, that is, relations between companies.
ERP	Unified system that integrates departments and functions of the company. Improves the flow of information chain in such a degree that it has become a standard operation.

Morais and Tavares [7] highlight several benefits provided by IT systems, as shown in table 2:

Table 2. Benefits of IT systems applied to SCM

Technology	Benefits
Barcode	- Replaces the process of collecting and exchanging information paper, with risks of error and rework constant. - Rapid deployment, - Easy to use - Compact Equipment
CAD	- Creation of movements in the drawing, allowing testing before production. - Reduced time for product development - Creating better quality drawings to facilitate communication with partners - Greater flexibility and faster responses in the design modifications - Offer data entry for computerized manufacturing
EDI	- Possibility of integration between organizations in applications like accounts payable, inventory control, shipping and production planning.
Fleet tracking	- Contribute to the management of the fleet and cargo and to control the hours of service of drivers
MES	- Flexible manufacturing process and high quality.
TMS	- Reduction of costs. - Efficient management and coordination of freight transportation efforts.
WMS	- Improvement of the distribution process.
CRM	- Satisfaction and Customer Loyalty
RF	Reduction of the costs of distribution warehouses, retail and handling stockouts.
SCP	Obtaining the real data demand, time and inventory.
ERP	Integrating and efficient flow of information in organization and / or between it and its partners.

Other authors reported the following benefits of the integration of IT and SCM:

Sanders et al. [8] showed a direct relationship between the use of technology in SCM and it was reported that organizations use IT more than normal in your industry, to achieve more operational benefits such as reduced costs and cycle times.

Levary [9] suggests that the benefits include: 1. Minimizing the bullwhip effect, 2 . Maximize the efficiency of conducting activities along the supply chain, 3 . Minimize inventory throughout the supply chain, 4 . Minimize cycle times along the supply chain, 5 . Achieve an acceptable level of quality throughout the supply chain.

Dias et al. [10] list the following benefits achieved by the use of IT in SCM: (i) sharing instant information , (ii) sharing programs that increase operational efficiency, (iii) real-time monitoring of the consumer load ; (iv) development of global sales channels (v) reduction of inventories , and (vi) greater flexibility .

These benefits can be obtained as the level of installation and use of IT systems, which directly affects the performance of the supply chain.

3   Methodology

Type of Research

To achieve the objective of this work was carried out a survey with consultants and professionals in IT and supply chain who work in large companies. To collect the data needed for analysis, we used the exploratory research of a qualitative nature.

For Gil [12], the exploratory research aims to provide greater familiarity with the problem in order to make it more explicit .

Zikmund [13] considers that exploratory studies are conducted to clarify ambiguous problems, research is needed to better understand the dimensions of the problems .

The qualitative approach presents a reality that can not be quantified or measured items and involves subjective reality research. You can work with the data without specific statistical treatment, seeking understanding of reality [14] .

The research can be categorized as "survey" as it involves the question directly to respondents, members of a significant sample of the research universe and whose behavior you want to know, because their results can lead to conclusions corresponding to the data collected [11].

Sample and Actors Research

The actors of the research are:

- IT Consultants
- Supply Chain Consultants.
- Employees of companies working with IT and Supply Chain.

Questionnaires were sent to 60 companies and 14 responded and, of these, most opted not to disclose the name or corporate fantasy for strategic reasons.

Research Instrument

For Gil [12] , most cases of exploratory research involves literature review and interviews.

The interview, at Gil [11], is a technique in which the researcher has investigated against him and asks questions, the objective of obtaining the data of interest to research.

The research instrument of this work consists of a questionnaire with closed and open questions. Some of the responses were directed by the interviewer, in the form of performance notes which aim to detect the degree of importance, according to the intensity of perception for that aspect.

4   Analysis of Results

The survey showed that all IT systems reported by Patterson et.al. [3], are used by some of the companies surveyed. The systems that are most commonly used by companies are those that provide greater operational benefits, as Sanders et.al. [8], including:

1) Barcoding and ERP, shown in Figure 01, were the most used systems in 11 of the 14 companies surveyed (78.5%). The companies surveyed confirmed the operational benefits that offer the use of the barcode as ease of use and elimination of paper in data collection and integration and efficiency in the flow of information in the organization and / or between it and its partners in the case of ERP [7].

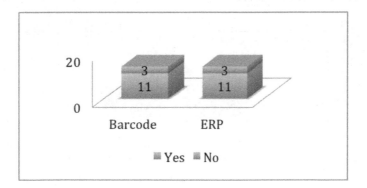

Fig. 1. Use of Barcode and ERP

2) Legacy systems, CAD, BI and WMS, had a use of 11 of the companies surveyed (71.4%) as noted in Figure 02. Legacy systems provide operational benefits as accesses to data and legacy systems, but are still used by companies. The BI organizes and structures the transaction data of an organization, facilitates the analysis in order to benefit the operations and support their decisions. To Morais e Tavares [7], the benefits obtained with CAD are creating movements in design allows testing before production, reduced time for product development, design creation of better quality to

facilitate communication with partners , greater flexibility and faster responses in the design modifications and offer input to the computerized manufacturing, whereas for the WMS, the benefit is the improvement of the distribution process.

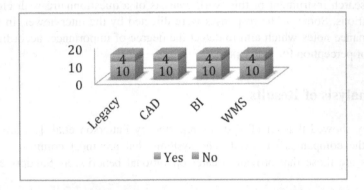

Fig. 2. Use of legacy systems, CAD, BI and WMS

3) The EDI and its use, as demonstrated in Figure 03, was reported by 9 of the 14 companies surveyed (64.2%). The main benefit presented is the possibility of integration between organizations in applications like accounts payable, inventory control, shipping and production planning.

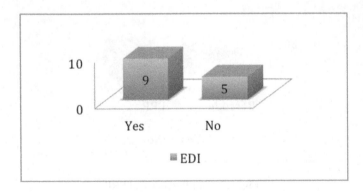

Fig. 3. Use of EDI

4) The use of CRM, DFS and SCP systems, as in Figure 04, are present in half of the companies surveyed (50%). Halves of the companies answered "No", this may indicate that these companies have caution in using these systems, or are not convinced about the benefits that they can provide since some benefits are geared more for planning than for operating as satisfaction and loyalty through CRM, obtaining the real data demand, time and inventory by SCP and forecast demand for products and services obtained from the DFS, as shown Morais and Tavares [7].

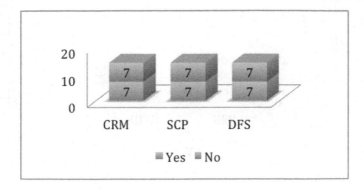

Fig. 4. Use of CRM, SCP and DFS

5) Among the seven fleet tracking systems, AQC, MES, TMS, WIS, PDM and RF, shown in Figure 05, five of the 14 companies surveyed - (35%) - answered "Yes" Tracking fleet, AQC, MES, TMS, WIS and 6 companies (42%) answered "Yes" to PDM and RF. Research has shown that the benefits offered by these systems as fleet management and cargo, flexible manufacturing process and high-quality, cost reduction and efficient management of freight, reducing expenses distribution warehouses, etc., relate to processes and management and not with the operational benefits, which does not make them attractive for use by all companies.

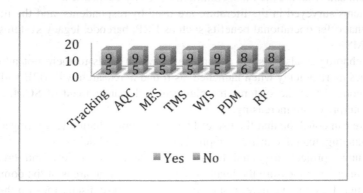

Fig. 5. Use of fleet tracking, AQC, MES, TMS. WIS, PDM and RF

6) In both B2B and RFID systems, shown in Figure 06, we note that the systems were less used by 14 companies surveyed, 4 for B2B companies (28.5%) and 3 companies for RFID (21.5%). It can be deduced that the low utilization is on the point that the two systems need specific equipment for deployment and the benefits are not operational.

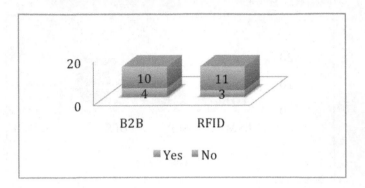

Fig. 6. Use of B2B and RFID

Questioned whether the respondents which would be applied to the IT systems of the future SCM. Two systems were cited VMI (Vendor Managed Inventory) - Stocks Managed by the Provider and ERP version 3.

5   Conclusions

The research achieved the objectives of verifying the main IT systems used in the supply chain and what are the most commonly used by businesses.

All systems surveyed in the literature are used by respondents, and the most used are those that offer operational benefits such as ERP, barcode, legacy systems, CAD , BI and WMS .

New technologies also " scare " companies which leads to them not adopt these technologies more quickly when launched, as found in research with B2B and RFID.

It was noticed that the systems for planning and management of SCM, and their usage in enterprises are increasing.

Thus, we can conclude that the use of IT in the supply chain directly impacts in the areas of planning, manufacturing   suppliers, customers and delivery.

As a future project, expected to use these items for review and creation of indicators in order to measure the level of impact in different areas of the company.

The matter does not end here, is a contribution to future discussions on the subject and quest for improvement of systems analysis of information technology in supply chain management .

Acknowledgment. CNPq, for making it possible and funded this research.

References

[1] Bandeira, R.A.M., Maçada, A.C.G.: Information technology in supply chain management: the case of the industry of gases. Produção 18(2), 287–301 (2008) (in portuguese)

[2] Ming-Lang, T., Kuo-Jui, W., Thi, T.N.: Information technology in supply chain management: a case study. Procedia - Social and Behavioral Sciences 25, 257–272 (2011)

[3] Prajogo, D.: Supply chain integration and performance: The effects of long-term relationships, information technology and sharing, and logistics integration. International Journal of Production Economics 135, 514–522 (2012)

[4] Davenport, T.H., Brooks, J.D.: Enterprise systems and the supply chain. Journal of Enterprise Information Management 17(1) (2004)

[5] Patterson, K., Grimm, C., Corsi, T.: Adopting new technologies for supply chain management. Transportation Research Part E 39, 95–121 (2003)

[6] Iguider, Y., Morita, H.: Toward Next Generation E-Marketplace for Small Business. International Journal of Computer Information Systems and Industrial Management Applications 5, 227–234 (2013)

[7] Morais, K.M.N., Tavares, E.: Use of information technology in managing supply chain in São Luís do Maranhão and opportunities for the development of local suppliers. Interações (Campo Grande). Campo Grande 12(2) (December 2011) (in portuguese)

[8] Sanders, N.R., Premus, R.: IT applications in supply chain organizations: a link between competitive priorities and organizational benefits. Journal of Business Logistics 23, 65–83 (2002)

[9] Levary, R.R.: Better supply chains through information technology. Industrial Management 42(3), 24–30 (2000)

[10] Dias, R., Pitassi, C., Joia, L.: Integrated management of the supply chain. Rio de Janeiro: FGV, EBAPE (2003) (in Portuguese)

[11] G.A.C.: Methods and Techniques of Social Research, São Paulo, Editora Atlas (1997) (in portuguese)

[12] Gil, A.C.: How to develop research projects. São Paulo. Editora Atlas (2002) (in portuguese)

[13] Zikmund, W.G.: Business Research Methods, 6th edn. The Dryden Press, Fort Worth (2000)

[14] Costa, M.A.F., Costa, M.F.B.: Research Methodology - Concepts and Techniques, Rio de Janeiro. InterCiência (2001) (in portuguese)

Managing Requirements: For an Integrated Approach from System Engineering to Project Management

Michel Malbert[1], Daniel Estève[2], Claude Baron[2,3], Philippe Esteban[2,4], and Rui Xue[2,3]

[1] Consultant, 24 rue Cartailhac, 31000 Toulouse, France
michel.malbert@outlook.fr
[2] CNRS, LAAS, 7 av. du colonel Roche, F-31400 Toulouse, France
{daniel.esteve,claude.baron,philippe.esteban,rui.xue}@laas.fr
[3] Univ de Toulouse, INSA, LAAS, F-31400 Toulouse, France
[4] Univ de Toulouse, UPS, LAAS, F-31400 Toulouse, France

Abstract. This paper puts forward several evolutions in methodological approaches to « project management ». Firstly, it aims to bring closer the founding models of different engineering approaches including systems engineering and project management recommendations to allow for a greater continuity and enhanced management coherence, from beginning to end of the project. It focuses on operating a generic process, called DECWAYS, based on handling management requirements: (1)analyze the requirements to arrive at a complete inventory of the final product ;(2)associate with each one of these requirements, an « indicator » setting a target objective for completion, supplemented by a risk function detailing the risk at hand based on the deviation relative to this target objective; (3) share and allocate the responsibility for requirements follow-up between the project team leaders; (4) organize and coordinate the follow-up of these indicators throughout the product development as proof of a good work management and,(5) finally, validate the total completion of the target objectives through the final prediction/completion conformity of these indicators. Based on this, several operational recommendations are explained and the practicality of DECWAYS embodying these principles is demonstrated using an experimental example for the design/planning of an electronic key.

Keywords: System Engineering, Project Management, Collaborative Engineering.

Introduction: In terms of « system », innovation defines an issue which is very difficult to address and still open to methodological progress in the management of multidisciplinary and complexity, prerequisite for success at all levels of the innovation process: from project definition and design stages to the finished product's end of life cycle. This issue is therefore grounded in all scientific and technical approaches built around this system innovation: « system engineering» which purports to formalize and comprehend the design of complex systems; «project management » which aims to organize step by step the smooth operation of project development (or program development when several projects have to be coordinated); « collaborative engineering » which intends to facilitate, optimize communication between all actors and

B. Grabot et al. (Eds.): APMS 2014, Part I, IFIP AICT 438, pp. 142–149, 2014.

therefore contribute to meeting coordination needs… Naturally, to master the difficulties inherent in multidisciplinary, it is first assumed that these various inputs get progressively aligned through a single "integrated" approach. These alignments are being carried out and have already given rise to meetings and joint documents [1, 2, 3]: they define a path of progress through terminological adjustments and a standardization of processes which will necessarily have to cut across various fields. This path is slow and arduous if only for the reason that it must be constructed on the operational ground, that of the company… Here, a more conceptual path is being proposed to move forward: we intend to rely on an innovation process, a unique federating process built on managing «systems requirements» only: this overall system development-innovation process can be defined as the set of basic processes enabling us to organize and handle the full completion of specifications and requirements, from the product definition phase to the product's end of life cycle… The prerequisite for success is that system requirements are complete in the sense that they have to address the whole innovation–development process one intends to manage: for simplicity's sake it is assumed that these requirements can be presented in the form of a List (R1, R2…). Based on these considerations, DECWAYS propose a complete innovative generic process build on the idea of sharing the requirements follow up between three specialized leaders (executing, controlling and planning), for structuring a permanent coordination. The presentation develop successively: the question of requirements to arrive at a complete inventory of the final product ; the association with each one of these requirements, an « indicator » setting a target objective for completion, supplemented by a risk function detailing the risk at hand based on the deviation relative to this target objective; the information system which organize and coordinate the follow-up of these indicators throughout the product development as proof of a good work management. Finally, we illustrate a first step of DECWAYS development on an experimental example for the design/planning of an electronic key.

1   Requirements, the Foundation for a «Product» Development Follow-Up Process

Requirements analysis is a 'critical' input at the start of an innovating project: based on the results of this analysis are all the prospective assessments that will play such an important part in the decision to launch the project… And it is worth underlining here how important these results are in the drawing up of a management methodology which on the basis of a complete inventory of these requirements, supports the definition of a consistent approach for product development construction and management. This approach consists of the following steps: (1) Analyze requirements to arrive at a complete inventory of the product life; (2) Associate with each one of these requirements an 'indicator' setting a completion target objective, supplemented by a risk function detailing the risk at hand as a function of the deviation relative to that target objective; (3) Assign responsibility for requirements follow-up among the project team leaders; (4) Organize the follow-up of these indicators throughout product development as proof of a sound work management; (5) Finally, validate the full completion of the target objectives through the final prediction/completion conformity of these indicators.

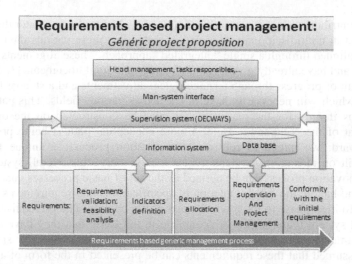

Fig. 1. Requirements-based project management

It appears that a requirements-based management lays the groundwork for a generic and complete project management process: generic because it does not imply that the nature of the project be specified as it may be a product or service; complete in the sense that it arises from an expression of ideas and objectives, through requirements and these target indicators, and finishes with an ending «selected» by the degree of conformity of the work result with these target objectives. Our ambition is to propose a «supervision system» associated with an «information system» related to this generic process whose assignment is to provide information and monitor automatically the evolution of "indicators" values throughout the work: thus emphasis is placed on the choice and quality of these indicators which more than ever must be fully defined, measurable, traceable and documented…

2   Indicators

In the approach put forward, **indicators are directly associated with the requirements** of which they are proof throughout the development work. Under this assumption, their evolution from the initial situation to the target objective must be programmed using milestone target values in relation to the overall progress of the development work. Let us call Δ the deviation, at a given step t, between target value and current value, our proposal being to associate with this deviation a «**risk function**» for the project. In most cases, this function will pertain specifically to the corporate policy and will therefore be perfectly known to all actors. Our recommendation is that, at the very least, this function, which will be involved in the decision choices, be concerted at the start of the project and then have its full part in the decision phases. In practice it may take the simple form of a conventional risk scale, typically Δ between 1 and 7, to calibrate the response between a low level of risk and a serious danger of failure. Indicators are simple and straightforward if they reflect requirements such as timelines, expenditures and certain performances, but they may also result from an aggregation of data selected following discussions to narrow down the number of parameters to be followed in the progress of the work or to express more clearly the corporate policy. These indicators will be computed online by the information system. In practice, the approach we recommend consists in collecting and recording during a step assessment (milestone) all indicator data on a «**management dashboard**» comparing the current reality with the «**strategic dashboard**» drawn up initially by the project management team. Any deviations found may then lead to management corrective actions partly guided by the risk functions analysis. This point is key for a sound management of the project and actors must necessarily be coordinated to ensure pertinence, coherence and efficiency in their corrective choices. In these choices, the corporate policy plays a decisional role which should already be known to all, given the calibrations of risk functions selected for each requirement. One may question the genericity of the proposal as a function of specificities in the choice of certain preferred industrial management options: for example, can this approach be applied indifferently, for a «conventional top-down» management and an «agile» management of project: in the latter case, the alignment of milestone deadlines and the need to factor in an added value for each one does not call for a change in the approach: at each new step in the project breakdown, a limited number of selected requirements will guide in the management of the new step, once the results of the previous step have been achieved.

3   Information System

During project development, a requirements-based management will basically consist in following up the indicators throughout the project life: thus any deviations in terms of completion between the current progress and the target objective initially defined

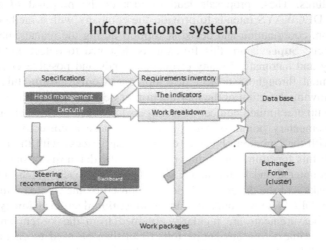

Fig. 2. Information system

by the requirements will be detected. Thus, looking at all the indicators (dashboards) one can accurately monitor the evolution of the project and detect at the earliest any possible drift relative to the target objectives and possible errors in operational management: this can be achieved by programming milestones or alternatively, it may spontaneously follow a project management decision to intervene. For complex projects necessitating a task breakdown, task managers will receive their roadmaps on the basis of a project requirements assignment and will be able to organize their task developments in accordance with our recommendations. Together they will have to complete during the milestones their progress file stating to senior management any progress that has been recorded under their guidance. An information system is essential for the collection and storage of all useful data: organizational choices, target data, current data, management decisions and exchanges between the different actors.

4   Supervision (DECWAYS)

Improving the methods and tools in project management is an industrial imperative clearly identified in the reviews dealing with assessment study: successes and failures of a large sample of projects. Here our ambition is to improve the dysfunction detection approach in project management and the ability of all project actors to coordinate their involvement. The idea is to propose a structured path for the actions to be carried out by apportioning the requirements follow-up tasks between a defined number of managers and thus oblige the latter to structurally make concerted decisions. This principle is supplemented by the choice, for project management, of a supervision system approach based on an automated detection of deviations or malfunctions during programmed management, by risk analysis in the choice or corrective decisions and by a systematic storage of all decisions made. This choice should facilitate implementation in practice since monitoring does not call for a modification of the tools already in use in companies but «only» to make them communicate towards the proposed procedures. These proposals lead in turn to the proposal of a new tool: DECWAYS. DECWAYS intends to provide the company with a method and a tool for supervision, coordination and decision support during the management of development projects: **Supervision**: this function is designed to detect and characterize systematically and automatically any erroneous trends and possible errors in design and management throughout project development. **Coordination**: this function is designed, following detection of the malfunction or deviation, to «oblige» the collegial body made up of a limited number of managers to consult each other on their structurally complementary points of view, and to propose a corrective consensus in accordance with the common objective of achieving success with the project. **Decision support**: this function which aims to support the diagnosis of the cause for the difficulty encountered and to formulate a corrective approach which anticipates the compared « risks » of the different solutions proposed by the limited number of partners in charge. DECWAYS is built around a **conventional supervision system architecture** [4]: measurements are regularly obtained from the system and compared with reference values. Any deviations found can then be used to check the proper functioning and detect possible «failures». But that can only be done if the reference values, that is the correct functioning model, are «fair». In practice, there exist two options: one is empirical based on value learning during periods of correct operation, the other relying on a theoretical model. In terms of project management, the model is necessarily theoretical: it results from an initial modeling which is predictive of the project progress.

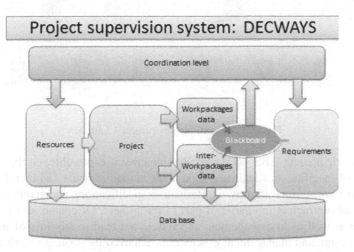

Fig. 3. – Project supervision system: « DECWAYS »

5   Example of DECWAYS Implementation and Application to the Design of an Electronic Key

Basic rules [5] condition the development of specialized tools furnishing supervision, coordination and decision support in project management. However, it turns out that these expert rules are in part the result of work conducted within the framework of the contract ANR/ATLAS [6] in which the three salient features of DECWAYS were being explored : supervision, coordination and decision support though the concept of risk functions associated with the deviations between current data and target objectives. A first result of this experiment: it is imperative that design and planning managers share the same Work Breakdown Structure (hereafter 'WBS') for the project. This structural framework formalizes and organizes exchange, coordination and decision needs shared at each level (milestones). A supervision software mockup [7] has been developed with an industrial support which validated the practicality of the approach. It is being investigated in depth in order to create a new DECWAYS tool including the previous proposals and puts forward a generalization of the notion of indicators in order to take into account the strategic objective of standardization between system engineering and project management processes. The tool ATLAS has been investigated within the framework of an «electronic key» project follow-up for the automotive industry. Look at Fig. 4 below: it depicts at the instant considered, the logic breakdown tree for the project's system design with a review of possible solutions in the case of a kcy-detector couple. The project management tree remains the same. This homomorphy results from the step-by-step construct logic reliant upon the generic process and illustrated in Fig. 5.

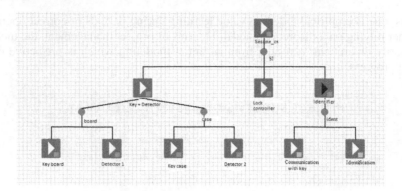

Fig. 4. The electronic key project « Sésame»

The generic process relies on the general idea that it is possible, on the basis of the initial set of specifications and its embodiment in requirements and therefore in indicators under constraints, to draw up derivative specifications and requirements for a group of subcontractors in charge of part of the project. Of course all this applies to the design as well as to management and should not lead to any loss of information. Coupling design and management processes is achieved by pooling together a number of indicators (allowing thus for the detection of any inconsistencies between the two parties) and sharing decisions (e.g., the decision to define a subcontractor workpackage calls for the approval by both partners as to the technical objectives and the means provided to reach them). Example of a situation handled by ATLAS: consider a joint design and management indicator, Nh the total number of work hours to reach the objective assigned to a subcontracted workpackage. This value is set by the prime contractor and assigned as objective to be reached by the subcontractor's management. The subcontractor's design will assess this value and submit the result to his management colleague: in the event of a dispute they will either look for a solution acceptable to them or contact the prime contractor to negotiate a settlement. Indicator values are known at each tree node (nodes being depicted as small squares in Fig. 4). Therefore it is possible to know the state of the system at each tree node via the associated dashboard: this information along with the formalized collaboration between these two major functions "design" and "management" are both a diagnostic support and beyond, a decision support. Note that the dashboard associated with a node yields for an indicator the local value and the aggregate value fed from the tree branch concerned This feature allows management to choose between several solutions the one which yields for example the best result for a key indicator. An operational prototype ATLAS has been drawn up and allows us to check 1/ the feasibility of the design – management coupling, 2/ the support in choosing the right solutions for the electronic key problem, 3/ the relevance of the choice of thin client-Web technology as an implementation environment.

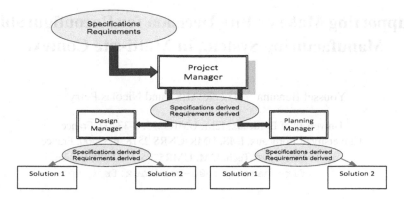

Fig. 5. Tree construction principle

Conclusions: Improving the methods and tools for project management is an industrial imperative that has been clearly identified in the analyses dealing with assessment reviews, successes and failures of a large sample of projects. The aim of the proposals made in this paper is to improve coordination and cooperation between all project leaders. The idea relies on putting forward a generic process built on the thorough management of the system requirements which is then used to build up information and supervision system referred to as DECWAYS. Thanks to a generalized follow-up of « indicators », this system supports automated detection of any deviations or malfunctions in the programmed management, risk analysis in the choice of corrective actions and systematic storage of these decisions… These proposals lead in turn to the proposed of a new tool DECWAYS which does not call for any modification of the tools already in use by companies but "simply" to have them communicate (information system) towards the proposed procedures. A simple example of a first development shows the feasibility and confirms the interest of the approach.

References

1. Sharon, A., de Weck, O.L., Dori, D.: Project management vs. systems engineering management: A practitioners' view on integrating the project and product domains. Syst. Eng. 14(4), 427–440 (2011)
2. Conforto, E., Rossi, M., Rebentisch, E., Oehmen, J.: Pacenza, Survey Report: Improving Integration of Program Management and Systems Engineering. MIT Consortium for Engineering Program Excellence (2013)
3. Systems Engineering – Project Management (SE – PM) Working Group — INCOSE Chesapeake Chapter Chesapeake Chapter of INCOSE, http://www.incose-cc.org/2012/04/systems-engineering-project-management-se-pm-working-group/ (last consult: February 27, 2014)
4. Bonhomme, S., Campo, E., Esteve, D., Guennec, J.: Methodology and tools for the design and verification of complex systems. In: IS 2008, Varna, pp. 24-2–24-7 (September 2008)
5. Malbert, M., Estève, D., Baron, C., Xue, R., Esteban, P.: DECWAYS, une nouvelle étape dans les approches de la conduite de projet. LAAS-CNRS (in press 2014)
6. ATLAS, Aides et assisTances pour la conception, la conduite et leur coupLage par les connAissanceS, Contrat ANR programme, Technologies Logicielles, 07-TLOG-002-05 (2007-2011)

Supporting Make or Buy Decision for Reconfigurable Manufacturing System, in Multi-site Context

Youssef Benama[1,*], Thècle Alix[2], and Nicolas Perry[3]

[1] University of Bordeaux, I2M, UMR5295, F-33400, France
[2] University of Bordeaux, IMS, UMR-CNRS 2518, F-33400, France
[3] Arts et Métiers ParisTech, I2M, UMR5295, F-33400, France
firstname.name@u-bordeaux.fr

Abstract. The make or buy decision is a strategic issue. When looking for finding out which components or products should be manufactured or externalized then buy, capacity for human and technical resources at the workshop level as well as costs of the externalization are key questions to be answered. In the case of mobile manufacturing systems that are movable between various locations, long term strategic aspects must be considered when addressing the make or buy decision problem. This paper aims to provide a structured make or buy decision model, adapted for reconfigurable manufacturing systems with strong mobility constraints. An industrial application case is provided to illustrate the presented method.

Keywords: Mobility, RMS, make or buy, multi-site context, MCDM.

1 Introduction

The make or buy decision problem also known as "sourcing", "outsourcing" or "subcontracting" problem, is among the most pervasive issues confronting modern organizations [1]. Making the right decision with regard to outsourcing can provide a major boost to a company's financial performance, although there is evidence that many companies do not achieve the advantages of outsourcing [2]. McIvor [3] demonstrates that decisions on outsourcing are rarely taken on the basis of particular strategic perspectives. Most of time the only intention is gaining short-term cost advantages [2].

The "make or buy" decision is a strategic decision and has implications for the overall corporate strategy of the organization by analyzing a number of strategic factors in case of short term cost reduction purpose, long-term strategic considerations, which have greater importance, should be considered [4]. Padillo[1] identified six disciplines covered by the make or buy problem: (1) industrial organization; (2) corporate/business strategy; (3) purchasing or supply management; (4) strategic operations management; (5) operations research; and (6) cost accounting or managerial economics.

---

* Corresponding author.

B. Grabot et al. (Eds.): APMS 2014, Part I, IFIP AICT 438, pp. 150–158, 2014.

Make or buy decision was argued most frequently by the economists. They have considered the "make or buy" problem especially with the perspective of costs. But the "make or buy" decision considerations should not only focus on costs [4]. Many authors, have noted the need to include multiple factors when performing a make or buy analysis [1]. They take into account strategic competitive performance, managerial performance, sourcing performance and financial performance. McIvor [5] proposed a model based on technical capability, comparison of internal and external capabilities, organization profiles and total acquisition costs.

On the other hand, manufacturing systems operating in a context characterized by: demand fluctuation, local production and site dependency, should cope with specifications such as mobility, scalability and functional adaptability. Those specifications allow fast and cost effectively adaptation to environment changes. In the literature, manufacturing systems meeting these specifications are referenced as Reconfigurable Manufacturing Systems (RMS) [6]–[9]. In the area of RMS, we notice a lack of models that takes into account the production system mobility, when addressing the "make or buy" problem. Furthermore, in multi-site context, a long term vision should be incorporated into the decision model in order to optimize the investments for the manufacturing mobile system respectively to the expected capacity and final product costs.

In the following sections we detail our proposed make or buy model adapted to RMS systems. Then, the industrial application case illustrates the model before concluding.

2   The Proposed Make or Buy Model for RMS Systems

The proposed decision model framework is adapted from the model proposed by van de Water and van Peet [2]. This framework highlights 3 decision model stages:

- Strategic analysis: the make or buy decision is based on the satisfaction of multiple objectives (e.g. cost, risk...). This stage deals with the importance of each objective. The given importance highlights the priorities of the decision maker. Decision situation has an impact on these priorities, for example, considering the purchasing situation classification presented by Faris [10].
- Alternative evaluation: this stage proposes a model to evaluate in house manufacturing or external sourcing alternatives. The evaluation model is based on indicators definition. Each of the four indicators proposed is depending on other parameters which we call attributes. This stage will be detailed in the next section.
- Providers selection: this stage is about contractual aspects in the provider selection process and collaboration nature definition. It's based on previous stage results. While our aim is to identify if manufacturing of a specified product will be achieved in house or via external sourcing. This stage is out of this paper scope.

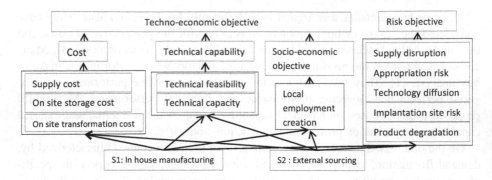

Fig. 1. Structure of the alternative's evaluation model

2.1   Alternative Evaluation Model

Assessment of Techno-economic Objective

Cost evaluation

We identify three attributes linked to cost objective. Supply cost (1): it takes into account material purchasing costs and shipping costs set from transportation costs and customs clearance fees. On site storage cost (2): it depends on component value, storage period and cost of all tools used in storage activity. On site transformation cost (3): concerns all costs linked to transformation operations and value added activities realized on site. For in house manufacturing case, it takes into account, machinery investment, cost relative to usual functioning like process configuration cost, maintenance cost and energy cost. In addition, for a mobile manufacturing system, the full workshop is shipped on site, so it's necessary to consider the shipping cost. On the other hand, external sourcing case concerns in most cases quality inspection operations when receiving materials, and reworking operations.

To assess the satisfaction of the cost objective, we use the satisfaction function proposed by Harrington [11] which appears to give satisfactory results in our case.

Technical capability objective

Internal technical capability

Internal technical feasibility describes the ability of in-house manufacturing alternative to ensure the know-how and process required to satisfy the product feasibility on site. It depends on:

System mobility: machinery and resources must be movable from one site to another.

Qualification availability: operators are needed to be hired locally.

Energy availability and accessibility: in the context of desertic location, energy accessibility may be difficult, that can limit the use of certain resources (welding...).

On the other hand, internal technical capacity is related to the ability to supply the necessary quantity of raw materials. Two factors are involved: (1) the availability of qualified suppliers, (2) their proximity from the geographical production location.

Supplier technical capability
McIvor and Humphreys [5] identified 6 criteria to evaluate the technological capabilities of supplier, which include manufacturing capabilities, technical support, design capability, investment in R&D, speed of development and new product introduction (NPI) rate. In our analysis, technical support, investment on R&D and design capability are embedded in technical feasibility. On the other hand, manufacturing capability, speed of development and NPI rate determine the technical capacity of suppliers.

Evaluation of technical capability satisfaction
Evaluation of each technical capability factor is realized by giving notation between 0 and 1. Non-compensatory aggregation strategy is needed because the failure of one technical capability factor could not be compensated by the well performance of another factor. GOWA (Generalized Ordered Weighted Averaging) aggregation operator could be used to make aggregation [12].

Socio-economic objective
In the case of public projects where clients are governments or official institutes, socio-economic issues must be considered. Öncü stated that "*A government concerned with economic growth cannot ignore the economic aspects of technology. Major purpose of national technology policy is the harnessing of technology to meet economic and social goals [...]. When one local-manufacture project is chosen rather than an import project, the choices have consequences for employment, [...]. Each local manufacture project will affect employment and wage payments.*" [4]. The socio-economic benefits in terms of promoting local employment have an impact on final decision. We propose to incorporate in our model a socio-economic objective, which is concerned with the direct employment creation. This objective will be directly linked to geographical production localization of the supplier: if the supplier is localized in the same country than client site, the satisfaction value is 1, otherwise, the satisfaction value is 0.1.

For a considered make or buy alternative, the assessment of the corresponding techno-economic objective is based on the aggregation of cost, technical capability and socio-economic objectives. For aggregation, we use GOWA operator [12]:

$$TEO_i(A_j) = \sqrt[s]{\omega_{TEO} * TEO_i^s + \omega_{RO} * RO_i^s} \qquad (1)$$

Risk Objective

Identification of risk factors
Padillo [1] identified 4 sourcing risk attributes: appropriation risk, technology diffusion risk, end-product degradation risk, and supply disruption risk. Appropriation and technology diffusion risks are relevant mostly for outsourcing alternatives. While Supply disruption is applicable to both in-house and outsourcing alternatives [1]. On the other side, end-product degradation risk is in relation with the outsourcing of an activity that is located between the firm and its customers. This type of risk is not present in our problem, but the risk about transportation activity remains dominant. Wagner [13] divided risk sources into five distinct classes: (1) demand side;

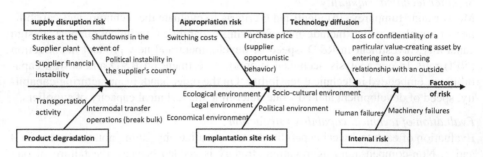

Fig. 2. Identification of risk factors

(2) supply side; (3) regulatory, legal and bureaucratic; (4) infrastructure; and (5) catastrophic. Srinivasan [14] focus on two types of factors that can impact the performance of supply chain, the first factors are internal to supply chain, which are demand and supply risks, like demand variability, lead-time variability supply delays, order cancellations, etc.). On the other hand, environment uncertainty which includes factors that are external to the supply chain. Those factors are strategic in nature, like, changes in product or process technology, competitor behavior, changes in consumer preferences, etc.

Production system mobility implies that the characteristics of the site where the production system will be implanted will vary. In consequent, the risk factors related to implantation site should be integrated in the analysis. We use a macro-environment analysis, like the PESTLE (Political, Economic, Social, Technological, Legal and Environmental analysis) approach to characterize risks related to the implantation site. In the other hand, either make or buy situations require realization of additional operations by the buying firm. Internal operations need human and machinery interventions and should be realized locally on site. In consequent, internal risks corresponding to human and machinery failures should be considered in both situations.

The assessment of each risk factor is firstly conducted using the FMECA (Failure Modes, Effects and Criticality Analysis). Each risk factor will be identified and quantified in term of likelihood of occurrence and in term of severity. Thereby, the overall risk criticality of will be defined by summing the corresponding criticality of risk factors. The next question is how to judge if the level of the risk criticality is acceptable or not. We define a satisfaction function that will express the preferences of the decision maker. We use Derringer function (Derringer, 1980); the decision maker expresses an interval of criticality levels among which the criticality level of the considered alternative will be acceptable.

Performance Evaluation

Local Performance evaluation
Local performance evaluation aims to find out the best alternative for each considered site localization. Each objective is evaluated as it was mentioned previously. The decision-maker should express it's preference between the importance of each

objective. Aggregation of the local performance is made using the GOWA operator [12]. This operator allow the DM to adapt the aggregation strategy, i.e. if compensation will be considered or not, to each situation decision, by setting the trade-off strategy parameter. For each site i, Local performance evaluation of alternative j is assessed:

$$LPE_i(A_j) = \sqrt[s]{\omega_{TEO} * TEO_i^s + \omega_{RO} * RO_i^s} \qquad (2)$$

TEO : Technical and Economical Objective value. RO : Risk Objective value

Global Performance evaluation
Global Performance evaluation aims to determine the best alternative in regard to overall sites. First condition that should be verified is the importance of each site. For strategic reasons, like the willingness to enter a new market, or for reasons of market size. Global Performance Evaluation (GPE) of the alternative j is given by:

$$GPE(A_j) = \sqrt[s]{\sum_{i=1}^{n} \omega_i * \left(LPE_i(A_j)\right)^s} \qquad (3)$$

n: number of sites where the production system will operate. ω_i is the importance of the site i. $LPE_i(A_j)$ is the local performance evaluation of the alternative j, for the site i. s is the trade-off strategy parameter. All alternatives will be ranked following the GPE value, and then the best alternative will have the high GPE.

3   Industrial Application

The Industrial application concerns an enterprise E, operating in solar energy sector. For confidentiality reasons, real values have been changed, but hypotheses and assumptions remain valid. The component analyzed is a steel part obtained by bending process. This part is critical because it contributes to mechanical resistance of the end-product. The production should be operated by the same reconfigurable manufacturing system sequentially on 5 different sites. The expected volume demands are: S1=20000, S2=18000, S3 = 16000, S4 = 5000, S5 = 11000. We consider 3 different alternatives. A1: part will be manufactured by the internal production system. A2: part will be realized by an external low cost supplier in Eastern Europe. A3: corresponds to an external supplier localized in North Africa.

3.1   Stage 1: Strategic Analysis

Objective's Weighting
Importance of each objective is set using a pairwise comparison. Therefore, the importance of each objective will be obtained by the eigenvector of the matrix: Cost Objective: 0.635, Technical capability=0.287 and Socio-economical objective=0.078. In order to assess local performance for each site, technical and economical objective and risk objective will be considered with the same importance: $\omega_{TCO} = 0.5$ and $\omega_{Risk} = 0.5$.

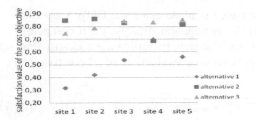

Fig. 3. Satisfaction of cost objective

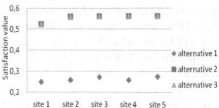

Fig. 4. Satisfaction of technical capability

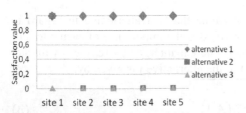

Fig. 5. Socio economic objective

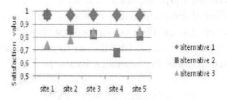

Fig. 6. Techno-Economic Objective

3.2   Stage 2: Evaluation of Alternatives

Evaluation of Techno-Economic Objective (TEO):

Technical and economical objective is assessed from cost (figure 3), technical capability (figure 4) and socio-economic objectives (figure 5). Compensation (s=100) has been made between these attributes. For alternative 1, poor satisfaction values of cost and technical objectives are compensated by the satisfaction of the socio-economic objective.

Evaluation of Risk Objective

Alternative 1 allows better control of risk factors, because in this case technology diffusion risk doesn't exist, supply disruption and product degradation risks are reduced because supplying raw materials has less value than supplying finite components. In the other hand, internal risks are more important in the case of internalization because more resources are needed. Consequently, human and machinery failures have more impact in this case.

Local Performance Evaluation

For each alternative, in order to assess the local performance, non compensatory aggregation (s=-100) is made between TEO and risk objective, and that for each site location. In the case study, figure 8 shows alternative 1 ranked 1.

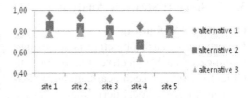

Fig. 7. Evaluation of risk objective

Global Performance Evaluation

The global make or buy decision must be made by accounting for all local performance evaluations. Compensation (s=100) is made between different sites. This implies that business 'strategic plan included that sites with negative financial results can be compensated by other sites with positive results. Figure 8 shows that alternative 1 presents in this case the best solution regarding the 5 sites. We note that all the 5 site locations are assumed to have the same importance : ω_{site} = 0.2.

Fig. 8. Local Performance Evaluation   **Fig. 9.** Global Performance Evaluation

4   Conclusion

The paper aims to propose a structured decision model adapted for reconfigurable systems in multi-site context. Although the financial objective traditionally dominated the analysis of make or buy alternatives, this research demonstrates that is possible to consider strategic and technological issues in connection with the decision. The study allows considering specific characteristics of the mobile manufacturing systems and provides a model that takes into account a longer term vision.

There are additional areas to investigate. We considered that all providers and production sites were well identified. However, it depends on the commercial strategy of the firm. Uncertainty about future clients and likely suppliers should be considered.

References

1. Padillo, J.M., Diaby, M.: A multiple-criteria decision methodology for the make-or-buy problem. International Journal of Prduction Research (1999)
2. van de Water, H., van Peet, H.P.: A decision support model based on the Analytic Hierarchy Process for the Make or Buy decision in manufacturing. J. Purch. Supply Manag. 12(5), 258–271 (2006)
3. McIvor, R.T., Humphreys, P.K., McAleer, W.E.: A strategic model for the formulation of an effective make or buy decision. Manag. Decis. 35(2), 169–178 (1997)
4. Öncü, A.A., Oner, M.A., Başoğlu, N.: Make or Buy' Analysis for Local Manufacture or Import Decisions in Defense System Procurements Using AHP: The Case of Turkey. In: Proceedings of PICMET, p. 2 (2003)
5. McIvor, R.T., Humphreys, P.K.: A case-based reasoning approach to the make or buy decision. Integr. Manuf. Syst. 11(5), 295–310 (2000)

6. ElMaraghy, H.A.: Flexible and reconfigurable manufacturing systems paradigms. Int. J. Flex. Manuf. Syst. 17(4), 261–276 (2006)
7. Bi, Z.M., Lang, S.Y.T., Shen, W., Wang, L.: Reconfigurable manufacturing systems: the state of the art. Int. J. Prod. Res. 46(4), 967–992 (2008)
8. Koren, Y., Shpitalni, M.: Design of reconfigurable manufacturing systems. J. Manuf. Syst. 29(4), 130–141 (2010)
9. Stillström, C., Jackson, M.: The concept of mobile manufacturing. J. Manuf. Syst. 26(3–4), 188–193 (2007)
10. Faris, C.W., Wind, Y., Institute, M.S., Robinson, P.J.: Industrial buying and creative marketing. Allyn & Bacon, Boston (1967)
11. Collignan, A.: Méthode d'optimisation et d'aide à la décision en conception mécanique: Application à une structure aéronautique. Université Bordeaux I (2011)
12. Yager, R.R.: Generalized OWA Aggregation Operators. Fuzzy Optim. Decis. Mak. 3(1), 93–107 (2004)
13. Wagner, S.M., Bode, C.: An empirical examination of supply chain performance along several dimensions of risk. J. Bus. Logist. 29(1), 307–325 (2008)
14. Srinivasan, M., Mukherjee, D., Gaur, A.S.: Buyer–supplier partnership quality and supply chain performance: Moderating role of risks, and environmental uncertainty. Eur. Manag. J. 29(4), 260–271 (2011)

Using Unitary Traceability
for an Optimal Product Recall

Thierno M.L. Diallo[1], Sébastien Henry[1], and Yacine Ouzrout[2]

[1] DISP Laboratory, University of Lyon, University Lyon 1, France
{Thierno.Diallo,Sebastien.Henry}@univ-lyon1.fr
[2] DISP Laboratory, University of Lyon, University Lyon 2, France
Yacine.Ouzrout@univ-lyon2.fr

Abstract. Product recall is a challenge which may have a significant financial impact. Incidents should be anticipated to improve responsiveness and reduce potential harm. In this paper, we propose a product recall approach following the detection of a critical fault. It is applicable to foodstuffs industry characterized by complex processes with high variability, high-speed manufacture and very large lots sizes. In such a case, usual strategy which consists of recalling entire lots is expensive and does not foster continuous improvement. The proposed approach in this paper allow to identify root causes and other products likely to present the same noncompliance in order to make a targeted recall. The root causes are searched based on an analysis of traceability data using a Bayesian model. A data model suitable for product and process traceability is also proposed. The originality of our approach lies on the reconstitution of the conditions of manufacturing of each item through the coupling of product and process unitary traceability data.

Keywords: Product Recall, Root Causes, Traceability, Bayesian Networks.

1 Introduction

Despite all the control means implemented in industries, the risk of shipping noncompliant products that do not meet consumer safety standard always exists [1-3]. When this nonconformity might cause serious and lasting health problems or death because of the use or exposure to the product then a recall is required. Due to globalization of exchanges (several suppliers and customers across all continents), product complexity (several ingredients and complex manufacturing processes) and regulations (accountability of the manufacturer on its product), product recall is nowadays a challenge that is facing more and more industries[4]. Although product recall may concern any type of product, but it is especially more frequent and critical in the field of food products. The causes of these recalls mainly come from materials, equipment or processes [1, 2, 4]. The usual strategy which consists of recalling entire lots generates direct and indirect costs especially on branding. These massive recalls are generally done without knowing the status (compliant or not) of recalled products. There are several examples where companies do very large recall because they cannot identify really defective items [2].

B. Grabot et al. (Eds.): APMS 2014, Part I, IFIP AICT 438, pp. 159–166, 2014.

The product recall scenarios are quite varied depending on the type of product, the type and scope of the supply chain and regulation. These scenarios also vary depending on the lifetime of the product, its manufacturing process and the actors involved in its life cycle (manufacturer, distributor, and retailer). The common point of all these scenarios is the need to trace the product to be recalled [5]. All recall scenarios use more or less traceability data to achieve the recall procedure. The knowledge of product life cycle from the origin of raw material is a key factor for the identification of products to be recalled and the definition of an effective recall procedure [4-6]. That is why traceability plays a crucial role in product recall. The determination of the causes of a nonconformity will depend in large part on the quality of the traceability system.

The use of deterministic tools for causal analysis in product recall procedure as reported in [4, 6] is not always justifiable. In this work, we devise a framework for optimal product recall following a nonconformity finding based on a probabilistic causal model using a Bayesian network (BN). To find these causes, the knowledge of product records is necessary. To our knowledge, the few published data models dedicated to the unitary traceability (see for example [7, 8]) have some restrictions in terms of actual material and process data registration. The unitary traceability system (enabling a serialized unique identification at the item level) and the proposed data model allow to know accurately the process parameters of each item. From this history, causal analysis is performed to identify potential causes for the noncompliance and other products that may be affected. Determination of the list of potentially noncompliant products thus enables a targeted recall.

This paper is organized as follow. The overall recall procedure proposed is presented in Section 2. In Section 3, we propose a data model for collecting traceability data required for the developed causal analysis framework. This causal analysis framework is presented in Section 4. And last we conclude with the mains contributions and perspectives of this work.

2   Traceability and the Proposed Product Recall Procedure

Traceability is an effective means for the mastery of the supply chain and for production optimization (scheduling and resources optimization). It enables to cope with urgent and unforeseen situations such as product recalls. When the element under consideration is a food product, the important elements to trace are raw materials and ingredients making up the product, the history of transformation processes and distribution and location of the product after delivery [9]. The traceability unit can be an aggregation of several articles (e.g. a lot or a pallet) or can be thinner and correspond to an article (unitary traceability).Within the framework of product recall, both types of traceability are required: tracking or forward traceability and tracing or backward traceability. Forward traceability is used to determine, for example, finished products containing a particular ingredient or having undergone a specific process. Backward traceability offers the possibility to identify suppliers and processes involved in producing a particular article [5]. In terms of visibility and management policy, there are two levels of traceability; internal and external traceability [10]. Internal traceability deals with private data stored within the company for internal use or in case of requests from the authorities. Among these data may be mentioned the process parameters, the origin of raw materials, quality records, etc. External traceability concerns public data that the different partners in a supply chain shall exchange between them to ensure end-to-end traceability. The recall procedure presented in this paper uses unitary and internal traceability data.

Unlike the conventional recall procedure, the aim of the proposed procedure is to restrict the number of items to recall by exploiting unitary traceability data. This strategy is especially relevant for products with high added value with large lot sizes (>1 million). The proposed recall procedure starts with the detection or the reporting of a noncompliance. Fig.1 illustrates graphically the main tasks of the proposed recall procedure.

Confirmation of the Noncompliance. This preliminary task enables the product manufacturer to establish unambiguously the noncompliance reported and to place the responsibilities between the different stakeholders (manufacturer, shipper, distributor, etc.). To do this, it may refer to historicized traceability data and tests. These traceability data must be reliable and usable.

Determine Possible Causes of the Noncompliance through Backward Traceability. Determine root cause (raw material /process / machine parameters) likely to be causing the noncompliance. This task corresponds to the backward traceability process. This is a challenging task due to the large number of parameters to be considered, their large variability and uncertainties. Causes other than process / machine parameters such as design defects may give rise to non-compliances. But in our study, we limit ourselves to causes related to process / machine parameters.

Determine the Duration of Abnormal Operation. Determines the range of time during which the manufacturing process has been in abnormal operation. This abnormal operation is characterized based on the identified root causes. Through the traceability data, the goal is to automate this task. Spite of the 100% control, the risk of shipping noncompliant products is nonzero especially in process industries.

Identify and Locate Items to Recall by Forward Traceability. The determination of the offending articles is crucial for an optimal recall. With a reliable unitary traceability, it is possible to restrict the number of recalled items. Through the unit traceability system, it is also possible to determine the position of each item in the supply chain by its identifier.

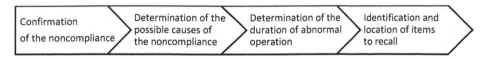

Fig. 1. Main tasks in our recall procedure

The implementation of this procedure depends largely on the traceability data and the causal analysis to determine root causes. This was two issues we have identified in this research work. The following two sections present our contribution to cope with these two challenges.

3   Data Model for Traceability

Through the development of automatic data collection tools and technologies (RFID, Data Matrix, etc.), it is possible to track each item and accurately determine its process parameters. The unitary traceability (unlike lot traceability) provides a more detailed knowledge of the process. It allows a finer search for the roots causes. To find the roots causes of noncompliant in the context of this research work, we mostly need the internal traceability data. A few data models dedicated to the unitary traceability have been published. Jansen-Vullers, M.H., et al. [7] and Khabbazi, M.R., et al.[8] develop an internal traceability data model with some restrictions in terms of actual material and process data registration. The traceability performed in the industrial area (including pharmaceutical and food) is usually managed by disconnected data models. The motivations are often compliance with regulatory in unusual situations. Root cause search is very tedious in these conditions. We aim to collect all the necessary data and facilitate the causal analysis to determine the root causes and facilitate data exchange. IEC 62264 [11] standard provides objects models and attributes of manufacturing operations. The GS1 EPC (Electronic Product Code) Global standards [12] allow end-to-end product traceability along a supply chain. We based on IEC 62264 and EPC Global standards to propose item-based traceability data model (Fig.2). The proposed model allows to know for each item, the process parameters of its manufacture. In our data model, the traceability data are organized by production order. The production order data is made up of data related to different process segments. For each process segment, production data, material consumed actual and material produced actual are recorded.

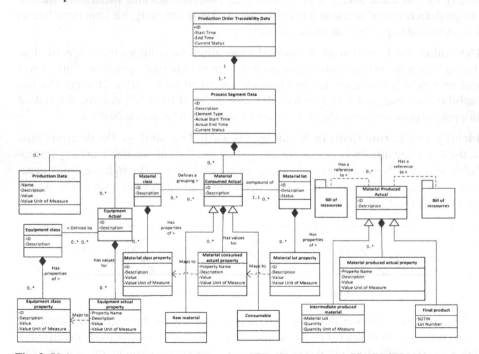

Fig. 2. Unitary traceability data model based on IEC 62264 [11] and GS1 EPCIS [12] standards

Usually, when a nonconformity is detected, one contents oneself with recalling the whole lot without seeking prior exact causes of this noncompliance. However, this search can promote an optimal recall focusing only on defective items and processes improvement. The benefits gained by a selective recall are considerable especially in the case of large lots sizes and a large dispersion of finished products. But identifying root causes of a recall is in some cases a complex task. The following section presents our contribution to the search for the roots causes related to process parameters.

4   Causal Analysis by Bayesian Modeling

Food industry often operate in a complex and difficult to model process. It is also characterized by a large number of parameters, a large variability and various types of failure. It is therefore difficult to diagnose a noncompliance. Various analytical tools have been used to determine the root causes of a noncompliance as part of a product recall procedure (see for example [4, 6]). Deterministic reliability engineering tools such as FMECA, HACCP, cause effect diagram and fault tree are often used. In the industrial context outlined herein, the use of deterministic methods with categorical decisions is not always justifiable [4]. In this paper, we propose a probabilistic causal model using Bayesian networks (BNs). BNs are graphical models for reasoning under uncertainty [13]. They allow to combine, on the one hand, certain and uncertain knowledge. On the other, they allow to exploit both data and expertise. A BN is Directed Acyclic Graph (DAG) represented by the pair (V, E) where V is a set of vertices and E a set of directed edges connecting vertices. It is associated with each node marginal or conditional probability distribution table of the corresponding variable. The main purpose of our model is to determine the parameters that might be responsible for the detected nonconformity.

We first present the construction of the model from the prior knowledge and historical data and then the use of the model with traceability data. Both historical and traceability data follow the data model developed in the previous section.

4.1   Structure of Our Model

The structure of the BN of our model is defined by background knowledge. Nodes and causal relationships are obtained from FMECA and fault tree produced by domain experts. The network is structured in 3 levels (see Fig.3): process parameters considered as root cause, product defect and nonconformity detected by end-users.

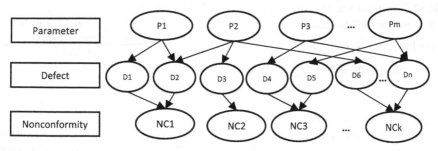

Fig. 3. The BN structure

The first level correspond to the different process/machine parameter considered that may impact the product quality. The product defect is any deviation from the specification of the product. The nonconformity represents a symptom or effect of one or many product defects.

Depending on its values (Normal or Abnormal), a process/machine parameter may generated (G) or not generated (NG) a product defect. As for the first two parameters, a nonconformity also has 2 states: observed or unobserved. Each of these nodes has a probability table.

4.2   Determination of Our Model's Probabilities

Let X be a random or uncertain variable. We denote $p(X = x|\xi)$ or $p(x \mid \xi)$ the probability that X = x with state of information[1] ξ. We assume that variable x is distributed according to f, where f is a parameterized probability distribution. This parametric model is noted $x \sim f(x|\theta)$ with θ the set of unknown parameters. The uncertainty on the parameters θ is modeled through a probability distribution $\pi (\theta)$ called prior distribution. The most critical point of Bayesian analysis is the choice of the prior distribution [14, 15]. Bayesian modeling has been adopted in several diagnostic and causal analysis applications. But the determination of f and the prior distribution of root causes has been little discussed. We start by addressing this issue.

We assume process parameters to be independent variables distributed according to a Gaussian distribution $f(x,\theta)$: $f(x,\theta) = \frac{1}{\sigma\sqrt{2\pi}}e^{-\frac{1}{2}(\frac{x-\mu}{\sigma})^2}$ with $\theta = \{\mu, \sigma\}$.

With prior knowledge through the process data historian and in order to meet the requirements of objectivity, as the normal distribution belong to exponential families, we proceeded with the conjugate priors approach.

From $f(x|\theta) \sim \mathcal{N}(\mu, \sigma^2)$, we deduce $\pi(\mu)$ and $\pi(\sigma)$ (the following development is based on [14-16]).

$$\pi(\mu|\mu_0, \delta_0) = \frac{1}{\delta_0\sqrt{2\pi}}e^{-\frac{1}{2}\left(\frac{\mu-\mu_0}{\delta_0}\right)^2}$$

$$\pi(\sigma|\sigma_0) = \frac{\sigma_0}{\sigma^2}$$

The hyperparameters $\mu_0, \delta_0, \sigma_0$ are determined by the Markov Chain Monte Carlo (MCMC) method and Maximum-Likelihood Estimation (MLE).

We use traceability data to update the prior belief by calculating posteriori probabilities. According to Bayes' theorem, $\pi(\theta|x, \mu_0, \sigma_0, \delta_0) = \frac{\pi(\mu|\mu_0,\delta_0)\pi(\sigma|\sigma_0)f(x|\mu,\sigma)}{f(x|\mu_0,\sigma_0,\delta_0)}$ where $f(x) = f(x|\mu_0, \sigma_0, \delta_0) = \int_{-\infty}^{+\infty}\int_{\sigma_0}^{\infty} f(x, \mu, \sigma|\mu_0, \sigma_0, \delta_0)d\sigma$

---

[1] Unlike the statistical probability, Bayesian probability varies according to background knowledge. But to make the notation less cluttered, we will ignore this conditionality that accompanies all Bayesian probabilities.

The best estimates of μ and σ are: $\hat{\mu} = \left\{\mu: \frac{dlog_e[\pi(\mu \,|x)]}{d\mu} = 0\right\}$ and
$\hat{\sigma} = \left\{\sigma: \frac{dlog_e[\pi(\sigma \,|x)]}{d\sigma} = 0\right\}$

Process/Machine Parameter or Root Causes. For each parameter, we divide the value space into two regions: Normal (N) and Abnormal (AN).

Let x_{up} and x_{low} the upper and lower bounds of definition range of parameter P_i.

$$P(P_i = N) = P(x_{low} \leq x \leq x_{up}) = \int_{x_{low}}^{x_{up}} f(x)\, dx \text{ and } P(P_i = AN) = 1 - P(P_i = N)$$

Product Defects or Intermediate Nodes and Nonconformities or Leaf Nodes. For each node representing a product defect or a nonconformity, its conditional probability table is leaned from historical data and background knowledge. These probabilities are updated based on new data or knowledge acquired on the process. These updates may also suggest a change in the structure of the Bayesian network.

4.3   Use of the Model

In the previous two subsections we have built the Bayesian network modeling the causal relationships of the studied system. Its use consist in updating the prior belief and inference calculations. When a nonconformity is detected, this causal analysis model is used to found the root causes. This is a diagnostic reasoning problem. In general, probabilistic inference in Bayesian networks is NP-hard. Despite the potentially large size of this type of graph, this inference problem can be addressed by techniques that are custom tailored to particular inference queries [17].Once the root causes behind the nonconformity have been determined, a search in the traceability data is conducted to determine the duration of abnormal operation and then the other items likely to be noncompliant.

5   Conclusion

In this paper, we have presented a holistic approach to product recall. This approach allows to optimize the recall procedure by a search of the roots causes. It thus allows to limit the recall solely to incriminated products. The proposed recall procedure is based on unitary product / process traceability. In order to facilitate the collection and exchange of traceability data, we have proposed a data model based on IEC 62264 and GS1 EPCIS standards. The search for causes of a recall is done by analyzing these data by means of a Bayesian model. This model allow to combine certain and uncertain knowledge and to exploit both data and expertise. In future research works, this approach will be implemented and evaluated in industrial context. Experimental results will be analyzed and discussed. An extension of variables' (parameter, defect, nonconformity) value spaces is also envisaged.

Acknowledgements. This work was supported by OSEO (French organization for innovation support and funding, Ministry for Economy, Finance and Industry, and Ministry for higher education and research) through the FUI Traçaverre project.

References

1. Potter, A., et al.: Trends in product recalls within the agri-food industry: Empirical evidence from the USA, UK and the Republic of Ireland. Trends in Food Science & Technology 28(2), 77–86 (2012)
2. Hora, M., Bapuji, H., Roth, A.V.: Safety hazard and time to recall: The role of recall strategy, product defect type, and supply chain player in the U.S. toy industry. Journal of Operations Management 29(7–8), 766–777 (2011)
3. Magno, F.: Managing Product Recalls: The Effects of Time, Responsible vs. Procedia - Social and Behavioral Sciences 58, 1309–1315 (2012)
4. Kumar, S.: A knowledge based reliability engineering approach to manage product safety and recalls. Expert Systems with Applications 41(11), 5323–5339 (2014)
5. Wynn, M.T., et al.: Data and process requirements for product recall coordination. Computers in Industry 62(7), 776–786 (2011)
6. Kumar, S., Budin, E.M.: Prevention and management of product recalls in the processed food industry: a case study based on an exporter's perspective. Technovation 26(5–6), 739–750 (2006)
7. Jansen-Vullers, M.H., van Dorp, C.A., Beulens, A.J.M.: Managing traceability information in manufacture. International Journal of Information Management 23(5), 395–413 (2003)
8. Khabbazi, M.R., et al.: Data Modeling of Traceability Information for Manufacturing Control System. In: International Conference on Information Management and Engineering, ICIME 2009 (2009)
9. ISO, E.,NF EN ISO 22005: Traceability in the feed and food chain - General principles and basic requirements for system design and implementation. 2007.
10. AISBL, G. GS1 Traceability Standard (2013), http://www.gs1.org/gsmp/kc/traceability (cited 2013 16 février 2013)
11. ISO/CEI, IEC 62264-2, in Enterprise-control system integration – Part 2: Model object attributes, p. 96 (2004)
12. GS1, The GS1 EPCglobal Architecture Framework, GS1 (2013)
13. Korb, K.B., Nicholson, A.E.: Bayesian Artificial Intelligence. Taylor & Francis (2003)
14. Armstrong, N., Hibbert, D.B.: An introduction to Bayesian methods for analyzing chemistry data: Part 1: An introduction to Bayesian theory and methods. Chemometrics and Intelligent Laboratory Systems 97(2), 194–210 (2009)
15. Robert, C.: The Bayesian Choice: From Decision-Theoretic Foundations to Computational Implementation. Government Printing Office, U.S (2001)
16. Sivia, D., Skilling, J.: Data Analysis: A Bayesian Tutorial. Oxford University Press, USA (2006)
17. Heckerman, D.: Bayesian Networks for Data Mining. Data Mining and Knowledge Discovery 1(1), 79–119 (1997)

Information Flow Management as Cornerstone for Streamlining Business Processes

Susanne Altendorfer-Kaiser

Industrial Logistics, Montanuniversitaet Leoben, Austria
susanne.altendorfer@unileoben.ac.at

Abstract. The purpose of this paper is to highlight the importance of an information flow management (IFM) and to show a way how IFM can streamline business processes. First a definition of relevant terms is given. Then the paper demonstrates how IFM can be applied to an industrial case in order to streamline and support the business processes.

Keywords: information flow, information systems, streamlining business processes, business software.

1 Introduction

Information flow management (IFM) and Information systems (IS) are crucial factors for companies in all lines of business. Within the years the requirements to do business have changed and got more complex. [6] Thus the companies' structures have to respond to these new situations with changing the way they are doing business. Traditional structures are no longer appropriate. New technologies and services, like location-based services, Internet of Things, Cloud Logistics and new technologies in the area of auto-ID technologies urge companies to adapt their processes and the way they do business. This change leads towards the introduction of Information flow management to optimize the effectiveness of companies. [6] Here, knowledge becomes an integral production factor. And knowledge is based on information.

This paper describes how IFM can be regarded as cornerstone for streamlining business processes. Therefore the paper sketches the value of IFM for companies described with a use case example from the automotive near industry.

2 Terms and Definitions

The competitiveness of companies in the future is strongly influenced by the way they do business. Here, knowledge becomes an integral production factor. And knowledge is based on information. Nowadays information is omnipresent – it is the time of the so-called information society. Not only in our private lives we are confronted with information also the daily business is formed by an information overload. Especially for companies the right information at the right time is nowadays a crucial asset.

B. Grabot et al. (Eds.): APMS 2014, Part I, IFIP AICT 438, pp. 167–174, 2014.

Barney [2] defines information as one resource (among others) that enables "the firm to conceive of and implement strategies that improve its efficiency and effectiveness". Nevertheless it is not the quantity that is important. It is the quality of information that comes into value.

In order to talk about the quality of information in general and for logistics in particular, it is important at this point to define the terms data, information and knowledge, to connect information and logistics in a more appropriate way.

— *Data*: The noun data is defined as facts and statistics collected together for reference or analysis. The term itself comes from the Latin plural of "datum".
— *Information*: For this paper the relevant definition of information is defined as something that is conveyed or represented by a particular arrangement or sequence. The term information origins in the Latin verb *"informare"* (in English" to inform"), which means 'to give from' or 'to form an idea of'. Furthermore the Latin noun *"informatio"* had already had the meaning of concept and idea".
— *Knowledge*: Knowledge comes from the verb "to know", which is of Germanic origin Knowledge means facts, information, and skills acquired through experience or education and can refer to theoretical and practical understanding of a subject. Furthermore it can be divided between implicit and explicit knowledge.

After having defined the terms it is furthermore relevant to bring these terms in a context, which is shown in Fig. 1.

Fig. 1. Definition of the term 'information' [1]

Characters are the main element and are the smallest unit. Characters in a special form become Data. Data with a special meaning (in an appropriate context) become Information. Finally information with relevance become knowledge for someone. For example in a company's context the numbers '123456' are meaningless data (every number itself is a character). If you put e.g. Art.No. in front of the numbers - Art.No.123456 – it is clearly defined what kind of information the numbers are. If this Art.No.123456 is then of relevance, for the employee dealing with it, the information become to intrinsic knowledge. At this point the employee has the knowledge what '123456' in his business context means.

Floridi defined the general definition of information (GDI) as a tripartite way: σ is an instance of information, as semantic context, if:

— (GDI.1) σ consists of one or more data;
— (GDI.2) the data in σ are well-formed;
— (GDI.3) the well-formed data in σ are meaningful [5].

For this definition "well-formed" means, as also shown in Figure 1, that the data are clustered together correctly, according to the syntax (order). And "meaningful" means that the data complies with the semantics (meanings). Referring to the Art.No. example, the single characters are meaningful in combination with the addendum of 'Art.No.'. And this meaningful information with relevance can then be defined as knowledge, which again is relevant for companies. Knowledge is not only relevant it is an essential factor for companies. Surveys state that the percentage of knowledge at the value creation within a company is above 60 % [1]. Nevertheless, surveys also reveal that employees use more than 40 % of their working time looking for the right information [1].

These circumstances lead to the necessity that an efficient information flow is necessary for every company nowadays. Out of the production point of view – as especially the production is dependent on the right information at the right time – the need for an information flow management, which can be subsumed to information logistics, comes up. Here the focus of information logistics is strongly on data and information, as shown in Fig. 2.

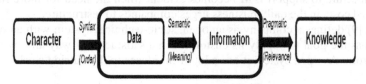

Fig. 2. Importance of the term 'information' for IFM

Especially data, its generation, storage and use in form of information is essential for the material flow. Thus the link between information and business processes can be set up.

3   Information Flow Management

Nowadays information is omnipresent – it is the time of the so-called information society. Especially for companies the right information at the right time is nowadays a crucial asset (That is what an efficient IFM is about). Barney [3] defines information as one resource (among others) that enables "the firm to conceive of and implement strategies that improve its efficiency and effectiveness". Nevertheless it is not the quantity that is important. It is the quality of information that comes into value. But it is not only the quality of information that matters. What's even as important is that the information is at the right time at the right place. Here the six R's of logistics matter for the proper information flow management.

The following table shows the six R's of logistics applied on information. [2]

Table 1. 6 R's of Logistics applied on Information [2]

Right Information	Necessary for the user
Right Time	Decision-supportive
Right Quantity	As much as necessary
Right Place	Accessible for the user
Right Quality	Detailed enough and usable
Right Costs	Reasonable PRice

To support the realisation of an adequate IFM within the company, the concept of IT as enabler of process change is still on the forefront although dates already back to [4] and [7]. A change in information systems is possible as the technological progress over the years has opened new possibilities to support the organizational reengineering. However, information system aspects have often been left out of consideration in reengineering projects. Information systems often have had and still have the status of being a matter of course and therefore their integration is often not thoroughly considered [8]. Thus companies are far too often behind in their information technologies. Software systems are often out-dated and poorly structured. The need for agile software architecture to support IFM becomes evident when the need for more flexibility and reduced costs in the daily business urges companies to restructure.

Martin [9] defines a company as an open, socio-technical system with an organisation that has the goal to supply its customers in a satisfactorily way and by doing so making profit. As open system it has a lot of interfaces to the outside world, as shown in Fig. 3.

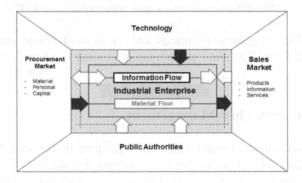

Fig. 3. Interfaces of a Company [translated to English based on [11]]

Highlighted in this figure is the information flow, which runs in parallel to the material flow. This already shows the importance of a defined information flow and a well established information flow management. And an IFM is not only necessary for intra-company flows but also for the whole supply chain. Vogt puts a lot of weight on the importance of information along the supply chain: „Information regarding the demand for, quality of the products, and other factors such as financing, and guarantees, will flow up and down the supply chain to keep every member informed of the current state of affairs pertaining to their products. This information must be timely and accurate as the manufacturing of the products must be adjusted to the demand as quickly as possible" [14].

This is just one statement pointing out the importance of the information flow. Thus the demand for information flow management and appropriate Information Systems is obvious. IFM has a great potential to support the processes of a company and the whole production area. Especially initiatives like "Cyber-physical Systems", "Internet of Things" and "Industry 4.0" are strongly heading in the direction of smart factory and horizontal and vertical integration along the supply chain. At this point IFM will be an essential cornerstone. And as technologies enable new software architectures, it makes sense to introduce not only standalone software systems but business software to support a proper IFM. In this context Sundblad [13] states that business software is often introduced for exactly one reason: "It should support the business and its activities to increase the productivity and efficiency of the business". The advantage of business software lies in the fact that business software can be integrated in all relevant business processes – like sales, production, after sales - to get a higher scale effect.

The following chapter will illustrate a use case where IFM – based on business software integration – is used to streamline business processes.

4   Use Case Domain

The research area for this use case is the automotive-near industry with a research partner that develops and sells engine test bed systems. These products are examples of automation systems. A test facility system basically measures, records, and visualizes numerous values provided by sensors according to test plans. The test facility requires appropriate parameterization for that purpose. Due to the various different use cases of test facilities, test facility systems have to be adapted according to customer-specific requirements. Typical test facilities consist of hundreds of thousands of components. According to Martyr "an engine test facility is a complex of machinery, instrumentation and support services, housed in a building adapted or built for its purpose. For such a facility to function correctly and cost-effectively, its many parts must be matched to each other while meeting the operational requirements of the user and being compliant with various regulations" [10].

A typical business process chain in the domain of this use case, shown in Fig. 4 as coarse-grained overview, covers aspects from product management, sales and order fulfillment (equal to production) to the customer service.

All processes are considered as a separate phase with several sub-processes, each having separate handover breaks and requirements.

Fig. 4. Schematic Process Chain

Taking a closer look however on the software systems in use along the process chain it becomes obvious that many different systems are used and many interfaces are needed to enable an information flow. Nevertheless all handover breaks and interfaces, even if they are automated, are a potential risk for information loss: These gaps cause a significant information loss and cause extra manual conversion and transfer efforts. Moreover relevant information might be lost throughout the process chain, and information needed in the progression of the project might not be available, as the importance of these data might not be clear upfront.

However, implementing an efficient information flow management that is supported by an integrated information system can streamline the business processes. This requires an information flow management that is implemented by integrated business software along all processes.

5   Benefits of an IFM Approach

Through the integration of a software system as business software, indicated as a constant banner in Fig.5, an efficient IFM can be established. Thus all essential processes will be supported and it will have predefined interfaces to other tools, which are relevant for the processes. While the new business software is the technical backbone for the information flow, the other tools, indicated as tool 1 till tool n, are mainly used for individual matters.

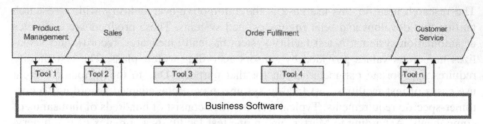

Fig. 5. IFM supported process chain

The application of this concept has individual benefits on the different processes within an organisation. Therefore all relevant information has to be added gradually to the software system. This constant information flow also enables a better fault management as the information flow is integrated along all processes.

An IFM achieves not only benefits through an integrated information flow along the processes. IFM has also effects on the processes themselves. In general there are two relevant points where first savings can be achieved:

1. a reduction of cycle times can either be achieved with an elimination of process steps or with
2. the shift of process steps to upstream processes.

The first one can be achieved, as the system offers the possibility that process steps are done automatically. The latter one enables a cost reduction as several process steps can be done earlier in the process for less costs.

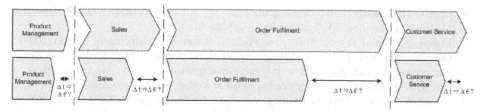

Fig. 6. Business Process Streamlining

First analyses show that savings between ten and fourteen per cent can be achieved. This first analysis, however, is only based on scenarios where the business software usage to enable IFM is mainly concentrated on the project execution phase. With a process-wide implementation, as shown in Fig. 6, even more savings can be achieved. Costs savings in a two-digit percentage range are expected.

6   Conclusion and Future Work

In this paper the benefits of an information flow management, realised by the use of integrated business software are described in the context of the automotive industry. It described the effects of a business software usage on the processes and on the company as a whole. Generally speaking it can be stated and also proven with first results, that an integrated business approach with IFM can have an enormous effect on the business process within an organisation. The applied research in the area of industrial automation systems proves applicable and undermines the positive effects of IFM. This approach promises to overcome information loss along the value chain and most important it supports business processes.

References

1. Auer, T.: Wissensmanagement: Reizwort oder zeitgemäße Notwendigkeit, Publikation im Controller-Leitfaden. WEKA Verlag (December 2008)
2. Augustin, S.: Informationswirtschaft und Informationslogistik im Industrieunternehmen. München (1990)
3. Barney, J.: Firm Resources and Sustained Competitive Advantage. Journal of Management 17 (1991)
4. Davenport, T.: Process Innovation: Reengineering Work Through Information Technology. Harvard Business School Press (1993)
5. Floridi, L.: Information: A Very Short Introduction, pp. 3–59. Oxford University Press (2010)
6. Hacker, W.: Informationsflussgestaltung als Arbeits- und Organisationsoptimerung. Jenseits des Wissensmanagements. vdf Hochschulverlag AG an der ETH Zürich (2007)
7. Hammer, M., Champy, J.: Reengineering the Corporation: A Manifesto for Business Revolution. Harpers Paperbacks. Rev. Upd. (2003)
8. Kawalek, J.: Rethinking Information Systems in Organizatons. Integrating Organisational Problem Solving. Routledge. New York (2008)

9. Martin, H.: Transport-und Lagerlogistik.Planung, Struktur, Steuerung und Kosten von Systemen der Intralogistik. Springer Vieweg, München (2011)
10. Martyr, A.: Engine Testing: Theory and Practice, Butterworth Heinemann, 3rd edn (2007)
11. Osterloh, M., Frost, J.: Prozessmanagement als Kernkompetenz: Wie Sie Business Reengineering strategisch nutzen können (Processmanagement as Core Competence: How to strategically use Business Reengineering). Gabler Verlag, Wiesbaden (2006)
12. Semar, W.: Weiss + Appetito Holding AG - Software für den ganzen Konzern. In: Wölfle, R., Schubert, P. (eds.) Dauerhafter Erfolg mit Business Software - 10 Jahre Fallstudien nach der eXperience Methodik, München, pp. S.51–S.64. Carl Hanser (2009)
13. Sundblad, S., Sundblad, P.: Business Improvement through better architected software. Microsoft Architect Journal (2007)
14. Vogt, J.J., Pienaar, W., de Wit, P.W.C.: Business Logisitics Management: Theory and Practice, 2nd edn. Oxford University Press, South Africa (2005)

Current Skills Gap in Manufacturing: Towards a New Skills Framework for Factories of the Future

Afroditi Skevi[1], Hadrien Szigeti[2], Stefano Perini[3], Manuel Oliveira[4], Marco Taisch[5], and Dimitris Kiritsis[6]

[1] Ecole Polytechnique Fédérale de Lausanne (EPFL), Lausanne, Switzerland
afroditi.skevi@epfl.ch
[2] Dassault Systémes, Paris, France
Hadrien.SZIGETI@3ds.com
[3] Politecnico di Milano (POLIMI), Rome, Italy
stefano.perini@polimi.it
[4] SINTEF, Trondheim, Norway
manuel.oliveira@sintef.no
[5] POLIMI
marco.taisch@polimi.it
[6] EPFL
dimitris.kiritsis@epfl.ch

Abstract. In the Factories of the Future framework, cutting-edge ICT developments have been accomplished by the industry, triggering new professional needs, which lead to new learning and training needs and new roles, especially regarding high-skilled labor force. Under this light, in this paper we define and analyze further the reasons triggering what is known as a "skills gap" in the world of European and global manufacturing, before reviewing applied solutions. Missing roles and related manufacturing skills, necessary for the development and progress of Factories of the Future, are then identified, based on surveys which reveal the voices of industrial stakeholders dispersed in the international market. The present analysis was conducted in the frame of the FP7 FoF project "ManuSkills", which aims to study the use of enhanced ICT-based technologies and training methodologies to facilitate an increase of young talent interest in manufacturing and to support their training of new manufacturing skills.

Keywords: Skills Gap, Manufacturing Skills, ICT for Manufacturing, Factories of the Future, ManuSkills.

1 Introduction

According to the Department for Education and Skills [1] in the UK a skills shortage is defined as "A situation where there is a genuine shortage in the accessible external labor market of the type of skill being sought, and which leads to a difficulty in recruitment". Additionally, we can find an internal skills gap, where existing employees with a certain skill set are insufficient to meet the constantly renewed business

B. Grabot et al. (Eds.): APMS 2014, Part I, IFIP AICT 438, pp. 175–183, 2014.
© IFIP International Federation for Information Processing 2014

objectives. From another perspective, given that most manufacturing positions today require at least basic STEM (Science, Technology, Engineering and Maths) skills, this phenomenon is often referred to as the STEM crisis, since not many students nowadays follow careers stemming from the STEM fields, creating thus an ominous future for manufacturing. This problem is said to be present at world-wide level; United States, Australia, China, Brazil, South Africa, India and of course Europe.

2   Skills Shortage: The European Case

Landing in Europe, skill deficiencies are already a critical issue. The European Company Survey [2] presents data, showing that in 2009 approximately 36% of firms belonging to EU-27 encountered trouble to hire (highly) skilled personnel. Figure 1 reveals that in 2009 a significant part of European firms experienced difficulties in tracing suitably skilled employees, especially in the domains mostly affected by the crisis. An important part of manufacturing employers (40%) reported a higher shortage of skilled labour force [3]. Cedepof [4] identified that green occupations, vital for innovation and sustainability, suffer from skills gaps, especially when it comes to STEM skills.

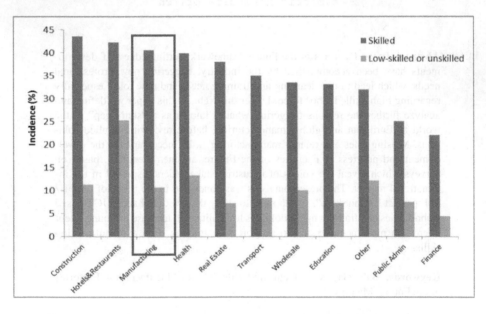

Fig. 1. Skills and labor shortages by economic sector in EU-27 (2009). Source: [3].

3   The Missing Roles

The global case does not seem more promising, as skills gaps seem to have an impact on the majority of the roles required in manufacturing. In the present survey we focus on roles related to highly skilled labor force. The Economist Intelligent Unit [5] conducted a global survey with executives from diverse industries. Almost 60% of them seemed to be worried about shortages found or anticipated in the technical or engineering field (Figure 2). Regarding the most significant skill shortages, deficient problem solving skills reached the top, with basic technical and industry-employability skills (ex. ICT literacy, self-directed learning, adaptability, communication, teamwork) following.

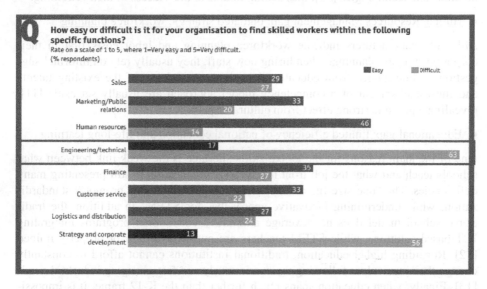

Fig. 2. Difficulty of skilled workers identification, based on specific functions. Source: [5].

The aforementioned situation rises a paradox, given the constantly increasing rate of unemployment. More specifically according to Eurostat data [6], between 2007 and 2012 most of the EU countries presented a raise above 2% in the unemployment rate of their active population with Ireland, Greece and Spain reaching peak numbers (from 10 to 18%). Only Malta, Austria and Germany lessened their unemployed population. Even if this statistical data do not refer exclusively to manufacturing, it is widely known that also candidates of the engineering areas – often overqualified – have a hard time finding the appropriate position. A skills mismatch is considered as the main factor defining this paradox, with long-term unemployment, recruitment hesitation due to economic uncertainty [7] and elastic labor demand [8] aggravating further the problem.

4   Skills Gap Root Causes

Many attempts have been made to explain and interpret the critical issue of skills gap. Our survey of the relevant literature identified 5 key gaps:

- Demographic gap: an aging workforce

The rapidly aging workforce leads to skilled-labor shortages. According to Eurofound in 2011 [9], the working population (Eu27) aged between 55 and 64 grew by approximately 17% from 2000 to 2010, with manufacturing absorbing the main percentage (14%) of the aged workforce. Employers tend to attribute the elderly staff with a high level of absenteeism, resistance to change, low flexibility and adaptability to new methods and technologies [10], thus setting doubts to the success of their retraining.

- Human Resources Management gap: outdated strategic workforce planning

Although manufacturers indicate workforce planning and labor costs first in their corporate strategy planning, when hiring new staff, they usually rely on informal suggestions, while advice from educational institutes, retraining of the existing talents and the establishment of a competency model approach are usually set aside [11], revealing a possible strong effect from cultural aspects.

- Educational gap: limited efficiency of national education and life-long learning

One of the main reasons for the global skills shortage is the weak link between what schools teach and what the job front needs. STEM education is still presenting many deficiencies. The "one-size-fits-all" approach often implemented promotes standardization, while undermining innovative approaches for STEM. In addition, the traditional school model does not leverage alternative educational programs integrating ICT-based solutions, while STEM teachers are not always fully or properly trained [12]. Regarding higher education, traditional institutions cannot afford to constantly change their curriculum following the continuously and fast-changing industrial needs [13]. Finally, when education spans much further than the K-12 frame, it is impossible for formal education to eternally claim responsibility for lifelong learners. Consequently, workers should independently self-direct their training throughout their career.

- Manufacturing Image gap: poor perception among the young generation

The widespread belief that "we don't make things anymore in Europe" [14] can discourage the younger generation from following an industrial career. Further, some of the media propagate such perceptions, ignoring the recent progress and the contribution of different manufacturing actors. Moreover, the social environment often prevents young talents from working in manufacturing, due to consolidated opinions based on experiences created by industrial standards of the past [15].

- Flexibility gap: the changing nature of work

During the last decades, the core of STEM working has radically changed. Long-term employment is hard to find, while the labor market is overwhelmed by temporary positions [16]. On the other hand, currently many companies –unwilling to invest time and money for training- favor too much outsourcing [16]. Thus, the volatility and rapid transformation consists an additional barrier for young people towards engineering.

5   Overview of Solutions

The critical issue of skills shortage, is not a new problem to industrial actors, having tackled with the challenge to a degree with different levels of success. Literature indicates that some companies, especially in the high-skilled level, rely on overtime or contingent labor (such as outplacement agencies), even by addressing new workforce segments such as former army members, housewives or immigrants [11].

However, overtime hours appears as a short term solution not effectively addressing the issue of unemployment. Outsourcing, mainly used to reduce operating costs, only seems to displace the problem to other companies engaging "experts" not exclusively devoted to a certain organization. Additionally, it has negative effects on the attractiveness of skilled jobs, and may lead to an eventual loss of control over the company's processes and sub-standard quality output, while in the case of offshore outsourcing, issues may raise regarding language and communication [17].

Some industrial domains have also taken local actions to face the problem by addressing national education or vocational training institutions for bilateral training programs, in order to customize their curricula to train effectively future candidates [18].

As a step further, following the German example [19], a global European initiative could scale up these local ones, thus providing a more sustainable solution to develop required manufacturing skills, with countries with an effective program of vocational education helping other weaker countries enforce their future skilled force

Trying to achieve a solution in the long-run, governments are spending billions of dollars every year to enhance the ranks of STEM workers [14, 20, 21]. The European Commission [3] has also shown an active engagement, in order to limit the impact of this phenomenon by giving guidelines, which aim to identify clearly the skill needs and supply, to effectively bridge the gap between the labor market and education.

However, the challenge here is to boost field oriented, competence based learning, scaffolded by innovative delivery mechanisms, which can raise training effectiveness. Skills standardization is a promising method, with employers communicating the skill standards they have defined to educational and technical training actors, so that they design and conduct effective training programs. As a result, employers can hire workforce with relevant skills, who boost productivity by returning faster the company's staffing investment. Further, relevant skills can be leveraged by promoting the role-model of life-long learners and encouraging professional mobility –if necessary with cross border skill policies and a better strategy to match people's skills to the industries' requirements.

6   New Skills Requirements

Behind this skills gap there is an opportunity: if education could provide more skilled workers and advanced manufacturing engineers to the industry, there would be an opportunity to radically transform the European factories, boost their competitiveness and profoundly renew the social image of manufacturing.

In order to efficiently transform the European factories, we should get rid of this XXth Century Taylorist vision of skilled worker roles. Definition of skills and competences of the workers is far too much enclosing them inside a single industry or process specialty -such as Assembly, Injection Molding, Surface Treatments or Die Casting- while engineering and technician positions are usually written in a way that leave them navigate from industry to industry or from specialty to speciality. It doesn't mean that skilled workers should not specialize in a given kind of process, but they should be given the necessary background to make it easy for them to move from one speciality to another based on job market demand.

As stated by Manufuture consortium, representing dozens of large and small manufacturing companies in Europe, in its 2007 proposed roadmap for Factories of the Future [22], the success of European manufacturing requires a new definition of manufacturing roles: *"Taylorism is contradictory to knowledge-based manufacturing. Manufacturers need to adapt to a new type of Taylorism which takes into account dynamic change and adaptation, specific human skills and the requirement of co-operation in networks. (...) Success of European manufacturing to date is mainly related to the great diversity and skills of personnel at all levels."*

Based on this observation our project proposed to infer from recent Factory of the Future roadmaps the skillsets that would enable a fast adoption of breakthrough industrial concepts in Europe. We can classify the value brought by each breakthrough into 3 broad categories, as proposed by ActionPlanT roadmapping project in 2010 [23].

- **On-Demand delivery of customized products through a network of manufacturing partners**

Factories of the Future require production engineers capable of rapidly prototyping new manufacturing systems in Engineering To Order (ETO) model, and continuously optimize manufacturing models. Production Engineers also need to be able to reconfigure an existing manufacturing system to adapt to a change in demand or a change in design. Eventually Production Engineers need to be capable of simulating the details of the manufacturing processes, machinery kinematics, ergonomics, with maximum accuracy to allow virtual and augmented reality.

Skilled workers as well as their management need to be trained in methodologies allowing frequent design and process changes, in a context of more and more complex and configured "Built To Order" products. More and more production systems will be self-optimizing with advanced monitoring and control: skilled workers need to be able to operate them.

Eventually more engineers and skilled workers need to be capable of using modern ICT solutions to plan and optimize manufacturing tasks taking into account their entire manufacturing systems as a single "Virtual Factory" (a.k.a "Global Plant Floor"), including the network of their suppliers and distributors in order to react in the best way to all unexpected changes that may happen internally, or from their customers, or from their suppliers.

- **Fast industrialization of innovative new product / process technologies**

Factories of the future also require manufacturing engineers and manufacturing managers capable of mastering the innovation life cycle in a manufacturing context, from laboratory assessment to ramp-up in production. Each new process or piece equipment will use intellectual property that it is important to identify, protect and monetize attached to new equipment and processes: this is another discipline that needs to be taught to manufacturing engineers and manufacturing managers. This leads also to training manufacturing engineers and manufacturing managers, so that they can design and launch new manufacturing business models relying on finance- and science-based entrepreneurial spirit.

As production and test equipment is also improving in flexibility and precision, skilled workers and engineers need to be trained to rapidly learn how to configure and operate new pieces of equipment at their full capacity from day one. This is especially true for new processes leveraging advanced, graded, bio-, nano- or hazardous materials. An initiative promoted as part of Factories of the Future is the concept of "Teaching Factory" capable of training employees for emerging manufacturing job profiles, and assessing their skills.

- **Enforcement of quality and sustainability compliance while minimizing cost**

Engineers are also required more and more to run lean assessments and optimize processes efficiency enterprise-wide. They need to learn how to reconfigure state of the art operations management ICT systems that are used to monitor and control the enterprise processes in real time. Similarly, aftersales Engineers and field Technicians are required to design, simulate and run new kinds of aftersales services, such as inspection, repair or upgrade of complex products.

Eventually Factories of the Future also require more skilled workers knowledgeable about ways to ensure compliance of products, processes and services with regulatory constraints, or with industry best practices or with internal company rules. Factories of the future will require Quality Technicians capable of planning and executing preventative maintenance plans and condition-based maintenance of manufacturing equipment. Eventually more Sustainability Technicians are required to optimize end to end energy consumption and other environmental costs factors of manufacturing processes.

7   Conclusion

The list of manufacturing skills proposed above is the result of our research and constitutes only an example that needs to be further matured and maintained with the help of industry representatives. However we demonstrated that it is possible to link all these definitions together to increase the attractiveness of manufacturing jobs, and ease the mobility of skilled workers across manufacturing specialties, industries and geographies.

There are already many regional and national initiatives in place, very often organized by industry but also more general sometimes. As a continuation to our work, we now would like to identify such organizations and involve a maximum of them in the dissemination activities of our project.

An alignment with the US Manufacturing Skills Certification System, would be a complementary approach that could help adoption by a majority of stakeholders. However as long as these job positions are not mapped with actual job offers from each industry segment, there will be little appeal for students and school program managers.

Within the ManuSkills project we plan to prototype a platform that will help the industry and the academics define these manufacturing skills, and develop awareness and training programs to attract young talents to manufacturing. Experiments conducted by the consortium partners in different European countries both in the secondary and tertiary level of education, in close collaboration with industrial stakeholders, will attempt to apply and evaluate the ICT tools developed and leveraged to raise awareness and sometimes facilitate the acquisition of the aforementioned skills. As a final step –stimulating though insights for further research-, results of our studies will be used to redefine a skills framework much closer to the vision set by Factories of the Future.

Acknowledgements. The research conducted in the frame of "ManuSkills" project leading to these results has received funding from the European Community's Seventh Framework Programme (FP7/2007-2013) under grant agreement n° 609147.

References

1. Hogarth, T., Wilson, R.: Employers Skill Survey: Skills. Local Areas and Unem-ployment, Nottingham: Department for Education and Skills, DfES Report SK 39 (2001)
2. European Foundation for the Improvement of Living and Working Conditions: European Company Survey (ECS) 2009. Eurofound (2009)
3. : European Commission: Employment and Social Development in Europe 2012 – The Skill Mismatch Challenge in Europe. Commission Staff Working Document, ch. 6, Brussels, vol. 8/9 (2012)
4. Cedepof, A.: strategy for green skills? Briefing Note (2011a)
5. Economist Intelligence Unit: Plugging the Skills Gap – Shortages among plenty. The Economist (2012)
6. Eurostat: Unemployment Statistics (2012)
7. Rampell, C.: An Odd Shift in the Unemployment Curve. The New York Times (2013)
8. Ozimek, A.: An Alternative Theory of the Skills Shortage. Forbes (2013)
9. European Foundation for the Improvement of Living and Working Conditions: Employment trends and policies for older workers in the recession. Eurofound (2011)
10. Armstrong–Stassen, M., Templer, A.: Adapting training for older employees: The Canadian response to an aging workforce, Journal of Management Development, Vol. Journal of Management Development 24(1), 57–67 (2005)
11. Deloitte Touche Tohmatsu & US Council on Competitiveness: 2010 Global Manufacturing Competitiveness Index (2010)

12. Burke, L., Mc.Neill, J.B.: Educate to Innovate: How the Obama plan for STEM education falls short. The Heritage Foundation (2011)
13. Yang, D.: Can we Fix the Skills gap? The Forbes (2013)
14. Lindsay, E.: President Obama Presented Ideas to Accelerate Job Growth and America's Competitiveness at Jobs Council Meeting. The White House Blog (2011)
15. Harris, S.: Teenagers shun manufacturing for more glamorous desk jobs. The Engineer (2013)
16. Charette, R.: The STEM crisis is a Myth. IEEE Spectrum (2013)
17. Flat World Solutions: The pros and cons of outsourcing (2014)
18. Sennekamp, P.: EU wind industry skills shortage: over 5.000 more workers needed per year. EurActive Press Release (2013)
19. Plüss, M.: Es darf keine billige Art sein, den Lehrlingsmangel zu überbrücken". Tages Anzeiger (2013)
20. The White House: Fact sheet: the State of the Union: President Obama's Plan to win the Future. The White House – Office of the Press Secretary (2011)
21. The LEVIN Institute: The evolving global talent pool: lessons from the BRICS countries. The State University of New York (2009)
22. Jovane, F., Westkämper, E., Williams, D.: The ManuFuture road: towards com-petitive and sustainable high-adding-value-manufacturing. Springer (2008)
23. Taisch, M., Tavola, G.: A roadmap of ICT for Manufacturing in the Horizon 2020 prospective. In: Zelm, M., Sanchis, R., Poler, R., Doumeingts, G. (eds.) Enterprise Interoperability: IESA 2012 Proceedings, ISTE Ltd & John Wiley and Sons, Great Britain (2012)

Agile Product Development Governance – On Governing the Emerging Scrum/Stage-Gate Hybrids

Anita Friis Sommer[1], Iskra Dukovska-Popovska[2], and Kenn Steger-Jensen[2]

[1] Engineering Design Centre, Department of Engineering, University of Cambridge, UK
afs35@cam.ac.uk
[2] Center for Logistics, Department of Mechanical and Manufacturing, Aalborg University, DK
{Iskra,Kenn}@celog.dk

Abstract. Product Development (PD) management is changing through the emergence and implementation of agile principles into existing PD frameworks. This process changes PD governance assets, even though this aspect is not yet described in existing literature. Thus, this paper introduces PD governance of agile/stage-gate hybrid solutions through a comparative study including five case companies supported by a review of existing literature. The results include an overview of applied governance assets including which are supportive for PD management. The study indicates that only assets not part of corporate governance are affected by the introduction of agile, and that unaltered corporate assets affect PD performance of the hybrid solutions negatively.

Keywords: Product development governance, agile product development, scrum, stage-gate models, case study.

1 Introduction

Globalization is believed to be a major driver of increasing competition, generating higher customer expectations and thus shorter product life cycles [1]. In this global-ized world, the competitive industrial company is the one that succeeds in being open and flexible to any customer demand, while still developing and producing high-quality products at low cost [2][3]. From a systems perspective we can see PD processes evolving from fitting the description of a closed deterministic system to approaching more the definitions of an open system. Indeed, complex PD processes are more accurately described through open-system models, including a number of un-determined influential external factors.

To support the PD management process the majority of large industrial companies have generic process models or process standards [4]. The generic process model includes a visual representation of the series of main activities in the PD process often sorted in a series of stages and gates [5]. The process model is accompanied by cor-responding PD methods describing how to use the model during the PD process. Fur-thermore, PD is enabled by PD process governance, which entails the supporting management processes and supporting mechanisms of the organization. While much research has been concerned with PD process improvement and PD management methods, only few articles focus on PD governance.

B. Grabot et al. (Eds.): APMS 2014, Part I, IFIP AICT 438, pp. 184–191, 2014.
© IFIP International Federation for Information Processing 2014

PD governance has emerged from project governance, among others, where a major and recent trend is concerned with governance from an institutional perspective [6]. In 2007 Patel [7] even used the phrase 'governance movement'. The aim of PD governance is to support the PD process in achieving long-term value [8]. Hence, PD governance is of major importance for PD performance, yet little research is concerned with governance of complex PD processes [9], which includes the open system PD processes of interest in this paper. One of the latest branches of research on PD management is agile PD, which has recently emerged (in the early 10's) on managing the increasing complexity of the PD process using agile methods. The agile methods originate from the software development industry and are now increasingly being adapted by, among others, research and development in industrial companies. Recent academic findings include Cooper [10], who shows that agile methods are applied within the context of existing stage-gate PD models, and Ovesen [11], who in 2012 conducted a multiple case study of industrial manufacturers implementing Scrum. Scrum is one of the dominant agile PD frameworks, including agile process model, methods and PD governance. The findings indicate that companies significantly improve PD performance after implementation, but that the agile framework is merged into the existing PD standards rather than replacing them.

This paper is concerned with exploring PD governance of the agile/stage-gate hybrid solutions, which are currently emerging in industry for the purpose of developing theoretical proposals for further research on PD governance. The paper includes a theoretical background of PD governance, agile PD with focus on Scrum, and an introduction to Scrum governance. Afterwards, is a presentation of a multiple case study method and the involved case companies, followed by an overview of the case study findings, discussion of the results, and finally proposals for further research.

2   Theoretical Background

Governance is an emerging aspect of PD management and an area of increasing attention [12-14]. Governance is a set of management systems, rules, protocols, relationships, and structures that provides the framework within which decisions are made to achieve the intended business or strategic motivation [15]. A PD governance system includes an overall governance structure with supporting governance assets (adapted from Weill and Ross [16]), which is illustrated in Figure 1.

Agile PD is one of the latest branches of research that recently emerged (in the early 10's) within industrial PD management. Agile methods are specialized in managing highly complex PD including active customer involvement. The agile methods originate from the software development industry and have now been adapted to new PD research in the context of the manufacturing industry. Recent academic findings include Cooper [10], who shows that agile methods are applied within the context of existing stage-gate models, and Ovesen [11], who in 2012 conducted a multiple case study of seven Danish manufacturers implementing the agile PD method called 'Scrum', which included an agile process model and governance of PD projects into

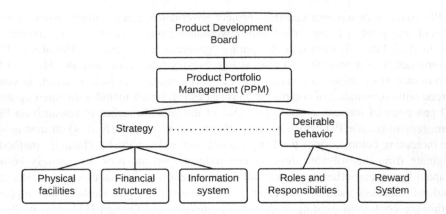

Fig. 1. Supporting governance assets Weill and Ross [16]

the existing traditional PD solution. The findings indicated that companies significantly improved PD performance after implementation. These findings are supported by Sandmeier, Morrison and Gassmann [17] reporting of increased PD performance and improved customer integration after implementation of the agile PD method 'Extreme Programming' at three large German manufacturers. Hence, empirical studies show that mass-producers can benefit significantly from implementation of agile/stage-gate hybrid PD methods. Furthermore, the agile methods support the trend of increased active customer involvement in especially the early phases of the PD process [18]. The trend encourages companies to engage in collaborative PD since the agile methods enable a flexible PD method supporting active involvement. Thus, the agile/stage-gate hybrid methods seem to fit managing PD as an open system (including the considerations for ongoing change and thus high uncertainty) and active customer collaboration. However, there are no prior case studies on the corresponding PD governance assets supporting these hybrid PD solutions.

2.1   Scrum Governance

Scrum was originally exclusively a software development framework or, rather, a generic PD standard. Scrum has recently gained interest in agile PD in industrial companies due to the positive impact on PD performance [11, 19]. The Scrum Guide, which is the official Scrum guidebook, includes a toolbox of interconnected project management methods and a process model. The process model is the visualization of the Scrum activity-flow which works as a visual coupling of the Scrum methods [20].

The governance assets within Scrum governance differ significantly from traditional PD governance. Generally, **physical facilities** are not well defined for traditional PD. However, Scrum includes a set of distinct required physical facilities. Each active scrum team must have a dedicated project room, where they are physically located throughout the development process. Furthermore, the project rooms are equipped with at least one large white board (called the scrum board), used for visually displaying the sprint process, burn-down chart, and product backlog. On the other hand **financial structures** are as little described in Scrum as is the case for traditional PD. Hence, it is relevant to notice that the goal for PD management frameworks is to improve PD performance including financial performance, and at the same time the determining financial structures are undefined. The same situation occurs for both **information systems** and **reward systems** for PD management, which generally remain undescribed in both Scrum and traditional PD frameworks. However, **roles and responsibilities** are well described in existing frameworks with distinct variations. The Scrum roles are the product owner, scrum master, and scrum team, which have a set of distinct responsibilities as described in Table 1.

Table 1. Scrum roles and responsibilities

Scrum Roles	Responsibilities
Product Owner	- Clearly express product backlog items - Order product backlog items to best achieve goals and missions - Ensure the value of the work the development team performs - Ensure that the product backlog is visible, transparent, and clear to all - Ensure the development team understands items in the product backlog
Scrum Master	- Clearly communicate vision, goals, and product backlog items - Teach participants to create clear and concise product backlog items - Facilitate Scrum events as requested or needed - Coach in self-organization and cross-functionality - Remove impediments to the Development Team's progress - Plan Scrum implementations within the organization; - Help employees and stakeholders understand and enact Scrum
Development Team	- Self-organize - turning product backlog into product increments - Cross-functional collaboration - Share accountability in the Development Team as a whole - Avoid sub-teams dedicated to particular domains

In contrast, traditional PD frameworks generally operate with a steering committee, a project manager, an a project team. The steering committee is responsible for strategic decisions, whereas the project manager is responsible for all tactical and operational decisions including both project and process management. The project team does not have management responsibilities and are only responsible for finalizing assigned tasks.

Hence, there are significant differences between traditional PD governance and Scrum governance, but some governance assets still remain undefined within both. Since companies increasingly implement Scrum in combination with traditional PD methods, it is relevant to explore how governance systems are correspondingly affected by the emerging hybrid solutions. Therefore, we ask the research question: *"What are the applied governance assets in practice, in cases of scrum/stage-gate hybrid methods for product development management?"*

3   Method

In order to answer the research question, an explorative comparative case study has been conducted including five large companies with different product types in different industries. The companies were selected based on their maturity in hybrid/stage-gate solutions to include companies with experience in using them, and thus the chosen companies had implemented their solutions between 2-5 years prior to the study. An overview of the companies is presented in Table 2.

Table 2. Case studies on agile PD governance

Company	Product types	Number of employees	Company type	Data
D	Pharmaceuticals	37,000	Industrial mass-producer	3SI, 1 GI, 1 OS, PM, ID.
E	Plastic Toys	10,000	Industrial mass-producer	2 SI, PM, ID
F	Electronics	170	Industrial mass-producer	2 SI, PM, ID
G	Windows	10,000	Industrial mass-producer	16 GI, PM, ID
H	Cross-country power lines	700	Energy Construction and service provider	24 SI, 6 GI, 1 WS, PM, ID.

SI= single interviews, GI= Group Interviews, OS=Observations studies, WS=Workshops, PM=Project Management standards, ID=Internal Documents.

A multiple case study approach was chosen to enhance the possibility of attaining rich data hence allowing greater depth and clarity [21]. Furthermore, a multiple case study creates the opportunity to compare results across the case contexts and develop a broader and more generalizable understanding of the phenomenon. The data was analysed through open coding and sampling according to governance assets into a conceptually ordered display. The interview study findings were strengthened through triangulation to company internal documents and company project management standards for PD.

4   Results

The results have been structures according to the five governance assets, and overview of applied assets in the case companies is presented in table 3.

Physical facilities include project rooms with scrum boards in four out of the five companies, which were implemented together with Scrum. These facilities enabled and enhanced process visibility and knowledge sharing both within the team and towards PD stakeholders. The company without dedicated facilities was in a process

Table 3. Case studies on agile PD governance

Cases	Governance assets in case companies				
	Physical facilities	Financial Structures	Information System	Reward System	Roles and responsibilities
D	Portfolio board, PR and SB	No Account	None	KPI	Hybrid
E	PR and SB	Dedicated	Rally	KPI	Hybrid
F	PR and SB	Dedicated	None	KPI	Hybrid
G	PR and SB	Dedicated	None	KPI	Hybrid
H	No dedicated facilities	Dedicated	None	KPI	Hybrid

PR = Project Room, SB= Scrum Board, Dedicated = Dedicated project account
No Account = No dedicated account within projects, owned and managed financially by R&D department. Hybrid = Scrum team with project manager as project owner and liaison to a steering committee.

of implementing these due to recognition of the possible benefits. Company D furthermore had a portfolio board displaying the PD projects publically within the company enhancing visibility across PD projects. Based on the cases, project rooms with scrum boards are regarded an essential part of PD governance of agile/stage-gate hybrids. Four of five cases have dedicated account to PD projects as part of the **financial structure.** The dedicated accounts allow for PD managers to purchase resources from the surrounding organization and make the project independent from other activities. Company D had no dedicated accounts, and based on this experienced difficulties in finalizing PD projects towards internal customers, and challenges in 'borrowing' specialized resources especially from manufacturing. Thus, dedicated accounts are considered to be the preferred financial solution for PD governance. Regarding the information system, only company E had implemented an **information system** to support the agile PD process, however the effects were still too immature to materialize. Hence, for information system asset it is deduced that this governance asset is not yet part of hybrid PD governance practice. The reward systems were not affected through implementation of scrum, and the Key Performance Indicators (KPI) system was applied in all five cases. Even so, this entailed challenges due to a mismatch between the rigidity of the system and the level of change in PD projects. Hence, even though the KPI system is present in all cases, it is not the ideal solution, and practitioners call for more flexible adaptable reward solutions. Finally, the **Roles and Responsibilities** included a hybrid between traditional PD and agile PD. For all companies, the Scrum terminology has been adapted including product owners, Scrum masters, and a self-organizing development team. However, all cases also had steering committees consisting of line managers and management stakeholders. Through the implementation process, the former project managers had become product owners, whereas selected team members had been trained scrum masters.

5   Discussion and Conclusions for Further Research

In a majority of the cases PD governance assets include; dedicated project rooms, Scrum boards, dedicated project accounts, and hybrid project roles as supporting governance mechanisms. Hence, these governance assets are relevant for further studies on advantages of hybrid PD including explanatory research developing theories to explain why these solutions work in practice. Furthermore, the cases suggest that there is potential for improving PD performance in further improvement of agile/stage-gate governance, and thus we call for further research on agile PD governance effects on PD performance.

However, some assets were not affected by the introduction of agile, which were the information system and a KPI reward system. These two assets are generally part of corporate governance, since they expand to the entire company. Based on this finding, we suggest that implementation of agile/stage-gate hybrids affect the PD governance system towards more agile governance assets, however only for assets not influencing corporate governance. Thus further research is recommended on the affect of corporate governance on PD performance especially in cases with agile/stage gate hybrids.

A final conclusion on the study is related to the generalizability of the emerging hybrid governance assets. The assets were identified across five companies in different markets, and based on this study we suggest that it is possible to develop a prescriptive generic model for hybrid PD governance, which is applicable across industries, and thus we also call for further applied research on this subject.

References

1. Jou, Y.T., Chen, C.H., Hwang, C.H., Lin, W.T., Huang, S.J.: A study on the improvements of new product development procedure performance–an application of design for Six Sigma in a semi-conductor equipment manufacturer. International Journal of Production Research 48, 5573–5591 (2010)
2. Soosay, C.A., Hyland, P.W., Ferrer, M.: Supply chain collaboration: capabilities for continuous innovation, Supply Chain Management. An International Journal 13, 160–169 (2008)
3. Hilletofth, P., Eriksson, M.D.: Coordinating new product development with supply chain management. Industrial Management & Data Systems 111, 6–6 (2011)
4. Haque, B.: Problems in concurrent new product development: an in-depth comparative study of three companies. Integrated Manufacturing Systems 14, 191–207 (2003)
5. Cooper, R.G.: Overhauling the New Product Process. Industrial Marketing Management 25, 465–482 (1996)
6. Clegg, S.R., Pitsis, T.S., Rura-Polley, T., Marosszeky, M.: Governmentality matters: designing an alliance culture of inter-organizational collaboration for managing projects. Organization Studies 23, 317–337 (2002)
7. Patel, D.: Why executives should care about project governance; What your peers are doing about it. PM World Today 9, 165–187 (2007)

8. Klakegg, O.J., Williams, T., Magnussen, O.M., Glasspool, H.: Governance frameworks for public project development and estimation. Project Management Journal 39, S27–S42 (2008)
9. Klakegg, O.J.: Challenging the Interface between governance and management in construction projects. In: 5th Nordic Conference on Construction Economics and Organisation (2009)
10. Cooper, R.G.: What's Next? After Stage-Gate. Research Technology Management 57, 20–31 (2014)
11. Ovesen, N.: The Challenges of Becoming Agile: Implementing and Conducting Scrum in Integrated Product Development. In: Department of Architecture & Design, Aalborg University, Aalborg (2012)
12. Sanderson, J.: Risk, uncertainty and governance in megaprojects: A critical discussion of alternative explanations. International Journal of Project Management 30, 432–443 (2011)
13. Baker, M., Bourne, M.: A Governance Framework for the Idea-to-Launch Process: Development and Application of a Governance Framework for New Product Development. Research-Technology Management 57, 42–49 (2014)
14. Sommer, A.F., Dukovska-Popovska, I., Steger-Jensen, K.: Barriers towards Integrated Product Development:-a holistic project management perspective. International Journal of Project Management (2013)
15. Bekker, M.C., Steyn, H.: Project governance for global projects. In: Technology Management for the Global Future, PICMET 2006, pp. 2195–2202. IEEE (2006)
16. Weill, P., Ross, J.W.: IT governance on one page. CISR WP 349 (2004)
17. Sandmeier, P., Morrison, P.D., Gassmann, O.: Integrating Customers in Product Innovation: Lessons from Industrial Development Contractors and In House Contractors in Rapidly Changing Customer Markets. Creativity and Innovation Management 19, 89–106 (2010)
18. Franke, N., Schreier, M.: Why Customers Value Self-Designed Products: The Importance of Process Effort and Enjoyment. Journal of Product Innovation Management 27, 1020–1031 (2010)
19. Schwaber, K.: Agile project management with Scrum. Microsoft Press, Redmond (2009)
20. Boehm, B., Turner, R.: Management challenges to implementing agile processes in traditional development organizations. IEEE Software 22, 30–39 (2005)
21. Yin, R.: Case Study Research: Design and Methods. Sage, CA (1994)

Ontology-Based Modeling of Manufacturing and Logistics Systems for a New MES Architecture

Luca Fumagalli, Simone Pala, Marco Garetti, and Elisa Negri

Department of Management, Economics and Industrial Engineering,
Politecnico di Milano, Piazza Leonardo da Vinci 32, 20133 Milano
{luca1.fumagalli,simone.pala,
marco.garetti,elisa.negri}@polimi.it

Abstract. The paper illustrates the role of modeling of shop floor to support an innovative solution for the control architecture of automated manufacturing systems. One of the main characteristics of manufacturing systems domain is, in fact, the variety of configurations that manufacturing systems can assume and this may prevent the possibility to easily adapt and reconfigure the control solution for advanced manufacturing systems. To this end, the paper presents a proposal on how to cope with this issue, coming from a collaborative project, where important European universities and companies are involved. The proposal is based on a structured modeling (i.e. ontology) of manufacturing systems. The paper proposes a practical example of the modeling, envisioning how this can be then exploited within the proposed architecture that defines a new concept of the Manufacturing Execution System of manufacturing equipment.

Keywords: Manufacturing Systems Ontology, Factory and process automation, Service Oriented Architecture, Manufacturing Execution System.

1 Introduction

Efforts of many researchers toward the generalization of methods for the design and management of manufacturing systems have been often limited by the variety of the context of their applications. On the other hand, many authors have addressed this issue in the past; nevertheless it has become available for better handling of modeling problems only in the more recent years thanks to the development of new information technology tools and languages. For instance, the Manufacturing Execution Systems Modeling Language (MES-ML) integrating all necessary views important for Manufacturing Execution Systems (MES) and pointing out their interdependencies has been developed by Witsch and Vogel-Heuser [1].

This paper presents a part of a research developed in the scope of an ongoing European funded project on this topic, named eScop (*Embedded systems Service-based Control for Open manufacturing and Process automation*). The central concept of eScop is to combine the power of embedded systems with an ontology-driven service-based architecture for realizing a fully open automated manufacturing

B. Grabot et al. (Eds.): APMS 2014, Part I, IFIP AICT 438, pp. 192–200, 2014.

environment. The innovation of the solution proposed by eScop is the fact that it merges the power of ontology knowledge and SOA control approaches; this allows the control to be automatically configured by the ontology to a specific manufacturing system. Thus, one result is the substitution of the traditional control model based on hierarchical hardware architecture, with a single level population of embedded systems plus a free series of pure software control levels. The deployment of such approach to manufacturing has been named Open Knowledge-Driven Manufacturing Execution System (OKD-MES). The kernel of the eScop platform will be presented in the remainder of this paper, showing the novelty that it introduces.

This document is structured in the following way: section 2 details the benefits for the overall approach proposed by eScop project introducing the new vision provided by the project research activity and the Representation Layer, namely the ontology modeling concept that is included in the proposed architecture. Section 3 explains how a demonstrator has been deployed for modeling, thanks to the eScop approach. Eventually, section 4 provides the conclusions and envisions future challenges in this field of research.

2   New MES Architecture for Manufacturing and Logistics Systems

In factory automation the evolutionary path of real-time control architecture is directed to overcome the rigidity of current traditional solutions. In fact, the current architecture of MES real-time control is based on fragmented and scattered information from the field, joined with a rigid hardware structure, hence being suitable and efficient only in stable contexts. In the remainder of the document this situation is called "AS-IS scenario" in contrast with the "TO-BE scenario" envisioned by the research. In the AS-IS scenario, in order to manage a production system, the supervisor generally requires an external input (i.e. information about product features and order portfolio), while business logic, scheduling algorithms and configuration data (i.e. information on process, transportation and storage equipment) are stored in the system database. Part of the required information is directly programmed in the Devices Control Units (DCUs) managing physical equipment. Depending on the hardware architectural solution, DCUs can be made of Manufacturing Control Units (MCUs), Computer Numeric Controls (CNCs) or Programmable Logic Controllers (PLCs). In the TO-BE scenario, in order to overcome the rigidity and limits of the traditional control architectures, the development of communication technologies is exploited to make it possible and affordable to integrate heterogeneous devices into a large network. To this end, specific attention is paid to web services protocols [2]. Web Services are "self-contained, self-describing, modular applications that can be published, located and invoked across the web" [3]. The scientific community has started to prove the validity of the use of web services and SOA for manufacturing automation and monitoring through industrial test-beds (e.g. [4,5]).

Due to the advent of SOA and Web service technologies, the task of monitoring and controlling locally distributed heterogeneous devices has become an effortless task.

However, knowledge is required about the physical and logical structure of the application domain, if the collected data must be transformed into useful information. In the AS-IS scenario, this knowledge is encapsulated into the machine control systems, according to the specific situation. Hence, due to its static implementation, this configuration does not allow easy re-configurability and also interoperability of components by different manufacturers [6]. To overcome this limit, one possible attempt is to abstract this knowledge and to store it, thus allowing quick and effortless reconfigurations [7]. To this end, ontologies are claimed as important to capture the conceptual structure of a domain [8,9].

Therefore, ontology seems to be a good solution for fulfilling the need of a dynamic knowledge base of the production system to be controlled. Nevertheless, if ontology is used just to describe the static aspect of a manufacturing system, most of its power is wasted and not used. The innovation about using ontology in factory automation is, in fact, to consider it within the tools in charge for the control of the manufacturing system. In this case, ontology highlights the unique feature to be queried and updated by web services with languages and tools belonging to the world of the semantic web [10]. Thus, ontology is definitely better than other databases to represent and manage web services, given that it can interact with them directly.

This research aims at showing the innovation in the ontology use for the control of the shop floor, with the ultimate aim of setting up the TO-BE scenario. Indeed, potentiality of knowledge-based semantic web services in factory automation has been already postulated by Lastra and Delamer [11]; the shift from the traditional control system architecture to the schema based on ontology and web services enables the transition towards a knowledge-based production control system (as previously postulated by Lobov et al. [12]), in which the key is the semantic coordination of standardized production components. To this end, Long [13] provided an overview on how to improve MESes, dealing with a generic ontology tier (level), even if not specifically detailed with manufacturing knowledge and Garetti et al. [14] further analyzed the integration of ontology and web services.

The platform proposed by eScop project is fully based on this research background. The platform architecture is represented in Figure 1 by a view of its kernel module, controlling the physical system and connecting it to the upper applications. The kernel is made by 3 main layers (Physical Layer, Representation Layer and Service Orchestration Layer), plus an Interface Layer to the applications part. Physical Layer corresponds to the hardware components of the production system, where each one of them is insulated by an embedded system providing intelligent device control to the physical equipment and acting as a SOA-based Remote Terminal Unit (RTU). Web services do not substitute RTUs (PLCs, CNCs and so on), but they are a layer above the machine-level controllers whose functionalities are seen as encapsulated, thus achieving a great degree of flexibility in various dimensions.

The main element for Representation Layer consists of the instance of the production system under control, taken from a reference ontology of production systems (i.e. the so called eScop Manufacturing System Ontology - MSO). This production system modeling allows to formally instantiate any specific production system, thus being able to drive the set of SOA based orchestration tools which act as the Supervisory Control System. eScop MSO is based on the Politecnico di

Milano - Production System Ontology, the P-PSO, which represented manufacturing systems as outcome of a large research activity carried out at Politecnico di Milano. The research started back in the 90's, while recently the P-PSO has taken shape aiming at a complete representation of a manufacturing reality. Details are available in Garetti and Fumagalli [15].

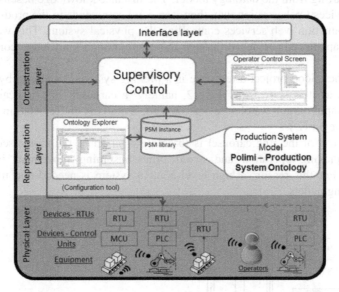

Fig. 1. Detail of the eScop Kernel

The eScop MSO can be considered as a meta-model of the manufacturing systems domain, since it specifies the entities (building blocks) it is made of, their attributes and their relations, thus defining a standardized data format for its description. The manufacturing system modeling in eScop MSO addresses three different aspects separately, i.e., the physical aspect, the process aspect and the control aspect.

eScop MSO ontology can directly interact with web services through SPARQL queries that allow to retrieve or update information stored within the ontology, activities needed for the successful run-time control of the system. The language in which eScop MSO is written and which allows querying and the related reasoning activities is OWL, as it is clearly explained by Pan [16].

Orchestration layer acts as the Supervisory Control System of the manufacturing equipments and it is made of two main components: i) the set of Orchestration Tools and Services which interact, via the Representation Layer models, with the shop floor (i.e. Level 1 devices) and ii) the Production Scheduler which feeds the Orchestration Tools and Services with work orders coming from the factory Order Entry System. The ontology is exposed as a service itself through the Ontology Service on the Orchestration platform.

The resulting architecture will be flexible, reliable and scalable and tailored for control (and even monitoring) in industrial environments.

3   Application Domain: Picking System Case

When the control system for a given shop floor system has to be established, the eScop MSO instance of the system is created by the operator through the Ontology Manager starting from the ontology model. The instance knowledge base is connected to Web Services Orchestration that, then, can send commands to the production layer through production web services controlling the physical system. This way, flexible command capability is achieved through the configuration knowledge content of the ontology.

Within the eScop project a test case is a picking system, composed by four main subsystems, as it is shown in Figure 2, namely: a carousel ring (indicated by "A" letter), an input/output warehouse station (B), a picking buffer station (C) and a gravity conveyor (D).

The purpose of the ring carousel is to create a buffer of the most used pallets to speed up picking operation and avoid time-consuming movement in/from the warehouse. For this reason, a high level control system is needed that manages the in/out coming pallets.

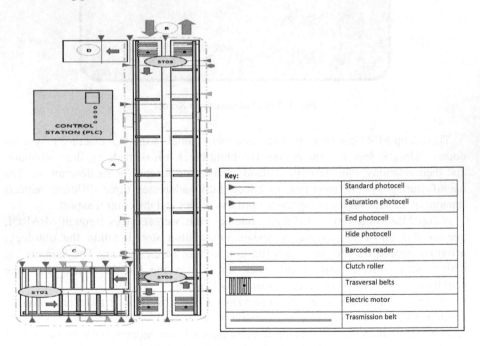

Fig. 2. Layout of the logistic system

The actual control system, the so called "AS-IS scenario", is based on a rigid and hierarchical structure on a three level control schema (according to the IEC 62264 [17]): level 0, 1 and 2. The level 0 is mainly composed by electro-mechanical devices and controllers that can autonomously take decisions (e.g. stop a pallet in a compartment on ring carousel because the next compartment is occupied by another pallet), level 0 can interact only with level 1. Level 1 is composed by the PLC that acts as the control station, its role is to coordinate the actions for correct sorting of pallets; level 1 interacts with level 0 by collecting information and coordinating the action of level 0 actuators, the "decision points" ST01, ST02 and ST03 has been identified as the main decision points of level 1. Level 1 also interacts with the supervisory level, level 2, which provides the orders of the goods to be picked by operators and coordinates the action with other parts of the system to allow the correct working (e.g. it requests to warehouse control system to deliver specified pallets to the ring carousel).

The behavior of the system in the "TO-BE scenario" will be the same as in the "AS-IS one"; this is an aspect that has to be taken into account during the model generation of the logistic line.

The complete model, based on eScop MSO ontology and drawn in UML class diagram notation, is shown in Figure 3. Each object that composes the logistic system, described above and shown in Figure 2, belongs to one class and can be linked by association, by inheritance or by aggregation to another class. Hereafter the main classes that compose the model are presented, explaining how they are logically linked together and providing comments to understand the rationale behind the presented model.

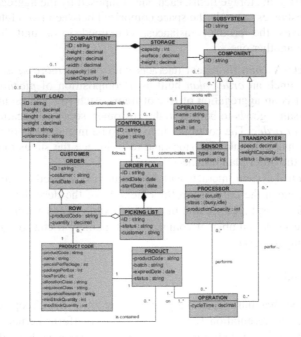

Fig. 3. Modeling of the logistic system through eScop MSO

Physical Aspect: The *subsystem* class allows creating customized building blocks that can be used everywhere in the object model. In this paper the class subsystem contains one item, that is the whole logistic line.

The *component* class: represents generic physical items of a production system. It can be further decomposed into subclasses according to the nature of the object: storage, transporter, processor, operator and sensor.

- o The *storage* class: comprises all the entities that perform a storage function, i.e. keeping material for later use into the production process.
- o The *transporter* class: groups the entities that physically move a product in the plant.
- o The *processor* class: is composed by the entities used to perform a production process function, i.e. transforming the material.
- o The *sensor* class: groups the items used to get physical information from the field, such as: position, status, temperature, etc.

An operator belonging to *operator* class performs an action on/with a component.

Process Aspect: An *operation* can be performed by a *transporter* or a *processor* on a *product,* the latter is identified through a ProductCode. Every product item is moved in the system thanks to a *unit load* that contains it and that is the pallet in this industrial case. Each *unit load* instance is stored in a *compartment* instance, that represents the single spaces for *storage.* To this end it is easy to see that the ring carousel (indicated by letter "A" in Figure 2) and the picking buffer station (letter "C") are two different storage items, each one composed by the aggregation of several compartment instances (namely the space comprised between two clutch rollers). The transporter moves the product instances, contained in a unit load, from one compartment to another one.

Control Aspect: A *controller* item interacts with one or more sensors and/or other controllers to launch an *order plan* built as a composition of *picking list* instances. The picking list is an aggregation of *row* of items, each row representing a specified quantity of the same goods to be sent to the customer, so an aggregation of *row* items builds a *customer order.* The controller item has to be intended not only as a PLC, but as every item capable to take decisions and to influence the status of the system and acting to fulfill the order plan instances.

Once the control system interacts with information structured as presented above, it is possible to control the entire shop floor flexibly of the described logistics system for picking. The control architecture, in fact, is flexible to any variation of the system (e.g. the change in the number of compartments, namely a change in the number of instances of compartment).

4   Conclusions

The present paper has introduced the general concept of the eScop research project, focusing on the Representation Layer of the eScop platform kernel. The theoretical use of modeling of a system for control logic has been addressed by a specific industrial case.

The case refers to an industrial domain, where automation is particularly important. In fact, automated logistic systems are systems that allow efficiency in many different companies. Moreover, they represent a typical case where the problem of flexibility for new configuration is crucial.

In order to cope with the problem, it has been demonstrated how the proposed approach is useful and can provide interesting results.

This paper aimed at introducing the possibility of a new vision of MES, providing a tangible example related to the modeling of the physical system. This fosters the dissemination for a larger research activity that is ongoing within eScop project and will provide new scientific results in the near future.

Acknowledgements. The research leading to these results has received funding from the ARTEMIS Joint Undertaking under grant agreement n° 332946 and from the Italian Ministry of Education, Universities and Research (MIUR), correspondent to the project shortly entitled *eScop, Embedded systems for Service-based control of Open Manufacturing and Process Automation*. The authors would like also to personally thank all the European partners of the project and, in particular, INCAS S.p.a that provided the material and support for the development of the presented case.

References

1. Witsch, M., Vogel-Heuser, B.: Towards a formal specification framework for manufacturing execution systems. IEEE Trans. Ind. Informat 8(2), 311–320 (2012)
2. HYPERLINK, http://www.w3.org/TR/ws-arch/
3. Tidwell, D.: Web services-the web's next revolution. IBM developer Works. HYPERLINK (2000), http://www.ibm.com/developerWorks/
4. Macchi, M., Fumagalli, L., Garetti, M., Tavola, G., Checcozzo, R., Rusina, F., Vidales Ramos, A., Jokinen, J., Popescu, C., Lastra, J.L.M., Karhumaki, O., Vainio, M.A.: Use case analysis method for the implementation of service-oriented solutions for monitoring and diagnostics. In: Proceedings of the 24th COMADEM International (2011) ISBN: 0-9451307-2-3
5. ESONIA, HYPERLINK, http://www.esonia.eu
6. Wong, A.K.Y., Ray, P., Parameswaran, N., Strassner, J.: Ontology mapping for the interoperability problem in network management. 10. IEEE J. Sel. Areas Commun 23, 2058–2068 (2005)
7. Cai, M., Zhang, W.Y., Zhang, K.: ManuHub: A Semantic Web System for ontology-Based Service Management in Distributed Manufacturing Environments. IEEE Trans. Syst. Man, Cybern. Syst, Part A: Systems and Humans 41(3), 574–582 (2011)
8. Brachman, R.J., Levesque, H.J.: Knowledge representation and reasoning. Elsevier (2003)
9. Chandrasekaran, R., Josephson, J.R., Benjamins, V.R.: What are ontologies, and why do we need them? IEEE Intell. Syst. (2009)
10. Hunter, J.: Enhancing the semantic interoperability of multimedia through a core ontology. IEEE Trans. Circuits Syst. Video Technol. 13, 49–58 (2003)
11. Lastra, J.L.M., Delamer, M.: Semantic web services in factory automation: fundamental insights and research roadmap. IEEE Trans. Ind. Informat., 2, 1–11 (2006)
12. Lobov, A., Ubis Lopez, F., Villasenor Herrera, V., Puttonen, J., Lastra, J.L.M.: Semantic Web Services Framework for Manufacturing Industries. In: IEEE International Conference on Robotics and Biomimetics, Bangkok, Thailand, pp. 2104–2108
13. Long, W.: Research on Development Method of MES based on Component and Driven by Ontology, JSW, vol. 5(11) (November 2010)

14. Garetti, M., Fumagalli, L., Lobov, A., Lastra, J.L.M.: Open automation of manufacturing systems through integration of ontology and web services. In: Proceedings of 7th IFAC Conference on Manufacturing Modelling, Management, and Control International Federation of Automatic Control, June 19-21, Saint Petersburg, Russia (2013)
15. Garetti, M., Fumagalli, L.: P-PSO ontology for manufacturing systems. In: 14th IFAC Symposium on Information Control Problems in Manufacturing, May 23-25, Bucharest, Romania (2012)
16. Pan, J.Z.: A flexible ontology reasoning architecture for the Semantic Web. IEEE Transactions on Knowledge and Data Engineering, vol 2 (2007)
17. ISO/IEC 19501:2005, Information technology—Open Distributed Processing—Unified Modeling Language (UML). IEC 62264:2013, Enterprise-control system integration

Towards Supplier Maturity Evaluation in Terms of PLM Collaboration

Sara Mahdikhah[1], Mourad Messaadia[1], David Baudry[1], Thierry Paquet[2], Anne Louis [1], Bélahcène Mazari[1], Richard David Evans[3], and James Xiaoyu Gao[3]

[1] CESI/IRISE, Rouen, France
{smahdikhah,mmessaadia,dbaudry,alouis,bmazari}@cesi.fr
[2] University of Rouen /LITIS, France
Thierry.Paquet@univ-rouen.fr
[3] University of Greenwich, Chatham Maritime, Kent, United Kingdom
{R.D.Evans,J.Gao}@gre.ac.uk

Abstract. The product lifecycle management (PLM) system has a significant role to support the collaboration and manage the partnership between OEM and supplier to enable the success of supplier integration. Today great rates of cooperation as suppliers have been dedicated to SMEs.

Since one of the PLM task is to control the collaboration between OEM and suppliers, this paper provide supplier (SMEs) a framework to find their level of relationship with OEM and the steps that they can improve it. To respond to this trend, we defined a methodology based on collaborative matrix maturity levels and four PLM axes of strategic, organization, process and tools levels. Finally according to this matrix, we proposed a structure of a proper questionnaire and example that shows suppliers how to evaluate their positions in terms of collaboration in PLM.

Keywords: PLM, OEM/Supplier Collaboration, Collaboration maturity.

1 Introduction

Technology of PLM is composed of complex process involve challenges of organization in terms of information flow, management of human resource and different relation levels between OEM and suppliers [1].

The integration of supplier in value chain of product is not a new challenge. Various researches and projects have been focused on this issue that seeks more efficient ways to improve integration. In this study we found researches with aspect of interoperability [2], data exchange [3] and those ones that consider organization between OEM and its supplier, through the development of different level of cooperation and integrate the suppliers in the network.

The suppliers in the field of automotive are looking for new innovative ways to propose high quality of product and platform while the costs are faire. According to high demand for rapid development of innovation, high quality and increased regulation, it will be apparent that the favorite suppliers are those ones who focus on

B. Grabot et al. (Eds.): APMS 2014, Part I, IFIP AICT 438, pp. 201–208, 2014.

leverage the innovative products with grow development in new platforms and programs. Therefore for OEMs, especially in the domain of automotive, it will be important to seek new trends of development that involves supplier integration into the product development process chain. To respond to this need of supplier integration, it seems to be necessary to deal with PLM framework and tools that focus on integration of supplier and on collaboration between OEM [4].

The classic works until the last few years have had a great revolution in industry. The evolution was characterized in the network of OEM and suppliers with a vertical cooperation method. This approach was the result of integration of supplier's equipment through the simultaneous process of development in automotive industries in different phases such as planning, design and education [5].

According to aims of BENEFITS project to understand the challenges relating to knowledge management and sharing cooperation of supplier and OEM, an industrial investigation was conducted during six months in UK. The result obtained from previous questionnaires persuaded us to investigate about different levels of collaboration between OEM and SMEs from begging steps to the optimal level. This framework can help suppliers (SMEs) to assess their positions in this cooperation and provide them perspective of an optimal cooperation. In addition more we will propose a structure of proper questionnaire that prepare the supplier's manager to benchmark the situation of level of collaborating and be able to answer some key questions such as:

- What are the activities of each level of co-PLM?
- What is the actual level of collaboration?
- What are the requirements elements to improve the level of collaboration?

The paper is organized as different sections. The next part addresses the PLM approach in term of collaboration between OEM and suppliers. Section three analyses the state of the art in term of collaboration level between suppliers (SMEs) and OEMs. The results of presenting a framework and assessment level of collaboration is presented in section forth. Finally, we conclude and discuss future works according to BENEFITS project in fifth part.

2   PLM Approach in Term of Collaboration between OEM & Suppliers

Nowadays the enterprises seek new collaborative business methods to solve their new challenges. They wish these solutions be able to change the global marketing of the product by leveraging the power of product collaboration across different parts of value chains such as partners, employees, suppliers, and customers. In addition more, the methods must provide them a faster product development, more efficiency in managing of their programs. Also this collaborative program that involve product and supply chain processes should be able to reduces development costs, increase product innovation, make the time of marketing faster and to have a significant result on revenue. It is expected that the methods of PLM collaborative programs impacts on technical advantages as to provide more effective partnership for PLM users, delete the barriers to innovation and finally increase the customer satisfaction [5].

In order to reduce the expenditure of collaborative programs, OEM -especially in automotive industries- prefer to have direct connection to suppliers with limit number of capable and effective suppliers that called system supplier. In this system, there is no direct link between other suppliers which calls sub –supplier with OEM but instead the system supplier works closer to OEM and in a another hand deals with sub-supplier and manage theirs task and coordination [6].

Many OEM and supplier networks in automotive industry which have been developed in 1980's are characterized by "vertical cooperation". This cooperation often starts with request of OEM to supplier for producing a product according to its precise specifications and OEM will keeps the industrial properties of their products, responsibility and the product band. In addition more, this relationship can be evolved to the level of co-development between OEM and suppliers.

In the automotive industry, vertical partnership has a significant effect in different aspects such as integration of equipment suppliers in a simultaneous development process of cars, planning, design and implementing.

More over in the aerospace industry, we will face three kinds of vertical partnerships (OEM/supplier) such as, classical relationship with OEM dominance that Boeing can be as an example, Cooperative model with example of Airbus and finally those ones that OEM's role is limited to the level of integration in purchased part [7]. The implementing of such collaboration requires organizing effective communication between enterprises through integration and interoperability on different levels (Fig. 1)

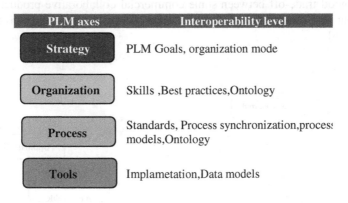

Fig. 1. Interoperability through PLM axes

In this paper, to keep up with these tasks above, a PLM collaboration framework is established, enabling supplier to assessment their actual level of collaboration to OEM and the steps to improve their partnership.

3   Levels of Collaboration in PLM

In order to reach to a successful developed business and issues related to PLM such as processes or information, it seems to be necessary that the actual situation of every unit of business, regional unit or product area be recognized and understood well. The PLM maturity model is a suitable tool for this evaluation and analysis [9].

The exist PLM maturity model refers to the generic maturity model CMM by means of COBIT standard [10]. This matrix with five rough levels describes how a company and its management team are able to use and extend a corporate-wide PLM concept and related processes and information systems. These stages represent the organizational growth, learning, and development and they allow analysing the maturity of the enterprises during this cooperation [10]. Although in concept of collaboration in PLM, benefit of PLM system in network of SMEs are rare but is an attractive subject for researchers of this domain in recent years [11, 12, 13, 14, 15]. Among them one study has investigated the adoption of PLM system in SMEs network by means of 11 case studies. This research tackles related problems and tries to accomplish a crucial task in PLM to evaluate the achieved benefits. In order to do this, they defined a methodology to assess PLM advantages according to a defined industrial target by means of some quantitative indicators such as time and cost. These SMEs are classified to three groups. The first stages related to those one that there are no use of advanced communication and management technology and Communication took place by traditional ways. In second stage, a commercial PDM system is conducted and data sharing improves in a standard way and finally in stage three the network of suppliers deals with evolution of exiting PDM tools toward a PLM approach which leads to a good trade-off between some commercial collaborative product definition management tools and the most advanced computer supported cooperative work applications [16].

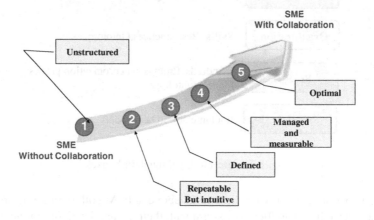

Fig. 2. Levels of SMEs collaboration through PLM based on [10]

Intense pricing and limit of time will force the OEMs to work with the suppliers that provide them faster and more accurate responses. A PLM system called NSK (Nanjing-Fiat Solution Kit) has been established to make the collaboration between an OEM called Nanjing-Fiat and suppliers, exchanging files and key information about vehicles faster and more efficient.

In this PLM system a web-based tool can be used by both OEM and suppliers for the operations such as uploading, browsing, exchanging, and downloading of data relates to product requirements for specific vehicle systems. NSK PLM system will present in three different levels of stagey, technique and operation level.

At the strategy level, the PLM strategy focusing on supplier integration. At the technical level the tools to enable supplier integration have been selected and finally at the operation level, the PLM system is going to be implemented [17].

In this study according to the investigation, different PLM system and existing maturity models, we presented a PLM framework in section 5, based on maturity models of PLM and four axes: strategic, organization, process and tools.

4   PLM Framework and Assessment the Level of Collaboration between OEM and Supplier

In this section we will introduce a framework of maturity level of collaboration between OEM and Suppliers which called SPOT. In continue we will present a structure of questionnaire to provide supplier's manager assess their place of collaboration in a better way. (Table1).

4.1   Discussion

For improving our framework we need to propose a structure of questionnaire and apply it to different enterprises (OEM/Supplier) to have Feedbacks. These feedbacks will be used to improve the table for the levels validation.

For this questionnaire we need to choose the right person for having the best answer. That's why we adopt different levels in our approach. These levels will be as:

- Strategic level: will address Top management.
- Organization level : will address managers, departments responsible,
- Process level: will address managers and engineers, and team head etc.
- Tools level: we will address all technical staff

We will formalize questions in order to replace the Supplier (SME) directly in the right level. As an example, in the strategic axe we have five levels; in each level we have some activities. One of these activities concerns the PLM concept, in which evolves from one level to another. In the level1, Unstructured Collaboration, we have "work must be done to define the PLM concept". In the second level, partial but intuitive collaboration, we have "PLM concepts are defined but not formalized", etc.

In order to identify the right level for each activity, questions will be addressed to the Boss/Managers and structured as follows:
In your opinion, what is the best definition of PLM concept?
Is it defined in your enterprise?

Table 1. PLM framework and assessment the level of collaboration of OEM and supplier

Level	Working Practice	PLM axes			
		Strategy	Organization	Process	Tools
1	Unstructured collaboration	Have started to recognize PLM topic in terms of collaboration and its importance have been agreed	Have begun to Select supplier after zooming potential ones	Work must be done to develop the PLM concept and standards	No advance communication and traditional management is used
		Work must be done to define the PLM concept	There is no defined organization concerning lifecycle management; all lifecycle and product management issues are resolved by individuals on a case-by-case basis.	Difficulties in finding past documentations	
		Have begun to identify potential supplier		There is no defined process concerning lifecycle management and collaboration	
2	Partial but intuitive collaboration	PLM concept is defined but not formalized	There is a high degree of reliance on individual knowledge and therefore errors occur	Lifecycle and product management processes have developed to the stage where similar procedures are followed by different people undertaking the same task(i.e. the processes function on ad hoc bases)	IT systems don't support processes of collaboration but they're defined
		Have begun to Identify PLM need concerning participation between supplier and OEM	An internal Organization concerning PLM is under structuration		
3	Collaboration needs Defined	The PLM concept is not uniform throughout the corporation but is formalized	The industrial partners accessed documents as external users with limited rights	Actors belonging to OEM upload data and files to specific areas of the PDM system to enable collaboration and is possible for them to remove data to end collaboration	OEM adopted a commercial PDM system properly customized to meet specific process requirements
		Have started to develop partnership between supplier and OEM and have begun to decision making for type of the supplier integration			
			Processes and basic concepts are standardized, defined, documented, and communicated through manuals and training	The PLM processes are not uniform throughout the corporation	IT systems support individual parts of processes
		Have begun to define extended enterprises needs		There is no end-to-end PLM process supporting IT systems, all work is completely or partially manual from the process point of view	
		Synchronized collaboration with other organizations is not in best practice	The human factor is still important		No PLM platform
4	Managed and measurable collaboration	The state of uniformity of PLM concept is formed	Numerous workshops have been organized to understand the main criticalities of actual processes, to choose how to evolve the adopted system to meet the extended enterprises needs and to define the technical specifications of the new PLM platform	It is possible to monitor and measure the compliance between processes and to take action where processes are not functioning well	IT systems support PLM processes well
		The state of uniformity of organization and processes are clear		Processes and concepts have been refined to the level of best practice, based on continuous improvement and benchmarking with other organizations	
		Concepts of PLM are developed through clear vision throughout the corporation		PLM process are formalized	
			There is best practice of synchronization with other organizations	Processes are developed through clear vision throughout the corporation	
5	Optimal collaboration	Use Execution plan ,PLM configuration and continual improvement	New system functionalities have been defined in cooperation with industrial partners	The implemented system can be considered a good trade-off between some commercial CPDm tools and the most advanced CSCW applications	Evolution of the existing PDM tools toward a PLM approach
					IT is used in an integrated manner
				New system processes (PLM) have been defined process automation exists on an end-to-end basis	There is a PLM platform

- If No = L1
- If Yes ≥ L2

Is it formalized in your enterprise?

- If No = L2
- If Yes ≥ L3

Is the PLM concept integrated uniformly throughout your enterprise?

- If No = L3
- If Yes ≥ L4

For taking decision, we need to develop all questions in the same way and cross different answers. Since the framework is based on existing states of the art reviews, we still need to improve the table and to validate previous questions by investigations.

Furthermore uniformity of questions is very important. As seen before, each question must be linked to the related level. In continue we will assign weights to questions according to their importance in the PLM adoption. This will give a unique result related to each level, even if it is arbitrary and we can give recommendation for the negative response.

Another important point is the PLM adoption by Suppliers (SMEs). Introducing PLM system can help them to tackle the challenges of their processes. The importance of the organizational aspect is reinforced by the fact that PLM is based on the cooperation of various businesses; collaboration that takes place at different levels (Informal collaboration, project/process collaboration and extended collaboration, etc.).

5   Conclusions and Further Work

In this study we analysed the maturity levels of SMEs collaboration with OEM. Based on our proposed PLM axes (Strategy, Organization, Process and Tools), we classified the activities of each maturity level. This kind of classification is important for the identification of domain and person concerns by the activity.

As future work, we will develop the questionnaire based on the levels of maturity. The future questionnaire will include the results of the PLM adoption base on the table. This part will give an assessment of the capacity of SMEs, especially the ability to adopt PLM or not. As an example, indirect costs, manager, type of communication, size of SMEs, etc. We will integrate elements for adopting ICT (especially PLM) technology. For example, we can see the negative aspect of "Informal communication mode" in the process axis. It's related to SMEs practices, because in the most cases SMEs have an informal communication mode (according to their small size) and this kind of communication impact the PLM adoption.

Acknowledgement. Acknowledgement is made to European Union for the support of this research through the European Program INTERREG IVA France-Channel-UK by funding project entitled "Building an Expertise Network for an Efficient Innovation & Training System (BENEFITS).

References

1. Mahdikhah, S., Messaadia, M., Baudry, D., Gao, J., Evans, R.: A Business Process Modelling Approach to Improve OEM and Supplier Collaboration. Journal of Advanced Management Science 2(3), 246–253 (2014)
2. Panetto, H., Berio, G., Benali, K., Boudjlida, N., Petit, M.: A Unified Enterprise Modelling Language for Enhanced Interoperability of Enterprise Models. In: 11th IFAC Symposium on Information Control Problems in Manufacturing, INCOM 2004, Salvador, Brazil (2004)

3. Xiao-li, Q., Hong, Y., Xi-ying, W., Ming-yuan, C.: Information shares of network manufacturing system based on STEP and XML. Journal of Computer Integrated Manufacturing System 8(7), 293–316 (2002) (Chinese)
4. Calvi, R., Le Dain, M., Harbi, S., Bonottoo, V.: How to manage Early Supplier Involvement (ESI) into the New Product Development Process (NPDP): several lessons from a French study. In: 10th International Annual IPSERA Conference, Jönköping, Sweden (2001)
5. Ming, X.G., Yan, J.Q., Wang, X.H., Li, S.N., Lu, W.F., Peng, Q.J., Ma, Y.S.: Collaborative process planning and manufacturing in product lifecycle management. Computers in Industry 59, 154–166 (2008)
6. Rangan, R.M., Rohde, S.M., Peak, R., Chadha, B., Bliznakov, P.: Streamlining product lifecycle processes: a survey of product lifecycle management. Journal of Computing and Information Science in Engineering Transaction of the ASME 5, 227–237 (2005)
7. PLM interest Group, http://www.plmig.com/
8. Messaadia, M., Belkadi, F., Eynard, B., Sahraoui, A.E.K.: System Engineering and PLM as an integrated approach for industry collaboration management. In: INCOM, Romania (2012)
9. Silventoinen, A., Papinniemi, J., Lampela, H.: A Roadmap for Product Lifecycle Management Implementation in SMEs. In: ISPIM Conference, Vienna, Austria, June 21-24 (2009) ISBN 978-952-214-767-7
10. Saaksvuori, A., Immonen, A.: Product Lifecycle Management. Springer, Berlin (2008)
11. Siller, H., Estruch, A., Vila, C.: Modeling workflow activities for collaborative process planning with product lifecycle management tools. J. Intell. Manufacturing 19, 689–700 (2008)
12. Denkena, B., Shpitalni, P., Kowalski, G., Molcho, G., Zipori, Y.: Knowledge Management in Process Planning. Annals of the CIRP 56(1) (2007)
13. Pol, G., Merlo, C., Legardeur, J., Jared, G.: Implementation of collaborative design processes in to PLM systems. Int. J. Product Lifecycle Management 3(4) (2008)
14. Sudarsan, R., Fenves, S.J., Sriram, R.D., Wang, F.: A product information modeling framework for product lifecycle management. Computer-Aided Design 37(13), 1399–1411 (2005)
15. Germani, M., Mengoni, M., Peruzzini, M.: A QFD-based method to support SMEs in Benchmarking co-design tools. Computers in Industry 63, 12–29 (2012)
16. Peruzzini, M., Mengoni, M., Germani, M.: PLM benefits for networked SMEs. In: PLM11 8th International Conference on Product Lifecycle Management (2012)
17. Tang, D., Qian, X.: Product lifecycle management for automotive development focusing on supplier integration. Computers in Industry 59, 288–295 (2008)

Global Value Chains in Shipbuilding:
Governance and Knowledge Exchange

Lise Lillebrygfjeld Halse

Molde University College, Specialized University in Logistics, Molde, Norway
lise.l.halse@himolde.no

Abstract. Over the last decades, the Norwegian shipbuilding industry has become increasingly globalized, with offshoring of production of to low cost locations. Globally dispersed production of complex and customized ships has proven to be challenging with respect to coordination of activities and exchange of knowledge. The paper investigates how different governance alternatives affect knowledge exchange in the global value chains of two shipbuilding groups. The findings indicate that vertical integration facilitates coordination and knowledge transfer to foreign shipyards. However, reverse knowledge transfer through these linkages seems to be limited. This may have implications for the future innovativeness of this industry.

Keywords: Global Value Chains, Supply Chain Management, Knowledge, Shipbuilding.

1 Introduction

The latest decades have been characterized by an increasing globalization, which has led to geographically dispersed production networks, pushed forward by intensified competition and cost focus. This development challenges companies in high-cost countries. Reducing production costs by introduction of automation, often combined with systems for production efficiency such as Lean, is one way of meeting this challenge. Another is to focus more on product differentiation and innovativeness [1]. The latter strategy has been pursued by the Norwegian Maritime cluster, which delivers complex and customized vessels for offshore purposes, and categorized as Engineer-To-Order (ETO) producers [2]. Furthermore, the innovative strength of this industry has been ascribed to close user-producer linkages between geographically proximate actors, where knowledge has been easily transferred [3]. Despite being leading in this market segment, price competition has led to increased offshoring of production to low-cost locations. Due to more geographically disperse value chains this development may represent a challenge for the innovativeness of this industry. On the other hand, global production networks can be considered as knowledge networks, where companies can access knowledge from foreign knowledge sources, which they can combine with their own internal knowledge base. A widespread view in the literature is that the most innovative firms access international sources of knowledge,

B. Grabot et al. (Eds.): APMS 2014, Part I, IFIP AICT 438, pp. 209–216, 2014.

where they merge a strong local knowledge base with high levels of connectivity to other regions in the global network [4, 5]. However, the type and amount of knowledge that is exchanged will depend on the form of cooperation established between the companies in the supply network. Little attention has been drawn to how the coordination of global supply networks will affect the knowledge sharing in those networks [6]. Furthermore, literature on management or coordination of global supply chains of ETO industry is scarce [2]

This paper aims at filling this gap in the literature by providing two case studies of two shipbuilding companies residing in the Norwegian maritime cluster. First, I apply the concept of governance to investigate the forms of coordination implemented by the two shipbuilding groups in their global linkages, associated with their core activities: design and production of ships. I then investigate how the choice of governance affects knowledge sharing in these linkages. The remainder of this paper is structured as follows: First, the theoretical framework applied in this study is presented. Thereafter, a brief description of the Norwegian shipbuilding industry and the research methodology is provided. Then the main shipbuilding processes are presented, shedding light on governance and knowledge flow in global linkages. Finally, the findings are discussed ending in conclusions and suggestions for further research.

2   Theoretical Background

The literature presented in this paper draws on a typology for governance of global value chains rooted in transaction cost economics, production networks theory and the concept of technological capability. This framework is then extended to capture what implications the choice of governance will have for knowledge sharing in global value chains.

2.1   Governance of Global Value Chains (GVC)

Transaction cost theory has provided an important theoretical base for conceptualizing the form of coordination within supply chains. The governance concept provides a theoretical explanation of the most efficient way of organizing transactions between companies [7]. Authors provide different typologies of governance, ranging from arm's length market dynamics at one end of the scale, to hierarchical structures on the other. Gereffi et al. [8] offer a typology that helps explaining governance patterns in global value chains. They identify three variables that play a large role in determining how global value chains are governed: the complexity of transactions, the codifiability of knowledge, and the capabilities in the supplier base. Based on different combinations of these, they separate between five ideal governance types, where the governance types represent different degrees of explicit coordination and power asymmetry: market, modular, relational, captive and hierarchical. In the market type of governance, product specifications are simple, knowledge exchange is mainly price information, and the number of possible suppliers is large. In modular value chains, the product complexity is greater, but it is possible to codify the information with the use of standards, which makes it possible to easily switch supplier. The relational form of governance is based on mutual dependence, loyalty and trust, which has its basis in a common culture, developed through shared history and experience of the agents. The relational form of governance emerges when the information associated with products is complex, when the transferred knowledge is typically tacit and requires face-to-face contact between actors, and when supplier capabilities are high. In captive value chains, the supplier is dependent on the much larger buyers, and relations are characterized by high degree of control by lead firm. This mode of governance will emerge when products are complex, when it is difficult to codify information and when supplier capabilities are low [8]. The hierarchal type of governance corresponds to vertical integration of suppliers, which is appropriate when products are complex and when the codifiability and the capabilities in the supplier base are low. As Gereffi et al. (2005) point out different industries may change between the different forms of governance in a dynamic manner.

2.2   Governance and Knowledge

Pietrobelli and Rabelotti [9] find that learning mechanisms can vary widely within the various forms of governance of global value chains (GVC), using the governance typology of Gereffi et al. [8]. Similarly, Isaksen and Kalsaas [1] analyze possibilities for knowledge upgrading and innovation activities in global production networks and argue that firms' possibilities for learning and knowledge upgrading depend on how the network is governed. Based on these theoretical frameworks, table 1 presents the forms of knowledge exchange and innovation opportunities associated with the different forms of governance in Gereffi et al.'s typology.

Table 1. Governance and knowledge flow in global value chains

Governance	Form of information/ knowledge	Knowledge exchange and innovation in supply chain
Market	Price, simple product specification	No deliberate knowledge transfer between companies, innovation through knowledge spillovers and imitation (competitors)
Modular	Standards, explicit knowledge	Knowledge transfer through standards, codes and technical definitions. Innovations related to development and improvements of standards and production processes.
Relational	Explicit and tacit knowledge	Intense knowledge transfer through face-to-face interaction, innovation of product through close interaction between companies in network having complementary competence.
Captive	Explicit and tacit	Deliberate knowledge transfer from lead firm typically related to narrow range of tasks, typically related to production.
Hierarchy	Explicit and tacit	Deliberate knowledge transfer, arenas for knowledge exchange, training programs. Cooperative innovation depends on power relations and competence.

3   The Norwegian Shipbuilding Industry

The Norwegian shipbuilding industry fosters innovations in the design, engineering and construction of offshore and specialized vessels to the offshore sector, creating a global niche through a focus on product innovation and management of complex projects. The vessels produced by this industry are built on a high degree of customization for individual customers. Despite of high cost associated with this strategy, the industry has proved to be successful, most probably due to high degree of innovativeness and being world leading in systems integration. One of the most important characteristic of Norwegian shipbuilding industry is its flexibility, which gives customers the possibility to decide many features of the vessel quite late during the shipbuilding process [10].

The actors in this industry can be divided into four major groups [11]: shipping companies (ship owner), design companies, shipyards, and equipment suppliers. The present study focuses on two shipbuilding groups. Both of these groups, however, have their own design companies delivering design to own and other shipyards.

4   Research Method

In order to investigate the link between governance and knowledge transfer in global value chains in an ETO setting, I chose an explorative multiple case study [12]. The two largest shipbuilding groups in the Norwegian maritime cluster in North West Norway were chosen as cases in this study. The main data collection was performed through in-depth, semi-structured interviews of key personnel and through observations in meetings in central cluster companies, subsidiaries, suppliers, and representatives in foreign locations in China, the Netherlands, Poland and Brazil.

Shipbuilding group 1 has a global owner and consists of four separate shipyards in the cluster, and four at foreign locations. During the last years the group has built up a design company delivering design to own shipyards. Shipbuilding group 2 is family owned, and has one shipyard in the cluster. The group has long experience in designing vessels for its own shipyard and for foreign shipyards. Expanding the design and project management activity of the company has been the primary strategy the last years, as the production capacity of their shipyard is limited.

5   The Shipbuilding Process

Figure 1 identifies the main stages in the shipbuilding process[1] discussed in this paper. The conceptual and basic design process takes place within the cluster. However, the subsequent stages in the supply chain differ with respect to localization, depending on the type of project undertaken, and the customer's needs. Two different

---

[1] This figure represents a simplified and sequential image of the shipbuilding process. In reality, engineering, procurement, and production activities are performed in near concurrency throughout the project execution (concurrent shipbuilding).

production processes can be identified, representing value chains with different degrees of outsourcing to low-cost locations (offshoring). In the first process, A, basic design is performed within the cluster, and detailed design is performed in the cluster and at foreign engineering companies. Production of hulls is outsourced to low cost country locations, while most part of the outfitting, testing and delivery is undertaken locally in the cluster. Parts of outfitting are in some cases performed at foreign shipyards, and the strategy is to increase this activity abroad. In the second process (B) only conceptual design, basic design and parts of detailed engineering is carried out locally in the cluster. Parts of detailed engineering and the complete fabrication of the vessel are carried out at foreign locations in low-cost countries. The focus of this study is the part of the processes that is associated with the transition between engineering and production, including outfitting.

In the following, governance and knowledge transfer in the linkages between the Norwegian shipbuilding groups and the foreign company in each of these processes is discussed separately.

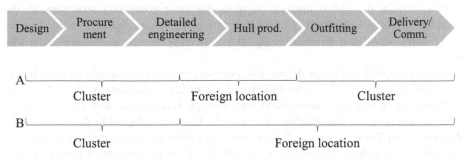

Fig. 2. Shipbuilding processes in the Norwegian maritime cluster

5.1 Process A

After the conceptual design phase, the contract is signed with a shipyard. A basic phase then follows where more detailed drawings of the vessel are made, before the ideas in the conceptual and basic design is translated into detailed engineering. The production of the hull is then started at a foreign yard. In this process, the main global linkage is between a Norwegian shipyard and the foreign hull yard. In principle, the production of hulls is not very complex, and the knowledge and information that needs to be transferred is mainly of explicit nature. Consequently, and according to Gereffi et al. [8], several modes of governance could be appropriate in the link towards the hull yards.

Shipbuilding group 1 has chosen to acquire foreign companies in low cost countries in order to perform the work intensive parts of the shipbuilding process, as construction of hulls. Since the 1990s, they have owned several foreign hull yards. Respondents in this company argue that this strategy allows for control over the supply chain with regard to capacity, work processes and knowledge flow. However, the first years after the acquisition, there were challenges regarding the quality of the hulls (e.g. welding). These problems have been reduced over the years. Today there is considerable information and knowledge exchange between the home yards and the foreign hull yards, in particular related to production planning. Knowledge and information is frequently exchanged between the regional shipyards and the foreign hull yards. To further reduce costs the shipyard is in a process of moving activities like simple equipping from the local shipyards to the hull yards. However, this process has proven to be challenging, due to quality issues and delivery time.

Shipbuilding group 2 has chosen not to own the foreign hull yards, but has sought to establish cooperation with some foreign shipyards. The reason for this strategy is mainly based on financial risk and market considerations. However, Shipbuilding group 2 has not been able to establish long-term relationship with a particular foreign hull yard. According to theory, this may hamper knowledge and information exchange between the companies.

5.2   Process B

In this process, the global linkages must handle more complex interactions, as the complete vessel is being built at a foreign location. The global linkages in this process is typically between a Norwegian design/engineering company and a foreign shipyard.

Both shipbuilding groups deliver complex and customized vessels and can be categorized as Engineer–To-Order (ETO) producers [2]. Traditionally, there has been exchange of dominantly tacit knowledge through face-to-face interaction between regional actors in the shipbuilding process, which is well adapted to this kind of production. From Table 1, we see that the relational form of governance corresponds to this form of knowledge exchange, which also has been the prominent form of governance regionally in the maritime cluster. This form of governance is, however, difficult to sustain over longer geographical distances. Consequently, the shipbuilding groups have to find other forms of governance towards foreign shipyards.

Shipbuilding group 1 owns wholly or partially the foreign shipyards (vertical integration). They have employees from their home yards stationed at foreign yards, which according to the respondents is critical in order to achieve project success. These persons have important roles in the knowledge transfer between the Norwegian design/engineering environment and the foreign shipyard. Vertical integration is in line with Gereffi et al. [8], as the production of complete offshore supply vessels is complex, the information to be transferred is difficult to codify, and the foreign shipyards are reported to have low competence in building such vessels.

Shipbuilding group 2 exerts looser ties to the foreign shipyards. Their strategy in this process is to take a supplier role, delivering design, equipment packages and project management. By using standards and specifications, they aim at making the interface between the design company and the foreign shipyard more 'clean', allowing for more flexibility in the selection of foreign shipyards, in accordance with the modular form of governance [8]. This implies transfer of knowledge associated with the shipbuilding process from tacit to explicit. Moreover, this approach requires codifiability of information related to building and equipping the vessel, which implies a development towards making standardized or simpler vessels compared to the advanced and customized vessels the cluster companies are renowned for. Furthermore, the complex and flexible nature of the ETO shipbuilding process represents an opportunity for selling project management competence to foreign shipyards. However, the mismatch between the competence and responsibility balance in the relationship with the foreign shipyards represents a challenge: With respect to competence, Shipbuilding group 1 is in power relative to the foreign shipyard, which resembles the captive form of governance in figure 1. The Shipbuilding group has, however, no formal responsibility in its relationship with the shipyards, as it only is a supplier of design and project management to the foreign shipyards. This mismatch may hamper knowledge exchange in the relationship.

Both shipbuilding groups report, independent of form of governance, that cultural barriers, and a different way of producing vessels at the foreign shipyards, represent challenges in carrying out shipbuilding projects at foreign shipyards. Cultural issues are in particular related to hierarchy and power distance [13]. The complex nature of the production process of these vessels represents a challenge in a hierarchical production environment where workers are used to receiving orders and detailed instructions. Consequently, the design and engineering departments have found it necessary to increase the level of detail in project plans and technical drawings.

6   Discussion and Implications

In this paper the choice of governance in global value chains of two shipbuilding groups has been studied. The paper identifies two dominant production processes with varying degree of offshoring of production. In the first (A), most of the complex work is still kept inside the cluster, which makes it possible to continue the traditional relational form of governance in large parts of the supply chain. In the second process (B), only design, some engineering and project management is kept within the cluster, while the production is carried out at foreign shipyards. This represents considerable challenges for coordination of activates along the value chain. The findings in this study largely confirms the theoretical framework provided by Gereffi et al. [8], which predicts that hierarchical governance is appropriate when complexity is high, supplier capability is low and codifiability is low. Regarding knowledge, the findings indicate that vertical integration may provide stable relationship and gradually building of knowledge at the foreign production facilities, whereas building a global value chain is challenging for a shipbuilding group taking the role as a supplier of design of such complex and customized vessels.

Independent of governance alternatives, findings indicate that the shipbuilding groups to a small extent acquire and take advantage of knowledge from the foreign production sites. This reflects that the innovation processes primarily takes place in the conceptual design phase, which still is regional, involving local demanding customers, design companies, shipyards and suppliers of advanced equipment [14]. The process is characterized by face-to-face contact and exchange of tacit knowledge. Personnel involved in this process often has a background from the construction of vessels, indicating that this knowledge is important also for the design process. From this perspective, increased global sourcing of production may hamper future innovativeness of this industry. This issue should be subject for further research.

References

1. Isaksen, A., Kalsaas, B.: Suppliers and Strategies for Upgrading in Global Production Networks: The Case of a Supplier to the Global Automotive Industry in a High-cost Location. European Planning Studies 17(4), 569–585 (2009)
2. Haartveit, D.E.G., Semini, M., Alfnes, E.: Integration Alternatives for Ship Designers and Shipyards. In: Frick, J., Laugen, B.T. (eds.) Advances in Production Management Systems. IFIP AICT, vol. 384, pp. 309–316. Springer, Heidelberg (2012)
3. Asheim, B.T., Isaksen, A.: Regional Innovation Systems: The Integration of Local 'Sticky' and Global 'Ubiquitous' Knowledge. Journal of Technology Transfer 27(1), 77–86 (2002)
4. Semlinger, K.: Cooperation and competition in network governance: regional networks in a globalised economy. Entrepreneurship and Regional Development 20(6), 547–560 (2008)
5. MacKinnon, D.: Beyond strategic coupling: reassessing the firm-region nexus in global production networks. Journal of Economic Geography 12(1), 227 (2012)
6. Iammarino, S., McCann, P.: The structure and evolution of industrial clusters: Transactions, technology and knowledge spillovers. Research Policy 35(7), 1018–1036 (2006)
7. Williamson, O.E.: Transaction-cost economics: the governance of contractual relations. Journal of Law and Economics 22(2), 233–261 (1979)
8. Gereffi, G., Humphrey, J., Sturgeon, T.: The governance of global value chains. Review of International Political Economy 12(1), 78–104 (2005)
9. Pietrobelli, C., Rabellotti, R.: Global Value Chains Meet Innovation Systems: Are There Learning Opportunities for Developing Countries? World Development 39(7), 1261–1269 (2011)
10. Semini, M., Haartveit, D.E.G., Alfnes, E., Arica, E., Brett, P.O., Strandhagen, J.O.: Strategies for customized shipbuilding with different customer order decoupling points. Proceedings of the Institution of Mechanical Engineers, Part M: Journal of Engineering for the Maritime Environment (2014)
11. Hervik, A., et al.: NCE Maritime klyngeanalyse 2012: status for maritime næringer i Møre og Romsdal. Møreforsking Molde AS. Molde (2012)
12. Yin, R.K.: Case study research: design and methods. Sage, Los Angeles (2009)
13. Hofstede, G., Hofstede, G.J., Minkov, M.: Cultures and organizations: software of the mind: intercultural cooperation and its importance for survival. McGraw-Hill, New York (2010)
14. Hammervoll, T., Engelseth, P., Halse, L.L.: The Role of Clusters in Global Maritime Value Networks. International Journal of Physical Distribution & Logistics Management 44(2) (2014)

Enablers and Disablers for Operational Integration in a Craft Oriented- versus a Mass Production Enterprise

Inger Gamme* and Catrine Eleonor Larsson

Gjøvik University College/Norwegian Science of Technology, Gjøvik/Trondheim, Norway
{inger.gamme,catrine.larsson}@hig.no

Abstract. Companies today are struggling to cope with ever changing requirements arising from environmental concerns and increasing competition. Hence it is important to innovate, improve, and increase efficiency by achieving streamlined value chains. In this paper we examine both a single craft-oriented leisure boat producer and a car component mass producer to find similarities and differences with regard to operational integration in these two types of organizations. The study is based on interviews and field studies carried out at the production line. From this study several common enablers for integration are found: informal culture and little hierarchy, little distance between process steps and mutual rewards. The differences were found in degree of standardization and formalization, connecting links between departments and knowledge of overall and departmental strategy.

Keywords: Craft, mass production, operational integration, information sharing, collaboration.

1   Introduction

The increasing challenges that production companies are facing nowadays must be met by corresponding improvement in the efficiency of the supply chain. To be able to cope with the complexity that continuous changes cause, it is important not only to focus on improving each process step, but also to ensure that there is integration between the process steps. Under these conditions, optimization of collaboration and information sharing could provide a competitive advantage [1]. In existing research there are few empirical studies focusing on antecedents to integration [2].This article focuses on the similarities and differences in operational integration between internal process steps in the production line of a craft-oriented manufacturer versus an industrialized mass producer (hereafter referred to as "CP" and "MP", respectively). Therefore, the overall aims of this article are as follows:

- What are enablers and disablers for operational integration?
- Is there a difference between these two sectors?

---

* Corresponding author.

B. Grabot et al. (Eds.): APMS 2014, Part I, IFIP AICT 438, pp. 217–224, 2014.

2   Theory

2.1   Craft Oriented vs Mass Production

Five different production paradigms are in use in modern times: Craft Production, Mass Production, Flexible Production, Mass Customization and a paradigm that has become relevant in recent years, sustainable production [3]. In this article we focus on Craft and Mass production.

Craft oriented enterprises are typically organized in a more informal way than larger companies and are characterized by the use of tacit knowledge and, typically, a flat organizational structure with few resources [4]. They often have a fire-fighting mentality with an emphasis on ad hoc decision making [5], and tend to have different needs and decision making process than larger firms [6]. Operational processes seem to be more acknowledged than managerial processes. Craft production can be defined as: "Skilled workers, using general purpose machines, making exactly the product that the customer paid for, one product at a time "[7].

Mass production can be defined as manufacturing a very large amount of identical products, and selling them to customers that the company is sure will be there to buy them. An increase in production volume requires more standardization of the processes. At the same time, an increase in production volume also makes it possible to reduce prices, thereby making it possible for more customers to buy the products [3] .

2.2   Operational Integration

Many authors have focused on the interdependencies between two different process steps, but the content and framing varies, and many authors refer to the topic of operational integration without presenting a specific definition[8]. The term "coordination" has been used to describe managing dependencies between activities, meaning arranging the work tasks of two or more groups so that the groups can work together efficiently and hence achieve a common understanding of the work done by each of the groups [9]. The common goals for the groups are aligned, but the groups are separately responsible for performing their own work tasks [10].

In the literature there has been considerable emphasis on the "why" of integration, but comparatively little focus on how to achieve good integration [2, 8]. Promoting a positive attitude towards other departments is one way in which line managers can enhance integration [2]. In addition, when departments are equally responsible for achieving their aligned company goals, this circumstance tends to improve operational integration. Degree of operational integration can depend on elements such as reward systems, amount of formal and informal communication, organizational structures, and even different company cultures might [8, 11]. Job rotation is also shown to be effective, and has been found to be mildly connected to integration in small companies, and strongly connected to integration in make-to-order companies [2]. Different companies may have different needs with respect to integration [12]. Aiming towards full integration is not always the answer, and as argued by Katz and Kahn [13], integration can be pushed too far.

3   Method and Material

The data presented in this article represent two different research initiatives. The two companies were chosen because they represent two different production paradigms, and the aim of this study was to examine the question of whether operational integration varies according to the type of organization.

The first case study was funded by the Norwegian Research Council, and was undertaken with the primary objective of developing effective, competitive and profitable production within a leisure boat and craft-oriented industry in Norway. The goal of preserving the craft tradition while moving towards industrialization was emphasized. The case company used primarily manual manufacturing processes.

The second case study was an independent research initiative by two PhD Candidates whose projects were funded by the Norwegian Research Council. The aim was to study mechanisms for operational integration in the production line. The company chosen was a car component producer for commercial vehicles, one that produced a high volume of products. This company was also located in Norway, but was part of a larger group with operations on four continents.

A case study is one of various ways of doing science. It is a useful approach to understand complex social occurrences and to achieve understanding of organizations [14]. Table 1 lists the essential characteristics of the two case companies.

Table 1. Case Company Characteristics

Characteristics	Craft Producer	Mass Producer
Years of study	2008-2012	2012-2013
Main product	Leisure boats	Commercial vehicle components
Number of employees	20	37
Formal interviews	12	11
Part of value chain included	Molding, pre-assembly, assembly	Injection molding, assembly
Type of informants	Operators, foremen, manager, production manager.	Operators, production manager, foremen, planner, tool manager, quality technician

This research is based on two single case studies. The use of fewer cases facilitates more in-depth analysis, but affords less opportunity to draw generalized conclusions. To increase the robustness of the research[15], data triangulation was used. It can be achieved by the use and combination of different methods such as surveys, interviews, observations and content analysis of documents to study the same phenomenon[16]. Prior to both studies a research protocol with an interview guide was worked out. Several semi-structured interviews were conducted to identify the operational integration for the production lines and its enablers and disablers. Semi-structured interviews are defined as planned interactions for which some predefined guidelines are outlined, so the informant can provide important insight into facts in addition to their opinions on a desired topic [16]. The informants were given the possibility to answer freely and to offer additional information. In addition to the interviews, content analysis of documents, formal and informal meetings and direct observations were performed. Most of the time at both companies was spent on the shop floor interacting with the workers. Typically the focus of these meetings was on clarifying questions and discussing findings and special issues.

The collected data were recorded on a dictation machine, analyzed and coded into main categories [16, 17] to identify the mechanisms for operational integration.

4   Findings and Discussion

To organize the data, categories are developed on the basis of previous work by different researchers who have found the overall mechanisms for integration to be culture at the plant, degree of vertical integration and formalization, facility and layout, degree of use of information systems, consensus on integration and measurements and rewards [2, 8, 12, 18]. The mechanisms from the different researchers are combined and further developed to form the basis for the organization of our data. These categories and findings are shown in Table 2. It should be mentioned that some of the enablers and disablers could fit into more than one group.'

Table 2. Enablers and disablers for integration in the MP and the CP

Categories developed from literature	Findings at Mass Producer	Findings at Craft Producer
Culture		
• Values, understandings, way of thinking	• Used to standardized work • Some lack of confidence in systems • Main focus on own work station, minor focus on overall value chain. • Prefers verbal communication	• Little information sharing mentality • Ad hoc culture • Lack confidence in systems • Standards rarely used
• Informal communication • Connecting links	• Informal culture • Foreman connects team boards	• Informal culture • Foremen main source for information
• Cross functional teams • Job rotation	• On higher levels • Not standard procedure	• Not standard procedure
Vertical integration		
• Informal culture between management and operators • Small organization and little hierarchy	• Informal culture, little hierarchy • Foreman connects team boards • Departmental meetings each week, separate days per dept.	• Small organization, little hierarchy • Informal culture • Meeting with all employees • Management not driving force to attain integration
Formalization		
• Policies, rules, certification • Job descriptions • Standard procedures, technical reports • Charts, information process practices etc.	• ISO/TS 16949, ISO 14001, lean • Standardized work descriptions • Shift log, mail, verbal communication etc. • Department meetings, team board meetings, shift overlap meetings • SAP, Excel sheets	• ISO 9001 - not maintained. • Not adequately maintained. • Team board meeting, foremen/management meeting, • Self-made system for production planning • Few KPI's, not decomposed into functional measures
• Strategic planning, functional plans, scheduling • Performance control • Visual systems	• KPI's established, some decomposed to functional measures • Kanban, visual logistics planning, visual tool status	• Some visual systems established

Table 3. continued. Enablers and disablers for integration in the MP and the CP

Categories developed from literature	Findings at Mass Producer	Findings at Craft Producer
Facility & Layout		
• Plant size	• Large plant, small value chain	• Small physical distances
• Physical distances	• Small physical distances.	• Small value chain - easier to
	• Intimate environment.	understand entire process.
• Partitions	• Physical hindrances to verbal	• Intimate environment.
	communication	• Physical hindrances
	• Functional silos	• Functional silos
Information systems		
• Degree of formalization of information flows	• Several systems in use such as ERP, document handling system,	• Few information systems in use, mainly used by man-
• Enhanced capacity of information processing	mail system etc.	agement
	• Some lack of trust in systems	• Lack of trust in IT systems
Consensus integration		
• Functional strategies must support the business strategy and each other.	• Operators know department strategy, less of company strategy	• Overall strategy well known, but focus differs
	• Some measures derived from	• Operators' main focus: own
• All functions support business strategy and each other, and all managers know this is going on.	strategy, visual via team board.	work
	• Operators' main focus: own work	• Overall strategy not trans-
		ferred to functional meas-
		ures.
		• Bonus upon achieving a
Measurement, rewards		certain number of produced
• Bonuses, rewards	• Verbal acknowledgment per num-	boats
	ber of improvement proposals	

Culture, Social mechanisms and creation of lateral relations
Company culture is found to affect integration. Thus, when problems arise in achiev-ing integration, it might be helpful to try to change the culture [11].

The culture at the two plants was experienced as quite similar, despite the different structures. At both plants the operators called for more information from the man-agement. In contrast, few of them saw the need for sharing/receiving information beyond their own process step, saying; "I have too much to do with my own work". The foremen played a superior role in information sharing, but even more at the CP than at the MP. This could make the foremen a bottleneck for information sharing.

Job rotation is found to contribute to achieving integration [2].At both plants there had occasionally been a rotation of workers, and this was experienced as providing more knowledge of the rest of the value chain.

Vertical integration
Both companies had an informal culture with respect to interaction between operators and management. However, the MP had more formal systems for this interaction.

The CP had one team board located in the molding department. Each morning the foreman and the operators met at the board to plan what was going to be produced. Prior to this meeting, the management and the foremen had their daily morning meet-ing, and the meeting in the molding area was based on output from this meeting.

The MP had one team board at each department, and the team leader participated in both these meetings. In this way the team leader acted as a connecting link between the team boards. The CP did not have the same degree of driving force for integration.

222   I. Gamme and C.E. Larsson

Formalization and standardization
Standardization is one mechanism that drives integration[18], and this was found to differ between the two companies. As a result of its decades of experience with certified quality systems, the MP had several standardized procedures for information sharing. Each department used a team board and several visual systems. Despite this, there seemed to be different perceptions among some of them in terms of how information should flow.

The CP had little bureaucracy. They had earlier been ISO 9001 certified, but the systems lacked updating. A visual system for material handling was established in the previous year. The overall impression was that information sharing was more verbal than written, and that information flow was mainly single sourced, where the foremen was referred to as the person primarily responsible for information sharing.

In both companies it was experienced that the operators lacked trust in systems and found it necessary to double check information. Some called to check if emails had been received, and some verbally verified the content of operation formulas as they perceived them as insufficiently trustworthy. To achieve integration it is essential that employees comply with established and standardized systems [18].

Facility & Layout
Both companies had small facilities, with short distances, but had separators between the process steps. The MP had a minor wall with an open connection, while the CP had a separation with a door. The presence of these partitions led to functional silos with separate cultures on each side of the partitions, and little understanding of each other's daily challenges. None of the companies had routines for job rotation, which could have contributed to increasing the understanding of the problems that occurred at the other stations and further contributed to a more holistic view of the company[2].

Information systems
The CP made little use of IT systems, and those that existed were uses primarily by the management. Some of the operators had earlier been responsible for updating the process descriptions, but in more recent years the production manager had updated them. At the MP, the operators used tools such as e-mail and registration of production data in the ERP system. But, according to one of the operators, approximately 90% of the communication was verbal. An explanation of why operators had mistrust of the IT systems at the MP could be, as claimed by one of the informants: "The IT strategy does not correspond with the overall company strategy". Use of information systems does not necessarily affect the integration positively, since how and if the information is being processed also is of importance[19).

Consensus / integration
To achieve the overall company goal, it is important to decompose the strategy into "subtasks" relevant for the employees [9]. At the CP the overall strategy was well known to all workers. However, there was little translation of this strategy into functional measures. At the MP some overall goals were decomposed into functional tasks at the production level and visualized on the team boards. Despite this, it did not seem as though the overall strategy was clear enough to all.

Measurement and rewards

Both companies used common rewards for the departments in their value chains. The CP had bonuses per boat produced, while the MP used verbal acknowledgements per number of improvement proposals. These practices are in accordance with research that notes the importance of having aligned goals for the departments[10].

4.1   Summary of Findings

Table 3 summarizes the similarities and differences from the findings in the study.

Table 4. Summary of similarities and differences from the findings in the study

Characteristics	Similarities	Differences
Culture	• Lack confidence in systems • Prefer verbal communication • Little information sharing mentality	• Experience with standardized work
Vertical Integration	• Foremen main source for information	• Foremen connecting link between team meetings
Formalization	• Informal culture • Little hierarchy • Little distances.	• MP more standardized than CP
Facility & Layout	• Physical hinders • Functional silos	
Information systems **Consensus integration**	• Lack of trust in IT systems • Several operators focus mainly upon their own process step	• Different use of IT systems • Company strategy well known in CP less in MP • Departmental strategy well known in MP minor in CP
Measurement, rewards	• Rewards includes more than one department	

5   Conclusion

The aim of this study has been to enable a better understanding of similarities and differences in mechanisms for operational integration in a craft-oriented versus a mass production enterprise. Although these companies belong to different production paradigms, they had several common enablers for integration: little hierarchy, informal culture, little distance between process steps, mutual rewards. The differences was found in degree of standardization and formalization, foremen functioning as connecting links between team boards   and   the fact that overall strategy is well known in CP, while departmental strategy is more known in MP. The common disablers for integration were found to be related to culture and physical hinders in location.

The study has focused on creating new insight into enablers and disablers for operational integration in two different production paradigms and how these differ. The experiences from this study could also contribute to providing operational guidance to similar types of companies who want to improve their operational integration.

Generalization from only two single studies can of course be open to critique, but this study should contribute to building a theory of operational integration. Future research should focus on attaining more empirical results to gain knowledge of mechanisms that contributes to achieving operational integration.

References

1. Zhou, H., Bentonjr, W.: Supply chain practice and information sharing. Journal of Operations Management 25, 1348–1365 (2007)
2. Basnet, C., Wisner, J.: Nurturing Internal Supply Chain Integration. Operations and Supply Chain Management 5, 27–41 (2012)
3. Jovane, F., Koren, Y., Boër, C.R.: Present and Future of Flexible Automation: Towards New Paradigms. CIRP Annals - Manufacturing Technology 52, 543–560 (2003)
4. Nonaka, I., Takeuchi, H.: The knowledge-creating company. Oxford University Press, New York (1995)
5. Garengo, P., Biazzo, S., Bititci, U.S.: Performance measurement systems in SMEs: A review for a research agenda. International Journal of Management Reviews 7, 25–47 (2005)
6. Shrader, C.B., Mulford, C.L., Blackburn, V.L.: Strategic and Operational Planning, Uncertainty, and Performance in Small Firms. Journal of Small Business Management 27, 45–45 (1989)
7. Koren, Y.: The global manufacturing revolution: product-process-business integration and reconfigurable systems, vol. 80. Wiley.com (2010)
8. Pagell, M.: Understanding the factors that enable and inhibit the integration of operations, purchasing and logistics. Journal of Operations Management 22, 459–487 (2004)
9. Malone, T.W., Crowston, K.: The interdisciplinary study of coordination. ACM Comput. Surv. 26, 87–119 (1994)
10. Cao, N., et al.: How are supply chains coordinated?: An empirical observation in textile-apparel businesses. Journal of Fashion Marketing and Management 12, 384–397 (2008)
11. Braunscheidel, M.J., Suresh, N.C., Boisnier, A.D.: Investigating the impact of organizational culture on supply chain integration. Human Resource Management 49, 883–911 (2010)
12. Turkulainen, V.: Managing cross-functional interdependencies-the contingent value of integration. Teknillinen Korkeakoulu (2008)
13. Katz, D., Kahn, R.L.: The social psychology of organizations (1978)
14. Eisenhardt, K.M., Graebner, M.E.: Theory Building from Cases: Opportunities and Challenges. The Academy of Management Journal 50, 25–32 (2007)
15. Patton, M.Q.: Qualitative evaluation and research methods. SAGE Publications, inc. (1990)
16. Yin, R.K.: Case Study Research. Design and Methods, 4th edn., vol. 5. Sage Publications, Beverly Hills (2009)
17. Tjora, A.: Kvalitative forskningsmetoder i praksis, 2nd edn. Gyldendal Akademisk (2010)
18. Bowersox, D.J., Closs, D.J., Stank, T.P.: 21st century logistics: making supply chain integration a reality. Michigan State University, Council of Logistics Management (1999)
19. Galbraith, J.R.: Competing with flexible lateral organizations. Addison-Wesley Reading (1994)

Towards a Spatiotemporal Ontology-Based on Mereotopological Theory in Assembly-Oriented Design

Elise Gruhier, Frédéric Demoly, Olivier Dutartre, Said Abboudi, and Samuel Gomes

IRTES-M3M, UTBM 90010 Belfort Cedex, France
{elise.gruhier,frederic.demoly,olivier.dutartre,
said.abboudi,samuel.gomes}@utbm.fr

Abstract. This paper presents a novel spatiotemporal ontology based on a mereotopological theory in the context of assembly-oriented design, which integrates assembly sequence planning in the early product design stages. Based on a brief literature review on ontology and existing spatiotemporal ontological models, the authors propose to go beyond by defining their own formal ontology in the domain of assembly-oriented design. The proposed ontology provides formal description of product-process information and information consistency checking through the product lifecycle. Here, the ontology covers the spatial, temporal and spatiotemporal dimensions. The ontology uses OWL language and is implemented in Prot´eg´e. The main objective is to provide a product design description by proactively considering its assembly sequence as early as possible in the product development so as to ensure information and knowledge consistency with preliminary information and later introduce a spatiotemporal reasoning layer.

Keywords: Formal description, Product-Process, Logic, Ontology, OWL.

1 Introduction

In complex product development environments, contributions from human can entail mistakes. That is the reason why information along the product lifecycle are currently managed by PLM (Product Lifecycle Management), a computer-based information system. A recurrent issue is that information or knowledge are lacking consistency due to a lack of reasoning capabilities in PLM systems [12]. Relationships between objects have to be simulated to avoid information inconsistency [14]. That is the reason why a theory based on this notion has already been proposed [8]. The theory describes product-process evolution by extracting knowledge from designer's experience. Designers need to be assisted by adavanced knowledge management tools in order to avoid mistakes. Semantic web technology has been considered with its language so as to formalize this theory and to represent information in a structured and understandable manner. Ontology is used to capture, represent and reuse knowledge in PLM systems and therefore ensure information and knowledge consistency in product design. The paper is focused on the development of a spatiotemporal ontology in AOD (Assembly-Oriented Design). The objective is to provide a product design description

B. Grabot et al. (Eds.): APMS 2014, Part I, IFIP AICT 438, pp. 225–232, 2014.
© IFIP International Federation for Information Processing 2014

by proactively considering its assembly sequence as early as possible in the product development so as to ensure information and knowledge consistency with preliminary information. The next step will be to add rules to the proposed ontology in order to check information consistency through PLM. Built on this, further efforts will be done so as to introduce DL (Description Logic) and SWRL (Semantic Web Rule Language) rules and then develop a specific reasoning layer.

Firstly, the paper presents, in section 2, a brief literature review on ontology and existing spatiotemporal models. Then, Section 3 describes the proposed formal ontology with OWL (Ontology Web Language) language, which provides product-process associations through semantics and logics. Section 4 introduces a mechanical assembly to illustrate the relevance of the ontology. In section 5, the advantages and limits of the model are described. Finally, in section 6, conclusions and future work are given.

2   Literature Review

2.1   Ontology Engineering

Ontologies address the semantic representation of information for the purpose of storing and exchanging shared knowledge over a worldwide network [6]. An interesting definition is proposed by Gruber [7]: "ontology is an explicit specification of conceptualization". Moreover ontology brings a common vocabulary [11] and a formal aspect enabling information models to be machine interpretable. Inference ontology uses logical deductions on information and ensures the information consistency of the product along the product lifecycle. In mechanical engineering domain, Kim et al. [9] developed an assembly design ontology and an ontology-based assembly design framework in order to facilitate collaborative product development. In this framework, design intent can be well understood among different designers, and applications can reason about assembly knowledge without any semantic ambiguity. Moreover Demoly et al. [2] described product relationships with mereotopological primitives and have implemented it into ontology with OWL-DL and SWRL languages, so as to be machine-interpretable.

2.2   Ontology Models

The NIST (National Institute of Standards and Technology) has developed CPM (Core Product Model) to support PLM information [3]. Purely functional reasoning about a product in the conceptual stages of design can be supported by CPM. Then CPM has been extended to cover assembly issues through OAM (Open Assembly Model), a standard representation and exchange protocol for assemblies. The NIST interest in knowledge ontologies has led to the transformation of CPM and OAM to an inference model [5]. Then CPM2 has been proposed to support a broad range of information relevant to PLM [4]. Moreover Matsokis et al. have developed an ontology model of the product data and knowledge management Semantic Object Model (SOM) [10] using UML class diagram. SOM is a product item oriented model achieving both an efficient description of the product as it is designed from the manufacturer point of view and a functional structure for storing data of the products lifecycle [12]. So it improves interoperability in PLM.

3   OWL Implementation of the Spatiotemporal Ontology

3.1   Product-Process Knowledge Description in AOD

A theory, called JANUS (Joined AwareNess and Understanding in assembly-oriented deSign with mereotopology), has already been proposed to describe product-process evolution during the assembly-oriented process with a mereotopologybased theory [8]. The approach formally represents the relationships between regions (Figure 1). Product design is composed of spatial objects (such as parts) linked together by spatial associations and assembly sequence planning is composed of temporal objects (such as assembly operations) linked together by temporal associations. By using spatiotemporal objects (such as swept volumes: space occupied by an object during its move or deformation) and spatiotemporal relationships, spatial objects evolution over time can be understood. Spatial, temporal and spatiotemporal primitives, summed up in Table 1 and Table 2, have been defined in [8] in order to describe possible evolutions during the assembly process. The object evolution depends on its position in space (i.e. give the localization compared to other objects), its position in time (i.e. give the temporal position of the object regarding to others) and its form (i.e. give the object structure). When one attribute (i.e. time, space and form) is modified, a change during the assembly design occurs. Objects and their relationships are considered as entities of information and this information is interconnected to create an ontology [14].

3.2   Overview of the Research Approach

The novel approach, called PRONOIA2 (PROduct relatioNships description based On mereotopological theory), is based on the PRONOIA approach [2] and extends it in the temporal and spatiotemporal dimension in order to have a more realistic model. The model aids the designer to check information consistency in the early design phases. Product information can be accessed, stored, served and reused throughout the entire product lifecycle [15] by using a dedicated ontology. The ontology is implemented using Prot´eg´e, an ontology management tool [13] and OWL2 (extention of OWL). As shown in Figure 1, the ontology model is divided into three levels, such as the meta-ontology, the domain-ontology and the application-ontology.

3.3   Meta-Ontology Description

This section introduces the meta-ontology representing objects and their relationships in the three dimensions: spatial, temporal and spatiotemporal. Classes, sub-classes and properties are described to build the knowledge base and illustrated in Figure 2.

Table 1. Spatial and temporal primitives described in [8]

Spatial primitive	Temporal primitive
Part of **P**	*TemporallyPart of* **Pt**
InteriorPart of **IP**	*StartTemporallyPart of* **Pts**
Crosse **X**	*FinishTemporallyPart of* **Ptf**
Overlap **O**	*TemporallyInteriorPart of* **IPt**
Discrete **D**	*TemporallyPrecede* <
Tangent **T**	*TemporallyTangent* **Tt**
Boundary **B**	*TemporallyOverlap* **Ot**
Straddle **St**	*TemporallyEqual* =**t**

Table 2. Spatiotemporal primitives described in [8]

Spatiotemporal primitives		
Kinematic joints	Other evolutions	Technological pairs	
Move	*SerialPermutation*	*InterferenceFit*	*BlindRivet*
CylindricalOP	*ParallelPermutation*	*GasWelding*	*ArcWelding*
PrismaticOP	*Addition*	*Soldering*	*SpotWelding*
SphericalOP	*Deletion*	*Brazing*	*Clinching*
RevoluteOP	*Split*	*AdhesiveBonding*	*Crimping*
PlanarOP	*Union*	*SnapIn*	*MechanicalFastening-*
PointContactOP	*ChangeOfForm*	*NailAssembly*	*ByThreadedFasteners*
LineContactOP	*Deformation*	*MetalStitching*	
ScrewOP	*Growing*	*SimpleRivet*	
Rotation	*Decrease*	*DoubleRivet*	

The model is composed of two top-level types of classes: the physical entity (i.e. region) and the relationship between these entities (i.e. primitive). Spatial and temporal regions and primitives are four different sub-classes of the meta-ontology. As the spatiotemporal dimension depends on the spatial and temporal dimensions, it has been considered as a sub-class of those two dimensions. Classes and sub-classes are linked with properties, which are semantic relationships to facilitate the reuse of existing data, find the inconsistency and errors in data and aids designers to make right decisions by considering complex criteria [1].

3.4   Assembly-Ontology Description

Based on the meta-ontology, assembly-ontology is defined on Figure 3 in terms of classes, sub-classes and properties in the AOD domain. New introduced classes and sub-classes are represented in bold. The primitive class is not shown as it has already been described in Table 2. This ontology has specific vocabulary linked to the assembly process (such as swept volume), which differentiates it with other domain-ontologies (e.g. manufacturing-ontology). Therefore spatiotemporal primitives, such as kinematic pairs, technological pairs and evolutions inferred during the assembly process, are formalized in this ontology.

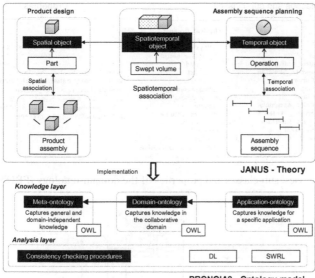

Fig. 1. Research approach of the JANUS theory and of the PRONOIA2 ontology model

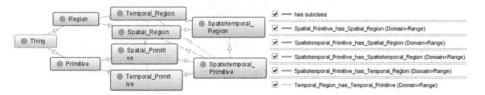

Fig. 2. Classes, sub-classes and properties of the meta-ontology (PRONOIA2)

4   Case Study: A Mechanical Assembly

This section presents a mechanical assembly (see Figure 4) with its related mereotopological descriptions and its related ontology. The case study is composed of six parts. The ASDA algorithm [2] has generated a relevant assembly sequence that is *[1,[3, 2, 4], 5, 6]*. Here the spatial regions *2, 3* and *4* are embedded in a sub-assembly (denoted SA). Product-process mereotopological description are described in Figure 5 and are based on graph developed in [8].

Spatial regions (i.e. oval), temporal regions (i.e. column) and spatiotemporal regions (i.e. rectangle) are represented and linked with primitives (i.e. line). The third level of the model is created by adding individuals to populate the ontology. A part of the individuals has been shown on Figure 6. The authors have checked that the ontology is composed of all concepts needed in the description of product-process evolution through AOD as well as their consistency.

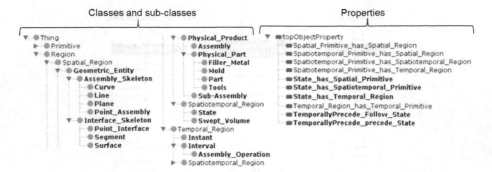

Fig. 3. Classes, sub-classes and properties of the domain-ontology (PRONOIA2)

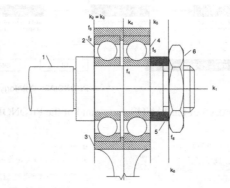

Fig. 4. Cross-section view of the considered mechanical assembly

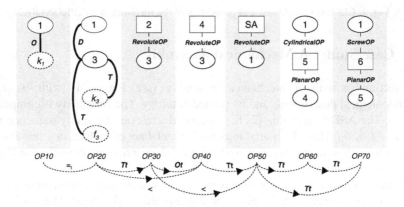

Fig. 5. Understanding product-process integration with semantics and logics

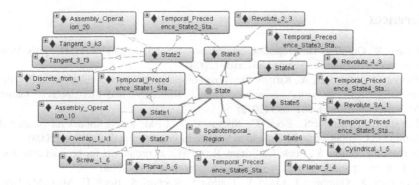

Fig. 6. Application-ontology (PRONOIA2) for the presented case study

5   Discussions

The proposed ontology is the result of an initial research effort, on which a full ontology covering the whole PLM could be defined. The ontology has been broken down into three levels so that some domain-ontologies (e.g. manufacturing-ontology...) can be added whenever the authors want. When the manufacturing-ontology will be added to the ontology, the authors will just have to import the meta-ontology into a new project file. So the proposed ontology has been developed in focusing on the long term.

6   Conclusions and Future Work

Based on a brief state of the art survey on ontology models, this paper has introduced a research effort towards a spatiotemporal ontology in AOD. The proposed PRONOIA2 ontology is based on a mereotopological theory (JANUS), which qualitatively describes product-process definition and evolution. As a consequence, the ontology covers three dimensions, such as spatial, temporal and spatiotemporal, so as to check information consistency issues in AOD. Here, the spatiotemporal dimension has been added in order to be able to describe product-process knowledge and information in a consistent and understandable manner. This dimension aids designers to understand changes during AOD. The ontology model is composed of a meta-ontology, a domain-ontology (in that case the assembly process) and an application-ontology. The JANUS theory is now formalised and machine-interpretable, since an OWL implementation has been done. The actual stake is to get a long term dynamic vision of the space in order to facilitate the understanding of assembly and design changes. In future work, rules will be added using SWRL and DL languages so as to reason on spatiotemporal associations within PLM systems (i.e. Product Data Management and Manufacturing Process Management systems). Such efforts will enable the introduction of novel procedures for consistency checking of product-process information and knowledge in PLM.

References

1. Chang, X.: Ontology Development and Utilization in Product Design. Ph.D. thesis, Virginia Polytechnic Institute and State University (2008)
2. Demoly, F., Matsokis, A., Kiritsis, D.: A mereotopological product relationship description approach for assembly oriented design. Robotics and Computer- Integrated Manufacturing 28(6), 681–693 (2012)
3. Fenves, S.J., Foufou, S., Bock, C., Sriram, R.D.: CPM: a core model for product data. Journal of Computing and Information Science in Engineering 5, 238–246 (2008)
4. Fenves, S., Foufou, S., Bock, C., Sriram, R.: CPM2: a core model for product data. Journal of Computing and Information Science in Engineering 8(1) (2008)
5. Fiorentini, X., Gambino, I., Liand, V., Foufou, S., Rachuri, S., Bock, C., Mani, M.: Towards an ontology for open assembly model, Italie (2007)
6. Fortineau, V., Paviot, T., Lamouri, S.: Improving the interoperability of industrial information systems with description logic-based models - the state of the art. Computers in Industry (2013)
7. Gruber, T.: Ontology (1993)
8. Gruhier, E., Demoly, F., Gomes, S.: A spatiotemporal mereotopology-based theory for qualitative description in assembly design and sequence planning. J.S. Gero, United Kingdom (2014)
9. Kim, K.Y., Manley, D.G., Yang, H.: Ontology-based assembly design and information sharing for collaborative product development. Computer-Aided Design 38(12), 1233–1250 (2006)
10. Kiritsis, D., Bufardi, A., Xirouchakis, P.: Research issues on product lifecycle management and information tracking using smart embedded systems. Advanced Engineering Informatics 17(3-4), 189–202 (2003)
11. Lee, J., Jeong, Y.: User centric knowledge representations based on ontology for AEC design collaboration. Computer-Aided Design, 735–748 (2012)
12. Matsokis, A., Kiritsis, D.: An ontology-based approach for product lifecycle management. Computers in Industry 61(8), 787–797 (2010)
13. Sun, W., Ma, Q.Y., Gao, T.Y., Chen, S.: Knowledge-intensive support for product design with an ontology-based approach. The International Journal of Advanced Manufacturing Technology 48(5-8), 421–434 (2010)
14. Witherell, P., Grosse, I., Krishnamurty, S., Wileden, J.: AIERO an algorithm for identifying engineering relationships in ontologies. Journal Advanced Engineering Informatics, 555–565 (2013)
15. Zhong, Y., Qin, Y., Huang, M., Lu, W., Gao, W., Du, Y.: Automatically generating assembly tolerance types with an ontology-based approach. Computer-Aided Design 45(11), 1253–1275 (2013)

BPRM Methodology: Linking Risk Management and Lesson Learnt System for Bidding Process

Juan Diego Botero, Cédrick Béler, and Daniel Noyes

Laboratoire Génie de Production / INPT-ENIT - University of Toulouse,
47, Avenue d'Azereix, 65016 Tarbes Cedex, France
{juan.boterolopez,cedrick.beler,daniel.noyes}@enit.fr

Abstract. The working relationship between industrial partners often begins with a bidding procedure by which a costumer chooses a provider of works or services. From the bidder point of view, there are several risks when responding because he must propose an offer for a future development. In this context, considering the whole project cycle is essential to identify all potential risks and take them into account during the development of the technical and commercial offer. In this paper, a methodology for bidding process risk management (BPRM) is presented. It is based on the experience acquired during past projects in order to manage the risks of current BP and make it more efficient.

Keywords: bidding process (BP), risk management (RM), project lifecycle, lesson learned system (LLS).

1   Introduction

In recent years, bidding process (BP) has become a key practice for almost all professional sectors. This practice is based on the competition of potential providers. Each one of them spends time and resources to make proposals that will not always be accepted or even, that will penalize the bidder during the product development. A successful BP is one that allows achieving both client and provider goals. To be efficient, proposals must meet client quality requirements while minimizing costs and time. These constraints make BP risky and complex. Since it is a widely used procedure, it is necessary to develop support management tools in order to assist this process.

Depending on the project advancement, two risk families are distinguished. The first one is associated to the BP itself in relation with the non-acceptance of the offer, and the second one is related with the project execution. An incorrect assessment by the bidder of the difficulties associated with the realization (inadequate estimation of development context, evaluation errors) can distort the offer. If it is accepted, the bidder may be engaged in a very penalizing process (cost overruns, non-compliance of technical requirements, non-compliance of deadlines...).

To effectively solve these major problems, a BP instrumentation is proposed by coupling a suitable risk management engineering with a dedicated lesson learnt system. This instrumentation and the underlying methodology (called BPRM "Bidding

B. Grabot et al. (Eds.): APMS 2014, Part I, IFIP AICT 438, pp. 233–240, 2014.

Process Risk Management") aims to assist BP by taking into account BP risks through a lesson learned system (LLS).

The central principle of BPRM approach is the capitalization of past BP cases including all project cycles, focusing on risks. This goal is achieved through a fact sheet featuring all relevant information to facilitate posterior exploitation. These fact sheets are called "experiences" and they include information about a project: its context, its analysis, its solution, its deployment and its closure. All these experiences are stored in a database to be reused, once adapted, in new cases.

The paper is organized in five sections.

— In section 2, the general principles of BP are presented. BP is positioned in a project management frame and set as the initial phase of the project.
— In section 3, the concept of BP risk is shown and a risk model called "CEMDEx" is proposed to store all relevant information dedicated to risk management.
— In section 4, the BP experience is presented and put in relation with the risk management process.
— The general approach of BPRM methodology is detailed in section 5. Here, the operating mechanisms of the proposed LLS are explained.
— Conclusion and perspectives are discussed in the last section.

2   Bidding Process and Project Cycle

Bidding is a global process in which two entities are involved. The first one is the customer who makes a call for tenders for works, supplies or services; and the second one are the different bidders who respond to this request based on formal client requirements [1]. This process includes the steps of receipt of invitation to tender, feasibility study, decision making (go / no go), technical offer development, cost estimation and negotiation [2].

BP is part of a more global process, which is the actual project cycle [3]. A descriptive BP model and its positioning in the project cycle are introduced in Fig. 1. This model presents the classic project steps (client process) and their correlation with BP extended to development cycle (supplier process). The project steps related to BP are: expression of needs, feasibility and, if the offer is accepted, development.

For a project that involves a call for tenders' procedure, the request is made during the phases of expression of needs and feasibility study (*cf.* Fig. 1). In these steps, formal requirements are established, criteria on which the project will be evaluated are defined, and the call for tenders is issued. This invitation is received by several bidders who respond depending on their capability and their interest in the project.

For bidder, BP includes the request analysis (from call for tenders to "go / no go" decision) consisting of a feasibility study and decision-making steps. This decision is based on the ability to meet customer demand but also on bidder competitive and commercial strategy. The next step, technical offer design, which consists in drawing up the client proposal, is essential because future design scenario must be considered in order to develop an adapted proposal that meet both client specifications and supplier constraints. Then, costs are estimated in order to establish the price of the offer based on resources to be used and on expected gain. The negotiation phase consists in sending the offer to the client and discussing with him on technical and economic issues that can arise. This last step leads to a positive or negative response from the client.

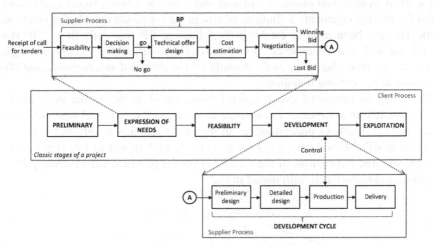

Fig. 1. BP and project cycle

If the bidder's offer is accepted, the development phase begins. This product development cycle includes the steps of preliminary design, detailed design, production and delivery [4]. A control phase from the client process to the bidder process occurs to inspect the expected characteristics. Finally, the product is delivered for its use by the client.

BP has several critical features. This process has a short duration (bidders often have little time to prepare the proposal) and, very especially, it is conducted under uncertainty (since the product does not exist yet and since the available information is not always reliable). It has a big impact on the whole project since BP set up the conditions for future development [5]. These characteristics impose severe constraints and expose the bidder to different kinds of risk. The first level of risk is associated with the client decision (acceptance or rejection) and the second one is related to the project development where bidder can be penalized (several reasons are possible: lack of skills, cost overruns, delays...). Note that an upstream risk can also be associated with the "go / no-go" decision in relation to the project interest the bidder may have.

3   BP Risk and CEMDEx Model

A classic view of risk is related to the perception causes / consequences of an unwanted event. Risk is associated to the occurrence of this event correlated with the consequences it induces [6]. The occurrence context of an unwanted event establishes the hazard and, depending on this, the potential consequences can be more or less serious. A risk model that integrates this characteristic has been developed in previous work [2]. This approach takes into account external factors present in the context (that may increase or reduce the consequences). In addition, the "control" aspect is integrated to represent actions carried out on causes and on consequences.

In order to manage BP risks, it is very important to define risk in this context. Since BP is an upstream phase of a project and since the whole project cycle is considered for risk management, definitions of risk in the broad sense and of project risk in particular have been used to establish the following BP risk definition: *"BP risk is associated with the occurrence of an unwanted event whose occurrence affects, firstly, acceptance objectives and, secondly (if the proposal is accepted), the objectives of quality, cost and timeliness".*

Regarding an unwanted event, several properties characterize the associated risk and its possible management. In this regard, an adapted risk model has already been developed [7]. It allows understanding all the useful features to inform the processes involved in BPRM methodology. Five aspects are highlighted in this representation, forming the five dimensions of the CEMDEx model (Causes, Effects, Mapping, Description, and Experience) introduced in Fig. 2.

$$R_{BP} = \{<C>, <E>, <M>, <D>, <Ex>\}$$

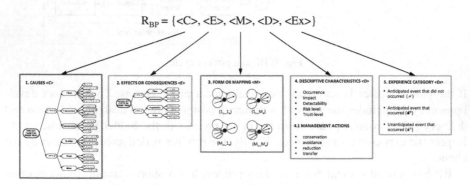

Fig. 2. CEMDEx model

Causes (<C>). According to the classification of risk factors for an unwanted event proposed in [8], a partition "external / internal causes" has been created. In this approach, external causes include all causes from the bidder outside context in relation with the current BP. Internal causes include all causes which are specific to the bidder context. Classes included in these two categories are respectively *client* causes, *competition* causes and *environment* causes for external causes, and *strategy* causes, *project* causes and *product* causes for internal ones. Each class may have other specific subclasses, which are typically: organizational, technical, financial, human and juridical ones.

Effects or consequences (<E>). As was done for the causes, effects of unwanted event are split up according to the partition "external / internal effects". In this case, external effects include all effects affecting the bidder outside context in relation with the current BP. The internal effects include all effects affecting the bidder context. Effects in relation to the *client* and the *environment* are identified as external effects, and effects related to the *project* and the *product* are identified as internal ones. Like for causes, subclasses (organizational, technical, financial, human and juridical) may be associated with each effect.

Form or "mapping" (<M>). This dimension allows clarifying the number and form of dependencies between the possible causes of an unwanted event and its effects. Four basic forms may be considered with respect to the generic risk representation: *i)* one cause to one effect, *ii)* one cause to multiple effects, *iii)* multiple causes to one effect, and *iv)* multiple causes to multiple effects. Considering "multiple causes to multiple effects", aggregation operators (conjunctive or disjunctive) must be defined and have an important impact on the adopted risk management strategy. For instance, the application of "cause avoidance" techniques is, a priori, more favorable to conjunctive causes than those of disjunctive (in the first case, avoidance of one possible cause is sufficient to exclude the occurrence of the unwanted event).

Descriptive characteristics (<D>). The main descriptive characteristics in quantitative terms are the following properties: *i)* occurrence (often expressed with probabilities), *ii)* impact or severity (often expressed with scale of values), *iii)* detectability (expressed as binary or gradual value), *iv)* risk level (often expressed by the product of occurrence and impact), and *v)* trust-level (confidence level expressed as gradual value). Qualitative characteristics are those that describe the management actions carried out (or likely to be carried out). This description combines classically choices and actions of conservation (passive risk acceptance), avoidance (actions to avoid causes), reduction (actions to limit consequences), and transfer (insurance).

Experience category (<Ex>). This last dimension refers to risk scenarios already found in past experiences; it is directly related to the LLS. In the context of past BP, several risk scenarios for the project development have been identified. Starting from risk associated with an unwanted event, a risk can be: *i)* anticipated and not occurred (a risk that should not have been considered or, on the contrary, a risk for which actions carried out avoided its occurrence), *ii)* anticipated and occurred (a risk for which actions carried out were not enough), and *iii)* unanticipated and occurred (a risk in which the analyst did not think).

This generic BP risk model can be refined according to the system to be developed (product/service). This representation is exploited in decision-making processes involved in the BP different phases. For more information about CEMDEx see [7].

4   Experience Concept and BP Guideline

In order to carry out activities related to LLS (capitalization, processing and exploitation) [9], an experience vector (set of structured information eventually nested) has been proposed. It allows to record all relevant information to the implementation of a LLS towards BP risk management and is made of five elements: *i)* the "context" describing the current BP framework, *ii)* the "analysis" conducting feasibility studies and risk analysis, *iii)* the "solution" describing the technical and commercial offer, *iv)* the "deployment" presenting the product development as well as the encountered difficulties (if the offer is accepted), and *v)* the "closure" giving the final risk analysis and synthesis of the project.

Fig. 3. Experience vector

This experience vector has been implemented in a LLS computerized fact sheet that allows capitalizing and exploiting experiences in a practical way. This sheet aims to trace BP (extended to the project) in order to facilitate the extraction of information and to simplify the mechanisms for its reuse during a new BP. A key aspect of this tool is to provide the full traceability of the expert reasoning when dealing with risks during a BP. In particular, special information fields have been developed to include (eventually) expert comments.

Based on this experience frame, a guideline with six stages for processing a new BP is offered: *i)* fact sheet assignment, *ii)* similar experiences lookup, *iii)* risks extraction and analysis, *iv)* offer estimation (quality, cost and timeliness), *v)* solution deployment, and *vi)* final risk analysis and project closing. Coupling between the BP stages, the experience vector and the offered guideline is given on Fig. 4.

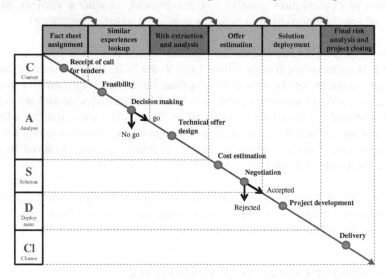

Fig. 4. Matching between Experience, RM and LLS

Note that correspondence between these three elements is straightforward. Each BP stage (extended to project) matches an element of the LLS fact sheet (the description of the experience) and a phase of the advisable guideline.

5   General Approach for BP Risk Management

The previous guideline for BP risk management allows both to lead BP effectively and to lead risk management in accordance with ISO 31000 [10]. Indeed, our BPRM methodology follows, in an original manner, the stages of risk management, which are: communication, context set up, risk appreciation (identification, analysis and evaluation), treatment and monitoring. Fig. 5 illustrates risk management mechanisms involved in the BPRM methodology via the LLS.

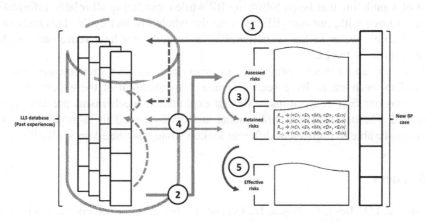

Fig. 5. Operating mechanisms of LLS database for risk management in BP

The first step consists in requesting the LLS database in order to find relevant experiences for a new case ❶. This request may use three lookup mechanisms: *i)* similarity of experiences (considered as a whole), *ii)* similarity of risks associated to specific context elements of experiences (stored in past experiences for each risk) *iii)* search for peculiar risks (according to the expert knowledge and know-how).

Step 2 returns inferred risks to be studied drawn up from full experiences and specific risks ❷. This risks list can be completed by letting the analyst add new risks (no previous occurrence). Such risks are conformant to the CEMDEx model.

The third step involves the transition from assessed risks to retained risks (risks to be considered in current BP) ❸. Each risk component must be adapted to the current case. This can be done through the analyst expertise (or eventually by using automated rules). Again, a particular attention has been paid to capitalize the analyst reasoning trace for each risk analysis ("risk trace" history is available) ❹.

Finally, step 5 concerns the transition between considered risks (in BP phase) to effective risks occurred during the project execution ❺. Here, the provider can see if the implemented risk strategy was adequate (pertinence of retained risks and effectiveness of the corresponding risk management actions).

Note that, even if last step of risk management cycle (monitoring) is not explicit in Fig. 5, it is implicit in the methodology because, through the LLS implemented, risks are under control, and revision and updates are systematically carried out when the risks adaptation for new cases of BP is made.

6   Conclusion and Perspectives

Bidding process (BP) is an unavoidable and risky practice for companies that respond call for tenders. The BPRM methodology was proposed so as to give such companies a tool to control the different kinds of risk associated to tenders. The originality of this work is the coupling of risk management with a lesson-learnt system (LLS).

The first contribution was to define what essentially is a BP Risk. A generic model called CEMDEx has been used for this purpose. The second contribution is the proposition of a guideline that helps following BP while capitalizing all related information in concordance with, not only BP, but with the whole product cycle. This ends up in an information vector called "experience" that is stored for later reuse and which is the central part of the LLS.

Up to now, a fact sheet representing an experience has been implemented and several lookup mechanisms have been designed. Capitalization of the expert reasoning (trace) was our first concern and although exploitation mechanisms are not yet implemented. The usage of a flexible model and its associated meta-model have been decided to be able to implement different lookup strategies (based on similarities).

References

[1] Botero, J.D., Béler, C., Noyes, D., Geneste, L.: Integration of experience feedback into the product lifecycle: An approach to best respond to the bidding process. Information Control Problems in Manufacturing 14, 1095–1100 (2012)

[2] Botero, J.D., Béler, C., Noyes, D.: Risk analysis in project early phase taking into account the product lifecycle: Towards a generic risk typology for bidding process. In: Manufacturing Modelling, Management, and Control (2013)

[3] Wang, J., Xu, Y., Li, Z.: Research on project selection system of pre-evaluation of engineering design project bidding. International Journal of Project Management 27(6), 584–599 (2009)

[4] Cross, N.: Engineering design methods: strategies for product design (2008)

[5] Chalal, R., Ghomari, A.: An approach for a bidding process knowledge capitalization. World Academy of Science, Engineering and Technology 19 (2006)

[6] Gouriveau, R., Noyes, D.: Risk management-dependability tools and case-based reasoning integration using the object formalism. Computers in Industry 55(3), 255–267 (2004)

[7] Botero, J.D., Noyes, D., Béler, C.: Modèle des risques pour les soumissionnaires aux appels d'offres. In: 10 Congrès International de Génie Industriel (CIGI) (2013)

[8] Alquier, A.M., Cagno, E., Caron, F., Leopoulos, V., Ridao, M.A.: Analysis of external and internal risks in project early phase. PRIMA Project, 147–155 (2000)

[9] Rakoto, H., Hermosillo, J., Ruet, M.: Integration of experience based decision support in industrial processes. In: International Conference on Systems, Man and Cybernetics, vol. 7, p. 6 (2002)

[10] ISO/31000, Risk management — Principles and guidelines. ISO (2009)

Development of Information and Communication Systems within the Building of Project-Oriented Manufacturing Organization

Anna Hamranova[1], Stefan Marsina[1], Pavol Molnar[1], and Frantisek Okruhlica[2]

[1] University of Economics in Bratislava, Slovakia
(anna.hamranova,stefan.marsina,pavol.molnar)@euba.sk
[2] Comenius University Bratislava, Slovakia
frantisek.okruhlica@fm.uniba.sk

Abstract. Project management (PM) has become a managerial discipline which is an inevitable prerequisite of managing modern business organizations, especially manufacturing ones. When applied properly it helps organizations to cope with permanently changing environment predominantly represented by customers, suppliers, competitors, and public authorities. Development of the project management methodology leads to increasingly effective implementation of strategic changes which is fundamental for being competitive on the marketplace. This PM development is in the center of building project orientation of an organization. But, developing just PM without development of overall organizational culture leads to low effectiveness of projects implemented in the organization. That is why development of projects and project management should be supported by development systems and areas of activities such as communications, knowledge, training and development of employees, and development of organizational standards and norms. The article focuses on the area of communication by using Business Intelligence systems.

Keywords: Project management, project-oriented organization, communications, knowledge, culture, Business Intelligence, project management office.

1 Introduction

Manufacturing companies more and more need projects and project management for being innovative, flexible, interoperable and efficient. Even quality standards take care of project management. For the field of project management the ISO 10 006 standards represent a clear definition of a project as a process that brings a planned change.[5] However the use of projects in manufacturing organizations is known, it is less known, that the programs and projects are the outcomes of strategic thinking of top management of the organization. [7] Transition from strategic thinking to the particular act of strategy implementation is expressed in the following brief idea: A project starts when the management authorizes it. [10]

A project itself is not only a tool for technological or organizational innovation, but also a tool for generation of new managerial culture in the organization.

B. Grabot et al. (Eds.): APMS 2014, Part I, IFIP AICT 438, pp. 241–248, 2014.

Communication techniques applied in project teams enable mutual share of professional information which is essential for building a knowledge-based enterprise. Also techniques for saving information during the project, and at the end of it, offer possibilities to maintain the database of knowledge which is subsequently used for next events performed in the enterprise. The acquired knowledge has to be available for authorized people, so that the enterprise should develop organizational standards and norms for managing acquired know-how. All this mixed with purposeful training and development of the employees, who are important for providing core organizational activities, creates a ground for project orientation development.

The project-oriented organization becomes a significant issue in the strategic thinking of top managers today. Concerning the problem of getting right professional information in right time, the information flood coming from internet does not help sufficiently to increase the knowledge of specialists throughout the organization. Equally, it seems to be not satisfactory just to establish a position of chief communication, information, or knowledge officer in the enterprise without development of supporting relations and activities. The aim of this paper is to offer a model how to build project orientation in a business organization with focus on communication as one of supporting areas within this comprehensive process. This contribution has been elaborated on the basis of partial results of the research project VEGA 1/0933/14 supported by the Slovak Ministry of Education and Sport.

2   Project Orientation of an Organization

2.1   Model of Building Project Orientation

The low strategic thinking level of the top management in business organizations often reveals the orientation just on operational issues, short-term goals, and overlooking trends. This is very risky, and often leads to deep problems in near future. These organizations do not use projects for curing their systems problems, but they would like to take advantage of co-financing them by the European supporting funds. The evidence of this finding is available from results of an institutional VEGA research project carried out in 2005. [6] It must be stated, that it is a long-term run for such a poorly project-oriented organization to become a mature project-oriented one with developed programming. Also, the common professional effort of both managers and owners is a prerequisite. Owners usually have a majority in the Board of directors. If a company is to function professionally, it is very important that members of the board are properly skilled. [9] An integrated model of the process of becoming strategically highly developed project-oriented organization is suggested in Table 1: Integrated model of transformation process leading to the project-oriented organization. [8]

The model suggests that beside Project management development, which is in the center of the transformation process; there are other areas in the organization to be developed: Communications, Knowledge development, Training and development of employees, and Organizational standards & norms. Table 1 shows the transformation of a current organization into a project-oriented one. Columns from left represent initial state of a company/organization, which is not yet developed in an area, and next five developing steps lead to a project-oriented, strategically mature organization.

The project development in Table1 starts from the state when projects, if any, are designed and implemented by external experts. No special organizational unit cares for this area. In most, this is a competence of one top manager or the functional manager authorized by him/her. Through the gradual involvement of internal personnel the enterprise establishes its own unit, a project management office, for the administration of design and implementation of projects.

The model was tested in real business environment independently by two diploma students while elaborating their theses. The first company was a manufacturing one operating in defense industry and its project-orientation in all areas oscillated on 3rd step of development. The second company was mixed construction and consulting one, and its state of project-orientation development was in four areas at 4th step and in knowledge development area at 5th step.

2.2   Communication and Knowledge Development Areas in an Organization

Knowledge development inevitably goes concurrently with development of communication culture and training and development of employees. At first, the knowledge of employees is exclusively connected with their profession. They have no idea about what is done by their colleagues in the next functional area. For example, people in technical area have no concern for economy and vice versa. Solution of a multidisciplinary problem is almost impossible. The third step proposes an interdisciplinary approach of people working in professionally different areas. In the fourth step the multidisciplinary knowledge is acquired during the project preparation and/or implementation. The multidisciplinary work on the project and intensive communications enable participants to learn much about the profession of a partner within the project team. The supporting role of top management to make communications in team effective is expressed by Yeatts: The managers' behaviors and what they said were the means of conveying this support. [13] The fifth step describes the managed activities of the project management office where specialists share professional information with partners. The project management office is becoming a consulting center of the organization. [2] It can even become the publisher of a professional journal issued regularly minimum once a year.

The acquired knowledge has to be saved and properly stored for using by others later on. In the organization, the area covering standardization and normalization takes care of it. Thereby, knowledge generated from communication can be formalized and positively influences the behavior and overall culture of an organization. [12]

Table 1. Integrated model of transformation process leading to the project-oriented organization

Initial state	Developed area	1st step	2nd step	3rd step	4th step	5th step	Desired state
Current organization	Organizational standards & norms	Standards & norms for routine processes	In general, organizational norms support operation of ICT and T&D of employees	Organizational norms include the project administration	Organizational norms specified for PM include utilization of Business Intelligence apps and outsourcing of selected ICT	Specific norms developed for the Project management office (PMO*)	Mature project-oriented organization
	Communications	Communication gaps between professional areas and managerial levels	Identification of activities to be supported by IS/ICT	Increased horizontal and vertical cooperation, start of implementing BI applications	Development of communication within the project teams; optional use of Business Intelligence applications	Communication of project professionals organized by PMO	
	Knowledge Development	Knowledge related to profession and position in the organization	Knowledge related not only to profession in the organization	Creating environment for interchanging of tacit knowledge	Multidisciplinary knowledge acquired on the project	Shared knowledge of PM professionals (PMP**) within the projects or PMO (+ Journal)	
	Project management development	Projects, if any, designed and implemented by external experts	Projects are designed and implemented prevailingly by external experts	Projects are designed and implemented prevailingly by internal experts	Internal experts are gradually certified as PM professionals and Project managers	PMO administers design and implementation of projects including pool of PM experts	
	Training and development of employees	T&D only in the profession given by external trainers	T&D only in profession given prevailingly by external trainers	T & D of mixed ex-pertise given prevailingly by internal trainers	T & D of mixed ex-pertise given prevailingly by internal trainers or is given within the project	T & D of mixed expertise given prevailingly by internal trainers leads to PMP certification	

* PMO – Project Management Office, ** PMP – Project Management Professional

Source: own

2.3   Communication Problems in the Manufacturing Organization

Communications in an organization is a complex system of technically supported and non-technically supported communication. Non-technically supported communication is verbal or nonverbal (face-to-face). Information is exchanged between groups or individuals. Technically supported communication can be included to the information and communication systems known as IS/ICT. For the support of building or development of project orientation of an organization we must analyze both technically and non-technically supported communications.

In general, communication problems in the organization can be viewed from horizontal and vertical perspective. Fig. 1 shows a model of hierarchical and functional problems in communications within the organization.

Both phenomena – the hierarchical and functional communication gaps work simultaneously. The result is the creation of communication islands within which specialists operate. For example, it is clear that to improve the mutual behavior of partners in a supply chain in specific situations means actually the change of behavior of individual partners, i.e. the change of their culture. Definitely, it is a key process and not a short-term one. The developed communication systems should remove the communication gaps which are shown in Fig. 1.

Communication   Communication gaps   Communication isles
gaps hierarchical   functional

Fig. 1. Implications of bad hierarchical and functional communications in the organization (adapted by [4])

Another communication problem has been defined by Schulte. He calls it "Conflicts of goals between functional departments in the manufacturing company". [11] The functional departments especially in manufacturing organizations speak different professional languages and follow different goals. For example, marketing managers thing about wishes of customers, production managers about low costs, lead times and quality, research and development people thing about most modern design of products, and financial managers about investment and financial sources. One of the places where they can understand each other is a project team, because they share the same common goal.

3   Business Intelligence Tools for the Development of Project-Oriented Manufacturing Organization

The evolutionary maturity model of Business Intelligence applications is well compatible with the Model of development of a project-oriented organization.

On the basis of study several models concerned with maturity of Business Intelligence systems it has been found that each model is focused on the development of a specific part of Business Intelligence systems. For further research the BIMM (Business Intelligence Maturity Model) was developed initially by Gartner Company, then published by authors Chamoni & Gluchowski. [1] This model was supplemented with elements from the TDWI (The Data Warehousing Institute) and Hewlett – Packard models. They served to determine the stages of BI maturity model evolution. Concurrently, criteria for measurement of maturity level of the individual enterprise were established. [3]

Starting from the above mentioned it is possible to describe BIMM as follows:

The BIMM consists of 5 levels, where each level covers 3 areas within which every level will be analyzed:

    a)   Business processes and reporting,
    b)   Information technologies,
    c)   Strategic management of an organization (the strategy in relation to BI)

1st level – pre-defined reporting
This level represents organizations, which start thinking about BI implementation, or those which have passed several bad starts and revalue they BI strategy.

2nd level – BI within the professional departments
Organizations on this level prefer manual solutions while creating analyses. They start planning and monitoring business processes, where they tend to apply new methods.

3rd level – BI expansion to all areas of organization
The third level of maturity model can be characterized by a need for integrating the subject or vertical oriented information solutions, which were implemented on the second level. Thereby organizations gain possibility to define metrics in more detail, e.g. metrics which require data from more than one area.

4th level – expansion the number of users and decision making support
Beside the top and middle management users of BI there is an extension of access for lower managerial levels of the organization, i.e. support of innovation and overall activity of employees.

5th level – the active knowledge management
The 5th evolutionary level of the BIMM is characterized by activities related to integration of IS/ICT within the organization with other external systems all focused on increasing the value of business organization. The critical factor of success is the knowledge management principles application together with full support for Business Intelligence systems utilization.

According to published research [1, 3] manufacturing companies' lag behind in Business Intelligence area compared to IT, financial and telecommunication companies. According to the BIMM the manufacturing companies reach only the 1st. or 2nd level maximally.

There are more suitable simpler and cheaper solutions for the manufacturing companies focused on basic business processes, whereas especially for small enterprises the BI solutions within information systems ERP (Enterprise Resource Planning), or the open source solutions are sufficient.

Further research for possible improvement of Building project-oriented organization model will take into account the above mentioned achievements and the 5 levels of BIMM will be tested against the 5 levels/steps of the Project-oriented organization model.

4   Conclusion

To become a mature project-oriented manufacturing organization means to undergo a process which is based on strategic thinking and systems approach of the owners and executives. The aim of this contribution was to offer a model for manufacturing organizations presenting how to build the project orientation not only through developing projects and project management but also with support of other four activity areas development. This comprehensive approach ensures better the sustainability of high level project-orientation of the organization. Communication as one of the four supporting areas in this comprehensive process was discussed in more detail.

In manufacturing companies communication problems occur not only as hierarchical gaps but as extreme functional gaps caused by diversity of professional orientation of organizational units. Building of project-orientation can be a remedy.

References

1. Chamoni, P., Gluchowski, P.: Integrationstrends bei Business-Intelligence-Systemen - Empirische Untersuchung auf Basis des Business Intelligence Maturity Model. In Wirtschaftsinformatik Ausgabe Nr. (February 2004)
2. Gareis, R.: Happy projects! Manz Verlag, Luchterhand, Stämpfli, Wien (2005)
3. Hamranova, A.: Aspekty implementácie Business Intelligence v slovenských podnikoch, pp. 41–47. Ekonóm, Bratislava (2013)
4. Kerzner, H.: Project Management. A Systems Approach to Planning, Scheduling, and Controlling, 9th edn. John Wiley and Sons, Inc., Hoboken (2006)
5. Lacko, B.: Strategic goals of project management. In: International Conference: Strategic Management and its Support by Information Systems. Technical University of Ostrava, Ostrava (2001)
6. Majtan, M., Marsina, S.: The evaluation of research questionnaire. In: Annual Report 2005 of the VEGA Research Project: Adaptation and Development Processes in Slovak Enterprises After the Slovak Republic Entry into European Union, Faculty of Business Management, University of Economics in Bratislava, Bratislava (2006)
7. Marsina, S.: Analýza pôvodu projektu v podnikovom prostredí. In: Economics, Finance and Management of Enterprise: Proceedings of the International Scientific Conference of the Faculty of Business Management, pp. 364–368. University of Economics, Bratislava (2003) (in Slovak)
8. Marsina, S.: Project Orientation Helps Business Organizations to Become Competitive. Economics and Management - the Scientific Journal of Faculty of Business Management, University of Economics in Bratislava, vol. 3 (2013)
9. Okruhlica, F.: The Responsibility of Boards is Unreplaceable. In: AmCham Connection. The Official Magazine of the American Chamber of Commerce in Slovakia, vol. 11, Bratislava (2006)

10. Rosenau, M.D., Githens, G.D.: Successful Project Management – A Step-by-Step Approach with Practical Examples, 4th edn., p. 22. John Wiley & Sons, Inc., Hoboken (2005)
11. Schulte, K.: Logistics, p. 78. Victoria Publishing, Prague (1994)
12. Thomasova, E.: Organizovanie, p. 112. Ekonóm, Bratislava (2007) (in Slovak)
13. Yeatts, D.E.,, Hyten, C.: High-performing self-managed work teams, p. 190. SAGE Publications, Inc., Thousand Oaks (1998)

Top-Down Definition of Design Spaces Based on Skeleton Modelling

Nicolas Petrazoller*, Frédéric Demoly, and Samuel Gomes

IRTES-M3M,
Université de Technologie de Belfort-Montbéliard (UTBM),
90010 Belfort Cedex, France

Abstract. This paper introduces a novel modelling approach based on the analogy to the incubator concept so as to provide a suitable support for designers through product design process. The main objective is to define a knowledge-intensive design context in the early product design stages. The main goal of the proposed approach is to provide a knowledge-based design context for designers by considering engineering knowledge in an appropriate and seamless manner. As such, the proposed design incubator will assist designers to make better-informed decisions by delivering knowledge and engineering information at the right time. A case study has been introduce to illustrate the relevance of the proposed approach.

Keywords: Assembly modelling, Skeleton-based modelling, Top-down assembly design, Proactive engineering, Design context definition, Knowledge-intensive design

1 Introduction

The current globalised competitive context requires industry to reduce development lead times at optimised costs and improve the quality and the efficiency of their products in order to fulfil customers' requirements. To reach these goals, a phase of architectural design is required. The role of product architects will be consider the numerous number of constraints (i.e. reliability, sustainability, ...) in the product design process. Product architects also have a global view on the system to be developed especially on functional, structural, behavioural, geometric and physical aspects which are associated to different viewpoints [6].

The fact of working collaboratively and remotely on the same product is part of a recurrent issues in large-scaled companies. As such, it is important to define a design context to assist designers through their activities. This paper is based on previous research works on proactive design for assembly and skeleton based modelling approaches ([7] [8] [9]). Built on this, the whole is to propose a proactive top-down modelling approach of layout elements based on an analogical

---

* Corresponding author.

B. Grabot et al. (Eds.): APMS 2014, Part I, IFIP AICT 438, pp. 249–256, 2014.

reasoning approach with incubator in the early product design stage. The incubator is composed of several layers of engineering information and knowledge (i.e. skeleton entities, functional surfaces, design spaces, parameters, knowledge and requirements to name a few). Compared to previous research efforts in this field [8], this approach will introduce the generation of design spaces from skeleton interface entities and functional surfaces.

Built on this, section 2 reviews some previous research works in the field of top-down and layout modelling design. In Section 3, a presentation of the design incubator concept is proposed and the overall approach is also presented. Then section 4 discusses about the deployment of the approach through a mechanical assembly. Finally, conclusions and future work are given.

2   Related Works

This section aims to give a brief overview of published research works on top-down and layout modelling design issues, so as to provide the foundation of the proposed approach based on current status and challenges.

2.1   Top-Down Design

Top-down approach starts with the formalisation of requirements and the establishment of general layout models, specifying but not detailing any first-level components. Then, components are refined in greater details until the overall definition of the product. Support for top-down design and multiple viewpoints is a key point of top-down design which should be take into account when developing computer environments for mechanical assembly design [15]. An overview in this research domain [22] highlights some issues such as assembly model representation for top-down product design and the reasoning method from conceptual model top parametric model which must be tackled. In addition, Mäntylä [16]state that the design process could be decomposed into several stages (i.e. functional, conceptual and detailed design) while a top-down design process should support multiple abstraction models.

2.2   Layout Modelling

The product design process is composed of several stages from the identification of customer needs to the detailed definition of product [18]. Layout design has a crucial role to play [3] in the embodiment design stage which is the focus of this paper. By using layout elements (featured by geometric entities and engineering information), it is possible to support designers activities and exchange design data with other teams. In literature, many attempts have been made to carry out various aspects of the layout design. [12] uses layout elements to define kinematics constraints between functional components.

Li et al. [14] capture all the feasible designs to find an optimal geometry by integrating user-defined constraints. Theodosiou et al. [20] developed full comprehensive models for spatial constraints, and in particular, for free space requirements. Ballu et al. [2] proposed a functional design method that early aides to identify and analyse functional geometrical entities and tolerance (Technologically and Topologically Related Surfaces). Mun et al. [17] proposed a solution to share skeleton model among companies working collaboratively in order to protect their intellectual property. Delgado et al. [5] uses spatial design to generate a structural solution inside it. Moreover, Gelston et al. [11] proposed a method for reconstructing boundary surfaces corresponding to skeletal curves, and then extend the method for reconstruction of boundary surfaces corresponding to skeletal surfaces. Kovacs et al. [13] describes the incremental development of a knowledge-based system for supporting floor plan design. Bai et al. [1] deployed tools based on Product Layout Feature concept to carry out collaborative design activities among multi-disciplinary teams. Skander et al. [21] proposed a skeleton-based method and models that tackle the issue of manufacturing processes selection and constraints integration , as soon as possible, into the product modelling stage. Csabai et al. [4] uses design spaces to analyse interferences between product components. Gane et al. [10] defined a methodology for building and managing requirements driven design spaces with parametric Computer Aided Design tools.

3 Proposed Approach

This section presents the proposed approach which introduces the design incubator concept (Fig. 1). Design incubator provides a knowledge-intensive and living support to designers by defining layout product geometry at the beginning of the embodiment design phase. Such analogical reasoning will enable the introduction of a novel paradigm in CAD modelling stage.

The incubator improve coordination and information flows between three systems, such as Product Data Management (PDM) system, knowledge base and CAD system. Its role is first to generate a design context to designers. Then, when designers start their activities, it will identify and analyse their intents. Once design intents are captured, a request to the knowledge base is process in order to get appropriate engineering information or knowledge for designers at the right time. Finally, when designers store their component, the incubator will generate design intents history. Such procedures will ensure understanding and traceability in design with new technical objects.

3.1 Overall Methodology Description

Based on the SKL-ACD approach[7] [19], an enriched flow chart is introduced to describe the proposed approach in a more detailed view (Fig. 2). An explanation of the different steps of the method is visible below:

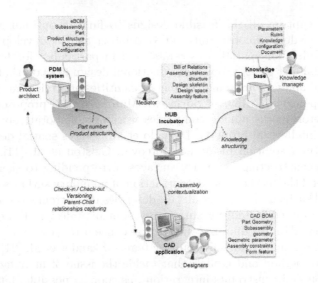

Fig. 1. Incubator concept

- Start: Starting from the early defined assembly sequence and product relational information embedded in graphs and matrices, the product architect defines kinematics/technological pairs in the directed graph;
- Steps 1 and 2. The product structure is automatically generated and assembly skeleton places are assigned inside (Steps 1 and 2 of Fig. 2);
- Steps 3 and 4. Based on these relationships, assembly constraints are automatically defined and geometric skeleton entities are generated in order to provide interface control elements for assembly modelling (Steps 3 and 4 of Fig. 2);
- Step 5. The product architect introduces new assembly constraints between the generated geometric skeleton entities (Step 5 of Fig. 2); A new graph, called skeleton graph, built upon these constraints, is defined by skeleton entities and their related assembly constraints;
- Step 6. This graph is simplified later on by the generalization and the concatenation of skeleton elements into a minimal skeleton graph (Step 6 of Fig. 2);
- Step 7. Based on this minimal skeleton graph and the early-defined assembly sequence, this step allows the structuring and regrouping of skeleton elements in assembly skeletons (Step 7 of Fig. 2);
- Step 8. An assembly coordinate system is defined for each assembly layer and associated to each identified base part. Therefore new constraints are introduced to link the defined assembly coordinate systems with the interface control elements from the minimal skeleton graph (Step 8 of Fig. 2);
- Step 2. The resulting assembly skeletons can be allocated to the initial product structure. At this stage, it is possible to assign rights to a skeleton entity which is at the interface of different assembly skeletons (Step 2 of Fig. 2);

- Step 9. Based on the kinematic pairs between components and product architect choice, the skeleton interfaces entities are defined (Step 9 of Fig. 2);
- Step 10. Supported by skeleton interfaces entities, functional surfaces are defined (Step 10 of Fig. 2);
- Step 11. From functional surfaces and skeleton interface entities, design spaces are generated (Step 11 of Fig. 2);
- End: As a result, the assembly skeleton CAD model, functional surfaces and design spaces are semi-automatically generated.

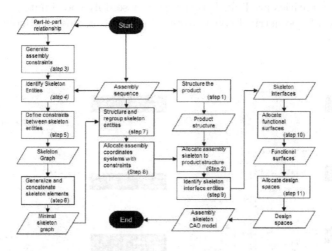

Fig. 2. Enriched flowchart of the proposed approach

4 Case Study

In this section, the proposed approach is illustrated with a mechanical system (Fig. 3). Each step of the method are described for a better understanding (Fig. 4 and Fig. 5).

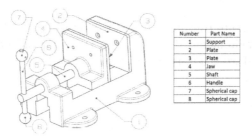

Number	Part Name
1	Support
2	Plate
3	Plate
4	Jaw
5	Shaft
6	Handle
7	Spherical cap
8	Spherical cap

Fig. 3. Case study : vice and parts list of the case study

4.1 Determination of the Skeleton Minimal Graph (Step 3 to 6 of Fig. 2) and Introduction of an Assembly Coordinate System (Step 7 to 8 of Fig. 2)

The product architect starts by defining the kinematic pairs between each parts. Based on the kinematic pairs, the skeleton entities and position constraints between each parts are deducted. At this point, to facilitate the management of the skeleton entities, it is possible to simplify the proposed skeleton graph by generalize and concatenate skeleton entities. Based on the minimal skeleton graph of the previous step, an assembly coordinate system is introduced. Each skeleton entities are linked to this new assembly coordinate system by the intermediate of geometrical constraints. Then, the geometrical constraints are concatenated.

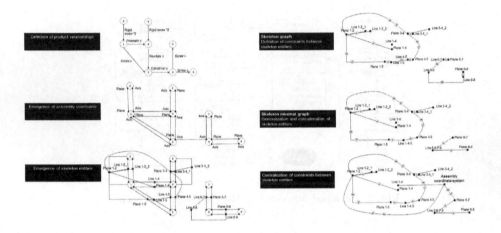

Fig. 4. Definition process of a minimal skeleton model

4.2 Allocation of Skeleton Interface Entities and Functional Surfaces (step 9 to 10 of Fig. 2) and Generation of Design Spaces (Step 11 of Fig. 2)

Based on previous steps, the skeleton interface entities are defined and associated to skeleton entities.

Then, it is possible to concatenate skeleton interface entities in order to simplify the design environment. Finally, after this simplification, the functional surface are deduced from the skeleton interface entities.

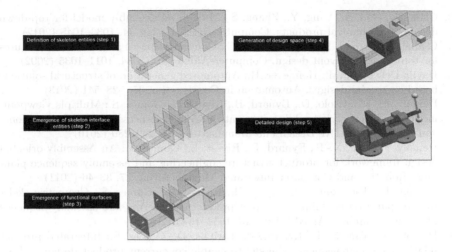

Fig. 5. Definition process of design spaces models

5   Conclusions and Future Work

In this paper, a novel approach to define a design context in the early phases of the design development has been proposed and described in detail. The current issue of the paper is to allocate design spaces to the assembly skeleton model. Defining design spaces based on skeleton modelling will permit a better understanding of "what to design" by designers. To illustrate the feasibility and the relevance of the proposed approach, a use case has been carried out. Finally, three main issues demand further research: the incorporation of knowledge; adding requirements; and create a link between the method and PDM system.

Acknowledgements. The research activity is part of the INGéPROD (Productiveness for Product-Process Engineering in a Design Chain context), which has been funded by French Automotive Cluster Pôle de Compétitivité Véhicule du Futur. The authors would like to thank General Electric for this collaboration and all the financial supports of this research and technology program: DRIRE de Franche-Comté, Communauté dAgglomération du Pays de Montbéliard, Conseil Général du Doubs and Conseil Régional de Franche-Comté.

References

1. Bai, Y.W., Chen, Z.N., Bin, H.Z., Hu, J.: Collaborative design in product development based on product layout model. Robotics and Computer-Integrated Manufacturing 21, 55–65 (2005)
2. Ballu, A., Falgarone, H., Chevassus, N., Mathieu, L.: New Design Method based on Functions and Tolerance Specifications for Product Modelling. Annals of the CIRP

3. Chen, X., Gao, S., Yang, Y., Zhang, S.: Multi-level assembly model for top-down design of mechanical products. Computer-Aided Design 44, 1033–1048 (2012)
4. Csabai, A., Stroud, I., Xirouchakis, P.C.: Container spaces and functional features for top-down 3D layout design. Computer-Aided Design 34, 1011–1035 (2002)
5. Davila Delgado, J.M., Hofmeyer, H.: Automated generation of structural solutions based on spatial designs. Automation in Construction 35, 528–541 (2013)
6. Demoly, F., Monticolo, D., Eynard, B., Rivest, L., Gomes, S.: Multiple viewpoint modelling framework enabling integrated product process design. International Journal on Interactive Design and Manufacturing 4, 269–280 (2010)
7. Demoly, F., Yan, X.-T., Eynard, B., Rivest, L., Gomes, S.: An Assembly oriented design framework for product structure engineering and assembly sequence planning. Robotics and Computer-Integrated Manufacturing 27, 33–46 (2011)
8. Demoly, F., Toussaint, L., Eynard, B., Kiritsis, D., Gomes, S.: Geometric skeleton computation enabling concurrent product engineering and assembly sequence planning. Computer-Aided Design 43, 1654–1673 (2011)
9. Demoly, F., Yan, X.-T., Eynard, B., Kiritsis, D., Gomes, S.: Integrated product relationships management: a model to enable concurrent product design and assembly sequence planning. Journal of Engineering Design 23, 544–561 (2012)
10. Gane, V., Haymaker, J.: Design Scenarios: Enabling transparent parametric design spaces 6, 618–640 (2012)
11. Gelston, S.M., Dutta, D.: Boundary surface recovery from skeleton curves and surfaces. Computer Aided Geometric Design 12, 27–51 (1995)
12. Kim, K.J., Sacks, E., Joskowicz, L.: Kinematic analysis of spatial fixed-axis higher pairs using configuration space 6, 279–291 (2001)
13. Kovfics, L.B.: Knowledge based floor plan design by space partitioning: A logic programming approach. Artificial Intelligence in Engineering 6, 162–185 (1991)
14. Li, C.G., Li, C.L., Liu, Y., Huang, Y.: A new C-space method to automate the layout design of injection mould cooling system 6, 811–823 (2012)
15. Libardi, E., Dixon, J., Simmons, M.: Computer environments for the design of mechanical assemblies: a research review. Engineering with Computers 3 (1988)
16. Mntyl, M.: A modeling system for top-down design of assembled products. IBM Journal of Research and Development 34, 636–659 (1990)
17. Mun, D., Hwang, J., Han, S.: Protection of intellectual property based on a skeleton model in product design collaboration. Computer-Aided Design 41, 641–648 (2009)
18. Pahl, G., Beitz, W.: Engineering design, a systematic approach, 2nd edn., p. 544. Springer, London (1996)
19. Petrazoller, N., Demoly, F., Deniaud, S., Gomes, S.: Towards a knowledge-intensive framework for top-down design context definition. In: Prabhu, V., Taisch, M., Kiritsis, D. (eds.) APMS 2013, Part I. IFIP AICT, vol. 414, pp. 210–218. Springer, Heidelberg (2013)
20. Theodosiou, G., Sapidis, N.S.: Information of layout constraints for product lifecycle management: a solid-modelling approach 6, 549–564 (2003)
21. Skander, A., Roucoules, L., Klein Meyer, J.S.: Design and manufacturing interface modelling for manufacturing processes selection and knowledge synthesis in design. International Journal of Advanced Manufacturing Technology 37, 443–454 (2008)
22. Wen Jian, L.: Tian guo J.: Research state and development directions of product top-down design. Computer Integrated Manufacturing Systems (2002)

Framework for Information Sharing in a Small-to-Medium Port System Supply Chain

Peter Bjerg Olesen[*], Cecilie Maria Damgaard, Hans-Henrik Hvolby,
Iskra Dukovska-Popovska, and Anita Friis Sommer

Centre for Logistics, Department of Mechanical and Manufacturing Engineering,
Aalborg University, Fibigerstræde 16, 9220 Aalborg Ø, Denmark
{pbo,cmd,hhh,iskra}@celog.dk

Abstract. Small-to-medium ports are characterised with inefficient, ineffective and resource intensive information sharing, which is not supporting their complex and dynamic environment. This creates challenges both for optimizing the internal planning of the activities at the port according to the demand, and for stronger supply chain integration with the external actors. This paper focuses on identifying the needs and criteria for an information sharing system, and proposes an approach for sharing operational data in port systems for improved supply chain integration, in the context of logistic engineering. The proposed approach has the potential to alleviate some of the problems when operating in a dynamic demand environment.

Keywords: Information sharing, supply chain integration, ICT, role based access, coordination, trust.

1 Introduction

Port systems are an important part of many supply chains, as a place for transport transformation and cargo consolidation. Ports are often characterised by a complex supply chain environment, including not only many external customers, but also many different companies within the port, making the coordination and planning even more complex. In addition, the environment is unstable because of the high variety and lack of knowledge about the timing of the activities of the different actors at the port system. This creates a need for information sharing to ensure an efficient supply chain. Literature on supply chain management states that the companies should optimise external coordination and collaboration with suppliers and customers to improve its performance and reduce uncertainties [1] [2], and to do this effectively information sharing is required. It is known that integration and coordination via information sharing in supply chains are beneficial [3], [4]. Information sharing is the act of sharing information between separate organisational units. A previous study dealing with how to enable information sharing in a port, found that there is a need to develop a system

---

[*] Corresponding author.

B. Grabot et al. (Eds.): APMS 2014, Part I, IFIP AICT 438, pp. 257–264, 2014.

to support the sharing of information [5]. The paper highlights the benefits of information sharing and finds that sharing more real-time data will ensure better planning, reduce waiting time and increase utilization of resources in port systems. The general level of integration and information sharing in small ports have not been developed much, even though it is possible [5]. Today, most information sharing in small ports is based on manual tools, such as phone calls and emails. This type of information sharing is not very flexible and is resource intensive, as all changes are propagated via manual communications methods. Therefore, an automatic IT system is required to ensure a higher level of information sharing in ports. Olesen et al. [5] finds that for such information sharing system to be usable in a small port, the system must address the issues of trust between actors of the supply chain, availability and quality of data and the complexity level of the system.

The paper is organized as follows: firs a literature presents the basic requirements and challenges for information sharing in supply chain. Further, a case study of small-to-medium port identifies the current information sharing and future needs of different actors at the port. Finally, an approach for sharing information in small-to-medium port system is proposed.

2   Theoretical Background and Analysis

To develop an information-sharing approach it is necessary to understand the challenges related to the process of sharing information between organisational units. Therefore, this section will describe some of the benefits and challenges related to information sharing. According to Zhou [6] the dynamism of demand and supply are the reasons that information sharing has a high potential value. The main benefit of information sharing in the dynamic environment is the ability to adapt plans and schedules to external input, if there is new information or the external systems behaves in an unexpected manner [7]. Furthermore, information sharing would allow the different supply chain partners to align their operations [4], making it easier to align the production system with the input and output based on the supply chains' requirements.

Information sharing challenges also include the quality and availability of information within companies. This applies to intercompany coordination of processes, but also use of information to internal planning, such as ensuring correct capacity plans. However, literature on information mainly discusses how to improve the data quality instead of the reason for bad or non-existing data [8], [9]. Besides ensuring the data quality, it is important to have the necessary data, thus the system should only contain the information required in order to keep partners updated on the events that affect them.

According to a review by Perego [10] information and communication technology (ICT) solutions for transport companies and supply chain communication is an under-developed area in both literature and industry. Zhang [11] also underline the need for a new approach to how ICT systems should operate based on whether it is intra or inter company operations the system should support. Another problem regarding ICT solution is the sometimes extreme complexity that is caused by cross-functionality and huge amounts of data. Overall, information sharing systems should be developed to be as simple as possible. Furthermore, both user interface and technical aspects affect the complexity as both can prevent a successful implementation.

Currently, most ICT systems employs sharing technology to some degree, and what is missing is from both literature and praxis is a method that enables sharing of data and acknowledges the special requirements of small and medium sized companies. Trust is one of the major hindrances for sharing information between companies [12], [13]. Trust between companies is one of the main challenges of information sharing. The trust level is often influenced by a lack of knowledge about the other companies' intentions and strategic direction [12]. A high level of trust is identified to enable: relational exchange of knowledge, facilitating parties to focus on long-term benefits of the relationship [1], supplier responsiveness [2], and collaboration [3].

It is stated by Olesen [5], that information sharing can be non-existent, manual or automatic, and that the true benefit is achieved with automatic sharing. There are some solutions that focus on the technical aspects of information sharing [14], [15], and some that discuss information sharing in a supply chain [6], [16]. However, it has not been adapted to fit systems like a port. Therefore, this paper focuses on how the information sharing systems should be adapted to support information sharing in port systems.

Based on the benefits, the requirements and the limitations of information sharing as is, the challenge moving forward is to realise why information sharing is not widely used in the industry. The main reasons are that most computer systems simply do not fit how the companies operate, and that there is no technical understanding of how companies are protective and secretive about even simple transaction data. The theoretical gap is not the technical solutions, but how they are applied in the organisation. To understand how an information sharing system can support a port system, the general setup of a port system is described.

3   Information Sharing Needs in a Small-to Medium Port System

The case is done in a medium-sized port in Denmark with around 1800 ship berths a year. The port is a collection of many services and companies, often many of these need to work together in order to move cargo from land to sea or the other way around. Examples of actors in the port are:

- Port system
  - Port authority
  - Port Terminal
- Transporters
  - Shipping lines
  - Truck carriers
- Customer
  - Shipping brokers
  - Direct customers

The **Port Authority** has central role mediating information to all companies in the port system. The Port Authority controls the approach and docking procedures of the ships, and is in contact with the approaching ship. Further, the Port Authority is the link between the ships and land services, sending the orders to the local partner. Lastly, the Port Authority communicates with the shipping brokers to book future ship arrivals and services. The Port Authority receives information related to orders and experiences challenges when this information changes or arrives late. The only up-to-date information comes from the GPS system that tracks the ships within ca. 200 km of the port, and the port authority would like to receive more updated information, about movement and timing, and be able to propagate this information to the rest of the port system. The port authority uses a lot of time to gather and distribute information about delays and other events, and feels a need for more automated approach.

The **container terminal** handles the movement of containers between land and sea. The information currently present here includes the timing of when the ships arrive and the defined deadline for when trucks arrive based on ship departures. This means that the information flow is limited and directly related to the physical flow. Information on the containers is not known by the terminal prior to the arrival, however all activities that follow the arrival are dependent on the freight letter following the container. Information about destination and time of arrival or departure is not available before the actual arrival of a truck. The information is available about containers arriving via ship, but only the ship arrival date and the number of containers. The information on containers going to or from the hinterland is only known at the terminal the day before ship departure, as orders for the ship are only final here. The terminal deals with many containers leading to high risks of waiting time and low resource utilisation. Furthermore, trucks tend to arrive around the latest deadline, creating queues and heavy peak hours. The container terminal often experiences rework from the lack of coordination of information. Improving the information sharing will improve its planning of slot times, capacity and placement in the storage area. Currently there is no way of sharing this information.

Shipping brokers are the connection between the customers needing transport of goods from one place to another and the different services available through a port. Their task is to book transport on both land and see. Their main challenge is when ships or cargo is delayed and this has influence on the booking of equipment or transport, so they would benefit from having access to this information directly and fast, instead of having to source the information through external partners. Further, a shipping broker would also benefit from having access to information about available capacity in the port, as they can use this to plan their next shipments.

A **Special Cargo supplier** producing large products for the offshore industry, often charters specials ships to transport its products to the installation sites. Since the ships are specially fitted for the job they are expensive to operate, and the equipment needed on the landside to load the ship is expensive. The problem here is that the company producing the elements, sometimes does not inform others that their production is delayed, which means that the ship waits at the dock until the cargo is ready. If the delays in production could be communicated earlier, the ship could take other tasks before, saving the company money, as a ship in dock is very expensive. Further shared information would also make the ship's approach available as a planning constraint.

There is a need to develop an approach that solves the issue of no or slow information sharing in a port system. A possible solution to this is proposed in the next section.

4   Information Sharing System at Small-to-Medium Ports

This section suggests an approach of how information sharing should be conducted in a small-to-medium port. However, it is the intention that the presented approach would allow the creation of an information sharing system. From the literature, it can be concluded that to overcome the issues of data quality, technical complexity and trust, it is necessary to make a sharing system simple. Therefore the information sharing system must:

1. Be relatively easy to use and implement.
2. Share only transactional data, reducing complexity and increasing understanding of the consequences of sharing information.
3. Easy to configure the access to the data, based on organisational position.

The focus is on the ability to update information about changes inside the previously received order information, keeping these up to date. The solution should therefore focus on sharing only limited amounts of relevant data, reducing the need for complex software. This is supported by research studies, which indicate that high level of trust is not sufficient to reach the full collaboration potential, and requires the support of electronically mediated data exchange [5].

4.1   ICT Approach

Fig. 1 illustrates the proposed system to share information in smaller ports. The important part of the system is its functionality in translating and sharing the *specific* and *correct information* needed by the supply chain partners. The system will function by having a set of standard information types that are relevant for the companies. The system will then map the chosen data types to the relevant data in a database, and be able to read changes when they happen. This allows customers and suppliers to exchange data between each other by implementing the same or similar systems. This proposed ICT solution can be a portal system that is either cloud based or installed on a local server; the specific solution is only relevant to the security setup of the ICT infrastructure in the companies.

The system will not use any new technology but will make use of a new approach to how technology and management work together. This is done by creating a new way of assigning access to specific data, and by creating an abstraction layer as seen in Fig. 1. The abstraction layer or information sharing system has several functions; 1) to secure data from the outside, by only allowing indirect specified access to databases, 2) creating a uniform API for data exchange and data presentation, 3) to filter the information based on which partner and which data this partner has access to. These functions are then based on the pre-existing agreements made between two companies' frontend office functions.

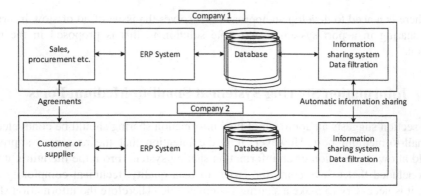

Fig. 1. Automatic information sharing through an add-on system or API that creates access control and information filtering

As a means to secure and segment access, *Role-based user control* is introduced to allow for easy configuration of access to the information in a way that gives the owner of the data full control and knowledge about the level of sharing. Role-based user control, means assigning access privileges on a per-user and user-group basis [17]. This allows an easy way of configuring exactly what information is available for whom, and gives the benefit of defining a unique sharing scheme for each user and user group, making it more configurable and understandable what information is shared with who. This will also meet the trust barriers to define a very specific amount of information that needs to be shared.

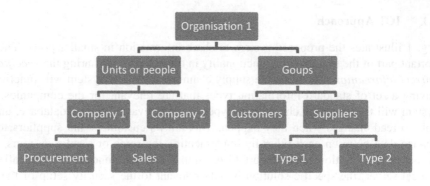

Fig. 2. Hierarchy of access and filtering

Fig. 2 shows the structure of groups and users. Each level can have a set of permissions that can be established for an entire group or for a specific user. This allows for segmentation of data, e.g. to customers giving access to capacity information and to suppliers access to inventory levels. It is therefore important that the access is controlled in a way that gives each company complete control and understanding of how the information is shared. Role-based access control also gives the benefit of defining a unique sharing scheme for each user or user group, making it more configurable and understandable what information is shared with whom. Stefansson[18] describes how to choose data that is relevant to the supply chain performance and how this transparency can increase the ability to track performance measurements. The solution described here does not consider any particular information as this is entirely configurable, and only requires a link to a database and a business decision about access restriction to this data.

This might seem simple, but the important realisation is that each company have full control over the information sharing on a level that should be understood by managers and not IT professionals. This enable the people with the organisational knowledge to

5   Discussion

The suggested setup, if implemented, will allow companies to share updated information without having to worry much about trust and about technological complexity, while keeping the critical information updated in close to real-time. The potential of the solution is to include some of the dynamic properties of any supply chain into the operations and planning of internal activities in companies. This includes already present and updated information in production planning, which makes it more likely that the committed production resources are used to produce according to the exact demand of customers, which is the ultimate mission for any operations. Also it is the primary principle behind the Lean philosophy, to only do what adds value to the customer [19]. By adhering to these concepts, it also helps reducing the impact of contingencies such as inventory etc. There are regular customers who deliver to the port several times a week and some who are one-off. The information system should therefore allow servicing these customers in different ways. Therefore, it is important that the system should have a web interface made available, where the customer has the possibility to book a time slot. There will be customers who will not make use of such a system. For more regular customers it would be more in terms of an application interface that can be connected to the companies' own planning systems and a central system in the port. Therefore, the IT solution should be able to translate the information from each actors IT system and make sure it will not influence other companies etc.

6   Conclusion and Further Research

This paper introduces an approach for creating an information sharing setup, usable for port supply chain integration. The information model takes the main barriers relating to information sharing into account and proposes a method to alleviate the impact of the barriers. The main contribution of this paper is to introduce a new abstraction layer between partner companies for sharing information based on identity and function. The proposed solution will help the trust issue by giving management insight and understanding about how and what they share and also making the benefits more clear, such as reducing the impact of dynamism. This allows an increased alignment of activities throughout the supply chain. The implication to theory is to bridge the gap between the literature showing the benefits of information sharing and the literature that shows how information can be shared over a public network, by considering the organisational issues. Further work will focus on operationalization of the approach, as in the current state only proposes the general aspect of the information approach. The implementation and evaluation of the performance effects of such a system are part of the future research. The ideas presented in this paper would also be relevant for other context such as manufacturing and it would be highly relevant to test a future information sharing system in this context as well.

References

1. Mentzer, J.T., DeWitt, W., Keebler, J.S., Min, S., Nix, N.W., Smith, C.D., Zacharia, Z.G.: Defining Supply Chain Management. J. Bus. Logist. 22, 1–25 (2001), doi:10.1002/j.2158-1592.2001.tb00001.x
2. Simatupang, T.M., Sridharan, R.: The Collaborative Supply Chain. Int. J. Logist. Manag. 13, 15–30 (2002), doi:10.1108/09574090210806333
3. Lee, H.L., So, K.C., Tang, C.S.: The Value of Information Sharing in a Two-Level Supply Chain. Manag. Sci. 46, 626–643 (2000)
4. Yu, Z., Yan, H., Cheng, T.C.E.: Benefits of information sharing with supply chain partnerships. Ind. Manag. Data Syst. 101, 114–121 (2001), doi:10.1108/02635570110386625
5. Olesen, P.B., Hvolby, H.-H., Dukovska-Popovska, I.: Enabling Information Sharing in a Port. In: Emmanouilidis, C., Taisch, M., Kiritsis, D. (eds.) APMS 2012, Part II. IFIP AICT, vol. 398, pp. 152–159. Springer, Heidelberg (2013)
6. Zhou, H., Benton Jr., W.C.: Supply chain practice and information sharing. J. Oper. Manag. 25, 1348–1365 (2007), doi:10.1016/j.jom.2007.01.009
7. Lee, H.L., Padmanabhan, V., Wang, S.: The Bullwhip Effect in Supply Chains. Sloan Manage. Rev. 38, 93–102 (1997)
8. Webster, J.: Networks of collaboration or conflict? Electronic data interchange and power in the supply chain. J. Strateg. Inf. Syst. 4, 31–42 (1995), doi:10.1016/0963-8687(95)80013-G
9. Holmqvist, M., Stefansson, G.: "smart Goods" and Mobile Rfid a Case with Innovation from Volvo. J. Bus. Logist. 27, 251–272 (2006), doi:10.1002/j.2158-1592.2006.tb00225.x
10. Perego, A., Perotti, S., Mangiaracina, R.: ICT for logistics and freight transportation: a literature review and research agenda. Int. J. Phys. Distrib. Logist. Manag. 41, 457–483 (2011), doi:10.1108/09600031111138826
11. Zhang, X., van Donk, D.P., van der Vaart, T.: Does ICT influence supply chain management and performance?: A review of survey-based research. Int. J. Oper. Prod. Manag. 31, 1215–1247 (2011), doi:10.1108/01443571111178501
12. Braziotis, C., Tannock, J.D.T.: Building the Extended Enterprise: Key Collaboration Factors. Int. J. Logist. Manag. 22, 4 (2011)
13. Fawcett, J.A.: Chapter 10 Port Governance and Privatization in the United States: Public Ownership and Private Operation. Res. Transp. Econ. 17, 207–235 (2006), doi:10.1016/S0739-8859(06)17010-9
14. Wiederhold, G.: Information sharing system and method with requester dependent sharing and security rules (2001)
15. Malone, T.W., Grant, K.R., Turbak, F.A., Brobst, S.A., Cohen, M.D.: Intelligent Information-sharing Systems. Commun. ACM 30, 390–402 (1987), doi:10.1145/22899.22903
16. Ha, A.Y., Tong, S., Zhang, H.: Sharing Demand Information in Competing Supply Chains with Production Diseconomies. Manag. Sci. 57, 566–581 (2011), doi:10.1287/mnsc.1100.1295
17. Sandhu, R.S., Coyne, E.J., Feinstein, H.L., Youman, C.E.: Role-based access control models. Computer 29, 38–47 (1996), doi:10.1109/2.485845
18. Stefansson, G., Lumsden, K., Mirzabeiki, V.: Smart Transportation Management Systems to Support Visibility of the Supply Chain Information Types (2009)
19. Womack, J.P., Jones, D.T.: Lean thinking: banish waste and create wealth in your corporation. Simon and Schuster (2003)

Preliminary Requirements and Architecture Definition for Integration of PLM and Business Intelligence Systems

Magali Bosch-Mauchand, Matthieu Bricogne, Benoît Eynard, and Jean-Philippe Gitto

Université de Technologie de Compiègne,
Department of Mechanical Systems Engineering,
CNRS UMR7337 Roberval
CS 60319, 60203 Compiègne Cedex, France
{magali.bosch,matthieu.bricogne,benoit.eynard,
jean-philippe.gitto}@utc.fr

Abstract. With the advance of information systems and business intelligence technologies, new possibilities and functionalities to measure, monitor and control processes have emerged in the research area and in the market. In the context of PLM system, not only KPI for strategic goals can be measure and indicators for decision but also operational metrics link to product, project and process to manage agility of companies.

Keywords: PLM, Business Intelligence, Project Management, Performance Measurement, Agile methods.

1 Introduction

According to Gröger *et al.*, "Agility is a critical success factor for manufacturers in volatile global environment and requires employees monitoring their performance and reacting quickly to turbulences." [1] An extrapolation can be drawn to the engineering processes, including engineering product and manufacturing process design, where actors and collaborators must have the means to monitor their performances, take decisions regarding them and react if required. This reaction can be necessitated to "respond to unpredicted changes like a late customer request, a designer failure, or some other external environmental impact" [2], but also to respond to poor performance detection. The performance measurement in engineering processes can be based on data shared by the Information System (IS) applications of Product Lifecycle Management (PLM). In fact, to be able to perform measurement on data, companies "will continue to face new and ever-increasing issues surrounding the quality of the data on which they rely", with companies incorporating data from a wider variety of sources [3]. In order to provide appropriated indicators for performance monitoring, in PLM system, the data integration is a crucial issue and it relies on various systems interoperability and their applications or data together [3]. A focus must be done on Business Intelligence (BI) systems enabling engineering process performance measurement and Integrated Decision System Support (IDSS).

B. Grabot et al. (Eds.): APMS 2014, Part I, IFIP AICT 438, pp. 265–272, 2014.

The paper proceeds as follows: the second section introduces a background in performance measurements (KPI - Key Performance Indicators and metrics), in BI as performance dashboard provider and in PLM as operational data sources. The third section is dedicated to PLM-BI systems requirements for performance management. Finally, the fourth section reports on a proposed architecture to manage data for operational decision making within PLM-BI application.

2   Background

2.1   KPI and Metrics for Performance Measurement

In order to improve competitiveness, companies measure, monitor, and analyze their performance. Performance Management Systems (PMS) are regularly implemented as "balanced and dynamic solutions requiring considerable human and financial resources, and offering support to the decision-making process" [4]. According to Neely *et al.* [5], Performance Measurement can be defined as "the process of quantifying the efficiency and effectiveness of action"; a performance measure can be defined as "a metric used to quantify the efficiency and/or effectiveness of an action"; a PMS can be defined as "the set of metrics used to quantify both the efficiency and effectiveness of actions".

Key Performance Indicators are global metrics largely used in manufacturing industries to assess the efficiency and effectiveness of production workflow and the MES - Manufacturing Execution System [6; 7]. Based on this type of metrics, most PMSs are mainly historical and static. They are not dynamic and sensitive to changes in the global environment of the company. As a result, the information reflected by KPI is not relevant, up-to-date or accurate [8; 9]. In order to make PMS more efficient, KPI need to become dynamic and process dependent.

KPI and PMS design need to be based on companies' strategies and operational process [10; 11]. In the same consideration, various methodologies aiming to determine relevant KPI in engineering design processes have arisen in the last few years for instance in New Product Development [12] or engineering department management [13].

In this section, dynamic metrics and KPI concepts have been presented to support performance measurement. These indicators are actually mainly used in the manufacturing field, but great perspectives are envisioned in the product design and in the manufacturing process design. In the next section, emerging BI concepts are presented to assist decision making process.

2.2   BI System as Performance Dashboards Provider

To monitor their performance, companies use specific performance dashboard derived from BI system. These BI systems are based on a set of models, methods, and tools that convert "raw" data into meaningful and useful information for business performance control. As defined by Negash [14], "BI systems combine data gathering, data storage, and knowledge management with analytical tools to present complex internal and competitive information to planners and decision makers." In BI technologies, three types of views of business activities can be provided: historical, current and predictive views. The most common functions of BI technologies are: reporting, On Line Analytical Processing (OLAP), analytics, data mining, process mining, complex event processing, business performance management, predictive analytics, and prescriptive analytics.

BI traditional components are data warehouse, data sources management, data marts, query and reporting tools. For instance, in the perimeter of supply chain management systems, information from various sources are collected and loaded through extract and transformation applications (ETL – Extract Transform Load) into the data warehouse [15].

According to Abdelfattah [16], the issue to select the right dashboard system architecture is to understand user requirements and the complexity of the metrics and applications that this dashboard needs to provide. It distinguishes seven dashboard architecture categories [16]: Direct Query; BI Tools; Mashboards; in-Memory Dashboards; Data Federation; Data Marts; Complex Event Processing (CEP). The competitive pressure of today's businesses has led to the increased need for near real-time BI. The goal of near real-time BI (also called operational BI or just-in-time BI) is to reduce the time latency between when operational data is acquired and when analysis over them is feasible, as CEP example in [17].

Dashboards are expected to "improve decision making by amplifying cognition and capitalizing on human perceptual capabilities" [18]. In this paper, the aim is to point out the expected benefits of the integration between design based dashboard and manufacturing based dashboards for decision support.

In this section, dynamic dashboard functionality of BI systems has been presented as a way to display appropriate indicators for performance measurement. In the next section, PLM systems, especially Product Data Management (PDM) and Manufacturing Process Management (MPM) functionalities are presented as interesting data sources for dashboard.

2.3 PLM as Operational Data Source

PLM is defined as "a strategic business approach that applies a consistent set of business solutions in support of the collaborative creation, management, dissemination, and use of product definition information across the extended enterprise from concept to end of life" [19].

PLM aims at integrating the various processes and phases involved during a typical product lifecycle with collaboration in product development processes [20]. PLM system has to be consider, from a technical point of view, as a collaborative IS platform, not a single tool or package. It shares product data among actors, processes and organizations in the different phases of the product lifecycle for achieving desired performances and sustainability for the product/project/process [21].

In PLM systems, information mainly relies on product data, design logic, assembly, tolerance information, the evolution of products and product families [22]. PLM systems are fully integrated with enterprise IS and maps with processes and organization. It takes into account needs of project team members and product end-users.

In PDM and MPM modules, static and predefined reports presented as dashboards are provided as standard functionality to follow change management and manufacturing process management. Some systems or complementary modules allow defining specific reports but few use the possibility of BI systems. A list of Product Development Metrics is given by Kenneth Crow from DRM Associates [23]. Some researches aim at defining KPI for PLM implementation and monitoring [24] and even if the objective is not the same, some of these KPI seems to be adapted to PLM system in-use monitoring. In most of PLM system, the statistical metrics are no up-to-date information, measured at regular times and stored for historical purpose. Two kinds of statistical metrics links to business report can be identified. The first one falls relates on data characteristics such as number, quantity and types of objects or documents (files, Engineering Change Request, Engineering Change Order, Computer Aided Design documents...). The second one related on the usage of each PDM/MPM functionality (query, create report, standard parts usage, parts reuse...).

There exists also a real need for monitoring metrics that are up-to-date information used for management and maintenance of the PLM system by IT Department. These monitoring metrics, such as IS supervision (Central Processing Unit (CPU), alive processes, disk space, bandwidth...) and system exploitation (connections number, number of opened sessions, license activation).

Other types of metrics can be useful in PLM system such as « Collaboration performance » metrics or Quality Assurance for Software setting metrics based on bug tracker tools [25] As an extension to [26], all engineering processes face the same challenges: dealing with technical complexity of product and process; understanding the interactions and dependencies between phases and partials model; and, evaluating the status of a product/project/process.

3   PLM-BI System Requirements for Performance Management and Architecture Definition

In the previous section, a focus was done on the operational data available in PLM system that are not relevantly use to monitor and control product/project/process: PLM systems are great IT support to capture data on products and engineering processes that have to be exploited to provide metrics/indicators of performance.

3.1   PLM-BI System Current Researches

Numerous researches point out how BI framework could be used in the context of PLM in order to refine information for better decision making [27]. Depending on the maturity level of PLM system, the use of BI in PLM environment can be considered as premature. Maturity models can be characterized as special types of roadmaps for implementing practices in an organization, and their purpose is to help in the continuous improvement of the capabilities of an organization in certain application or management areas [28].

Liu *at al.* point out that "a limitation of current BI-concepts is the neglecting of engineering data and technical process attributes" [29]. Relevant and accurate data and information integration is the most fundamental issue for all integration aspects in IDSS and this integration is crucial for the construction of relevant analysis based on estimated indicators because data is the basic format for decision variables, constraints and objective functions [30].

In [31], Do focuses on PDM system and the monitoring of ongoing product development process based on KPI regarding quality, cost and delivery metrics for product and design activities. He proposes a specific Product Data Model and a specific Multidimensional Product Data Model to structure the data in the BI system used for predefined metrics. But this type of architecture does not insure flexibility for the KPI dashboard management; the structure and metrics model is predefined and thus static.

The dashboards integrated within PLM systems that provide current and historical product and process data, allow comprehensive, reliable monitoring and control of product/project/process [6]. Also, in [6], authors highlight the needs for indicators management solutions, integrated within a PLM system, to manage three main areas: Design for X (product-oriented indicators such as cost, weight, space requirement, energy consumption, assembly etc.), project controlling (time or cost efficiency indicators) and PLM performance improvement ("Process Indicators for Product Engineering").

3.2   PLM-BI System Needs, Uses and Requirements

The companies have understood the importance of metrics-driven management to estimate the goals defined by their strategy [15]. As for manufacturing process, the proposed levels of dashboards are modelled on company's organization levels [1]. Three types of dashboard must be set: strategic/enterprise control, tactical/project control and operational/process dashboards. In the tactical/project control dashboard, monitoring for IS expert and Product Development manager has to be set. At each level, specific dynamical metrics have to be measured.

A survey and synthesis paper on the current research efforts with regard to the development of IDSS was written by Liu *et al.* [30]. This paper underlines that such system must be compatible with new BI systems and allows more flexibility and agility. The process improvement is not limited to the efficiency and effectiveness of the decisions, but has to integrate collaborative support and virtual team working improvement. Such a system must be characterized by its responsiveness and its agility [9]. The responsiveness of a PLM-BI system is its ability to provide real time reports on PLM processes. The agility of a PLM-BI system is defined by its ability to adapt itself to changes or organizational modifications.

3.3   Proposal for Data Extraction, Transformation and Loading: The Workers

For each of involved components of IS, the goal is to extract the required data and to store it in the Data Repository (DR). This functionality is performed by a specific machine, called in this paper a worker (Fig. 1) [34].

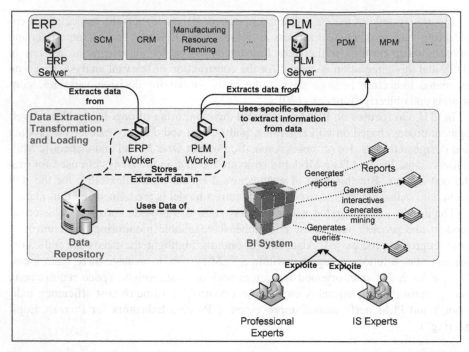

Fig. 1. PLM metrics extraction and storage for performance measurement thanks to BI system

Each worker is dedicated to a specific IS: it takes advantage of the extension's capabilities of every component in terms of chosen programming language, available Application Programming Interface (API), data model, etc…[33]

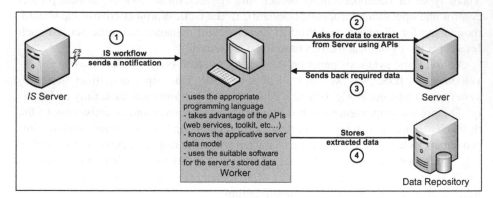

Fig. 2. Workers' processes for data extraction

Sometimes, the data stored in the IS component need to be managed by specific application. In this case, this application can be installed in the worker system in order to extract the desired information and to store it in the DR. For instance, in a PDM system, CAD data can be retrieved, opened and analyzed in order to store the proper information (e.g. the mass of the product) in the DR (Fig. 2).

4   Conclusion

In this paper, the issue of enhancing PLM systems monitoring by performance control by applying BI concepts has been introduced. Needs of specific and relevant metrics for engineering process and PLM IS monitoring has been highlighted. Future work aims at defining a case study aiming to monitor product quality factor based on PLM-BI system.

Acknowledgements. This work was carried out in the framework of the LabCom DIMEXP, funded by the French Government, through the program " Investments for the future" managed by the National Agency for Research (Reference ANR-13-LAB1-0006-01).

References

1. Gröger, C., Hillmann, M., Hahn, F., Mitschang, B., Westkämper, E.: The Operational Process Dashboard for Manufacturing. Procedia CIRP 7, 205–210 (2013)
2. Bricogne, M., Troussier, N., Rivest, L., Eynard, B.: Agile design methods for mechatronics system integration. In: Bernard, A., Rivest, L., Dutta, D. (eds.) PLM 2013. IFIP AICT, vol. 409, pp. 458–470. Springer, Heidelberg (2013)
3. Isık, O., Jones, M.C., Sidorova, A.: Business intelligence success: The roles of BI capabilities and decision environments. Inf. & Manag. 50, 13–23 (2013)
4. Vukšić, V.B., Bach, M.P., Popovič, A.: Supporting performance management with business process management and business intelligence: A case analysis of integration and orchestration. Int. J. of Inf. Manag. 33, 613–619 (2013)
5. Neely, A., Gregory, M., Platts, K.: Performance measurement system design: A literature review and research agenda. Int. J. Oper. Prod. Manag. 25, 1228–1263 (2005)
6. Kickstein, J., Drewinski, R.: Systematic indicator management as a component of a PLM environment Controlled product and process. Product Data Journal, 28–31 (2012)
7. Kemper, H., Baars, H., Lasi, H., Kemper, H.-G., Baars, H., Lasi, H.: An Integrated Business Intelligence Framework. In: Rausch, P., Sheta, A.F., Ayesh, A. (eds.) Business Intelligence and Performance Management, pp. 13–27. Springer, London (2013)
8. Đurić, Ž., Maksimović, R.: Efficiency of applying a model for measuring key performance indicators in an industrial enterprise. Sc. Research and Essays 8(14), 554–574 (2013)
9. Nudurupati, S.S., Bititci, U.S., Kumar, V., Chan, F.T.S.: State of the art literature review on performance measurement. Comput. Ind. Eng 60, 279–290 (2011)
10. Lohman, C., Fortuin, L., Wouters, M.: Designing a performance measurement system: A case study. European Journal of Operational Research 156, 267–286 (2004)
11. Neely, A., Gregory, M., Platts, K.: Performance measurement system design: developing and testing a process-based approach. Int. J. Oper. Prod. Manag. 20, 1119–1145 (2000)
12. Cheng, Y.-T., Chou, H.-H., Cheng, C.-H.: Extracting key performance indicators (KPIs) new product development using mind map and Decision-Making Trial and Evaluation Laboratory (DEMATEL) methods. African J. of Business Manag. 5, 10734–10746 (2011)
13. Beisheim, N., Stotz, F.: Key Performance Indicators for Design and Engineering. In: Concurrent Engineering Approaches for Sustainable Product Development in a Multi-Disciplinary Environment, pp. 341–351 (2013)

14. Negash, S.: Business Intelligence. Communications of the Association for Information Systems 13, 77 (2004)
15. Sahay, B., Ranjan, J.: Real time business intelligence in supply chain analytics. Information Management & Computer Security 16, 4–28 (2008)
16. Abdelfattah, M.: A Comparison of Several Performance Dashboards Architectures. Journal of Intelligent Information Management 5, 35–41 (2013)
17. Chaudhuri, S., Dayal, U., Narasayya, V., D'Atri, A.: An overview of business intelligence technology. Communications of the ACM 54, 88 (2011)
18. Yigitbasioglu, O.M., Velcu, O.: A review of dashboards in performance management: Implications for design and research. Int. J. of Accounting Inf. System 13, 41–59 (2012)
19. CIMdata, Product Lifecycle Management – Empowering the Future of Business. CIMdata Inc., USA (2003)
20. Sharma, A.: Collaborative product innovation: Integrating elements of CPI via PLM framework. Comput. Aided Des. 37(13), 1425–1434 (2005)
21. Terzi, S., Bouras, A., Dutta, D., Garetti, M., Kiritsis, D.: Product lifecycle management – from its history to its new role'. Int. J. of Product Lifecycle Manag. 4(4), 360–389 (2010)
22. Rachuri, S., Fenves, S.J., Sriram, R.D., Wang, F.: A product information modeling framework for product lifecycle management. Comput. Aided Des. 37(13), 1399–1411 (2005)
23. Product Development Metrics,
    http://www.npd-solutions.com/metrics.html
24. Alemanni, M., Alessia, G., Tornincasa, S., Vezzetti, E.: Key performance indicators for PLM benefits evaluation: The Alcatel Alenia Space case study. Comput. in Ind. 59(8), 833–841 (2008)
25. Kenny, E., Meneses, D.: Common Framework for Extracting Information and Metrics from Multiple Change Trackers, EGI Community Forum 2012/EMI Second Technical Conference (2012)
26. Hahn, A., Austing, S.G., Strickmann, J.: Metrics – The business intelligence side of PLM. In: Int. Conf. on Product Lifecycle Management, PLM 2007, pp. 11–20 (2007)
27. Myllärniemi, J., Jussi Okkonen, H.K.: Utilizing Business Intelligence Framework for Leveraging Product Lifecycle Management. In: 9th Int. Conf. on Elect. Business (2009)
28. Kärkkäinen, H., Myllärniemi, J., Okkonen, J., Silventoinen, A.: Assessing Maturity Requirements for Implementing and using Product Lifecycle Management. In: 9th Int. Conf. on Elect. Business (2009)
29. Koch, M., Baars, H., Lasi, H., Kemper, H.-G.: Manufacturing Execution Systems and Business Intelligence for Production Environments. In: Proc. of the 16th AMCIS (2010)
30. Liu, S., Duffy, A.H.B., Whitfield, R.I., Boyle, I.M.: Integration of decision support systems to improve decision support performance. Knowledge and Information Systems 22, 261–286 (2009)
31. Do, N.: Application of OLAP to a PDM database for interactive performance evaluation of in-progress product development. Comput. in Ind., 1–10 (2014)
32. Lasi, H.: Industrial Intelligence - A Business Intelligence-based Approach to Enhance Manufacturing Engineering in Industrial Companies. Procedia CIRP 12, 384–389 (2013)
33. Kickstein, J., Drewinski, R.: Systematic indicator management as a component of a PLM environment Controlled product and process. Product Data Journal, 28–31 (2012)
34. Bricogne, M., Belkadi, F., Bosch-Mauchand, M., Eynard, B.: Knowledge based Product and Process Engineering enabling Design and Manufacturing Integration. In: Vallespir, B., Alix, T. (eds.) APMS 2009. IFIP AICT, vol. 338, pp. 473–480. Springer, Heidelberg (2010)

Logistical Causes of Food Waste: A Case Study of a Norwegian Distribution Chain of Chilled Food Products

Lukas Chabada[1], Cecilie Maria Damgaard[2], Heidi Carin Dreyer[1],
Hans-Henrik Hvolby[2,1], and Iskra Dukovska-Popovska[2]

[1] Norwegian University of Science and Technology,
Department of Production and Quality Engineering, Trondheim, Norway
{lukas.chabada,heidi.c.dreyer}@ntnu.no
[2] Aalborg University, Centre for Logistics,
Department of Mechanical and Manufacturing Engineering, Aalborg, Denmark
{cecilie,hhh}@celog.dk, iskra@m-tech.aau.dk

Abstract. This study discusses logistical planning and handling activities contributing to food waste in the food distribution chain of chilled products with fixed shelf life and with an age dependent deterioration rate. The study has exploratory character and all the findings are based on the case study investigation from six Norwegian companies. The causes of food waste as identified in the case companies are grouped into four areas, namely planning decisions, data utilisation, execution of plan, and damaged products. Quantitative data indicates that for chilled products with fixed shelf life, logistical planning seems to have higher impact on financial losses from food waste than physical handling.

Keywords: logistics, causes, food waste, distribution chain, chilled products.

1 Introduction

Managing the physical flow of chilled products with short shelf life and sensitiveness to physical handling is challenging for the actors in the food distribution chain (FDC). The FDC includes the wholesalers, stores and logistical and transport provides which takes part in the delivering of food to end customers. The main priorities are to make sure of short lead times and sufficient conditions during the physical distribution. In the food distribution chain products are being wasted stages (Beretta et al., 2012; Eriksson et al., 2012). A study by Hanssen et al. (2013) revealed food waste of around 5-8% for chilled products at the retail stage in Norway. Such waste has economic, environmental and social impacts (Mena et al., 2011). Therefore, managers have an intention to reduce food waste. However, methods and concepts systematically approaching food waste reduction are scarce (Garrone et al., 2014). This might be because food waste related costs have been undervalued or hidden (Mena et al., 2011).

Identifying the causes of food waste is the first step towards food waste reduction. Studies by Mena et al. (2011), Beretta et al. (2012) or Muller (2013) have indicated several causes of food waste. For example, as food companies strive for a high service

B. Grabot et al. (Eds.): APMS 2014, Part I, IFIP AICT 438, pp. 273–280, 2014.
© IFIP International Federation for Information Processing 2014

level under varying demand, they often maintain too high inventories and safety stock levels, which subsequently lead to food waste. For food products, due to its perishable nature and restricted shelf life, it is significantly important that supply and demand is aligned and that the planning and control mechanisms are designed according the characteristics of the product, market and process involved. Until now, research on food waste has mainly focused on quantifying volumes, where in the food chain waste is created and what product category which most frequently is being created. The planning and control of the FDC and the effects on food waste is still area which needs to be explored in order to understand how food waste could be reduced.

The aim of this study is to explore logistical causes of food waste in the FDC of two types of chilled products; products with fixed shelf life and products with age dependent deterioration rates. The reasons for differentiating the products are the different planning and handling practices used for the above mentioned types, as similarly used by Bakker et al. (2012). The scope of this study is on food distribution chains in Norway, whose geography is characterized by long transportation distances, scattered population centers, and challenging climatic conditions which increase lead time and lead time variability (Romsdal et al., 2011). Since the phenomenon under study is relatively new, a case study research has been selected (Yin, 2009).

Current research identifying causes of food waste is described in the section 2 followed by section describing methods of data collection and analysis. After that case description, findings and discussion on identified challenges in logistical planning and physical handling captured from interviews in case companies are presented. In the last chapter, several concluding comments are made and future work is proposed.

2   Connecting Logistics and Food Waste

The main reasons for food being wasted is insufficient quality and expired date (Mena et al., 2011). Setting this in relation to logistics, it can refer to time and quality which are among the main performance indicators of logistics (Shapiro et al., 1985). According to APICS (2013) logistics system consists of planning and coordination of the physical movement aspects of a firm's operations such that a flow of raw materials, parts, and finished goods is achieved in a manner that minimizes total costs for the levels of service desired. Model of food waste have been recently presented by Garrone et al. (2014) where they considered different management practices handling surplus food to define food waste from environmental, zootechnical and social perspectives. Inspired by their study and food waste definitions used by Beretta et al. (2012) or Gustavsson et al. (2011) our understanding of food waste in this study is: *finished food products that are manufactured, wholesaled and retailed but not sold to the intended customer or which are sold but to a price lower than the intended price due to insufficient quality or short remaining shelf life.* For example discounts due to short remaining shelf life are considered as waste. The intended customer for the wholesaler is the store and for the store the intended customer is the paying consumer.

For in-depth analysis of food waste and its logistical causes a need for locating food waste in the processes of the FDC has been recognized. Eriksson et al. (2012)

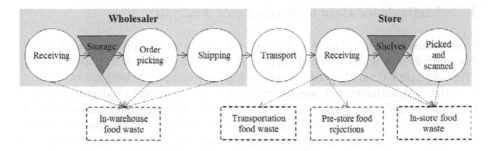

Fig. 1. Categories of food waste in the food distribution chain

defined two main types of food waste in the stores on the process level, namely in-store and pre-store food waste. This study extends on their work and adds transportation and in-warehouse food waste to the analysis (see Fig. 1).

In-warehouse food waste includes all food products wasted during the processes in the warehouse of the wholesaler. Transportation food waste includes the food waste created during transportation between wholesaler and stores. Pre-store food rejections include food products rejected by the store within 24 hours after delivery. After this period it is considered as in-store food waste. This waste belongs to the supplier in accounting terms, but usually becomes physical waste at the store (Eriksson et al., 2012). Finally, in-store food waste includes all products wasted inside the store.

The number of studies identifying the causes of food waste at different stages of the food supply chain in different countries has increased during the last couple of years. Mena, Adenso-Diaz, and Yurt (2011) have looked at the causes of food waste in the supplier-retailer interface at British and Spanish companies. They categorized the causes into mega-trends, natural constraints and management root causes where only the latter can be fully under the control of the managers, and includes issues such as inaccurate planning and forecasting, poor information sharing, poor ordering, poor handling or poor promotions management. Similarly, Muller (2013) presented a root cause analysis of food waste in Norwegian food supply chains. In that study, overproduction and over-ordering, large distribution packages, high inventory levels, inappropriate stock rotation or inadequate handling have been among the mentioned logistical causes of food waste. Finally, Beretta et al. (2013) presented causes of food waste considering the whole food supply chain in Switzerland, and categorized the causes into avoidable, possibly avoidable and unavoidable considering. They mention overproduction or high stock levels among the avoidable causes.

All of the above mentioned studies indicate that food waste could be reduced by better planning and handling of logistical activities. Since the current studies present mainly qualitative data of different causes on quite an aggregated level one can only assume, based on the frequency of evidence, that planning has a greater impact on food waste than physical handling. Moreover, the studies indicate that physical handling, decisions made by planners, and data used during the planning process could have an impact on food waste. This study investigates for the evidence of food waste causes in the case companies that can support these hypotheses.

3   Methods for Data Collection and Analysis

Investigation of logistical causes of food waste is still an unexplored area, therefore, this study undertook the case study approach outlined by Yin (2009). Case companies have been selected based on their relatively high impact in the Norwegian market.

Different quantitative and qualitative data has been collected to identify causes of food waste in the case companies. Quantitative data showing the redistribution of the main causes has been collected for in-warehouse food waste and pre-store food rejections since the wholesaler is the only company that registers them. The in-house ERP system and the internal documents of the wholesaler have been used for this purpose. Since the data is registered differently in pieces, boxes and kilos depending on the product type, financial losses have been used to compare the relative values of registered causes. Quantitative data aggregates amounts from a 12 –month period and consider food waste as defined by the case companies and not as defined in the section 2. The impact of different causes has been analyzed in relation to the total food waste.

Second, qualitative data supplements the quantitative findings by discussing underlying causes of the main causes identified in the case companies. The data has been collected via semi-structured interviews, mapping and personal observations of planning and handling processes. Causes of transportation and in-store food waste have been collected via interviews and observations at two transporters and three stores. In order to highlight the main problematic areas the identified underlying causes of food waste were grouped using the fishbone diagram (Stevenson et al., 2007).

The scope of the investigation is on chilled products, as these have been identified as the main wasted category (Gustavsson et al., 2011). This study includes product groups like dairy, meat, fish, fruit and vegetable products (F&V) and the main focus is on the planning and handling causes of food waste in the FDC. During the study it has been recognized that planning and handling practices of products with fixed shelf life varies from products with age dependent deterioration rate, therefore this study differentiates between these two categories when discussing causes of food waste. *Products with fixed shelf life* are wasted when the due date is exceeded or close to be exceeded. Besides F&V, majority of chilled products have fixed shelf life. *Products with age dependent deterioration rate* are wasted when the quality is perceived to be insufficient. The majority of F&V have an age dependent deterioration rate.

4   Case Description and Findings

The wholesaler is a major wholesaler in Norway distributing around 5500 products. Three stores are direct customers of the wholesaler consisting of one store with low and two stores with high turnover. Together with two transportation companies delivering food products between the wholesaler and the stores the companies are part of the same supply chain. First analysis of data indicates 90% of food waste in this FDC comes from wasted chilled products. Two main causes of food waste are registered at the wholesaler, namely insufficient quality and short remaining shelf life. Quantitative data on causes of food waste revealed that in two thirds of cases of in-warehouse food waste of products with fixed shelf life, short remaining shelf life is the main cause leaving one third for damaged products. In more than 90% of cases the main cause of in-warehouse food waste for products with age dependent deterioration rate is insufficient quality (this information comes from discussions with planners and operators in the warehouse). Similar findings can be observed for pre-store food rejections where 96% of products with age dependent deterioration rate have been rejected by stores due to insufficient quality while 64% of products with fixed shelf life have been rejected due to short remaining shelf life (see Fig. 2).

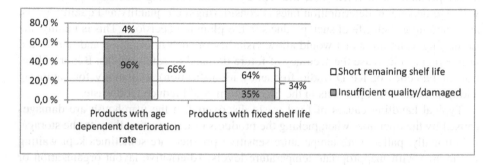

Fig. 2. Registered causes of pre-store food rejections

Fig. 2 also illustrates that around two thirds of food waste come from products with age dependent deterioration rate. This might be due to several reasons like different biological deterioration rate of products, higher margin or different planning and handling procedures of products with age dependent deterioration rate and fixed shelf life. Analysis of causes of food waste registered at the wholesaler revealed that "insufficient quality" represents mainly handling failures and "short remaining shelf life" represents mainly planning failure when considering food products with fixed shelf life. Based on this, logistical planning seems to have higher impact on financial losses than physical handling of products with fixed shelf life.

5 Causes of Insufficient Quality and Short Remaining Shelf Life

Company visits and interviews with planners and operators confirmed the existence of food waste categories defined in Fig. 1. Moreover, several underlying causes of insufficient quality and short remaining shelf life have been revealed. These are discussed in this chapter per food waste category, supported by previous studies when relevant.

In-warehouse food waste of products with fixed shelf life is mainly created due to short remaining shelf life. As the potential underlying causes have been pointed high inventory and safety stock levels, and quite aggregated planning and coordination of promotions with stores. For promotions the stock levels are set high in order to prevent stock outs and because demand is unpredictable, thus increasing food waste. Food waste is also increased due to product cannibalization (Taylor et al., 2009).

Ordered amounts are sometimes increased also due to low ordering frequency and big batch sizes, when the wholesaler orders more than is needed to fit the batch size. Increased uncertainty due to promotion planning or ordering frequency has been identified also by Mena et al. (2011). More frequent deliveries and information exchange could thus reduce food waste (Kaipia et al., 2013; van der Vorst et al., 1998).

Products with age dependent deterioration rates have insufficient quality as the main registered cause of food waste. This is expected as most of the products do not have due dates to be judged by. Many of the underlying causes are, however, similar as for products with fixed shelf life. An additional planning challenge for products with age dependent deterioration rates is considering their quantity and quality levels, and remaining shelf life of such products in the planning decisions. This is mainly due to missing technology that would allow visibility of such information and that would utilize them to increase the accuracy of future demand or safety stocks. Better utilization of barcodes or RFID (radio frequency identification) technology for capturing additional data about products in the ERP system could reduce food waste.

Typical handling causes of food waste discovered in the warehouse are damages caused by the operators when picking the products or transporting them to the storage. Additionally, pallets with temperature sensitive products are sometimes kept waiting in the area with inappropriate temperature levels. Alternative layout organization or training of operators could improve the physical handling of such products.

Transportation food waste created for both products with fixed shelf life and age dependent deterioration rates is mainly due to inappropriate handling during the loading and unloading process or during the transportation. Among the main challenges is the organization of pallets inside the trucks with frozen and chilled temperature zones, mostly organized based on the order of the stores. Temperature sensitive products placed against the isolated partition panel between two temperature zones, or against an outer wall whilst outside temperatures are very low might be exposed to either too low or high temperatures, thus reducing quality level. This is an even bigger challenge for deliveries to distant stores with longer delivery times. Including information about product sensitivity in route planning could identify optimal trade-offs between space allocation and potential level of food waste created in different scenarios.

Pre-store rejections occur mainly due to insufficient quality (products with age dependent deterioration rate) or short remaining shelf life (products with fixed shelf life). The underlying causes lie at the wholesaler warehouse. For example, time and quality decrease for products that are picked at the stock of the wholesaler and kept in the temporary waiting area before they are dispatched to stores. The temperature in the temporary area is either higher or lower than is required by the products and the time spent in this area sometimes exceeds two days. This information is, however, not considered when planning the picking orders and deliveries to stores. Pre-store rejections could be thus reduced by considering the shelf life, waiting time and temperature information during the planning and control of deliveries in the warehouse. This would consequently lead also to saving additional transportation and disposal costs.

In-store food waste of products with fixed shelf life and products with age dependent deterioration rate is created due to similar reasons. From a planning perspective it is lack of data captured and utilized in replenishment process that causes the most problems. Information about current volumes or expiration dates of products in shelves are checked only manually without using suitable information technology that captures and utilizes the mentioned data. Forecasts and safety stock levels are therefore calculated only based on an experience of planners who sometimes consider historical sales. High order and delivery frequency allow high turnover stores to plan without very precise forecast. For the smaller stores higher ordering frequency and smaller batch sizes could reduce food. Capturing and utilizing data about the current product volumes and remaining shelf life of the products in the shelves could increase visibility of the products, and reduce uncertainty and food waste. Other causes of in-store food waste have been indicated mechanical damages caused by customers or operators. Utilizing equipment ensuring the right temperature and display of the products in the shopping area could lead to reduction of mechanical damages in the stores.

The above discussed causes are summarized and grouped in the fishbone diagram under four areas, namely planning decisions, data utilization, execution of plan and damaged products, in order to highlight the main problematic areas (see Fig. 3).

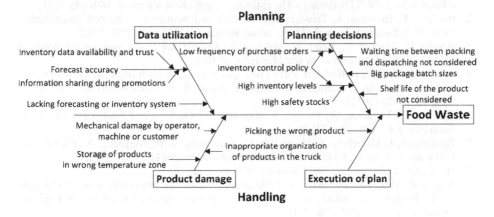

Fig. 3. Planning and handling causes of food waste

6   Conclusion

The study presents the main and underlying causes of food waste for products with fixed shelf life and age dependent deterioration rates as identified in the case companies. The underlying causes of food waste are structured into four areas, namely planning decisions, data utilization, execution of plans, and damaged products. More research is necessary to validate the findings of this study. Some of the identified causes might not be that relevant for other countries. For example, companies in other countries might be able to cope with low delivery frequency or big batch sizes better than companies in Norway, as they do not face the challenges such as long delivery lead times or long distances traveled due to fjords, ferries or temporary closed roads during the winter period. Future research could focus on deeper analysis and quantification of identified causes in order to understand the relative impact of individual causes on food waste and so to better identify improvement options. The main focus could be on quantifiable causes of food waste as forecasting accuracy, inventory and safety stock levels and promotions which have been highlighted also by other researchers. Furthermore, trade-offs between food waste and availability should be investigated and discussed. The study contributes to the literature by in-depth analysis of quantitative and qualitative data on planning and handling causes of food waste in the FDC which is still rare in the current research. Practitioners in a similar industry may use the findings as a baseline for identification of food waste causes in their companies.

Acknowledgement. Authors of the paper would like to express a deep gratitude to the case companies involved, to the researchers Peter Falster and Chris Martin, and to research organization NordForsk which funds the LogiNord project.

References

1. APICS (ed.): APICS Dictionary - The essential supply chain reference, 14th edn. (2013)
2. Bakker, M., Riezebos, J., Teunter, R.H.: Review of inventory systems with deterioration since 2001. European Journal of Operational Research 221(2), 275–284 (2012)
3. Beretta, C., Stoessel, F., Baier, U., Hellweg, S.: Quantifying food losses and the potential for reduction in Switzerland. Waste Management (2012)
4. Eriksson, M., Strid, I., Hansson, P.A.: Food losses in six Swedish retail stores: Wastage of fruit and vegetables in relation to quantities delivered. Resources, Conservation and Recycling 68, 14–20 (2012)
5. Garrone, P., Melacini, M., Perego, A.: Opening the black box of food waste reduction. Food Policy 46, 129–139 (2014)
6. Gustavsson, J., Cederberg, C., Sonesson, U., van Otterdijk, R., Meybeck, A.: Global food losses and food waste. FAO of the United Nations, Rom (2011)
7. Hanssen, O.J., Møller, H.: Food Wastage in Norway (2013)
8. Kaipia, R., Dukovska-Popovska, I., Loikkanen, L.: Creating sustainable fresh food supply chains through waste reduction. International Journal of Physical Distribution & Logistics Management 43(3), 262–276 (2013)
9. Mena, C., Adenso-Diaz, B., Yurt, O.: The causes of food waste in the supplier–retailer interface: Evidences from the UK and Spain. Resources, Conservation and Recycling 55(6), 648–658 (2011)
10. Muller, S.: Food waste in Norway: Root causes analysis at the producer - retailer stage (Master Thesis). BI Norwegian Business School, Oslo (2013)
11. Romsdal, A., Thomassen, M., Dreyer, H.C., Strandhagen, J.O.: Fresh food supply chains; characteristics and supply chain requirements. Paper Presented at the 18th International Annual EurOMA Conference, Cambridge, UK (2011)
12. Shapiro, R.D., Heskett, J.L.: Logistics Strategy: cases and concepts. West Publishing Company St., Paul (1985)
13. Stevenson, W.J., Hojati, M.: Operations management, vol. 8. McGraw-Hill/Irwin, Boston (2007)
14. Taylor, D.H., Fearne, A.: Demand management in fresh food value chains: A framework for analysis and improvement. Supply Chain Management 14(5), 379–392 (2009)
15. van der Vorst, J.G.A.J., Beulens, A.J.M., de Wit, W., van Beek, P.: Supply Chain Management in Food Chains: Improving Performance by Reducing Uncertainty. International Transactions in Operational Research 5(6), 487–499 (1998)
16. Yin, R.K.: Case study research: Design and methods, vol. 5. Sage Publications, Inc. (2009)

Requirements Engineering for Cyber-Physical Systems

Challenges in the Context of "Industrie 4.0"

Stefan Wiesner[1], Christian Gorldt[1], Mathias Soeken[2,3],
Klaus-Dieter Thoben[1,4], and Rolf Drechsler[2,3]

[1] BIBA – Bremer Institut für Produktion und Logistik GmbH,
Hochschulring 20, 28359 Bremen, Germany
[2] Deutsches Forschungsinstitut für Künstliche Intelligenz, Cyber-Physical Systems,
Bibliothekstr. 1, 28359 Bremen, Germany
[3] Faculty of Mathematics / Computer Science, University of Bremen, Germany
[4] Faculty of Production Engineering, University of Bremen, Germany
{wie,gor,tho}@biba.uni-bremen.de,
{mathias.soeken,rolf.drechsler}@dfki.de

Abstract. According to a widely shared view, manufacturing is currently undergoing its fourth industrial revolution, termed "Industrie 4.0" in the high-tech strategy of the German government. Smart Factories with vertically and horizontally integrated production systems are enabled through the realization of machines, storage systems and utilities as Cyber-Physical Systems (CPS), which are able to share information, act, and control each other autonomously. The development of CPS requires the collaboration of different disciplines, like mechanical engineering, electrical engineering and computer science. This creates new challenges for Requirements Engineering (RE), which needs to establish a common perception of the targeted CPS for the involved stakeholders. This paper will elaborate the specific challenges in RE for CPS based on a literature review. Natural Language Processing (NLP) is used as an approach to automatically translate shared informal requirements specifications to formal domain specific models for the involved disciplines, to develop a comprehensive RE methodology for CPS.

Keywords: Requirements Engineering, Industrie 4.0, Cyber-Physical Systems, Natural Language Processing, MSEE Integrated Project.

1 Introduction

Three industrial revolutions have led to paradigm changes in the domain of manufacturing so far: mechanization through water and steam power, mass production in assembly lines, and automation using information technology. However, for the last years researchers and policy makers have increasingly advocated an upcoming fourth industrial revolution. For example, the German government promotes the computerization of manufacturing industries in their "Industrie 4.0" program [1], while in the

B. Grabot et al. (Eds.): APMS 2014, Part I, IFIP AICT 438, pp. 281–288, 2014.

United States the Smart Manufacturing Leadership Coalition (SMLC) facilitates the broad adoption of manufacturing intelligence [2]. In order to follow these trends, elements like machines, storage systems and utilities need to be able to share information, as well as act and control each other autonomously. Such systems are called Cyber-Physical Systems (CPS) [3]. CPS emerge through the complex networking and integration of embedded systems, application systems, and infrastructure, enabled by human machine interaction. In contrast to conventional systems used for production or logistics, they can be seen as *systems of systems*, which require the collaboration of different disciplines such as mechanical engineering, electrical engineering, and computer science for their realization [4].

For the development of today's conventional production systems, methods and tools from the field of systems engineering are applied, which deal with the development of complex solutions, consisting of a large number of components whose interactions shall produce a desired result [5]. Systems have to be both appropriate and cost effective [6], which makes understanding the requirements of the customer and other affected stakeholders a prerequisite for successful systems engineering [7]. They are needed for planning the development process, assessing the impact of changes and testing the acceptance of the outcomes [8]. Inadequate Requirements Engineering (RE) is one of the main sources for the failure of development projects and culminates in exceeding budgets, missing functionalities or even the abortion of the project [9]. Consequently, in concordance with the principles of concurrent engineering, RE continues along the development process of a system and secures a consistent and traceable elicitation and management of requirements. There is an ongoing interaction be- tween RE and the development phases in systems engineering [8].

Therefore, adequate RE is also the key to success or failure of every CPS development project. However, CPS differ from conventional production systems in various aspects, leading to new challenges for the RE process. CPS are open systems, which have to be aligned with dynamic user needs in a global context. Furthermore, requirements towards CPS underlie evolutionary changes. The scope and emphasis of the relevant requirements change with respect to the final application and environment of the CPS [4]. Finally, CPS are based on integrating hardware, software, and service components, covering the whole life cycle, from ideation to decommission. The required competencies for CPS development and their support in all life cycle phases have to be included through collaboration with partners from the different disciplines [10].

The objective of this paper is to elaborate the specific challenges of RE for CPS in detail and give first recommendations for their solution. Therefore, in Section 2 the state-of-the-art in CPS and systems requirements engineering is described. Based on this theoretical background, the detailed challenges are extracted from a literature review in Section 3. Natural Language Processing (NLP) is used as an approach to overcome the language barriers between the involved disciplines in Section 4. The conclusion in Section 5 gives an outlook, how a comprehensive RE methodology for CPS could be developed.

2   Theoretical Background

In this chapter, the main characteristics of Cyber-Physical Systems are explained, followed by the state-of-the-art in Requirements Engineering for systems, in order to be able to identify the challenges of RE for CPS.

2.1   Cyber-Physical Systems

Cyber-Physical Systems (CPS) can be seen as systems of integrated computational elements interacting with physical entities. In contrast to embedded systems where the focus is more on the computational elements, CPS emphasize the link between the computational and physical elements. In this sense, CPS represent a network of inter- acting elements with physical input and output instead of as standalone devices. CPS are therefore complex systems and can be characterized by five distinct characteristics [4].

1. **Merge of physical and virtual world:** CPS involve a multitude of parallel and in-terlinked sensors, computers, and machines, which collect and interpret data to decide on this basis and control real world physical processes. Thus, systems engineering needs to integrate industrial process and control systems with information technology [11].
2. **System of systems with dynamic system borders:** Depending on application and task, different CPS are arranged into a system of systems for a limited time. Con-sequently, CPS have to be able to actively configure services and networks with other systems or parts of systems, which may be unknown in the beginning, and provide new and composite components and services in a controlled way [12].
3. **Context-aware, partially or fully self-governed, with active control in real-time:** Relating to their specific task, CPS use the relevant services to capture their application environment and situation to coordinate a useful and valuable system behavior for all involved stakeholders. This requires continuous monitoring and as-sessment of environmental and application data [13].
4. **Collaborative systems with distributed and alternating control:** The CPS has to be able to perceive and assess the situation, the activities to be executed and the lo-cal and global goals of the actors. Decisions are based on this information and lead to a cooperative learning process [14].
5. **Comprehensive human-system interaction:** CPS have to incorporate human be-havior also on a physical level, which requires the use of sensor and actuator tech-nology, e.g. in the form of artificial limps. This leads to an extension of the human capacity to act and human cognition, supported by multimodal control interfaces, recognition, and interpretation of human behavior and interactive decision making between the system and single persons or groups [15].

2.2   Systems Requirements Engineering

Requirements define the needs of organizations, groups, or people along with their surroundings and describe what a solution must offer in order to satisfy those needs.

Their formulation, documentation, and maintenance are the main objectives of Requirements Engineering. It describes *"a process, in which the needs of one or many stakeholders and their environment are determined to find the solution for a specific problem"* [16]. Systems engineering involves RE as an independent activity not restricted to a specific development phase or project. There is an ongoing interaction between RE and the development phases in systems engineering, as can be shown with the V-Model [17] in Fig. 1:

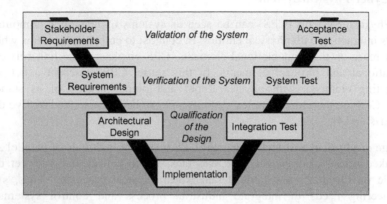

Fig. 1. Requirements engineering in the V-Model, according to [8]

Fig. 1 shows the activities performed during the individual phases of system devel- opment in separate layers. Requirements are important for all layers in systems engi- neering. It is necessary to validate requirements from lower layers against require- ments from upper layers and the stakeholder needs in order to check that the require- ments represent the original goals for the system development. Furthermore, the de- sign and implementation of the system has to be verified to check that it fulfills the requirements. In order to support the different tasks, the specification of requirements has to follow several contradictory objectives. To minimize the time to write require- ments and make them understandable for all of the involved stakeholders, often an informal approach is used without any constraints on how requirements are specified e.g. in natural language. However, to minimize the time needed to validate require- ments and verify the system design, a formal specification is required. Abstract se- mantics and syntax enable automatic checks like formal verification. Often a trade-off between formal and informal specification is implemented, e.g. by using controlled languages [18] or boilerplate techniques [19].

3   Challenges of Requirements Engineering for Cyber-Physical Systems

In their research agenda for CPS, Geisberger and Broy [4] identify engineering challenges for Cyber-Physical Systems. They emphasize the central role of

Requirements Engineering for CPS development, integration, maintenance and evolution. Involving users and other stakeholders from different domains actively into CPS development from the beginning and adaption of CPS to needs, habits and competences of the users, would require a more informal approach for requirements specification. However, the specification of formal requirements models is requested for detailing of requirements and mapping them to system elements, integration of mechanical engineering models with digital models from software and systems engineering for the collabora- tive description of requirements, as well as their implementation, validation, evolution and communication between stakeholders from different disciplines.

Penzenstadler and Eckhardt [20] agree that ensuring communication and consistency of requirements for CPS is a challenge due to the variety of stakeholders involved. Furthermore, viewing CPS as a system of systems, the independence of the constituent systems and their evolutionary nature leads to exceptionally distributed RE activities for a multitude of stakeholders with isolated RE approaches. The authors propose a RE content model for requirements elicitation and documentation at different levels as a solution. However this requires the adoption of a formal model by all stakeholders involved. Ncube [21] focuses on the systems of systems aspect. RE needs concepts and techniques to specify key interoperation influencing requirements. Furthermore, the complexity of systems of systems leaves requirements fragmented among many disciplines and sometimes conflicting, unstable, unknowable or not fully defined. Finally, the properties of systems of systems emerge from the cumulative interactions of the single systems. Therefore, RE methods and tools have to be able to verify emergent effects against requirements with predictable results.

The analyzed literature shows that Requirements Engineering for CPS creates specific challenges, especially for requirements specification and verification. On the one hand, a way has to be found to involve the system user into the development process and dynamically exchange requirements between a multitude of stakeholders from different disciplines. This demands for a more informal, generic requirements specification. On the other hand, for the identification of the system elements and emergent effects for the verification of requirements, more formal and domain specific modeling of requirements is needed. A solution could be the application of both, formal and informal requirements specification, connected by a (semi-)automatic translation. Natural Language Processing (NLP) could be used in such an approach.

4   Natural Language Processing

The CESAR project provides an overview of different Requirements Specification Languages (RSL) for systems engineering, according to their degree of formality [22]. In textual form, formality is increased from Guided Natural Language, over boilerplate RSL up to pattern based RSL. Guided Natural Language specifications are achieved by checking free text descriptions with a domain specific dictionary, highlighting ambiguous terms. Boilerplates are pre-formulated requirements, which are parameterized to describe stakeholders, capabilities or attributes, while patterns use a stronger formalism with fixed semantics. In graphical form, SysML is a visual modeling language for system design based on UML, which can cover multiple degrees of formality with its various underlying diagrams.

In the development of large and complex CPS one is highly interested in a high degree of automation. This becomes accessible, although not easy, when formal descriptions are used that are readable by machines. Conversely, formal descriptions are often not accessible for end users and differ heavily between the disciplines involved in CPS development. The most basic format, understood by the end user and all stakeholders is natural language. Therefore, at higher levels of abstractions, e.g. for stakeholder and system requirements, most of the descriptions are given in natural language text. However, they are therefore barely accessible for automation.

Natural language processing techniques can be utilized to overcome this problem and support requirements exchange between the system user and the stakeholders in CPS development. Several algorithms and tools for syntax [23] and semantics analysis [24] have been proposed for this purpose. Due to ambiguities that are contained in natural language one needs to take into account a trade-off between the degree of automation and the restrictions that are assumed on the text. In order to achieve 100% automation, all ambiguities need to be avoided which can e.g. be achieved by controlled languages [18] or boilerplate techniques [19]. This comes to the cost of basically learning a new language, which may not be practical implementable when texts are written by many stakeholders from different disciplines, which prohibits the application of domain specific ontologies or boilerplates.

Alternative approaches employ a dialog system between the designer and the machine in order resolve possible ambiguities [25]. The machine tries to process as much information as possible automatically and whenever no reliable conclusion can be implied the designer is asked for assistance. This approach has e.g. been used to extract formal models in UML or SysML to represent structure from natural language use case scenarios [26]. Also for translating natural language requirements to formal expressions, NLP techniques have been used [27]. Finally, NLP techniques can assist specification engineers when writing texts. Simple techniques such as spell checking and grammar checking are already common practice in state-of-the-art word processing applications. Techniques that go beyond these are the automatic detection of requirement sentences, measuring the clarity of a sentence, or measure the validity of the sentence with respect to specification guidelines.

The application of NLP to Requirements Engineering for CPS could help to solve some of the challenges identified in the previous section. User involvement would be supported, as requirements and validation feedback could be informally specified in natural language and callback in the case of ambiguities. Furthermore, information exchanged between stakeholders of different disciplines, e.g. in requirements workshops, could be semi-automatically transformed into the correct formal models for each discipline involved.

5   Conclusion

The development of CPS creates new specific challenges for Requirements Engineering, in contrast to conventional production systems. Relevant characteristics of CPS that have to be observed are the integration of physical and virtual elements, the constitution of CPS as systems of systems, context awareness, distributed control and human-system interaction. This results, on the one hand in intensified user collaboration and on the other hand in the involvement of many different disciplines during system development. In spite of distributed RE activities, communication and con- sistency of requirements have to be secured. Interoperability of the CPS elements has to be guaranteed by specific requirements. Dynamically changing and emergent behavior must be included in the CPS specification. Natural language could be used as an informal requirements specification for exchange between the system user and stakeholders from various disciplines, but is often unclear and ambiguous. Further- more, it can barely be handled automatically. As an approach to keep natural language as the form to exchange requirements, while still having unambiguous and automatically processible formal specifications, Natural Language Processing is proposed. The application of NLP could establish a dialog system, which supports resolving ambiguities and semi-automatically transform requirements in natural language into formal domain specific models. Further research in this area will be conducted to concretize NLP application in RE for CPS and propose first practical methods and tools.

Acknowledgements. This work has been partly funded by the European Commission through the FoF-ICT Project MSEE: Manufacturing SErvice Ecosystem (No. 284860) and the German Federal Ministry of Education and Research (BMBF) through the project SPECifIC (01IW13001).

References

1. Kagermann, H., Wahlster, W., Helbi, J.: Deutschlands Zukunft als Produktions-standortsichern—Umsetzungsempfehlungenfür das ZukunftsprojektIndustrie 4.0. Ab-schlussberichtdes Arbeitskreises Industrie 4.0 (2013)
2. Smart Manufacturing Leadership Coalition, Implementing 21st Century Smart Manufacturing. In: WorkshopReport, SMLC and USDOE (June 2011)
3. Baheti, R., Gill, H.: Cyber-physicalsystems. In: The Impactof Control Technology, pp. 161–166 (2011)
4. Geisberger, E., Broy, M. (eds.): Agenda CPS: Integrierte Forschungsagenda Cyber-Physical Systems, vol. 1. Springer DE (2012)
5. Sage, A.P., Rouse, W.B.: Handbook of systems engineering and management, 2nd edn. John Wiley & Sons, Hoboken (2009)
6. Kossiakoff, A., Sweet, W.N., Seymour, S., Biemer, S.M.: Systems engineering principles and practice, 2nd edn. John Wiley & Sons, Hoboken (2011)
7. Elgh, F.: Modelling and management of manufacturing requirements in design automation systems. In: Loureiro, G. (ed.) Complex Systems Concurrent Engineering, pp. 321–328. Springer, London (2007)
8. Hull, E., Jackson, K., Dick, J.: Requirements Engineering, 3rd edn. Springer, London (2011)
9. Hauksdóttir, D., Mortensen, N.H., Nielsen, P.E.: Identification of are usable requirements structure for embedded productsina dynamic market environment. Computers in Industry 64(4), 351–362 (2013)

10. Blanchard, B.S.: System engineering management, 4th edn. John Wiley & Sons, Hoboken (2012)
11. Rajkumar, R.R., Lee, I., Sha, L., Stankovic, J.: Cyber physical systems: The next computing revolution. In: Proceedings oft he 47th Design Automation Conference, pp. 731–736. ACM (June 2010)
12. Colombo, A.W., Bangemann, T., Karnouskos, S.: A systemof systems view on collaborative industrial automation. In: 2013 IEEE International Conference on IndustrialTechnology (ICIT), pp. 1968–1975. IEEE (February 2013)
13. Furno, A., Zimeo, E.: Context-Aware Security Solutions for Cyber Physical Systems. In: Vinh, P.C., Hung, N.M., Tung, N.T., Suzuki, J. (eds.) ICCASA 2012. LNICST, vol. 109, pp. 18–29. Springer, Heidelberg (2013)
14. Zhou, K., Ye, C., Wan, J., Liu, B., Liang, L.: Advanced Control Technologies in Cyber-Physical System. In: 2013 5th International Conference on Intelligent Human Machine Systemsand Cybernetics (IHMSC), vol. 2, pp. 569–573. IEEE (August 2013)
15. Schirner, G., Erdogmus, D., Chowdhury, K., Padir, T.: The future of humanin- the-loop cyber-physical systems. Computer 46(1), 36–45 (2013)
16. Nuseibeh, B., Easterbrook, S.: Requirements Engineering: A Roadmap. In: Proceedings of the Conference on the Future of Software Engineering, Limerick (2000)
17. Rausch, A., Broy, M.: DasV-Modell XT –Grundlagen, Erfahrungen, Werkzeuge. Dpunkt. Verlag, Heidelberg (2007)
18. Funk, A., Tablan, V., Bontcheva, K., Cunningham, H., Davis, B., Handschuh, S.: CLOnE: Controlled Language for Ontology Editing. In: Aberer, K., et al. (eds.) ASWC 2007. LNCS, vol. 4825, pp. 142–155. Springer, Heidelberg (2007)
19. Farfeleder, S., Moser, T., Krall, A., Stålhane, T., Zojer, H., Panis, C.: DODT: Increasing requirements formalism using domain ontologies for improved embedded systems development. In: 2011IEEE 14th International Symposium on Design and Diagnostics of Electronic Circuits & Systems (DDECS), pp. 271–274. EEE (April 2011)
20. Penzenstadler, B., Eckhardt, J.: Arequirements engineering content modelfor cyber-physical systems. In: 012 IEEE Second Workshopon on Requirements Engineering for Systems, Services and Systems-of-Systems (RES4), pp. 20–29. IEEE (September 2012)
21. Ncube, C.: On the Engineering of Systems of Systems: key challenges for there quirements engineering community. In: 2011 Workshop on Requirements Engineering for Systems, Services and Systems-of-Systems (RESS), pp. 70–73. IEEE (August 2011)
22. Rajan, A., Wahl, T. (eds.): CESAR: Cost-efficient Methods and Processes for Safety-relevant Embedded Systems (No. 978-3709113868). Springer (2013)
23. Jurafsky, D., Martin, J.H.: Speech & Language Processing. Prentice Hall (2008)
24. Miller, G.A.: WordNet: A Lexical Database for English. In: CACM, vol. 38, pp. 39–41 (1995)
25. Drechsler, R., Soeken, M., Wille, R.: Towards Dialog Systems for Assisted Natural Language Processing in the Design of Embedded Systems. In: IEEE Design andTest Symposium (IDT) (2012)
26. Soeken, M., Wille, R., Drechsler, R.: Assisted Behavior Driven Development Using Natural Language Processing. In: Furia, C.A., Nanz, S. (eds.) TOOLS Europe 2012. LNCS, vol. 7304, pp. 269–287. Springer, Heidelberg (2012)
27. Soeken, M., Harris, C.B., Abdessaied, N., Harris, I.G., Drechsler, R.: Automating theTranslation of Natural Language Assertions Using Natural Language ProcessingTechniques. In: Forum on Specification & DesignLanguages (FDL) (2014)

WeKeyInnovation, A Wiki Based on Crowdsourcing to Share Information about Innovation Support

Jérémie Faham[1], Nawel Takouachet[1], and Jérémy Legardeur[1,2]

[1] ESTIA, F-64210 Bidart, France
{j.faham,n.takouachet,j.legardeur}@estia.fr
[2] IMS, UMR 5218, Talence, France

Abstract. One of the challenges to foster innovation is to understand the existing practices and the real needs to help companies when they initiate and develop innovative projects or new ideas. This paper addresses this question by proposing a new interactive and collaborative support based on the crowdsourcing approach. We pro- pose a collaborative wiki platform *WeKeyInnovation* (WKI), which will be used and enriched progressively by companies, consulting and institutional. To identify specific companies' needs, we introduce how this guide has been developed promoting a collaborative environment to share and evaluate good practices, tools, software or theories about creativity and innovation. Furthermore, our WKI solution will allow building a dynamic observatory by collecting empirical and valuable ground data on their real practices and needs. The final purpose is to define most efficient policies and enhance the formulation of a real regional strategic plan toward an economical growth based on innovation.

Keywords: Innovation, Small and Medium Enterprises, Crowdsourcing, Interactive Platform, Open Innovation, Collaboration, Entrepreneurship.

1 Introduction

It is now a well-established fact that creativity and innovation stimulation is a key issue for company's development and competitiveness. This topic has been widely studied either in the social, economic and management sciences or in the engineering fields. Most of the times global analysis are based on questions and surveys that are push to companies in order to have a feedback on their needs and practices, aiming to identify their barriers and levers faced to innovation processes [14].These approaches are often promoted by different stakeholders (researchers, governmental institutions…) and lead to the publication of different documentation [13] that provides global information according to the situation of the country, the size and the type of the company, the field of activity…On the other hand, research-action based on empirical studies within companies also produces qualitative results about the deep understanding of sociotechnical and economical aspects of innovation processes [1]. However, classical methods (enquiries, surveys, soundings, diagnostics…) commonly used in Social and Human Sciences and Engineering Sciences are limited

B. Grabot et al. (Eds.): APMS 2014, Part I, IFIP AICT 438, pp. 289–297, 2014.
© IFIP International Federation for Information Processing 2014

regarding to methodological (lake of reliability, insufficient answers rates…) and operational aspects (waste of time, duplications, lake of interest for the organizations investigated…).

In this paper, we attempt to overcome these limitations by proposing *WeKeyInnovation* (WKI), an open interactive and collaborative support based on the crowdsourcing approach [2]. Indeed, it can be used and enriched progressively by any individual or organization interested in innovation processes.

Our open and collaborative platform is designed according to two main objectives:

- The first is to give an online access to information related to existing methods, tools, software, funding, consulting… that can be used by companies to manage and support their creativity and innovation processes. This information is progressively proposed and updated by all the stakeholders. This raw information is reviewed and classified by advanced users or experts in the field of creativity and innovation management that can be composed of researchers, consulting, associations… It has to offer an intuitive front office providing a free access to qualita- tive information reviewed by experts.
- The second objective is to provide a dynamic observatory to allow some specific statistics and elicitations concerning the practices, the needs, the levers and the barriers for companies faced to innovation challenges. This collected ground data is helpful to define new innovation policies and politics enabling then the implementation of better designed strategic plans toward an economical growth based on innovation.

This paper is structured as follows. In Section 2 we suggest 10 key points we identified throughout the existing literature about creativity and innovation processes within en- terprises. In section 3 we show how our WKI features answer those 10 key points we underlined. In section 4 we present the technical prerequisites that our WKI must inte- grate to satisfy our objectives and insure a successful implementation. In section 5 we discuss the future implications of this work before concluding with some directions for future work.

2   Background Literature Review

We reviewed existing literature regarding levers, confines, difficulties and limits of innovation processes in companies [3,4,5,6,7,8,9,10,11,12,13,14]. We identified and selected ten significant key points that may reduce the existing gap between the real needs and the usual tools or measures commonly used to answer enterprises desires to implement creativity and innovation processes, as following:

1. Consider innovation as a collective and iterative process.
2. Open and crowd innovation driven by the promotion of partnerships and a free access to knowledge to enhance the creation of new skills and solutions which didn't exist until now.

3. Introduce both educational and entrepreneurship values based on a broad creativity mindset to develop "innovation culture" outside and within organizations. This implies a wide demystification and democratization of "innovation perception" by the education of individuals and especially SMEs owners, showing them that innovation is surely not only a technologic high added value process restricted to big enterprises and always requiring wide ID capabilities.

4. Increase interdisciplinary projects and diversified culture within organizations by building real "cross-disciplinary innovative teams".

5. Create the conditions to promote a smart collaboration outside, within and between organizations, aiming to enhance an economic sustainable growth based on the knowledge.

6. Reinforce collaboration with a better networking and circulation of information to stimulate exchanges and links between all innovation stakeholders and elaborate a real "innovative ecosystem".

7. Design efficient strategic innovation policies, based on real enterprise's needs, weaknesses or strengths. This involves relying on a qualitative and qualified raw data collection.

8. Pay attention to "societal innovation" by focusing on advances for the society and highlighting the new collaborative innovation development models to satisfy societal challenges implications.

9. Insure a central role of public authorities and regions in strategic innovation policies definition and implementation to ensure good spillovers on the wider national and thus international economic society.

10. Introduce new tools that catalyze the needs, the skills and centralize the best know-how. This should allow creating an open network and a common language by arranging the contributions of different fields. Those new tools have to support both human resources and technologic advances bringing together new sustainable development paradigm and numeric revolution challenges to design new sustainable development models and growing strategies for SMEs.

Those ten key points lead us to design our *WeKeyInnovation* to reduce the gap existing between company's needs, practices and classical supports traditionally used. The main purpose is to help defining better policies to foster innovation.

3   WeKeyInnovation Features

The purpose is to develop a collaborative platform opening creativity and innovation processes to all individuals and companies with a special focus on SMEs. In this section, in order to illustrate and answer the key points we presented in the previous section, we will introduce our main proposal: the design of an interactive and collaborative opened platform **(1) (2) (4) (10)** designed to support SMEs in their operational daily tasks and enhance the creativity and innovation processes they would like to start, improve or implement. The idea is to develop a way toward a real "innovation culture" based on a broad creativity mindset within the WKI community we created (3) (10).

One of the main key point we assert to answer implementing WKI is to better under- stand the practices of all the organizations by collecting raw data without having to resort to traditional methods. Hence, our solution attempts to help designing efficient and adequate strategic innovation policies starting from real enterprise's needs, customs, weaknesses or strengths automatically collected in real time on our WKI (7) (9). Via this automatic treatment of information raised from the observed interactions, the followed trajectories and inputs provided or filled on the web platform by the WKI users, we expect a better understanding of real enterprises and individuals confines or needs to design then better policies and satisfy societal challenges implications (8) (9) (10). Already in the elaboration stage of the process, the *WeKeyInnovation* is comprehended as an interactive platform dedicated to support enterprises in both their operational needs and innovative processes, based on serious play and crowdsourcing concepts (1) (2) (4), usable online by enterprises, individuals, institutional and consulting organizations via a pioneering web portal (6) (10). We pay a particular attention to SMEs as they constitute the core of the European but also international economic and productive network. Regarding to this requirement, our platform will create a smart supportive environment (5) enabling an efficient networking to stimulate exchanges and links between all innovation participants (6) (10).

4   Technical Prerequisites

As a first stage of *WeKeyInnovation* design, we intend to insure a set of technical features to develop an efficient framework enable to further a qualitative, fast and intuitive enrichment of the platform.

4.1   Scalable and Flexible Arborescent Architecture

To allow a smart collaborative interaction between users and stimulate a progressive auto-enrichment, we design an open architecture enabling to process, rank, comment or rate users contributions. But to insure a successful implementation we first need to integrate a pre-organization of data collected during our "state of the art" process. A first classification has been proposed according to the literature (innovation guides, creativity methods, norms, web sites links, skills reports, solutions, existing software platforms, free open data bases...). On the other hand, contributions proposals are organized in a tree categories structure composed by information about the whole supporting and consulting measures, tools or helps existing to support innovation at large, such as: Methods, Tools, Expertise, Diagnostics, Suggestions, Events, Testimonies, Good practices... The arborescence is flexible enough to be later progressively and collectively enriched or expanded by all the users of the community. Indeed, according to his/her profile, each user can investigate, add, qualify, evaluate or approve contributions. He can also classify or modify contributions categories. The figure (Fig.1) shows the example of the possible reviewer actions on WKI.

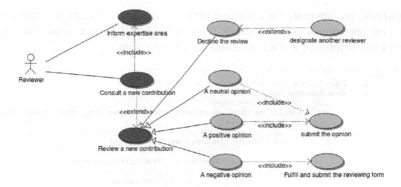

Fig. 1. UML use case diagram of the reviewer role

Those contributions are filled in the WKI by users through predefined templates we already designed to ensure an easy flow of information (Fig. 2).

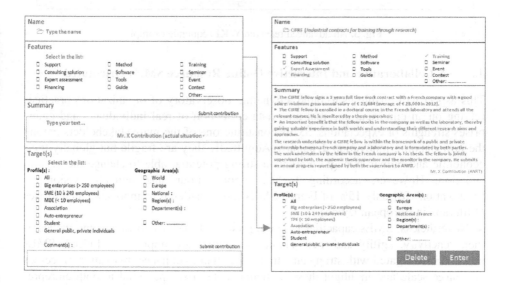

Fig. 2. An example of the WKI template

4.2   An Intuitive Front Office Interface

Another challenge is to provide a fast and efficient use compatible with all kinds of computer supports. WKI must ensure pertinent answers according to the user's operational needs, while leading them to implement progressively innovation processes. This feature brings us to think on a smart design which promotes an intuitive browsing easily understandable "by and for the whole stakeholders", especially for our main specific target: SMEs owners. In addition of classical research functions based on keywords, we integrate an advanced research browser offering a smart intuitive and precise need formulation to satisfy each individual's expectations. The figure 3 illustrates an example of a WKI advanced research sequence.

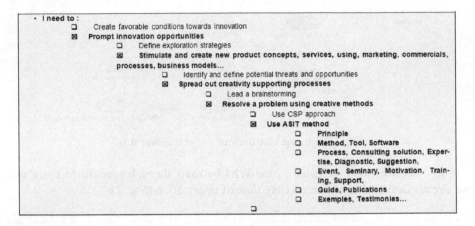

Fig. 3. An advanced research WKI sequence example

4.3   A Collaborative and Interactive Online Resource SMEs-Orientated

This aspect will enable us to build a dynamic observatory of organizations practices relying on an empirical and real-time data collection of real individual's and enterprises strengths or expectations. SMEs constitute one of the main stakeholders among the new ongoing innovation dynamics. Admittedly they are fragile but globally their economic and human strength presents a strong potential able to change the general situation. However, according to the report "Pour une nouvelle vision de l'innovation" [6] only 15% of French SMEs are considered as innovative enterprises (14th rank in European Union).

Nevertheless, SMEs capacities to learn, product, transfer knowledge and values as their reactivity, agility and their adaptive potential are impressive. Indeed, SMEs must be investigated with strong attention if we plan to enhance innovation processes at a large scale and highlight those particular enterprises potential in both entrepreneur and academic worlds. Constituting one of the main targets of WKI, we reviewed a consistent state of art focusing on creativity and innovation processes within SMEs [3,4] [7]. Relying on these findings, we design the WKI contents towards SMEs characteristic obligations to release their strong innovative potential. Our WKI features take into account real SMEs needs and obstacles being as well a smart support to communicate around their strengths and good practices.

4.4   Securing Environment

Our wish for an open and free-access to useful knowledge for the society at whole shouldn't mask the importance we attach to confidentiality and data securing, being both essential requirements for our tool. Indeed, the maximal reduction of the risk is a necessary prerequisite to achieve the creation of a secure environment. This must absolutely be seriously considered, especially when dealing with economic organizations and SMEs to ensure a free flow of information exchanges and the development of innovation processes in a safe climate based on confidence within the new community.

Regarding to this topic, we design so a controlled access for users by making them log in to WKI using their professional e-mail address or their professional social networks account. A beta test of WKI is already planned within a selected community. The objective is to guarantee its proper functioning in operating conditions and select skilled professionals intended to assume the role of reliable "reviewers" when we will launch WKI into its real environment. This reviewers-selection-process is a key issue to implement in order to help the administrators to detect and filter intentional misinformation or misdirection and ensure the quality of all data published on this collaborative platform.

In another hand, being aware that companies consider collected content as a strategic asset, one reference person per organization is designated to be in charge of the validation of the information filled about his organization.

4.5   Integration of a Data-Extraction System to Drag Up Information

We integrate a back-office module to collect qualitative and quantitative data concern- ing contributors' profiles, their web pages research, the evolution of their consultations and the nature of the information they filled on the WKI. In a second time, the data collected will be processed to build a global diagnostic. The purpose is to build statisti- cal outputs to implement most efficient regional policies toward innovation incentives relying on a qualified raw organization's needs, practices and individuals expectations.

4.6   Validation Process of the Information

Each new information created by contributors on WKI passes through a multi-phase validation process which lead to an eventual blending or selection of ideas submitted. In this way, we implement in addition with the reviewers system described above, a voting system for each contribution filled on our WKI to give more details regarding to the success of each contribution. The purpose is to provide another tool to the administrators to help them in their final validation and classification of the contents. In addition, we highlight that a part of this information will be already filtrated by an automatical integrated robot to reduce nuisances and the risk of intrusions.

4.7   Users Motivating Process

To motivate users, we intend to offer an incentivizing system by unlocking "premiums functions" all along their evolution toward new status and through an incremental in- formation filling process of their profiles and affiliated organizations. We offer so a plurality of users profiles starting from the simple "contributor" to most knowledgeable expert ones as "reviewers", having then the possibility to qualify others users contributions in order to facilitate the validation work dedicated to the "administrators". This attempts to enhance progressively the pertinence and the quality of the contributions provided by the users. Indeed, the evolution within the WKI community will be motivated by reaching progressively the access to refined data and much more pertinent and personalized information.

5   Conclusions and Future Work

In this paper we have presented our principles for designing WKI, an open and collab- orative platform dedicated to support innovation and creativity processes. We de- scribed its features and technical prerequisites that might answer the difficulties we identified in the previous related works. The objective is to offer an innovative way of processing raw information to broadcast a new perspective and horizons to consider differently innovation processes in enterprises, especially within SMEs. WKI is already in the developing stage. First, we design it to be used initially in Aquitaine region but we expect to export it in others regions or countries to provide then a benchmarking enabling to produce comparative statistics and analysis for all the stakeholders involved within the community. Secondly, the open and scalable dimension of WKI is destined to implement it as a collaborative platform to reduce the existing gap between the specifics SMEs needs and the actual traditional answers usually given to them. In addition, by developing the information-crossing potential and the contacts it enables between both academic and entrepreneurial worlds, WKI is expected to reduce the lack of collaboration existing, in France maybe more than anywhere else, between those two environments.

Acknowledgements. Authors would like to acknowledge our partner AGEFA PME for its support concerning the Chair on SMEs 3.0 and the TRANSCREATIVA project which has been co-financed by the "Fonds européen de développement régional" (FEDER) in the frame of the Interreg IV B program, "le programme de coopération territoriale de l'espace Sud-ouest européen" (SUDOE).

References

1. Boujut, J.F., Tiger, H.: A socio-technical research method for analyzing and instrumenting the design activity. Journal of Design Research 2(2) (2002)
2. Howe, J.: The Rise of Crowdsourcing. Wired Magazine. Issue 14.06 (2006)
3. Borter, S., Nyffeler, N., Bergeron, L.: Analyse d'une Démarche Transdisciplinaire Favorisant l'Innovation au Sein des PME. In: 10ème Congrès International Francophone en Entrepreneuriat et PME (CIFEPME), Bordeaux (2010)
4. Gallais, M., Bayad, M.: Accompagner Autrement le Dirigeant de PME Vers l'Innovation: Une Exploration du Rapport de Prescription. In: 10ème Congrès Interna-tional Francophone en Entrepreneuriat et PME (CIFEPME), Bordeaux (October 2010)

5. AFNOR: Management de l'Innovation — Guide de Mise en Œuvre d'une Démarche de Management de l'Innovation. Technical report, FD X 50-271 (Décembre 4, 2013)
6. Pascal Morand, P., Manceau., D.: Pour une Nouvelle Vision de l'Innovation. Techni-cal report, ESCP Europe (Avril 2009)
7. Bpifrance: PME 2013, Rapport sur l'Évolution des PME. Technical report, L'Observatoire des PME (2014)
8. Publications Office of the European Union: Horizon 2020 In Brief, The EU Framework Programme for Research and Innovation. Technical report, European Commission (2014)
9. ADE (Aide à la Décision Économique), LL&A (Louis Lengrand Associés).: Étude sur l'Évolution des Diagnostics et des Stratégies Régionales d'Innovation Dans les Régions Françaises Dans le Cadre des PO FEDER 2007-2013. Technical report, Rapport Final (Synthèse) (Juillet 2010)
10. Direction Générale de la Compétitivité, de l'Industrie et des Services (DGCIS): L'Innovation Dans les Entreprises Moteurs, Moyens et Enjeux. Technical report, Minis-tère de l'Économie des Finances et de l'Industrie (Mai 2011)
11. European Commission: Guide to Social Innovation. Technical report, Regional and Urban Policy (February 2013)
12. ARF (Association des Régions de France), Avise (Ingénierie et Services pour Entreprendre Autrement).: L'Innovation Sociale, Un Levier Pour le Développement Des Territoires - Repères et Bonnes Pratiques pour Développer des Politiques Régionales de Soutien à l'Innovation. Technical report, (Juillet 2012)
13. Organisation de Coopération et de Développement Économiques, Office Statistique des Communautés Européennes.: Manuel d'Oslo: Principes Directeurs pour le Recueil et l'Interprétation des Données sur l'Innovation - Troisième Edition, la Mesure des Activités Scientifiques et Technologiques. Technical report, OECD (2005)
14. Eurostat: The Community Innovation Survey (CIS, The Harmonized Survey Question-naire. Technical report, Final Version (July 9, 2010)

Mobile Personalised Support in Industrial Environments: Coupling Learning with Context - Aware Features

Nikos Papathanasiou[1,2], Dimitris Karampatzakis[2],
Dimitris Koulouriotis[1], and Christos Emmanouilidis[2]

[1] Democritus University of Thrace, Greece
jimk@pme.duth.gr
[2] ATHENA Research & Innovation Centre, Greece
{npapatha,dkara,chrisem}@ceti.athena-innovation.gr

Abstract. The human response time to events in a manufacturing environment depends both on the available skills and competencies of technical staff but also on the extent to which actionable and task-relevant content is readily available when and where is needed. Relevance itself is determined by the task situation context, which in turn is influenced by many factors. This paper presents the development of a context-aware mobile support system for personalised assistance in industrial environments. Combining the individual strengths of learning and content management systems with the ubiquity of delivering relevant content to users carrying NFC (Near Field Communication) enabled mobile devices, the system aims at both enhancing personnel competences as well as their work efficiency. The developed solution is customised to serve an industrial maintenance-support application scenario, wherein the relevant context is determined through location and asset identification, as well as through task and user profiling, offering practical on the spot mobile support.

Keywords: NFC, mobile support, e-maintenance, context awareness.

1   Introduction

The continuous increase in the inherent complexity of modern industrial production environments exerts greater pressure on personnel, required to operate in a safe and efficient manner to meet overall production and task-specific goals. This is especially the case for personnel involved in maintenance tasks, where high technical skills and competences are sought. Specific sectors, involving safety critical processes, such as aerospace or nuclear industries, have reached a level of maturity which is not tolerant to human errors or unforeseen events. But while safety concerns can be of paramount importance in such cases, a much wider potential impact on improving technical personnel response time in most typical manufacturing sectors has been less well explored [1]. Maintenance staff is required to possess a wide, multi-disciplinary and constantly up-to-date skill set in order to efficiently perform their everyday work tasks. On the individual worker level, a steadily updated set of competences can improve work opportunities in a global volatile job market. Technology-enhanced

B. Grabot et al. (Eds.): APMS 2014, Part I, IFIP AICT 438, pp. 298–306, 2014.

solutions should support agile production and work roles so as to meet challenges in a fast changing manufacturing environment [2].

The complexity of modern production lines may be overwhelming for both new employees and older generation ones, thus preventing them from unfolding their true capacities. An obvious improvement would be the provision of on-site support for their work activities, providing the right supporting content to the right personnel at the right time. The appropriate alignment of supporting content and services to the real needs of a specific situation would be a key enabler for making a mobile support solution to be of practical use. This paper presents a context-aware mobile support system, which employs NFC identification and performs basic context data acquisition, such as location, time and user information, as well as a Learning Management System (LMS) for content handling and user roles management. The developed solution provides personalised support to industrial maintenance personnel, thus enabling them to improve their task response time, while also supporting their overall job-related skills development.

The paper is structured as follows. Section 2 outlines the need for providing documentation support in industrial environments, highlighting past efforts and challenges. The importance of involving context identification and context-aware adaptation mechanisms is then discussed and the incorporation of Near Field Communication (NFC) is identified as an indirect method for supporting context identification in industrial settings. Section 3 presents an integrated solution that fuses the benefits of Content Management Systems (CMS) and LMS with NFC-enabled context identification mechanisms, in order to provide fast, intuitive and on the spot support to technical teams, thus supporting their work efficiency. Finally, Section 4 presents the main conclusions of the present work and highlights further research and development directions.

2   Contextualised Documentation Support in Industrial Environments

The readily access to technical documentation and practical guidelines is considered critical in order to support maintenance technicians during their job. This information is equally important to be accurate and closely related to the task assigned to technical staff. Employing mobile computers, wireless networks and identification-supporting technologies can facilitate the integration and delivery of task-relevant content on the spot, by applying context adaptation based on different context parameters. A key requirement for this context-driven adaptation is a method to acquire and fuse context information.

The concept of context was introduced in computing to provide an abstraction of the factors that need to be taken into account in delivering content to users, thereby personalising service delivery. An application can be considered as context-aware if it uses context to provide relevant content and services to the user [3]. What is deemed to be relevant depends on several factors, which may be classified in broad categories, such as user, system, environment, service and even social context [4]. In handling context, many issues can be taken into account. A basic context management loop includes acquisition of primary context data, their fusion for context identification or reasoning, and finally the dissemination of the identified context to the respective context-aware applications [5], which are responsible for the contextually-relevant presentation of content and services to the user. Context data acquisition and processing can be supported by a modelling abstraction, a form of context-widget or context engine that persistently collects and fuses context information, in order to disseminate it to any application that has been declared as interested for this context [6]. This continuous data acquisition on a hardware level is usually performed by networked sensors, which collect raw data from the environment and transmit them to the aforementioned widget to extract useful context information. An alternative to this continuous context information acquisition is to trigger this procedure based on user actions. This explicit initiation of context data acquisition has the benefits of lower power consumption and reduced volume of unprocessed context data [7].

Context-aware service delivery presupposes an efficient way of acquiring and understanding context. In the simplest case, context is often linked to localisation and identification, both which can be served by NFC technology. NFC is a wireless communication technology between coupled inductive devices which is regulated by standards such as ISO/IEC 14443 and ISO/IEC 18092. According to these standards, the range of the antenna is short, usually less than 10 cm and the operational frequency is 13.56 MHz. The NFC standardized data rate of 424 kbps is limited compared to other protocols but it is still an efficient means of transferring credentials, short messages or initiating relationships [8]. The format of the NFC exchanged data is the NFC Data Exchange Format (NDEF), which is common to all NFC devices. An NFC message contains one or more records of the following types: simple text, URIs, smart posters or signatures [9]. NFC communicating devices can be active or passive. An active device can act as initiator, whereas a passive device that can emulate a NFC card, using the RF field of an active device to communicate [10]. NFC identification offers a deterministic input modality as opposed to the probabilistic sources such as speech recognition which makes it appropriate for a deterministic and usually time-crucial industrial environment. NFC identification poses little overhead on the power consumption of the mobile device, thus rendering it suitable to be continuously executed. Embedded in low-cost mobile devices, NFC is essentially the evolution of short range RFID technology and has become a de facto standard, facilitating the emergence of new, context-aware applications [11].

Certain industrial sectors with relatively high demands in human technical expertise and relatively complex maintenance procedures were the first which attempted to introduce technology-enhanced support for personnel. In the aerospace sector, the replacement of workcards containing detailed guidelines on how to perform each maintenance task, with computer-based documentation systems was one of the first e-maintenance applications [12]. Part of their initial concerns was to verify the quantitative and qualitative benefits of the new systems. A method to offer digital support material to technical staff operating at the shop floor that has been suggested by many authors is the use of Augmented Reality (AR) to superimpose computer-generated information on top of the real world environment. A major issue with AR is tracking, namely the accurate determination of the user's location, gaze direction, proximity and head pose estimation in reference to the surrounding objects and environment. Two prevalent solutions that have been proposed for this problem are either pre-applied tracking markers, or pre-built CAD models of the machinery positioning. Other methods that can be used for tracking but demand highly specialized hardware are strapped down systems with accelerometers and gyroscopes, ultrasonic pulse acoustic trackers or electromagnetic trackers. AR implementations require complex equipment and hardware intensive procedures, a substantial amount of preparatory work, requiring previous knowledge of the exact machinery placement [13] and/or sophisticated image processing and rendering capabilities.

While AR usage is well-justified in certain cases, when generic supporting solutions with minimal customisation requirements are sought, there is a considerable potential in investing in the development of technician-centric applications that employ mobile devices and exploit the NFC identification technology coupled with content management offered by a customised Learning Management System, in order to provide on-the-spot context-aware learning and support to maintenance technicians. This work outlines the development of a mobile and context-aware supporting solution that instead of traditional workcards, employs e-support entries that are able to combine different interfacing options offered by modern mobile devices, as tablets, to provide an intuitive and interactive experience. The innovative point of the developed solution is the use of a Learning Management System as the base for the development of a new module that takes advantage of the offered user management and content editing capabilities and combines it with NFC identification for basic level context data acquisition, so as to provide context-adaptive mobile learning and task support. In previous research [14], the structure of the LMS based e-support system was described. The present work focuses on the context-awareness capabilities that are realized by processing stored knowledge and information acquired by NFC identification.

3   Building Context-Aware Mobile Support for Asset Management

In order to provide any kind of context-adaptive service it is necessary to receive some input from the environment that when appropriately fused can guide this adaptation. An industrial setting may impose particular limitations in relation to non-industrial environments. For example, GPS is rarely supported inside a building that may be shielded against electrical interference and noise levels may be too high to support voice recognition. Conversely, the developed solution involves specific identification capabilities, either for machine parts or for the involved technicians, combined with an LMS as the base platform for learning and content management (Fig. 1).

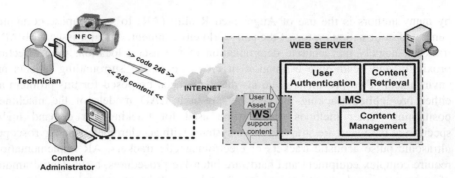

Fig. 1. Schematic Representation of E-Support Functionality

A simple format for the stored information is considered sufficiently flexible and easy to process; therefore the selected NFC record type for this implementation is "Simple Text". The native mobile support application scans this information and parses the data. For the deployment of the mobile application an Android Nexus device was selected mainly due to the open-source tools available and NFC identification capabilities. An example of an NFC tag that is used is "asset:246" where the number 246 refers to the code of an asset. The information within the tag is transferred through web services to a Learning Management System on a Web Server that is mainly responsible for:

- Authenticate users and authorize user requests,
- Locate the right support content to send to the mobile device,
- Provide an environment for editing and handling this content.

The selected LMS is Moodle (www.moodle.org), known for customization and expandability flexibility. Aiming to reduce power consumption on the mobile device, a lightweight NFC identification component with minimal processing requirements is developed, instead of a comprehensive context-widget. Thus, a large part of reasoning and processing is being delegated to the corresponding web server component. The latter is a custom-built Moodle module, responsible for handling content delivery service requests through web services and storing information derived from the mobile device such as new photos, voice comments, user bookmarks and interactions. This material can be used by authorized users to further enrich the system's content. The support information is delivered to the technician through intuitive and user-friendly mobile application interfaces, employing a simple and intuitive interaction model, as shown in Fig. 2.

The communication between the mobile native application and the Moodle module is bi-directional, offering a two-fold benefit. First, the technician's feedback, acquired as annotated photos and voice comments, is stored to the server and can be used to further enrich the e-support content by the creation of new support entries. Second, the technician's profile is constantly updated, so as to have an integrated overview of all the tasks that have been dealt with when relevant support is requested. The coupling of a native mobile e-support application with a Learning Management

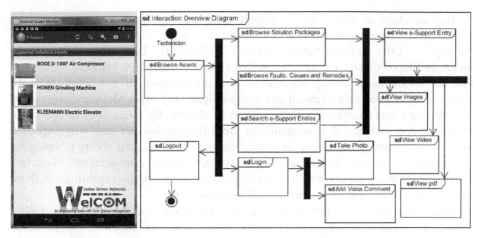

Fig. 2. E-support mobile application and Interaction overview diagram.

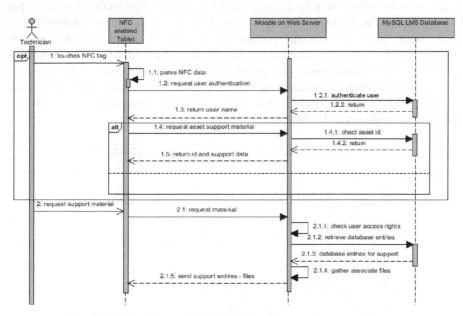

Fig. 3. Mobile e-Support with NFC Identification Sequence Diagram

System for the handling of all the recorded support content has some unique benefits. The LMS is literally a fully functional content management system dedicated to learning, which provides also a full set of user management capabilities. It is easy and intuitive to consider technicians as trainees with different levels of access to the learning content and the e-support entries as e-learning objects. These objects follow a predefined structure, enabling easier support information recording and retrieval. The following sequence diagram shows the basic NFC identification, web service requests and content retrieval actions (Fig. 3).

The structure of the stored e-support data was designed to meet industrial requirements, based both on personal meetings with the industrial project partner, namely a Lifts manufacturing industry (Kleemann Lifts SA, http://www. kleemannlifts.com) and on a subset schema of the MIMOSA standard [15]. The internal requirements set by Moodle for the development of new plug-ins were followed so as to be able to install and communicate with other Moodle components. The structure was completed with the aim to be flexible for future content additions, regarding new technical documentation or input from authorised staff with expertise on a specific type of machinery. A critical design factor was the ability to integrate the mobile e-support system to larger comprehensive e-maintenance systems, providing a wide spectrum of web-service-based interconnectivity capabilities both on the Moodle module and on the native mobile application.

The diagram in Fig. 4 depicts the overall information model. The e-support table stores the e-support component installation data, the user comments table stores information provided by the technicians and the entries table stores all the basic support content, which may be accompanied by relevant files, such as images, pdf files or videos. The FMECA (Failure Modes, Effects and Criticality Analysis) table stores input from an external processing application enhancing the module interconnectivity within an integrated e-maintenance platform [16]. The remaining tables target the categorization and easier extraction of the content. The many-to-many relation between entries and other tables enables content reusability. The actual implementation required some extra tables, ensuring compatible with Moodle component installation and future platform upgrades.

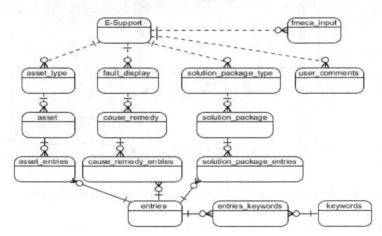

Fig. 4. Mobile e-Support Database Schema

4   Conclusions and Further Work

The complexity of modern industrial asset facilities and the rapid adoption of technological changes require from technical personnel to maintain an up to date often multi-disciplinary skills-set. To reduce staff response time to events occurring at the shop floor, methods for the storage, management and delivery of task-relevant support content and services are needed. In this paper, the provision of context-aware maintenance support though mobile devices is presented. The mobile support system utilizes NFC identification to acquire basic location and asset information and employs a customized module within a Learning Management System for user and content management. Information acquired via NFC suffices to cover explicitly three out of five minimum parameters that are necessary to understand context, namely who, where and when [5]. The other two, namely why and what, are derived from the user interaction with the mobile device. The processing of such information along with task profiling are performed by a dedicated LMS-customized module. A joint benefit of the LMS-based content management and the NFC-based context-awareness approach is the overall concealment of the technical communication and context processing details from the end-user, facilitating system acceptance, through the use of simple and user-friendly interfaces. Another benefit is the enrichment of the stored data about learners and their context, which is a key step for the implementation of Learning Analytics as part of further research. A mobile support system that combines an LMS, NFC identification and context-awareness, is an efficient and cost-effective basis to offer on-the-spot maintenance support, assisting maintenance personnel to improve their competencies as well as their work speed and efficiency.

Acknowledgements. Mobile support requirements and relevant content were offered by Kleemann Lifts and Mr Aggelos Papadopoulos contribution to this end is gratefully acknowledged. The project received financial support through GSRT grant 09SYN-71-856 (WelCOM project).

References

1. Ab-Samat, H., et al.: Reduction of response time during machine breakdown: a case study in semiconductor industry. International Journal of Logistics Systems and Management 16(2), 167–185 (2013)
2. Meixner, G., Petersen, N., Koessling, H.: User interaction evolution in the SmartFactory. In: Proceedings of the 24th BCS Interaction Specialist Group Conference, pp. 211–220. British Computer Society, Dundee (2010)
3. Abowd, G.D., Dey, A.K.: Towards a Better Understanding of Context and Context-Awareness. In: Gellersen, H.-W. (ed.) HUC 1999. LNCS, vol. 1707, pp. 304–307. Springer, Heidelberg (1999)
4. Emmanouilidis, C., Koutsiamanis, R.-A., Tasidou, A.: Mobile guides: Taxonomy of architectures, context awareness, technologies and applications. Journal of Network and Computer Applications 36(1), 103–125 (2013)
5. Perera, C., et al.: Context Aware Computing for The Internet of Things: A Survey. IEEE Communications Surveys & Tutorials 16(1), 414–454 (2014)
6. Dey, A.K.: Understanding and Using Context. Personal Ubiquitous Comput. 5(1), 4–7 (2001)

7. Bravo, J., et al.: From implicit to touching interaction: RFID and NFC approaches. In: 2008 Conference on Human System Interactions (2008)
8. Trottmann, U.: NFC-Possibilities and Risks. Network, 35 (2013)
9. Igoe, T., Coleman, D., Jepson, B.: Beginning NFC: Near Field Communication with Arduino, Android, and PhoneGap, p. 246. O'Reilly Media (2014)
10. Vauclair, M.: NFC. In: van Tilborg, H.A., Jajodia, S. (eds.) Encyclopedia of Cryptography and Security, pp. 840–842. Springer US (2011)
11. Garrido, P.C., et al.: A Model for the Development of NFC Context-Awareness Applications on Internet of Things. In: 2010 Second International Workshop on Near Field Communication (NFC) (2010)
12. Drury, C.G., Patel, S.C., Prabhu, P.V.: Relative advantage of portable computer-based workcards for aircraft inspection. International Journal of Industrial Ergonomics 26(2), 163–176 (2000)
13. Zhu, J., Ong, S.K., Nee, A.Y.C.: An authorable context-aware augmented reality system to assist the maintenance technicians. The International Journal of Advanced Manufacturing Technology 66(9-12), 1699–1714 (2013)
14. Papathanasiou, N., Emmanouilidis, C., Pistofidis, P., Karampatzakis, D.: Context Aware E-Support in E-Maintenance. In: Emmanouilidis, C., Taisch, M., Kiritsis, D. (eds.) APMS 2012. IFIP AICT, vol. 397, pp. 574–581. Springer, Heidelberg (2013)
15. MIMOSA - Machinery Information Management Open Systems Alliance, http://www.mimosa.org/
16. Pistofidis, P., Emmanouilidis, C., Papadopoulos, A., Botsaris, P.N.: Modeling the Semantics of Failure Context as a means to offer Context-Adaptive Maintenance Support. In: Second European Conference of the Prognostics and Health Management Society, PHME 2014, Nantes, France (PHM Society), July 8-10 (2014)

Alarm Management at Operators Workstations

Patrik Urban and Lenka Landryová

Department of Control Systems and Instrumentation,
VSB-Technical University Ostrava, 17. listopadu, Ostrava - Poruba, 708 33, Czech Republic
{patrik.urban,lenka.landryova}@vsb.cz

Abstract. This contribution deals with issues regarding alarm management at the operator workstations of industrial automated systems. It is focused on the Object Oriented Programming techniques and data acquisition from controlled processes provided for the human machine interface of these systems, the possibilities to configure the monitored variables of the processes and their parameter definition. It shows the different aspects of decision making over the options for using system functions in applications of operator environments on concrete examples.

Keywords: Alarm, System, Management, HMI, Automation.

1 Introduction to Techniques Applied for Work of Operator Workstations

Operators of control systems work in a field, in which emerging technology is characterized by features allowing implementation of control into processes without direct human intervention. However, automation and supervisory control do not fully exclude all human activity, those who supervise the automatic work of machines, in which it is still required to participate in a task for machine setup, the program upload, optimization of processes and similar areas.

1.1 Component Object Model Techniques and Server – Client Architecture

The technology, which has enabled bringing data to an operator workstation, is based on the principle of object-oriented modeling, which allows two or more components of applications to cooperate with each other even if they are created in different programming languages and designed for the use in different operating systems.

This Component Object Model (COM) technology works on the server – client communication principle, where the server sends data only when the client requests them, and uses the already mentioned object- oriented architecture, which brings one of the advantages of the "encapsulated" feature of programs into reusable software components that allows them to hide data and functions into the objects.

The object is an instance of a class, which is linked to a set of member functions and data. The component is a part of the program in a binary form, and as such, it

B. Grabot et al. (Eds.): APMS 2014, Part I, IFIP AICT 438, pp. 307–314, 2014.

must meet a certain binary standard. As already mentioned above, this object can be connected to different applications or other program components. Due to the packaged data and functions of the object, the client does not care about the internal implementation but the external object behavior, for example, the provided functions, which are defined for the application by COM technology (Bajgar, 2000).

1.2   Communication Standards in Control Systems

Integration of business plans and the control systems in the industry would not be possible without standards developed for their communication. Manufacturers rely on the use of Supervisory Control And Data Acquisition (SCADA) or Distributed Control Systems (DCS) to implement their plans into production. This is enabled by open and effective communication architectures with OLE (Object Linking Embedding) for Process Control (OPC) standard, which focuses on data access and not the data type.

The idea of the OPC server is implemented into OPC Historical Data Server, as well as Alarm & Event Handling Server. OPC is a standard for both hardware providers and software developers. It provides a standard mechanism for the transfer of data from hardware devices to any client application, the highly optimized communication of software applications with the data sources, and it defines a mechanism for efficient data exchange between software and hardware.

Together with OPC interface allowing any client to access their device using OLE and COM techniques allow developers to use software components in their programs written in different languages.

2   Hierarchy of Industrial Control

The industrial control systems work in a hierarchical structure and consist of levels, see Fig. 1 (Bajgar, 2000):

- The level of **direct** control, from where "smart" sensors and smart devices provide the system with their data through the interface. This data collected from the equipment together with its configuration parameters are presented to the software applications.
- **Process** level, where the data is used by DCS and SCADA systems with Human Machine Interface (HMI). The user of these systems is able to monitor, manage and evaluation processes, from which the data are obtained and can be further used at the information level.
- **Information** level, where data are analyzed and processed by tools and used for management and information systems or economic applications. At this level the users are able to work and connect with SCADA software, databases, word processing, spreadsheets in conjunction with the production system.

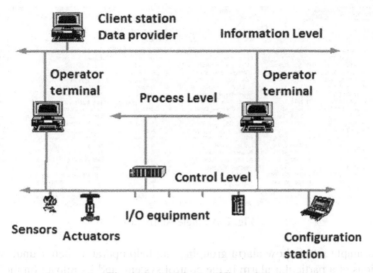

Fig. 1. Control System Hierarchy

3   Services of Control Systems

The service is the OPC server concept, which allows many different OPC servers to be placed under one common server that unifies access to data from different sources. This common server provides one set of OPC compliant interfaces, eliminating the need for client applications to know which OPC server to use for each data item.

The service provides an interface compatible with OPC client applications to use the data. In this case, the control system is designed in functional hierarchical structure for each manufacturing operation and the procedural parts (involving equipment such as engines, tanks, etc.). This enables operators to configure an alarm system, a basic operator support system for managing abnormal situations, and create a simple alarm list of each monitored variable. The control system automatically adds the alarm from an object into a specific section in each alarm list.

It's a very effective and fast way from the point of view of cost, and also easier for operators, who are able to monitor "their" alarms, alarms in their competence under their login into a system, and not long unsorted list of alarms of all control systems. When a new alarm appears, it is added to the functional structure of the object automatically. Operators can monitor unacknowledged alarms recorded in the event list. The visible part of the control system alarm list also contains a "live tracking values" feature, which displays actual values and parameters that triggered the alarm, for example when the level in the tank falls below a certain minimum.

In the list it can also be seen, what the current value of a monitored variable is, which carried out the alarm. This feature can be identified as Alarm Grouping, meaning drawing up lists of key attributes, and thus creating manageable lists. The result is the one alarm in the alarm list for all alarms in the whole group presented to the operator screen.

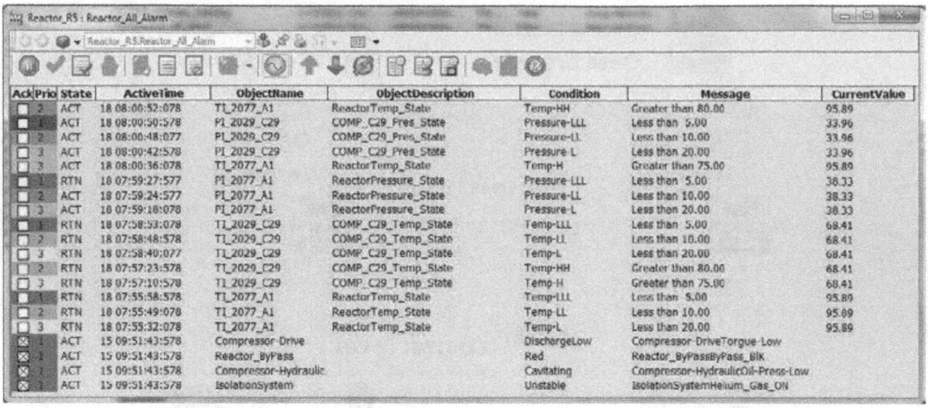

Fig. 2. A Single Alarm List

This example shows how alarm grouping can help operators better understand the implications of a particular alarm in the control system, and its impact on the process. In systems without this feature, the decision and resolution of the alarm conditions rely on the knowledge of an operator, and under circumstances when several processes are monitored at the same time it is quite time consuming and/or risky.

Fig. 3. Alarm Grouping Tool Applied for Alarm List

4   Alarm Issues Which Operators Deals with in Control Systems

The basis for the work is to describe the situation and processes in which the alarm system is deployed. The correct description of the system facilitates further work with alarms and their management. An important idea of the methodology is a combination of the qualitative and quantitative approach to the research applied to the alarm system development. Data collection in the form of alarm records from different applications and process systems help us to find weaknesses in the management of alarms.

The data here are evaluated from two different process systems, resulting in a different number of events in them. This also shows that it is necessary to obtain the largest amount of findings possible to be able to evaluate better the management of alarms. The first records are taken from 15 minutes of monitoring, during which 27 alarms came, 25 of which were alarms on values exceeding the limits, and 2 were system failures alarm in first control system. Another system was examined as well and for the same period of 15 minutes the operator received 500 events on the workstation screen. This is an increased burden for the operator. Of the 500 events, 433 events were acquired as changes of monitored values and confirmed alarms, remaining events were alarms that showed an exceeded limit of 25 monitored variables, and a group of other system alarms, which consisted of changes in the valves/actuators of manual → automatic mode, a small change of reference values, changes from true → false values of binary variables.

Rationalization of alarm issues, listed in Table 1, should help operators manage stressful situations. The objective of configuration of the alarm management system is to allow operators to remove standing or nuisance alarms that are re-occurring on the main alarm list of their screens.

Table 1. Alarm Issues (Atkinson, T. , 2011)

Alarm Issues	Symptoms	Effects	Implications
Alarm Load	High number of alarms per operator per minute, 1 per minute is unacceptable, Highest seen 40 per minute, Operators accept alarms without review	Devaluing of the Alarm System Decision making impaired Poor operator responses Adds to operator stress Masks high priority alarms More outages Loss of protective layer	Texaco Milford Haven Alaska North Slope Esso Longford explosion
Burst Alarms	High number of alarms from a single cause e.g. Compressor trip Shutdown/Startup Often see 100+ Occasionally see 500+	Incorrect/delayed diagnosis of causal event Incorrect response to incident Delayed response to incident Miss key alarms hidden in list E.g. failure to shut down safely Poor operator 'situational awareness' following event Increased likelihood of subsequent errors	Three Mile Island

Table 2. (*continued*)

Alarm Issues	Symptoms	Effects	Implications
Nuisance alarm handling	High number of alarms per operator per minute Repeating alarms Instrument Fault alarms System alarms	Alarms defeated Safety alarms 'Unofficial' defeats Ignoring the alarm system Poor control room environment High operator stress Devaluing of work request system	BP Prudhoe Bay Maryland rail Accident BP Grangemouth Esso Longford
Poor Design	High numbers of high priority alarms Safety alarms not differentiated No defined operator response Standing Alarms Out of use or standby equipment	Operators respond to inappropriate alarms Delayed or no response to important alarms Inconsistent or incorrect operator response	BP Texas city explosion Helios crash Explosion at Texaco Milford Haven
Poor management	Alarms disabled inappropriately Without risk assessment Without regular review Alarms ignored Faulty alarms not addressed	Removal of a layer of protection Safety Environmental Economic Regulator attention	BP Texas city explosion Maryland Rail Accident

Therefore two functions were configured for the above mentioned control system: Alarm Hiding and Alarm Shelving. Alarm shelving lets operators decide whether or not to put an alarm 'on the shelf' for a defined period of time or a certain occurrence. This temporarily removes it from the main alarm list to a special list, but the alarm itself is not affected. It will later require attention from the operator. In the meantime, the operator can concentrate on tasks judged to require their immediate focus. The question remains if alarm shelving makes a valuable and much-appreciated tool that helps operators work with maximum efficiency. The shelving is time limited to prevent important alarms to be removed or forgotten

Alarm hiding is set up during the engineering phase. Its main purpose is to suppress alarms that are either expected or not relevant in a particular situation, or that are based on a known process state, e.g. low temperatures or flow during a controlled shutdown. As the name suggests, 'hidden' alarms are never visible to operators. They only see alarms that require action on their part.

5   Conclusion

Automation is the field, in which modern technology is being developed, characterized by features allowing implementation of control processes without direct human intervention. However, automation and supervisory control do not fully exclude people, who supervise the direct work of machines. The motivation for the research is fill in the gap between practice – the daily operation of operators supervising control systems, and an analysis of such processes. As an example of supervisory control we describe here the area of an alarm management system. Such system is dealing with alarm logs giving a feedback for better understanding at the level of the human-machine interface in order to improve and support the engineering work on the design, configuration and implementation of the system for an operator supervising the production and managing alarms. As the production processes get very complex, there are increasing numbers of things, which can go wrong when controlling them. This research was also aimed to find out about the alarms from actual cases, how they are defined, what types are used, and how much their configuration in practice matches the ISA 18.2 standard, which defines alarm management for conditions in different control systems. The operators who are the immediate users and the engineers who configure the control systems features at the site during their implementation need to cooperate. The evaluation of process alarms in the control system from system operator point of view was described. Alarms are displayed, depending on whether the configured monitored variable exceeds the set limits. The alarm prioritizing during their configurations and design in terms of the frequency for requests for alarm acknowledgement by a single operator and alarm handled by operators during stressful situations remains a big task of control systems engineers to prevent hazardous consequences.

References

1. AAMD, Advances in Alarm Management (cit. May 2014)
   http://www.ece.ualberta.ca/~aamd/ (retrieved)
2. ABB. 2014. ABB data in progress (cit. May 2014), http://inside.abb.com/ (retrieved)
3. Alarm management problem solved (cit. May 2014),
   https://www.asmconsortium.net/Documents/Alarm%20Management%2
   0Wasnt%20that%20problem%20solved%20years%20ago_DeWildeReisin
   g_2011HUGAmericas.pdf (retrieved)
4. Atkinson, T.: Human Factors in the Process Industries Blog (cit. December 2011),
   http://www.abb.com/blog/gad00540/3F0E.aspx (retrieved)
5. Bajgar, D.: Administration of alarm events with the use of OPC object technology. Ostrava: Department of Control Systems And Instrumentation, Technical University of Ostrava, 62 pages Final thesis, Supervisor: Landryová, L (2000)
6. Crawford, W., Hollifield, B.: Energy-tech (cit. May 2014), http://www.energy-tech.com/article.cfm?id=28019 (retrieved)

7. Data analysis (cit. May 2014),
   http://ori.hhs.gov/education/products/n_illinois_u/datamanag
   ement/datopic.html (retrieved)
8. Data analysis example (cit. May 2014), http://www.ats.ucla.edu/stat/dae/
   (retrieved)
9. Data Collection Method (cit. May 2014),
   http://people.uwec.edu/piercech/researchmethods/
   data%20collection%20methods/data%20collection%20methods.htm
   (retrieved)
10. Difference between Scada and HMI (cit. May 2014),
    http://www.indusoft.com/blog/2013/04/19/what-is-the-
    difference-between-scada-and-hmi/ (retrieved)
11. ISA norm 18.2 (cit. May 2014),
    https://www.isa.org/.../DownloadAsset.aspx?id=1233...(retrieved)
12. Marchelli, M.: Situation Awareness in Scada, 2011 (cit. May 2014),
    http://www.emmos.org/prevconf/2011/Training_2_Situational%20
    Awareness%20in%20SCADA%20_EMS_GMS_DMS_Rev3_1.pdf (retrieved)
13. Research in alarm management communication (cit. May 2014),
    http://ieeexplore.ieee.org/xpls/abs_all.jsp?arnumber=6339920
    &tag=1 (retrieved)
14. What do mean Scada (cit. May 2014),
    http://www.reliance.cz/cs/products/what-does-scada-hmi-mean
    (retrieved)

MDA Based Tool for PLM' Models Building and Evolving

Onur Yildiz[1,2], Nada Aouadi, Aimad Karkouch, Philippe Pernelle[3],
Lilia Gzara[2], and Michel Tollenaere[2]

[1] Audros Technology
F-69003 Lyon, 41 rue de la cit´e, France
oyildiz@audros.fr
[2] INP Grenoble, Laboratory G-SCOP F-38000 Grenoble, France
lilia.gzara@grenoble-inp.fr, Michel.Tollenaere@inpg.fr
[3] University of Lyon 1, Laboratory DISP F-69621 Villeurbanne Cedex, France
philippe.pernelle@univ-lyon1.fr

Abstract. Product Lifecycle Management (PLM) systems are sufficiently generic to propose models adapted to companies' specific needs without additional development. However, the implementation of such systems and their multiple reconfigurations may introduce coherence problems. To ensure structural and functional coherence while creating and evolv- ing PLM models, a methodological approach is described in this paper. The proposed approach is based on Model Driven Architecture (MDA) principles in order to allow : [1] models' creation while respecting syntac- tic and semantic constraints, [2] models' evolution while respecting de- pendencies between the various PLM syste' components. This approach is being prototyping based on Eclipse framework.

Keywords: PLM system, MDA, metamodel, constraint, OCL, trans- formation, ATL.

1 Introduction

Nowadays, industrial companies using PLM systems need to deploy models which are adapted to their requirements. PLM are information systems ded- icated to managing the entire lifecycle of a product, from inception, through engineering design and manufacture, to service and disposal of manufactured products. In this research, we are focusing on these models' building and recon- figuration, more precisely from a PLM editor/integrator point of view. These models are generic enough to propose ones that can be adapted to each com- pany' needs by doing some additional developments. However, in the case of initial PLM deployment, the elaboration of a PLM system that complies with the company's activities often requires one or more specific data models and a set of specific functions (processing).

B. Grabot et al. (Eds.): APMS 2014, Part I, IFIP AICT 438, pp. 315–322, 2014.
© IFIP International Federation for Information Processing 2014

Usually, the idea is to adapt the generic model, based on a set of templates which correspond to typical business needs (such as Catia data management, ProEng data management, MS Office reporting, etc.) so to reduce workload. Data model definition must be validated in order to avoid inconsistencies. This validation step consists of respecting a set of structural and functional predefined constraints. Thus, any new data model creation can be used permanently after the validation of data coherency.

Similarly, the various evolutions of already deployed systems made to adapt or add new functions in the data model are very difficult to perform for a com- pany. In order to achieve this, companies are often accompanied by an editor or an integrator. In fact, a company must adapt to the ongoing development of its market or to any changes in its working methods. Therefore, it's often required to change the existent data model or system functionalities. But, in most often cases, these companies are not able to identify the impact of these changes ; there isn't any tool allowing them to have a global vision of the deployed PLM sys- tem in terms of components' dependencies. Without this global vision, changes may cause coherence problems or side effects. Thus, the phases of models' cre- ation and evolving imply setting up a methodological approach for creating or maintaining the implemented system with a structural and functional coherence.

This research work aims at helping companies when they configurate or evolve their PLM system. The proposed approach consists of building a generic busi- ness model and providing a set of mechanisms to transform this generic business model into specific models according to each company' specificities. This ap- proach is based on MDA. The rest of the paper is organized as follows. Section 2 describes the foundations of proposed approach using MDA. Section 3 gives the principles of proposed approach deployment. Section 4 describes the software prototype developed to support eh approach and finally section 5 gives some conclusions and perspectives.

2   Proposed Approach Foundations

MDA [6] [7] [1] is an architecture derived from MDE (Model Driven Engineer- ing) approach proposed by OMG (Object Management Group). MDA uses the concepts of MOF (Meta-Object Facility) [8] and UML (Unified Modeling Lan- guage). It is based on multilevel modeling (or metamodels) and mechanisms for models' transformations. The MDA logic is to propose a refinement of models from a high level of abstraction to executable code. The fundamental rule of MDA is to separate the business logic from the implementation one. According to the three level approach proposed in MDA, models or metamodels are defined by a process of abstraction towards target platforms : Computation Independent Model (CIM), Platform Independent Model (PIM) and Platform Specific Model (PSM). In the rest of this section, we will describe these levels and mechanisms of transition between models of different levels.

2.1   Metamodeling within MDA

A metamodel aims to define the main concepts to be used in the PLM models [11] [5] . These concepts must be independent of the PLM system. They are used to characterize the conformity of the lower level models. The proposed elements in our metamodel [12] (fig. 1) describe the structural, behavioral and invariant concepts to be used in a PLM system. The diagram below shows the generic reduced metamodel with basic concepts for modeling business model.

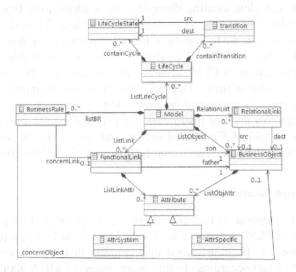

Fig. 1. Extract from Business metamodel

The fundamental metamodel elements make it possible to structure concepts in order to be used and deployed in a company. These concepts are structured according to descriptive elements (BusinessObject, AttrSpecific), structural re- lationship (FunctionnaLink), dependency relationship (RelationalLink) and Life cycle Management elements (LifeCycle). Business Rule concepts (BusinessRule) have to be considered as constraints that ensure business model consistency.

These concepts would enable building compliant business models. The busi- ness model includes business as in the activity sector and information system. This is justified by the fact that final implementation should respect PLM con- cepts (regardless of the platform). Therefore we believe to be consistent with the MDA approach "spirit" (the CIM is independent of execution platforms).

2.2   Validation and Conformity of Models

The metamodel described in previous section is part of the proposed approach for building and reconfigurating PLM models process.It is one element among others that allow developing consistent models . There is no standard metamodel. How- ever, several studies have attempted to propose reference models [10] [4] .The proposed metamodel in this paper is generated from an abstract approach of these reference models . Concepts defined in metamodel are not always enough for the construction of robust models (they are not very sensitive to the con- text modifications). In fact, we used constraints in order to successfully express restrictions on built models [2], constraints must be defined.

A constraint represents a boolean-valued expression which can be attached to any metamodel element. It generally indicates a limitation, or gives further information on the model. They are used in most cases to specify invariants on the meta classes. These constraints complete existing diagrams by implementing business rules and making relationships more precise (without ambiguities). To add constraints on proposed models, we choose to use the Object Constraint Language (OCL) [9].

The model is a level (PIM) of modeling which has to enable implementing business concepts within a PLM system. In the context, the modeling is not unique and can evolve in time. The business concepts defining the models of this level characterize a contextual business terminology. Here the contextual meaning implies a low level of invariance for two reasons. On one hand concepts treated are very specific for industrial sector and the concepts used involve a certain ambiguity, on the other hand concepts treated are evolving over time

2.3   Model Transformations

The aim of our proposal is to facilitate the conception and implementation of business models in PLM systems. Therefore, Meta Models of proposed approach (PIM level) have to be transformed into models that are dependent on target platforms (PSM level) according to the main steps of MDA approach. The last level, achieved by PSM generation, is then obtained by transformations between different levels, from CIM to PIM and from PIM to PSM

A PIM to PIM transformation consists of transforming a metamodel while respecting associated constraints. Likewise, a PIM to PSM transformation corre- sponds to the transformation of an independent functional model into a platform compliant model (with constraints specific to the chosen platform).

The transformation process could be described as a succession of 2 stages. In the first stage, the target metamodel is defined, and then mapped with the source meta-model. Mapping task is implemented using transformation rules. These rules allow producing a target model (conform to the target metamodel) starting from a source model (conform to the source metamodel). The second stage consists of executing the model transformations rules in a particular lan- guage (in our case, in SQL (Structured Query Language) script). Indeed, the PLM system configuration and data are stored in a database. Then, the last step of transformation process should make it possible to add, delete and up- date these data within the database. To sum up, a source model allows producing a target code thanks to the transformation process with Atlas Transformation Language (ATL).

3   Proposed Approach Deployment

As stated previously, providing generic concepts is not of much help when it comes to identifying enterprise's business concepts. This is because, most of the time, the experts to set up the PLM, are either business experts or IT experts but rarely both. On the one hand, our modeling's approach is independant of software tools and highlights the generic concepts of a PLM information system and business domains. On the other hand, we strongly believe that it should be supported by a methodological approach where various experts may simultane- ously contribute to the business models' construction.

The suggested approach is based upon business-domain segmentation. Some business objects are well standardized to be used, as they are, in the enterprise. The main existent systems offer preconfigured models to ease building enterprise own business models and thus accelerating domain-specific model creation. The above-mentioned approach consists of building, progressively, parts of models by IT and business experts using each domain's invariant elements and business rules validation.

Specific Templates

The domain is used to group concepts with adaptable granularity. In addition, some domains are sufficiently invariant (or normalized) in companies to be used as they are. We could mention for example : changes management domains, En- gineering Change Request (ECR), Engineering Change Order (ECO) are CAD (Computer Aided Design) data management domains (part, assembly, ...). These domains can be elaborated by IT or business experts and then integrated pro- gressively into the construction of the global PIM.

Business Rules

Business rules Business rules characterize PIM or PSM concepts constraints and are, as mentioned before, described using OCL [3]. In the proposed method- ological approach, they are used during the explicit validation, in addition to metamodels' implicit validation. Thus, business rules can be defined during ev- ery step during PIM and PSM construction. Similarly to domains, there could be two types of business rules : information system rules, business activity rule.

Models Updates

In order for a company to continuously take into account economical environment changes, its information system and therefore its PLM system should be adapted. Updates can be identified at two levels : PSM's level and particularly its instance within the PLM (for example : adding some specific script) , PIM's level (for instance : business object modification, adding links, ...)

The advocated methodological approach is dual. On one hand, it is to make reverse transformations from instantiated PSM to PIM. On the other hand, it is to provide PIM comparisons. This approach will enable experts to measure the impact of changes applied to the PLM.

4   Application

The suggested approach based on MDA is supported by a framework implement- ing models transformations and constraints validation mechanisms [13]. This framework is built on top of Eclipse platform and its extending capabilities likes EMF (implementation of the MOF providing tools for implementing DSLs (Domain-Specific languages). This framework is a way to verify and validate concepts introduced in the first part of this article.

Business Model Modeling

The construction of business model is done thanks to a graphical editor based on Eclipse GMF (Graphical Modeling Framework). This editor allows user creating his own business concepts based on a generic metamodel. The following diagram (Fig. 2) represents a business model with constraints. A violated constraint is marked with a red cross (i.e a BusinessObject can not have an empty name).

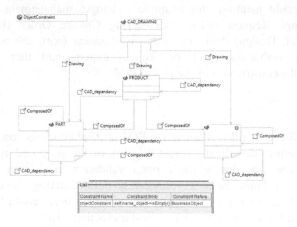

Fig. 2. Business model with constraints

Audros Metamodel

In order for the model to be exploitable, an SQL script needs to be generated and applied to the PLM system. To achieve this, a metamodel defining Audros PLM's concepts have been created

The main goal is to generate an Audros model conform to the Audros meta-model from a business model edited with GMF and conform to the business metamodel (introduced in the first part) by means of ATL transformation. The transformation results in a compliant Audros model. The transformation is done by iterating over the input model's content, comparing this content with the source patterns (correspondence rules defined in the .atl file) and producing target patterns in the target model whenever a matching occurs.

The following figure (Fig. 3) shows a case of ATL correspondence rule de- fined between the two metamodels. This rule takes a BusinessObject (defined by Audros metamodel) as an input and transforms it into an Object Class (defined by Database metamodel). The whole transformation process is used to translate and inject the Business Model into the database, to become accessible and usable within the PLM.

```
-- Règle de transformation d'un objet du modèle métier en une classe du modèle BD
lazy rule BusinessObject2Class {
    from
        b : Business!BusinessObject
    to
        c : DB!Class (
            name <- b.name_object,
            attribute <- b.ListObjAttr->collect(attr | thisModule.BusinessAttribute2Attribute(attr))
        )
}
```

Fig. 3. ATL rule

The obtained specific model is not yet exploitable in Audros PLM. It needs to be transformed into an SQL script to inject into the system database using existent tools in Eclipse (Acceleo and Liquibase).

The following figure (Fig. 4) illustrates Audros PLM's final state after the transformations' sequences applied to the model introduced earlier in this paper (the objects are usable within the PLM).

Fig. 4. Audros PLM result

5   Conclusion

The research work described in this paper aims at helping companies when they configurate or evolve their PLM system. The proposed approach consists of building a generic business model and providing a set of mechanisms to trans- form this generic business model into specific models according to each company' specificities. The proposed approach is based on a model-driven architecture

322   O. Yildiz et al.

(MDA). One of the main goals of this approach, besides creating adequate mod- els, is providing controlling mechanism in case of models evolution in order to keep total consistency in PLM systems. In the proposed approach, companies' specific needs are implemented through a refinement of models from a high level of abstraction to executable code. For that aim, three modeling levels are defined (CIM, PIM, PSM) and a set of transition mechanisms between levels is given. This approach is supported by software prototype which allows implementing concepts proposed in this paper. In this article, we concentrated on business model creation methodology. Now, a reflexive posture is conducted to address business model evolution methodology that ensures semantic and syntactic co- herence with already existing PLM components.

References

[1] Bezivin, J., Gerbe, O.: Towards a precise definition of the omg/mda framework. In: 16thIEEE International Conference on Automated Software Engineering, San Diego, USA (November 2001)
[2] Cabot, J., Teniente, E.: Transformation techniques for ocl constraints. Science of Computer Programming 68(3), 152–168 (2007)
[3] Dang, D.H., Cabot, J.: Automating inference of ocl business rules from user scenarios. In: Muenchaisri, P., Rothermel, G. (eds.) APSEC- 20th Asia-Pacific Software Engineering Conference 2013. IEEE, Bangkok (2013),
http://hal.inria.fr/hal-00869234,atlanModAtlanModITM-Factory,FrenchFUI14
[4] Eynard, B., Gallet, T., Roucoules, L., Ducellier, G.: PDM system implementation basedonuml. Mathematics and Computers in Simulation 70(5-6), 330–342 (2006)
[5] Le Duigou, J., Bernard, A., Perry, N.: Frameworkfor plm integrationin smes networks. Computer-Aided Design and Application 8(4), 531–544 (2011)
[6] OMG: Omg model driven architecture (2001), http://www.omg.org/mda/
[7] OMG: Mda guidev1.0.1 (2003), http://www.omg.org/mda/
[8] OMG: Meta object facility (MOF) (2011),
http://www.omg.org/spec/MOF/2.4.1/
[9] OMG: Object constraint language OMG available specification version (2014),
http://www.omg.org/spec/OCL/2.4/PDF
[10] Sudarsan, R., Fenves, S., Sriram, R.: A productin formation modeling framework for product lifecycle managemen. Computer Aided Design 37(13) (2005)
[11] Terzi, S., Panetto, H., Morel, G., Garetti, M.: Aholonic meta model for product lifecycle management. International Journal of Product Lifecycle Management 2(3), 253–289 (2007), http://hal.archives-ouvertes.fr/hal-00120019
[12] Yildiz, O., Gzara, L., Pernelle, P., Tollenaere, M.: An MDA approach for plm system design. In: Emmanouilidis, C., Taisch, M., Kiritsis, D. (eds.) APMS 2012. Part II. IFIP AICT, vol. 398, pp. 216–223. Springer, Heidelberg (2013)
[13] Yildiz, O., Pernelle, P., Gzara, L., Tollenaere, M.: A frame work for plm model design. In: Bernard, A., Rivest, L., Dutta, D. (eds.) PLM 2013. IFIP AICT, vol. 409, pp. 159–169. Springer, Heidelberg (2013)

General Use of the Routing Concept for Supply Chain Modeling Purposes: The Case of OCP S.A.

Mohamad Degoun[1,4,5], A. Drissi[2], Pierre Fenies[1,3], Vincent Giard[1,4],
K. Retmi[1,3,5], and J. Saadi[1,5]

[1] Mohammed VI Polytechnic University – EMINES, Benguerir, Maroc
{mohammed.degoun,kawtar.retmi}@emines-ingenieur.org
[2] Managing Director OCP S.A
a.drissi@ocpgroup.org
[3] Paris Ouest Nanterre University
pierre.fenies@u-paris10.fr
[4] PSL –Paris-Dauphine University
vincent.giard@dauphine.fr
[5] Hassan II University – ENSEM – LISER
janah.saadi@ensem.ac.ma

Abstract. This paper proposes a modelling and formalizing approach to field-work-collected data in order to develop a set of tools to both direct and increase industrial production. The OCP ("Cherifian Office of Phosphate") provided authentic data for the construction and use of an inductive approach. This approach enabled us not only to give details about the problems encountered but also to have the necessary level of granularity required for a number of ex ante management decisions. Several instances of the suggested modelling applications are given in the real context of the OCP's supply chain reengineering. They equally allow the reader to obtain a feedback on the implementation of a twofold modelling generated by a unique collection of knowledge.

1   Introduction

The purpose of this paper is to analyze the solutions to the methodological problems that arose in the first phase of our research aiming to create a dual decision-making support system (DMS) dedicated to Supply Chain management and management control system. This phase has to do with gathering and formalizing the required knowledge to design simulation models on which to base the DMSs. Supply Chain (SC) generally refers to the logistics chain of multinationals. The different subsidiaries of these companies participate in the SC, both from within the organization, and as « satellites » involving multiple third party providers of logistics services and subcontractors whose operations are coordinated by the multinational company [1]. The SC object of our study is that of Cherifian Office of Phosphates (OCP S.A.),

B. Grabot et al. (Eds.): APMS 2014, Part I, IFIP AICT 438, pp. 323–333, 2014.
© IFIP International Federation for Information Processing 2014

owned by the kingdom of Morocco[1]. Both the DMSs rely on complementary models of the SC, used to simulate its activities dynamically. In this context, management is focusing i) on the tactical decisions to negotiate the terms of new agreements (limited number of customers) and so maximize the margin generated by the SC and ii) on the operational decisions to fulfill its obligations under the current agreements while keeping costs down. This paper focuses mainly on the operational management aspect. Highlighting the consequences in terms of time and space of the contemplated operational decisions is largely achieved through the simulation tool, which of course does not preclude recourse to complementary approaches (optimization…) to identify the best course of action. Ex ante assessment of the decisions should be complemented by an ex post assessment by management control, through a tailored management accounting scheme to make a proper economic analysis of the decisions. In the context of production to orders, the management control referential cannot be efficient if it only refers to legacy data. Indeed, the use of simulation techniques is needed in order to obtain a truly relevant referential, one that is built dynamically. We start by delimiting the context of this work (§ 2), and then consider (§ 3) the key concept of routing in order to present (§ 3) some principles of collecting and using the gathered data that we will illustrate (§ 4) with applications in the OCP context before making any conclusion.

2   Research Context

Any modeling / simulation (M / S) research on production systems is determined by the objectives sought and by the general characteristics of the system. We shall therefore begin (§2.1) with a description of the objectives of the research as they determine the choice of relevant information to be gathered and the level at which the model is to be designed. (§2.2) analyses the information gathering approaches proposed in extent literature showing their limits for the purposes of this research.

2.1   Objectives of the "Dual" Modeling

The Figure 1 summarizes our chosen approach. The combined gathering of field information by SC management experts and management control / management accounting players should make for two consistent and complementary representations of the SC's activities. The basic inputs are technical documents used in the field, complemented by observation, particularly of decision-making practices, where the required information is not set out in writing. Such basic inputs (which are not availa-

---

[1] It is made up of a complete industrial sector (described in figure 5) from ore extraction (more than half of world reserves belong to OCP S.A.), to production of phosphoric acid and fertilizers. The Jorf site located at the end of this SC is characterized by its production plants, owned by OCP as well as by a number of technically similar plants, jointly managed by OCP and its foreign partners under joint ventures (JV). Moreover, the adjunction of 300 km of pipeline (for minerals transfer) will entirely change the SC to enable implementation of production to orders.

ble in the public domain (and therefore not listed in the bibliography)) are processed in order to design a dual model of SC activities, with an adequate granularity for the DMS to be designed. The desired model is intended for use by a discrete event simulator, which is a relevant technical solution for our purpose. The primary data gathering process and its processing in order to build the foundations of a simulation model poses a number of difficult methodological problems.

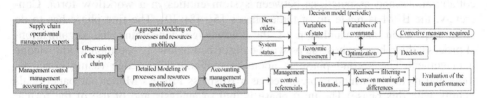

Fig. 1. Complementarity and use of Operational Management & Management Control Models

The M / S created for the operational DMS does not call for a fine detail of SC process mapping; on the other hand, it presupposes a good understanding of the main levers available to decision-makers and a proper modeling of the domino effect of consequences of these decisions in time and space. The first step, therefore, consists in an accurate plotting of the concerned physical activities. In order to further inform the decision-making process, beyond the anticipation of consequences of alternative decisions, one needs to measure their economic impact. This implies recourse to a management accounting scheme based on the second M / S. The M / S created for the Management Control DMS stems from a detailed mapping of the productive entities of the SC, using a rather local focus. This should enable a better assessment of cost factors and therefore the design of a relevant management accounting scheme, for use both for decision-making purposes to assess the economic aspects and for subsequent control purposes. The economic assessment aspect is not the focus of this paper which will only implicitly refer to costs drivers. It is to be used at a later stage in the operational management DMS to fine tune operational decisions and for tactical decision-making purposes. Moreover, the fact of being able to produce to order should drive the development of a dynamic referential for use by the Management Control DMS.

2.2   BPM, Supply Chain Costing and Supply Chain Management

In 1980's and '90s, a number of technical and managerial innovations took place simultaneously, along with sweeping economic environment changes that led to root and branch changes in the organization and management of Western businesses. These gradually shifted the traditional approach to functional line management and process reengineering" [3], activity costing, project management [4], management software packages were all managerial and technological breakthroughs stemming from a process approach of organization and the associated software. Accordingly, there was a perceived need to systematically draw up models for almost every aspect of the organization so as to identify the good practices and to organize the acquisition of information concerning the organizational processes. A number of authors and actors have defined [5] the Business Process Management (BPM) as one which enables the modeling of the business process. Using collected information about the activities of a complex system such as a SC [6], a representation of the organizational processes is designed in the form of a knowledge model (KM) of this system. The KM is defined as the translation in natural or graphic language of the structure of the system's activities. A number of authors [7] suggest a definition of the system process' KM as the aggregation of information and data used to plot interactions, collaborations and associations between system entities in a workflow form. Concretely, the BPM is made up of three phases [5]; [8]; [9]. The first phase has to do with acquisition and validation of the knowledge concerning the organizational process; this phase, whose steps will be described below, is common to knowledge management. The second phase is about formalizing knowledge (using concepts, tools and methods) which is presented as a Business Process Model(our paper deals mainly with this phase).The third phase is that of analysis and of use of the formal models developed in the previous phase [10]. During the analytical phase, corporate actors analyze, use and expand the KM. Four steps have been identified for knowledge acquisition through partial analysis of extent literature: (*i*) the first phase is about the choice of knowledge acquisition mode; the choice of method is bound up with the system and with available information. Moreover, a number of approaches may be used simultaneously; (*ii*) the second phase is about translating the knowledge acquired in the form of rough basic documentation in digital format ; it is key [9] to store the information in digital format so as to improve productivity and traceability; (*iii*) the third phase serves to validate the rough translation of the collected information; (*iv*)the fourth phase concerns the development of basic documentary knowledge to enable the subsequent formalization of the system's organizational process. Note some authors consider this basic documentary knowledge, often presented in natural language, as a model in itself of the corporate processes [11]. Using an iterative approach, basic process knowledge is then expanded as the process is started all over again from phase 1 [12]. Research [12] on corporate use of structured and formalized basic process knowledge highlighted the five following applications (figure 2): (*i*) the knowledge model is used to design the Information System (data storage, basic data, ERP), [11]; (*ii*) the knowledge model is used to design decision-making applications (Advanced Planning and Scheduling, optimization models, simulation models) [13] ; (*iii*) the knowledge model is used to design the performance assessment system (Management Control systems as part of SC Costing), [14,15]; (*iv*) the knowledge model is used to design and validate the current or future corporate organizational process through interaction with target system players [3]; (*v*) the knowledge model is used for organizational process certification purposes under the quality management approach.

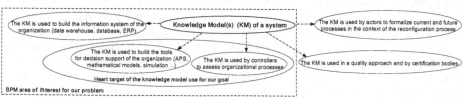

Fig. 2. Multiple uses of knowledge model systems.

Research by [14] showed that a given model may be used by different users; one may suppose that the productivity of the formalization process would be greater if it were centralized and performed once and for all, since the knowledge model draws on the same basic knowledge regardless of use. Indeed, this single process mapping performed as part of the modeling exercise of a complex system may be used, for our purposes, indifferently to design the information system, the decision-making rules and the process valuation/optimization system [7]. In light of SC complexity, introducing a BPM approach serves to formalize the logistical process between and within the systems making up the SC [12] and serves as a pre-requisite for operational collaboration in the long run. As shown in figure 2, BPM activity, which consists in formalizing process system knowledge, also involves producing a documented model useful for different purposes. Nevertheless, in light of our objectives of design of SC Management decision-making support applications, we will focus on use of the knowledge model geared to the routing concept of an SC, and to the creation of a DMS integrating economic metrics.

3   Knowledge Use: Routing Based Modeling of SC Processes

The gathering of the technical information yields multiple items of different forms and formats, from which one has to extract the relevant information for modeling/simulation purposes. Methodological considerations lead to a detailed analysis of the notion of routing (§3.1) and to to generate the relevant information from the detailed information gathered (provided one relies on properly defined aggregation rules (see §3.2)). One must also achieve the relevant level of detail by keeping the number of objects created in the model down to a minimum (§3.3).

3.1   Routing Components and Routing Breakdown

Routing is central to technical information. Generally speaking, production routing is defined by use of one or several products matching the required characteristics, combined in predetermined quantities, to obtain, after a certain time (processing time), with the help of multiple material (equipment, machinery...) and human resources (operators), all being viewed as components of a processor, the desired product (or products in the case of linked productions). Figure 3 shows the components of a Routing and their « combination ». To every reference i of an input is associated a bill of materials coefficient q_i; symmetrically, to every reference j of an output is associated the quantity q_j produced by the operations. These quantitative data (q_i and q_j) are structurally consistent.

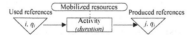

Fig. 3. Representation of a Routing

The above general definition helps to breakdown production operations into the different elementary steps, each characterized by an elementary routing. This is referred to as a detailed routing. These elementary steps are connected by logical relationships of precedence (a downstream step may not start until the upstream step has been completed), in which a product made upon completion of an elementary upstream step is used by the next elementary step downstream. These different routings are generated to satisfy different needs (real time order, ordering, scheduling). Detailed routings may be viewed as a description of the production process. Detailed routings gathered in the field generally do not match the required level of detail for a dual modeling/simulation of the SC under review. They, however, enable one to generate the relevant information from the detailed information gathered, provided one relies on properly defined aggregation rules (see §3.2). One must also achieve, in the required model, the relevant level of detail by keeping the number of objects created in the model down to a minimum (§3.3).

3.2   Aggregation Rules

Aggregated activities encompass all of the elementary steps of the detailed routing, together with the products exchanged between these elementary steps. Four rules are relevant to the elementary routing aggregation:

(i) The rule of legacy as to time sequence: The time sequence relationship linking the different elementary steps that are merged into an aggregated activity will disappear, as does any trace of the products exchanged between these elementary steps. The aggregated activity inherits the time sequence relationship linking an elementary step to another lying upstream or downstream, but that are not included in the aggregated activity (figure 4).

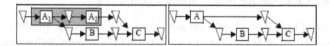

Fig. 4. Rule of time sequence relationship legacy

(ii) The rules of consolidation duration: The above analogy with project management helps define the duration of aggregated activity as equal to the duration of the critical path calculated on the flowchart of the detailed routing, where cycles are not noted. This duration consolidation rule is subject to the following three constraints:

(1) In discrete production, the processor which performs an activity handles a single batch (or unit) at a time and only processes the next one once the first has been completed. A transposition of this principle to aggregated activity distorts the representation of reality, since the processor performing the first elementary activity of the aggregated activity is in a position to handle a new batch as soon as it has finished the previous batch, without having to wait for the batch it has processed to leave the processor performing the last elementary activity of the aggregated activity.

(2) adaptation to line production is straightforward if one considers that the line production process can be approximated by a discrete process handling small batches (for example, a batch corresponding to product volume manufactured in k minutes by the processor, k being the number of minutes).

(3) The duration of aggregated activity is only valid provided there is no interruption in supplies, preventing an elementary activity on the critical path from being performed

(iii) The rules of resource consolidation: The resources mobilized by every elementary activity are all mobilized by the aggregated activity. Application of this principle in project management poses a problem as it is obvious that the mobilization of a non-storable resource by an aggregated activity does not imply its use throughout the activity. In the context of modeling/simulation of a production process, this objection should be dropped if the proposal described above to allow the process to handle simultaneously n batches is adopted as, at any time, all the non-storable resources are simultaneously consumed by the n batches.

(iv) The flow conservation rules: The aggregation method should respect the principle of flow conservation: at cruising speed, what enters the plant (expressed in weight or otherwise…) is necessarily equal to what goes out, knowing that some output may be waste.

3.3   Definition of the Granularity Level

The risk of modeling is that of adopting too fine a level of detail. Two principles should guide this effort: define a model that is relevant for the decisions to be taken (*i*) and limit the number of model components to a minimum (*ii*).

(i) Modeling relevant for the decisions to be taken: The level of detail of each of the two M / S should be consistent with the objective of the DMS using it and enable the exchange of relevant information between the two DMSs. Note the issue of a possible decoupling between certain SC sub-systems which serves to circumscribe in time and space the scope of analysis of the consequences of certain decisions. The economic aspect will be looked at subsequently with reference to the management accounting scheme, which is linked to the second DMS. Its aim is to globally minimize overall costs. The tactical management goal of the first DMS is to maximize the margin generated by the new orders, through a contribution to the negotiation process, and, in particular through provisional production capacity, possibly subject to availability of certain raw materials. This corresponds to a wider scope and different missions which may call for the mustering of other approaches, such as mathematical scheduling, to complement the simulation approach. The level of M / S detail for management control purposes is clearly different than that geared to operational management. The complementarity of the two DMSs implies that the basic production unit used for modeling is not shared by other units of the model on which the operational management DMS is based.

(ii) Limitation of the number of components consumed in the modeling: To facilitate comprehension and maintenance, the proposed model should be as dense as possible (for a required level of detail). The M/S applications enable the design of components from basic components (processors, inventory...), which may be used as new basic components to be reused to build new components. M/S applications also enable use of parameterized routings that may be used in a particular productive subsystem to describe its use by different types of production. Finally, these enable pinpointing a single processor to describe multiple identical processors working side by side. These different possibilities shall be leveraged, taking into account the different aggregation rules proposed.

4   Examples of Application of These Principles in the Formalization of the Gathered Data

We present below the application of the principles developed in our research with examples of information gathering and processing. Figure 5 describes the configuration of OCP S.A.'s SC and offers a representation of the information gathered, processed and formalized. The primary information is made up of textual descriptions of the process and its resources, but excludes part of the implicit routing information. A flowchart with a list of additional required information is obtained. The system processes three types of flow; a zoom is proposed on one of these. The granularity level presented here is for information purposes.

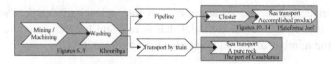

Fig. 5. Macro modeling of OCP S.A.'s Supply chain

The process documentation of an ore washing chain (text, tables, maps) supplied was quite exhaustive and we noted that the washing site comprises six identical washing chains. The documentation highlighted differences related to the type of ore transformed, in terms of system and resources used as well as flow path. The first phase of translation of this data was the creation of a detailed routing for each type of ore input, with the output ("wash concentrate", as it is called) being always the same. Figure 6 represents one of the 4 detailed routings. It features rate and average processing time. The principle of flow conservation is respected. The average processing time is approximately of 26.1; the fact that the process is a cycle complicates the calculation somewhat (the result was obtained by simulation). Figure 7 illustrates the aggregated routing derived from the detailed routing. It should be highlighted that this information is valid in cruising speed and that this is also true for the following examples. A juxtaposition of the 4 detailed routings yields figure 6, which shows a parameterized routing model. The numbered arcs of table 1 serve to identify the rate information (for example, line C_2 corresponds to information of figure 6; the possible neutralization of an arc is noted by a dash.

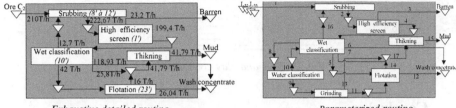

Exhaustive detailed routing   *Parameterized routing*

Fig. 6. Exhaustive and parameterized routing - C_2 ore washing

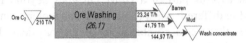

Fig. 7. Example of exhaustive aggregated routing - C_2 ore washing

Table 1. Rates (tons/hour) of the parameterized routing of figure 6

Intrant N°Flux	1	2	3	4	5	6	7	8	9	10	11	12	13	14	15	16	17
C_2	300	318	33	285	60	170	37					37		23	60	18	60
C_{31}, C_{32}, C_{33}	300	335	30	305	73	77	60	137	60	77	42	71	18	44	122	35	122

Super components may be designed through recursive construction, thus appearing as a specific category of components. On the Jorf platform, OCP S.A. owns three workshops organized as a flow shop (figure 8). The phosphoric acid and fertilizers production workshops are each represented by a component obtained through the same creation process as that used to build the sulfuric workshop component. The sulfuric and phosphoric acid productions are shown as external inventory as they may be used indifferently by the OCP S.A.'s workshops and those of Jorf's Joint Venture. The super-component is represented synthetically as in figure 9. Jorf's JVs are characterized by production units that are derived from OCP S.A.'s. They may be "grafted" onto the sulfuric acid supply, (which they do not produce) or onto the phosphoric acid supply, in which case, they only manufacture fertilizers, or onto both. The Jorf platform, therefore, is made up of the OCP S.A. production plant onto which the JV's production plants are grafted.

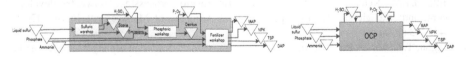

Fig. 8. Example of recursive modeling   **Fig. 9.** Example of super-component

This plug and play type configuration leads to the model described in figure 10, where the Indian JV (IMACID) (producing phosphoric acid), the Brazilian JV (BUNGE) (producing phosphoric acid and fertilizers) and a JV project under study are integrated, thus illustrating the modularity of the approach. In terms of modeling, it suffices to parameterize the OCP S.A. component to be able to describe the Jorf industrial complex with an adequate level of granularity for management purposes.

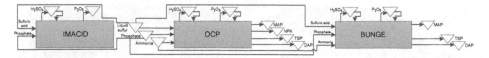

Fig. 10. *Plug and play* configuration

5   Conclusion

This paper proposes a routing-based modeling approach to a complex logistics process. This approach forms part of a BPM but goes beyond it as the knowledge gathered may be used in different ways (both for management control and operational management purposes through a combination of the physical flows, see fig 2). It therefore stands out as an innovative approach with multiple scientific and management implications. Though its relevance is clearly limited to SCs of the type under review (where DMS may be modeled on activities that are interconnected and where a single totally integrated organization exercises control), our proposed approach appears promising for a wide variety of applications: coupled modeling of "operational levels" should yield decision-making applications including physical and financial aspects; construction of a single referential to measure logistics performance of operations throughout the production process; the construction of real time **activity valuation scheme** feed into industrial management control referential. In short, there are multiple prospects for implementation of our model.

References

1. Lee, H.L., Padmanabhan, V., Whang, S.: Information distortion in a Supply Chain: The bullwhip effect. Management Science 43(4), 546–558 (1997)
2. Giard, V.: Gestion de la production et des flux. Economica (2003)
3. Hammer, M., Champy, J.: Le Reeingineering: Réinventer l'entreprise pour une amélioration spectaculaire de ses performances. Dunod (1993)
4. Giard, V., Midler, C. (eds.): Pilotages de projet et entreprises. Economica (1993)
5. Weske, M., Van der Aalst, W.M.P., Verbeek, H.M.W.: Advances in business process management. Data & Knowledge Engineering 50, 1–8 (2004)
6. Hult, G.T.M., Ketchen Jr., D.J., Slater, S.F.: Information processing, knowledge development, and strategic supply chain performance. Academy of Management Journal 47(2), 241–253 (2004)
7. Raghu, T.Z., Vinze, R.: A business process context for Knowledge Management. Decision Support Systems (2005)
8. van der Aalst, W.M.P., ter Hofstede, A.H.M., Weske, M.: Business process management: A survey. In: van der Aalst, W.M.P., ter Hofstede, A.H.M., Weske, M. (eds.) BPM 2003. LNCS, vol. 2678, pp. 1–12. Springer, Heidelberg (2003)
9. Seshasai, S., Gupta, A., Kumar, A.: An integrated and collaborative framework for business design: A knowledge engineering approach. Data & Knowledge Engineering 52, 157–179 (2005)
10. Gartner, 2014 Application Development and Maintenance Research Note M-16-8153, The BPA Market Cathes another Major Updraft, http://www.gartner.com

11. Scheer, A.W.: ARIS – Des processus de gestion au système intégré d'applications. Springer, Heidelberg (2002)
12. Madhusudan, T., Zhao, L.J., Marshall, B.: A case-based reasoning framework for workflow model management. Data & Knowledge, Engineering 50, 87–115 (2004)
13. Danese, P., Romano, P., Vinelli, A.: Managing business processes across supply networks: The role of coordination mechanisms. Journal of Purchasing & Supply Management 10, 165–177 (2004)
14. Grigoria, D., Casati, F., Castellanos, M., Dayal, U., Sayal, M., Shan, M.: Business Process Intelligence. Computers in Industry 53, 321–343 (2004)
15. Davies, I., Green, P., Rosemann, M., Indulska, M., Gallo, S.: How do practitioners use conceptual modeling in mpractice? Data & Knowledge Engineering (2005)
16. Cooper, R., Kaplan, R.: The Design of Cost Management System, 2nd edn. Prentice Hall International, London (1991)

Inspection Interval Estimation: A Fuzzy Logic Based RBI Analysis Approach

R.M. Chandima Ratnayake

Department of Mechanical and Structural Engineering and Materials Science,
University of Stavanger, Stavanger, Norway
chandima.ratnayake@uis.no

Abstract. Risk based inspection analysis (RBIA) on offshore oil and gas (O&G) production systems optimize level of in-service inspection. The potential failure risk of a system, a sub-system or a thickness measurement location (TML) of O&G production systems comprise the consequence of failure (CoF) and probability of failure (PoF). A tailor-made risk matrix supports the estimation of maximum inspection intervals. When the inspection intervals are calculated using a risk matrix, suboptimal classification tends to occur as there are no means to incorporate actual circumstances at the boundary of the input ranges or at the levels of linguistic data and risk categories. This manuscript suggests a fuzzy inference system (FIS) to overcome the aforementioned. Membership functions and the rule base development have been carried out in alignment with a tailor-made risk matrix which has been utilized by a production plant owner operator organization. A rule view and a calculation result have been demonstrated to illustrate the methodology.

Keywords: Risk based inspection analysis, production system, inspection interval, fuzzy inference system.

1 Introduction

The performance of production and/or process plants are sustained by appropriate inspection planning and scheduling [1,2]. However, in this context, it is vital to determine the optimal inspection intervals in terms of a criteria of interest [3,2]. Consequently, risk based inspection analysis (RBIA) has been accepted over the last few years as a method for prioritizing the in-service inspection of a plant as well as for estimating corresponding inspection intervals [4]. These methods have been developed nationally (e.g. American Petroleum Institute (API), a number of private organizations (particularly in the petrochemical industry), etc.) [5] and internationally (e.g. RIMAP – Risk based inspection and maintenance procedures for European industries) [6]. The importance of risk was recognized principally as an important measure in assuring system safety [7]. However, there is a fundamental challenge in the mathematical modeling of RBIA to perform optimum maintenance as a subject [8].

The mathematical modeling enables mitigating subjective judgments based on limited information and also, some of the inherent challenges present in the current

B. Grabot et al. (Eds.): APMS 2014, Part I, IFIP AICT 438, pp. 334–341, 2014.
© IFIP International Federation for Information Processing 2014

RBIA [8, 9]. Alternatively, it mitigates the significant variability and discrepancy present in the current inspection interval estimations. For instance, a report published on a case study evaluation of an onshore process plant revealed that "subjective judgments based on limited information did lead to some significant differences in inspection periods" [5]. It also revealed that although "generally, the inspection periods reflected the assessed risk", "considerable scatter was apparent in the data and some participants exhibited greater conservatism in their assessments than others" [5]. The same report suggests that "software, expert systems and expert judgment all have merits, greater integration of these elements might be beneficial" [5]. Hence, it is vital to develop expert systems to support expert judgments and alternatively to develop sophisticated software to minimize the variability present in estimating inspection periods (i.e. inspection intervals).

This manuscript proposes a fuzzy logic based expert system for estimating in-service inspection intervals [10]. The estimation of in-service inspection intervals is based on PoF, CoF and currently established values of inspection intervals with respect to different risk levels.

2   Industrial Challenge

Currently, recommended practices, standards (e.g. DNV-RP-G101), operator company procedures, etc., provide decision matrices for estimating inspection intervals (i.e. time to inspect) [11]. However, when the classifications are carried out, there is no formal mechanism to incorporate data and information at the boundaries of the risk categories (i.e. alternatively at the boundaries of the ranges and levels of linguistic data). This is mainly due to the fact that there are no means to incorporate real data (qualitative or quantitative) in a consistent manner in estimating the maximum allowable time intervals. For instance, along a boundary, the spontaneous jumps of risk classification together with recommended inspection intervals (e.g. VH to H: the recommended inspection interval changes from 6 months to 48 months) hinder realistic values depending on the estimated PoF and CoF, leading to suboptimal inspection interval estimations (see Fig. 1). Fig.1 illustrates such a risk matrix along with relevant maximum inspection intervals that have been utilized for piping RBISIA (i.e. in an operator organization which owns a production and process plant).

Due to the lack of a consistent approach, the inspection interval recommendations made are mostly confined to the PoF intervals, CoF intervals, and corresponding inspection interval values in an *ad hoc* manner dependent on the person who is involved in the analysis. Hence, it is vital to have a consistent approach to incorporate PoF, CoF and inspection intervals.

3   Methodology

In order to cater for rapid changes (in inspection interval) at the boundaries of each risk level (see Fig.1), fuzzy membership functions have been introduced for each PoF, CoF and inspection interval. The introduction of fuzzy membership functions enables the inspection interval estimation to be made more realistic. Furthermore, a fuzzy inference system (FIS) enables the mitigation of discrepancies that may occur during the risk assessment process as a result of simultaneous consideration of different PoF and CoF ranges of values for estimating maximum inspection intervals.

3.1   Risk Matrix

During the detailed risk analysis process, the static mechanical pressure systems are subject to an investigation of PoF and CoF according to the categorization presented in Fig.1. This is a 5x5 matrix, indicating levels of both PoF and CoF whilst providing five risk levels (i.e. VL, L, M, H and VH). These risk levels represent a combination of PoF and CoF based on the relevant numerical value ranges. The numerical value ranges for PoF and CoF have been retrieved from the documentation pertaining to the case study plant operator's organizations (see Fig. 1). In addition, the corresponding maximum inspection interval (in months) has been indicated within the parenthesis under each risk level.

	Category	PoF (per year)	Time to release (years)	Risk level [maximum inspection interval (MII) in months]								
PoF	VH	> 1E-2	< 3	VL (144)	L (120)	M (72)	VH (6)	VH (6)	VH (6)	VH (6)	VH (6)	VH (6)
	H	(1E-2 – 1E-3)	(3 - 7)	VL (144)	L (120)	M (72)	H (48)	H (48)	H (48)	VH (6)	VH (6)	VH (6)
	M	(1E-3 – 1E-4)	(7 - 15)	VL (144)	VL (144)	L (120)	M (72)	M (72)	H (48)	H (48)	H (48)	H (48)
	L	(1E-4 – 1E-5)	(15 - 30)	VL (144)	VL (144)	L (120)	L (120)	M (72)	M (72)	M (72)	M (72)	M (72)
	VL	< 1E-5	> 30	VL (144)	VL (144)	VL (144)	L (120)	L (120)	L (120)	M (72)	M (72)	M (72)
*Potential loss of life		Safety CoF (*PLL due to a release)		< 1E-5	(1E-4 – 1E-5)		(1E-3 – 1E-4)			(1E-2 -1E-3)		> 1E-2
**'000' Norwegian Krone		Economical CoF (**KNOK)		< 50	(50 – 500)		(500 – 5000)			(5000 – 50000)		> 50000
		CoF Category		VL	L		M			H		VH
				CoF								

Fig. 1. RBI matrix (maximum inspection interval in months)

3.2   Probability of Failure Assessment

In essence, the piping equipment is organized into corrosion groups which can contain several degradation mechanisms. Two models have mainly been used for evaluating the probability of failure (PoF) of piping equipment due to degradation: I. a susceptibility model for stainless steels; and II. a rate model for carbon steels.

Susceptibility models are used when the PoF is related to operating conditions. In this context, for a given set of conditions that are constant over time, the PoF also remains constant over time. This indicates that it is not easy to monitor the development of damage mechanisms by using inspection. Hence, actions are related to the monitoring of key process parameters, which are used as a trigger for inspection. DNV-RP-G101, Appendix A [11] provides guidance about typical materials and environmental conditions where this model is expected to be applicable and suggest values for PoF for typical conditions. For the susceptibility models there are two governing conditions required for degradation: I. wet environment; and II. temperature. The results from the monitoring of these conditions are the most important in setting the probability.

Rate models have increasing probability over the time, which makes it difficult to express as one probability value. Even though 'time to release' is itself not a probability expression, it explains the speed at which the probability increases, and therefore represents a useful profile of the probability. Hence, the development of degradation is measured by inspection. Then, the PoF is documented as an estimated 'time to release', based on the wall thickness and degradation rate on the area found to have the shortest time to release. In corrosion loops, both stagnant and varying flow conditions indicate very different estimated time to release (leak). Hence, the time to inspection is split among them in order to obtain the optimal time to inspection and this is reflected in the RBI analysis.

This manuscript provides a knowledge based engineering approach with the help of a fuzzy logic based inference system for estimating the inspection interval using a tailor-made risk matrix.

3.3   Fuzzy Logic Based Inference System

A 'pure fuzzy logic system' consists of a fuzzy rule base, which comprises a collection of fuzzy IF–THEN rules. These rules are utilized by the fuzzy inference engine to determine a mapping from fuzzy sets in the input universe of discourse $U \subset R^n$ to fuzzy sets in the output universe of discourse $V \subset R$ based on fuzzy logic principles. The fuzzy IF–THEN rules follow the form below:

$$R^{(1)} : \text{IF } x_1 \text{ is } F_1^1 \text{ and } \dots x_n \text{ is } F_n^1 \text{ THEN y is } G^1 \tag{1}$$

where F_i^j and G^j are fuzzy sets, $x = (x_1, x_2, \dots, x_n)^T \in U$ and $y \in V$ are input and output linguistic variables which belong to the input and output universes, respectively, and $j=1, 2, \dots, m$. Practical experience reveals that these fuzzy IF–THEN rules provide a convenient framework to incorporate human expert knowledge. In Eq. (1), each fuzzy IF–THEN rule defines fuzzy set $F_1^j, F_2^j \dots F_n^j => G^j$ for $i = 1, 2, \dots, n$, in the product space $U \times V$. Expert opinions and data/information retrieved from different sources are taken into the mathematical model using the aforementioned rules. The main focus is to enhance the discerning power in the risk analysis process, whilst minimizing the uncertainties that may occur in dealing with the linguistic variables of the risk levels (i.e. H, VH, VL, etc.) at the boundaries of quantitative ranges. Essentially, membership functions (MFs) are developed with experienced personnel who are familiar with the risk analysis process [12]. Then, along with a rule base, MFs provide the possibility of recycling experts' knowledge in a consistent manner.

In 1975, Mamdani built one of the first fuzzy systems which used a set of fuzzy rules supplied by experienced human operators to control a steam engine and boiler combination [13]. To date, Mamdani's approach has been successfully applied to a variety of industrial processes and consumer products [14]. Fig. 2 illustrates the work process of the proposed fuzzy inference system.

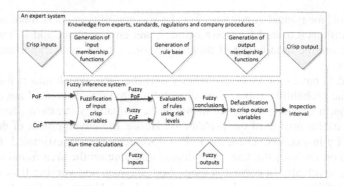

Fig. 2. An expert system for estimating maximum inspection intervals

The PoF, time to release (TTR), safety consequence of failure, which is estimated by potential loss of life (PPL) (i.e. CoF_{PPL}) and economic consequence of failure (i.e. CoF_{Econ}) have been selected as the input variables. The inspection interval has been selected as the output. These variables consist of quantitative, qualitative and judgmental (i.e. linguistic) data. For each of the aforementioned variables, there is an associated membership function, which is established with the help of data, information and expert opinion [13]. The fuzzification process aids fuzzifiying the inputs by determining the value of the membership functions corresponding to the different inputs. Furthermore, instead of restricting the user to a single, crisp, input value, this process allows an interval of values to be given, with values near the center of the interval being assumed to be 'more certain' than those near the edges, and the width of the interval indicating the amount of uncertainty present in the different input variables. The aforementioned has been achieved by associating appropriate membership functions (MF) for the input variables. Using an appropriate MF, the user has 'more confidence' that the input parameter lies relatively closer to the center of the interval than at the edges. In this study the author has incorporated triangular membership functions [15].

The fuzzy inference system (FIS) parameters were selected as follows: 'And' method with 'minimum', 'Or' method with 'maximum', 'Implication' with 'minimum', 'Aggregation' with 'maximum' and 'Defuzzification' with 'centroid' algorithm. Fuzzy rule bases were developed using the table-look-up approach (see Fig. 1). The toolbox simulator of the MATLAB (R2011a) tool was utilized to implement a fuzzy criticality ranking system [16].

4   Fuzzy Logic Based Modeling

4.1   Membership Functions for PoF

In essence, the PoF per year has been related to degradation mechanisms in the susceptibility model. At the same time, the TTR has been utilized in the rate models to express the speed at which the probability increases (note: the probability related to rate models is a variable with time). The PoF is also subjected to an analysis for both external and internal failure mechanisms. The membership functions (MFs) for inputs PoF and TTR have been developed based on data, information and expert opinions (see Fig. 3 and Fig. 4).

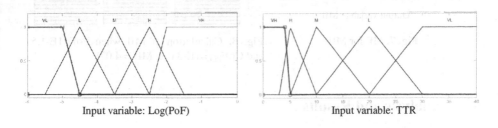

Input variable: Log(PoF)   Input variable: TTR

Fig. 3. MF for PoF   **Fig. 4.** MF for TTR

4.2   Membership Functions for CoF

The CoF$_{PPL}$ values are estimated by quantitative risk analysis. The COF$_{Econ}$ values are determined based on the inputs from relevant operation and process personnel (production loss) and from piping/vessels discipline engineers (repair costs). Fundamentally, COF$_{Econ}$ covers costs related to loss of production and costs for repair in the case of a leak. Consequence of loss of functionality is also considered as an economic loss due to reduced or lost production and/or major repair cost, not necessarily given a leak or shutdown of equipment. For instance, typical loss of functionality is mostly related to failure of internals in vessels and coolers. However, in this manuscript the values of CoF$_{PPL}$ and COF$_{Econ}$ have been retrieved from the tailor-made company specific topside inspection manual of the case study operator company. The MFs for inputs CoF$_{PPL}$ and COF$_{Econ}$ have been developed based on data, information and experts' opinions (see Fig. 5 and Fig. 6).

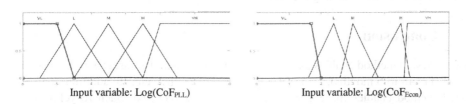

Input variable: Log(CoF$_{PLL}$)   Input variable: Log(CoF$_{Econ}$)

Fig. 5. MF for CoF$_{PPL}$ **Fig. 6.** MF for COF$_{Econ}$

The membership function for maximum inspection interval (MII) is illustrated in Fig. 7.

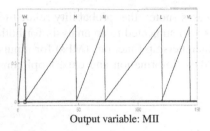

Fig. 7. MF for MII

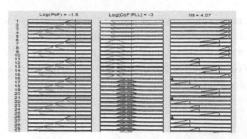

Fig. 8. Calculation of MII when PoF=1E-1.5 and CoF_{PLL}=1E-3 (i.e. MII = 4.07)

5   Analysis and Results

PoF and CoF_{PLL} have been utilized to illustrate the calculation of MII (see Fig. 8). Using the table look-up approach (see Fig.2) to estimate MII in relation to different PoF and CoF_{PLL} levels, 45 rules have been generated. Fig. 8 illustrates approximately 29 rule views and the corresponding calculation of MII (i.e. MII = 4.07) for PoF=1E-1.5 and CoF_{PLL}=1E-3.

It is possible to use a similar approach for PoF & CoF_{Econ} vs. MII; TTR & CoF_{PLL} vs. MII; and TRR & CoF_{Econ} vs. MII. All the combinations can be merged into a single workspace using the 'Simulink' facility available in 'Matlab' (MATLAB, 2011).

6   Discussion

The suggested approach enables the quantitative values in a range to be distributed in relation to their significance. For instance, the left-hand side and right-hand side of a quantitative range have more relation to the previous and following qualitative category (i.e. VH, H, M, etc.) respectively. In the suggested approach, the aforementioned relationship is consistently established with the help of MFs. Using a rule base, the different MFs are consistently interrelated incorporating the practical significance of the PoF and CoF in calculating the MII.

7   Conclusion

The suggested method enables gaps present to be mitigated, for instance in-between H to VH (i.e. 48 to 6 months), L to M (i.e. 120 to 72 months), etc. In addition, the suggested method enables the experts' knowledge to be recycled. Such recycling provides the opportunity to reduce variability present in the analysis due to human error, inconsistency of awareness, lack of experience, etc. Alternatively, the use of the suggested approach facilitates the improvement of the quality of the MII calculation process in terms of time and accuracy. However, special attention should be paid to developing the MFs.

Future research should be carried out to investigate the effect of triangular vs. Gaussian MFs on the accuracy of the MII analysis process.

References

1. Ratnayake, R.M.C., Markeset, T.: Maintaining Technical Integrity of Petroleum Flow-lines on Offshore Installations: A Decision Support System for Inspection Planning. In: Proceedings of the ASME 2010 29th International Conference on Ocean, Offshore and Arctic Engineering, OMAE2010-20035 (2010)
2. Wang, W.: A Model of Multiple Nested Inspections at Different Intervals. Computers and Operations Research 27(6), 539–558 (2000)
3. Ratnayake, R.M.C.: A Decision Model for Executing Plant Strategy: Maintaining the Technical Integrity of Petroleum Flowlines. International Journal of Decision Sciences, Risk and Management (IDJRSM) 4(1/2), 1–24 (2012)
4. Ratnayake, R.M.C., Samarakoon, S.M.S.M.K., Markeset, T.: Maintenance Integrity: Managing Flange Inspections On Aging Offshore Production Facilities. In: Proceedings of the ASME 30th International Conference on Ocean, Offshore and Arctic Engineering, ISBN: 978-0-7918-4435-9
5. Geary W.: Risk Based Inspection - A Case Study Evaluation of Onshore Process Plant, HSL/2002/20, Engineering Control Group (2002),
   http://www.hse.gov.uk/research/hsl_pdf/2002/hsl02-20.pdf
   (accessed on February 9, 2013)
6. Kauer, R., Jovanovic, A., Angelsen, S., Vage, G.: Plant Asset Management RIMAP (Risk-Based Inspection and Maintenance for European Industries) The European Approach, ASME PVP-Vol. 488, Risk and Reliability and Evaluation of Components and Machinery, PVP2004-3020, (2004), http://www.tuvreales-tate.com/uploads/
   images/1134986959023229878962/ASME-RIMAP_SanDie-go2004.pdf
   (accessed on September 2, 2013)
7. Brown, S.J., May, I.L.: Risk-based Hazardous Protection and Prevention by Inspection and Maintenance. Trans. ASME Journal of Pressure Vessel Technology 122(3), 362–367 (2003)
8. Scarf, P.A.: On the Application of Mathematical Models in Maintenance. European Journal of Operational Research 99(3), 493–506 (1997)
9. Ratnayake, R.M.C.: Utilization of Piping Inspection Data for Continuous Improvement: A Methodology to Visualize Coverage and Finding Rates. In: Proceedings of the 32nd International Conference on Ocean, Offshore and Arctic Engineering (OMAE 2013), OMAE 2013-10025 (2013)
10. Ratnayake, R.M.C.: Plant Systems and Equipment Maintenance: Use of Fuzzy Logic for Criticality Assessment in NORSOK Standard Z-008. In: Proceedings of the IEEE International Conference on Industrial Engineering and Engineering Management (IEEM) (2013)
11. DNV-RP-G101: Risk Based Inspection of Offshore Topsides Static Mechanical Equipment, Det Norske Veritas (2010)
12. Lapa, C.M.F., Guimaraes, A.C.F.: Effect Analysis Fuzzy Inference System in Nuclear Problems using Approximate Reasoning. Annals of Nuclear Energy 31(107), 107–115 (2004)
13. Mamdani, E.H., Assilian, S.: An Experiment in Linguistic Synthesis with a Fuzzy Logic Controller. International Journal of Man-Machine Studies 7(1), 1–13 (1975)
14. Wang, L.X.: Adaptive Fuzzy Systems and Control—Design and Stability Analysis. University of California at Berkeley, PTR Prentice Hall (1993)
15. Juang, Y.T., Changa, Y.T., Huangb, C.P.: Design of Fuzzy PID Controllers using Modified Triangular Membership Functions. Information Sciences 178(5), 1325–1333 (2008)
16. MATLAB: MATLAB 7.12.0 (R2011a): Fuzzy Logic Toolbox, 1984-2011 The MathWorks, Inc. (2011)

Knowledge-Based Planning
and Scheduling

Multi-agent Approach for Personnel Scheduling and Rescheduling in Assembly Centers

M. Sabar

Groupe ISCAE: Institut supérieur de commerce et d'administration des entreprises
Km 9,500 Route de Nouasseur BP. 8114 - Casablanca Oasis, Casablanca, Maroc
msabar@groupeiscae.com

Abstract. This article presents a multi-agent based algorithm for personnel scheduling and rescheduling in the dynamic environment of a paced multi-product assembly center. Our purpose is, on the one hand, to elaborate daily assignment of employees to workstations to minimize the operational costs as well as the personnel dissatisfactions and, on the other hand, to generate an alternative planning when the first solution has to be rescheduled due to disturbances related to operators' absenteeism. The proposed approach considers the individual competencies, mobility and preferences of each employee, as well as the personnel and competency requirements associated with each assembly activity given both the current master assembly schedule and the line balancing for each product. To benchmark the performance of the multi-agent approach, we use solutions obtained through a simulated annealing algorithm. Experimental results show that our multi-agent approach can produce high-quality and efficient solutions in a short computational time.

Keywords: Personnel shift scheduling, Multi-agent systems, Coalition, Kernel stability, Cross-training, Flexible assembly lines.

1   Introduction

Personnel scheduling problems are particular cases of resource allocation problems (Hao et al. 2004). They aim to construct a working timetable for each employee by defining start time periods, duration of work, break intervals, as well as the tasks to be fulfilled. The objective is for the timetable to optimize one or several criteria while respecting a set of constraints such as labor requirements, individual preferences, or specific competencies (Thompson, 1995; Ernst et al. 2004). Typical classifications of personnel scheduling problems tend to separate problems in three categories (Ernst et al. 2004): shift, days-off and tour scheduling problems.

In this article, the focus is on shift-scheduling problems in a large assembly line environment where the pace setting takt time between individual product units is pre-set, equal to at least a few minutes. We consider an assembly line with multiple workstations responsible to sequentially assemble different product-models. Each assembly task requires one or several employees with a specific competency profile.

B. Grabot et al. (Eds.): APMS 2014, Part I, IFIP AICT 438, pp. 345–354, 2014.

In addition, concerning the manpower pool, we take into account individual competencies, mobility and preferences. Specifically, we consider that:

- Each worker has a specific degree of cross-training, enabling them to carry one or several types of assembly activities during a work shift.
- Workers are allowed to move between workstations in order to fulfill specific assembly activities according to the product assembly schedule.
- Workers can be assigned to secondary activities, which can be either productive, administrative or learning, when the employees are not assigned to an assembly workstation.
- Each worker has a set of individual preferences related to (1) the shift duration, (2) the assignable activities and (3) the number of transfers between activities.

Due to product changeovers and the specific manpower competency requirements associated with each product at each station, there are often large waves of personnel moves among stations. This causes significant disruptions to operations, deterring the overall productivity of the line and causing dissatisfactions among the personnel (Sabar et al. 2008, Sabar et al. 2012). Also, this paper considers that if a disturbance related to operators' absenteeism occurs at a given time period, the variables representing the personnel' scheduling up to this period are fixed to the matching values from the original plan and, the disturbance' parameters are considered for the remaining time periods. Then, a new rescheduling has to be performed on the global level through complete regeneration of personnel schedule. Concerning the operators' absence, we distinguish full absenteeism (operator absents from work during the entire shift) from partial absenteeism (operator arriving late to work or leaving work during working hours due to sickness or personal affairs). In both cases, the rescheduling aims to generate a new allocation plan which replaces absent operators by transferring activities to the available and on-call workers.

In this context, we present a multi-agent based approach that aims to tackle the complexity of our targeted personnel scheduling / rescheduling problem through distributed problem-solving. The proposed approach is based on cooperation among several rational agents which encapsulate individual competencies and preferences of employees. In this approach, the agents negotiate to form coalitions which allow them to improve their individual schedules, and consequently to iteratively improve the global solution of personnel scheduling problem. To benchmark the performance of the multi-agent approach, we use solutions obtained through a simulated annealing approach.

The remainder of the article is organized as follows. Section 2 defines multi-agent settings and presents in detail the multi-agent architecture and principles retained to sustain our scheduling/rescheduling approach. Section 3 presents the formal description of the proposed multi-agent approach. The experimental setup and results are discussed in section 4. Finally, section 5 presents conclusive remarks.

2   Multi-agent Architecture Proposed for Personnel Scheduling and Rescheduling Problem

In this research, the real environment to model is an assembly line system. It is made up of several workstations which constantly require a mix of skilled employees. In order to model such a system, we developed a multi-agent system composed of heterogeneous and autonomous agents, which cooperate with one another to produce a personnel schedule. Each agent represents a physical entity of the assembly system, or encapsulates a planning and decision making function. Our multi-agent system includes four categories of autonomous agents: a production-agent; a station-agent for each workstation; a coordinating agent; and an employee-agent representing each employee. These agents are autonomous, rational and able to communicate with each other.

(1) Production-agent: elaborates and manages the production planning. It determines the dynamic sequence and quantity of the product models to be assembled. The production plan is then communicated to stations-agents. The Production agent uses a set of priority rules to decide which job orders are to be planned. Its objective is to optimize criteria such as the maximization of the workstations' utilization or the minimization of delays. In this article, we consider that the production planning decisions are independent of the influence of human resources management.

(2) Station-agent: manages and controls the assembly activities of a workstation. Based on the production planning, this agent defines the needs of the workstation concerning number of employees and their required competencies, which it sends to the coordinator-agent.

(3) Coordinator-agent: is responsible for coordinating the employee-agents. First, it elaborates an initial solution of personnel scheduling. Then, it takes the active role of mediator in the negotiation process among the employee-agents who will try to improve their initial work plans through activities swapping.

(4) Employee-agent: represents the individual interests of an employee. It encapsulates the state as well as the main characteristics of the matching employee, in particular his competencies, his preferences and his allocation history. These agents can negotiate and cooperate among them in order to maximize their profit and their satisfaction. In the proposed architecture, they are coordinated by the coordinator-agent which plays a mediator's role.

In our approach, the personnel scheduling process is supported by the Coordinator-agent and the Employee-agents. In the first step, the coordinator-agent uses priority rules to produce an initial solution taking into account employees 'needs and competencies. Next, the initial work plan of each employee is transmitted to the corresponding Employee-agent. Considering that the initial solution is often mediocre quality in terms of total cost and employees' satisfaction, we use coalitions to improve the performance of the schedule. The issue of coalition formation has been studied in the game theory literature in the context of cooperative N-person games (Rapoport, 1970).

In our approach, coalitions are formed among Employee-agents who negotiate a potential mutual agreement on what activities to swap in order to increase their individual profits and ultimately improve the global personnel scheduling solution. Each Employee-agent is rational and self-interested. It has interest in forming coalitions which releases him from less satisfying assembly activities and/or allows him to get a more satisfying set of activities. The proposed coalition approach is round based. In each round at most one coalition is formed. Each round involves two phases:

- Phase 1 aims to generate a stable coalitional configuration, which consists of a partition of the set of employee-agents into disjoint stable coalitions. To maintain polynomial complexity of the formation process, we restrict our research on coalitions of size two. At the beginning of each round, each employee-agent contacts other employee-agents with whom it has common competencies. It seeks to identify whether there are assembly activities that can be swapped and sends coalition offers. In the scheduling case, all activities' exchange possibilities are tested. However, in the rescheduling case, only activities which are not carried out yet are taken into consideration. A coalition offer contains the list of tasks that may be switched, and the corresponding payoff. For each received coalition-offer by an employee-agent, it uses the Kernel stability concept (Davis and Maschler, 1965) to test the coalition equilibrium. The Kernel is based on the idea that the members of a coalition should be in an equilibrium concerning their power to object to each other's payoff. If an employee-agent finds that it can outweigh the other according to the initial payoff, it uses the Transfer Scheme proposed in Streans (1968) to demand a side payments transfer. Using a stable payoff distribution, the employee-agents can compare different coalition structures. In fact, each employee-agent compares the payoff of all received proposals. It chooses the coalition which is most beneficial for the employee it represents (i.e. the one that maximizes his utility function), and informs the Coordinator-agent about the accepted coalitions.

- Phase 2 proceeds to select the coalition to enact. Once all accepted coalitions have been received by the Coordinator-agent, it randomly selects a coalition among the group of coalitions that have a bilateral acceptance of the two members. In a rescheduling case, the priority is given to a coalition among those which disengage completely or partially an agent-employee of his activities during his absence periods. Next, the Coordinator-agent informs the two coalition's members about the agreement. These two agents complete the process by exchanging tasks. Based on the new task distribution, the employee-agents start a new round of coalition formation.

These two phases are structured within the framework of an anytime algorithm. Such a type of algorithm improves gradually the quality of its solution as computation time increases and can be interrupted at any time during computation to provide a solution (Russell & Zilberstein, 1991).

3   Multi-agent Approach for Personnel Scheduling and Rescheduling

In this section, we formally present our multi-agent approach for personnel scheduling. We describe on one hand the algorithm for initial solution generation, and on the other hand, sequentially the algorithm to generate coalitions with K-stable payoff distributions and the algorithm for coalition selection. It should be noted that whenever the process of solution improvement by coalition formation is stopped, it produces the best currently available solution. This process is generally interrupted when the desired state is reached or when having to answer an immediate need of assembly lines about some employee's allocation, for example when an employee becomes out-of-kilter.

The initial solution of employee allocation is performed at the coordinator-agent level based on a priority dispatching rule. Using the production planning, each station-agent has a view of local requirements concerning the number of employees and their competency profile. The used dispatching rule involves the selection, period by period, of the workstation with the least extra number of employees that have the required competency profile. At a given period, the extra number of employees is equal to the difference between the number of available employees and the required number of employees. For each selected workstation, the coordinator-agent assigns the least cross-trained employee available among those who have the required competency profile.

At the end of the first stage, each employee-agent $i \in N = \{1,...,n\}$ possesses a vector of activities to perform $\rho^i = [a^i_{nm,0},...,a^i_{kl,t}]$, where $a^i_{kl,t}$ is the activity k to execute on station l in the period t by the employee-agent i. To evaluate the utility of each employee-agent $i \in N = \{1,...,n\}$, we use a linear function: $V_i(\rho^i) = S - f_i(\rho^i)$, where S is a constant which corresponds to an initial amount allocated to each employee-agent, it represents an artificial gain that each employee earns if it succeeds to totally release himself from duty. f_i is an increasing linear function of work duration and dissatisfaction of employee i . In fact, $f_i = F1 + F2 + F3 + F4 + F5 + F6 + F7 + F8$, where[1] :

- $F1$: Salary cost of employee i ;
- $F2$: Activity assignment cost of employee i;
- $F3$: Idleness penalty cost of employee;
- $F4$: Cost savings generated by the assignment of employee i to secondary activities;
- $F5$: Transfer cost of employee i ;
- $F6$: Penalty cost associated to the deviation from the number of transfers preferred by employee i ;
- $F7$: Penalty cost associated to the deviation from the total work duration preferred by employee i ;
- $F8$: Penalty cost (positive or negative) associated to the dissatisfaction or satisfaction of employee i for its assignment to a set of activities.

---

[1] For more details concerning the function f_i , see Sabar et al. 2008.

The algorithm to generate coalitions with K-stable payoff distributions (**Phase 1**) is as follows:

Each agent-employee i

1. Maintains a register concerning the references of the employee-agents with whom it can exchange certain activities.
2. For each employee-agent j indexed on its register, i tests all possible permutations of activities and calculates the value of each potential coalition $v(C_{ij}) = V_i(\rho_{new}^i) + V_j(\rho_{new}^j)$. In case of several permutation possibilities with an agent j, i retains the one which generates the highest coalition value. In rescheduling case, the coalitions are based on the exchange of the activities which are not carried out yet (i.e. activities planned between the periods of absence' notification and the shift-end). Activities carried out are considered fixed and cannot be changed. However, they are taken into account in assessing the total cost of personnel staff scheduling.
3. If $v(C_{ij}) \geq V_i(\rho^i) + V_j(\rho^j)$, then i sends a coalition proposal PR_{ij} to j. The proposal encapsulates the set of activities to be permuted; the coalition value $v(C_{ij})$ and the initial proposed payoff $u_j = V_j(\rho^j) + \dfrac{v(C_{ij}) - (V_i(\rho^i) + V_j(\rho^j))}{2}$ (i.e. Dividing the profit generated by the coalition into two equal parts).
4. Receive coalition proposals from the other employees-agents.
5. Evaluate the received coalition proposals:
   (a) Use the Kernel concept to test the proposals coalitions equilibrium;
   (b) If employee-agent i dominates any other agent, it uses the Streans' transfer scheme to evaluate the side-payment demand and informs the concerned agent.
6. For each instable coalition, send or receive a part of payoff equal to the side-payment demand.

The utility function V_i is designed so as to generate more profit for an employee who succeeds to release himself from duty or acquire a set of activities which creates a higher satisfaction.

Given a pair of employee-agents (i, j) with the activity vectors ρ^i and ρ^j, we define the potential value of the coalition $C_{i,j}$ as: $v(C_{i,j}) = V_i(\rho_{new}^i) + V_j(\rho_{new}^j)$, where ρ_{new}^i and ρ_{new}^j are the new activity vectors of i and j if they agree to form the coalition by permuting a part of their initial activities. To accept a coalition, the payoff of each agent after the redistribution of the coalition value must be at least equal to its initial self-value, i.e. $v(C_{ij}) = u_i + u_j$; $u_i \geq V_i(\rho^i)$ and $u_j \geq V_j(\rho^j)$.

Each employee-agent uses the Kernel concept to evaluate the offered payoff and to assess its power to object to its partner's payoff. A general strategy used by employee-agents for coalition formation and payoff distribution is defined as follows.

3.1. Initialization of the regression coefficient : $\eta = 1$

3.2. Each employee agent $i \in \{1,...,n\}$:

- Elaborates the list $\Lambda_{i,\eta}$ of K-stable coalitions that give him a payoff at least equal to $\eta \times u_{i,\max}$;

- Sends the list to the coordinator-agent.

3.3. Based on all the received lists, the coordinator-agent selects the set BC of coalitions which have a bilaterally acceptance from the two members i.e. the coalitions $C_{ij} \mid (C_{ij} \in \Lambda_{i\eta}) \wedge (C_{ij} \in \Lambda_{j\eta});\quad \forall i, j \in \{1,...,n\}$. At this level, there are two possible scenarios :

- $BC \neq \phi$: several coalitions have a bilaterally acceptance of their two members:
  - In scheduling cases, the Coordinator-agent randomly selects a coalition from BC. In rescheduling cases, it selects in priority a coalition among those which release completely or partially an agent-employee of duties during his absence periods. Then, informs the two coalition's members about the agreement.
  - These two agents finalize the process by exchanging tasks. Based on the new tasks distribution, the employee-agents start a new round of coalition formation (return to Stage 2).
- $BC = \phi$: no consensus is reached, then the regression coefficient will be decreased $\eta \leftarrow \eta - \varepsilon$:
  - If $\eta \geq 0$ return to 3.2.
  - If $\eta < 0$ the global solution has reached a local optimum (i.e. given the current activities distribution, employee-agents have no benefit by forming coalitions), then we introduce an artifice for fictitious payoffs distribution. This artifice randomly generates and attributes factitious profits to a certain number of employee-agents in such manners as to incite them to form coalitions. Return to stage 2 in order to generate new K-stable coalitions.

Fig. 1. Algorithm for coalition selection (Phase 2)

At the end of this stage, we obtain a set of potential coalitions with stable payoff distributions. Each employee-agent may have several offers of coalitions with various profits. Since each employee-agent i is rational, it tries to form the coalition, among all possibilities, in which it earns the greatest payoff $u_{i,\max}$. However, if an agent i chooses to form a coalition with the agent j, nothing guarantees that agent j will accept because j may earn more by forming another coalition with a third agent k . In case of conflicts of interest between employees-agents, we introduce a regression function f_{reg} which allows agents to reduce the value of their aimed payoff in order to reach a consensus. For an employee-agent i , this function is defined as $f_{reg}(i,\eta): u_{i,\max} \to \eta \times u_{i,\max}$, where $\eta \in [0,1]$ represents the rate of payoff's decreasing. Considering the reduced payoff, each employee-agent $i \in \{1,...,n\}$ chooses among its K-stable coalitions those which give him a payoff at least equal to $\eta \times u_{i,\max}$. After that, it communicates the results to the coordinator-agent which randomly selects a coalition among the group of coalitions that have a bilaterally acceptance of the two members. The detailed procedure for coalition's selection is defined as detailed on Figure 1.

4   Computational Experiments

In this section, we present experimental results concerning several shift scheduling problems in the context of a paced multi-product assembly center. A set of five problems is conducted to test the performance of the proposed multi-agent approach. For each problem, the production planning is spread out over 60* 9-hour shift. Experiments have been performed in an assembly line consisting of 40 workstations. The takt time between two product units is preset equal to 15 minutes. For each workstation, the employee requirements in a given period are determined according to the assembly activities to be fulfilled on the scheduled product according to the preset line balancing. Concerning the staff, we consider that the offer and the demand per shift for employees vary between 150 and 200 employees. The daily absenteeism rate varies according to the shift number, from a minimum of 1% to a maximum of 5% of total employees.

To evaluate the quality and the efficiency of the proposed multi-agent approach, we report solutions obtained on the same problems through the simulated annealing approach (SA). A detailed description of the proposed simulated annealing algorithm and its use for resolution of personnel scheduling problems can be found in (Sabar 2008, Sabar et al. 2012). For each shift s, we report the cumulated deviation CD_s between the best solutions founded by these two approaches for a computation time equal to 10 minutes for scheduling and 3 minutes if rescheduling is required.

$$CD_s = \frac{MAS \text{ cumulated cost at } (s) - SA \text{ cumulated cost at } (s)}{SA \text{ cumulated cost at } (s)}.$$

Figure 2 exhibits the evolution of this deviation between SMA and SA results. It shows clearly that for the five test problems the proposed SMA approach leads to high quality solutions in comparison with the SA approach. It is interesting to observe that SMA systematically outperforms SA for all shift results. Indeed, we notice that the deviations of the SMA approach solutions from SA range between -4.2 % and -0.7 %. These results demonstrate that the proposed multi-agent approach for personnel scheduling is effective and can generate high-quality solutions fast and reliably.

5   Conclusion

In this article, we developed a multi-agent approach for the personnel scheduling/rescheduling problem in the context of a paced multi-product assembly center.

The proposed approach is based on cooperation among several rational agents which encapsulate individual competencies and preferences of workers. The experiments we have performed demonstrate that the multi-agent approach can produce high-quality and efficient solutions in comparison with simulated annealing approach.

Our future research will focus on the impact of dynamic random events such as product quality issues on the line, and probabilistic operation times potentially depending on the operator's skill level. In addition, we will investigate the impact of modeling employee preferences on the quality of the scheduling solutions obtained.

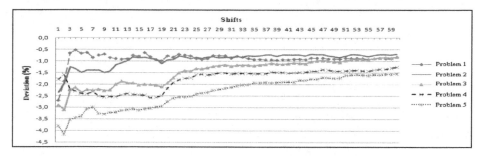

Fig. 2. Deviation between MAS and SA results

References

1. Schuldt, A.: Multiagent coordination enabling autonomous logistics. Springer, Berlin (2011)
2. Davis, M., Maschler, M.: The Kernel of a cooperative game. Naval Research Logistics Quarterly 12, 223–259 (1965)
3. Ernst, A., Jiang, H., Krishnamoorthy, M., Sier, D.: Staff Scheduling and Rostering, A review of applications, methods and models. European Journal of Operational Research 153, 3–27 (2004)
4. Hao, G., Lai, K.K., Tan, M.: A Neural Network Application in Personnel Scheduling. Annals of Operations Research 128, 65–90 (2004)
5. Leitão, P., Barbosa, J., Trentesaux, D.: Bio-inspired Multi-Agent Systems for Reconfigurable Manufacturing Systems. Engineering Applications of Artificial Intelligence 25, 934–944 (2012)
6. Oliveira, E., Fischer, K., Stepankova, O.: Multi-agent systems: Which research for which applications. Robotics and Autonomous Systems 27, 91–106 (1999)
7. Rapoport, A.: N-person game theory: concepts and applications. University of Michigan Press (1970)
8. Russell, S.J., Zilberstein, S.: Composing Real-Time Systems. In: Proceedings of the Twelfth International Conference on Artificial Intelligence, pp. 212–217 (1991)
9. Sabar, M., Montreuil, B., Frayret, J.-M.: Competency and preference based personnel scheduling in large assembly lines. International Journal of Computer Integrated Manufacturing 21, 468–479 (2008)
10. Sabar, M.: A multi-agent based approach for personnel scheduling in assembly centers, Doctoral Thesis, Université Laval, Canada (2008)

11. Sabar, M., Montreuil, B., Frayret, J.-M.: An agent-based algorithm for personnel shift-scheduling and rescheduling in flexible assembly lines. Journal of Intelligent Manufacturin 23(6), 2623–2634 (2012)
12. Stearns, R.E.: Convergent Transfer Schemes for N-Person Games. Transactions of the American Mathematical Society 134, 449–459 (1968)
13. Thompson, G.M.: Improved implicit optimal modeling of the labor shift scheduling problem. Management Science 41, 595–607 (1995)
14. Wooldridge, M.: An Introduction to Multi-agent Systems. Published by John Wiley & Sons, Chichester (2002)

Designing Interdisciplinary Scheduling Decision Support Systems in Small-Sized SME Environments: The i-DESME Framework

Christos Dimopoulos[1,*] and Julien Cegarra[2]

[1] EUC Research Center, Nicosia, Cyprus
c.dimopoulos@euc.ac.cy
[2] University of Toulouse, Toulouse, France
julien.cegarra@univ-jfc.fr

Abstract. This paper introduces i-DESME, an interdisciplinary framework for the design of IT scheduling Decision Support Systems in small-sized SME industrial environments. The proposed framework adopts a structured software engineering design approach, which has been suitably modified in order to explicitly identify and model the interdisciplinary characteristics that dictate the implementation of scheduling processes within an SME industrial environment. The framework aims to help practitioners design support systems which are not only effective, but are also being trusted and adopted for use by human schedulers. An overview of the framework's application within the environment of a typical micro-sized food manufacturing company is provided.

Keywords: Scheduling, Decision Support Systems, Function Allocation, Interdisciplinary Design, Case Studies.

1 Introduction and Background

The implementation of scheduling processes in realistic industrial environments consists of a large number of interpersonal, interdepartmental tasks, which are carried out dynamically by a human scheduler (or a team of human schedulers) in cooperation with other human or non-human 'actors', including IT systems [1]. These actors exchange information in various formats (electronic, printed, hand-written, verbal), in a manner which is not necessarily standardised or coordinated. In addition, this implementation is subject to various organisational, cognitive, psychological, and sociological characteristics, which cannot be readily incorporated within a typical mathematical process model.

Since 1992, when Kerr published his seminal article on a failed implementation of a production scheduling system [2], the research community about human and organizational factors in scheduling paved the way for successful implementations of interdisciplinary DSS. More precisely, during the last decades a considerable number of researchers have questioned the usability of scheduling algorithms and the level of trust placed to off-the-shelf IT scheduling decision support systems (DSS) within

B. Grabot et al. (Eds.): APMS 2014, Part I, IFIP AICT 438, pp. 355–362, 2014.
© IFIP International Federation for Information Processing 2014

realistic industrial environments. In addition, IT decision support is rarely provided to human schedulers in micro and small-sized SME (Small to Medium Enterprises) industrial environments, even though SMEs (and especially micro-sized SMEs) constitute a large part of the financial basis of the industrialised world. As a result, significant research efforts in the area of scheduling are currently devoted to the investigation of the following questions:

i. *Can we design scheduling DSS which provide effective support to human schedulers in realistic industrial environments? (including micro and small-sized environments)*

ii. *Can we design scheduling DSS which are adopted and trusted by human schedulers during the implementation of scheduling tasks?*

iii. *Can we design scheduling DSS which efficiently exploit the operation of production research algorithms for the benefit of the human scheduler?*

Various approaches have been suggested for improving the efficiency, usability and adaptability of scheduling DSS in realistic industrial environments. However, a structured software development framework for their implementation which simultaneously addresses the previous considerations is considered as scientifically challenging [3] and has yet to be proposed. The research presented in this paper provides a contribution towards this goal by introducing i-DESME (i-nterdisciplinary DEsign for SMEs), a structured interdisciplinary framework for the design of scheduling DSS in micro and small-sized SME manufacturing environments. The intuition behind the development of the i-DESME framework has its origins in the works of [1] and [4,5,6,7].

The remainder of this paper is organised as follows: The activities of the proposed i-DESME framework are described in detail in Section 2. The application of the i-DESME framework for the case of a typical micro-sized manufacturing SME is overviewed in Section 3. Finally, the conclusions of this research effort are discussed in Section 4 of the paper.

2   The i-DESME Framework

2.1   Overview

The i-DESME design framework introduces a case-based structured approach to the design of scheduling DSS in micro and small-sized SME industrial environments. The main features of the i-DESME framework are the following:

i. Structured, modelled-driven software engineering approach to system development.

ii. Interdisciplinary modelling and analysis of the scheduling environment (organisational, technological and cognitive modelling).

iii. Function allocation between the support system and the human scheduler.

iv. Interdisciplinary evaluation of the suitability of scheduling algorithms for the support of specific scheduling tasks / subtasks.

v. Modelled-driven specification of the system's functional, non-functional and data requirements

vi. Modelled-driven specification of the system's architecture

The main operational phases and the information flow of the i-DESME framework are presented in figure 1.

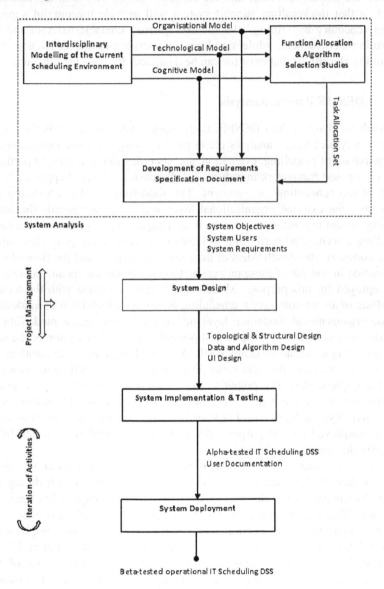

Fig. 1. Overview of the i-DESME framework

Standardised software engineering phases are defined for the development of the scheduling DSS. These phases have been suitably modified and enhanced in order to explicitly consider the interdisciplinary characteristics of the scheduling environment, the presence of the human scheduler, the possible algorithms which can provide support on the implementation of scheduling subtasks, and the allocation of functions between the human scheduler and the support system. The intuition behind this approach is that the resulting support system will provide meaningful support to the human scheduler by "fitting" the interdisciplinary characteristics of the particular scheduling environment, while simultaneously exploiting the efficiency of research scheduling algorithms that exist (or can be designed) for her / his scheduling tasks.

2.2   i-DESME Phases: Analysis

The analysis phase of the i-DESME framework covers and extends the conventional scope of a typical SDLC analysis phase by suggesting the implementation of a comprehensive set of modelling, evaluation, and specification activities. In particular:

The proposed framework introduces a 3-dimensional layered approach to the modelling of the scheduling environment. The modelling of the scheduling processes starts from the external organisational layer and progress towards the inner layers utilising modelling information which is progressively generated. Organisational modelling activities primarily aim to identify the scheduling processes implemented by the company, the stakeholders of their implementation, and the flow of scheduling information in and out of these processes. Organisational charts and context diagrams are employed for this purpose. Modelling activities continue with the technological modelling of all the company's scheduling processes which have been identified during the organisational modelling layer activities. Technological modelling activities provide an unambiguous (to the largest possible extend) description of the scheduling processes' implementation using UML Activity Diagrams, mathematical programming models, and data flow diagrams. The framework's modelling activities conclude with the implementation of cognitive modelling activities, which provide a detailed examination of the company's scheduling processes from the human scheduler's perspective. Typical hierarchical task analysis and cognitive task analysis methodologies are employed for this purpose. An analytical description of i-DESME's modelling activities can be found in [8].

At the culmination of the interdisciplinary modelling activities an interdisciplinary representation of the current ('as-is') implementation of the scheduling processes within the environment of the micro / small-sized SME company has been generated. This modelling information provides the basis for the implementation of function allocation and algorithm selection studies on the future ('to-be') implementation of the scheduling processes based on the suggestions of van Wezel et al. [9]. The proposed studies initially evaluate the interdisciplinary characteristics of the tasks which are carried out by the decision maker during the current implementation of the scheduling processes. This evaluation leads to a description of the suggested control mode for the future ('to-be') implementation of these tasks. In addition, scheduling algorithms which 'fit' the characteristics of scheduling tasks are identified and their interdisciplinary characteristics are evaluated. The result of the function allocation / algorithm selection studies is a task allocation set for the future implementation of scheduling processes.

The final stage of the analysis phase shifts the focus of the framework's efforts from the current ('as-is'), to the future ('to-be') implementation of the scheduling processes within the micro / small-sized SME industrial environment. This is achieved through the iterative development of the software requirements specification document which describes unambiguously how the future implementation of these processes will take place with the aid of the scheduling DSS. The specification is generated by explicitly considering the interdisciplinary modelling characteristics of the particular micro / small-sized industrial environment. The finalized requirements specification document describes the new system's objectives, potential benefits, as well as its anticipated users and stakeholders. In addition, it specifies the system's functional (through UML Use Case Diagrams) and non-functional requirements. A detailed description of i-DESME's requirements specification process can be found in [10].

2.3   i-DESME Phases: Design

The requirements specification document provides the basis for the development of the design specification of the scheduling DSS. The design specification document is developed in an iterative way, using draft artifacts as communication tools between the system developers, the system analysts and the system stakeholders. This specification focuses on generating an architectural representation of the scheduling DSS which will be able to offer the services outlined in the requirements specification document. In particular, it specifies the topological, structural, algorithmic, data and user interface (UI) parameters of the system to be implemented.

2.4   i-DESME Phases: System Implementation and Testing

The specification of the support system's requirements and architecture provide the necessary input for the initiation of the framework's implementation and testing phase. Coding and documentation activities lead to the construction of the system's operational software version which will be deployed within the industrial environment of the micro / small-sized SME company. While coding activities do not directly benefit from the interdisciplinary artifacts of the proposed framework, the development of the user documentation is founded on the support system's analytic use-case descriptions, as these are outlined in the requirements specification document. The same descriptions provide the basis for the validation and verification of the DSS's functional and non-functional specifications, through the implementation of alpha-testing activities.

2.5   i-DESME Phases: Deployment

The smooth deployment of the scheduling support system within the company's environment is a crucial step towards its successful adoption by the human scheduler. The generation of trust (from the human scheduler's point of view) requires a gradual introduction of its functions within the manufacturing environment. The i-DESME framework employs the topology diagram design model for the installation and deployment of the support system within the environment. The system functions are subsequently beta-tested in off-line mode by the human scheduler using realistic production data from past production periods and the corresponding use-case descriptions. After the implementation of improvements and corrections based on the results of the beta-testing process, the scheduling DSS is ready to enter its first operational phase in the company's environment.

3   The i-DESME Case-Study

The i-DESME framework was applied in the industrial environment of a company which specialises in the manufacturing of food products. The target company was a family-run micro-sized SME, which has been in operation since the beginning of the 20th century. The company produces various types of traditional sweets in a purpose-built manufacturing facility. The company employs 10 workers for the implementation of its manufacturing processes.

The presentation of the full case study results is not possible within the size constraints of this paper; however, it is interesting to note some of findings of the interdisciplinary modelling process which can be considered typical for the scheduling environment of a micro-sized industrial SME. In particular:

- No long-term scheduling processes (aggregate production planning, material requirements planning) are implemented by the company in an organised manner. Raw materials are ordered and stored in adequate quantities whenever they are available, due to the peculiarities of the local supply chain
- The principal actor during the implementation of scheduling processes is the company's CEO, who is also responsible for the implementation of most other company's business processes, facing an extremely heavy daily cognitive load
- The CEO does not employ any form of IT support for decision-making purposes.
- All scheduling information is communicated on a hand-written, non-standardised format
- The company has not developed any cost models for the implementation of its manufacturing processes
- The human scheduler (the company's CEO) utilises information during the implementation of the scheduling processes which is not readily available in a 'visible' format. The scheduler calculates this information cognitively, based on his experience

A scheduling DSS was subsequently specified, based on the previous findings. The developers and the system stakeholders agreed on a support specification with clearly articulated objectives and anticipated benefits. In particular, the aim of the new system would be to help the human scheduler make informed, reliable scheduling decisions, with a lower cognitive load, through the interactive generation and evaluation of potential scheduling solutions. The system would provide an electronic repository of all scheduling information, allowing the long-term improvement of scheduling processes. In this way, the system would offer effective support to the human scheduler for the future ('to-be') implementation of scheduling processes, while 'fitting' the characteristics of his environment and exploiting the efficiency of scheduling algorithms.

The specification of the support system's requirements provided the necessary input for the realisation of the system through the implementation of the framework's subsequent phases, namely the design, system implementation and testing phases. The final phase of i-DESME's framework concerned the deployment of the support system within the company's scheduling environment. The system was beta-tested for a limited amount of time using realistic scheduling information, operating in parallel with the existing manual system of the scheduling processes' implementation. The IT scheduling DSS has since become an integral part of the implementation of the scheduling processes within the company's environment. From a usability perspective, this stresses the usefulness of the proposed approach in order to design an adopted DSS.

It should be noted that a proper scientific evaluation of the applicability and benefits of the proposed framework will require its application on multiple industrial environments of various types and sizes, as well as the long-term operation of the developed support systems within these environments. However, the implementation of the IT scheduling decision support system for the case of a typical micro-sized SME company provides encouraging indications on the usefulness of the proposed approach in similar environments especially in relationship to the three highlighted questions, as well as valuable information for the improvement of its suggested activities in future applications.

4   Conclusions

While there are many publications about scheduling DSS, they tend to focus on the mechanical process of generating a schedule and are too limited to provide comprehensive solutions to real-world problems [4]. Indeed standardized software engineering phases have already been separately adapted for the interdisciplinary development of scheduling DSS (e.g., [5] for interface design, [9] for function allocation). But an integrated framework had yet to be proposed and unrolled in a realistic industrial environment. In this way, the i-DESME framework introduces a structured interdisciplinary model-driven approach to the development of scheduling Decision Support Systems in micro / small-sizes SME industrial environments. The application of the proposed framework leads to the development of IT scheduling decision support systems which 'fit' the environment of the human scheduler and can therefore be trusted and adopted for use during the realistic implementation of scheduling processes.

Acknowledgments. The research presented in this paper is funded by the Cyprus Research Promotion Foundation's Framework Programme for Research, Technological Development and Innovation 2009-2010 (DESMI 2009-2010, TEXNOLOG/ MHXAN/0609(BIE)/05). This framework is co-funded by the Republic of Cyprus and the European Regional Development Fund.

References

1. Riezebos, J., Hoc, J.-M., Mebarki, N., Dimopoulos, C., Wezel, W.M.C., van, P.G.: Design of Planning & Scheduling Algorithms: A Critical Discussion. In: Fransoo, J.C., Wafler, T., Wilson, J.R. (eds.) Behavioral Operations in Planning and Scheduling, pp. 299–322. Springer, Heidelberg (2011)
2. Kerr, R.M.: Expert systems in production scheduling: Lessons from a failed implementation. Journal of Systems and Software 19(2), 123–130 (1992)
3. COST Action A29: Human and Organisational Factors in Industrial Planning and Scheduling – HOPS: Memorandum of Understanding. COST, http://w3.cost.eu/fileadmin/domain_files/ISCH/Action_A29/mou/A29-e.pdf (accessed April 1, 2014)
4. Wiers, V.C.S.: A review of the applicability of OR and AI scheduling techniques in practice. OMEGA - The International Journal of Management Science 25(2), 145–153 (1997)
5. Higgins, P.G.: Architecture and interface aspects of scheduling decision support. In: MacCarthy, B.L., Wilson, J.R. (eds.) Human Performance in Planning and Scheduling, pp. 245–281. Taylor and Francis, Oxford (2001)
6. Jackson, S., Wilson, J.R., MacCarthy, B.L.: A New Model of Scheduling in Manufacturing: Tasks, Roles, and Monitoring. Human Factors: The Journal of the Human Factors and Ergonomics Society 46(3), 533–550 (2004)
7. McKay, K.N., Black, G.W.: The evolution of a production planning system: a ten-year case study. Computers in Industry 58(8-9), 756–771 (2007)
8. Dimopoulos, C., Cegarra, J., Gavriel, G., Chouchourelou, A., Papageorgiou, G.: Interdisciplinary Modelling of Scheduling Environments: A Case Study. In: The 4th Production & Operations Management World Conference (P&OM 2012), Electronic Proceedings, Amsterdam (2012)
9. van Wezel, W.M.C., Cegarra, J., Hoc, J.-M.: Allocating Functions to Human and Algorithm in Scheduling. In: Fransoo, J.C., Wafler, T., Wilson, J.R. (eds.) Behavioral Operations in Planning and Scheduling, pp. 339–370. Springer, Heidelberg (2011)
10. Dimopoulos, C., Cegarra, J., Gavriel, G.: Developing Interdisciplinary Specifications for the Design and Implementation of IT Scheduling Decision Support Systems: An SME Case Study. In: 10th International Conference on Manufacturing Research (ICMR 2012), Electronic Proceedings, Birmingham (2012)

Optimum Arrangement of Taxi Drivers' Working Hours

Takashi Tanizaki

Department of Informatics, Faculty of Engineering,
Kinki University, Hiroshima, Japan
tanizaki@hiro.kindai.ac.jp

Abstract. We propose optimum arrangement of taxi drivers' working hours. In Japan, income of taxi vehicle is decreasing about 11 thousand yen in the past 15 years. Then some taxi companies are investing to gain more customers. But there are many small taxi companies that are difficult to invest with much money. Therefore we have been researching the other method to gain more customers by little investment for small companies. In this paper, we analyze present situation of the Taxi Company which we research, research optimum arrangement of taxi drivers' working hours so as to increase sales amount using mathematical model, and verify validity of our method with numerical calculation.

Keywords: optimum arrangement, mathematical model, taxi company, staff scheduling, Weighted Constraint Satisfaction Problem.

1   Introduction

Financial condition (ex. Income of taxi vehicle per day) of taxi companies in Japan from 1995 to 2011 is shown in Fig.1. The annual number of customer is decreasing by about 800 million people, the annual transportation income is decreasing by about 860 billion yen, the number of taxi vehicle is decreasing by about 13 thousand cars, and income of a taxi vehicle per day is decreasing about 11 thousand yen. It is thought

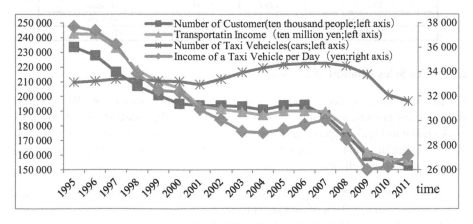

Fig. 1. Financial condition of taxi companies [1]

B. Grabot et al. (Eds.): APMS 2014, Part I, IFIP AICT 438, pp. 363–370, 2014.
© IFIP International Federation for Information Processing 2014

that this factor is in the collapse of the bubble economy and the failure of Lehman Brothers. Then taxi companies introduce various methods to gain more customers. Some companies begin to introduce new taxi operation system using GPS and smartphone to shorten taxi waiting time. But there are many small taxi companies that are difficult to introduce above system. So we have been researching the other method to gain more customers by little investment for small companies as follows [2][3].

- Rearranging taxi drivers' working hours using computer simulation so as to work many taxis with many taxi delivery demands by telephone requests.
- Optimum allocation of standby taxis at taxi stands so as to minimize total millage between taxi stands and the place where customer takes a taxi.

In this paper, we analyze present situation of the Taxi Company which we research (we call Company A in this paper), research optimum arrangement of taxi drivers' working hours so as to increase sales amount using mathematical model, and verify validity of our method with numerical computation results.

2   Present Situation of Company A

2.1   Taxi Drivers' Working Hours of Company A

Taxi drivers' working hours according to service pattern of Company A is shown in Table 1. Taxi driver's service pattern consists of four groups, such as Shift, Day, Fixed time, and Night. Details of each service pattern are described in [2].

Table 1. Working hours

Service pattern		Start	End	Total working hours
Shift	1	7:00	1:00	18hours
	2	8:00	2:00	18hours
	3	8:00	3:00	19hours
	4	12:00	8:00	20hours
Day		7:00	19:00	12hours
Fixed time		7:00	21:00	14hours
Night		20:00	4:00	8hours

2.2   The Sales Amount of Company A

We get sales data between 2011/12 and 2012/11 from Company A. We calculate average sales amount according to time by the day of the week shown in Fig.2, by week shown in Fig.3, respectively.   Average sales amount values are normalized so that the minimum value is equal to 1.0. From Fig.2, the characteristics of average sales amount are as follows.

- Fhe sales amount differs by the day of the week. The Sales amount of Friday and Saturnday are high. That of Sunday is low.
- The sales amount according to the week is the almost same.

- The sales amount from 8:00 to 9:00 and from 17:00 to 24:00 is high, from 2:00 to 7:00 is very low, from 10:00 to 11:00 and from from 13:00 to 16:00 is low.

The sales amount is different depend on time and the day of the week. We research optimum arrangement of taxi drivers' working hours so as to increase sales amount using mathematical model.

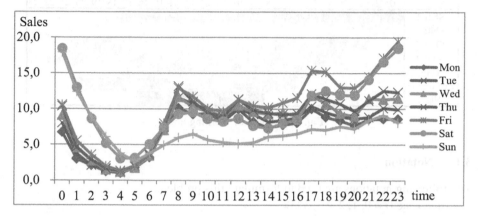

Fig. 2. Average sales amount according to time by day of week

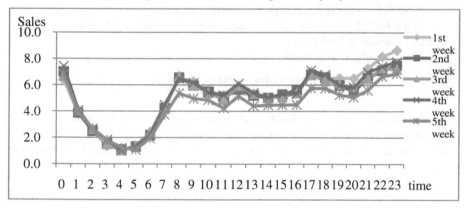

Fig. 3. Average sales amount according to time by week

3   Formulation

There are differences in the sales amount by time, the day of the week. This reason is because the number of customers and the taxi operation number vary according to time and the day of the week. Therefore we research optimum arrangement of taxi drivers' working hours so as to increase sales amount using mathematical model. Basic idea for arrangement of taxi drivers' working hours is putting the belt of continuous working time in the day under the following constraints (Fig.4).

- Taxi drivers must work working hours for each service pattern continuously.
- Working hours for every service pattern is the same every day.
- There is at least one service pattern "Shift" in every time zone.
- Service pattern "Night" differs in the day of the week which works in odd weeks and even weeks. Therefore we formulate two week model.

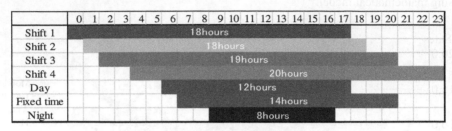

	0	1	2	3	4	5	6	7	8	9	10	11	12	13	14	15	16	17	18	19	20	21	22	23
Shift 1									18hours															
Shift 2									18hours															
Shift 3									19hours															
Shift 4									20hours															
Day									12hours															
Fixed time									14hours															
Night									8hours															

Fig. 4. Example of working hours

3.1   Notation

The following notations are used to formulate this problem.

i:time zone ($i = 0, 1, 2, \cdots, 335$)

j:service pattern ($j = 0, 1, \cdots, 7$)

0; Shift 1,   1;Shift 2,   2;Shift 3,   3;Shift 4,   4;Day,
5;first half of Fixed time,   6;second half of Fixed time,   7;Night

C_i:Sales amount in time zone i

C_i is calculated as follows

$$C_i = \frac{\text{Annual sales amount in time zone i}}{\text{Annual days of time zone i}}$$

N_{ij};The number of taxis which can work in time zone i for service pattern j

T_j:Continuation working hours for service pattern j

x_{ij}:0-1 integer variable which denotes taxi operation in time zone i for service pattern j

$$x_{ij} = \begin{cases} 1 \text{ (working)} \\ 0 \text{ (not working)} \end{cases}$$

3.2   Formulation

The objective is to maximize total sales amount.   Problem is formulated as follows:

$$\text{Maximize} \sum_{i=0}^{335} \sum_{j=0}^{7} C_i * N_{ij} * x_{ij}. \tag{1}$$

Subject to

$$\sum_{j=0}^{3} x_{ij} \geq 1, \tag{2}$$

$$\sum_{i=0}^{335} x_{ij} = 14 * T_j, \tag{3}$$

$$\sum_{i=1}^{335} x_{ij} x_{i-1,j} = 14 * (T_j - 1), \tag{4}$$

$$x_{ij} = x_{i+24*n,j} \quad (n=1,2,\ldots,13). \tag{5}$$

Constraint (2) shows that at least one service pattern "Shift" exits in each time zone. Constraints (3) and (4) shows service pattern j continues T_j hours. Constraint (5) shows taxi operation in each time zone is the same every day.

3.3   Solution Method

This model is nonlinear programming problem. It is difficult to calculate the optimum solution in short time. We reformulate the problem as Weighted Constraint Satisfaction Problem (WCSP) because variables are 0-1 integer, and solve WCSP by taboo search. WCSP is a problem which assigns a value in order to satisfy important constraints as much as possible [4]. In WCSP, the importance of constraints is set up as weight parameter. Therefore it is possible to calculate solution in which the model maker's intention was reflected about the sufficiency condition of constraints. An optimization problem is formulated as WCSP by changing objective function $f(x_1, x_2, \cdots, x_n)$ into the constraints introducing the target value μ as follows:

- In case of Minimization problem

$$\mu - f(x_1, x_2, \cdots, x_n) \geq 0$$

- In case of Maximization problem

$$f(x_1, x_2, \cdots, x_n) - \mu \geq 0$$

An objective function is treated as soft restrictions. Although soft restrictions must not necessarily be satisfied, they are satisfied as much as possible. In our problem, objective function (1) is changed constraint (6) in WCSP.

$$\sum_{i=0}^{335} \sum_{j=0}^{7} C_i N_{ij} x_{ij} - \mu \geq 0 \tag{6}$$

WCSP will end calculation, if one of the following conditions is satisfied.

(1)The solution which satisfies all the constraints is solved.
(2)The specified iteration count is exceeded.
(3)The specified computation time is exceeded.

We choose (3) and computation time is made into 3600 seconds. The solution procedure is as follows.

Step 1   Set up of computation time.
Step 2   Set up of target value μ.
Step 3   Solve WCSP using taboo search.

Step 4   When a solution comes out within computation time, a target value is increased and back to Step 3.

Step 5   When it exceeds computation time, calculation is ended. The solution at the
time is adopted.

4   The Application Result to Company A

4.1   Numerical Computation Case

We calculate quasi-optimum solution using procedure in chapter 3. We compare the
solution result of the problem in chapter 3 and the problem added constraints including heuristics to which sales amount may become high based on data analysis. Company A requests us to study the new service pattern which become the sales amount
high not adhering to the present service pattern. Therefore we compare the solution
result of the problem added the constraints with new service pattern (Table 2).

- Pattern 0

[Method] Solve problem in chapter 3.
[Purpose] Calculate quasi-optimum solution, and compare with the present condition

- Pattern 1

[Method] Add the constraints which change working hours "Fixed time".
[Purpose] Increase the number of taxi operation after 20:00 with high sales amount.

- Pattern2

[Method] Add the constraints which divide working hours of "Fixed time".
[Purpose] Increase the number of taxi operation after 20:00 and decrease the number
of taxi operation between 14:00 and 16:00 with low sales amount.

- Pattern 3

[Method] Add the constraints which change the day of the week of "Fixed time".
[Purpose] Increase the number of taxi operation on Friday and Saturday with high
sales amount.

4.2   Computation Results

Numerical computation results using sales data between 2011/12 and 2012/11 from
Company A is in Table3. The annual sales amount of case 17 of pattern 3 is the
highest. On the whole, the sales amount of the pattern 3 are high. Furthermore, it is a
result of the tendency which reduces the number of taxi operation in time zone of low
sales amout (9:00 to 16:00) , and increases the number of taxi operation in time zone

Table 2. Numerical computation case

Pattern	Case	Working hours
0	0	No changes
1	1	From 8:00 to 22:00
	2	From 9:00 to 23:00
Change working hours of "Fixed time"	3	From 10:00 to 0:00
	4	From 11:00 to 1:00
	5	From 12:00 to 2:00
2	6	From 7:00 to 14:00, From 17:00 to 0:00
	7	From 8:00 to 15:00, From 17:00 to 0:00
Devide working hours of "Fixed time"	8	From 8:00 to 14:00, From 18:00 to 1:00
	9	From 7:00 to 13:00, From 16:00 to 0:00
	10	From 8:00 to 14:00, From 16:00 to 0:00
	11	From 8:00 to 14:00, From 17:00 to 1:00
3	12	A:Mon, Fri, Sat, B:Tue, Fri, Sat
	13	A:Mon, Fri, Sat, B:Wed, Fri, Sat
Change the day of the week of "Fixed time"	14	A:Mon, Fri, Sat, B:Thu, Fri, Sat
	15	A:Tue, Fri, Sat, B:Wed, Fri, Sat
	16	A:Tue, Fri, Sat, B:Thu, Fri, Sat
	17	A:Wed, Fri, Sat, B:Thu, Fri, Sat

Table 3. Computation results

	case	Shift				Day	Fixed		Night	Sales ammout[*)]	rank
		1	2	3	4						
	Now	7:00 1:00	8:00 2:00	8:00 3:00	12:00 8:00	7:00 19:00	7:00 21:00		20:00 4:00	base	15
	0	8:00 2:00	12:00 7:00	6:00 1:00	6:00 2:00	18:00 6:00	13:00 3:00		20:00 4:00	106.0%	5
pattern 1	1									No feasible solution	
	2	8:00 2:00	8:00 2:00	7:00 2:00	17:00 13:00	14:00 2:00	9:00 23:00		17:00 1:00	102.3%	13
	3	3:00 21:00	7:00 1:00	7:00 2:00	8:00 4:00	14:00 2:00	10:00 0:00		13:00 21:00	99.2%	16
	4	8:00 2:00	16:00 10:00	8:00 3:00	8:00 4:00	15:00 3:00	11:00 1:00		20:00 4:00	105.9%	6
	5	7:00 1:00	14:00 8:00	1:00 20:00	5:00 1:00	17:00 5:00	12:00 2:00		23:00 7:00	105.5%	9
pattern 2	6	19:00 13:00	7:00 1:00	8:00 3:00	7:00 3:00	15:00 3:00	7:00 14:00	17:00 0:00	19:00 3:00	105.7%	8
	7	8:00 2:00	8:00 2:00	8:00 3:00	16:00 12:00	8:00 20:00	8:00 15:00	17:00 0:00	18:00 2:00	101.9%	14
	8									No feasible solution	
	9	8:00 2:00	8:00 2:00	7:00 2:00	13:00 9:00	13:00 1:00	7:00 13:00	16:00 0:00	19:00 3:00	103.8%	11
	10	15:00 9:00	8:00 2:00	10:00 5:00	7:00 3:00	14:00 2:00	8:00 14:00	16:00 0:00	20:00 4:00	105.9%	7
	11	5:00 23:00	9:00 3:00	9:00 4:00	1:00 21:00	14:00 2:00	8:00 14:00	17:00 1:00	15:00 3:00	102.4%	12
pattern 3	12	2:00 20:00	20:00 14:00	8:00 3:00	16:00 12:00	20:00 8:00	20:00 10:00		15:00 23:00	107.7%	2
	13	14:00 8:00	22:00 16:00	6:00 1:00	4:00 0:00	14:00 2:00	11:00 1:00		7:00 15:00	106.5%	4
	14									No feasible solution	
	15	0:00 18:00	7:00 1:00	14:00 9:00	23:00 19:00	15:00 3:00	3:00 17:00		20:00 4:00	104.9%	10
	16	8:00 2:00	8:00 2:00	11:00 6:00	5:00 1:00	18:00 6:00	13:00 3:00		20:00 4:00	106.7%	3
	17	7:00 1:00	10:00 4:00	21:00 16:00	6:00 2:00	16:00 4:00	12:00 2:00		20:00 4:00	108.7%	1

*) Contract with "case now".

of high sales amount (18:00 to 0:00). We get some hints which consider new working hours as follows.

- The number of taxi operation from Monday to Thursday is reduced, and it from Friday to Saturday is increased.
- The number of taxi operation from 9:00 to 16:00 is reduced, and it from 18:00 to 0:00 is increased.

5   Conclusions

We research optimum arrangement of taxi drivers' working hours to gain more customers by little investment for small companies. For the above purpose, we analyze present situation of Taxi Company A using sales data, and formulate mathmatical model so as to increase sales amount. This model is nonlinear programming problem and difficult to calculate the optimum solution in short time. Therefore we reformulate the problem as WCSP, and solve WCSP by taboo search. We verify validity of our method with numerical computation results. As a result, it turns out that it is effective strategy to reduce the number of taxi operation in time zone of low sales amout (9:00 to 16:00) , and increases the number of taxi operation in time zone of high sales amount (18:00 to 0:00).

References

1. Ministryof Land, Infrastructure, Transport, andTourism: Aboutthepresentconditionof national taxienterprise, http://www.mlit.go.jp/common/000226517.pdf (in Japanese)
2. Tanizaki, T.: Improvement Method of Service Productivity for Taxi Company. In: Emmanouilidis, C., Taisch, M., Kiritsis, D. (eds.) APMS 2012, Part II. IFIP AICT, vol. 398, pp. 329–336. Springer, Heidelberg (2013)
3. Tanizaki, T.: Optimum Allocation Method of Standby Taxi Vehicles at Taxi Stands. In: Prabhu, V., Taisch, M., Kiritsis, D. (eds.) APMS 2013, Part II. IFIP AICT, vol. 415, pp. 3–10. Springer, Heidelberg (2013)
4. Nonobe, K.: Development of general purpose solvers by meta heuristics. Communications of the Operations Research Society of Japan, 257–262 (2011) (in Japanese)

Supply Chain Management Strategies in Terms of Decoupling Points and Decoupling Zones

Joakim Wikner

Jönköping University
joakim.wikner@decouplingpoints.org

Abstract. Supply chain management is concerned with decisions related to the physical perspective of the enterprise and how the flow of goods and services is arranged. A wide set of strategies have evolved over time to provide guidelines for the decision makers but many of these strategies share a common foundation in process management that is based on decoupling points and decoupling zones. The strategies concerned here are segmentation, leagility, customization, postponement, servitization, sustainability, outsourcing, and visibility.

Keywords: Decoupling points, segmentation, leagility, customization, postponement, servitization, closed-loop, outsourcing, visibility.

1   Introduction

Several concepts related to strategies for production and supply management, hereafter referred to as supply chain management strategies, have been developed over the years covering a wide range of scenarios. As the market requirements change the concerned businesses have to evolve to stay competitive. Through this process the concept of supply chain management (SCM) has become fragmented and created a need for a more knowledge on fundamental properties that are shared between different concepts and strategies. A monolithic approach to SCM covers a wide range of issues that are complex and challenging to handle simultaneously. The decisions involved can be categorized from a transformation perspective into three layers as suggested by Wikner [1]. At the company layer a legal perspective is dominant since this involves the issue about who is actually the sponsor of the transformation. This is the layer where the financial transactions are in focus. The financial transactions are however a consequence of activities being performed at a physical layer where the type of transformation, such as manufacturing, transportation or distribution are handled by SCM. The physical layer does, however, rest on a generic process foundation represented by a logical layer based on generic transformations. This generic layer is the foundation for process management and consist of four decision categories [1] that can be used at the logical layer and this is the foundation below. First a short summary of the logical layer is provided based on process management. Thereafter eight SCM strategies are outlined and finally the SCM strategies are interpreted in terms of the generic decoupling framework.

B. Grabot et al. (Eds.): APMS 2014, Part I, IFIP AICT 438, pp. 371–378, 2014.

2   Process Management Decoupling Framework

Process management as used here refers to a generic approach to managing flow based on some fundamental and generic decision categories. Four flow based decision categories are used below based on [1]:

1. Flow driving involving the separation of speculation from commitment to customer order through the customer order decoupling point (CODP) and the customer order decoupling zone (CODZ).
2. Flow differentiation related to the uniqueness of the product ranging from standard, market unique, product to customer order unique special product which are separated by the customer adaptation decoupling point (CADP) and the customer adaptation decoupling zone (CADZ).
3. Flow delimitation concerns the reach of controllability. The flow can be separated into logical entities and the separation interface is related to the purchase order decoupling point (PODP) and the purchase order decoupling zone (PODZ).
4. Flow transparency is the fourth category and covers the availability of information where the demand information decoupling point (DIDP) limits the extension of demand information and the supply information decoupling point (SIDP) limits the extension of supply information.

These four categories are illustrated in Fig. 1 in combination with the strategic lead times that are critical for positioning these decoupling points and decoupling zones.

3   Supply Chain Management Strategies

The physical perspective is related to the physical transformation performed in the supply chain. The intention here is not to give a comprehensive and all-encompassing view of a set of SCM strategies but rather to outline some insights on key properties in preparation for the discussion about how they can be interpreted in terms of the generic process management layer.

I. Segmentation
Segmentation is related to that the supply chain should be designed to fulfil specific customer requirements [2], which may require that separate supply chains are designed for different markets. This has been an important part of supply chain design since the early days of materials management and this field of research has evolved over time to segmented supply chain design [3]

II. Leagility
Whereas segmentation mainly targets the customer service aspect of SCM a separate stream of research has put more emphasize on the properties of supply. Leagility is focusing on the fundamental issue of how to combine lean, with emphasis on heijunka and levelled flow with agile, with emphasis on flexibility and speed. The combination has been referred to as "leagility" [4, 5]. Leagility in this context basically represents how to balance efficiency with responsiveness.

III. Customization

Leagility is a concept that decouples the supply chain but does not include any explicit consideration of customization, i.e. to which extent the product is made unique for a specific customer. Lampel and Mintzberg [6] provided a comprehensive framework for categorization of customization. Note that this strategy encompasses a wide range of customization related strategies ranging from mass-customization [7] to engineer-to-order [8].

IV. Postponement

In parallel to segmentation, leagility, and customization a separate stream of research has progressed and is referred to as postponement where decisions are postponed to as late as possible for better decision support. In the literature, postponement dates back to the 1950's when the concept was introduced [9]. The concept of postponement was then developed further [10] in terms of time, form, and place. Pagh and Cooper [11] outlined a framework emphasizing speculation and postponement in terms of manufacturing as well as distribution to identify a set of strategies.

V. Servitization

The four strategies outlined above all originates in the context of physical goods. Goods only has turned out to be a difficult strategy for many companies with limited access to low-cost manufacturing. An alternative strategy is to deliver a package of goods and services to the customers [12]. This approach has also been termed servitization [13] and is a subset of the more general concept of services.

VI. Sustainability

By including services in the SCM strategy it is possible to take a more comprehensive approach to supply chains and to involve the whole life cycle of a product. SCM strategies are generally based on the forward supply chain but also a closed-loop perspective has emerged involving reverse flows. This topic originates in recycling which has evolved into product recovery management and the integrated supply chain [14]. This is also referred to as the closed-loop supply chain [15] which encompasses both forward flows and reverse flows and in addition is closely related to the topic of sustainability [16].

VII. Outsourcing

Considering the resources performing the processes in the supply chain it is relevant to make a strategic choice related to the ownership of the resources. Originally the logical choice was to obtain vertical integration [17] to obtain control but in many cases this is not possible, nor desirable. Instead the emphasis on core competence [18] grew stronger and as a consequence the intent was to outsource activities not considered as based on the core competence of the business [19]. This approach creates a better focus in each individual business but also contributes to the overall complexity of the supply chain as more actors are involved in the supply network.

VIII. Visibility

Competitive SCM requires access to information about the actual state of the supply chain. The information basically concerns information about demand that creates requirement for resources and information about supply and the available resources.

In the SCM context the main focus has been on demand information where demand visibility has turned out as an important factor for e.g. mitigation of the bull-whip effect [20]. Visibility for resource capacity, i.e. supply, has evolved over time from simple sharing of information to a strategic element [21] where visibility across several dimensions can be important [22].

4   Supply Chain Management Strategies Interpreted in Terms of the Process Management Decoupling Framework

The eight SCM strategies outlined above have been associated with decoupling related aspects by different researchers and below follows a summary of this work. Fig. 1 illustrates the connection between the physical perspective represented by the SCM strategies and the logical perspective represented by the decoupling framework based on [1]. Each strategy is expressed in terms of "level of" since the decoupling framework is based on positioning of decoupling points and decoupling zones across a lead-time based scale.

I. Level of segmentation
The explicit connection to market segments was emphasized by Hoekstra and Romme [23 p. 65] when they introduced the concept of "product-market combination". They also introduced the concept of decoupling points for designing integral logistics structures and consequently they early realized the critical link between segmentation and decoupling points. Thereafter segmentation using decoupling points have emerged as a separate path of research, see e.g. [24]. In particular the aspect of flow driver (related to CODP and CODZ) is emphasized but implicitly this is also closely connected to how to create offerings that are adapted to specific market requirements and hence there is also a strong dependence on flow differentiation (related to CADP and CADZ).

II. Level of leagility
Leagility was coined by Naylor, Naim [5] and was basically defined using the CODP as a point of reference. Over time this idea has been further developed but still it is mainly the flow driver that is used as a point of reference (related to CODP and CODZ). The CODP has been emphasized by different authors in both lean and agile.

III. Level of customization
Customization involves making a product unique for a particular market or even an individual customer. The topic of customization is broad but in particular two distinct approaches can be identified. First, it has been suggested that the flow driver should be considered from both a production perspective and an engineering perspective [25], which has also been interpreted from a mass customization perspective [26]. Second, the issue of customization and uniqueness provides additional complexity when the perspectives of customer and supplier are treated separately [27]. Hence customization is mainly concerned with flow differentiation (related to CADP and CADZ).

IV. Level of postponement

Postponement is a successful model for reduced risk exposure in both production and distribution. Central distribution and postponed product differentiation enables critical decisions to be postponed and to a larger extent become customer order driven. This provides an obvious connection to the flow driver (related to CODP and CODZ) as pointed out by e.g. [28]. Postponement is however also related to flow differentiation (related to CADP and CADZ) which is explicitly stated in [29] as point of product differentiation and by [30] as differentiation point.

V. Level of servitization

The level of servitization was, until relatively recently, not interpreted in terms of decoupling points. This is however appropriate when considering that there are many similarities between customer-order-driven activities and services. This analogy was first noted by Fließ and Kleinaltenkamp [31] and later further developed by [32] and [33]. In both these cases the emphasis were on flow drivers (related to CODP and CODZ) but obviously a fundamental aspect of services is the uniqueness of the offering and that it is differentiated for the customer (related to CADP and CADZ).

VI. Level sustainability

Recycling, reverse flows, product returns, and closed loop supply chains are all terminology related to sustainable supply chains. To a large extent the theory development for this field has been separate from theory for forward flow supply chains. Reverse flows are usually more prone to stochastic events and consequently of much more uncertain character. Blackburn, Guide [34] did however highlight that many concepts used in forward flow supply chains have a great potential also for reverse flows. One area they mentioned was postponement and [35] developed this line of thinking in terms of decoupling points and in particular the flow driver was considered (related to CODP and CODZ).

VII. Level of outsourcing

The first inclusion of purchased material into a decoupling point framework was by Hoekstra and Romme [23] when they identified Purchase and make to order (PMTO) as a separate product-market combination. In this sense they considered purchasing as something taking place before production activities and hence included this in flow driving (related to CODP and CODZ). An alternative was developed by [36] that used two-dimensional CODP with production and engineering dimension and extended this approach to also include purchasing as a separate dimension making it into a three dimensional flow driver. An additional approach was suggested by [37] that instead focused on if resources are within or outside the scope of control. In this sense they combined the flow driver with flow delimitation (related to PODP and PODZ) to more explicitly capture the controllability of the flow. In this context different scenarios of customer-supplier interaction can be defined by combining flow driving and flow delimitation.

VIII. Level of visibility in demand and supply

Visibility is a supply chain strategy with a slightly different approach compared to the above. Instead of focusing on the decision maker and how to use information when making a decisions, visibility is focused on the availability of information for the decision maker. For demand visibility Mason-Jones and Towill [38] introduced the concept of information decoupling point. Since different types of information are involved in visibility this is here referred to as demand information decoupling point (DIDP). Supply visibility has not received the corresponding interest from a decoupling perspective since availability of this kind of information is usually assumed. A corresponding decoupling point for supply information was suggested by [1] and is referred to as supply information decoupling point (SIDP).

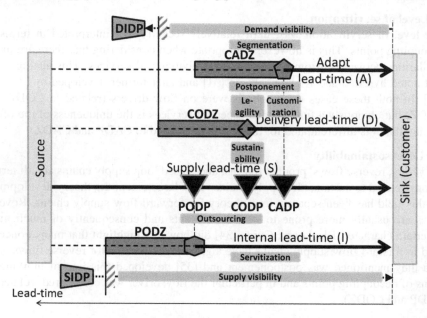

Fig. 1. SCM strategies and the decoupling framework

This short overview of how the eight SCM strategies can be interpreted in terms of decoupling points and decoupling zones has highlighted some key similarities between the SCM strategies and also illustrated that the decoupling framework represent some fundamental aspects of SCM. It is, however, important to note that even if the analogy identifies some fundamental similarities between the different SCM strategies there are still many other aspects of the SCM strategies that are not covered here.

Acknowledgement. This research has been performed in collaboration with six companies in the projects KOPeration and KOPtimera. The projects are funded by the Swedish Knowledge foundation (KKS), Jönköping University and the participating companies.

References

1. Wikner, J.: On decoupling points and decoupling zones. Production & Manufacturing Research, 167–215 (2014)

2. Sharma, A., Lambert, D.M.: Segmentation of markets based on customer service. International Journal of Physical Distribution & Logistics Management 20(7), 19–27 (1990)
3. van der Veeken, D.J.M., Rutten, W.G.M.M.: Logistics service management: Opportunities for differentiation. International Journal of Logistics Management 9(2), 91–98 (1998)
4. Mason-Jones, R., Naylor, B., Towill, D.R.: Engineering the leagile supply chain. International Journal of Agile Management Systems 2(1), 54–61 (2000)
5. Naylor, B., Naim, J.M.M., Berry, D.: Leagility: Integrating the lean and agile manufacturing paradigms in the total supply chain. International Journal of Production Economics 62(1-2), 107–118 (1999)
6. Lampel, J., Mintzberg, H.: Customizing Customization. Sloan Management Review 38(1), 21–30 (1996)
7. Davis, S.M.: Future perfect (1987)
8. Hicks, C., McGovern, T., Earl, C.F.: Supply chain management: A strategic issue in engineer to order manufacturing. International Journal of Production Economics 65(2), 179–190 (2000)
9. Alderson, W.: Marketing Efficiency and the Principle of Postponement. Cost and Profit Outlook 4 (September 1950)
10. Bucklin, L.P.: Postponement, speculation and the structure of distribution channels. Journal of Marketing Research 2(1), 26–31 (1965)
11. Pagh, J.D., Cooper, M.C.: Supply chain postponement and speculation strategies: How to choose the right strategy. Journal of Business Logistics 19(2), 13–33 (1998)
12. Wise, R., Baumgartner, P.: Go Downstream: The New Profit Imperative in Manufacturing. Harvard Business Review 77(5), 133–141 (1999)
13. Vandermerwe, S., Rada, J.: Servitization of business: Adding value by adding services. European Management Journal 6(4), 314–324 (1988)
14. Thierry, M., et al.: Strategic issues in product recovery management. California Management Review 37(2) (1995)
15. Daniel, V., Guide Jr., R., Wassenhove, L.: Closed-loop Supply Chains. In: Klose, A., Speranza, M.G., Wassenhove, L. (eds.) Quantitative Approaches to Distribution Logistics and Supply Chain Management, pp. 47–60. Springer, Heidelberg (2002)
16. Linton, J.D., Klassen, R., Jayaraman, V.: Sustainable supply chains: An introduction. Journal of Operations Management 25(6), 1075–1082 (2007)
17. Ford, H., Crowther, S.: Today and tomorrow, 281 p. Doubleday, Page & Company, Garden City, NY (1926)
18. Prahalad, C.K., Hamel, G.: The core competence of the corporation. Harvard Business Review 68(3), 79–91 (1990)
19. Bettis, R.A., Bradley, S.P., Hamel, G.: Outsourcing and Industrial Decline. The Executive 6(1), 7 (1992)
20. Forrester, J.W.: Industrial dynamics: a major breakthrough for decision makers. Harvard Business Review 36(4), 37–66 (1958)
21. Lamming, R.C., Caldwell, N.D., Harrison, D.A., Phillips, W.: Transparency in supply relationships: Concept and practice. Journal of Supply Chain Management 37(4), 4–10 (2001)
22. Hultman, J., Axelsson, B.: Towards a typology of transparency for marketing management research. Industrial Marketing Management 36(5), 627–635 (2007)
23. Hoekstra, S., Romme, J. (eds.): Integral logistic structures: developing customer-oriented goods flow, xii, 164 p. Industrial Press, New York (1992)
24. Hilletofth, P.: How to develop a differentiated supply chain strategy. Industrial Management & Data Systems 109(1), 16–33 (2009)

25. Wikner, J., Rudberg, M.: Integrating production and engineering perspectives on the customer order decoupling point. International Journal of Operations & Production Management 25(7/8), 623–641 (2005)
26. Rudberg, M., Wikner, J.: Mass customization in terms of the customer order decoupling point. Production Planning & Control 15(4), 445–458 (2004)
27. Wikner, J., Bäckstrand, J.: Decoupling points and product uniqueness impact on supplier relations. In: 4th World Conference P&OM, Amsterdam (2012)
28. Towill, D.R.: Decoupling for supply chain competitiveness (material flow decoupling). Manufacturing Engineer 84(1), 36–39 (2005)
29. García-Dastugue, S.J., Lambert, D.M.: Interorganizational time-based postponement in the supply chain. Journal of Business Logistics 28(1), 57–81 (2007)
30. Wikner, J., Wong, H.: Postponement based on the positioning of the differentiation and decoupling points. In: Olhager, J., Persson, F. (eds.) APMS 2007. IFIP AICT, vol. 246, pp. 143–150. Springer, Heidelberg (2007)
31. Fließ, S., Kleinaltenkamp, M.: Blueprinting the service company: Managing service processes efficiently. Journal of Business Research 57(4), 392–404 (2004)
32. Moeller, S.: Customer Integration—A Key to an Implementation Perspective of Service Provision. Journal of Service Research 11(2), 197–210 (2008)
33. Wikner, J.: A service decoupling point framework for logistics, manufacturing, and service operations. International Journal of Services Sciences 4(3), 330–357 (2012)
34. Blackburn, J.D., Daniel, V., Guide Jr., R., Souza, G.C., Van Wassenhove, L.N.: Reverse supply chains for commercial returns. California Management Review 46(2), 6–22 (2004)
35. Wikner, J., Tang, O.: A structural framework for closed-loop supply chains. The International Journal of Logistics Management 19(3), 344–366 (2008)
36. Mello, M.H., Semini, M., Haartveit, D.E.: A framework to integrate engineering, procurement, and production on the customer order decoupling point. In: Proceedings of the 17th International Working Seminar on Production Economics, Innsbruck, Austria, February 20-24 (2012)
37. Wikner, J., Bäckstrand, J.: Aligning operations strategy and purchasing strategy. In: EurOMA Conference, Cambridge, UK (2011)
38. Mason-Jones, R., Towill, D.R.: Using the information decoupling point to improve supply chain performance. International Journal of Logistics Management 10(2), 13–26 (1999)

Logistic Operator Selection with Capacity of Storage and Transport Frozen Product Using Multicriteria Decision

Geraldo Cardoso de Oliveira Neto, André Henriques Librantz,
and Washington Carvalho de Sousa

Nove de Julho University-UNINOVE, Industrial Engineering Post-graduation Program,
Av. Francisco Matarazzo, 612, São Paulo, Brazil
geraldo.prod@ig.com.br

Abstract. The aim of this work consisted in applying the Analytic Hierarchy Process (AHP) by considering the generic criteria and sub-criteria to select logistic operator to store and transport frozen products. The outcome of the AHP analysis is a preference priority for each alternative operator describing the expected performance level. Results pointed that the proposed model could be considered as a good alternative to this problem, thus contributing to achieve the goals of the organization.

Keywords: Selection, Logistic Operator, Multicriteria decision, Analytic Hierarchy Process.

1 Introduction

The analytic hierarchy process (AHP) is a structured technique for organizing and analyzing complex decisions, The AHP method was developed during the 70's by Thomas Saaty [1] to solve complex problems that involves multicriteria decisions [2] and has been extensively studied and refined since then. The applications of AHP to complex decision situations have produced extensive results in problems involving planning, resource allocation, priority setting, and selection of logistic operators, among alternatives.

AHP's use for logistic operator selection consists in an important aspect to identify and consider the criteria [3, 4, 5, 6], by knowing the contractor demands in order to achieve the main goal [7, 8], and evaluate alternatives and contract logistic operators that are more efficient [9] adding value to the supply chain [10], by using a evaluation method of analysis before the contractual formalization [11, 12, 13], to verify whether it is worth to outsource or internalize the activities [8].

Usually the focus is on selecting a service provider that has the relational capacity to facilitate the business integration, operation and quality treatment [14], that turns out more feasible to collaboration [15], including establishing common goals to control the performance and the strategic alignment of the partnership [16] to manage the service level [17].

B. Grabot et al. (Eds.): APMS 2014, Part I, IFIP AICT 438, pp. 379–386, 2014.

Regarding the quality analysis, it was developed a model based on SERVQUAL (quality dimensions), taking into account the criteria utilized for logistic operator selection [18].

It has been found some works, in which the AHP method was used to select logistic service providers to operate reverse logistic that could be considered a complex decision, once it is a recent operation, that needs reliability [19, 20, 21,22], with contractual renegotiation guaranteed politics [22] and mainly, really contributes with sustainability by reducing waste on transport and storage [15]. Other researchers used the AHP to select logistic operators to act on manufacturing of contractor [23, 24].

In Table 1 it is shown the logistic operator selection generic criteria and sub-criteria developed by action research in logistic services outsourcing processes on Brazil in the last six years. But, with a deep revision in literature it was possible to identify the researches that corroborate with the criteria and sub-criteria established on practice, making it possible to assure that it is made of a 15 criteria and 67 sub-criteria basis consolidated on theoretical research field.

In the literature review it wasn't identified researches that utilize the AHP to select logistic operators that storage and transport frozen refrigerated products and it was noted that it misses a more complete criteria and sub-criteria basis to apply the multicriteria analysis in outsourcing processes. Some researches produced fragmented results [3, 8, 9, 14, 18, 22] that makes it impossible to make decision.

In this context, the aim of this work consists in applying the AHP with support of the generic criteria and sub-criteria basis of logistic operator selection of storage and transport of frozen products.

2   Methodology

At first, the literature revision [25] was performed in the following data bases: Proquest, Ebsco, Science Direct, Emerald, Capes and academic Google, with the following keywords: (i)"Analytic hierarchy process" AND "outsourcing" AND "logistics"; (ii) "Analytic hierarchy process" AND "selection" AND "third party logistics"; (iii) "Analytic hierarchy process" AND "selection" AND "third-party logistics" e (iv) "Analytic hierarchy process" AND "selection" AND "service provider" with the objective of electing the articles that utilized the AHP to select the logistic operators, summarizing 24 researches, that were submitted to content analysis to categorize the data in a spread sheet [26] of the main themes and criteria utilized.

The utilized method was action research, in which the researcher is involved, along with the members of the analyzed organization, to deal with a problem, specifically in the appropriate selection of a logistic operator of storage and transport of frozen load [27], with that, the researcher participates in the process [28, 29, 30].

The process of action research involves five stages [28, 29, 30]:

(i)   Action research planning: – in this step, it was identified along with the contractor, the insecurity in selecting a logistic operator to move and transport frozen products, which brought up the following research's question: how to select a logistic operator appropriate to store and transport frozen products.

(ii) Instruments to collect field data: – active participation in meetings, focal groups and documents analysis. The focal groups or observation groups generate important lessons about the observed phenomenon [30].

(iii) Action Plans: - the decision making relative to logistic operator selection inevitably includes a consideration and evidence based in multiccriteria for the decision making [3, 4, 5, 2, 6]. With that in mind, we adopted 16 criteria and 67 sub-criteria of logistic operator selection [31].

Table 1. Criteria and Sub-criteria of logistic operator selection

Criteria	Sub-criteria	Corroborating Researches
Cost	Transport; Storage and handling; Delay on supplying and Devolutions.	[23, 21, 7, 17, 9, 8]
Financial stability	Investment Capacity; Financial Health and Indebtedness.	[3, 14, 22, 9, 8]
Adaptability	Logistic Operator *in lócus* with the Contractor; Flexibility in the treatment, Cultural Compatibility and Common Planning.	[17, 8]
Operation Infrastructure	Distribution Centers Location; Facilities Adequacy; Work Security; Loading; Truck Conditions; Equipment required for loading; Receipt in JIT without fault in the Logistic Operator; Equipment required in receipt; Equipment required for Moving; Handling Pallets without fault; Storage and Stacking in the warehouse; Equipment required in the warehouse; Separation to dispatch without fault; Uniting and Own cars; Equipment required to transport and dispatch of the order without fault in JIT.	[18, 3, 22, 16, 17, 8, 20, 6]
Operation Management	Management of: people; loading; receipt; storage; transport; quality and information.	[14, 22, 19]
Flexibility	Treatment capacity; Negotiated nuances and Treatment Service to the Clients.	[23, 3, 21, 15, 9, 19, 8]
Credibility	Business Reputation; Logistic Partnership and amount of Contracts per year.	[3, 14, 22, 6]
Experience	Service efficiency; Product's amount of experience; Amount of time in the market and Clients range.	[14, 7, 20, 6]
Quality	Quality Certification; Physical Integrity Compatibility; Logistic Operator seeks improvement in the process and Traceability.	[23, 14, 21, 22, 9, 8]
Information Technology	Easy Communication (Electronic Data Interchange - EDI); (Enterprise Resource Planning - ERP); (Warehousing Management System-WMS); (Transport Management System TMS) and Routing (Global Positioning System - GPS).	[23, 9, 19, 17, 20]
Human Resources	Employees Qualification; Capacity of Working in Group; Capacitation and practical test, Clothing and neatness of the employees.	[14, 21, 22]
Reliability	Complete Order Dispatching; Classified Information Leaking; Security against load stealing and Fines due to no-treatment.	[18, 8]
Responsibility	Operation in JIT and Dispatch in short term.	[18, 23, 21, 22, 15, 16, 17, 8]
Empathy	After-Sell and Commitment	[18, 14].
Environmental	Certification ISO 14000; Cleaner Production; Reverse Logistic and Training in environmental education	[3, 22, 15, 16, 19, 20]

Source: [31, 32] corroborated with some researches.

In fact the process of decision making is commonly complex. The multiccriteria Decision Analysis could support the decision maker to solve problems in which there are many goals to be reached at the same time. Three sets are initially considered in the formulation of multiccriteria decision problems: the set of alternatives, the set of criteria and the set of consequences [33]. The process consists of the following stages:

(1) Define the alternatives; (2) Define the relevant criteria to the decision problem; (3) Evaluate the alternatives related to the criteria; (4) Evaluate the relative importance of each criteria and (5) Determine the global evaluation of each alternative.

Along the methods developed in the Multiccriteria Decisions research, the most well-known is the Analytic Hierarchy Process – AHP, developed by Thomas Saaty [1] to identify the relevant criteria through binary correlation, which allows to associate a priority value above other elements in a numerical scale, merging an hierarchical structure of the problem of decision with support of the mathematical modeling.

As an example, when using the decision matrix A, the AHP method calculates the partial results of the A set inside each criteria $v_i(A_j)$, $j = 1, ..., n$, called impact value of the j alternative in relation to the i alternative, in which these results represent numerical values of the given data by the decision maker in each alternative comparison. The results are standardized by the expression 1:

$$\Sigma_i = 1 \ v_i(A_j) = 1, \text{ for } j = 1, ..., n; \tag{1}$$

where n is the number of alternatives or compared elements. Each part of the sum consists in: $v_i(A_j) = a_{ij} / \Sigma_i = 1 \ a_{ij}$, for $j = 1, ..., n$.

This expression relates the priority vector of the alternative *i* in relation to the C_k criteria be: $v_k(A_i) = \Sigma_j = 1 \ vi(A_j) / n$, for $i = 1, ..., n$

After having the priority vector or the impact value of the alternatives under each C_k criteria, the next step is the criteria levels. In this case, we adopt again the verbal scale to the classification pair-to-pair of the criteria, that are standardized by the expression 2:

$$wi(C_j) = C_{ij} / \Sigma_i = 1 \ C_{ij}, \text{ for } j = 1, ..., m; \tag{2}$$

where m is the number of criteria in the same level. The priority vector is obtained by:

$$w_i(C_i) = \Sigma i = 1 \ w(Cj) / m, \text{ for } i = 1, ..., m; \tag{3}$$

Finally, the final values of the alternatives are obtained through an aggregation process, standardized by the expression 4, in which:

$$f(A_j) = \Sigma i = 1 \ w(C_i) * v_i(A), \text{ for } j = 1, ..., n; \tag{4}$$

where n is the number of alternatives
(iv) Implanting Actions – scale selection for decision making to identify the most relevant contractual criteria. The Table 2 shows the scale.

Table 2. Criteria Evaluation Scale

Value	Definiton	Explanation
1	Same Importance	Both criteria contribute in the same way to the objective.
3	Little more Important	The analysis and experience prove that a criteria is a little more important than the other.
5	Much more Important	The analysis and experience prove that a criteria is much more important than the other.
7	A lot more Important	The analysis and experience prove that a criteria is a lot more important than the other.
9	Hugely more Important	Without doubt, a criteria is predominant over the other one.

Source: based on Saaty [1].

(v) Discuss Results – the final stage implies in learning through reflection among the results of the action of the participants [29] to verify which logistic operator can successfully fulfill the operational capacities (criteria) required as described in the following stage.

3   Results and Discussion

The main focus of the corporation is the product industrialization. Thus, they decided to outsource its storage and frozen product transport processes, taking into account the dispatching capacity of the operators. So, three logistic operators have been chosen to be analysed by AHP method.

Numerical Application
In this section, the multi-criteria group decision model is applied to a procedure for selecting logistic operators. In order to obtain the Multicriteria numerical application it was used the AHP method based on the 16 criteria and 67 sub-criteria, allowing an identification of seven more critical criteria. The main criterion to be observed in the logistic operators' evaluation is the transport responsiveness. However, to make the responsiveness capacity better to the market, it was required criteria of infrastructure (physical resources) to improve the storage capacity, that was missing physical space in the appropriate floor to allocate 134 tons a day – 4 freezing tunnels that allocate 26 docks and infrastructure criteria (physical resources) to improve the transport capacity – strategic localization near the beltway to deliver the products quickly.

This way, the main concern of the contractor was the complementation of storage and transport capacities, variables associated to the responsiveness and infrastructure criteria. It is important to note that the contractor was not only worried about analyzing the physical resources to store and transport, as well, but the managing capacity of the logistic operator within these activities, by considering the efficiency indicators implantation required integrated with fee applications in case of non-effectiveness.

The results pointed that the qualitative analysis should precede the AHP application with the objective of knowing the demands of the contractor regarding the capacities. In most published works, decision makers applied the multicriteria analysis [3, 4, 5, 6, 8, 9, 10, 11, 12, 13, 21, and 32], neglecting the qualitative evaluation. Many authors pointed out the need of relational capacity without a deeper analysis of the other required capacities [14, 15, 17, and 28]. The relational capacity and the quality capacity can be considered generic, because this is a common necessity in any outsourcing process, being required a deeper analysis on the operational routine of the contractor to identify specific capacities, as shown in the results.

Table 3 shows the consequence matrix with critic criteria obtained after the model application. The numbers were normalized to obtain the relative importance (pair-wise comparison).

Table 3. Consequence Matrix

Criteria	Operation Infrastructure	Operation Management	Quality	Tech-nology	Human Resources	Relia-bility	Respon-siveness
Operation Infrastructure	1,000	1,000	0,111	0,111	0,111	0,111	0,111
Operation Management	1,000	1,000	0,111	0,111	0,111	0,111	0,111
Quality	3,000	1,000	3,000	0,333	0,333	0,333	0,333
Technology	3,000	1,000	0,600	0,333	0,333	0,333	0,333
Human Resources	3,000	1,000	0,600	0,333	0,333	0,333	0,333
Reliability	3,000	1,000	0,600	0,333	0,333	0,333	0,333
Responsiveness	9,000	1,000	1,800	1,000	1,000	1,000	1,000

Based on the seven critical criteria, the three logistic operators were analyzed. Table 4 presented the decision matrix and the results obtained for each alternative.

Table 4. Decision Matrix

Alter-native	Operation Infrastructure	Operation Management	Quality	Tech-nology	Human Resources	Relia-bility	Respon-siveness
LO 1	0,195	0,210	0,397	0,162	0,302	0,250	0,203
LO 2	0,520	0,519	0,503	0,543	0,397	0,491	0,593
LO 3	0,284	0,271	0,101	0,295	0,302	0,259	0,203

Once obtained the decision matrix, it was possible to evaluate the score and classify the logistic operators, indicating which of them was considered more able to store and transport frozen products.

The logistic operator 2 (score 0.41) was considered more able to improve the dispatch responsiveness of the contractor in the metropolitan region of São Paulo, because it is in a strategic localization near the beltway, allowing better product outflowing, among having better consolidated infrastructure concerning equipment, as for an example, term kings to control the temperature, and freezing tunnels in the warehouse.

The second-best (score 0.23) was the logistic operator 1 that presented low capacity of infrastructure that could prejudice the dispatching responsiveness.

Finally, the logistic operator 3 (score 0.21), that presented lack of control in the efficiency of the provided services, making it impossible to analyze the punctuality indicators of dispatch.

Both logistic operators 1 and 3 were not localized near a beltway, which was considered, by the contractor, a crucial aspect.

This results corroborate with the researches of [19, 20] related to the development of a ranking to avoid the opportunist behavior of logistic operator regarding the possibility of offering sets of generic services that do not meet the contractor demands and could lead to the outsourcing failure.

4   Conclusions

In this work, the AHP technique was used in the selection of logistic operators to store and transport frozen products. The AHP is a structured technique for organizing and analyzing complex decisions, and coub be useful, especially in complex decision processes, once it enables people to make decisions involving many kinds of concerns including planning, setting priorities, selecting the best among a number of alternatives, and allocating resources. Complex problems or issues involving value or subjective judgments are suitable applications of the AHP method. Its approach of division in hierarchical criteria and alternative correlation with criteria, allows an easy comprehension and better evaluation of the problem. Taking into account that many strategic decisions, such as logistic operator selection, are many times, made without any methodical support, the proposed model can be considered as a good alternative to the investigated problem, since it can support the decision process, which can contribute to increase efficiency of the supply chain of the organization.

References

1. Saaty, T.L.: Decision Making with the Analytic Hierarchy Process. International Journal of Services Sciences 1, 83–98 (2008)
2. Almeida, A.T.: O conhecimento e o uso de métodos multicritério de apoio à decisão. Editora Universitária UFPE (2011)
3. IÃNez, M.M., Cunha, C.B.: Uma metodologia para a seleção de um provedor de serviços logísticos. Revista Produção Online 16, 394–412 (2006)
4. Kasture, S., Quresh, M.N., Kumar, P., Gupta, I.: FAHP Sensity Analysis for selection of Third party Logistics (3PL) service providers. Journal of Supply Chain Management 4, 41–60 (2008)
5. Chen, Y.M., Goan, M.-J., Huang, P.-N.: Selection process in logistics management – a view from third party logistics provider. Production Planning and Control 22, 308–324 (2011)
6. Asuquo, M., Coward, L., Yang, Z.: Modeling selection of third party ship management services. Case Studies on Transport Policy. Journal of Manufacturing Technology Management 2, 25–28 (2014)
7. Daim, T.U., Udbye, A., Balasubramanian, A.: Use of analytic hierarchy process (AHP) for selection of 3PL providers. Journal of Manufacturing Technology Management 24, 28–51 (2013)
8. Reis, L.P., Ladeira, M.B., Fernandes, J.M.: Contribution of the analytic hierarchy Process (AHP) method for supporting the decision to outsource or internalize activities in the context of technology-based company. Revista Produção Online 13, 1325–1354 (2013)
9. Ho, W., He, T., Lee, C.K.M., Emrouznejad, A.: Strategic logistics outsourcing: An integrated QFD and Fuzzy AHP approach. Expert Systems With Applications: An International Journal 39, 10841–10850 (2012)
10. Routroy, S.: Selection of Third Party Logistics Provider in Supply Chain. International Journal of Services Technology and Management 12, 23–23 (2009)
11. Rajesh, R., Pugazhendhi, S., Muralidharan, C.: Development of a composite model for selection of third party logistics service provider. International Journal of Electronic Customer Relationship Management 3, 375–375 (2009)
12. Bansal, A., Kumar, P.: 3PL selection using hybrid model of AHP-PROMETHEE. International Journal of Services and Operations Management 14, 373–373 (2013)
13. Bayazit, S., Karpak, B.: Selection of a third party logistics service provider for an aerospace company: an analytical decision aiding approach. International Journal of Logistics Systems and Management 5, 382–404 (2013)

14. Gol, H., ÇAtay, B.: Third-party logistics provider selection: insights from a Turkish automotive company. Supply Chain Management: An International Journal 12, 379–384 (2007)
15. Sasikumar, P., Haq, A.N.: A multi-criteria decision making methodology for the selection of reverse logistics operating modes. International Journal of Enterprise Network Management 4, 68–79 (2010)
16. Xiu, G., Chen, X.: The Third Party Logistics Supplier Selection and Evaluation. Journal of Software 7, 1783–1790 (2012)
17. Peng, J.: Selection of Logistics Outsourcing Service Suppliers Based on AHP, Energy Procedia. International Conference on Future Electrical Power and Energy Systems 17, 595–601 (2012)
18. Soon-Hoo, S.O., Kim, J., Cheong, K., Cho, G.: Evaluating the service quality of third party logistics service providers using the analytic hierarchy process. Journal of Information Systems and Technology Management 3, 261–270 (2006)
19. Senthil, S., Srirangacharyulu, B., Ramesh, A.: A decision making methodology for the selection of reverse logistics operating channels. Revista Produção Online 38, 418–428 (2012)
20. Senthil, S., Srirangacharyulu, B., Ramesh, A.: A robust hybrid multi-criteria decision making methodology for contractor evaluation and selection in third-party reverse logistics. Expert Systems with Applications: An International Journal 41, 50–58 (2014)
21. Chiang, Z., Tzeng, G.-H.: A third party logistics provider for the best selection in Fuzzy dynamic decision environments. International Journal of Fuzzy Systems 11, 1–10 (2009)
22. Bhatti, R.S., Kumar, P., Kumar, D.: Analytical Modeling of third party service provider selection in lead logistics provider environments. Journal of Modelling in Management 5, 275–286 (2010)
23. Rosa, E.P.S., Sellito, M.A., Mendes, L.W.: Avaliação multicriterial de desempenho e separação em aglomerados de fornecedores críticos de uma manufatura OKP. Revista Produção Online 16, 413–428 (2006)
24. Grewal, C.S., Sareen, K.K., Gill, S.: A multicriteria logistics-outsourcing decision making using the analytic hierarchy process. International Journal of Services Technology and Management 9, 1–13 (2008)
25. Cooper, H.M., Lindsay, J.L.L.: Research synthesis and meta-analysis. Sage Publications (1998)
26. Bardin, L.: El análisis de contenido. Ediciones akal. Madrid (1986)
27. Bryman, A.: Research Methods and Organization studies. Unwin Hyman, London (1989)
28. Westbrook, R.: Action Research: a new paradigm for research in production and operations management. International Journal of Operations and Production Management 15, 6–20 (1995)
29. Coughlan, P., Coghlan, D.: Action research for operations management. International Journal of Operations & Production Management 22, 220–240 (2002)
30. Thiollent, M.: Metodologia da pesquisa-ação, 15th edn. Cortez. São Paulo (2007)
31. Oliveira Neto, G., Godinho Filho, C., Memorian, M., Costa, M.A.G., Silva, B.K., Estratégia, D.: em Terceirização para contratação de Operador Logístico: uma abordagem teórica sob a ótica da teoria baseada em recursos. Revista Gestão & Produção (2014)
32. Oliveira Neto, G.C.: Integração complexa entre empresa contratante e operador logístico: Critérios para contratação. Dissertação. UNIP, São Paulo (2008)
33. Deng, Y., Chan, F.T.S.: A new fuzzy dempster MCDM method and its application in supplier selection. Expert Systems with Applications: An International Journal 38, 9854–9861 (2011)

A Multidisciplinary Model of Problem Solving in Complex Production Systems

Ralph Riedel[1], Ulrike Starker[2], and Rüdiger von der Weth[3]

[1] Technische Universität Chemnitz, Factory Planning and Factory Management, Germany
ralph.riedel@mb.tu-chemnitz.de
[2] University of Bamberg, Department of Educational Research, Germany
ulrike.starker@uni-bamberg.de
[3] Dresden University of Applied Sciences, Business Administration, Human Resources
Management and Industrial Science, Germany
weth@htw-dresden.de

Abstract. Future production systems, if they want to remain competitive, need the capability to autonomously adapt to new challenges, to learn new behavior and to solve complex problems. This leads to a changing role of the employees as part of sociotechnical (production) systems, because it's mainly their capability to cope with complex problem situations that determines the capabilities of the whole system. The paper presents a multidisciplinary, holistic approach to model and to design production systems from a problem solving perspective. The modelling architecture comprises of three interacting levels. Those are described in detail as well as the propositions which could be derived from the model and its parts.

Keywords: production system, modelling, simulation, problem solving.

1 Introduction

Industrial companies, and therefore production and logistics systems, face new challenges such as an increasing level of globalization and networked production, a reduced and diversified workforce potential, shorter product lifecycles, etc. This leads to a changing role of humans in production systems – they need to continuously adapt to new situations, new technology, new processes and new organizations [1]. Therefore, production systems need to be designed in a way that they facilitate learning processes and that they foster the motivation and competence of workers to cope with changes, deviations from normality and disturbances. Beside cognitive capabilities, emotional factors like anxiety or confidence also play a decisive role. As a consequence certain design strategies for work systems, working processes and for the whole production systems have to meet the aforementioned requirements.

As a prerequisite a sound understanding of the basic psychological processes and their interactions with system's characteristics is absolutely necessary. Therefore, qualitatively improved models of production systems are needed to support the

B. Grabot et al. (Eds.): APMS 2014, Part I, IFIP AICT 438, pp. 387–394, 2014.

analysis and design of sophisticated solutions. In this paper we present a conceptual framework for such an integrated model by which it will be possible to map and to integrate the problem solving and learning capabilities of workers in production systems based on basic emotional factors and psychological mechanisms. This extended sociotechnical model will also be able to close a transaction gap between planning and reality.

The paper is organized as follows: First we will discuss briefly the state of the art of production system modelling. In a second part we will refer to the basics of problem solving and problem solving capability. In the main part of the paper we will explain our concept of a multidisciplinary, integrated model of production systems. After a short overview of the model's architecture we will unfold its single components. Finally we will draw some conclusions and we will give an outlook on future research, also addressing some hypotheses about the behavior of the extended model.

2   Modelling of Production Systems

The planning of production systems as well as operations management is usually based on a system modelling approach, i.e. the analysis, evaluation and design of such systems is done with the help of models [2]. Such models normally cover the elements of the system (like technical equipment, products and material, workers) and their interaction (material flow, processing time etc.). Often the models are used for simulations [3] where experiments are conducted to test for example different parameter settings. Simulation-ready models can be found in a multitude of applications in production systems planning, e.g. in supply chain management and for the optimization of logistics processes [4], for transportation processes in micro- and macrologistics [5], for planning and scheduling problems [6], for the configuration of production networks and for ramp-up processes [7, 8], etc.

Usually such models cover mainly technical aspects and mirror the modelled system at its normal operation mode. Although recent approaches of artificial intelligence [9] make use of certain concepts of human information processing, the human itself as an autonomous subject and the dynamic interaction of such subjects has not yet been addressed. Also other sophisticated approaches like the person oriented simulation [10], the analysis of decision systems [11], the integration of human performance models (circadian rhythm) in simulation tools [12] or learning-capable and communicative agents in socio-cultural processes [13] have not been able to fill the gap.

It can be concluded that the demand for integrating human behavior into production system's models has already been identified [12] [14, 15]. However, there are only a few concrete modelling approaches so far and even fewer approaches with a profound psychological background which can be used for predicting human behavior in such systems. Emotional regulation, complex problem solving processes and the interaction of several subjects haven't been included in production systems models so far.

3   Problem Solving and Problem Solving Competence

The main challenge in integrating human behavior in production systems emerge from modelling human behavior, which is able to solve the complex problems described above. The ability to solve complex problems refers to several demands. E.g. the most accurate test for cognitive sub-functions in complex problem solving is about "decision making", "system analysis" and "searching for mistakes" [16]. Moreover it is basic knowledge in psychology that success in problem solving is not only based on cognitive abilities and skills. In critical situations coping with problems depends highly on the actual level of subjective control [17, 18]. If problems are increasingly new, opaque and complex, the chance to derive plans and decisions from consolidated knowledge becomes more and more improbable and this itself is a stressor by reducing the level of control. Because of that typical mistakes were found in experiments simulating complex situations. These mistakes are far beyond the intellectual level of the actors and their probability is high [19]. Generally a lower performance occurs in decision making under stress [20]. However, empirical studies show that a general high level of self-efficacy improves the performance of problem solvers [19], [21, 22]. Erpenbeck & Rosenstiel [23] have the hypothesis that a high level of self-efficacy is also improving the tendency and ability to act autonomous in difficult situations. Self-efficacy in work situations is not a personal trait. It depends on learning in problem solving situations. In work context it depends on several aspects [24]:

- knowhow in the specific domain
- general problem solving experience
- integration in well performing organizational processes
- social support.

Studies by Starker [25] show that successful entrepreneurs have the ability to develop strategies for emotion regulation in complex situations. Students who have the ability to change actively their mood in problem solving situations have significantly better results in a computer simulated management game.

The interaction of emotion and cognitive processes in problem solving behavior was also tested in cognitive science research about action regulation. Basing on the PSI-model of Dörner [26] virtual agents have been programmed to develop strategies for survival in a fictitious micro-world [27, 28]. Different types of computer programs (emotional vs. non-emotional) and real subjects have controlled the agents in the micro-world. Artificial agents with simulated emotional functions and real subjects were more similar and showed a different behavior compared to non-emotional programs. They were also more successful. The basic principles of the emotional agents of these studies were used for developing an emotional problem solver in our own work described now.

4   Multidisciplinary Model of Production Systems

4.1   Architecture

To integrate human behavior in a dynamic model of the production system we have to understand the processes at three levels.

- *Production model*: The production system level describes the activities and interaction of machines and workers as a whole. Human behavior is the central resource for problem solving and therefore also for innovation, change and the management of dysfunctional processes. Human behavior is unique, that means two persons can behave differently in the same situation and one person will not repeat automatically the same behavior in the same situation. The production model describes, which forms of organization and processes fosters problem solving activities and which kind of human problem solving activities are improving performance and problem solving capability of the whole production system
- *Incentive model:* On the work system level it is described how a specific work situation impacts a specific individual. Which part of the reality is experienced on a specific work place? Which incentives and affordances exist in this work situation and how do they differ depending on the knowledge and the emotional state of the specific person? How can the work place be improved to encourage and enable people to more problem solving activity?
- *Behavior model:* The behavior model describes how the incentives influence the individual regulation of behavior and how this behavior influences the performances of the production system and changes it. The behavior model is dynamic. Actual control, self-efficacy, learning processes and problem solving strategies are changing in the process. This influences performance and the kind and intensity of problem solving activities.

The model shall allow insights which organizational structures, formal processes and work place designs encourage workers to solve problems autonomously and which are the prerequisites that these autonomous activities improve the problem solving capability of the whole production system.

4.2   Production Model

The core of the extended production model covers the interaction between design parameters of the production system, the capability for problem solving and learning as well as central system indicators. The approach is presented in fig. 1.

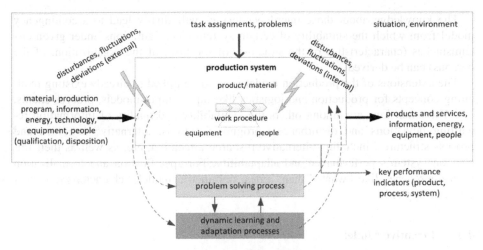

Fig. 1. Extended model of production systems

The description of problem solving and learning processes are crucial for the extended production model. Those are dependent on parameters of the situation, the task itself as well as the person. Those problem solving and learning processes are triggered by external (or even internal) assignments. Hereby, unexpected events resulting from internal or external dynamics, for instance changes in the production program, technology changes, disturbances, etc., play an important role. The problem solving and learning processes themselves lead to certain results which have an impact on the processes and stages in the production system. The system, esp. its behavior, can then be evaluated by key indicators like robustness, resilience, adaptability, productivity etc.

As the influence of structural and process parameters on economic and logistics performance indicators is already well known, the innovative core of the extended production model lies in the impact of system's design parameters on indicators for the efficient and effective reaction on disturbances, deviations and changes – see fig. 2.

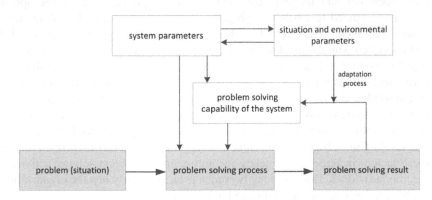

Fig. 2. Variables in the extended production model

The knowledge about those interdependencies will finally lead to a contingency model from which the suitability of certain system's configurations under given circumstances (characteristics of the situation, of the task, of the organization, of the persons) can be derived.

The extensions of the production model need to be linked to already existing modelling concepts for production and logistics like input-output-models, process chains, etc. The extensions are among others the availability and quality of information regarding deviations and disturbances, prognosis options, alternative activities and process structures, including alternative resource allocation, etc. as well as their impact on system's performance and adaptability. For specification and formalization such approaches like "what-if-then" rules, parametric models, characteristic curves could be applied.

4.3   Incentive Model

The incentive model is based upon classical work Lewin [29], Gibson [30] and Norman [31]. The input for this level is both the actual data of the production system and the actual state and position of the respective worker. Depending on the production data and his actual coordinates the actual perceptual field can be computed. The incentives for activities which are in this field depend on his knowledge (e.g. about the correct use of a certain tool) and his actual plans and mood. The authors are especially interested in incentives for autonomous problem solving activities. The amount of incentive varies from person to person, depending on knowledge, problem solving abilities and self-efficacy. On the other hand there exist organizational restrictions like the amount of time, which can be used for a problem solving activity, the formal rules for work in the production system for the handling of incidents and dysfunctions. Additional factors are the availability and motivation for colleagues´ support.

4.4   Behavior Model

The behavior model describes the internal processes of action regulation and how the external incentives and the cognitive and emotional prerequisites of the specific workers are computed to a behavior program. The program is an adapted version of the general PSI-agent described before. It is changed for the specific purposes of the production-system-simulation. The most important internal variable is the actual level of subjective control and the possible changes which occur when a worker follows the respective incentives of the possible alternatives. The results of his activities depend on his knowledge and his actual mood. There are three kinds of results: a change in the production system, a development of his knowledge and maybe a change in the workers mood. For starting problem solving activities the person needs an acceptable internal level of self-efficacy, knowledge and appropriate problem solving strategies. All these factors increase the tendency for autonomous problem solving activity for the specific individual. This tendency becomes even stronger when the organizational framework supports social interaction and mutual help.

5   Conclusion and Outlook

As discussed the proposed model should be able to allow better prognoses about autonomous problem solving behavior of workers in corresponding production
processes in reality. The next important step will be to develop the validity and explanatory capability of the model. At the moment a real production system in a laboratory setting is planned which should serve as benchmark towards the prognoses of an
also more sophisticated simulation model. A first simulation based upon the model
produced plausible results about fictitious workers´ behavior in a production system
[32] and proofed the feasibility of the approach. Planned experiments will lead to
insights on how certain configurations of production systems and workers with specific prerequisites influence the readiness for problem solving activities. By comparing
the prognoses of the model with real human behavior in the laboratory production
system, the model will be improved step by step (so called corner stone method). The
long term objective of the presented and continuing research work is a better understanding in which way the organization of production systems and the design of work
places, processes and working conditions influence problem solving in production
systems.

References

1. Rösio, C., Säfsten, K.: Reconfigurable productionsystem design – theoreticaland practical
   challenges. J. of Manufacturing Technology Management 24(7), 998–1018 (2013)
2. VDI 5200: Factory planning - Planning procedures. VDI, Düsseldorf (2011)
3. VDI 3633: Simulation of systems in materials handling, logistics and production. VDI,
   Düsseldorf (1993)
4. Chang, Y., Makatsoris, H.: Supply Chain Modelling Using Simulation. International Journal of Simulation 2(1), 24–30 (2001)
5. Dangelmaier, W., Mueck, B.: Using Dynamic Multiresolution Modeling to Analyze large
   Material Flow Systems. In: Ingalls, R.G., Rossetti, M.D., Peters, B.A., Smith, J.S. (eds.)
   Proceedings of the 2004 Winter Simulation Conference (WSC 2004), pp. 1720–1727
   (2004)
6. Hildebrandt, T., Heger, J., Scholz-Reiter, B.: Towards improved dispatching rules for
   complex shop floor scenarios: A genetic programming approach. In: Proceedings of the
   12th Annual Conference on Genetic and Evolutionary Computation, Portland/ Oregon, pp.
   257–264 (2010)
7. Weiler, S., Páez, D., Chun, J.-H., Graves, S., Lanza, G.: Supply chain design for the global
   expansion of manufacturing capacity in emerging markets. CIRP Journal of Manufacturing
   Science and Technology 4(3), 265–280 (2011)
8. Fleischer, J., Lanza, G., Ender, T.: A Dynamic Business-Process Based Production Ramp-
   up Simulation Model. In: Production Engineering Research and Development, vol. XIII
   (2), pp. 107–110. Hannover (2006)
9. Scholz-Reiter, B., Rippel, D., Sowade, S.: A Concept for Simulation of Autonomous Logistic Processes. International Journal of Systems Applications, Engineering & Development 5(3), 324–333 (2011)
10. VDI 3633/6: Representation of human resources in simulation models. VDI, Düsseldorf
    (2001)

11. Zülch, G.: Modelling and Simulation of Human DecisionMaking in Manufacturing Systems. In: Perrone, L.F., Wieland, F.P., Lawson, J., Liu, B.G., Nicol, D.M., Fujimoto, R.M. (eds.) Proceedings of the 2006 Winter Simulation Conference (2006)
12. Baines, T.S., Mason, S., Siebers, P.-O.: Humans: The missing link in manufacturing simulation? Simulation Modelling Practice and Theory (12), 515–526 (2004)
13. Sun, R.: The CLARION cognitive architecture: Extending cognitive modeling to social simulation. In: Sun, R. (ed.) Cognition and Multi-Agent Interaction. Cambridge University Press, New York (2006)
14. Grabot, B., Marsina, S., Mayere, A., Riedel, R., Williams, P.: A socio-technical view on Supply Chain Management problems. In: Karwowski, W., Trzcielinski, S. (eds.) Value Stream Activities Management: HAAMAHA 2007 - Managing Enterprise of the Future, pp. 240–253. IEA Press, Poznan (2007)
15. Riedel, R., Fransoo, J., Wiers, V., Fischer, K., Cegarra, J., Jentsch, D.: Building Decision Systems for Acceptance. In: Fransoo, J.C., Waefler, T., Wilson, J.R. (eds.) Behavioral Operations in Planning and Scheduling, Springer, Heidelberg (2010)
16. Leutner, D., Fleischer, J., Wirth, J., Greiff, S., Funke, J.: Analytical anddynamicalproblem-solving.... Psychologische Rundschau 63, 34–42 (2012) (in German)
17. Selye, H.: Stress and disease. Science 122, 625–631 (1955)
18. Lazarus, R.S.: Emotion and adaption. Oxford University Press, New York (1991)
19. Dörner, D.: The logic of failure. Metropolitan Books, New York (1996)
20. Cannon-Bowers, J.A., Salas, E.: Makingdecisions under stress: Implications for individual and teamtraining. American Psychological Association, Washington DC (1998)
21. Bandura, A.: Self-efficacy: Toward a unifying theory of behavioral change. Psychological Review 84, 191–215 (1977)
22. Jerusalem, M., Pekrun, R.: Emotion, Motivation and Performance. Hogrefe, Göttingen (1999) (in German)
23. Erpenbeck, J., Rosenstiel, L.V.: Handbook competence measurement: Recognizing, understanding and evaluating competencies in organizations, pedagogy and psychology. Schäfer-Poeschel, Stuttgart (2007) (in German)
24. Von der Weth, R., Starker, U.: Integrating motivational and emotional factors in implementation strategies for new enterprise planning software. Production Planning and Control 21(4), 375–385 (2010)
25. Starker, U.: Emotional Adaptivity. Pabst, Lengerich (2012) (in German)
26. Dörner, D.: Blueprint of a soul. Rowohlt, Reinbek/Hamburg (1999) (in German)
27. Dörner, D., Starker, U.: Should successful agents have emotions? In: Proceedings of the Sixth International Conference on Cognitive Modelling, pp. 344–345. Lawrence Erlbaum, Mahwah (2004)
28. ElKady, A., Starker, U.: Simulating different human Action Strategies in Uncertain Environments. In: Opwis, K., Penner, I. (eds.) Proceedings of Kogwis 2005, Schwabe, Basel (2005)
29. Norman, D.A.: The psychology of everyday things. Basic Books, New York (1988)
30. Lewin, K.: Main Features of a topological Psychology. Huber, Bern (1969) (in German)
31. Gibson, J.J.: The Theory of Affordances. In: Shaw, R., Bransford, J. (eds.) Perceiving, Acting, and Knowing: Toward an Ecological Psychology, pp. 67–82. Lawrence Erlbaum, Hillsdale (1977)
32. Riedel, R., Müller, E., von der Weth, R., Pflugradt, N.: Integrating Human Behaviour into Factory Simulation – a Feasibility Study. In: Proceedings of the IEEE International Conference on Industrial Engineering and Industrial Management, Hong Kong (2009)

Serious Play as a Method for Process Design

Mary Dempsey[1], Ralph Riedel[2], and Martina Kelly[1]

[1] National University of Ireland Galway, College of Engineering and Informatics,
Galway, Ireland
{mary.dempsey,martina kelly}@nuigalway.ie
[2] Technische Universität Chemnitz, Factory Planning and Factory Management, Germany
ralph.riedel@mb.tu-chemnitz.de

Abstract. As motivating and including people is a crucial aspect in any planning, design and change process there is always a need for appropriate methods and tools to support this. Lego Serious Play (LSP) is such a method which was developed to facilitate among others communication, creativity and shared mental models. In this paper the application of LSP is demonstrated for the case of re-designing a product development lifecycle process. With the case study we pursue a qualitative approach to seek for support that LSP is able to support team building and team decision processes, to avoid typical pitfalls of group-think which will finally lead to solutions of higher quality, to efficient processes and to satisfied participants.

Keywords: Lego Serious Play, new product development, process design, participative design processes.

1 Introduction

Due to current challenges from a dynamic and global economy enterprises are forced to maintain and improve competitiveness. This requirement for improvement is mainly based on effective and efficient processes as well as innovative products and services. The need for flexible and competitive processes encompasses not only production and logistics but also the necessary supportive and administrative processes. It also extends to early activities in the product lifecycle such as product development. Well-established principles already exist for the efficient design of production and logistics processes, many of which have been developed within the Lean Management paradigm. With respect to supportive and administrative processes, business process re-engineering (BPR) and business process management (BPM) techniques are well supported. However, when faced with new product development and the product development lifecycle process, greater challenges exist. Due to the inherent complexity of process analysis and process design, enterprises tend to follow heuristic principles. These principles are based predominately on the knowledge of the people involved in the processes. Moreover, in every process and organizational design endeavor the people affected need to be involved not only for their specialist know-how but they must identify with and accept the solution in order to guarantee a successful outcome.

B. Grabot et al. (Eds.): APMS 2014, Part I, IFIP AICT 438, pp. 395–402, 2014.
© IFIP International Federation for Information Processing 2014

As motivating and including people is a crucial aspect in any change process there is always a need for methods and tools to support this. Serious Play approaches are one approach to not only unleashing people's creativity but also including them actively in the creative problem solving processes and thereby building identity with the developed solution. LEGO® SERIOUS PLAY ® (LSP) was developed to be an innovative, experiential process and has been shown to extend players' awareness of problems and ideas, and to enhance creativity and enable teamwork. This paper details the results of a case study which uses LSP as a tool to support the development of an effective New Product Development Life Cycle (NPDLC) process.

2   Theoretical Background and Methodology

2.1   Process Reengineering and Implementing Change

Evaluating, rethinking and reengineering are increasingly seen as a way to improve the productivity, product quality and operations of a company [1]. Hereby, it is widely agreed that the implementation phase of a newly designed process is of major concern [2]. Solving technological and project planning issues are necessary, but not sufficient, preconditions for the success of a process reengineering endeavor [2]. Reengineering processes, especially creative and collaborative processes like product development or production planning, are complex, involving numerous factors and especially people from different, heterogeneous backgrounds [2]. The literature suggests that the main factors in ensuring successful change are giving ownership to people, providing and communicating a clear vision, empowering people, and leadership [3, 4, 5, 6].

Although there is wide agreement that empowering people, facilitating team work and (autonomous) team decisions are necessary in the decision-making process, many well-known pitfalls exist. These include self-censorship, higher risk-taking behavior, and stereotyping which can lead to defective decision-making and reduced performance.

However, communication, shared mental models and beliefs can help to avoid those problems and therefore are seen as crucial aspects in team decision-making [7]. As a consequence, suitable methods and tools must be provided to ensure such beneficial conditions when empowering teams to participate in process (re)engineering. One of the methods that may support team decision making in this way is LEGO® SERIOUS PLAY® (LSP).

2.2   The LSP Method

Lego Serious Play® (LSP) was originally developed to facilitate the strategy building process of the LEGO Company. LSP can best be described as a facilitated workshop where participants respond to tasks by building symbolic and metaphorical models with LEGO bricks and subsequently presenting them to the other participants. The LSP method is built on some basic values, like "The answer is in the system", "Everyone has to express his/her reflections" and "There is no ONE right answer".

Participants are enabled to interact in a non-judgmental, free-thinking and playful way and can therefore work towards developing a common understanding, creative ideas etc. [8, 9]. LSP is founded on four main constructs:

1. the importance of play as a way to learn through exploration and storytelling
2. constructionism
3. the hand-mind connection as a path for creative and expressive thinking
4. the role of the different kinds of imagination

In a typical LSP workshop the participants are first asked to build their perception of a particular problem. In the creative and spontaneous building process that follows, the participants give meaning to their models. Afterwards each participant explains the underlying story of his or her model to the others. Participants must respect the model and its meaning but they are allowed to ask questions to clarify details. In an LSP workshop the individual models can be used to build a shared model, to draw connections, and to create a landscape with so called 'external agents'. In a concluding reflection part the group creates insights [8, 9, 10]. The whole model can be the basis for playing, for analyzing particular scenarios, and finally extracting guiding principles [8].

The LSP method has already been applied to a multitude of problems [9, 10, 11, 12, 13]. Considering the mechanisms and theories inherent in the method it can be expected that it also lends itself to positive team decisions in the context of re-engineering any kind of processes.

Table 1. Research design

Component	Equivalents
The study's questions	Is LSP a suitable tool to support also the collective / participative reengineering of a more or less creative process like product development?
The study's propositions	LSP supports collective decision making when reengineering a design process – typical deficiencies are avoided. Participants are satisfied with the process. Participants show a high identity with the result.
The study's units of analysis	The reengineering of a "product development lifecycle" process with a certain number of participants from different departments.
The logic of linking the data to the propositions	Observed and self-reported qualitative variables lead to conclusions regarding the propositions.
The criteria for interpreting findings	Number of observed groupthink events during the reengineering process, self-reported satisfaction, identification and acceptance from the participants, tangible outcome of the reengineering process.

2.3   Methodology and Propositions

A case study approach was chosen as the research methodology. A case study can be described as the "detailed examination of a single example of a class of phenomena" [14, p. 34]. It is useful in providing hypotheses, which may then be tested systematically later on with a broader empirical basis [15].

A case study research design usually has the following components displayed in table 1 [16, 17, 18] with its equivalents in our particular case.

3   Case Study Analysis

3.1   Case Description

This case study examines the impact of LSP as a tool in creating an effective Product Development Life Cycle (PDLC) process in which it is necessary to clearly define each functional role and respective responsibility. The company involved in the case study is a global medical device development and manufacturing business with head-quarters in the USA and a number of operations worldwide including Ireland. The company had undergone a period of rapid growth and this resulted in functional areas roles and responsibilities both overlapping and separating from each other. The result of this rapid growth led to confusion around functional roles and responsibilities. However, development teams are required to work very closely together to support PDLC processes in order to reduce time to market. Of interest to the researchers was whether or not improvements to the PDLC process could be made using LSP tools and techniques. To this end, a one-day workshop was convened. The workshop was conducted off-site, over a seven-hour period and was facilitated by a certified LSP facilitator. Detailed observations were made throughout the workshop by another independent person. At the end of the day feedback was elicited from participants using group reflection exercises and an individual questionnaire survey. The workshop design followed the typical LSP setup as explained in chapter 2.2.

At the outset, the participants declared that they had an open mind and no particular expectations at the start of the workshop. They were aware that the workshop involved the use of Lego and that the theme was defining functional roles and responsibilities during New Product Development Life Cycle (NPDLC) processes. The purpose was to create collaborative clusters working together towards a common goal. The challenge included how best to provide an authentic collaborative environment through learning activities to achieve a set of objectives. The Groups involved in the workshop were from three functional areas in the company and involved eight senior management participants (2 female and 6 male). The groups comprised the following:

- Research & Development (4 personnel)
- Regulatory Affairs (2 personnel)
- Design Assurance (2 personnel)

The workshop program involved (1) the introduction of participants and a brief introduction to LSP rules; (2) LSP skills building; (3) the building of individual and shared model(s) of the as-is- product development cycle; (4) the building of role models (group work); (5) the building of a shared model of a future product development lifecycle (aspiration) and the assignment of the different roles and their responsibility; (6) a final discussion with a conclusion and reflection and the agreement on further steps.

Each member was allocated an LSP kit and very quickly became familiar and comfortable with the workshop requirements. The 3D models built by each individual/group served as a communication tool and provided for a collaboration space to develop group responses and to trigger questions, see as an example fig. 1. From an observer's perspective this provided for peer-input and evaluation exercises and allowed knowledge sharing amongst the wider cohort. Obviously the 3D models acted as useful representations of proposed processes and allowed areas of overlap, redundancy, gaps and complications to be identified in a transparent way.

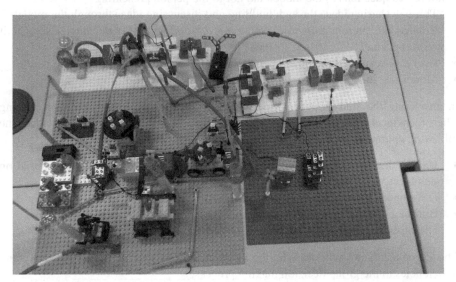

Fig. 1. Shared model of the future product development lifecycle

3.2   Evaluation Results

The feedback from the participants provided in the questionnaire centered around the following themes of collaboration challenges, resolution techniques and the resulting benefits. In answering the question "Is LSP a suitable tool to support the collective/participative reengineering of a more or less creative process like product development?" the following comments can support that this is the case.

- "Getting the group to engage openly and honestly with each other"
- "Ensuring everyone engaged openly and honestly in group discussions"
- "A lot of conflict within the group - was aware of this before the session and wasn't sure if it would work"
- "Pre-defined opinions strongly held"

- "Integrating models developed individually with the group models"
- "Differing views on process descriptions"
- "Definition of roles and responsibilities. Understanding of the process steps and stages from different departmental prospective in the PDLC"
- "Understanding/not knowing other members needs and perspectives"
- "Lack of clarity of roles"
- "Not all aligned back at the day job"

The participants explained how they resolved the challenges of working in a group:

- "Using the Lego we built models current and future that facilitated very good discussion"
- "Open communication, respect the viewpoint of others, spoke about the model and addressed questions to the model and not to the person presenting"
- "Through sharing ideas through building and discussing ideas through the models"
- "Rotated the presentation role, ensured everyone spoke to the model so that it wasn't personal"
- "Everyone respected the others opinion within the context of the exercise"
- "Model was independent of personalities and functions/departments"

In answering the study's proposition that LSP supports collective decision making when reengineering a design process and hence typical deficiencies are avoided, the following comments were made with respect to group/team engagement.

- "Having the three groups working together without any disruption and focused on one objective"
- "Developed closer ties between individuals and teams".
- "Building on the existing relationship between all members of the team"
- "Establishing group views for later discussion"

Those comments are supported by the independent observer who didn't identify any deficiencies in the group decision making process.

With respect to understanding roles and responsibilities, the participants rated understanding of each other's roles and responsibilities as a benefit and also highlighted the positive aspects of the experience. In terms of shared understanding for future growth, the participants recognized the need for growth and progress and felt this could be achieved through LSP. Benefits gleaned from the LSP experience included: "Listening to current state of affairs and preferred future state"; "Hearing other ideas and perspectives"; "Individuals take visual ideas from one another"; "Discussing ideas and challenges"; "Agreeing that future/continued actions are necessary to create an agreed strategy"; "More focus on the bigger picture"; "Bonding and alignment of views"; "Shared understanding was developed".

3.3   Advantages and Disadvantages

Whilst the participants appreciated working with visual tools and clearly identified the 'real-world' relevance of replicating industry scenarios and problem-solving activities through 3D models they were aware of the time required by this process. They also stressed the need for follow-up to implement the new model in the form of a written plan of action. It was also suggested that non-attendees may not take the process seriously so translating the output to the organization in a suitable manner would be important.

All the participants were satisfied with the workshop experience and agreed that working with LSP provided them with a deep learning experience and engagement with the group. The positive dynamic and confidence of all grew and they came to a shared understanding on the team goals as a result. The reasons for the positive outcomes fit with former research results proofing that the LSP methodology gives ownership to people, provides the possibility to express clear visions and leads to a shared understanding by an easy modelling technique.

4   Conclusion and Future Research

The responses from the participants indicate that incorporating LSP as a support tool for NPDLC resulted in extremely engaged and creative managers who became absorbed in a process of improvement. The responses also highlight that the objectives set at the start of the workshop were achieved. The results suggest a deeper understanding of NPDLC roles and responsibilities than previously. Also engagement with the process was enhanced as participants were required to use higher level cognition. The groups also rotated the leadership role and this facilitated group problem solving, communication and improved leadership skills. Perceived disadvantages of LSP were minimal.

The company intends to address and resolve gaps and misconceptions in the current PDLC process with respect to roles and responsibilities. It was agreed that an action plan would be developed and that a follow-up LSP workshop and review would take place in 12 months' time to determine what process improvement if any was achieved.

Further research will focus on evaluations on whether or not teams can function more effectively under different conditions. Variables to be considered may be problem's complexity and tangibility, group's heterogeneity, individuals' background, experiences and attitudes, situational parameters etc.

References

1. Lee, R.G., Dale, B.G.: Business process management: a review and evaluation. Business Process Management Journal 4(3), 214–225 (1998)
2. Grover, V., Jeong, S.R., Kettinger, W.J., Teng, J.T.C.: The implementation of business process reengineering. Journal of Management Information Systems 12(1), 109–144 (1995)
3. Paton, R.A., McCalman, J.: Change Management. Sage, London (2008)
4. Fritzenschaft, T.: Critical Success Factors of Change Management. Springer Gabler, Wiesbaden (2014)

5. Cameron, E., Green, M.: Making Sense of Change Management. Kogan Page Ldt. (2012)
6. Trkman, P.: The critical success factors of business process management. International Journal of Information Management 30, 125–134 (2010)
7. Neck, C.P., Manz, C.C.: From Groupthink to Teamthink: Toward the Creation of Constructive Thought Patterns in Self-Managing Work Teams. Human Relations 47(8), 929–952 (1994)
8. Kristiansen, P., Hansen, P.K., Møller Nielsen, L.: Articulation of tacit and complex knowledge. In: Schönsleben, P., Vodicka, M., Smeds, R., Riis, J.O. (eds.) 13th International Workshop of the IFIP WG 5.7 SIG, pp. 77–86. Eidgenössische Technische Hochschule Zürich (2009)
9. Hansen, P.K., Mabogunje, A., Haase, L.M.: Get a Grip on Sense - Making and Exploration Dealing with Complexity through Serious Play. In: Sun, H., Jiao, R., Xie, M. (eds.) IEEE International Conference on Industrial Engineering and Engineering Management, pp. 1593–1597. IEEE Press (2009)
10. Frick, E., Tardini, S., Cantoni, L.: LEGO®SERIOUS PLAY® - A state of the art of its applications in Europe. White Paper, Università della Svizzera italiana, Lugano, Switzerland (2013)
11. Hadida, A.: Let your hand do the thinking! Lego bricks, strategic thinking and ideas generation within organizations. Strategic Direction 29(2), 3–5 (2013)
12. Jentsch, D., Riedel, R., Müller, E.: Strategy and Innovation for the Production Systems of SME. In: Doolen, T., Van Aken, E. (eds.) Proceedings of the 2011 Industrial Engineering Research Conference (IERC), Reno (2011)
13. Jentsch, D., Riedel, R., Mueller, E.: Flow and Physical Objects in Experiential Learning for Industrial Engineering Education. In: Emmanouilidis, C., Taisch, M., Kiritsis, D. (eds.) APMS 2012. IFIP AICT, vol. 397, pp. 566–573. Springer, Heidelberg (2013)
14. Abercrombie, N., Hill, S., Turner, B.S.: Dictionary of sociology. Penguin, Harmondsworth (1984)
15. Flyvbjerg, B.: Five Misunderstandings About Case-Study Research. Qualitative Inquiry 12(2), 219–245 (2006)
16. Darke, P., Shanks, G., Broadbent, M.: Successfully completing case study research: combining rigour, relevance and pragmatism. Info. Systems J. 8, 273–289 (1998)
17. Rowley, J.: Using Case Studies in Research. Management Research News 25(1), 16–27 (2002)
18. Yin, R.K.: Case study research; design and methods. Sage, Thousand Oaks (2003)

Planning Nervousness in Product Segmentation: Literature Review and Research Agenda

Ann-Louise Andersen, Nicolai Præstholm, Kjeld Nielsen, and Thomas Ditlev Brunø

Department of Mechanical and Manufacturing Engineering,
Aalborg University, Denmark
annlou.andersen@gmail.com

Abstract. Differentiated planning is one of the means for today's companies to accommodate the increasing needs for product variety, delivery responsiveness, and cost-efficiency. Even though, product segmentation is the foundation for such planning, planning nervousness has not yet been addressed from this perspective. This paper seeks to establish a relation between planning nervousness and segmentation by analyzing the current body of literature with the objective of identifying overlaps between the two areas. The literature characteristics are assessed and directions for future research are provided.

Keywords: Planning, Nervousness, Product Segmentation.

1   Introduction

In today's business environment, one of the means to achieving competitive advantage is to offer a wide range of differentiated products in a cost-efficient and responsive manner, as customers have increasingly different needs [1]. As a result, companies need to design supply chains that can cope with conflicting demand, e.g. the need for providing both low-cost and customized product solutions, which means that supply chains must operate different setups simultaneously. The key to this is differentiated planning and control, where products are assigned to relevant product segments, which are subject to different planning methods, e.g. make-to-stock or make-to-order. The underlying foundation for practicing differentiated planning is the segmentation of products and items flowing in the supply chain. When this process is managed properly, a stable basis for securing product and item availability at the right levels of inventories is secured. In contrary, if the segmentation process contains instability, uncertainty is likely to ramify throughout the supply chain and through planning levels.

Thus, the purpose of this paper is to identify current state-of-art knowledge and unravel critical points on planning nervousness, in order to identify possible relations to item segmentation that can broaden knowledge of how to manage uncertainty in differentiated planning.

B. Grabot et al. (Eds.): APMS 2014, Part I, IFIP AICT 438, pp. 403–410, 2014.
© IFIP International Federation for Information Processing 2014

2   Literature Review Methodology

The objective of this literature review is to identify major tendencies in current literature on planning nervousness and possible connections to segmentation. Relevant research concerning nervousness was identified by searching the Web of Knowledge, Science Direct, Scopus, and Google Scholar databases. In order to ensure that relevant studies were not missed, four rather broad search terms were used: nervousness, planning nervousness, scheduling nervousness, and re-scheduling. Publications for the review were included if a) the study included one of the search terms in the title or abstract and if b) planning nervousness was included as a central element in the research. Through a qualitative assessment of these criteria, studies that primarily use nervousness as a term for uncertainty in general was excluded, as well as studies in which a specified planning level was not the primary context for the research or planning nervousness was only a minor parameter addressed. A total of 21 publications from 1979 to present were included and used as primary research in the review. In the following section, a brief review of the concept of planning nervousness is presented, followed by an assessment of the nervousness influencers that have been identified in literature.

3   Planning Nervousness

Planning nervousness is a term that has existed in research since the late 70's and was initially established for describing instability of plans on MRP level. MRP nervousness is defined as instability and frequent rescheduling of orders in terms of timing and quantity [2] [3] [4]. Later studies extend the concept of nervousness to MPS level, highlighting that nervousness propagates in the planning hierarchy [5] [6] [7]. Most recently, the concept of planning nervousness is broadened and covers multiple planning levels as well as multiple entities within supply chains [8] [9] [10]. In this sense, planning nervousness can be defined as the counterpart to planning stability, which is defined as the situation where plans do not change and equal the actual requirements imposed on the system [11]. Moreover, recent studies point out that nervousness has both vertical propagation in the planning hierarchy and horizontal propagation within the supply chain, which makes the phenomena highly critical to multiple performance aspects [12] [9] [13]. In connection to this, planning or system nervousness can be defined as a specific planning performance parameter, which magnitude should be evaluated when determining planning policy, e.g. inventory control policy or lot size policy [14] [15] [16].

Nervousness can be described as a consequence of planning flexibility and the ability to continuously respond to changing customer requests, where an essential trade-off between responsiveness and nervousness exists [17] [18]. However, this trade-off is primarily dealt with in the discussion of how often to re-plan, where frequent re-planning results in more updated parameters and ability to respond to urgent and changing customer needs, while nervousness increases in relation to the transition from the original plan to the updated plan. This relation emphasizes that planning nervousness cannot be approached in a vacuum, as it is a direct consequence of the applied planning policy and decisions within the planning system and therefore is interrelated with other planning outcomes e.g. service, responsiveness, and cost.

As the definition of planning nervousness has broadened, so has the discussion of its impact. In early works the consequence of MRP nervousness is primarily described as being confusion in shop floor priority, fluctuations in capacity utilization and incurring high rescheduling cost [19]. However, gradually the outcome of nervousness has been related more and more to the bullwhip effect, resulting in the two phenomena being used virtually as synonyms [9] [10] [12]. The bullwhip effect can basically be described as demand amplifications throughout the supply chain, where upstream links experience more fluctuating demand than downstream links, even when actual sales is rather stable [20]. The results of this are increased inventory buffers throughout the chain, fluctuating inventory levels, low capacity utilization, and delivery problems [12]. The similarities with nervousness are evident, as both the bullwhip effect and planning nervousness result from uncertainty generated by actions and policies applied within the planning system. However, when relating planning nervousness and the bullwhip effect, only the horizontal propagation of nervousness is considered, even though planning nervousness propagates both horizontally in the supply chain and vertically through planning hierarchies and product structure levels [10] [12]. Therefore, planning nervousness is in this paper considered as the broadest applicable term for system and planning uncertainty, defined as instability of plans in terms of timing and quantities requiring frequent rescheduling activities.

Some of the currently most addressed consequences of planning nervousness are disruptions in production plans and deliveries, increased inventory buffers, and increased planning cost [19] [11] [12]. Moreover, as plans become more and more unstable and predictability decreases, both planners and operators have reduced confidence in the planning system [2]. When the planning system does not reflect actual requirements on the operating system, humans are compelled to make manual adjustments in order not to damage customer service. However, such human planning adjustments and manipulations have actually proved to reinforce rather than mitigate planning nervousness, which creates a vicious circle of increased nervousness [10].

4   Planning Nervousness Influencers

Planning nervousness is addressed in various different planning contexts, which implies that various different influencers of nervousness are addressed as well. In Table 1, nervousness influencers addressed in central research are listed and divided as being either operational or environmental. The operational variables are directly controllable as they are internally generated and can be managed through planning policies, while the environmental variables are set by the operating environment and incontrollable by the planning system [19]. Some of the influencers included here are discussed primarily as means to dampen nervousness in the specific papers. However, recognizing a variable's dampening effect on nervousness is highly related to recognizing it as an influencer on nervousness.

In Figure 1, the influencers are classified under relevant groups that cover the meaning of the specifically mentioned influencers in Table 1. The aim of this is to unravel critical points in current knowledge and identify potential connection with product segmentation. In line with this, the findings suggest that there are currently two major tendencies in nervousness literature. The first is the discussion of how demand uncertainty and demand characteristics, e.g. in the timing and quantity of orders, influence the degree of nervousness experienced in the planning system. However, despite the inevitable impact of demand uncertainty, research in this area focuses solely on parameters that are difficult to control by companies. The second tendency in nervousness literature is the discussion of the impact of planning horizon, planning frequency, and lot-sizing rules on planning nervousness. The great main part of current research focuses on these parameters in inventory or MRP contexts. Despite the relevancy of such research, it has limited relevancy to product segmentation processes, where nervousness is believed to have as severe consequences as in the already treated planning contexts.

Table 1. Overview of Nervousness Literature

	Operating Variables	Environmental Variables	Context
[2]	Lot-sizing, planning horizon		MRP
[15]	Lot-sizing, order releases	Demand Variability	MRP/LRP
[4]	Planning frequency, planning horizon, lot-sizing	Demand Uncertainty Cost Structure	MRP
[21] [22]	Rolling horizon (planning frequency and planning horizon), lot-sizing, reordering method		Inventory Control
[19]	Lot-sizing, length of lead-time, length of planning horizon, component commonality	Demand variability, capacity utilization, cost structure in regards to delivery performance	MRP
[12] [23]	Planning horizon, planning frequency, varying planning processes	Demand variability, supply chain integration/collaboration, delay in information flow	Supply chain planning
[9] [10]	Planning Frequency, ease of representation (e.g. complexity of planning system), intervention/adjustments made by human planners, planning horizon	Number and structure of (organizations) planning levels, planning inertia (e.g. time to react), degree of interrelations in planning system	Planning hierarchy
[11]		Changes in customer orders, availability of raw materials, capacity/production uncertainty	MPS
[7] [6]	Length of planning horizon, length of frozen schedule, re-planning frequency, non-frozen interval strategy	Natural order cycle length, vendor flexibility, demand range, demand lumpiness	MPS

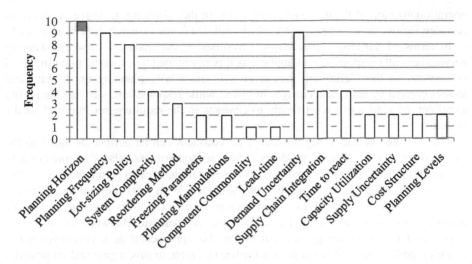

Fig. 1. Grouping of Nervousness Influencers

From the literature discussed above, it can be concluded that planning nervousness has received only limited attention in literature even though the term has existed for more than three decades. Moreover, research is limited to specific contexts, even though planning nervousness is considered a relevant property of planning system in general and undoubtedly has severe consequences in planning contexts other than those already addressed in literature. This also indicates a lack of explicit connection between planning nervousness and product segmentation.

The lack of connection between the two areas is critical, as product segmentation is an underlying process that secures a solid foundation for various planning activities both within single companies and integrated supply chains. Determining whether products are make-to-order or make-to-stock highly impacts how products are planned, replenished, and controlled. As nervousness propagates throughout planning levels, it is important to assess how this segmentation process impacts planning stability throughout the entire system. As in inventory management systems, where nervousness already has been well-addressed and quantified, decisions within the segmentation process and their impact on planning nervousness need to be assessable and measurable as well. This will constitute a highly improved foundation for decision-making, rather than merely relying on subjective intuition when addressing and handling nervousness issues in companies.

5   Nervousness in Product Segmentation

In order to broaden the context of planning nervousness and establish a connection with product segmentation, the definition, causes, and consequences of nervousness needs to be assessed from a segmentation context, as this will increase the operationalization of the nervousness concept. In the following, tentative connections between the two areas are proposed, which indicate future research directions as well.

In terms of defining segmentation nervousness, the trade-off between planning nervousness and responsiveness applies, as it is not related to a specific planning level or context. In this definition, nervousness is essentially planning uncertainty and shocks created by shifts and changes in plans, while responsiveness covers the ability to reflect the reality and react timely to changes in the requirements imposed on the system.

Thus, in the context of segmentation, nervousness can be defined as shifts in the assigned groups for specific products, while responsiveness relates to immediately and continuously updated segmentations based on changes in segmentation criteria e.g. demand variability, demand volume, etc. With this definition, planning nervousness in the context of segmentation is directly assessable, as it can be quantified by the number of shifts made in the segmentation between to successive runs. As a result, planning nervousness can be approached as a parameter under planning performance. It is a topic for further research, to investigate and empirically test if this relation between nervousness and segmentation holds. Moreover, studying the exact consequences of nervousness in segmentation should be on future research agendas, as literature on neither nervousness nor segmentation explicitly addresses this issue. It is expected that segmentation nervousness has both direct consequences as well as ramifications to other planning levels. A direct consequence is that stocking strategies for specific products change frequently, which causes either excess inventories or material unavailability. Olhager [24] describes both the negative and positive effects of shifting customer-order-decoupling point (CODP), which is related to the overall segmentation. However, he discusses CODP shifts solely from the perspective of strategic positioning and not from the perspective of frequent shifting caused by the planning processes. The strategic CODP shift effects are reduced or prolonged lead-times, increased or decreased production efficiency, and reduction or increases in WIP and inventory levels. In the context of frequent shifting, uncertainty in all of these areas is expected, which should be subject to further research.

In the literature review, rolling horizons were identified as one of the major sources of planning nervousness. The rolling horizon can be assessed through planning frequency and planning horizon, which are directly controllable parameters within the planning system. As the impact of these is highly acknowledged and they are both directly related to how segmentations are carried out, investigating their impact on nervousness is considered a viable first step in making a quantitative connection between the two areas. This will constitute a useful quantification and operationalization of key segmentation parameters in relation to planning nervousness.

6   Conclusion

Even though planning nervousness has existed as a research term for more than three decades, it is still limited to a few research contexts, being primarily MRP and inventory systems. However, planning nervousness is a relevant attribute of planning performance in general, meaning that other planning contexts should be considered in relation to nervousness as well.

In this paper, attention is drawn to the area of differentiated planning where a theoretical and tentative relationship to planning nervousness is established. The importance of such relation is based on the notion that companies are required to offer an increased variety of products, where differentiated planning and control is the key in terms of operating different supply chain setups simultaneously. Currently, there is no explicit connection between the two areas, which has two consequences. First of all, with no directly assessable connection, companies have to rely on subjective intuition when battling nervousness in planning systems. Secondly, as the connection between nervousness and segmentation is currently not emphasized sufficiently in research, companies are likely to treat symptoms rather than the root causes of nervousness, as nervousness ramifies through planning levels where segmentation is the overall differentiated planning foundation. Therefore, a quantification and verification of the relationship between nervousness and item segmentation should be subject to further research.

References

1. Fisher, M.: What is the right supply chain for your product? Harvard Business Review (March-April 1997)
2. Blackburn, J., Kropp, D.H., Millen, R.A.: A comparison of strategies to dampen nervousness in MRP systems. Management Science 32(4), 413–429 (1986)
3. Minifie, J.R., Davis, R.A.: Interaction effects on MRP nervousness. International Journal of Production Resources 28, 173–183 (1990)
4. Carlson, R.C., Jucker, J.V., Kropp, D.H.: Less nervous MRP systems: a dynamic economic lot-sizing approach. Management Science 25(8), 754–761 (1979)
5. Sridharan, V., Lawrence LaForge, R.: The Impact of Safety Stock on Schedule Instability, Cost and Service. Journal of Operations Management 8(4) (1989)
6. Robinson Jr, P., Sahin, F., Gao, L.-L.: Master production schedule time interval strategies in make-to-order supply chains. International Journal of Production Research 46(7) (2008)
7. Sahin, F., Powell Robinson, E., Gao, L.-L.: Master production scheduling policy and rolling schedules in a two-stage make-to-order supply chain. International Journal of Production Economics 115, 528–541 (2008)
8. Genin, P., Lamouri, S., Thomas, A.: Improving the robustness of a supply chain tactical plan. Supply Chain Forum 8(2) (2007)
9. Moscoso, P.G., Fransoo, J.C., Fischer, D.: An empirical study on reducing planning instability in hierarchical planning systems. Production Planning & Control 21(4), 413–426 (2010)
10. Moscoso, P.G., Fransoo, J.G., Fischer, D., Wäfler, T.: The Planning Bullwhip: A Complex Dynmaic Phenomenon in Hierarchical Systems, pp. 159–186 (2011)
11. Pujawan, N.: Schedule nervousness in a manufacturing system: a case study. Production Planning & Control 15(5), 515–524 (2004)
12. Kaipia, R., Korhonen, H., Hartiala, H.: Planning nervousness in a demand supply network: an empirical study. The International Journal of Logistics Management 17(1), 95–113 (2006)

13. Tunc, H., Kilic, O.A., Tarim, A.S., Eskioglu, B.: A simple approach for assessing the cost of system nervousness. International Journal of Production Economics 141, 619–625 (2013)
14. Jonsson, P., Mattsson, S.-A.: Inventory management practices and their implications on perceived planning performance. International Journal of Production Research 46(7), 1787–1812 (2008)
15. van Donselaar, K.H., Gubbels, B.J.: How to release orders in order to minimize system inventory and system nervousness? International Journal of Production Economics 78, 335–343 (2002)
16. Kazan, O., Nagi, R., Rump, C.M.: New lot-sizing formulations for less nervous production schedules. Computer & Operations Research 27(13), 1325–1345 (2000)
17. Schönberger, J., Kopfer, H.: Schedule Nervousness Reduction in Transport Re-Planning, http://www.sfb637.uni-bremen.de/pubdb/repository/ SFB637-B7-08-004-IJ.pdf
18. Ganeshan, R., Boone, T., Stenger, A.J.: The impact of inventory and flow planning parameters on supply chain performance: An exploratory study. International Journal of Production Economics 71, 111–118 (2001)
19. Ho, C.-J.: Evaluating the impact of operating environments on MRP system nervousness. International Journal of Production Resources 27(7), 1115–1135 (1989)
20. Lee, H.L., Padmanabhan, V., Whang, S.: The bullwhip effect in supply chains. Sloan Management Review 38(7), 93–102 (1997)
21. Inderfurth, K.: Nervousness in inventory control: analytical results. OR Spektrum 16, 113–123 (1994)
22. de Kok, T., Inderfurth, K.: Nervousness in inventory management: Comparison of basic control rules. European Journal of Operational Research 103, 55–82 (1997)
23. Kaipia, R.: Coordinating material and information flows with supply chain planning. The International Journal of Logistics Management 20(1), 144–162 (2009)
24. Olhager, J.: Strategic positioning of the order penetration point. International Journal of Production Economics 85, 319–329 (2003)

Planning Nervousness in Product Segmentation: Empirical Analysis of Decision Parameters

Nicolai Præstholm, Ann-Louise Andersen, Kjeld Nielsen, and Thomas Ditlev Brunø

Department of Mechanical and Manufacturing Engineering, Aalborg University, Denmark
annlou.andersen@gmail.com

Abstract. Previous research presents a theoretical relation between planning nervousness and product segmentation and indicates that the concept should be subject to further research. This paper seeks to empirically confirm this relation, by developing hypotheses and testing these on a specific case. Three hypotheses related to historical planning data, planning frequency, and demand variability are developed and tested using data from three-echelons in a case company. A key finding is a confirmation of the relationship, providing operational tools that can assist organizations in battling planning nervousness.

Keywords: Planning, Nervousness, Product Segmentation.

1   Introduction

In response to increased need for variety in products, supply chains need diverse operating strategies that can provide these responsively and cost-efficiently [1]. The variety of products is controlled through differentiated planning, where items are planned and controlled according to their characteristics. The segmentation of items is the core in differentiated planning, and thus the foundation for securing stable and effective planning processes. The objective of this paper is to investigate planning nervousness in relation to item segmentation, which is treated only to a limited extent in current research [2]. Existing research on planning nervousness relate to specific planning contexts, primarily MRP and inventory systems, where nervousness is evaluated in connection to determining planning policy [3]. However, as nervousness is a property of planning systems in general, this paper seeks to quantify a relationship between segmentation parameters and nervousness. This constitutes an improved foundation for decision-making, rather than merely relying on subjective intuition when handling nervousness problems in companies.

2   Planning Nervousness in Product Segmentation

Planning nervousness was introduced in the late 70's in order to describe instability and rescheduling of MRP plans in terms of quantity and timing [4] [5]. Later, the discussion of nervousness has broadened to cover multiple planning levels and

B. Grabot et al. (Eds.): APMS 2014, Part I, IFIP AICT 438, pp. 411–418, 2014.

entities, highlighting that nervousness propagates horizontally within supply chains and vertically within planning systems [6] [7] [8]. As a result, nervousness can be defined as the counterpart to planning stability, which is defined as the situation where plans do not change and equal the actual requirements imposed on the planning system [9]. A trade-off between responsiveness and nervousness exists, where frequent re-planning results in more updated parameters and ability to respond to changing customer needs, while nervousness increases in relation to the transition from the original plan to the updated plan [10].

As nervousness propagates throughout planning levels, it is important to assess how product segmentation affects planning stability and provides a solid foundation for differentiated planning. In recent research, a tentative relationship between the two areas is proposed, based on the nervousness-responsiveness trade-off, where nervousness is defined as shifts in the assigned groups for specific products between two successive versions of the segmentation [2]. In contrary, responsiveness relates to immediately and continuously updating segmentations based on changes in segmentation criteria e.g. demand variability or demand volume. The aim of this paper is to further investigate this relation and develop an assessable connection between three key segmentation criteria and nervousness. More specifically, historical planning data, planning frequency, and demand variability in relation to threshold values in the segmentation will be tested, as all three parameters were recognized as main influencers of nervousness in previous research [2].

3   Hypotheses

Three hypotheses are developed to test the relationship between nervousness and segmentation. In all hypotheses, nervousness is defined in the context of segmentation, referring to the number of shifts in the assigned segments.

The first hypothesis is built on planning horizons, which is recognized as a key influencer on nervousness [9]. However, as existing research focuses on MRP, MPS, and inventory contexts, planning horizon refers to the number of future time periods determined in the plan. The key notion is that when the planning horizon is prolonged, nervousness is mitigated [5]. In a segmentation context, this concept of planning horizon do not apply, as it is merely a foundation for planning rather than an actual time-phased plan. Nevertheless, the planning horizon has a direct link with the length of historical data periods included, as longer planning horizons require more historical data as the planning foundation [11]. This means that if the objective is to forecast or plan only on a short horizon, less data should be included than for longer horizons [12]. In a segmentation context, planning horizon can thus be compared to the number of periods in the segmentation data foundation. Therefore, the first hypothesis focuses specifically on the data foundation and its relationship to nervousness. The data foundation can be selected based on various reasons, but a relationship where the planning period constitutes a larger period when rolling the plan forward is expected to be more vulnerable to nervousness. This means that the more data that is included, the more nervousness is mitigated. This notion is encapsulated in the first hypothesis.

Hypothesis 1: As the number of historical data periods included in the segmentation is increased, nervousness is decreased.

The second hypothesis relates to the frequency of continuous segmentations. How often the segmentation is run, is expected to have a direct effect on nervousness in terms of segmentation changes. The notion of planning frequency impacting planning nervousness is already established and acknowledged in research on nervousness [13] [], but as in the former hypothesis, not in relation to segmentation. In this context, planning frequency refers to how often products are segmented and planning parameters re-calculated. A relationship is expected, as the possibility of excessive re-scheduling is anticipated to increase with planning frequency.

Hypothesis 2: As the time between re-planning is increased, planning nervousness decreases.

The third hypothesis focuses on demand variability, often measured by the coefficient of variance. This is one of the most commonly used segmentation criteria and is expected to have an effect on nervousness in relation to the selected threshold values set through the segmentation. These values are the limits that separate segments from one another. Demand variability have been frequently mentioned in relation to nervousness [4], but not considered in relation to the chosen threshold values. However, a relationship with low nervousness for both low and high values of demand variation and high for medium values is expected. This is based on the reasoning that low values of demand variability are stable enough to produce stable planning results with few shifts. Likewise, unstable products will also have few shifts, as they will always be treated as make-to-order.

Hypothesis 3: Nervousness peaks if demand variability corresponds to the threshold values selected in the segmentation method.

4   Methodology

In order to test the hypotheses, demand data from a case company is applied. The case company is a Danish utility company with global reach that serves a variety of market segments ranging from domestic use to industrial application. Currently, the case company is introducing new supply chain planning processes, including a new process for item segmentation and assignment of control methods. The aim of this process is to balance inventories and secure product availability in response to pressure of reducing cost and increasing customer service.

The segmentation process at the case company consists of a classification of products to three different groups, two make-to-stock groups and one make-to-order group. More specifically, the three groups are denoted plan-based (P), consumption-based (C), and order-based (O) and are named in accordance with their planning method. The segmentation is based on the number of order lines and the monthly demand coefficient of variance (CoV) of products, where P products have a CoV less than 0.3, C products have a CoV between 0.3 and 0.6, and O products have a CoV above 0.6. For simplicity, only the CoV's as a determinant for the segmentation is considered here.

In order to be able to empirically test the hypothesis, a specific supply chain at the case company is selected as the unit of analysis. This supply chain consists of three echelons: two supplying factories producing parts and assembly-ready-components, and one assembly site. All of the echelons are internally owned companies, but are separated in terms of management and planning activities.

In each of the three sites, 3-years of historic sales data is extracted for three part numbers belonging to different part types. The selection of part numbers is based on a combination of their initial segmentation and ranking on share of total sales volume. For instance, in the collection of a specific component type, the part number representing the median of the sorted sales volume data in both the P, C, and O group is selected, in order to increase how representative the tested part numbers are. For the finished products, part numbers are selected based solely on sales volume being high, medium, or low, due to lack of data foundation in regards to segmentation of finished products, but medians were likewise chosen. Median sampling is chosen to increase the generalizability of the results despite a relative small number of data points. In total, 24 part numbers representing different levels and types of sales is selected for the quantitative testing.

In order to test the three hypotheses, different assumptions are made. First of all, in all hypotheses nervousness needs to be quantified. As mentioned, nervousness is in this context defined as the number of shifts in overall segmentation, that is when a products shifts from being a plan-based (P) product to consumption-based (C) and order-based (O) product and vice versa.

In order to determine the category of each product, the CoV's are calculated on monthly buckets, with a specific number of months of historic sales included in the calculation and a varying planning frequency. Initially, hypothesis 1 and 2 regarding historical data periods and planning frequency are tested, as they represent a foundation for testing hypothesis 3. In each hypothesis, all part numbers are tested individually, but only the average results are presented and discussed in the following.

5   Results

5.1   Hypothesis 1

In order to test the relationship between the number of historical data periods and nervousness, varying amounts of historical data periods are tested with a constant re-planning frequency of 1 month. In Figure 1, the average result for all part numbers is depicted. The expected relationship is a decreased number of shifts with an increased amount historical data periods.

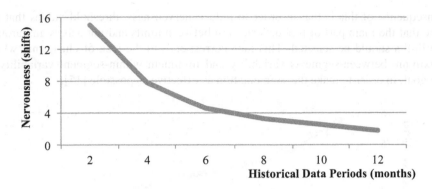

Fig. 1. Test Results For Historical Data Periods

As seen in Fig. 1., this hypothesis has strong empirical support. Moreover, there are indications that the relationship is exponentially decreasing, which mean that the benefits from increasing the amount of included historical data periods are considerable in the beginning and then decreases as more periods are included.

5.2   Hypothesis 2

In order to test the relationship between planning frequency and nervousness, varying planning frequencies are tested with a constant number of 6 months historical data points. In Figure 2, the average result of the testing is depicted. Again, there is empirical support for the hypothesis concerning a decrease in nervousness when planning frequency decreases. It may seem that planning frequency do not impact nervousness as strongly as the included historical data. However, the absolute number of planning shifts would have been considerably higher, if less than 6 months of historical data was applied. In other words, the absolute number of shifts is not as interesting as the relationship between the two tested parameters, which indicates an approximate decreasing exponential relation.

5.3   Hypothesis 3

In order to test the impact of the chosen threshold values in the segmentation, all the tested part numbers and their respective number of shifts and monthly CoV's are plotted in Fig. 3. The shifts are computed, as the average results for each part number that were used in Fig. 1 and Fig. 2.

In the segmentation approach applied in the testing of the hypothesis, the limits for the three different segments are CoV's of 0.3 and 0.6. In the empirical test, it is seen that nervousness peaks for products that has demand variability similar to these threshold values. In particular, a peak in nervousness is indicated around a CoV of 0.6, which is the limit between consumption-based and order-based segments. In other words, products that have a natural demand variability close to the chosen threshold values is expected to have the highest number of shifts between segments. A natural

consequence of this is that in order to reduce nervousness, threshold values that secure that the main part of products stays in between limits and not across and around
the limits should be selected. This idea corresponds to the idea of clustering, where
maximum between-segments variability and minimum within-segment variability is
the goal, in order to make the segmentation as effective as possible [15].

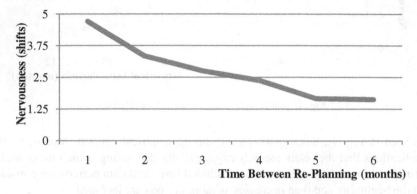

Fig. 2. Test Results For Planning Frequency

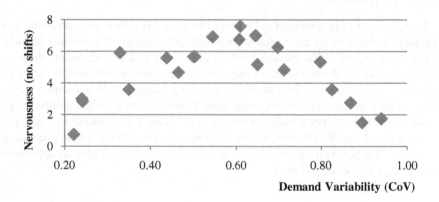

Fig. 3. Test Results for Threshold Values

6   Discussion and Managerial Implications

With the data foundation from the case company, it is concluded that the three hypotheses can be accepted for this specific case. However, when considering the sparse
data foundation and the fact that only one specific case supply chain is tested, the
need for further testing is stressed. For instance, only 24 different part numbers have
been tested, which even though they are selected as median representatives, only
make up less than a 1 ‰ of the total number of part numbers in the tested supply
chain. Therefore, it is suggested that future research should focus on empirically

validating these hypotheses on a broader data foundation cutting across both organizations and industries.

Another point that should receive more attention is the criticality of shifts. In this paper, the number of shifts in the segmentation quantifies nervousness, where the criticality of shifts is overlooked. This criticality is perceived to have larger consequences if a product changes directly from being a P product to an O product, without transitioning through the C group. Therefore, it could be argued that some shifts are more intense than others, thereby causing increased nervousness. This should be addressed in future research, where it is suggested that e.g. inventory limits in relation to segment changes are considered.

Validation of the three hypotheses implies that some degree of planning nervousness can be mitigated through changes in the product segmentation processes. As a result, it is expected that for this specific case, nervousness can be battled through changes in the segmentation setup. However, the objective of reducing nervousness by all means should be questioned, as this may create an inflexible setup with little emphasis on responsiveness. Therefore, nervousness reductions should always be considered in relation to the desired level of operational responsiveness. In this paper, only the mitigation of nervousness is considered, without measurable connections to responsiveness. However, nervousness should not be approached in a vacuum but must be addressed with emphasis both to the desired goals and the environment of the organization.

The confirmation of the hypotheses examined in this paper has led to findings on how the relationship between the amount of historical planning periods and planning frequency affects nervousness, and how it can be accelerated or alleviated through changes in the segmentation process. Additionally, the selection of threshold values poses a direct consequence on nervousness. A negative consequence is experienced if these threshold values are improperly chosen around the values. This outcome is seen as an initial step in operationalizing the measures causing and possibly mitigating planning nervousness within the process of segmentation. Nevertheless, no generalizable conclusions can be derived from this analysis, as the empirical evidence should be broadened, but indications strongly suggest a direct and controllable relationship between segmentation and planning nervousness.

7   Conclusion

The contribution of this paper should be seen as an initial step in the direction of explaining the relationship between nervousness and planning processes on a general level. Three hypotheses concerning key decision parameters within product segmentation have been established and tested for a specific case. The hypotheses are indented to operationalize the concept of nervousness, by allowing for quantitative evaluation of the amount of data periods included in the segmentation, the frequency of the segmentation, and the segmentation limits. In conclusion, it can be stated that for the case tested here, a relation between these segmentation parameters and planning nervousness exists. Evidence suggests that planning nervousness can be minimized through

418   N. Præstholm et al.

changes in the segmentation process. In other words, the degree of nervousness and planning instability experienced in companies can be controlled and is not solely determined by the incontrollable environmental factors. Though, it should be emphasized that in order to generalize the findings, these hypotheses should be tested on different cases in alternate environments. This paper therefore strengthens the field of knowledge-based production planning by operationalizing the concept of nervousness through establishing a direct relation between nervousness and product segmentation.

References

1. Fisher, M.: What is the right supply chain for your product? Harvard Business Review, pp. 105–116 (March-April 1997)
2. Andersen, A.-L., Præstholm, N., Nielsen, K., Brunoe, T.: Planning Nervousness in Product Segmentation: Literature Review and Research Agenda. Submitted to APMS 2014 Conference (2014)
3. Carlson, R.C., Jucker, J.V., Kropp, D.H.: Less nervous MRP systems a dynamic economic lot-sizing approach. Management Science 25(8), 754–761 (1979)
4. Ho, C.-J.: Evaluating the impact of operating environments on MRP system nervousness. International Journal of Production Resources 27(7), 1115–1135 (1989)
5. Blackburn, J., Kropp, D.H., Millen, R.A.: A comparison of strategies to dampen nervousness in MRP systems. Management Science 32(4), 413–429 (1986)
6. Kaipia, R., Korhonen, H., Hartiala, H.: Planning nervousness in a demand supply network: an empirical study. The International Journal of Logistics Management 17(1), 95–113 (2006)
7. Moscoso, P.G., Fransoo, J.C., Fischer, D.: An empirical study on reducing planning instability in hierachical planning systems. Production Planning & Control 21(4), 413–426 (2010)
8. Genin, P., Lamouri, S., Thomas, A.: Improving the robustness of a supply chain tactical plan. Supply Chain Forum 8(2) (2007)
9. Pujawan, N.: Schedule nervousness in a manufacturing system: a case study. Production Planning & Control 15(5), 515–524 (2004)
10. Schönberger, J., Kopfer, H.: Schedule Nervousness Reduction in Transport Re-Planning, http://www.sfb637.uni-bremen.de/pubdb/repository/SFB637-B7-08-004-IJ.pdf
11. Silver, E., Pyke, D., Peterson, R.: Inventory Management and Production Planning and Scheduling, 3rd edn. John Wiley & Sons, New York (1998)
12. Vollmann, T., Jacobs, F., Whybark, D., Berry, L.: Manufacturing Planning & Control, 6th edn. McGraw-Hill, New York (2011)
13. Sahin, F., Powell Robinson, E., Gao, L.-L.: Master production scheduling policy and rolling schedules in a two-stage make-to-order supply chain. International Journal of Production Economics 115, 528–541 (2008)
14. Robinson Jr, P., Sahin, F., Gao, L.-L.: Master production schedule time interval strategies in make-to-order supply chains. International Journal of Production Research 46(7) (2008)
15. Everitt, B., Landau, S., Leese, M.: Clyster Analysis, 4th edn. Wiley, New York (2009)

Quantifying the Bullwhip Effect of Multi-echelon System with Stochastic Dependent Lead Time

Ngoc Anh Dung Do[1], Peter Nielsen[1], Zbigniew Michna[2], and Izabela Ewa Nielsen[1]

[1] Aalborg University, Department of Mechanical and Manufacturing Engineering
{ngoc,peter,izabela}@m-tech.aau.dk
[2] Wroclaw University of Economics, Department of Mathematics and Cybernetics
zbigniew.michna@ue.wroc.pl

Abstract. Considering a multi-echelon system, the bullwhip effect is recognized as a significant factor with regards to the inventory management. This paper focuses on the effect of stochastic dependent lead time on the bullwhip effect. Simulation based approach is used to quantify the bullwhip effect with different demand and lead time distributions. The experiment results show that the dependent lead time has much effect on the 2nd echelon (from the downstream to the upstream) and bullwhip effect decrease significantly if the variance of this echelon decreases.

Keywords: bullwhip effect, multi-echelon supply chain, dependent lead time, reorder point, inventory management.

1   Introduction

The bullwhip effect occurs when the demand variance in the supply chain is amplified as demand prorogates up the supply chain (Lee et al., 1997). The variance of demand increases upstream in the supply chain. In general, to deal with the variance of demand, safety stock is used. The level of safety stock is proportional to the demand variance and the service level. This means that the safety stock increases toward the upstream of supply chain due to the amplification of demand variance. Higher level of safety stock has to be carried with consequently more investment, extra production capacity, and increased storage space (Chatfield et al., 2004). Therefore, bullwhip effect reduction can bring benefit to the supply chain.

Several studies have been focused on the variation of demand. Nielsen et al. (2010b) considered the time dependent demand and the interdependent of demands of multiple products and developed a method to model the time dependent demand rate profiles by using the estimations of multivariate density distributions, and then to evaluate the interdependence of demand rates of products. Many studies have been investigated on the bullwhip effect and a number of these studies identify the causes of bullwhip effect, for example Lee et al. (1997). Some studies analyze the bullwhip effect by using simulation and show the causes of variance amplification (Forrester, 1958 and Bhaskaran, 1998). Croson and Donohue (2003) concluded that the bullwhip

B. Grabot et al. (Eds.): APMS 2014, Part I, IFIP AICT 438, pp. 419–426, 2014.
© IFIP International Federation for Information Processing 2014

420   N.A.D. Do et al.

effect can be decreased by information sharing. Several papers focus on quantifying the bullwhip effect in a more analytical framework. Chen et al. (2000) quantified the bullwhip effect of a multi-stage supply chain with constant lead time and stochastic demand and concluded that the variance of orders of a retailer will be greater than variance of demand when that retailer updates the mean and variance of demand based on observed customer demand data. Moreover, they also pointed out that the customer demand information sharing can significantly reduce the bullwhip effect. The impact of lead time is considered in some studies. Wickner et al. (1991) noted that a twenty percent reduction in peak amplification can be achieved if lead time is reduced. Metters (1997) identified the magnitude of the bullwhip effect by establishing an empirical lower bound on the profitability impact of the bullwhip effect and found that eliminating the bullwhip effect can increase product profitability by 10–30% and significantly save inventories and other costs. Chen et al. (2000) showed that the increase in lead time will increase the variability of orders from retailer to manufacturer.

Nielsen et al. (2010a) offers an approach to improve supply chain planning through the use of RFID technology to track and thus be able to provide higher quality information, while Sitek and Wikarek (2013) offers approaches for improving planning through optimization. The main issue in applying optimization methods for supply chain management is the quality of the information available for the methods.

Most research to date has considered deterministic lead time and two echelons systems. A few papers have been investigated on stochastic lead time and multi-echelon system, for example Chatfield et al. (2004). Nielsen et al. (2013) considered the reorder point inventory management models sensitivity to demand distributions, demand dependencies and lead time distribution with four different versions of service level and concluded that the skew of demand distribution is the most significant with regards to the service level. However, no paper has been focused on the effect of stochastic lead time of the upstream echelon to that of the downstream one. All papers assumed that the lead times of echelons are independent. This is not practical because the variance of lead time of a downstream echelon can be longer due to the variance of lead time of an upstream echelon. Moreover, the variance of lead time affects the amount of safety stock of an echelon. Therefore, the reorder point (ROP) of an echelon is adjusted based on the historical data of lead time.

In this paper, the impact of stochastic lead time on the bullwhip effect of a multi-echelon system using an inventory policy is investigated. This paper differs from the previous studies that the dependence of lead times of echelons is considered. The problem description is presented in Section 2. Numerical experiment is shown in Section 3 and Section 4 points out the conclusions.

2   Problem Description and Methodology

2.1   Problem Description

A multi-echelon system is considered as in Figure 1. Li denotes the lead time of the echelon of order i. The variance of lead time is assumed unchanged. The lower echelon will place an order to the next upper echelon when the inventory level lower than or equal the ROP. The ROP is computed as the sum of expected demand during expected lead time and the safety stock. The safety stock is calculated based on the variance of lead time and service level. It is assumed that the continuous review policy is applied for the inventory system of each echelon. The ROP is updated when a new lead time is recorded. Order-up-to is used to determine the order quantity. This means that when the inventory level downs to the ROP, the order quantity can full fill the inventory level up to a desired value. The incoming replenishment and total demand which is not satisfied are considered when review the inventory level. In details, an order will be made when current inventory level + total incoming replenishment – total unsatisfied demand < ROP

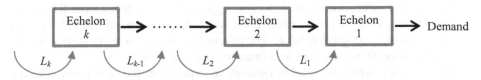

Fig. 1. The description of considered system

If the left hand side of the above inequality is denoted as the relative inventory level, then the order quantity will be

$$\text{order quantity = desired up-to-value – relative inventory level} \qquad (1)$$

To decide when an order should be placed, the manager of a lower echelon needs to know the ROP. However, the ROP is calculated based on the expected lead time. If the expected lead time is higher, the ROP is higher. Unfortunately, in practice, the manager cannot know exactly the expected lead time of the next order. Therefore, the manager estimates the expected lead time based on historical data of lead times of previous orders. In our experiment the expected lead time is estimated using a moving average with n = 3. This means that the expected lead time is the average of actual lead time of three consecutive orders which is closest to the time point to estimate the expected lead time. For example, at a certain time in planning horizon, an echelon placed N orders to the next upper echelon. The actual lead time of order i is denoted as LA_i. The expected lead time is estimated by using the following formula

$$\text{expected lead time} = (LA_N + LA_{N-1} + LA_{N-2}) / 3 \qquad (2)$$

Because the expected lead time is changed when a new order is made, the ROP of an echelon is also changed. As a result, the order quantity also changes in each order of an echelon. Due to the variance of order quantity, bullwhip effect will be expected to occur. The aim of this paper is to answer two questions. First, is there a bullwhip effect when the lead time of a lower echelon depends of that of the next upper echelon? In this paper, the bullwhip effect is defined as the ratio between the variance of order of the upper echelon and that of the next lower echelon. If all ratios are greater than 1, meaning that the variance of order of the upper echelon is higher than that of the next lower echelon, then the bullwhip effect exits. Secondly, if the bullwhip effect exists what is its size? Furthermore, through quantifying the bullwhip effect, we can see the effect of variance of lead time on the bullwhip effects of each echelon and the supply chain as a whole.

2.2   Methodology

To answer the two mentioned questions, Monte Carlo simulation is implemented on this multi-echelon system. Firstly, the possible events for each echelon are analyzed. The events at an echelon include:

- Order placing: when the relative inventory level is lower than or equal the ROP, an order is placed at the next upper echelon. The order quantity is calculated by equation (1). The information sent to the next upper echelon includes order ID and order quantity. Following this, information about the lead time of this order is sent back from the next upper echelon. The information about this order is recorded including order ID, release date, lead time, and order quantity.
- Order receipt: when the echelon receives an order from the next lower echelon. The lead time for this order is generated and sent back to the next lower echelon. Information about this order is recorded including order ID, order quantity, and delivery date.
- Order delivering: an order is considered to be delivered when its delivery date comes or is over and the current inventory level is higher than the quantity of this order. The upper echelon will sent information about order ID and actual delivery date. Current inventory level is updated and the order is removed out of the list of order receipt.
- Order replenishment: when the lower echelon receives the information about order delivery from the next upper echelon, the replenishment quantity is added to the current inventory. The lead time of this order is updated (in case it is different from the estimated lead time). Following this, the expected lead time is updated.
- Inventory review: investigates whether the relative inventory level is less than or equal to the ROP or not.
- Delivery check: to check whether an order in the list of order receipt is delivered or not. The condition for an order to be delivered includes delivery date of this order comes or is over and the current inventory level is higher than the quantity of this order.

For practical purposes there are some differences for the first and last echelon.

- Order receipt at the first echelon (echelon 1 in Figure 1): when the demand is received, the information is recorded to the list of order receipt following which the order delivery happens instantaneously.
- Order placement at the last echelon (echelon k in Figure 1): the lead time is generated when placing the order.
- Order replenishment at the last echelon: the order is replenished at the delivery date. This means that the order is replenished at the time which equals release date plus lead time

The simulation is terminated after the last day of planning horizon has been considered. After that, the variance of order of each echelon is calculated. Finally, the bullwhip effect of each echelon is computed.

3   Numerical Experiment

Some scenarios are conducted in the numerical experiment. Four echelons are considered. The scenarios are the combination of the different cases of demand and lead time shown in Table 1. It is assumed that all echelons have the same lead time. The target service level is 90%. All echelon will order up to 1000 units. The initial inventory level follows a uniform distribution U(0,500). The planning horizon is 365 days. There are 30 runs for each scenario. The result of the experiment is shown in Tables 2a, 2b, and 2c.

Table 1. The cases of demand and lead time

	Constant	Normal	Exponential	Uniform
Demand	D = 50	N(50, 10²)	-	U(40,60)
Lead time	L = 2	N(2,1)	Expo(2)	U(1,3)

Table 2. a. Average and std. deviation of bullwhip affect when demand is constant

	L = 2 days		L ~ N(2,1)		L ~ Expo(2)		L ~U(1,3)	
	Avg	Std	Avg	Std	Avg	Std	Avg	Std
Echelon 2	219.1721	0.8834	141.1904	120.0914	4.1726	0.9078	161.6278	127.3034
Echelon 3	4.4194	0.0011	1.9649	0.4869	1.8175	0.3010	2.4348	1.2051
Echelon 4	2.1398	0.0001	1.7096	0.6015	1.4620	0.2013	1.7175	0.4353

Table 2. b. Average and std. deviation of bullwhip affect when demand follows normal distribution

	L = 2 days		L ~ N (2,1)		L ~ Expo(2)		L ~U(1,3)	
	Avg	Std	Avg	Std	Avg	Std	Avg	Std
Echelon 2	107.6928	52.0421	121.3375	65.2603	5.0435	3.5167	93.0544	67.9523
Echelon 3	6.6632	16.3278	2.2906	1.6281	2.1476	1.0915	2.6482	2.3497
Echelon 4	2.2414	0.6832	1.7408	0.4810	1.5531	0.3856	1.8278	0.6581

Table 2. c. Average and std. deviation of bullwhip affect when demand follows uniform distribution

	L = 2 days		L ~ N (2,1)		L ~ Expo(2)		L ~U(1,3)	
	Avg	Std	Avg	Std	Avg	Std	Avg	Std
Echelon 2	88.4235	57.4673	97.0613	80.6057	5.1346	3.4074	155.8594	102.6469
Echelon 3	28.9540	63.5392	2.4675	1.2501	2.0744	0.7872	1.8746	0.6705
Echelon 4	2.3754	0.8439	1.6630	0.4460	1.7812	0.5060	1.6923	0.4614

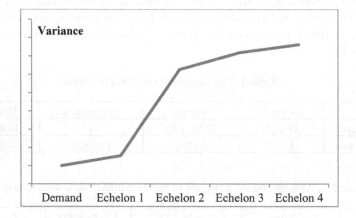

Fig. 2. Variance of order of each echelon

It can be seen from the experiment result that the bullwhip effect exists when lead time is stochastic and dependent. The different cases of demand do not affect the decrement in bullwhip effect when moving to the upstream (upper echelon) of the multi-echelon system. It shows that the second echelon has big bullwhip effect. The bullwhip effect becomes smaller when moving to the upper echelon. This shows that the bullwhip effect tends to have the value of 1 when more echelons are considered. Figure 2 shows the variance of order of each echelon

Figure 2 shows an interesting result. In echelon 1, the echelon closest to the demand and hence the natural demand, variance is very low. This seems reasonable as at this echelon the demand should be easy to observe and thus estimate. However, the orders sent to echelon 2 has an effect on the variance of order of echelon 2. Due to the amplification of demand variance, the upper echelon will have higher variance on demand. Figure 3 shows the direction of the increase of demand variance for a 4-echelon system where echelons 1 and 2 are considered as retailer and manufacturer and other echelons are the subsequent material suppliers. On the other hand, the cumulative effect of the lead time variance seems to directly impact the upper echelons, specifically the manufacturer. This is shown as the increase of lead time variability in Figure 3. The result is that the manufacturer experiences a very large bullwhip effect, much more so than any other echelon to echelon combination. The conclusion must

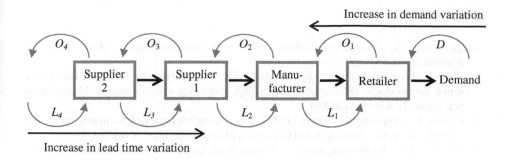

Fig. 3. Effect of the variances of lead time and demand on a 4-echelon system

be that the manufacturer especially absorbs the variance effect due to both the variance of lead time and demand. This underlines that the bullwhip effect of this system can be significantly reduced if the inventory policy of the manufacturer is carefully investigated. Furthermore, it can be concluded that the effect of lead time variation dominate that of demand variance in a multi-echelon system with dependent lead time. This means that decision making relate to inventory management is much different when lead time is uncertain and dependent. The study on inventory management with dependent lead time is very promising and can be put in future research.

4   Conclusion

In this paper, the stochastic and dependent lead time is considered in a multi-echelon system. The lead time of downstream (lower) echelon is assumed to be affected by that of upstream (upper) echelons. A simulation based experiment is run to determine and quantify the bullwhip effect in this type of system. Some scenarios are proposed for numerical experiments. The result of experiments shows that there is bullwhip effect in the system and the bullwhip effect is significantly decreased if the bullwhip effect of the 2nd echelon decreases. Several issues can be investigated for further study. Studying an optimal inventory policy for the 2nd echelon with considering stochastic and dependent lead time is very promising to decrease bullwhip effect of the whole system. Information sharing in the system is another issue which can show how much bullwhip effect can be reduced. The study also underlines that lead times and their variations are in fact critical for supply chains, especially if the lead times to some extend are dependent on each other.

Acknowledgement. The presented research is partly supported by the Polish National Centre of Science under the grant UMO-2012/07/B/HS4/00702.

References

1. Bhaskaran, S.: Simulation analysis of a manufacturing supply chain. Decision Sciences 29(3), 633–657 (1998)
2. Chen, F., Drezner, Z., Ryan, J.K., Simchi-Levi, D.: Quantifying the Bullwhip Effect in a simple supply chain: The impact of forecasting, lead times, and information. Management Science 46(3), 436–443 (2000a)
3. Croson, R., Donohue, K.: Impact of POS data sharing on supply chain management: An experimental study. Production and Operations Management 12(1), 1–11 (2003)
4. Forrester, J.W.: Industrial dynamics—A major breakthrough for decision makers. Harvard Business Review 36(4), 37–66 (1958)
5. Chatfield, D.C., Kim, J.G., Harrison, T.P., Hayya, J.C.: The Bullwhip Effect—Impact of Stochastic Lead Time, Information Quality, and Information Sharing: A simulation Study. Production and Operations Management 13(4), 340–353 (2004)
6. Lee, H.L., Padmanabhan, V., Whang, S.: The Bullwhip Effect In Supply Chains. Sloan Management Review 38(3), 93–102 (1997a)
7. Lee, H.L., Padmanabhan, V., Whang, S.: Information distortion in a supply chain: The bullwhip effect. Management Science 43, 546–558 (1997b)
8. Metters, R.: Quantifying the bullwhip effect in supply chains. Journal of Operations Management 15, 89–100 (1997)
9. Nielsen, P., Davoli, G., Nielsen, I., Rytter, N.G.: A Design of Experiments Approach to Investigating the Sensitivity of the Re-Order Point Method. In: Emmanouilidis, C., Taisch, M., Kiritsis, D. (eds.) APMS 2012, Part II. IFIP AICT, vol. 398, pp. 646–653. Springer, Heidelberg (2013)
10. Nielsen, I.E., Lim, M., Nielsen, P.: Optimizing Supply Chain Waste Management Through the Use of RFID Technology. In: Proceedings of the IEEE International Conference on RFID-Technology and Applications. Electrical Engineering/Electronics, Computer, Communications and Information Technology Association, pp. 296–301 (2010a)
11. Nielsen, P., Nielsen, I., Steger-Jensen, K.: Analyzing and evaluating product demand interdependencies. Computers in Industry 61, 869–876 (2010b)
12. Sitek, P., Wikarek, J.: A hybrid approach to modeling and optimization for supply chain management with multimodal transport. In: IEEE Conferrence: 18th International Conference on Methods and Models in Automation and Robotics (MMAR), pp. 777–782 (2013)

Warehouse Capacities in the Pharmaceutical Industry – Plan or Outsource?

Felix Friemann[*], Manuel Rippel, and Paul Schönsleben

ETH Zürich, BWI Center for Industrial Management,
WEINBERGSTRASSE 56, 8092 ZÜRICH, Switzerland
{ffriemann,mrippel,pschoensleben}@ethz.ch

Abstract. The pharmaceutical industry is undergoing a change. Different future developments such as the increasing amount of biopharmaceutical products and even stricter regulations increase the need for a reliable long range warehouse capacity planning. Results from a literature analysis indicate that managing these operations will mainly remain the responsibility of the pharmaceutical company itself and may not be outsourced. Hence, the capabilities must be built up within the pharmaceutical companies itself, too. However, none of the models identified in the literature can fulfill all requirements of a reliable and detailed long-range planning process in the pharmaceutical industry. Providing suggestions for further research areas, the paper contributes to the further development of more reliable planning processes.

Keywords: Supply Chain Management, Pharmaceutical Industry, Long-Range Warehouse Capacity, Strategic Planning, Outsourcing.

1 Introduction

Global medicines spendings will increase from $965Bn in 2012 to $1Tn in 2014 and exceed $1.17Tn by 2017 according to IMS Health showing the size of the pharmaceutical industry [1]. The industry can be divided into the market segments of ethical (prescription) and "over-the-counter" products [2]. This paper focuses on researching pharmaceutical companies (RPC) which are making most of their revenue from ethical products.

Due to various future trends, supply chain managers in this industry will increasingly face challenges: The market of biologics (complex macromolecules with some form of polymer structure) will grow above average and amount to approx. 19-20% of the overall pharmaceutical market in 2017 [1]. These products are generally more sensitive to environmental changes (e.g. temperature) on transports and in the warehouse than traditional solid products (e.g. tablets). With the BRIC markets (Brazil, Russia, India, China) being key growth drivers, these capacities are needed at different locations than before, in sometimes challenging settings [3]. All this has to be done under the umbrella of the highly regulated pharmaceutical industry where most

---

[*] Corresponding author.

B. Grabot et al. (Eds.): APMS 2014, Part I, IFIP AICT 438, pp. 427–434, 2014.

428   F. Friemann, M. Rippel, and P. Schönsleben

process changes require new approvals of different authorities and warehouse security (anti-counterfeiting) is becoming more and more important [4]. The new European "Guidelines of 7 March 2013 on Good Distribution Practice of Medicinal Products for Human Use (2013/C 68/01)" further increase the requirements for qualification, temperature control and traceability in the distribution [5].

Increasing supply chain transparency by better monitoring warehouse capacities and their development in the long-term seems one answer to better cope with these challenges. Expert interviews indicated that several pharmaceutical companies lack this capability. To exploit the reasons of this discrepancy, this paper firstly analyzes whether there can be a trend identified that capacities are outsourced and, consequently, warehouse planning will not be an issue anymore in the future. This is reviewed in a semi-structured interview series within 11 out of the 2012 TOP20 pharmaceutical companies (according to revenue) [6]. Secondly, the paper summarizes the findings of a literature analysis identifying relevant planning processes and models in academic publications.

2   Methodology

Originating from a case study with supply chain experts of a leading pharmaceutical company, different alternatives to increase transparency for warehouse capacities were evaluated. A basic question that arose was whether the company should estimate capacities on its own or whether the general trend is to outsource it in the industry. The derived hypothesis was that companies outsourcing this task to logistics providers face less limitations with regards to warehouse capacities. To answer this, a semi-structured interview series with supply chain managers from 11 out of the 2012 TOP20 researching pharmaceutical companies was used [6]. The interview guideline used contained both qualitative and quantitative questions. The interviews were conducted between 04'13 – 05'13. All interviewees were senior managers in a Supply Chain Management position. For reasons of validation, the survey results were sent to all participants with the request of approval. All results were approved. If a company differentiates between business units (animal health, generics branch, etc.), our study focused on the research-oriented pharmaceutical branch whenever possible to ensure comparability of the answers.

Secondly, to answer the question whether good models and practices exist to plan warehouse capacities in the pharmaceutical industry, the state-of-the-art is evaluated by a literature analysis. Scopus (www.scopus.com) was used as the main database. The findings of this literature search were further analyzed using scientometrics ([7], see [8] for an application example).

3   Pharmaceutical Supply Chains

The American Production and Inventory Control Society (APICS) define supply chain management as the design, planning, execution, control, and monitoring of supply chain activities with the objective of creating net value, building a competitive infrastructure, leveraging world-wide logistics, synchronizing supply with demand, and measuring performance globally [9].

Drug development can take around 15 years before it comes to the market. These phases can be divided into discovery-phase, clinical (exploratory) and registration (full development) phase ([2]). The earlier the stage in the drug development process, the bigger the uncertainty for a supply chain manager on whether to consider this product in the corresponding long-range capacities (i.e. how probable it is that it passes on to the next stage) and which logistics requirements this drug will actually have (i.e. temperature range, volume, special characteristics).

Within the product life cycle of a drug, the development phase is followed by an introductory, growth, maturity and decline stage. Production / capacity planning and inventory management becomes especially important in the growth and maturity stage [10] as products at these stages consume most of the warehouse capacities.

The general pharmaceutical manufacturing supply chain (Fig. 1) consists of the stages primary manufacturing where the active pharmaceutical ingredient (API) is produced, secondary manufacturing formulating the drug (e.g. producing a tablet), 3) packaging and 4) finished product distribution [11]. These stages are globally distributed.

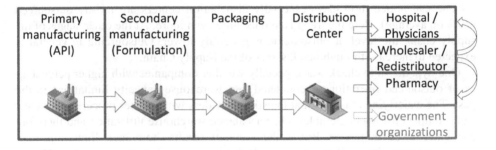

Fig. 1. General pharmaceutical supply chain structure (material flow)

4   Outsourcing at Research-Focused Pharmaceutical Companies

Interviews with experts of one case study company in a TOP5 researching pharmaceutical company ([6]) indicated that no high-level process is in place to monitor global warehouse capacities. Limitations happened in the past and are expected to increase in future due to previously mentioned developments. One argument not to spend resources on capacity planning might be that the operations tend to be further outsourced in future. Outsourcing means that parts of the value-added chain are turned over to other companies [12].

Fig. 2 illustrates the results of a semi-structured interview series with 11 out of the TOP20 pharmaceutical companies. It shows the mentioned level of outsourced activities (in percent and in terms of volume) throughout the supply chain indicated by the interviewees. It also expresses whether this percentage is expected to change in future (absolute value indicated by the black arrows).

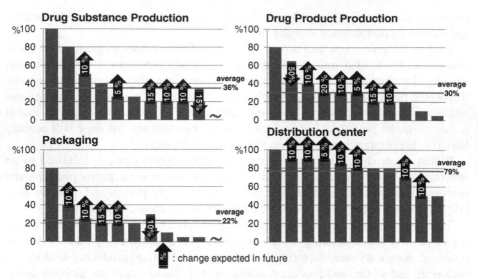

Fig. 2. Percentage of outsourced operations in the various stages of the Supply Chain and future change in percentage points (in terms of volume)

As one can notice, nowadays especially distribution centers are mostly outsourced (79% on average). Here the trend is to outsource even more. At the other stages of the supply chain, the level of outsourcing is generally lower. Outsourcing in general is expected to increase throughout all stages of the Supply Chain.

One hypothesis to check was especially whether companies with higher percentages of outsourced operations encountered less warehouse capacity limitations in the past. The underlying reason is that logistics providers with greater process knowledge and multiple customers are able to better balance warehouse utilization and therefore encounter fewer limitations. But, as the interview results show, most limitations (e.g. not enough capacity available when needed) occur at the distribution centers. Hence, the hypothesis cannot be confirmed. The explanation can be manifold. One reason might be that there are different characteristics in the pharmaceutical industry (long lead times, high equipment costs and corresponding high utilization) that make planning difficult downstream the supply chain.

The degree of outsourcing within the packaging stage seems to be the lowest. Reasons for this might be the complexity e.g. with regards to product variety or counterfeiting risks at this stage. Anti-counterfeiting is still a very important topic in the industry.

As outsourcing reasons, the most common answers were 1) strategic decision - decide based on strategic importance of the product, 2) not core competence - outsource when the operation is not a core competence, 3) risk mitigation - outsource production and distribution to ensure supply and increase flexibility, 4) external know-how - outsource when internal competence is not available.

Overall, it can be stated that even though outsourcing seems to generally increase, it will still be on a comparably low level at the production facilities from drug substance production until packaging making it necessary for pharmaceutical companies to establish a reliable process in order to estimate the required warehouse capacities and therefore ensure supply chain reliability. At a next step, the literature is analyzed for corresponding processes and models to help the pharmaceutical industry in this matter.

5   Warehouse Capacity Planning in the Pharmaceutical Industry

To identify streams and applicable literature in the field of warehouse capacity planning, keyword combinations 1) "supply chain", 2) "supply chain" AND "capacity", 3) "supply chain" AND "planning" and 4) "warehouse" AND "planning" were used in the Scopus database. Whether or not pharmaceutical supply chains should be treated with different tools than other industries is discussed in a controversial manner. Nevertheless, one can acknowledge that the pharmaceutical supply chain is more regulated than any other industrial sector and decisions can become ethical if a failure of the supply chain may have a severe impact on patients' lives, especially when dealing with ethical (prescribed) medicines like in this paper [2]. This imposes specific requirements on pharmaceutical supply chain planning. To identify the documents mentioning pharmaceutical issues, the keyword "pharmaceutical" was added to the previous keyword combinations. The number of results and especially the relation between general and pharmaceutical-specific literature is illustrated in Fig. 3.

The primary y-axis (n=1 to 6000) with the corresponding dotted lines show the results of a generic keyword search. The secondary y-axis (n=1 to 90) with the corresponding continuous lines show the same keyword search limited to papers mentioning the pharmaceutical industry.

A first interesting finding is that the relation between general literature and literature mentioning pharmaceutical keywords is more or less continuously around 1.5 % (1.6%, 1.3%, 1.5% resp. 0.9% for the keyword searches mentioned before) over the given timeframe. Some literature is stating that many papers concentrate on a handful of industry sectors, automobile being among them [13]. So repeating the keyword search for the automotive sector, using "automotive" instead of "pharmaceutical" as a keyword, doubles the overall number of papers found (factor 2.0 – 2.5 for all keyword combinations compared to the previous search). It leaves the conclusion, that pharmaceutical supply chain planning tends indeed to be underrepresented compared to other industries. The reasons for this were not further analyzed and might be a good area for further research.

When analyzing collaboration of authors in the pharmaceutical field using the scientometrics method ([7]), the area seems rather fragmented. Two groups identified are L. Patrono, Mainetti, De Blasi et al. publishing about RFID-tracking in the pharmaceutical supply chain or Westenberger, Buhse et al. dealing with quality monitoring throughout the supply chain ([14], [15]).

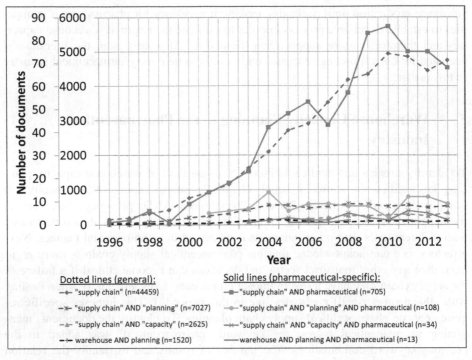

Fig. 3. Keyword search, timeframe 1990 – 2013 (shown: 1996-2013). Source scopus.com/. Updated: 04/2014

From the above streams, exemplary papers can be highlighted that deal with capacity planning in the context of supply chain managament. Gu et al. provide an extensive literature analysis with regards to warehouse operation planning whereas they do not discuss the global context within supply chain planning [16]. Heragu et al. discuss intra-warehouse improvements of the functional areas and propose an algorithm [17]. Susarla et al. or Levis et al. discuss integrated planning for a globally operating pharmaceutical companies, not considering warehouse requirements specifically though [18], [19]. Chen et al. discuss a simulation-optimization of the clinical trial supply chain [20]. Aghezzaf generally discusses strategic capacity and warehouse location planning including uncertainty and proposes a model [21]. For production capacity planning, several models exist. A profound general overview is provided by Mula et al. [22].

However, literature dealing with warehouse capacity planning in the context of a global supply chain and specifically fulfilling the requirements of pharmaceutical capacity planning (e.g. pallet spaces within different temperature zones) could not be identified by the literature research.

6   Discussion and Conclusion

This paper has introduced the reasons why warehouse capacity planning in the pharmaceutical industry will gain relevance in the future. The main production steps are still performed in-house at the interviewed pharmaceutical companies and this will stay mainly in-house in the future. Different developments will make it more difficult for supply chain managers to correctly plan the warehouse capacities in the long-range in order to get the right products to the right place in the right condition. With emerging markets getting more and more important in future, warehouse capacities will get even more difficult to correctly estimate.

Analyzing the current literature, this paper states that specific, highly automatable, readily applicable models for long-term warehouse capacity planning in the pharmaceutical industry could not be identified.

Further research has to be done in specifying requirements of such a model in the pharmaceutical industry, analyzing in greater detail how warehouse capacity planning is done in other industries and whether this can be leveraged for the pharmaceutical industry.

References

1. IMS Institute for Healthcare Informatics, The Global Use of Medicines: Outlook through 2017 (2013)
2. Savage, C.J., Roberts, K.J., Wang, X.Z.: A Holistic Analysis of Pharmaceutical Manufacturing and Distribution: Are Conventional Supply Chain Techniques Appropriate? Pharm. Eng. 26(4), 1–8 (2006)
3. Altmann, T., Werner, K.: Die Entwicklung des internationalen Pharmamarktes. Pharm. Ind. 75(9), 1418–1421 (2013)
4. Efrati, A., Loftus, P.: Lilly Drugs Stolen in Warehouse Heist. The Wall Street Journal (March 17, 2010)
5. Sponheimer, A.: Supply-Chain-Trends und Regularien in der Pharmalogistik. Pharm. Ind. 75(9), 1422–1428 (2013)
6. IMS Health: IMS Health, IMS MIDAS, Top 20 global corporations 2012 (2013)
7. Sci2 Team: Science of Science (Sci2) Tool. Indiana University and SciTech Strategies (2009)
8. Gram, M.: Equipment efficiency metrics in production systems. A literature review and survey. In: Book of proceedings of 9th International May Concefernce on Strategic Management – IMKSM 2013, pp. 468–478 (May 2013)
9. APICS — The Association for Operations Management, APICS Dictionary 13th edn. American Production & Inventory Control Society, Incorporated, Chicago (2010)
10. Laínez, J.M., Schaefer, E., Reklaitis, G.V., Lainez, J.M.: Challenges and opportunities in enterprise-wide optimization in the pharmaceutical industry. Comput. Chem. Eng. 47, 19–28 (2012)
11. Friemann, F., Verhasselt, S.: Best Practices for Supply Chain Management Techniques and Concepts across Industries. In: POMS 23rd Annual Conference, p. 16 (2012)
12. Schönsleben, P.: Integral Logistics Management, 4th edn., vol. 15(3), p. 1040. Auerbach Publications (2011)
13. Burgess, K., Singh, P.J., Koroglu, R.: Supply chain management: a structured literature review and implications for future research. Int. J. Oper. Prod. Manag. 26(7), 703–729 (2006)

14. Keire, D.A., Ye, H., Trehy, M.L., Ye, W., Kolinski, R.E., Westenberger, B.J., Buhse, L.F., Nasr, M., Al-Hakim, A.: Characterization of currently marketed heparin products: key tests for quality assurance. Anal. Bioanal. Chem. 399(2), 581–591 (2011)

15. Kauffman, J.F., Gryniewicz-Ruzicka, C.M., Arzhantsev, D.J.D., Spencer, S.J.A., Wolfgang, X., Li, S., Pelster, L.N., Westenberger, B.J., Buhse, L.F.: Pharmaceutical surveillance with rapid spectroscopic screening technologies. Am. Pharm. Rev. 13(1), 58–62 (2010)

16. Gu, J., Goetschalckx, M., McGinnis, L.F.: Research on warehouse operation: A comprehensive review. Eur. J. Oper. Res. 177(1), 1–21 (2007)

17. Heragu, S.S., Du, L., Mantel, R.J., Schuur, P.C.: Mathematical model for warehouse design and product allocation. Int. J. Prod. Res. 43(2), 327–338 (2005)

18. Susarla, N., Karimi, I.A.A.: Integrated supply chain planning for multinational pharmaceutical enterprises. Comput. Chem. Eng. 42, 168–177 (2012)

19. Levis, A.A., Papageorgiou, L.G.: A hierarchical solution approach for multi-site capacity planning under uncertainty in the pharmaceutical industry. Comput. Chem. Eng. 28(5), 707–725 (2004)

20. Chen, Y., Mockus, L., Orcun, S., Reklaitis, G.V.: Simulation-optimization approach to clinical trial supply chain management with demand scenario forecast. Comput. Chem. Eng. 40, 82–96 (2012)

21. Aghezzaf, E.: Capacity planning and warehouse location in supply chains with uncertain demands. J. Oper. Res. Soc. 56(4), 453–462 (2004)

22. Mula, J., Poler, R., García-Sabater, J.P., Lario, F.C.: Models for production planning under uncertainty: A review. Int. J. Prod. Econ. 103(1), 271–285 (2006)

An Empirical Investigation of Lead Time Distributions

Peter Nielsen[1], Zbigniew Michna[2], and Ngoc Anh Dung Do[1]

[1] Aalborg University, Department of Mechanical and Manufacturing Engineering
{peter,ngoc}@m-tech.aau.dk
[2] Wroclaw University of Economics, Department of Mathematics and Cybernetics,
zbigniew.michna@ue.wroc.pl

Abstract. This paper proposes a methodology for analyzing lead time behavior. The method focuses on identifying whether lead times are in fact identically independently distributed (i.i.d.). The method uses a combination of time series analysis, Kolmogorov-Smirnov's test for similar distributions and data sampling to arrive at its result. The method is applied to data obtained from a manufacturing company. The conclusions are that while the lead time to customers can for some products be assumed to be i.i.d. this is not uniformly true. Some products' lead times are in fact neither independently nor identically distributed.

1 Introduction

Supply chain management has long been one of the leading topics in both management and academia. The focus is the management of activities a cross a chain of companies and thus partitioning the supply chain into a number of echelons. As with all fields there are number of assumptions build in to the way supply chain management literature addresses the planning and control activities (Otto and Kotzab, 2003). This paper investigates lead times and the associated assumptions found in Supply chain literature.

In practice most research into supply chain management assumes that lead times follow one of two forms. Either lead times are assumed to be constant (see e.g. Chen et al. 2000) or they are assumed to be i.i.d. (Kim et al., 2006; Michna et al., 2013). Rather than attempt to model the impact of a given type of lead time behavior on a supply chain, this paper investigates the actual lead time behavior in a manufacturing company. The aim is to identify the actual lead time behavior and subsequently in further research model this behavior and its impact on supply chain performance.

The remainder of the paper is structured as follows. First, a brief literature review of the current-state of supply chain management with regards to modeling lead time behavior is presented. Second, a method for analyzing the distributions of lead times is presented before it is applied to data from a company. Finally implications from the case investigation and future avenues of research are presented.

2 State-of-the-Art

Otto and Kotzab (2003) define six specific approaches to address supply chain management with varying focus. This paper focuses on the perspective Otto and Kotzab

B. Grabot et al. (Eds.): APMS 2014, Part I, IFIP AICT 438, pp. 435–442, 2014.

(2003) would term Systems Dynamics and papers related to this perspective. Systems Dynamics is characterized by focusing on distortion of demand patterns for various reasons (demand forecasting, non-zero lead time, supply shortage, order batching, and price fluctuation (Duc et al., 2008) and typically this distortion is quantified by the bullwhip effect (variance of downstream orders / variance of upstream demand e.g. Chen et al. (2000)).

This research is narrowly focused on lead times and the assumptions build into analytical or simulation based models for determining the bullwhip effect in a given supply chain. It is also based on the notation that IT can be used to estimate and register lead times in real supply chains (Arshinder and Deshmukh, 2008). Chen et al. (2000) is one of the main contributions to quantifying the bullwhip effect in supply chains. However, in the work of Chen et al. (2000) lead times are actually assumed to be constant. The same goes for the control theory approach used in Dejonckheere (2003). This is not the case in the more recent work of Duc et al. (2008). Here the bullwhip effect is quantified for a system with stochastic lead times. The lead times are assumed to be stationary and i.i.d.. The same assumption is found in the work by Kim et al. (2006), who in their work use a similar analytical approach to Chen et al. (2000) and Duc et al. (2008). This is very significant as Chattfield et al. (2004) note that stochastic lead times are major source of bullwhip effect. Kim et al. (2006) choose another approach by assuming that both demand and lead times are stochastic, but rather than predict demands and assume stochastic lead times they choose to predict lead time demand. Another interesting aspect addressed by Chaharsooghi and Heydari (2010) is determining for a specific supply chain what has the largest effect; reducing the average lead time or reducing the variance of lead time? Chaharsooghi and Heydari (2010) use simulating and multivariate models to conclude that lead time variance is in fact a major cause of bullwhip effect. This underlines the importance of determining actual lead time behavior to reduce the bullwhip effect in supply chains. If lead times are not in fact i.i.d. the bullwhip effect will in all likelihood be higher than expected, and also higher than standard models will be able to explain.

Nielsen et al. (2010a) offers an approach to improve supply chain planning through the use of RFID technology to track and thus be able to provide higher quality information, while Sitek and Wikarek (2013) offers approaches for improving planning through optimization. The main issue in applying optimization methods for supply chain management is the quality of the information available for the methods.

It is interesting to note that there is very limited research that actually investigates lead times, regardless the fact that quite some research has been conducted assuming a given lead time behavior. This research addresses this gap and suggests a method for determining whether lead times are in fact i.i.d..

3   Method of Analysis

The method for analysis is composed so that it addresses both the independence of observations (in this case only investigated as L_i is independent of L_j, where L_j is a lead time observations lagged arbitrary to L_i) and whether any set of observations stem from the same distribution as any other set.

The data used is from a manufacturing company and represents the sales for the ten most frequently sold (in terms of number of order lines) make-to-stock products over a two year period. The most frequently sold product has 6,967 orders in the period and the tenth most sold has 2,158 orders. So no testing is done on less than 2158 observations. Data is only cleaned in so far that any lead time that is more than six standard deviations from the mean are removed as the tests methods tend to over fit to the few extreme distributions. The outliers are removed in one step.

The analysis methodology addresses both the aspect of identical distributions and independently distributions. From literature two combined assumptions have been identified and thus the analysis methodology must address both these aspects. This means that there are two hypotheses that must be tested:

1) Lead times are identically distributed, i.e. for any given practical purpose it is possible to assume that for a given planning horizon the lead time distribution is the same for the whole period.

2) Lead times are independently distributed. This may have different implications, but is typically taken to mean that any lead time observation does not depend on any previous observed lead time value. It may however also be taken to mean that lead times is not dependent on any other variable. In this research only the first aspect is investigated.

To investigate both these aspects the analysis methodology shown in Figure 1 is used.

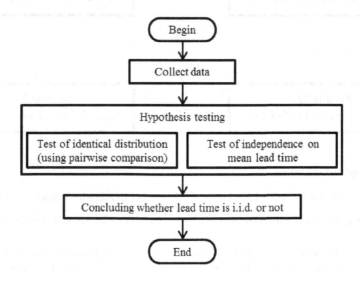

Fig. 1. Analysis methodology for investigating whether lead times are i.i.d

Kolmogorov-Smirnov's (KS) test is used to determine whether or not the lead times stem from identical distributions. The KS test is a widely used robust estimator for identical distributions (Conover, 1971) and does not suffer from some of the weakness of other tests such as Chi-squared. The method (as seen in Figure 1 and 2) relies on comparing samples of lead times and using KS test to determine whether not these pairwise samples are identical. In this research a 0.05 significance level is used and the ratio of pairwise comparisons that pass this significance test is the output from the analysis. Different sample sizes are used to determine if the lead times can be assumed to be similar distributed in smaller time periods, and thus if it is fair to sample previous lead time observations to estimate lead time distributions for planning purposes.

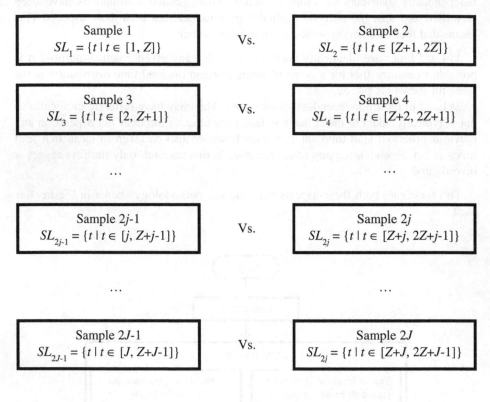

SL: a sample of lead time

Z: sample size of a sample of lead time   J: number of pairs for pairwise comparison

Fig. 2. Sampling for pair-wise comparison of similar lead time distributions

For the (in)dependence tests Box-Jenkins autocorrelation function is used (Box and Jenkins, 1976). In this case the test of independence is run on the mean lead time achieved on any given actual delivery date. The mean value is used as it makes no sense to chronologically order lead times for individual orders in smaller time intervals than one day. It is for all practical purposes not reasonable in most manufacturing environments to discuss manufacturing lead time in smaller intervals than whole days, as the data is not sampled with that level of detail. Only the first lag is considered as no systematic behavior is expected beyond piecewise increasing/decreasing lead times in the particular case study. In other contexts seasonality or customer order cycles could be incorporated and other lags should be included in the analysis.

4   Case Application of Method

The following section explores the results of the case study, with the results from applying the methodology to the case data shown in Figure 3.

1 period lag AC vs. ratio of pairwise samples significant on 0.05 or better level

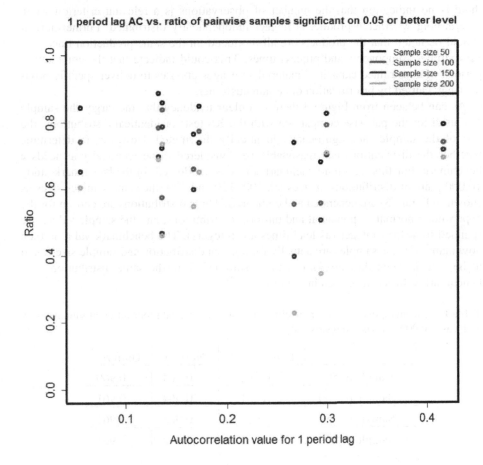

Fig. 3. An overview of first order autocorrelation

As seen in Figure 3 the first order autocorrelation values for the ten products range from 0 to 0.4. For practical purposes it would reasonable to assume that lead time set that have first order autocorrelation values below 0.2 is in fact independently distributed. Out of the ten products, six products have first order autocorrelations less than

0.2, while the remaining ten products have first order autocorrelations in the interval 0.25-0.42 indicating some form of dependence in the mean values of the lead times. It is also interesting to note that all the first order autocorrelation values are positive, indicating that to some extend large average lead times are follow by large average lead times. This clearly underlines that the average lead times may be linked to capacity issues, despite the products being purely make-to-stock. If capacity constraints are periodically present, one would expect to find that the average lead times are in fact dependently distributed, with positive autocorrelation values for a number of lags. In this aspect it is also interesting to note that the four products that are not independently distributed are in fact the third, fourth, seventh and tenth most sold products. So there is no indication that the number of observations is a relevant criterion when determining whether a product is in fact independently distributed. Furthermore it should be noted that the products are all produced on the same production line, with very similar components and process times. This could indicate that the company in periods of constrained capacity / material shortages chooses to deliver specific products, e.g. caused by prioritization of certain customers.

As can be seen from Figure 3 there is a clear tendency that the larger the sample size used for the pairwise comparison with the KS test for identical distributions, the less of the samples are significantly identically distributed. However, to determine whether the distributions can reasonably be considered to be identical one needs a benchmark. For this reason a benchmark study is conducted. In the benchmark study 10,000 pairs of distributions in sizes 50, 100, 150 and 200 (the same samples sizes as shown in Figure 3) are generated and compared. Three distributions are chosen for the experiment; normal, exponential and uniform distributions, and the sample values are rounded to nearest integer (as lead times are integers). The benchmark value is then how many of these samples are actually for a given distribution and sample size found to be similar when they are known to be sampled from the same distribution. The benchmark values can be seen in Table 1.

Table 1. Benchmark overview of three different distributions, with four different samples of in each case 10,000 pairwise comparisons

	Exponential	Normal	Uniform
Sample of 50	0.962	0.964	0.960
Sample of 100	0.961	0.964	0.961
Sample of 150	0.959	0.962	0.961
Sample of 200	0.960	0.962	0.961

The indication from the values in Table 1 is that even for small samples (50 observations) more than 95% of the comparisons should be significantly the same using a KS test. None of the sampled lead times achieve this high level of confidence. It is noteworthy that the KS test performs equally well for all three benchmark distributions, so no bias can be expected in the test due to the shape of the lead time distribution. It would be fair to conclude that most of the products exhibit a behavior that indicates that for reasonable sample sizes the lead times actually stem from the same distribution. The data covers around 500 work days of observations, meaning that even the product with the highest order frequency only has approximately 15 orders/day, assuming a lead time of 7 days, that would mean that on average 105 orders can be observed during a normal lead time and thus in c. 80% of the cases the lead time distribution for the next 7 days would be the same as for the previous average lead time period. This means that for most of the products it is actually fair to assume that the lead time distribution for the next lead time period can be estimated from the lead times observed during the last lead time period. It however also means that lead time distributions should be updated with relatively high frequency, which can lead to nervous planning systems. It is also interesting to note that the products with high first order autocorrelation values exhibit the poorest performance on the test for identical distributions as well. This is not unexpected as the KS test for similar distributions also tests the mean of the samples. If there is a tendency that lead times increase /decrease systematically, it is also fair to assume that the distributions change. Here it is critical to note that the shape of the lead time distribution may actually be the same, an obvious subject for further research. Taking together with the knowledge that demand distributions may exhibit similar time dependent distributions even within a planning period (Nielsen et al., 2010b) the planning problem is very much more complex that the assumptions allow for.

5   Implications and Further Research

There are a number of implications that can be inferred from the presented analysis for both academia and practitioners. First, it is obvious that lead times are, in the presented case, not constant as assumed in most supply chain models (see e.g. Chen et al. (2000)). Second, some of the products exhibit lead times that neither stem from identically nor independently distributions, while a number (six out of ten) can in fact reasonably be assumed to be i.i.d. For research purposes this indicates that even assuming that lead times are i.i.d. may be an oversimplification compared to real-life conditions. It also underlines the folly of assuming that lead times are constant, as this is a gross oversimplification. For practitioners there is also a significant implication. Specifically that lead times are in all likelihood not constant and thus that this uncertainty should be included in the planning and control approaches used. Another interesting implication is that the more information used to estimate the lead time distribution, the worse the estimate of the distribution in fact becomes. This is due to the pairwise comparison of identical distributions indicating that large sample sizes seldom lead to the same lead time distributions. In practice this means that companies should update their lead time information frequently and disregard old observations. This is completely contrary with the conclusions in e.g. Chen et al. (2000) and Michna et al. (2013) when stationary behavior is assumed on demand.

Future research will focus on investigating lead time distributions dependence on other parameters, specifically whether lead times depend on order sizes.

Acknowledgement. The presented research is partly supported by the Polish National Centre of Science under the grant UMO-2012/07/B/HS4/00702.

References

1. Box, G.E.P., Jenkins, G.: Time Series Analysis: Forecasting and Control. Holden-Day (1976)
2. Chaharsooghi, S.K., Heydari, J.: LT variance or LT mean reduction in supply chain management: Which one has a higher impact on SC performance? International Journal of Production Economics 124(2), 475–481 (2010)
3. Chatfield, D.C., Kim, J.G., Harrison, T.P., Hayya, J.C.: The bullwhip effect - Impact of stochastic lead time, information quality, and information sharing: A simulation study. Production and Operations Management 13(4), 340–353 (2004)
4. Conover, W.J.: Practical Nonparametric Statistics. John Wiley & Sons, New York (1971)
5. Dejonckheere, J., Disney, S.M., Lambrecht, M.R., Towill, D.R.: Measuring and avoiding the bullwhip effect: A control theoretic approach. European Journal of Operational Research 147(3), 567–590 (2003)
6. Duc, T.T.H., Luong, H.T., Kim, Y.-D.: A measure of the bullwhip effect in supply chains with stochastic lead time. International Journal of Advanced Manufacturing Technology 38(11-12), 1201–1212 (2008)
7. Kanda, A., Deshmukh, S.G.: Supply chain coordination: Perspectives, empirical studies and research directions. International Journal of Production Economics 115(2), 316–335 (2008)
8. Kim, J.G., Chatfield, D., Harrison, T.P., Hayya, J.C.: Quantifying the bullwhip effect in a supply chain with stochastic lead time. European Journal of Operational Research 173(2), 617–636 (2006)
9. Michna, Z., Nielsen, I.E., Nielsen, P.: The bullwhip effect in supply chains with stochastic lead times. Mathematical Economics 9(16) (2013)
10. Nielsen, I.E., Lim, M., Nielsen, P.: Optimizing Supply Chain Waste Management Through the Use of RFID Technology. In: Proceedings of the IEEE International Conference on RFID-Technology and Applications. Electrical Engineering/Electronics, Computer, Communications and Information Technology Association pp. 296–301 (2010a)
11. Nielsen, P., Nielsen, I., Steger-Jensen, K.: Analyzing and evaluating product demand interdependencies. Computers in Industry 61(9), 869–876 (2010b)
12. Otto, A., Kotzab, H.: Does supply chain management really pay? Six perspectives to measure the performance of managing a supply chain. European Journal of Operational Research 144, 306–320 (2003)
13. Sitek, P., Wikarek, J.: A hybrid approach to modeling and optimization for supply chain management with multimodal transport. In: IEEE Conference: 18th International Conference on Methods and Models in Automation and Robotics (MMAR), pp. 777–782 (2013)

An Optimization Tool for Process Planning and Scheduling

Mathieu Bettwy[1], Karine Deschinkel[2], and Samuel Gomes[1]

[1] IRTES-M3M, Université de Technologie Belfort Montbéliard (UTBM), France
mathieu.bettwy@utbm.fr
[2] FEMTO-ST Institute, UMR 6174 CNRS-University of Franche-Comté, France

Abstract. Process planning and scheduling are one of the most important functions to support flexible planning in a manufacture. The planning and scheduling should be solved simultaneously and not sequential for productivity improvements in manufacturing. In this paper, we propose an optimization tool based on genetic algorithm (GA) approach to help person in charge of process planning and scheduling to find the most promising sequence of operations considering a choice of machines on which to perform the operations. Minimizing makespan is the evaluation criteria.

Keywords: Process planning, Scheduling, Genetic algorithm.

1 Introduction

Many industries are trying to best optimize the whole system to deal with a global manufacturing industry more competitive. This will require to reconsider the supply chain. As a result, companies must migrate from separated planning processes toward the integrated planning process to provide competitive products while reducing costs and / or production time.

We define the problem as an integrated problem of process planning and scheduling (IPPS). A lot of work has been done on this subject and various approaches have been used to solve the problem.

Chryssolouris (1985) [1] is a precursor domain. He develops projects that are the basis to study the problems and interactions within a factory.

Tan (2000) [7] presents a review of the research in the process planning and scheduling area and discusses the extent of applicability of various approaches. They show that the efficient planning considering the alternative machines results in reduced lead-time and in improved overall machine utilization.

Moona and Seo (2005) [5] develop an evolutionary algorithm (EA)-based to solve some flexibility problems on shop floor.

Yuan and Xu (2013) [8] show an heuristic algorithm to figure out large-scale shop floor problem.

Li, Shao, Gao and Qian (2010) [4] develop a hybrid algorithm (HA) based-approach has been developed to facilitate the integration and optimization of process planning and scheduling in same time.

B. Grabot et al. (Eds.): APMS 2014, Part I, IFIP AICT 438, pp. 443–450, 2014.

Kim and Choi (2014) [3] propose to solve the backward on-line job change scheduling problem, a production system-based simulation methodology.

However, the main weakness of the models introduced from this two decades is that they consider alternative machines for each operation for a fixed assembly sequence. The originality of this paper is to consider a set of alternative assembly sequences and to provide the best one optimizing multiple criteria (Processing time, processing cost, both, ...). These criteria values are obtained through the resolution of the IPPS based on genetic algorithm method. In this paper, we consider a IPPS problem for a plant composed of a set of alternatives machines, multiple product flows and various assembly sequences. The alternative machines have different capabilities and require unequal processing time for an operation. Section 2 is dedicated to the problem definition. Section 3 gives details of our approach. The paper ends with a conclusion where our contribution is summarized and planned future work is discussed.

2 Problem Definition

In many manufactures, operations have a different possible way to be done with a set of alternative process plans. Fig. 1 shows an example of different flow to produce in a shop floor.

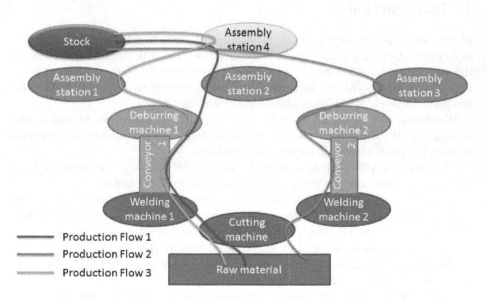

Fig. 1. Production flows in a shop floor

Shoop floors include several machines, which have different functions, processing time, and capabilities. Therefore, actual optimization should be done by considering the available machines and their ability. Fig. 2 shows the different steps of our proposed methodology for determining process planning and scheduling.

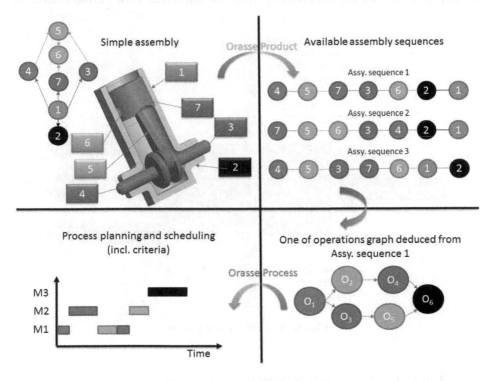

Fig. 2. Proposed Methodology

Our study is based on previous work done by ROBERT [6] concerning the tool "Orasse Product". This tool aims to guide the users during the definition of the assembly sequence of the generic product of a family. It goes from the concept with its list of components and the modular product architecture (from the adaptation of the FAST diagram) to the assembly sequence defined by the assembly planner thanks to Orasse Product features. From an assembly and kinematic scheme (first quarter of Fig. 2), "Orasse Product" helps assembly planners to build promising assembly sequences. In this tool, physical contacts and precedence constraints between components are modeled by a directed graph and algorithms based on partitioning matrix and graph theory are developed in order to guide the assembly planner during the constitution of the best assembly sequence. Based on the same methodology, we intent to develop "Orasse Process" (Fig. 3). In case of "Orasse Process", we consider an operations graph deduced from an assembly sequence generated by "Orasse Product". Next step consists in determining a process planning and a process scheduling associated to this operations graph regarding to specific criteria. Due to beta version we will work only on processing time : the makespan, and we will duplicate algorithm to others criteria in the future works. Once the method validated with the makespan, we will consider the processing cost, and the ability to maximize the processing cost and time, by delimiting the solutions from the algorithm by a Pareto efficiency.

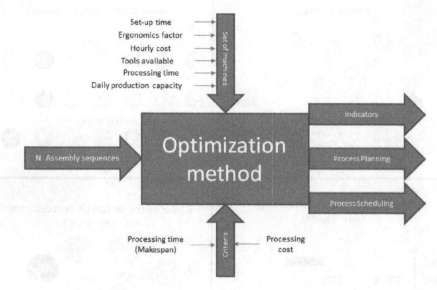

Fig. 3. Aims of Orasse process

3   Algorithms to Solve IPPS

Genetic algorithm (GA) is well suited to deal with optimization problem with a large searching space as in the IPPS (several assembly sequences, alternatives machines, mutli selection criteria, multi machines criteria). As we can see with Fig. 3, we can add a lot of criteria to each machines of the set (ergonomics, series, rentability, ...) the GA is the best way to find the better solution in short time by considering all input data. Moreover GA produces a set of near optimal solutions compared to other optimization methods which give only one solution. This can be useful for a person in charge of the shop floor production to select a solution among a reduced number of acceptable solutions taking into account particular criteria. A theoritical foundation of GA and their convergence to an optimal solution can be found in [2].

In this work, each chromosome is represented by a string of priorities: one distinct priority value for each operation. This string of priorities induces a specific order to derive a feasible schedule. The **Makespan algorithm (AF)** explains in details how the schedule is constructed and how the assignment of machines on operations is determined. The value of the resulting makespan is used as the fitness of the chromosome in the **Genetic Algorithm**.

3.1   Makespan Algorithm

The **Makespan algorithm (AF)** computes the fitness function by considering the priorities P_i assigned to each operation i. Input data is a directed graph of operations denoted by $G = (O, E)$ where O is the set of nodes and E is the set of arcs. Each node corresponds to an operation and a precedence constraint between two operations is modeled by an arc. The set of machines and their processing time for each operation are assumed to be known (filled or modified by the user) and data are saved in a matrix T where $T(i, j)$ is the time to operation i on machine j and $T(i, j) = 0$ if operation i is not feasible on machine j. The **Makespan algorithm (AF)** processes the operations in the order given by the priorities and assign a machines with the minimum time among available machines for the corresponding operation. An unique sequence with a given makespan σ is generated.

3.2   Genetic Algorithm

Genetic Algorithms (GAs) are stochastic, population-based search algorithms to deal with multiobjective optimization problems. GAs start by initializing a set (population) containing a selection of chromosomes (individuals). A fitness associated to each individual allows to distinguish between better and worse individuals. A GA iteratively tries to improve the average fitness of a population by construction of new populations. A new population consists of individuals (children) built from the old population (parents) by the use of re-combination operators (crossover and mutation operators). Better individuals have higher probability to be selected for re-combination than other individuals. After some criterion is met, the algorithm returns the best individuals of the population.

In our case, each chromosome is represented by a string of priorities (an integer between 1 and the number of operations). Figure 4 gives an example of chromosome. The initial population contains individuals randomly generated. The crossover and mutation operators are represented in figure 5. The fitness (here the makespan) of each chromosome of the population is evaluated through the execution of algorithm (AF). After a given number of iterations without improvement of the average fitness of the population, the algorithm stops and provides the best individuals.

As we consider a set of alternatives assembly sequences and consequently a set of alternatives operations sequences, we have to repeat the optimization process for different populations. At the end, our optimization tool will provide a set of promising schedules to the person dealing with the shop floor production.

Algorithm 1. AF Algorithm

Input:

G: Operations Graph (with O : set of nodes, and E set of arcs)

M: Set of Machines

T: Operating time

	Machine 1	Machine 2	...	Machine j	...	Machine M
Operation 1	T(1,1)	T(1,2)	...	T(1,j)	...	T(1,m)
Operation 2	T(2,1)	T(2,2)	...	T(2,j)	...	T(2,m)
...	...	...	...	...	...	...
Operation i	T(i,1)	T(i,2)	...	T(i,j)	...	T(i,m)
...	...	...	...	...	...	...
Operation N	T(n,1)	T(n,2)	...	T(n,j)	...	T(n,m)

P: set of priorities; P_i = priority associated with operation i

Output:

Process scheduling

S_i: Starting time of operation i

F_i: Ending time of operation i

D_j: Date of availability of machine j

Assignment $A(i,j) = 1$ if operation i is assigned to machine j else $A(i,j) = 0$

σ : Makespan

 1: **Initialization :**
 2:    $G'(O', E') \leftarrow G(O, E)$
 3: **for all** *machine* $j \in M$ **do**
 4:      $D_j = 0$
 5:      **for all** *operation* $i \in O'$ **do**
 6:        $A(i,j) = 0$
 7:      **end for**
 8: **end for**
 9: **Process scheduling :**
10: **while** $O' \neq \varnothing$ **do**
11:    **if** all nodes $\in O'$ have predecessor **then**
12:        Impossible assignment
13:    **else**
14:        Select $i \in O'$ with no predecessor and with the highest priority (minimum value of P_i)
15:        Select machine j with smallest $T(i,j)$
16:        $A(i,j) = 1$
17:        $S_i = D_j$
18:        $F_i = S_i + T(i,j)$
19:        $D_j = F_i$
20:        $O' \leftarrow O' \setminus i$
21:        $E' \leftarrow E' \setminus (i,v), v \in O'$
22:    **end if**
23: **end while**
24: $\sigma = \max_{j \in M} D_j$

O1	O2	...	Oi	...	ON
5	1	2	8	7	3

Fig. 4. Chromosome representation

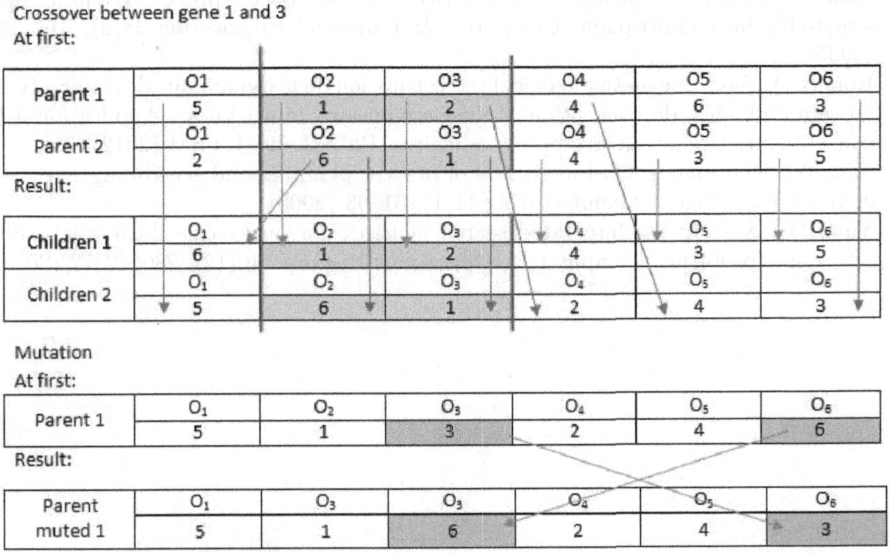

Crossover between gene 1 and 3
At first:

	O1	O2	O3	O4	O5	O6
Parent 1	5	1	2	4	6	3
Parent 2	O1	O2	O3	O4	O5	O6
	2	6	1	4	3	5

Result:

	O_1	O_2	O_3	O_4	O_5	O_6
Children 1	6	1	2	4	3	5
Children 2	O_1	O_2	O_3	O_4	O_5	O_6
	5	6	1	2	4	3

Mutation
At first:

	O_1	O_2	O_3	O_4	O_5	O_6
Parent 1	5	1	3	2	4	6

Result:

	O_1	O_3	O_3	O_4	O_5	O_6
Parent muted 1	5	1	6	2	4	3

Fig. 5. crossover and mutation

4   Conclusion

In this paper, a methodology based on genetic algorithm is proposed to solve IPPS problem by considering various assembly sequences for a same product and a set of machines for a same operation.

We intent to enrich our model by introducing many other criteria as transportation times for all pairs of machines, set-up times between operations, ergonomy and so on. Subsequently we will incorporate specific knowledge of the IPPS in the GA, so which generally improves its efficiency. A software "Orasse Process", proposing users the whole method, is under development. Orasse process cess will be test as beta version in Technifen, a company of Saint-Gobain, to help in the development of new products.

References

1. Chryssolouris, G., Chan, S., Suh, N.P.: An integrated approach to process planning and scheduling. {CIRP} Annals - Manufacturing Technology 34(1), 413–417 (1985)

2. Goldberg, D.E.: Genetic Algorithms in Search, Optimization and Machine Learning. Addison-Wesley Longman Publishing Co., Inc., New York (1989)
3. Kim, T., Choi, B.K.: Production system-based simulation for backward on-line job change scheduling. Simulation Modelling Practice and Theory 40, 12–27 (2014)
4. Li, X., Shao, X., Gao, L., Qian, W.: An effective hybrid algorithm for integrated process planning and scheduling. International Journal of Production Economics 126(2), 289–298 (2010)
5. Moon, C., Seo, Y.: Evolutionary algorithm for advanced process planning and scheduling in a multi-plant. Computers & Industrial Engineering 48(2), 311–325 (2005)
6. Robert, A.: Vers une méthodologie de structuration de la dynamique des interactions au sein dumodéle de conception Multi-Domaines et Multi-Vues - Application á la conceptionde familles de produits modulaires. PhD thesis, UTBM (2012)
7. Tan, W., Khoshnevis, B.: Integration of process planning and scheduling a review. Journal of Intelligent Manufacturing 11(1), 51–63 (2000)
8. Yuan, Y., Xu, H.: An integrated search heuristic for large-scale flexible job shop scheduling problems. Computers & Operations Research 40(12), 2864–2877 (2013)

Optimal "Sporadic" and Systematic Preventive Maintenance Policy for Leased Equipment under Various Operating Conditions

Jérémie Schutz

Université de Lorraine, LGIPM, EA 3096, Metz, F-57045, France

Abstract. In this paper, the considered system corresponds to a specific equipment proposed for leasing. This equipment is leased to several lessees who use it under various working conditions. The aims of this paper consist in determining optimal maintenance plans which minimize maintenance costs. Two maintenance policies are compared : systematic policy (imperfect preventive maintenance actions are performed, with the same effectiveness factor, after each mission) and "sporadic" policy (imperfect preventive maintenance action can be performed after a mission with its optimal effectiveness factor).

Keywords: Leased equipment, Working conditions, Maintenance policy, Finite horizon.

1 Introduction

In this research area, the first work on the themes of maintenance is usually attributed to Barlow and Hunter [1]. In this work, these authors were interested in determining an optimal time for replacement equipment thanks to the development of two major strategies known under the name "Age-Based Maintenance" and "Block-Based Maintenance". Subsequently, many authors have determined, for these periods of renewal, maintenance policies in order to minimize maintenance costs. Also, we can refer to the work of Nakagawa [7] who has made a very significant contribution in this area with periodical and sequential policies. Periodic policies are characterized by preventive maintenance actions performed at constant time intervals. Sequential policies consist in determining the optimal interval between each preventive action. Generally, for these policies, preventive maintenance actions are considered perfect (the equipment is restored to a state "As Good As New"). Corrective actions are considered minimal (the failure rate of equipment remains unchanged "As Bad As Old"). In 1988, Kijima et al. [5] proposed a first model for imperfect maintenance. It is characterized by an age reduction of the system. This reduction corresponds to a proportional amount of the time elapsed since the previous preventive maintenance activity. Nakagawa [8] proposed an alternative approach to modeling imperfect maintenance. It is characterized by an intensity increase in the failure rate after every

B. Grabot et al. (Eds.): APMS 2014, Part I, IFIP AICT 438, pp. 451–458, 2014.

preventive maintenance. However, after each imperfect action, the failure rate is reduced to zero ; the system can be considered new. All these models assume that the working of the studied system is constant over time. Alas, in reality, an equipment can operate under different operational conditions (e.g. production rate) or environmental conditions (e.g. temperature). Therefore, the degradation of the system depends on these conditions and the equipment can thus degrade faster or more slowly. In the literature, two models are used to represent the degradation variations. Accelerated Life Model (ALM) and Proportional Hazards Model (PHM) influence the reliability function (or hazard function) by adding a risk function [6][3]. The ALM changes the age of the system while the PHM defines a variation of the failure rate proportional to the working conditions.

Thanks to over half a century of research work and considering many important economic crises in recent years, recent work has sought to develop and implement maintenance policies for leased equipment. In recent work, the most notable contributions are those of Jaturonnatee *et al.* [4], Pongpech and Murthy [9] and Yeh *et al.* ([11], [12], [13], [14]). In these works, we find the usual policies such as sequential and periodic ones with imperfect maintenance based on the age reduction or failure rate increase. In 2007, Yeh and Chang offered an innovative policy where preventive maintenance actions are realized when the failure rate reaches a preset threshold.

Based on these observations, the aims of this paper consist in determining optimal maintenance plans which minimize maintenance costs for a leased equipment. This equipment is leased to several lessees with various working conditions. The remainder of this paper is organized as follows. Section 2 gives a studied system description, notations and working assumptions. In section 3, mathematical formulations of the maintenance policies and resolution methods are proposed. A numerical example is presented in the section 4. Finally, section 5 gives the conclusion and the future work.

2   Problem Description

In this paper, the considered system corresponds to a specific equipment proposed for leasing. Lessees are placed in a queue and obtain equipment for the desired period (duration of the mission) as it becomes available. Between two missions, this equipment can undergo imperfect preventive maintenance actions (based on age reduction) performed by the lessor (owner). These actions do not have negligible durations unlike the minimal corrective maintenance activities. The duration to perform preventive actions is a time percentage a of the length of all missions. The minimal corrective maintenance actions are performed during the missions by the lessor, when the system fails. The effect of working conditions, for a mission m, is based on the proportional hazard model (PHM) where they are modeled by a risk function g_m [2]. So, the hazard function is given by $g_m \cdot \lambda(t)$.

2.1   Notations

Throughout the paper, the following notations will be used:

- $\mathcal{M}$: Missions Vector to perform
- δ_m: Duration of the mission m
- $\lambda(t)$: Hazard function for nominal conditions
- $\Gamma(\cdot)$: Total cost of maintenance policy
- $\Phi(\cdot)$: Average number of failures
- ρ: Effectiveness factor of preventive maintenance action
- C_{CM}: Corrective maintenance action cost
- $C_{PM}(\rho)$: Preventive maintenance action cost based on effectiveness factor ρ

Other notations used in this document are defined below equations.

3   Mathematical Formulation

3.1   Minimal Maintenance Policy

The purpose of this policy consists only in maintaining the system in a state of working to assess the contribution of preventive maintenance policies. This maintenance policy consists solely of minimal corrective maintenance actions. These activities are carried out to overcome the immobilizing failures that arise over time. Maintenance total cost is given by:

$$\Gamma(\mathcal{M}) = C_{CM} \cdot \phi(\mathcal{M}) \tag{1}$$

Usually, when the system operates under constant working conditions during a period $[0, T]$, the average number of failures corresponds to the cumulative hazard function at the time T. However, in this research, the missions have various operating conditions and the failure rate evolves with the latter. So, the reliability of the system depends also on the working conditions but with minimal maintenance activities, the reliability must be continuous over time. In Schutz et al. [10], a functional age was defined to ensure a continuous reliability. To illustrate this functional age, let's consider two consecutive missions i and j. The reliability at the end of the mission i (at time $\nu_i + \delta_i$) under condition z_i must be equal to the reliability of the functional age (denoted ν_j) under condition z_i. The functional age is given by:

$$\nu_m = R^{-1}\left([R(\nu_{m-1} + \delta_{m-1})]^{\frac{z_m}{z_{m-1}}}\right) \tag{2}$$

where $R(\cdot)$ and $R^{-1}(\cdot)$ respectively denote the reliability function and its inverse. Therefore, from the equation (1), the average number of failures can be expressed by:

$$\phi(\mathcal{M}) = \sum_{m=1}^{\dim(\mathcal{M})} \left(z_m \cdot \int_{\nu_m}^{\nu_m + \delta_m} \lambda(t)\, dt\right) \tag{3}$$

3.2   Systematic Preventive Maintenance Policy

The first improved maintenance policy consists in planning preventive maintenance activities systematically after the completion of each mission. More precisely, the same preventive maintenance actions must be achieved after the $(\dim(\mathcal{M}) - 1)$ first missions. Indeed, after the last mission, a perfect preventive maintenance action is carried out. For this policy, total maintenance costs are specified by the following equation:

$$\Gamma(\mathcal{M}, \rho) = C_{CM} \cdot \phi(\mathcal{M}, \rho) + C_{PM}(\rho) \cdot (\dim(\mathcal{M}) - 1) \tag{4}$$

where the average number of failures is given by:

$$\phi(\mathcal{M}, \rho) = \sum_{m=1}^{\dim(\mathcal{M})} \left(z_m \cdot \int_{\nu_{m,\rho}}^{\nu_{m,\rho} + \delta_m} \lambda(t)\, dt \right) \tag{5}$$

From the equation (5), the average number of failures may seem identical to the equation (3) (minimal maintenance policy). However, the difference is in functional age expression. As preventive maintenance (system age reduction according to the effectiveness factor ρ) are carried out after the missions, functional age is expressed by:

$$\nu_{m,\rho} = \begin{cases} (1 - \rho) \cdot R^{-1}\left([R(\nu_{m-1,\rho} + \delta_{m-1})]^{\frac{z_m}{z_{m-1}}} \right) & \text{if } m > 1 \\ 0 & \text{else} \end{cases} \tag{6}$$

Determination of the Optimal Effectiveness Factor

The effectiveness factor "plays" a role in the quality of preventive action implementation. Due to this factor, preventive maintenance is considered imperfect and the system is returned to a state between ABAO (As Bad As Old) and AGAN (As Good As New). Therefore, it seems logical that this factor may also be involved in modeling the costs and lengths of preventive maintenance. For example, the competence of the operators can influence the quality of maintenance activities, but the maintenance action cost also depends on these skills.

Although costs may depend on the effectiveness factor, they are not necessarily proportional to the latter. Consequently, the cost of preventive action is based on a fixed one (e.g. parts and products used) and a variable one (qualification level, experience, etc.). Similarly, the length of preventive maintenance is composed of a fixed and a variable duration based on ρ. In this research, the cost and duration are modeled by:

$$C_{PM}(\rho) = C_{PM,F} + C_{PM,V}(\rho) \tag{7}$$

$$\mu_{PM}(\rho) = \mu_{PM,F} + \mu_{PM,V}(\rho) \tag{8}$$

where $C_{PM,F}$ and $C_{PM,V}$ correspond respectively to the part of fixed and variable costs. Similarly, the fixed and variable durations are $\mu_{PM,F}$ and $\mu_{PM,V}$.

As mentioned in section 2, the total time allocated to preventive actions is a percentage (noted α in the equation (9) of cumulative duration of all missions. For this systematic maintenance policy, the effectiveness factor is the same for all preventive actions. Thus, the maximum value of rho is obtained from equation (8) and its interval is given by:

$$
\rho \in \left] 0, \min \underbrace{\left(1, \frac{\log \left(-\frac{C_{PM,F} \cdot (\dim(\mathcal{M})-1) - \alpha \cdot \sum_{m=1}^{\dim(\mathcal{M})} \delta_m}{(\dim(\mathcal{M})-1)} \right)}{\log \left(C_{PM,V} \right)} \right)}_{\text{maximum value of } \rho} \right]
\tag{9}
$$

Integral limits of the function $\phi_{\text{sys}}(\mathcal{M}, \rho)$ are too complex to analytically determine the ρ factor. The latter will be determined by a numerical resolution.

This maintenance policy, compared to the minimal maintenance policy, can be further improved by determining the optimal value of the effectiveness factor for each preventive action.

3.3 "Sporadic" Preventive Maintenance Policy

This preventive maintenance policy is called "sporadic" because after each mission, preventive actions can be (or not) performed with diverse effectiveness factors. Basically, this model expression is very similar to the previous model. The total maintenance cost is given by:

$$
\Gamma(\mathcal{M}, P) = C_{CM} \cdot \phi(\mathcal{M}, P) + \sum_{m=1}^{\dim(\mathcal{M})-1} C_{PM}(\rho_m) \cdot \lceil \rho_m \rceil
\tag{10}
$$

with P the effectiveness factors vector of the first $(\dim(\mathcal{M}) - 1)$ missions and $\lceil \rho_m \rceil$ represents the ceil of the factor ρ_m. So, if the effectiveness factor is equal to 0, no preventive maintenance is performed (one of type ABAO has no interest).

The average number of failures, for this policy, is expressed by:

$$
\phi(\mathcal{M}, P) = \sum_{m=1}^{\dim(\mathcal{M})} \left(z_m \cdot \int_{\nu_{m,\rho_m}}^{\nu_{m,\rho_m} + \delta_m} \lambda(t)\, dt \right)
\tag{11}
$$

and the expression of the functional age remains unchanged (cf. equation (6))

This model resolution is more difficult. Indeed, there is not one decision variable but... $\dim(P)$ decision variables. Here again, the determination of these effectiveness factors cannot be computed analytically. Given the duration

allocated to preventive maintenance actions, effectiveness factors must satisfy
the following relationship:

$$\sum_{m=1}^{\dim(P)} \mu_{PM}\left(\rho_m\right) \leq \alpha \cdot \sum_{m=1}^{\dim(\mathcal{M})} \delta_m \tag{12}$$

Unlike the systematic maintenance policy, the ρ factor can take any value in
the interval $]0,1[$.

The next section presents a numerical example where the objective consists
in determining the effectiveness factor of preventive maintenance in the case of
systematic and sporadic policies.

4   Numerical Example

Let's consider the following arbitrarily chosen input data to illustrate our model:

- $\lambda(t) = \frac{2.5}{300} \cdot \left(\frac{t}{300}\right)^{(2.5-1)}$ (Weibull distribution, shape = 2.5, scale = 300)
- $C_{CM} = 500$ mu (money unit)
- $C_{PM} = 300 + (600)^{\rho}$ mu
- $\mu_{PM} = 2 + (8)^{\rho}$ tu (time unit)
- $\alpha = 0.05$

Various missions are presented in Table 1.

Table 1. Missions to perform during the lease period

Mission	1	2	3	4	5	6
δ_m	106	107	82	104	108	121
g_m	1.24	1.48	1.41	1.42	1.28	1.12

When maintenance actions performed are only of minimal type, the average
number of failures is about 6.66 and the total cost of maintenance activities is
3331.5 mu. With this cost, it will be possible to estimate profit from the two
preventive policies described in the previous section.

4.1   Systematic Maintenance Policy

As the total duration of all missions is 628 tu, the duration for preventive maintenance actions is 31,40 tu ($\alpha \cdot 628$). After each mission, preventive activities
can last, at the maximum, 6.28 tu ($\frac{\alpha \cdot 628}{6-1}$). During this period allocated to (imperfect) preventive maintenance, the maximum value of effectiveness factor is
0.69. Based on maintenance costs given above, the total cost of maintenance
activities amounted to 2289,7 mu with $\rho = 0.58$ and an average number of failures about 1.17. This first improved policy generates a profit of 31 %. When the
effectiveness factor is less than 0.19, this maintenance policy is less interesting
than the minimal policy. This is due to the slight decrease in the number of
failures compared to preventive actions cost.

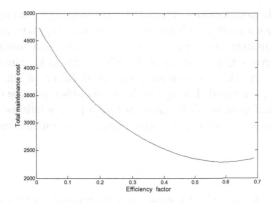

Fig. 1. Evolution of the total maintenance cost based on the effectiveness factor

4.2 "Sporadic" Maintenance Policy

As this preventive maintenance policy is more flexible, results are even better. From the numerical resolution, the best choice is to perform preventive maintenance activities after the second mission (with $\rho = 0.74$) and after the fourth mission (with $\rho = 0.78$). With these optimal decision variables, total maintenance cost is reduced by 46 % compared to the minimal maintenance policy. The average number of failures is 1.87, the cumulative duration of preventive maintenance actions is 13.72. In this case, extra time $(31, 4 - 13.72)$ can be used to add preventive maintenance actions to reduce the number of failures. However, total cost will be higher.

5   Conclusion and Prospects

In this paper, we considered a leased equipment for a defined horizon. During the lease period, the system was used in various working conditions. The latter affected the system, which degraded differently. To maintain a continuous reliability, functional age was introduced to generate equivalences between different operational conditions and working times. Thanks to this functional age, three maintenance policies have been studied. The first maintenance, minimal, is used to assess preventive maintenance policies benefit. Systematic preventive maintenance policy, characterized by the same preventive activities after each mission, give the best economical result. However, this result depends on the ratio between preventive and corrective costs (in the section referring to the numerical example, if $\rho < 0.19$, this policy should be avoided). The " sporadic" policy allows preventive maintenance action after the chosen missions. It is therefore more flexible but the determination of the decision variables requires much more time. It would be interesting to use a meta-heuristic for solving this problem when the number of missions increases.

Among possible perspectives, it would be interesting to study the case where the maximum duration after each preventive mission depends directly on mission duration. These maintenance policies may also be more realistic considering imperfect corrective actions and no negligible duration for these activities. The lessee can impose criteria such as equipment availability. In this case, preventive actions could be performed during missions. Another perspective would be to consider a set of different possible missions (with time windows). The aim would be to select missions to perform and to determine an optimal maintenance plan.

References

1. Barlow, R.E., Hunter, L.C.: Optimum Preventive maintenance policies. Operations Research 8(1), 90–100 (1960)
2. Cox, D.: Regression Models and Life-Tables. Journal of the Royal Statistical Society 34(2), 187–220 (1972)
3. Doyen, L., Gaudoin, O.: Classes of imperfect repair models based on reduction of failure intensity or virtual age. Reliability Engineering and System Safety 84(1), 45–56 (2004)
4. Jaturonnatee, J., Murthy, D.N.P., Boondiskulchok, R.: Optimal preventive maintenance of leased equipment with corrective minimal repairs. European Journal of Operational Research 174(1), 201–215 (2006)
5. Kijima, M., Morimura, H., Suzuki, Y.: Periodical replacement problem without assuming minimal repair. European Journal of Operational Research 37, 194–203 (1988)
6. Martorell, S., Sanchez, A., Vicente, S.: Age-dependent reliability model considering effects of maintenance and working conditions. Reliability Engineering and System Safety 64(1), 19–31 (1999)
7. Nakagawa, T.: Periodic and Sequential Preventive Maintenance Policies. Journal of Applied Probability 23(2), 536–542 (1986)
8. Nakagawa, T.: Sequential Imperfect Preventive Maintenance Policies. IEEE Transactions on Reliability 37(3), 295–298 (1988)
9. Pongpech, J., Murthy, D.N.P.: Optimal periodic preventive maintenance policy for leased equipment. Reliability Engineering & System Safety 91(7), 772–777 (2006)
10. Schutz, J., Rezg, N.: An integrated strategy for efficient business plan and maintenance plan for systems with a dynamic failure distribution. Journal of Intelligent Manufacturing 24(21), 87–97 (2013)
11. Yeh, R.H., Chang, W.L.: Optimal threshold value of failure-rate for leased products with preventive maintenance actions. Mathematical and Computer Modelling 46(5-6), 730–737 (2007)
12. Yeh, R.H., Kao, K.C., Chang, W.L.: Optimal preventive maintenance policy for leased equipment using failure rate reduction. Computers & Industrial Engineering 57(1), 304–309 (2009)
13. Yeh, R.H., Lo, H.C., Yu, R.Y.: A study of maintenance policies for second-hand products. Computers & Industrial Engineering 60(3), 438–444 (2011)
14. Yeh, R.H., Kao, K.C., Chang, W.L.: Preventive-maintenance policy for leased products under various maintenance costs. Expert Systems with Applications 38(4), 3558–3562 (2011)

Integrated Assembly Line Balancing
with Skilled and Unskilled Workers

Ilkyeong Moon[1,*], Sanghoon Shin[2], and Dongwook Kim[1]

[1] Department of Industrial Engineering, Seoul National University, Seoul 151-744, Korea
ikmoon@snu.ac.kr
[2] Postal Technology Research Center, ETRI, Daejeon, Korea

Abstract. In this paper, we extend the general assembly line balancing problem by designing an integrated assembly line and addressing the number of workstations and simultaneous assignments of skilled and unskilled workers. We develop a mixed integer program that minimizes the sum of total annual workstation costs and annual salaries of skilled and unskilled workers within a predetermined cycle time. Because this problem is NP-hard, we also develop a genetic algorithm to obtain efficient solutions for large problems. Numerical experiments demonstrate the efficiency of the random key-encoded genetic algorithm.

Keywords: assembly line balancing, genetic algorithm, skilled/unskilled workers.

1   Introduction

Most manufacturing companies employ workers based on their experience or skill set while also trying to reduce production costs. Therefore, assembly line problems have been widely researched during the latest period of industrial development. In his graduate thesis, Bryton (1954) introduced the idea of line balancing, and many studies have undertaken this subject over the subsequent 60 years. Various new assembly line balancing problem types such as two-sided, parallel, mixed-models and others, have emerged as have effective solution algorithms. Hoffmann [5] presented optimal line balances by operation on a matrix of zeros and ones called a precedence matrix.

Because the installation of an assembly line requires large investments, assembly line balancing problems can be distinguished based on objectives addressed through such as cost- or profit-oriented models. One of the cost-oriented models involves selecting equipment specific to the tasks assignments to workstations. The manufacturing of a product depends on resources such as equipment and manpower as well as processes. The term assembly line design problem is frequently used where these decisions are related. Pinto et al. [7] considered a model that combines the balancing problem with process alternatives that reduce task time. Bukchin and Tzur [2]

---

* Corresponding author.

B. Grabot et al. (Eds.): APMS 2014, Part I, IFIP AICT 438, pp. 459–466, 2014.

suggested a model of equipment alternatives that minimizes the total equipment costs for a given cycle time. The cost-oriented model can be extended by considering.

Since Salveson [8] formulated the assembly line balancing problem (ALBP) mathematically, numerous heuristic methods and procedures have been introduced. Corominas et al. [4] considered the process of rebalancing the line at a motorcycle assembly plant. They suggested a mathematical model based on a binary linear program to minimize the number of unskilled workers required. Chong et al. [3] compared a heuristics-treated initial population and a randomly generated initial population of genetic algorithm for solving ALBP. Moon et al. [6] introduced the integrated assembly line balancing problem with resource restrictions. They considered multi-skilled workers as resources and formulated a mixed integer linear program.

In this paper, we deal with the problem of designing an integrated assembly line with simultaneous assignment of skilled and unskilled workers. Although Corominas et al. [4] considered labor, they did not consider integrated assembly line balancing at the same time. Their objective was to minimize the number of unskilled workers for each workstation. Moon et al. [6] studied an integrated assembly line balancing problem, but they did not consider reducible task times through cooperation, a problem that arises when limited resources affect the operation time for every task. The selection of both skilled workers, whose salaries depend on their competencies, and unskilled workers, who can reduce operation time to perform tasks, is addressed in this study. In addition, the assignment of tasks to workstations with precedence restrictions is also considered as the resource issues are evaluated.

2   Mathematical Model

For the integrated assembly line balancing with skilled/unskilled workers, the following assumptions were made:

(1) The skilled workers are multi-skilled with different salaries.
(2) The skilled workers must be assigned to one workstation.
(3) The skilled workers can be assigned to tasks depending on their skills.
(4) The unskilled workers cannot be assigned alone to any workstations.
(5) The task time can be reduced by assigning an unskilled worker to a task.
(6) An unskilled worker can be assigned to only one task.
(7) A skilled worker can be assigned to a single workstation.
(8) The precedence constraints determine the sequence in which the tasks can be processed.
(9) There is a limitation for assigning tasks at a station.

Using these assumptions, we present a mixed integer linear program for an integrated assembly line balancing problem with skilled and unskilled workers. The following notation is used to explain the model:

Notation

i, j	indices of tasks (i,j = 1, 2, ..., I, J)
s	index for workstations (s = 1, 2, ..., S)
w	index for skilled workers (w=1,2, ..., W)
C	cycle time
O_i	operating time for task i when performed by a skilled worker
γ_i	reducible time for task i when performed by a skilled worker and a un-skilled worker together
$P_{(i,j)}$	set of task pairs (i,j) such that there is an immediate precedence relation between them
A_w	set of available tasks that can be assigned to skilled workers
FC	operating costs of a workstation
LC_w	salary for skilled worker w
LA	salary for unskilled worker
n	upper bound of number of tasks that can be assigned to a workstation
M	a sufficiently large number

Decision Variables

F Number of workstations to be used in the assembly line

X_{isw} $\begin{cases} 1, \text{ if task } i \text{ is performed by skilled worker } w \text{ at workstation } s \\ 0, \text{otherwise} \end{cases}$

Y_{sw} $\begin{cases} 1, \text{ if skilled worker } w \text{ is assigned to workstation } s \\ 0, \text{otherwise} \end{cases}$

Z_{isw} $\begin{cases} 1, \text{ if task } i \text{ is performed by an unskilled worker with skilled worker } w \\ \quad \text{at workstation } s \\ 0, \text{otherwise} \end{cases}$

Objective function

$$Min \quad FC \cdot F + \sum_{w=1}^{W} LC_w \left(\sum_{s=1}^{S} Y_{sw} \right) + LA \cdot \sum_{i=1}^{I} \sum_{s=1}^{S} \sum_{w=1}^{W} Z_{isw} \tag{1}$$

Subject to

$$\sum_{s=1}^{S} \sum_{w=1}^{W} X_{isw} = 1 \quad \forall i \tag{2}$$

$$Z_{isw} \leq X_{isw} \quad \forall i, s, w \tag{3}$$

$$\sum_{s=1}^{S} Y_{sw} \leq 1 \quad \forall w \tag{4}$$

$$\sum_{s=1}^{S} \sum_{w=1}^{W} (s \cdot X_{isw} - s \cdot X_{jsw}) \leq 0 \quad \forall (i, j) \in P_{(ij)} \tag{5}$$

$$\sum_{i=1}^{I} \sum_{w=1}^{W} (o_i \cdot X_{isw} - r_i \cdot Z_{isw}) \leq C \quad \forall s \tag{6}$$

$$\sum_{i=1}^{I} X_{isw} \le M \cdot Y_{sw} \quad \forall s, w \tag{7}$$

$$\sum_{i=1, i \ne A_w}^{I} \sum_{s=1}^{S} X_{isw} = 0 \quad \forall w \tag{8}$$

$$\sum_{i=1}^{I} \sum_{w=1}^{W} (X_{isw} + Z_{isw}) \le n \quad \forall s \tag{9}$$

$$\sum_{s=1}^{S} s \cdot X_{isw} \le F \quad \forall i, w \tag{10}$$

$$X_{isw}, Y_{sw}, Z_{isw} \in \{0,1\} \tag{11}$$

The objective function (1) is to minimize the sum of the total annual workstation costs and the annual salaries of the skilled and unskilled workers. Constraints (2) ensure that every task is performed by one skilled worker at exactly one workstation. Constraints (3) restrict that an unskilled worker might be assigned to task i when a skilled worker is assigned to task i. Constraints (4) restrict that a skilled worker is assigned to exactly one workstation. Constraints (5) ensure the implementation of the precedence relationships between the precedence task sets identified by $P_{(i,j)}$; for example, if task i is the immediate predecessor of task j, it must be assigned a higher operating index than task j. Constraints (6) represent that the total maximum operating time of each workstation within a given cycle time. Constraints (7) define the task assignment at the workstation with a worker. $X_{(isw)}$ can be greater than zero when skilled worker w is assigned to a workstation. Constraints (8) guarantee that a skilled worker cannot be assigned to a workstation with a task that the worker cannot perform according to the skilled worker's available task set A_w. Constraints (9) restrict the number of skilled and unskilled workers to the predetermined number for the workspace. Constraints (10) determine the total number of workstations to be used. Constraints (11) express the binary nature of the variables.

3   Genetic Algorithm

We developed a random key-encoded genetic algorithm with a procedure that slightly differs from the general one. The suggested genetic algorithm is summarized in following sentences.

Step 1. Generate an initial population of randomly constructed chromosomes with random keys for task and unskilled worker assignments that represent solutions to the problem.

Step 2. For the task arrangement chromosome, the offspring is generated using the convex hull crossover.

Step 3. Subject the offspring to mutation based-on probability to create slight changes in offspring structure. This mutation procedure can avoid premature convergence to a local optimum.

Step 4. Reorder the offspring to obtain fitness values, which are used for measuring the quality of each chromosome in comparison with others.

Step 5. Apply a selection procedure. The chromosome with the best fitness value joins the population and the one with the poorest fitness value is removed

Step 6. Terminate the algorithm when predetermined generations were reached or when the best individual does not improve more than 0.01% for predetermined generations.

3.1   Representation Chromosomes

The proper representation of a solution plays a key role in the development of a genetic algorithm. A string that consists of real integers is a solution (a chromosome). Traditionally, chromosomes are simple binary strings; however, this simple representation is not well suited for reproduction and other procedures. In this study, we use a chromosome that consists of two parts to represent task precedence and unskilled worker assignments. One of these offers solutions for assigning the tasks to the workstations through a random key, while the other offers solutions for unskilled worker assignments through randomly generated binaries as shown in Figure 1.

We used a random key to the task assignment for maintaining precedence relationships. If tasks do not have any predecessors, then their random keys are compared for selection and assigned to a workstation. For example, because Tasks 1 and 2 do not have any predecessors, as shown in Figure 1, they are candidates for selection. However, Task 2 is selected for a workstation assignment because the random key of Task 2 is larger than that of Task 1. After selection, the value of the random key is assigned a negative value to prevent it from being selected again.

For the skilled worker assignment, we used a simple heuristic that sorts on the basis of task precedence restrictions and the skilled workers' available task sets. The steps for the simple heuristic are as follows:

Step 1. Calculate operating time of cumulative tasks by observing the chromosome and divide workstations using the predetermined cycle time.

Step 2. Arrange the skilled worker candidates for each workstation.

Step 3. Select the workstation with the fewest candidates. If a tie occurs, select a workstation arbitrarily.

Step 4. Select the worker with the lowest salary.

Step 5. If the index of skilled worker candidates is empty for any workstations, find the appropriate combination of skilled workers.

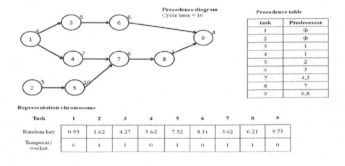

Fig. 1. Representation and initialization for a sample problem

3.2 Objective and Fitness Functions

The evaluation function in a genetic algorithm plays a role similar to that of the environment in natural evaluation. Each individual in the population represents a potential solution to the problem. A fitness function is computed for each string in the population and the objective is to find the string with the minimum fitness function value. For a given string, one can locate the minimum relevant cost. Equation (1) is used as a fitness function in the proposed genetic algorithm.

3.3 Reproduction, Crossover, and Mutation

The genetic operators such as crossover and mutation produce a second generation population of solutions. The method of the genetic operators -reproduction, crossover, and mutation- can change the set of the next population.

Reproduction is the biological process of producing new offspring from parents. In this study, parents are chosen by a rank mechanism. Unlike other reproduction approaches, a ranking approach offers a smoother selection probability curve. This prevents organisms from being dominated at early points in evolution. The crossover operation is a diversification mechanism that enables the genetic algorithm to examine unvisited regions and generate a solution. In this paper, we show the convex hull crossover operator for the task assignment and the one-cut point crossover operator for the unskilled worker assignment. We select two relative chromosomes for the crossover. Figure 2 shows an example to illustrate it. For the unskilled worker assignment, the position of the cut point is randomly generated from the range [1, (length of the chromosome − 1)]. We generate the offspring simply by exchanging the appropriate parts of their parents.

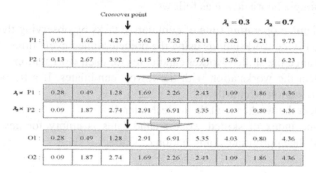

Fig. 2. Example of the convex hull crossover procedure

In a genetic algorithm, mutation is a background operator that produces a spontaneous random change in various chromosomes. Mutation plays the crucial role of replacing genes lost from the population during evolution so that they can maintain diverse populations, thereby preventing the population from being too rigid to adapt to a dynamic environment. In this paper, we used a swap mutation operator for the task assignment and a random point mutation operator for the unskilled worker assignment. The random point mutation selects a random point from the range [1, (length of the chromosome − 1)] where the gene is subsequently changed.

3.4   Termination

The terminating condition was determined when 50,000 generations are produced or when individual fitness was not bettered by more than 0.1% over 2,000 generations. For the parameters of the proposed genetic algorithm, the crossover and mutation operators were employed with the parameters listed in Table 1. A pilot test was conducted to find appropriate parameter values.

Table 1. Parameters of genetic operators

Parameters	*Value*
Population size	100
Convex hull crossover probability	0.7
One-cut point crossover probability	0.6
Swap mutation probability	0.4
One point mutation probability	0.4

4   Computational Experiments

The mixed integer linear program was implemented and solved using LINGO version 10.0. The proposed random key-encoded genetic algorithm was developed using C# with .Net framework version 4.0. Both numerical experiments were conducted on a Pentium IV 3.2GHz processor with 2GB RAM on the Microsoft Windows XP

Table 2. Comparison of mathematical model and proposed genetic algorithm

No	Examples		Mathematical Model		Genetic Algorithm	
			Objective	Time(sec)	Objective	Time(sec)
1	9 Tasks	8 Workers (1)	390,000	105	390,000	30
2	9 Tasks	8 Workers (2)	406,000	110	406,000	33
3	9 Tasks	8 Workers (3)	358,000	201	358,000	25
4	11 Tasks	8 Workers (1)	523,000	190	523,000	21
5	11 Tasks	8 Workers (2)	473,000	85	473,000	63
6	11 Tasks	8 Workers (3)	476,000	187	476,000	52
7	12 Tasks	8 Workers (1)	578,000	153	578,000	68
8	12 Tasks	8 Workers (2)	509,000	221	509,000	96
9	12 Tasks	8 Workers (3)	572,000	427	572,000	111
13	21 Tasks	15 Workers (1)	746,000	2,807	746,000	155
14	21 Tasks	15 Workers (2)	746,000	3,848	746,000	109
15	21 Tasks	15 Workers (3)	-	-	756,000	91
16	32 Tasks	15 Workers (1)	-	-	1,191,000	434
17	32 Tasks	15 Workers (2)	-	-	1,118,000	598
18	32 Tasks	15 Workers (3)	-	-	1,148,000	572
19	61 Tasks	29 Workers (1)	-	-	3,188,000	1,533

operating system. The mathematical model requires significant time to find an optimal solution. Moreover, this model was not able to solve problems as large as those with 32 tasks. To validate results, the mathematical model was compared with the proposed genetic algorithm for small problems.

The experiment was conducted for large problems: 61 tasks and 29 workers. The predetermined cycle time is 350 minutes and the annual operating cost for each workstation is $180,000/year. This assembly line is composed of 12 workstations, 23 skilled workers, and 23 unskilled workers. The total operating cost, which combines expenses of workstations as well as those of skilled and unskilled workers, is $3,188,000. The average computational time of 10 evaluations is 1,533 seconds. In addition, we solved 19 different examples. The result of the mathematical model and proposed genetic algorithm is shown in Table 2.

5   Conclusions

Moon et al. [6] proposed the concept of integrated assembly line balancing problem, and this study extends the idea by considering skilled and unskilled worker assignments. The skilled workers have multiple competencies and commensurate salaries, and unskilled workers, with lower salaries, are assigned to help them. We developed a mathematical model as an MILP for the integrated assembly line balancing problem with skilled and unskilled workers based on a task precedence relationship. Furthermore, we developed an efficient genetic algorithm based on random key-encoded chromosomes. The proposed genetic algorithm overcame the computational burden of the MILP. Therefore, the genetic algorithm has been shown to be a more helpful alternative than an MILP for designing a cost-effective assembly line with suitable worker assignments.

Acknowledgments. This work was supported by the BK21 Plus Program (Center for Sustainable and Innovative Industrial Systems) funded by the Ministry of Education, Korea.

References

1. Bryton, B.: Balancing of a continuous production line. M.S. Thesis, Northwestern University, Evanston, IL (1954)
2. Bukchin, J., Tzur, M.: Design of flexible assembly line to minimize equipment cost. IIE Transactions 32, 585–598 (2000)
3. Chong, K.E., Omar, M.K., Bakar, N.A.: Solving Assembly Line Balancing Problem using Genetic Algorithm with Heuristics-Treated Initial Population. In: Proceedings of the World Congress on Engineering 2008, July 2-4, London, U.K. (2008)
4. Corominas, A., Pastor, R., Plans, J.: Balancing assembly line with skilled and unskilled workers. The International Journal of Management Science 36, 1126–1132 (2008)
5. Hoffman, T.R.: Assembly line balancing with precedence matrix. Management Science 9, 551–562 (1963)
6. Moon, I.K., Logendran, R., Lee, J.H.: Integrated assembly line balancing with resource restrictions. International Journal of Production Research 47, 5525–5541 (2008)
7. Pinto, P.A., Dannenbring, D.G., Khumawala, B.M.: Assembly line balancing with processing alternatives: an application. Management Science 29, 817–830 (1983)
8. Salveson, M.E.: The assembly line balancing problem. The Journal of Industrial Engineering 6(3), 18–25 (1955)

Integration of Maintenance in the Tactical Production Planning Process under Feasibility Constraint

Martin Géhan, Bruno Castanier, and David Lemoine

Ecole des Mines de Nantes,
4 Rue Alfred Kastler, 44300 Nantes, France
{martin.gehan,bruno.castanier,david.lemoine}@mines-nantes.fr

Abstract. This paper deals with the problem of the joint optimization of the master production schedule and maintenance strategy for a manufacturing system. An efficient production planning and maintenance policy will allow to minimize the impacts of the potential random failures and will let the plan to be feasible. We present a modelisation where we take into account a feasibility constraint; the optimization problem is formulated as a linear program. We propose a heuristic algorithm to solve it and we show the impact of the feasibility constraint on different criteria.

Keywords: production planning, maintenances, feasibility.

1   Introduction

To be sustainable, a manufacturing company should take the right decisions to satisfy on time the customer demands, while minimizing the production costs. Thus, the production planning should be determined: the production goals are fixed according to the estimation of the available resources for a midterm horizon. That involves to determine the lot-sizes to produce: the aim is to calculate in function of the estimated production capacity the quantities which should be produced for each item and for each period of the given horizon to satisfy the customer requests, at the lowest cost (including the production, holding and setup costs). Many mathematical models can be used to solve this problem, [5] gives a classification of these ones.

However, some authors [3] shown that the production capacity of the system is often wrongly estimated: there is a difference between the estimated capacity and the real available capacity during the production process. This gap can lead to the infeasibility of the production plans. The authors identified several factors for this problem, and underline the main one: the consumption of capacity by maintenance actions. They consider two kinds of capacity loses: the capacity consumed by the preventive maintenance actions (the system should be maintained regularly) and the one consumed by the corrective maintenance actions, which are carried out every time that a breakdown occurs during the production. The figure 1 illustrates how the failures which occur during production (so the corrective maintenances) turn the production plan to be infeasible. In order to minimize and to anticipate the impact of

B. Grabot et al. (Eds.): APMS 2014, Part I, IFIP AICT 438, pp. 467–474, 2014.

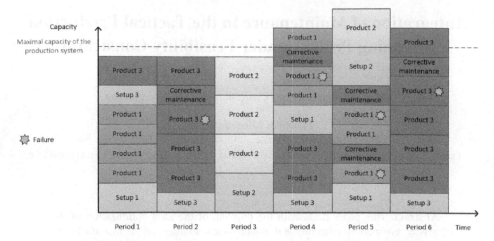

Fig. 1. Failures during production turn the production plan to be infeasible

the failures and of the maintenance actions on the production plan, making a joint planning of the production and the maintenance planning seems to be a reliable solution.

2   Review of the Literature

Tactical planning problems are usually classified according to several criteria: the number of items (single or multi items), the nature of the capacity (limited or unlimited), or the typology of the demand (constant or variable) [5]. This last criterion is known to be the most structuring one. Indeed we can sort the literature models into two categories:

- the Economic Production Quantities (EPQ) based models (where the demand is constant). The main objective is to find the fixed quantity to produce periodically which minimizes the total cost (including the storage costs and the setup costs) to meet the customers' demand. Generally, the production is resumed periodically when the concerned stock is empty,
- the Lot-Sizing Problem (LSP) based models (where the demand is variable, but known). Here, the temporal horizon is split in several periods, and the demand varies at each period. The aim is to find the quantities to be produced at each period in order to meet the customer demands while minimizing the total logistic cost.

We propose to focus on the study of the integration of maintenance concerns in the production planning when the demand is assume to be variable.

We found only nine papers devoted to the integration of maintenance into LSP-based models. [7] presents a model with an infinite production capacity with only one item, and a constant failure rate which implies no preventive maintenance. He studied two failures modes for which the price of the resuming of the production varies, and proposed a dynamic programming model to study the two cases and to provide a dynamic production plan. All the others authors [1, 8, 10, 12, 4, 9, 6, 2] propose to determine jointly a production plan and a preventive maintenance policy.

[1, 8, 10] propose a policy of periodic maintenance where preventive maintenances can only be carried out at the beginning of the periods. This strategy is basic and takes into account only a single criterion: the time. The main advantage of the use of this method is its simplicity when applied: preventive maintenance dates are determined in advance (when the production plan is established), and not dynamically. However, the fact that this policy is periodic can lead to several problems: the lack of flexibility of the planning of the preventive maintenance does not allow to carry-out them at the optimal times, either maintenance are planned too often, that will generates a significant maintenance cost ; or not often enough, that will let the system degrades and will generate many failures during production. [12] propose a periodic maintenance policy, but this one is based one the produced quantities. [9] uses a similar policy: the preventive maintenances are planned into time windows, and these ones are periodical in the time. Even if this policy has the same drawbacks than the previous presented ones, it is more flexible and allow to profit a little bit more of the opportunities of the production plan for maintenance. For [6, 2] maintenance could be planned only at the beginning of the periods, but not necessary periodically. Finally [4] propose a model, where the failure rate depends of the degradation of the system, which increases randomly with the amount of produced quantities. They propose a method to determine jointly a degradation threshold for which a preventive maintenance is applied, and a production planning which the feasibility probability is parametrizable.

The proposed maintenance policies are based only on a single criterion, and most authors do not consider the problem of feasibility of production plans they establish. Developping new models taking into account a feasibility constraint, with a maintenance policy based on several criteria seems to be a interesting solution to answer to our problem.

3   Problem Statement and Mathematical Formulation

We consider a time horizon of T periods. The production system can produce N items, noted i. A the end of each period t, a quantity $d_{i,t}$ of each item i should be available to satisfy the customer demand, shortages are not allowed. The production system, which is composed of only one machine, has a production capacity of c_t at each period t. The production of an item i consume p_i units of capacity. The various setup operations which are needed to launch the production of the item i consume τ_i units of capacity.

The system is ageing when it produced, the consequence of this ageing is the increase of the failure probability during the production. The age of the system increases by p_i units when one item i is produced. We note A_t the age of the system at the end of the period t. The failures are assumed to be Weibull distributed, with the parameters (β, η). The cumulative failure rate is noted Λ. We consider it increases with the system age, so $\beta > 1$. During the production, the system is ageing from a_1 to a_2 (the capacity consumed by the production is therefore $a_2 - a_1$), the cumulative hazard rate function is:

$$\Lambda(a_1, a_2) = \int_{a_1}^{a_2} \frac{\beta}{\eta} \left(\frac{u}{\eta}\right)^{\beta-1} du = \left(\frac{a_2}{\eta}\right)^{\beta-1} - \left(\frac{a_1}{\eta}\right)^{\beta-1} \tag{1}$$

When a failure occurs, the production stops. A corrective maintenance should be carry out to resume the production. These corrective maintenances are classified as *minimal*: they do not affect the system age, which remain the same than after the failure. We assume that a corrective maintenance consumed c_{cm} units of the capacity. When a period starts, a preventive maintenance can be carry out, these ones are considered *perfect*: they restore the age of the system to the new condition, so the failure rate becomes zero. The capacity consumed by these maintenances is c_{pm}.

At the end of each period, the manufactured products which are not dedicated to answer the demand of the current period can be stocked. In this case a unitary holding cost h_i should be payed for each unit of the item i. The stocked quantity of item i at the end of the period t is noted $I_{i,t}$. The setup operations involve a cost s_i each time that the production of items i is launched. A preventive maintenance involved a cost of pm, and we consider that corrective maintenances are costless. The aim of the problem is to minimize the sum of the production and maintenance cost.

We consider a feasibility constraint for the production plan. A period will be said to be ε-*feasible* if and only if the probability that the capacity consumed by all the production actions and by the maintenance actions (preventive et corrective) will be less than or equal to the available capacity of the period, is greater than or equal to a threshold ε. A production plan will be said to be ε-*feasible* if and only if each of its period is ε-*feasible*.

Objective

The decision problem is the joint determination of a production plan ε-*feasible* (therefore the determination of the quantities $Q_{i,t}$ to produce and the quantity $I_{i,t}$ to stock for each product for each period) and a preventive maintenance policy Π (ie to determine when preventive maintenance should be carry out). The production plan and the maintenance policy should minimize the total cost of the production, which is the sum of the holding costs, the setup costs, and the preventive maintenances costs:

$$z = \min \sum_{t=1}^{T} \left\{ \sum_{i=1}^{N} \left(s_i X_{i,t} + h_i I_{i,t} \right) + pm\, M_t \right\} \tag{2}$$

Main constraints

Our model consists the classic constraints of the CLSP [11]:

- the material balance equation (the stock of a period is equal to the previous period one, plus the produced quantities and minus the demand),
- the requirement of the setup operation to produce one item,
- the capacity constraint is included in the *ε-feasibility* constraint that we present further.

The following constraints ensure that A_t is equal to the age of the system at the end of the period t:

$$A_t \leq A_{t-1} + \sum_{i=1}^{N} p_i \, Q_{i,t} \quad \forall t \in [1, T] \tag{3}$$

$$A_t \leq \sum_{i=1}^{N} p_i \, Q_{i,t} + (1 - M_t) \cdot M \quad \forall t \in [1, T] \tag{4}$$

Modelization and linearization of the ε-feasibility constraint

As the failures follow a Poisson distribution with parameter Λ and if we set $a = A_t - \sum_{i=1}^{N} p_i \, Q_{i,t}$ the probability that k failures occur when the system is ageing from a to A_t during the production is:

$$P\big[N_f(a, A_t) = k\big] = e^{-\Lambda(a,A_t)} \cdot \frac{\Lambda(a, A_t)^k}{k!} \tag{5}$$

For a period t, the maximum number of failures that could occur is:

$$N_{f_{max}}(t) = \left[\frac{c_t - \sum_{i=1}^{N}(p_i \, Q_{i,t} + \tau_i \, X_{i,t}) - c_{pm} \, M_t}{c_{cm}} \right] \tag{6}$$

The *ε-feasibility* constraint for a period can be expressed as follow:

$$P\left[\sum_{i=1}^{N}(p_i \, Q_{i,t} + \tau_i \, X_{i,t}) + c_{pm} \, M_t + c_{cm} \, N_f\left(A_t - \sum_{i=1}^{N} p_i \, Q_{i,t}, A_t\right) \leq c_t \right] \geq \varepsilon \tag{7}$$

We can rewrite this probability as a function of the maximum number of failures allowed for the whole production (in terms of capacity):

$$P\left[N_f\left(A_t - \sum_{i=1}^{N} p_i \, Q_{i,t}, A_t\right) \leq N_{f_{max}}(t) \right] \geq \varepsilon \tag{8}$$

And finally we have:

$$\sum_{k=1}^{N_{fmax}(t)} e^{-\Lambda\left(A_t - \sum_{i=1}^N p_i \, Q_{i,t}, A_t\right)} \cdot \frac{\Lambda\left(A_t - \sum_{i=1}^N p_i \, Q_{i,t}, A_t\right)^k}{k!} \geq \varepsilon \qquad (9)$$

4   Resolution of the Model and Sensitivity Analysis

We linearised the previous constraint and tried to solve our linear program with CPLEX. We could not solve any data sets: the memory consumed by CPLEX was too huge. Therefore we chose to develop an heuristic algorithm to solve it. In this section we will describe the heuristic resolution method we developed.

Creation of an heuristic algorithm for the resolution

As we do not allow shortage product, for some cases the problem can have no solution, or maybe a few number. We developed an heuristic algorithm which try to found those solutions. It carries out those three tasks until that a ε-*feasible* production plan will be found or that no production plan can be determined in the first task:

- calculate a production plan (not ε-*feasible* but including preventive maintenances), to do that we choose a simple but efficient preventive maintenance policy: the age of the system must not exceed the value a_{max} ; the solver calculates jointly the production planning and the maintenance one whom minimize the costs,
- determine if the production plan is ε-*feasible* and calculate the violation of the constraint (in terms of capacity for each period) if it is not,
- change the capacity of periods of a plan in order to try to make it ε-*feasible*

This algorithm is carried out for several values of a_{max}: we divided the set $[1, \sum_{t=1}^N C_t]$ (which is the set of the possible values for a_{max}) into several partitions (the number of partitions is a parameter of the algorithm). The bounds of the partitions are the values that we tried for a_{max}. When no ε-*feasible* production plan can be associated to a value, we divided the partition where the best solution was found and we launch again the algorithm for the new values. In this way we tried to find the values of a_{max} from which we deduce low cost production plans.

Sensitivity analysis

We present in this section the experiments we done with the developed method. As we cannot find any dataset in previous researches we decided to build our own ones. We propose to study the influence of the parameter ε on different critera:

- the total cost,
- the mean number of preventive maintenances,
- the feasibility of the problem.

The cost of the production increases with the value of the parameter ε (because of the production levelling which makes the plan to become feasible). The sharp increase in the cost function presented in the figure 2 that occurs from the value $\varepsilon = 0.8$ is interesting: the cost increases linearly until this point, then to obtain a better feasibility level for the production plan will be very expensive. The number of preventive maintenance also increases with the parameter ε: it is necessary to regularly perform preventive maintenance to reduce the probability that failures occur and so increase the feasibility probability. The number of solutions decreases fast with the increase of the parameter ε, then the problem becomes impossible to solve because the ε-*feasibility* constraint becomes to strong.

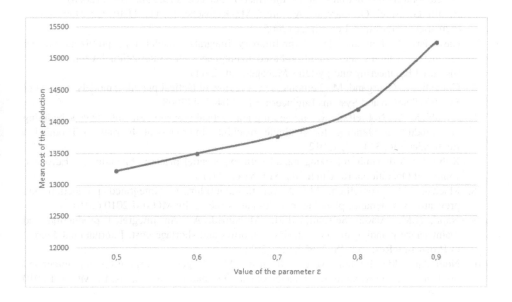

Fig. 2. Variation of the total cost of the production with the parameter ε

5   Conclusion and Perspectives

In this paper, we discussed about the problem of the integration of maintenance in the tactical planning process under a feasibility constraint. We presented a linear mathematical model, and explained why a classic solver could not solve it. Then we suggested an heuristic algorithm, this one used an age based policy which consist to apply a preventive maintenance before that the system reach a maximum age. Besides the interest of ensuring a feasibility level for the production plan, the joint optimization algorithm ensures a certain optimal aspect in terms of cost by the a priori allocation of capacity for the best suited maintenance according to the expected production levels. We test this algorithm on different benchmarks in order to evaluate the influence of the feasability parameter on different criteria, and shown that the insurance to have a good feasibility threshold for the production plan generate a significant cost.

References

1. Aghezzaf, E.H., Jamali, M.A., Ait-Kadi, D.: An integrated production and preventive maintenance planning model. European Journal of Operational Research 181, 679–685 (2007)
2. Aghezzaf, E.H., Najid, N.M.: Integrated production planning and preventive maintenance in deteriorating production systems. Information Sciences 178, 3382–3392 (2008)
3. Baglin, G., Bruel, O., Garreau, A., Greif, M., Kerbache, L., van Delft, C.: Management industriel et logistique. Economica (2005)
4. Castanier, B., Lemoine, D.: A preliminary integrated model for optimizing tactical production planning and condition-based maintenance. In: International Conference on Industrial Engineering and Systems Management (2011)
5. Comelli, M., Gourgand, M., Lemoine, D.: A review of tactical planning models. Journal of Systems Science and Systems Engineering 18, 204–229 (2008)
6. Fitouhi, M.-C., Nourelfath, M.: Integrating noncyclical preventive maintenance scheduling and production planning for a single machine. International Journal of Production Economics 136, 344–351 (2012)
7. Kuhn, H.: A dynamic lot sizing model with exponential machine breakdowns. European Journal of Operational Research 100, 514–536 (1997)
8. Machani, M., Nourelfath, M.: A genetic algorithm for integrated production and preventive maintenance planning in multi-state systems. In: MOSIM 2010 (2010)
9. Najid, N.M., Alaoui Selsouli, M.M., Mohamed, A.: An integrated production and maintenance planning model with time windows and shortage cost. International Journal of Production Research 48, 2265–2283 (2011)
10. Nourelfath, M., Fitouhi, M.-C., Machani, M.: A genetic algorithm for integrated production and preventive maintenance planning in multi-state systems. In: MOSIM 2010 (2010)
11. Trigeiro, W., Thomas, L., Mc Clain, J.: Capacited lot sizing with setup times. Management Science 35, 353–366 (1989)
12. Weinstein, L., Chung, C.: Integrating maintenance and production decisions in a hierarchical production planning environment. Computers & Operations Research 26, 1059–1074 (1999)

Optimal Storage Assignment for an Automated Warehouse System with Mixed Loading

Aya Ishigaki and Hironori Hibino

Tokyo University of Science, 2641, Yamazaki,
Noda, Chiba, 278-8510, Japan
ishigaki@rs.noda.tus.ac.jp, hibino@rs.tus.ac.jp

Abstract. In this study, an automated warehouse system with mixed loading is considered. The majority of previous studies considered assumptions that were similar to those for a single-shuttle system with single loading. Due to the increased number of items in recent years, storage assignment strategies with single loading are not feasible because of the shortage of storage racks. This study adopts a storage policy with mixed loading for an automated warehouse system, which enables the use of one warehouse. Additional movement and transshipment operations, which involve mixed loading, are considered in this paper.

Keywords: Automated warehouse, storage assignment policy, mixed loading.

1 Introduction

In this study, an automated storage and retrieval system (AS/RS) for multiple items is considered. The basic components of an AS/RS are the input/output (I/O) locations, storage racks, and automated stacker cranes (Fig. 1). An important measure of system performance is the cycle time of a stacker crane, which is the sum of the expected travel time and pickup/deposit time. The expected travel time is dependent on the storage assignment strategy. A low expected travel time is critical in the selection of the storage assignment strategy for an AS/RS.

In the past 30 years, studies of AS/RSs have addressed storage policies to reduce the travel time of a stacker crane. Hausman et al. [1] analyzed the cycle time of a stacker crane in a single-shuttle system in an AS/RS using a mathematical model. They analyzed different storage assignment strategies (dedicated storage policy and randomized storage policy) and demonstrated that full turnover-based dedicated storage was a suitable assignment policy. Hackman and Rosenblatt [2] considered the allocation of items to an AS/RS when it has insufficient space to store all of them. Using a dedicated storage policy, a set of storage locations is reserved for each product for the duration of the planning horizon. While the literature deals mostly with dedicated storage policies. Francis et al. [3] discussed about the four storage policies. They are: dedicated storage policy, randomized storage policy, class-based dedicated storage policy, and shared storage policy. A shared storage policy, allows

B. Grabot et al. (Eds.): APMS 2014, Part I, IFIP AICT 438, pp. 475–482, 2014.

units of different products to successively occupy the same location, and can provide substantial benefits when precise information is available concerning the timing of storages and retrievals.

Maximal benefits of this type of system are dependent upon the optimal system design. Eynan and Rosenblatt [4] and Wen et al. [5] demonstrated the influence of the system design (e.g., the length and height of the storage racks and the horizontal and vertical speeds of the stacker crane) on the optimal storage assignment policy. They clearly showed that the system design does not influence an optimal storage assignment policy.

The manufacturing industry is converting to multi-item small-sized production. Thus, a dedicated storage policy requires numerous storage racks because of the increased number of items. In addition, a dedicated storage policy may lack a storage rack. However, the replenishment factor for a storage rack is decreasing. In recent years, many companies load two or more items together to prevent shortage of storage racks. The influence of mixed loading on the optimal storage assignment strategy remains ambiguous.

In this study, an AS/RS with mixed loading is designed. High-performing storage assignment strategies are analyzed using a simulation technique.

2   The Model

2.1   Nomenclature

I	the number of items
N	the number of orders (I/O)
K	the number of storage locations
t_f	forking time
t_k	S/R machine travel time from the I/O point to the storage location k ($k = 1,\ldots,$ K) for $K < I$
t_p	time to mix items or divide items
λ_k	the turnover of a single loading pallet in the storage location k
μ_k	the turnover of a mixed loading pallet in the storage location k

2.2   Model

The assumptions of Hausman et al. [1] are employed throughout the paper:

- The analyzed single-shuttle system consists of a single stacker crane serving as a single one-sided aisle.
- A "First In First Out (FI-FO)" storage strategy was implemented in this system.
- The length and height of the storage rack and the S/R machine velocities in the horizontal v_x and vertical v_z directions ($v_x > v_z$) are known. The acceleration and deceleration of the S/R machine are not considered.
- The pickup and deposit times are assumed constant and equivalent to the forking time.

- The location number is set to in the order of early arrival from an I/O point ($t_1 \le t_2 \le \cdots \le t_K$).

The following assumptions are added to consider mixed loading:

- One pallet is deposited by a storage location. The replenishment factor of the storage location per item is less than 50%.
- If two or more items are deposited on the same pallet, these items will be mixed to create one pallet. If an item is picked up from the mixed loading pallet, the pallet will be divided into two pallets.

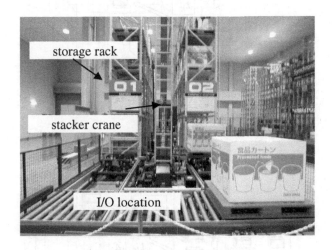

Fig. 1. Configuration of an AS/RS

2.3   Cycle Time of a Stacker Crane with Mixed Loading

Fig. 2 shows the movement of a stacker crane with single loading. When depositing a pallet with single loading, a stacker crane receives the item at the I/O point and carries it to a previously determined storage location (t_k). After depositing the pallet in a storage location (t_f), the stacker crane returns to the I/O point (t_k). In the case of a pallet with single loading, the required time for depositing and picking up for movement to location k is

$$\omega_k = 2 \times t_k + t_f . \tag{1}$$

Fig. 3 shows the movement of a stacker crane with mixed loading. When depositing a pallet of mixed loading, it is necessary to pick up a pallet with single loading from the storage location (ω_k) and to mix these items at an I/O point (t_p). A stacker crane receives the pallet at the I/O point, carries it to a storage location, and returns to the I/O point (ω_k). Thus, the movement of the stacker crane with mixed loading consists of the movement of the pallets with single and mixed loading. In the case of the pallet with mixed loading, the required time for depositing and picking up for movement to the location k is

$$\omega_k + (\omega_k + t_p). \tag{2}$$

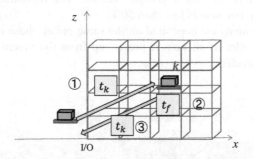

Fig. 2. Movement of a stacker crane with single loading

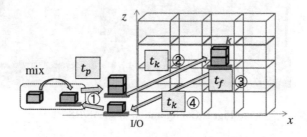

Fig. 3. Movement of a stacker crane with mixed loading

As previously mentioned, the average cycle time is expressed using λ_k and μ_k as follows:

$$CT = \frac{1}{N}\left\{\sum_{k=1}^{K}\omega_k \times \lambda_k + \sum_{k=1}^{K}\left[(\omega_k + t_p) \times \mu_k\right]\right\}. \tag{3}$$

$$N = \sum_{k=1}^{K}\lambda_k. \tag{4}$$

Here, if k_1 is smaller than k_2, ω_{k1} is smaller than ω_{k2} because the relation of $t_{k1} \leq t_{k2}$ is consistent with the assumption. As the first terms of Eq. (3) decrease, the turnover of the location near an I/O point increases for the condition of Eq. (4). Hausman et al. [1] proposed full turnover-based dedicated storage using an item's turnover. That is, the first term of Eq. (3) can be minimized by assigning items with larger turnover to the order near the I/O point. The results of a numerical experiment indicate that a full turnover-based dedicated storage policy was an acceptable assignment policy compared with a randomized policy. Items with a large turnover are combined and assigned near the I/O point to effectively minimize the first terms.

The second terms of Eq. (3) decrease when the movement of a mixed loading pallet does not occur. However, if items with a large turnover are combined, the number of movements for a mixed loading pallet will also increase.

2.4   General Model Formulation

In the study by Housman et al. [1], the discrete function t_k was approximated by a continuous function, and the turnover at the storage location λ_k was estimated using the mathematical method. They considered warehouse system configurations, such as square-in-time (SIT), and estimated the S/R machine travel time using the following equation:

$$t(j) = \sqrt{j} , (0 < j \le 1).$$ (5)

Here, j is the index of a pallet in a rescaled rack and $j \in (0,1]$. However, when considering mixed loading, the travel time to the storage location k needs to be considered a discrete function. We can then estimate the S/R machine travel time using the following equation:

$$t_k = \sqrt{x_k^2 + y_k^2} , (k = 1,2,\cdots,K).$$ (6)

and calculate the turnover of the storage rack k (λ_k and μ_k) using a simulation technique.

The results for the different policies for different s-parameter values of the ABC curve are shown in Fig. 3. The ABC curve is formulated by

$$G(i) = i^s , (0 < s \le 1).$$ (7)

Assuming that the total demand = 1, a demand of item i is shown by the following equation:

$$D(i) = si^{s-1} , (0 < i \le 1).$$ (8)

We created eight demand patterns using different values of s (1.000, 0.748, 0.569, 0.431, 0.317, 0.222, 0.139 and 0.065). If s increases, the demand for every item will be equivalent. In contrast, as s decreases, the demand differs significantly.

3   Comparison with the Storage Policy with Mixed Loading

In this section, the performance of the full turnover-based dedicated storage policy is compared with the performance of the randomized storage policy. The formulas for the full turnover-based dedicated and randomized storage policies are derived from Hausman et al. [1].

In a randomized policy, every item can be deposited to the vacant rack of the nearest neighborhood from an I/O point. If a shortage of empty racks occurs, a pallet will be loaded with various items together and deposit the rack near an I/O point. In a full turnover-based dedicated storage policy, the storage location of all items is determined in advance. Thus, even when the empty rack remains, it loads various items together at the previously determined location.

In Fig. 4, the average cycle time is plotted along the vertical axis, and the pattern number of demand is plotted along the horizontal axis. The pattern number of demand p was set to the descending order of s. Fig. 4 shows the results for three different values of t_p (0.0, 1.0, and 2.0) for each policy. In this study, t_p was set to 0 for simplification. The number of order N was set to 50,000.

In the case of single loading, the full turnover-based dedicated storage policy is optimal [1]. However, in the case of mixed loading, the randomized storage policy is optimal when the demand of items are similar (s is small). Fig. 5 and 6 display the average travel time and the number of mixed loading movements when $t_p = 0.0$ and 2.0. If a full turnover-based dedicated storage policy is used, the average travel time decreases and the number of mixed loading movements increases when p is large. However, if the randomized storage policy is used, the average travel time and the number of mixed loading movements have a slight influence on the variation of p. Furthermore, the number of mixed loading movements is small in the case of the randomized storage policy, and the randomized storage policy becomes effective when t_p is large.

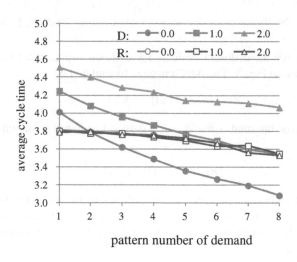

Fig. 4. Average cycle time for different values of demand (D: full turnover-based dedicated storage policy; R: randomized storage policy)

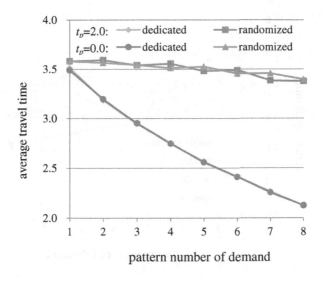

Fig. 5. Average travel time for each policy ($t_p = 0.0$ and 2.0)

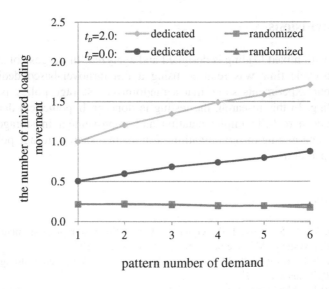

Fig. 6. Number of mixed loading movements for each policy (tp = 0.0 and 2.0)

Fig. 7 shows the comparison results for single and mixed loading using a full turnover-based dedicated storage policy. The mixed loading is effective when p is small. If p is small, many empty racks occur near the I/O point. Therefore, despite permitted mixed loading, the movements by single loading and the distance have decreased. This finding shows that a mixed loading of items is effective not only when a shortage of a storage location occurs but also when the demand of items is similar.

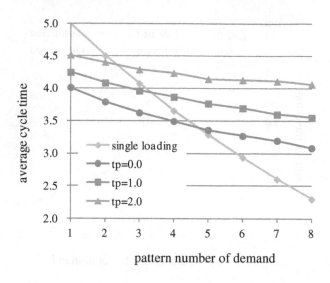

average cycle time

pattern number of demand

Fig. 7. Comparison results for single and mixed loading

4   Conclusions

An AS/RS with mixed loading is designed and analyzed. In the case of single loading, the average cycle time was reduced using a full turnover-based dedicated policy. However, our experiments show that a randomized storage policy is effective for mixed loading. In this research, the testing is done on hypothetical data. The future issues include a real-life implementation and improvement in storage policy. The method for determining the combination of items in a shared storage policy is critical for future operations.

References

1. Hausman, W.H., Schwarz, L.B., Graves, S.C.: Optimal storage assignment in automatic warehousing systems. Management Science 22, 629–638 (1976)
2. Hackman, S.T., Rosenblatt, M.J.: Allocating items to an automated storage and retrieval system. IIE Transactions 22, 7–14 (1990)
3. Francis, R.L., McGinnis, L.F., White, J.A.: Facility layout and location: an analytical approach. Prentice-Hall, Englewood Cliffs (1992)
4. Eynan, A., Rosenblatt, M.J.: Establishing zones in single-command class-based rectangular AS/RS. IIE Transactions 26, 38–46 (1994)
5. Wen, U.P., Chang, D.T., Chen, S.P.: The impact of acceleration/deceleration on travel-time models in class-based automated S/R systems. IIE Transactions 33, 599–608 (2001)

Routing Management in Physical Internet Crossdocking Hubs: Study of Grouping Strategies for Truck Loading

Cyrille Pach[1], Yves Sallez[1], Thierry Berger[1], Thérèse Bonte[1],
Damien Trentesaux[1], and Benoit Montreuil[2,3]

[1] Université Lille Nord de France, UVHC, Tempo-Lab., F-59313 Valenciennes, France
[2] CIRRELT, Université Laval, Québec, Canada
[3] Canada Research Chair in Interconnected Business Engineering
{firstname.lastname}@univ-valenciennes.fr,
Benoit.Montreuil@cirrelt.ca

Abstract. The aim of the innovative Physical Internet (PI) paradigm-shifting initiative is to reverse the unsustainability situation existing in current logistic
systems. In the Physical Internet, the efficient management of crossdocking
hubs is a key enabler of quick and synchronized transfer of containers across interconnected logistics networks. The paper focuses on the distributed control of
truck loading protocols in a rail-road crossdocking hub. It proposes grouping
strategies for truck loading based on the exploitation of active containers. The
grouping approach, the simulation platform and the obtained results are successively detailed.

Keywords: Crossdocking hubs, Routing, Physical Internet, Interconnected Logistics, Supply chain.

1   Introduction

Montreuil [1] points out that current logistic systems are unsustainable economically,
environmentally and socially. The aim of the innovative Physical Internet (PI or π)
paradigm-shifting initiative is to reverse this situation from three points of view:

- The economic goal is reducing by an order of magnitude the global costs induced by logistics and unlocking significant business opportunities;
- The environmental goal is reducing by an order of magnitude the logistics induced global energy consumption, greenhouse gas emission and pollution;
- The societal goal is enhancing the quality of life of the different actors (e.g.
  truckers, logistic workers…) implied in the logistic systems, and of society at
  large through better goods accessibility and mobility.

The PI concept is based on a metaphor of the Digital Internet. By analogy with data
packets, the goods are encapsulated in modular, reusable and smart containers, called
π-containers. The π-containers range in modular dimensions from large to small. The
ubiquitous usage of π-containers will make it possible for any company to handle and
store any company's products because they will not be handling and storing products

B. Grabot et al. (Eds.): APMS 2014, Part I, IFIP AICT 438, pp. 483–490, 2014.

per se. The efficient management of PI crossdocking hubs is a key enabler of quick and synchronized transfer of π-containers through interconnected logistics networks. It has been shown in a previous study [2] that truck loading activities in PI crossdocking hubs are crucial activities that should be studied in depth. The aim of this paper is to focus on this issue and to propose an approach and strategies for pre-loading grouping of π-containers to reduce the overall loading time.

The paper is structured as follows. The management issues of PI crossdocking hubs are introduced section 2. Section 3 focuses on the grouping approach and introduces alternative strategies. The simulation platform, protocol and results are then detailed in section 4. Finally a conclusion and some prospects are offered in section 5.

2   Physical Internet Context

The specificities of the Physical Internet crossdocking hubs (denoted π-hubs hereafter) are introduced in the following sections.

2.1   From the Classical Crossdock to π-hub

In a usual crossdocking approach, supply and demand chains are coupled and synchronized, replacing or greatly minimizing inventory buffers [3]. However usual crossdocking hubs are not designed for supporting the Physical Internet. Several points differentiate a π-hub from a usual crossdocking hub. The main difference is based on the foundation principles of the PI: usual crossdocking hubs are restricted to some suppliers and/or clients of a company, while the PI proposes an open meshed approach. The π-hubs are conceived by default to be open to any π-certified users and to handle multiple dynamically selected sources and destinations.

From a technical point of view, several other differences can also be noticed:

- First, existing crossdocking hubs handle all kinds of freight (e.g. cartons, shrink-wrapped pallets) while π-hubs are specifically designed to deal with modular and standard π-containers.
- In usual hubs, depending of the type of freight, the transportation is executed manually (e.g. by workers using forklifts for palletized freight) or based on dedicated automated systems [4]. As a π-hub handles only smart, standardized modular π-containers, it opens the way for high automation and high reactiveness. An automated π-hub can be mainly composed of a flexible network of π-conveyors, allowing decomposition, sorting and re-composition of the π-containers. The π-conveyors allow moving π-containers in the four directions (front, back, left and right) as depicted in Figure 1.
- In a π-hub, a π-container must not be considered as only a standardized container with a cargo as in usual crossdocks. It has informational, communicational and decisional capacities and can play an "active" role in the crossdocking process.

2.2   Illustration of a Road-Rail π-hub

Different π-hub combinations may exist: road-road, road-rail, etc. In order to make clear the nature of π-hubs, Figure 1 presents an illustrative example of a rail→road π-hub, inspired from the works of [5]. This rail→road π-hub aims to realize smooth interconnections between trains and trucks in shortest time. It allows the unloading of five wagons simultaneously and is composed of a sorting area and a manoeuvring area.

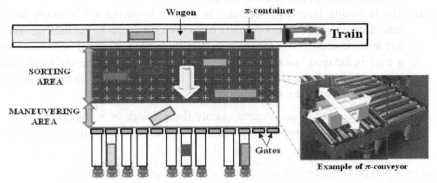

Fig. 1. Example of a rail→road π-hub (inspired from [5])

The sorting area is used to sort the inbound π-containers and to route them toward the manoeuvring area. The sorting area is composed of a grid of π-conveyors as depicted in Figure 1. The manoeuvring area allows returning the π-containers and moving them towards the different gates, where trucks are located. Note that this rail→road π-hub can be extended into a bilateral rail-road π-hub by adding to the right a road→rail π-hub section.

2.3   Current Issues in π-hub Management

In the recent PI research field, the management of π-hubs constitutes an important issue [5]. The quick and flexible transfer of π-containers from one transporter to another is the core activity of a π-hub. Different modal transfers (e.g., road to rail, road to road, ship to rail) are currently distinguished in PI networks and several problems must then be considered in the crossdocking process:

- Transporter scheduling in short term horizon: the π-hub gates are considered as resources (used by the trucks by example) that have to be scheduled. This problem requires deciding on the succession of inbound and outbound transporters (trucks, ships, etc.) at the gates of a π-hub.
- Allocation of π-containers to transporters: this problem consists in choosing the most appropriate loading of trucks with the π-containers unloaded from inbound train or trucks.
- Routing of π-containers across the π-hub: Once the π-containers have been unloaded from their inbound transporter, they are engaged in a preparation process that will get them composed appropriately with other π-containers and brought in time to be loaded in their outbound transporter.

The management of a π-hub as studied in this paper must concurrently deal with two types of perturbations:

– The external perturbations, taking into account the following degrees of variability and uncertainty:

   o The flow of π-containers to be treated can vary through time, both in terms of quantity, size mix and destination mix.

   o The incoming flow will normally be known to arrive a few hours ahead of time. Considering a train coming from a preceding π-hub, the information relative to its load is forwarded upon its departure. However in a rail→road hub, if a train is delayed, another train may enter the π-hub while the trucks are already positioned for the delayed train. Thus the control system should reactively solve a problem that was unknown until that moment.

– The internal perturbations concern mainly the network of π-conveyors: A part of the flexible conveying network can be out of order due to breakdowns or curative maintenance operations.

The next part presents a literature review in the field of π-hub control.

2.4   Short Survey of π-hub Control

In the recent PI field, a few studies have been already done on π-hub control. In [5] and [6], the authors propose respectively a specific design of a rail→road π-hub and of a road-based π-hub. The primary goal of these studies was to produce a functional design that performed at an acceptable level in terms of user key performance indicators and to explore its robustness with various flows. A simulation study has allowed to model and to validate the normal functioning of a π-hub. However, no perturbation on the conveying system or on the loading/unloading processes has been taken into account.

Moreover, at this point of development of the PI, very few research works have also addressed the routing problems in a π-hub [5, 7]. Recent works [8, 9] have proposed decentralized control to prevent deadlocks on a grid of π-conveyors. However these previous works deal with only small-size goods located on a unique conveying module and do not take into account different sizes of containers.

In [2], the authors study the routing of π-containers in a road-rail π-hub inspired from [5, 10]. They aimed to find the parameters that have a significant impact on the π-hub effectiveness. The parameters studied were the π-containers' size, their number of movements in the system, the numbers of conflicts between π-containers and the loading time of π-containers in trucks. The works presented in the next section are in the continuity of [2] and focus more precisely on the grouping of π-containers. Only the routing problem is treated in this paper. Interested readers can refer to [11] for a study of the allocation problem and a proposition of a formal model for the π-hub.

3   Grouping Approach and Strategies

Simulations presented in [2] have shown that the loading of trucks is the bottleneck activity of the π-hub. Thus to optimize the transfer of π-containers, an interesting solution is to assemble several small π-containers in front of the truck prior to loading and to load them as a single composed π-container. This section proposes a grouping approach using active π-containers.

Several approaches can be adopted (i.e. distributed or centralised) to solve the truck loading problem in a rail→road π-hub. In this paper, the concept of active product [12] is chosen for reactivity and adaptability reasons to face uncertainties and perturbations. Usually, distributed approaches can suffer from myopic behaviors [13]. In this case study, myopic behaviors cannot occur because each π-container already knows its destination truck. Moreover, for each truck a sole initiator can exist at a given time. In the retained approach, communicational and decisional capabilities are embedded in π-containers. These play an active role by creating groups of π-containers before being loaded onto a truck to reduce the loading queue.

The grouping approach, aiming at loading several π-containers while respecting a determined grouping size, is detailed below and depicted in figure 2 for a three-container group (initiator and two other containers).

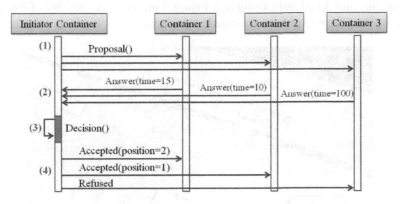

Fig. 2. Example of container grouping approach

(1) <u>Proposal</u>: The first π-container (the initiator) that arrives in front of its destination truck sends a "grouping proposal" to know the π-containers that could be grouped and loaded with it.

(2) <u>Answer</u>: The concerned π-containers answer to it by giving their arrival time.

(3) <u>Decision</u>: The initiator chooses the π-containers based on two parameters:
  - the grouping size limit (defined by the strategy chosen), that provides the maximum number of π-containers in the group,
  - the arrival times sent by the other π-containers. The initiator container chooses the π-containers with the earliest arrival times to form the group until the size limit.

(4) <u>Choice diffusion</u>: The initiator container sends to the chosen π-containers their specific location in the group formed at its right. It also sends a refusal to the unselected π-containers.

Using this approach, three strategies can be used to determine the grouping size limit (used in step 3 of Figure 2). First, all the containers going to the same truck are grouped and loaded at once (i.e. infinite limit). Second, the number of containers in each group is limited statically to avoid disturbing the loading of the neighbor trucks. And third, the number of containers in each group is limited dynamically by extending them if the gates on the right are not used (no truck allocated to the neighbor gates). Figure 3 presents a view of the simulator during this grouping approach and the location of containers within the π-hub.

To validate our approach, the next section presents the simulation environment, protocol and the results for each one of these strategies.

4   Simulation Protocol and Results

The grouping approach is evaluated through a simulation experiment by using the Netlogo multi-agent environment. This environment is well adapted for rapid prototyping of reactive multi-agent systems and provides user-friendly interfaces. The behaviors of the active π-containers are represented by agents with processing, communicational and decisional capabilities. Figure 3 presents a screenshot of the simulator during the grouping process presented in Figure 2.

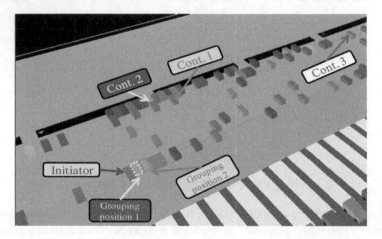

Fig. 3. View of the simulator describing a three-container grouping

Four series of simulations were performed: the first one presents a basic truck loading without grouping and the three others respectively concern the three grouping strategies presented above. Each simulation experiment contains 2000 runs of the simulator with a random positioning of trucks and π-containers. The train is assumed loaded with only small unitary π-containers that constitute the more interesting case study as highlighted in [2]. The different simulation experiments are as follows:

Sim. #1: π-containers route themselves into the π-hub and are loaded without grouping (i.e. grouping size limit = 1).

Sim. #2: the first π-container that reaches a truck waits for all the containers that go to the same truck to be loaded at once (i.e. grouping size limit = remaining space in the truck).

Sim. #3: the groups of π-containers are limited to three containers to avoid disturbing neighbor loading gates (i.e. grouping size limit = space between two gates = 3).

Sim. #4: the grouping size limit is now dynamic and can be extended if the neighbor loading gate is not used (i.e. $3 \leq$ grouping size limit $\leq$ remaining space in the truck).

The performance indicator is the evacuation time that represents the time between unloading the first π-container from the train and loading the last π-container onto its truck. Table 1 summarizes the different simulation results.

Table 1. Simulations results

Evacuation Time for 2000 runs (sec)	Simulations			
	#1	#2	#3	#4
Average	963	634	628	623
Standard Deviation	122	46	42	43
Min	664	524	520	504
Max	1744	816	800	828

First these simulations show that the grouping of containers is efficient. The evacuation time for simulation experiment #2 is around 30% lower than the one for the first baseline scenario (without grouping). The grouping of containers greatly reduces the evacuation time with several containers going in the same truck. Thus the maximum value is divided by two, which implies a lower standard deviation for the simulation experiment.

However, the simulations in experiment #2 exhibit some blocking situations where some truck loading is delayed because the place in front of the truck is occupied by the π-container grouping of the truck on the left. In simulation experiment #3, these blocking situations were avoided because the group size limit was set to 3. The extension of the grouping size limit in simulation experiment #4 does not impact most of the simulations. But in some cases, the evacuation time was lowered by 120 seconds (i.e. one loading time). Indeed, with this modification six containers can be loaded at once (if the gate on the right is not used) instead of two times three containers.

If the scenario includes a lot of π-containers going to the same truck, the strategies tested in experiments #3 or #4 have to be chosen. If there are some gates that are not used in the scenario, the strategy simulated in experiment #4 should be used to provide better results. So the strategies proposed consider an increasing number of specific cases without impacting the overall results. Indeed, the enhanced strategies respectively lower the evacuation time of simulation experiment #2 by 1% to 2% in average over 2000 runs, while taking into account the specific scenarios.

5   Conclusion

This paper presented a study of routing inside a π-hub and focused more particularly on the loading of π-containers onto trucks. The aim of this paper was to show the impact of different grouping strategies using the concept of π-container activeness.

The simulations proposed showed that the grouping of containers has significant value. It lowers the evacuation time of the system by 30%. The grouping of containers could be made using different parameters like the number of containers grouped or the time waited by containers before loading. This paper illustrated this with some grouping strategies dedicated to specific scenarios.

Next studies should first consider other performance indicators like the departure time of each truck or π-container. It could make easier the evaluation of specific scenarios and of the corresponding strategies. Another perspective is to include internal perturbations to prove the robustness of the routing mechanism in a disrupted environment. Finally, the routing approach could be extended for example by taking into account future states of the system in the decisional and grouping mechanism.

References

1. Montreuil, B.: Towards a Physical Internet: Meeting the Global Logistics Sustainability Grand challenge, CIRRELT-2001-03 Research rapport (2011)
2. Pach, C., Berger, T., Adam, E., Bonte, T., Sallez, Y.: Proposition of a potential fields approach to solve routing in a rail-road π-hub. Accepted in the 1st International Physical Internet Conference (IPIC), Québec City, Canada, May 28-30 (2014)
3. Kulwiec, R.: Crossdocking as a Supply Chain Strategy. TARGET (Association for Manufacturing Excellence) 20(3) (2004)
4. Van Belle, J., Valckenaers, P., Cattrysse, D.: Crossdocking: State of the art. Omega 40, 827–846 (2012)
5. Ballot, E., Montreuil, B., Thivierge, C.: Functional Design of Physical Internet Facilities: A Road-Rail Hub. Progress in Material Handling Research: 2012, MHIA, Charlotte, NC (2012)
6. Montreuil, B., Meller, R.D., Thivierge, C., Montreuil, Z.: Functional Design of Physical Internet Facilities: A Unimodal Road-Based Crossdocking Hub. Progress in Material Handling Research: 2012, MHIA, Charlotte, NC (2012)
7. Meller, R.D., Montreuil, B., Thivierge, C., Montreuil, Z.: Functional Design of Physical Internet Facilities: A Road-Based Transit Center. Progress in Material Handling Research, MHIA, Charlotte, NC (2012)
8. Gue, K.R., Furmans, K., Seibold, Z., Uludag, O.: GridStore: A Puzzle-Based Storage System with Decentralized Control. IEEE Transactions on Automation Science and Engineering (99) (2013), doi:10.1109/TASE.2013.2278252
9. Mayer, S., Furmans, K.: Deadlock prevention in a completely decentralized controlled materials flow systems. Logistics Research 2, 147–158 (2010)
10. Ballot, E., Montreuil, B., Thémans, M.: OPENFRET: Contribution à la conceptualisation et à la réalisation d'un hub rail-route de l'Internet Physique, MEDDAT, Paris (2010)
11. Walha, F., Bekrar, A., Chaabane, S., Loukil, T.: A rail-road PI-hub allocation problems: model and heuristic. Accepted in the 1st International Physical Internet Conference (IPIC), Québec City, Canada, May 28-30 (2014)
12. Sallez, Y., Berger, T., Deneux, D., Trentesaux, D.: The Life Cycle of Active and Intelligent Products: The Augmentation concept. Int. J. of Comp. Int. Manuf. 23(10), 905–924 (2010)
13. Zambrano, G., Pach, C., Aissani, N., Bekrar, A., Berger, T., Trentesaux, D.: The control of myopic behavior in semi-heterarchical production systems: A holonic framework. Eng. Appl. Artif. Intell. 26, 800–817 (2013)

Multi Layer Modeling of Socio-Technical Production Planning and Control Systems

Adrian E. Specker[1,*], Dieter Fischer[1], and Toni Waefler[2]

[1] University of Applied Sciences Northwestern Switzerland, School of Engineering
Bahnhofstrasse 6, CH-5210 Windisch, Switzerland
{adrian.specker,dieter.fischer}@fhnw.ch
[2] University of Applied Sciences Northwestern Switzerland,
School of Applied Psychology, Riggenbachstrasse 16, CH-4600 Olten, Switzerland
toni.waefler@fhnw.ch

Abstract. This paper discusses an approach and a proposal of modeling socio-technical production systems. During the analysis and the development of new concepts the need for suitable representation methods emerged. Especially we had to grasp and document varied system aspects and make these aspects understandable for our project team. Surprisingly no standardized, uniform, comprehensive and especially quite complete system modeling standard exists up to the present day. The modeling frame which we developed and which is presented in this paper corresponds first of all to the approach of General System Theory after which complex socio-technical systems a) can be modeled in a hierarchical structure (called "subsystems") and b) aspect-wise (called "aspect systems"). Within the scope of the project we developed several aspect systems, as for example the formal organization, flow of information, knowledge network and social network.

Keywords: socio-technical systems, modeling, production planning and control, manufacturing.

1 Introduction

During a project in several manufacturing companies which has been supported by the Swiss Confederation (KTI), the need for suitable representations and a model method emerged in order to support our analysis and conceptual tasks. The project has been about decision support and the optimization of production planning and control tasks and related decisions. During our project work it became (once more) clear, that in an interdisciplinary project regarding production planning and control, unfortunately, one has to develop inevitably "ad hoc" and individually favored representations and modeling technologies. Surprisingly up to the present day no standardized, uniform, comprehensive and "complete" system modeling method exists as an established standard. It is not clear at all with which methods one has to document

---

* Corresponding author.

B. Grabot et al. (Eds.): APMS 2014, Part I, IFIP AICT 438, pp. 491–498, 2014.

socio-technical production systems in an integrated way, and how these systems are to be modeled or to be explained. That is, no real methodical certainty exists when a project has to deal with many system aspects. Rather originate within the scope of such projects - in the absence of alternatives and of necessity - more or less new situation-related visualizations. This shows an attempt to do justice to the complexity and diversity of the systems to be described. Meanwhile most representation and modeling methods lack an integrating frame, which is why one has to use different and quite separate representations - which lack a clear and recognizable relation between different aspects of the system. The mental integration of different and especially separate representations can therefore not succeed in an optimal way.

Modeling methods, like CIMOSA [1], ARIS [2], SCOR [3], Viable system model - VSM [4], UML [5], Value Stream Method - VSM [6] etc. lay their focus mainly on the technical or organizational side. Especially social and cognitive aspect models are not an integrated part of those methods, like e.g. MTO-Analysis [7], Rasmussen [8], Hierarchical Task Model [9], or Knowledge Networks [10].

2   Problem Statement

The deficit we face in projects concerning the investigation of "production planning and control systems" depends in fact on our view, to sum it up, that there is no general accepted method to model socio-technical systems which is broad enough to deal with all social, cognitive and technical aspects in an adequate way - or that the methods in use rather negate important social and cognitive aspects. However, the success of projects in such a field depends on the fact, how well the project partners succeed in grasping all those aspects of the production system in order to form a comprehensive conceptual model. Today every successful project like e.g. in construction engineering would be totally inconceivable without high quality, comprehensive construction blueprints.

Models and representations of a socio-technical manufacturing system are not only a topic in the project area. Adequate models would also be valuable for employees who are active in the daily business - as with adequate models they could better understand their enterprise. To eliminate a misunderstanding in advance: Business processes are in many ways mapped or modeled in ERP systems and furthermore there exist quality manuals. However, on the other hand, we found that central factors about the work system are not well documented neither in ERP systems nor in quality manuals (s. below).

3   Goals and Requirements

On account of the problem formulation described above and the ascertained deficits, from our point of view the need of a method which documents socio-technical manufacturing systems has arisen. The method should permit therefore in particular taking into account the most different aspects (aspect systems) and integrate them without losing the internal relations to the overall system. The goals are:

- a model of the system hierarchy and its respective levels (system / subsystem)
- an integrated framework for various subsystem and aspect systems
- suitable to model technical and social aspect systems and their interrelations
- expansible to new aspects according to the user's needs
- easy navigation between different aspects and views of the system

4   Multilayer Modeling Approach

One purpose of the project consisted in creating an integrating representation meta frame in which different aspect systems at alternatively different system levels can be arranged, without the respective mutual relation gets lost. The system to be visualized must be integrated in a stable frame. As a base of the system representation and in analogy to an architect's plans or construction blueprint a so called "floor plan of the enterprise" served us here. This "floor plan" shows the overall system with his accompanying subsystems. Here, the possibility exists, to illustrate already several layers of the system. In support of the black box representation, known from the system engineering approach quite an easy representation with rectangles was chosen [11].

4.1   System Hierarchy: Systems and Subsystems

The uppermost representation level shows the overall system, which is called "S(0)". On the level "S(-1)" the system is shown with its subsystems (Fig. 2). In the example (Fig. 1) the system shows an overall system S(0) of our project partner. Eight departments, like painting, prototypes, logistics, etc., illustrate the according subsystems. With the change of the level S(0) to the level S(-1) the level of detail increases - this step is called "Drill-Down". The requirement of the Drill-Down has been realized in our software tools with the help of hyperlinks as the software tool we used did not support the generation of a hierarchy. In this feature is a major weakness of most graphic tools. Our prototype was provided in Microsoft Visio.

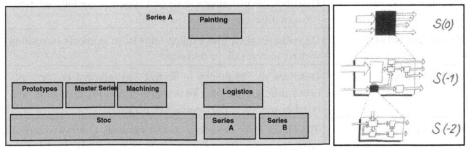

Fig. 1. Example of a Level S(-1) system

Fig. 2. System levels (s. Züst [11])

4.2   Aspect Systems - Aspect Layers

The system to be visualized has to be modeled - in order to understand its complexity - with its aspect systems or aspect layers (s. Fig. 3). These aspect layers should be integrated into the pre-existing floor plan as described above. During our project we have been able to derive a first set of these so called aspect layers. They emerged from our different perspectives of the planning and logistics system. There is no sequence in these layers, it is just a set which can vary according to the needs.

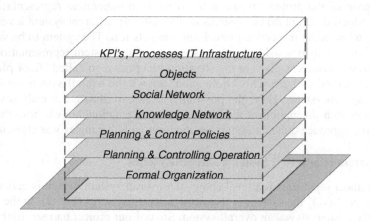

Fig. 3. Aspect Layers of the Socio-Technical System

Table 1. Aspect Layers

Layer	Description
Formal Organization	The formal organization is a mapping of the hierarchical leading structures of the company ("floor plan").
Planning and Control Operations & Policies	Describes the planning and control system, especially relations between different elements (push, pull).
Knowledge Network	Describes implicit and explicit knowledge elements in relation with a concrete task or decision.
Social Network	Describes the frequency of formal and informal contacts between different people. The frequency and importance is analyzed by ratings of the interviewed person.
Object Layer	The object layer describes system elements like raw material, products.
Process Layer	Describes the relevant business or work processes

The number of the aspect layers which can be illustrated is arbitrarily extendable, at least in principle (Tab 1.). Essential is not primary which symbols or which form a single representation uses - here personal preferences may rule. It is much more vital that different aspects in any combination can be faded in and out. This helps the understanding of the system and the successive mental integration of different system aspects and views.

Of course one has to determine well understandable symbols for the representation of these aspect layers. Besides, we tried hard not to invent new symbols or new methods but to use wherever possible already well known symbolic libraries like these from e.g. "Value Stream Modeling" [6]. This simplifies the general intelligibility of the system representation.

5   Examples of Realized Aspect Layers

In the following section exemplarily some of the aspect representations realized in the project are described in a more detailed way. An entire documentation of all used representations is not possible, because countless combinations of levels and aspects are possible what leads to a very high number of visualizations of the system [12]. It matters for us to illustrate the basic and fundamental principles of the provided representation method. That is to focus on the internal relation between the different aspect models with the underlying "floor plan".

5.1   Aspect of Planning and Control

An essential aspect of the analysis of the production system concerns the analysis of "work order relations" between different shop floors and departments. Work orders can be generated either from of a central planning and control department or as an alternative they can be initialized in a co-operative way (s. Fig. 4). In order to understand the planning and control philosophy one has to analyze the order relations between different systems. In particular we tried also to differentiate so called "push" and "pull" relations. As a "push relation" (straight arrows) we defined in our project relations, where the order-taking department has only a minimal autonomy concerning the timing of the order sequence as a central planning department releases these orders. On the other hand in "pull" relations (circle within the arrow) the order taking place is autonomous. The example below shows the differentiation between several places and departments. According to our notation it becomes evident that some workshops plan with push relations while others maintain only pull relations. We have defined different types of relationships concerning the work orders and have been relating these relations on the preexisting "floor plan". Every line could be augmented by some attributes in order to describe the exact type and purpose. This has been one starting point to document our analysis results. It shows how we have been able to relate our findings into the pre-existing floor plan.

5.2   Aspect of the Knowledge Network

As an example of the analysis of a social aspect system, we will illustrate how the so called "knowledge network" [10] could have been integrated into the same "floor

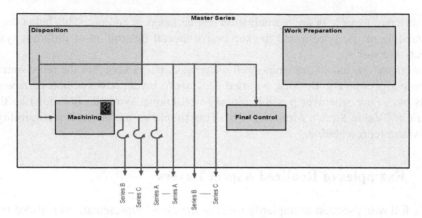

Fig. 4. Relations concerning planning and control - Push- und Pull-relations

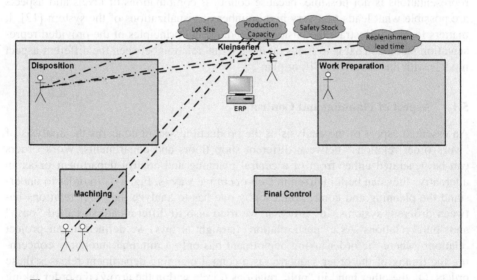

Fig. 5. Knowledge Network in Connection with the Organization and the "Floor Plan"

plan" as other elements without loosing the representation of the overall system. This analysis concerns the description of existing "knowledge items", that is, which relevant knowledge elements are "instantiated" at the same time for a very specific task. The result is illustrated in Fig. 5. The clouds show "knowledge elements" whereas the lines determine which person uses a certain concept or knowledge element.

In our specific project, the analysis of a "knowledge network" representation has been conducted for several selected specific tasks - in Fig. 5. the task of dealing with a "machine breakdown" is described. This analysis has been carried out by the work psychologists of our group. The results concerning the crucial knowledge and data items could be key to the design of the new ERP-system. This example indicates clearly how one can succeed in inserting a preexisting representation method - the one of the "knowledge network" - into a preexisting "floor plan", without the relation would have gone lost to the overall systems.

5.3   Aspect of the Social Network

In the area of planning & control of work orders almost always a so called "secondary network" can be identified [13]. This secondary network is established in order to fulfill the task of coordination of work order as e.g. the optimal timing of work orders. This network maps e.g. the distribution of decision-making competencies or the flow of certain information throughout the company (s. Fig. 6). It can be analyzed by interviews, e.g., by analyzing the frequency and the importance of bilateral relations.

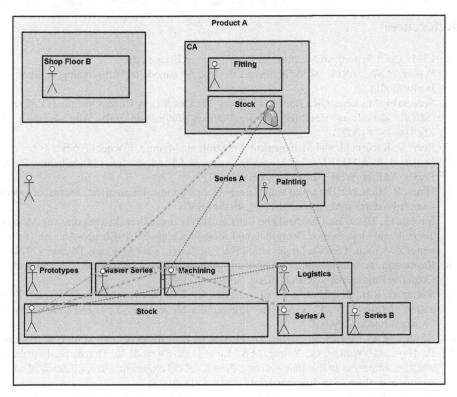

Fig. 6. Social Network

5.4   Experiences of Practice

The first experience concerns the software-technical implementation. The second category concerns the aspects of the shown content. The technical category can be characterized by the fact that the chosen software tool used had limited capabilities and supported certain demands only with considerable expenditure - the possibility of a hierarchical and comfortable drill-down was not supported adequately. The chosen software tool (Microsoft Visio) permitted it rather well, to select different aspects layers and to fade them in and out. However, a bigger problem consisted in the fact that new information could be integrated only with quite an effort into the pre-existing "floor plan". The "experience of practice" showed many positive aspects as we have been able to integrate results of work psychologists and industrial engineers.

6   Conclusion

The need for an integrated representation method which makes modeling of different aspects of a socio technical system on different layers possible could be fulfilled. It could have been shown that many - otherwise rather disjointed representations and models - can be integrated in an overall meta frame. Late changes of the floor plan can cause an effort in order to maintain the picture.

References

1. CIM - Open System Architecture, http://www.cimosa.de
2. Scheer, A.W.: ARIS: Modellierungsmethoden, Metamodelle, Anwendungen. Springer, Berlin (2001)
3. Schnetzler, M., Lemm, R., Bonfils, P., Thees, O.: Das Supply Chain Operations Reference (SCOR)-Modell zur Beschreibung der Wertschöpfungskette Holz. Allg. Forst- u. J.-Ztg 180, 1–14 (2009)
4. Beer, S.: Kybernetik und Management; Frankfurt am Main: S. Fischer (1962)
5. Burkhard, R.: UML – Unified Modeling Language: Objektorientierte Modellierung für die Praxis. Addison Wesley Longman, Bonn (1997)
6. Hines, P., Rich, N.: The seven value stream mapping tools. International Journal of Operations & Production Management 17(1), 46–64 (1997)
7. Strohm, O., Ulich, E.: Ganzheitliche Betriebsanalyse unter Berücksichtigung von Mensch, Technik und Organisation. Vorgehen und Methoden einer Mehr-Ebenen-Analyse (Schriftenreihe Mensch, Technik, Organisation Bd. 10); Zürich: vdf / Stuttgart: Teubner (1997)
8. Rasmussen, J.: Information Processing and Human-Machine Interaction. An Approach to Cognitive Engineering. North Holland, New York (1986)
9. Stammers, R.B., Shepherd, A.: Task Analysis. In: Wilson, J.R., Corlett, E.N. (eds.) Evaluation of Human Work: A practical Ergonomics Methodology, pp. 144–168. Taylor & Francis, London (1990)
10. Stanton, N.A., Stewart, R., Harris, D., Houghton, R.J., Baber, C., McMaster, R., Salmon, P., Hoyle, G., Walker, G., Young, M.S., Linsell, M., Dymott, R., Green, D.: Distributed situation awareness in dynamic systems: theoretical development and application of an ergonomics methodology. Ergonomics 49, 1288–1311 (2006)
11. Züst, R.: Einstieg ins Systems Engineering, kurz und bündig. Zurich, Verlag orell fuessli; 3. Auflage (2004)
12. Specker, A.: Modellierung von Informationssystemen: Ein methodischer Ansatz zur Projektabwicklung. p. 115. vdf Hochschulverlag, Zurich (2004)
13. Wäfler, T.: Planning and Scheduling in Secondary Work Systems. In: MacCarthy, B., Wilson, J. (eds.) Human Performance in Planning and Scheduling, pp. 411–447. Taylor & Francis, London (2001)

Industrial Implementation of Models for Joint Production and Maintenance Planning

Marco Macchi, Alessandro Pozzetti, and Luca Fumagalli

Department of Management, Economics and Industrial Engineering, Politecnico di Milano,
Piazza Leonardo da Vinci 32, 20133 Milano
{marco.macchi,alessandro.pozzetti,luca1.fumagalli}@polimi.it

Abstract. The paper aims at investigating the industrial applicability of models for joint production and maintenance planning. Scientific community has paid attention to this issue for decades and more recently many researchers proposed models to optimize such kind of planning. Nevertheless each scientific work is based on its peculiarities and hypothesis, which might prevent the applicability within different industrial contexts. This is also due to the very theoretical roots of many models, often tested only within numeric or simulation scenarios. This paper aims at presenting a case study analysis where the industrial test-bench is analysed to understand how these types of model are adaptable and extendable to a real context. To support the case study analysis, the main literature on the topic is reviewed, with the purpose to provide the background for the model deployment and test within the selected industrial context.

Keywords: Production Planning, Maintenance planning, Economic Production Quantity (EPQ), Manufacturing Industry.

1   Introduction

Production and maintenance management are responsibilities of different functions often corresponding to different departments of a manufacturing company. This could lead to an un-optimized management that does not seek for the overall maximization of operations performance, but only of production and maintenance. Conversely, a joint vision would allow to get an optimized management, in coherence with the single objectives of the two departments, but also aligned with the overall goal of the company. In this regard, all practices, rules and, in general, models that allow a joint and coordinated management are herein considered as "models" for joint production and maintenance planning in different time horizons; further on, within this research, a specific concern is given to mathematical models for optimization.

Considering these models, it is worth pointing out that in literature many works are dedicated to the optimization of production and the optimization of maintenance, but a practical point of view on a joint approach is not so diffused. Recently, models have been distinguished based on the time horizon they refer to in their planning scope. In particular, according to [1], models are used for the (i) long term strategic and maintenance concept, (ii) medium term planning (i.e. tactical level) and (iii) short

B. Grabot et al. (Eds.): APMS 2014, Part I, IFIP AICT 438, pp. 499–506, 2014.
© IFIP International Federation for Information Processing 2014

term scheduling; besides, another category of scientific works is specifically focused on control and performance indicators.

This paper deals with models supporting decisions at tactical level and it is based on a case study. The case allows studying the industrial applicability of such kind of models within a real context. This is aligned with the long-term objective of our research: contributing to fulfill the gap between the scientific theories and industrial practices with regard to the joint production and maintenance management. After a brief literature review (section 2), the model developed for industrial applicability is presented with related testing cases (section 3) and then used within a manufacturing industry case study (section 4); conclusions are eventually provided (section 5).

2   Literature Review

2.1   Brief State of the Art Analysis

Literature background is mostly based on two papers which revise the state of the art [1,2], presenting a classification of models for aggregate planning and scheduling.

According to [1], a first group of models – strategic decision models – is used during the system design phase, in order to identify at a high level the type of maintenance policy that should be applied in view of the production requirements of the designed system. The second group of models – tactical decision models – is focused on decisions over a mid-term (i.e. between one month and one year as time horizon). Such models support decisions for important maintenance interventions, deciding whether and when they should be performed based on their impact on the production plan for what concern the delivery of the demand of the planned period; this kind of models often considers the finite capacity of the maintenance crew in terms of hours that they make available for the activities of the maintenance plan. The last group of models – short term scheduling – considers a short time horizon, in order to schedule the interventions on lines or on singles machine based on an elaborated plan; this type of models takes care of deciding when a planned intervention must be scheduled within (often) one day timeframe.

[2] propose to analyze the scientific works by means of three areas of interest: Quality, Maintenance, Production. The authors then divide the works based on how these areas of interest are considered, by a joint approach, within the mathematical models provided by the papers surveyed from literature. Focusing on the relationships between two areas, Production and Quality are worth to be firstly discussed. They are intrinsically linked, considering that a production process is imperfect. This implies that scraps and WIPs are generated in an un-optimized manner, thus economically impacting on the performances of the production process. A quality factor is then included in models for the Economic Production Quantity (EPQ). These models are a variant of models for Economic Order Quantity (EOQ), defined when a production process is considered (instead of acquisition process). The imperfection of the process is generally modelled by its deterioration as a function of time with, for instance, a linear or exponential model. Quality problems might be then detected by inspections, often considered by the models, including their cost. This approach allows to optimize

the EPQ and the inspection interval to minimize the overall costs. Instead, for what concern the joint approach on Production and Maintenance areas, the main highlight concerns the relationship between production and maintenance in planning, often seen by separated approaches, pursuing an optimal maintenance plan, given the production plan or vice-versa. Also in this case, the EPQ models are used, considering the trade-off between preventive maintenance cost and the cost associated to the risk of corrective maintenance during the production period (in some cases also including the risk of defective products, that is the lack of quality). Further on, still within the relationship between Production and Maintenance areas, it is worth considering that the negative effect of stoppages might be also mitigated by the material kept on stock, which can be used to supply a given demand when production is not possible: in this regard, a good number of models considering the production systems with buffer capacity is proposed in literature. Eventually, the Maintenance and Quality areas are also sometime jointly addressed while neglecting the Production area. This is done basing on typical approaches as the following ones: a study of how maintenance, as an imperfect activity, impact on quality; an orientation towards using maintenance to reduce the quality gap with respect to a target value.

2.2   Selection of Reference Models from Literature

Starting from the literature surveys of [1,2,3], their references have been considered for more in depth analysis (respectively, [1] cited 88 papers, [2] 116 papers, [3] 45 papers). The references, integrated with other papers published during the more recent years, allowed us to select a sample of 90 papers as background for our research. Firstly, the analysis of this sample allows to assert that not all the scientific works provide a validation or verification of the proposed model. Moreover, only few of the sampled papers verify the models by means of an application in real world (6 papers, out of 90 papers of the sample), while the large amount of works considers validation only through numeric example (59 out of 90) or simulation (15 out of 90). This result further justifies our intention to concentrate on industrial applicability. Moreover, the objective of this analysis was to identify some reference models to be used for the definition of a model candidate to be tested in the industrial case study. Thus, as the 90 papers present optimization models for joint maintenance and production planning and scheduling, models were initially classified according to 7 clusters. The clusters are primarily inspired by the classification of [1]. Amongst them, 3 clusters are grouping the tactical models, as main concern of our research: EPQ models with quality issues; EPQ models with failure issues, Models considering systems with buffer capacity. EPQ with failure issues is the cluster of models this research has been concentrating on: more than a quarter of papers in our sample presents EPQ models with failure issues; based on this simple statistic, these models can be reasonably considered as the most addressed by the scientific community.

Thus, focusing only on the EPQ models with failure issues, we identified some decision drivers in order to fine-tune the selection of models. The linearity and easy understandability of the models have been considered as relevant properties for the industrial application, assuming that they would enable a more transparent approach to the industrial user. Moreover, production and maintenance have been focused as main target, not neglecting necessarily models that consider also quality as third area covered by the model. Eventually, the type of production system assumed by the model was also taken into account, in order to select the joint planning models that apply on properly detailed systems, thus at least comparable to real industrial systems.

3   Deployment of the Proposed Model

3.1   Overview of the Proposed Model

Literature analysis led to select some of the most recent models: [4,5]. [4] propose a model oriented to follow a given production optimization. The maintenance plan is subordinated to a strict constraint: the realization of the entire demand of each type of product. Backlog is not considered and demand must be strictly respected. The model considers a series of machines (a production line), introducing flexibility to represent both the system as a whole and the single phases and stations. Finally, each machine is subject to a Preventive Maintenance (PM) only once within the production planning bucket. [4] has been selected as good reference of a model that properly takes care of production priorities. [5] propose a model oriented to follow a given maintenance plan. Optimal PM frequency is then fixed and must be respected. Based on a certain maintenance behavior of the system, represented through failures' models, the model optimizes the production plan of orders, provided within a given time window (i.e. defined by the earliest and latest time for production). Backlog is considered through the related backorder costs; also overtime, if needed, can be exploited. Finally, the system is represented as a whole, even if failures' models provides a good lever for detailed modelling of the system. [5] was selected as good reference of a model that give adequate priority to maintenance plan. The two models are, thus, representative of two different attitudes, that is priority to production and priority to maintenance. Both models then reveal pros and contra. [4] model is good for a well deployment of the production system model by considering the machines / subsystems, while it lacks in a detailed modelling for overtime work and flexibility in the number of PM within a production time (only one PM is allowed). [5] model, instead, is good for its modelling capability of overtime work, but does not allow decomposition of the system and represents PM as fixed in its scheduling. Hence, this research aimed at the preparation of a new model as a fusion of the features provided by the two models. Hence, based on their pros and contra, requirements for a new model were firstly elicited. Requirements come from the need to support a decision maker within a manufacturing industry with a good flexibility to cope with both production and maintenance planning issues. A company producing white-goods offered a test-bench to this end. The company operates a mass-production. The production system of the test-bench is a manufacturing line; therefore, the system reliability is in accordance to a series logic: a stoppage of one of the machines in the line implies the stoppage of the entire line. This strongly requires an accurate maintenance planning, coordinated with production, to optimize availability of the line with the purpose to guarantee the production targets. Further details of the application of the model in the case study are proposed in section 4. Then, the following are the requirements identified for the deployment of a new model: i) frequency of PM is not fixed a-priori; ii) one PM always occur at the first period in order to restore the system at an "As-Good-As-New" state; iii) PM can occur more than once (generally twice) within the production time horizon; iv) the production system is considered divided in sub-systems, like machines, for quantifying the maintenance performances; v) the production system is considered as a whole for the production performance; vi) backlog is allowed; vii) overtime work is also exploitable. Overall, according to the requirements, the [4]'s model has been extended by the introduction of two decision variables – overtime work and backlog – and some new specific constraints (derived from [5]).

3.2   Testing Scenarios

An experimental plan was defined for a numerical validation of the developed model. From the literature, considering the typical variables involved in the analysis, the followings have been considered for the plan: production mix variability, demand predictability, aggregate planning strategy. Each variable can be considered with two levels: high (H) or low (L) value for variability and predictability, Level or Chase for the planning strategy. Thus, with the two levels and three variables, 2^3 scenarios are possible. Nevertheless, some key scenarios have been considered, out of all possible scenarios, envisioning their meaningfulness in some real industry. This led to identify three experimental conditions: i) Level strategy, high demand predictability, low mix variability; ii) Chase strategy, high demand predictability, low mix variability; iii) Chase strategy, low demand predictability, high mix variability. These scenarios were then created with numerical examples and applied to the proposed model, after representing the uncertainty (subsequent to demand predictability) based on Monte Carlo simulation. The numerical examples helped validating the new model, which has achieved similar or even better performances than the original models of [4,5].

Indeed, the case study corresponds to one of the scenarios used for numerical testing, namely the first one featuring a Level strategy, high demand predictability and low variability of the production mix (like working under conditions of a "quasi-constant" mix, with a low uncertainty for what concern the demand prediction). In this scenario, it has been seen that stocking material is a solution to prefer than requiring overtime work. To this end, the model proposed by [5] is not able to flexibly manage the preventive maintenance scheduling and result in a schedule that cut considerably available working time, forcing than to consider overtime working (even in a scenario where nominal capacity can satisfy a stable demand). The new model, instead, manage the risk of possible stoppages, balancing such risk, creating a scheduling that more reasonably consider the exploitation of the production capacity of the system. The new model was, thus, considered ready for an application in industry and judged as good reference in order to further work on a test in a real case.

4   Manufacturing Industry Case Study: Analysis and Results

By applying the model to the case the results theoretically achieved are equal to an overall saving of 57% of maintenance costs, compared with the AS-IS situation. This seemed a very interesting result, considering that in literature models for optimization of maintenance and production scheduling are claimed to be able to provide a saving of around 30% [6]. Starting from this potential, the analysis of the case was further directed to critically understand the reasons, identifying the hypothesis laying behind this behavior. Indeed, what is worth to be herein discussed is the sensitivity analysis, performed on the model with the purpose to check how it behaves. The methodology for case study analysis, that has been thus applied, followed some steps related with sensitivity analysis: i) the results given by the model have been compared with the actual practices of the company, ii) great differences between what suggested by the model and what presently ongoing as practices in the company were carefully checked, iii) the weaknesses of the model, namely some restrictive hypothesis not originally identified, were highlighted as a final outcome.

4.1   Analysis on Production Capacity Variation

First variable checked by sensitivity is production capacity. Production capacity has been intended by the company as a reduced time available for operations (shortly, in the remainder, operating time), resulting from either a reduction of shifts or closure days. This was compliant with the hypothesis of use of the model.

As a general consideration on the model behavior, it has been observed that the production capacity results correlated with production system utilization: a decrease of production capacity corresponds to an almost linear increase of utilization. Further on, the proposed model considers the PMs scheduled within operating time; their further impact should be then measured: subsequently, when decreasing production capacity, it has been noted that the model suddenly proposes to use overtime work in order to guarantee the demand; on the other hand, the variation of production capacity does not show any correlation with the plan of PMs suggested by the model, that remains unchanged. This can be explained basically considering the ratios of costs adopted for experimentation: the overtime work is costing less than backlogs and PMs; then, the model shows a capability to adapt its planning strategy based on cost minimization. In other words, in order to counterbalance the decreasing capacity, the overtime work is the resource used because is the less costing.

In comparison with the actual practices of the company, what suggested by the model was instead judged as not properly aligned. In fact, the practice of the company is to try to avoid the overtime work when the nominal production capacity is reduced and, instead, to neglect some PM interventions in comparison with the original plan, in order to save some operating time for production. This has been proved, based on experience over the years, not impacting on availability of the line. After discussing such a behavior, the root cause of misalignment of the model with the real conditions was identified: the reliability of the machines is in fact considered by the model as independent from the production capacity, hence the operating time of the line. More precisely, our model followed what normally proposed in literature: to consider the reliability only as a function of the calendar time. But reliability is also a function of the type of use, hence the operating time and other minor variables, especially true with electromechanical systems, as the machines of the line, that should be normally assumed behaving under so called Operating Dependent Failure (ODF). Thus, the case study highlighted how the type of use and the operating time should not be neglected, but instead should be taken into account by the model in order to represent a reliability behavior that is influenced by the capacity that the system deploys for achieving the production targets.

4.2   Analysis on Maintenance Parameters Variation

Maintenance parameters, time and costs, are the second type of variables checked by sensitivity analysis, to verify their effect on the comprehensive cost of the plan, and the number of maintenance interventions. In this regard, it is worth underlining that the failure distribution model adopted for the case is a Weibull function, according to well-known reliability theory, while the parameters of the Weibull have been derived based on an analysis of the historical data recorded in the company's maintenance information system at machine level. Considering an increase of cost of Corrective Maintenance (CM) interventions or of time needed to fix problems (equivalent to say that failures become more critical events), the model pushes to carrying on more PMs. More specifically, this trend is observed for the machines of the production system whose occurrence of failure is modelled by a Weibull with a form factor larger than 1, representing the behavior in a wear-out phase of the bathtub curve, well-known in the reliability theory. Conversely, for other machines, where the form factor is equal to 1 (i.e. the failure occurs based on a memory-less phenomenon, modelled by an exponential distribution), the model does not suggest PM, that practically would be not necessary, being the failures not depending on the elapsing of time. Eventually, when the form factor of the Weibull is minor than 1, the model leads to reduce as much as possible the number of PMs, that has not positive impact on the reduction of failures. All in all, the behavior observed with different Weibull models, changing based on different form factors, is aligned with expectations from reliability theory, in particular, with literature on maintenance cost optimization models.

Nevertheless, a misalignment with actual practices of the company was detected, in the cases of Weibull with form factor minor than 1. Further investigation then aimed at checking whether practices of the company might be considered wrong, or if some data introduced in the model were not aligned with the actual hypothesis. Indeed, the machines whose failures are characterized by a Weibull distribution with form factor minor than 1 are currently maintained with much more PMs than what suggested by the model. The mathematical formulation behind our optimization model, instead, considers that for these machines it is not worth carrying out PMs. In particular, according to how the model behaves based on its laying assumptions, the machines are considered "As-Good-As-New" after each PM and, in this case, they would start to suffer of more failures due to the case of infant mortality (i.e. the wear-in phase of the bathtub curve, correspondent to a form factor of the Weibull function minor than 1). According to this behavior, the model thus suggests to carry out less PMs than the ones presently carried out in the company. Nevertheless, this is a blind application of the mathematical model that risks to create a bias and even errors in maintenance planning. The most reasonable root cause of the error is using the Weibull analysis at a machine level. This hides the different failure modes that the machine can suffer from, and how the PMs contrast such failure modes. In effect, in reality, not all the PMs are an overhaul intervention on the machine; instead, they are of different types (e.g. minor regulations, cleaning, etc…) and address only few failure modes, thus being far from the hypothesis of returning the machines to an "As-Good-As-New" condition. Therefore, the model certainly shows one of its drawback when the overall behavior of the machine is modelled with Weibull with factor form < 1, while some PMs are carried out just to contrast few failure modes that, at a detailed level, could result modelled by a Weibull with factor form > 1. Making a detailed modelling of behavior of the machine is well discussed in reliability analysis, and, from our result, it seems worth of consideration within models for joint production and maintenance planning. Indeed, by the herein presented case study, it has been verified the strong impact it can have on the industrial usability of such kind of optimization model.

5   Conclusions

The paper introduced the topic of joint production and maintenance planning and scheduling by summarizing three main surveys in the research area. A new model based on existing scientific works has been presented by means of a brief explanation, neglecting the mathematical formulation, out of the scope of the present dissertation while focusing on its use in an industrial application. Indeed, the industrial application revealed some quite relevant differences between the recommendations resulting from the model and the actual practices carried on by the company. This has allowed to highlight some weaknesses of such kind of models, that we deem quite interesting in terms of possible future research.

On the whole, the analysis revealed how the impact of variance or uncertainty of inputs related with maintenance issues can be quite serious, possibly more relevant than the uncertainties due to production inputs. Unfortunately, the maintenance data are the ones that are often less considered, hence less modelled, in the companies. The case study then arises a warning on a proper management of maintenance data and, in particular, on maintenance performance, which can be really affecting overall plant performance and, more specifically, a coordinated production and maintenance plan.

Acknowledgements. The authors would like to thank Alessandra Del Centina for her support in the research through the deployment of her master of science thesis.

References

1. Budai, G., Dekker, R., Nicolai, R.P.: Maintenance and Production: A Review of Planning Models. In: Complex System Maintenance Handbook, pp. 321–344. Springer, London (2002)
2. Ben-Daya, M., Rahim, M.: Integrated production, quality & maintenance models: an overview. In: Rahim, M., Ben-Daya, M. (eds.) Integrated Models in Production Planning, Inventory, Quality, and Maintenance, pp. 3–28. Kluwer Academic Publishers (2001)
3. Schimdt, G.: Scheduling with limited machine availability. European Journal of Operational Research 121, 1–15 (2000)
4. Sitompul, C., Aghezzaf, E.H.: An integrated hierarchical production and maintenance-planning model. Journal of Quality in Maintenance Engineering 17(3), 299–314 (2011)
5. Najid, N.M., Alaoui-selsouli, M., Mohafid, N.: An integrated production and maintenance planning model with time windows and shortage cost. International Journal of Production 49, 2265–2283 (2011)
6. Cassady, C.R., Kutanoglu, E.: Integrating Preventive Maintenance Planning and Production Scheduling for a Single Machine. IEEE Transactions on Reliability 54(2), 304–309 (2005)

Exploring the Integration of Maintenance with Production Management in SMEs

Marco Macchi, Alessandro Pozzetti, and Luca Fumagalli

Department of Management, Economics and Industrial Engineering,
Politecnico di Milano, Piazza Leonardo da Vinci 32, 20133 Milano
{marco.macchi,alessandro.pozzetti,luca1.fumagalli}@polimi.it

Abstract. The paper presents the results of an exploratory research based on 10 SMEs used as case studies with the purpose to observe the state of practices with regard to the integration of maintenance with production management. The research intends to provide an evaluation of the quality of integration by means of a maturity assessment method. The resulting evidences allow an initial concern on strengths and weaknesses of maintenance management and its relationship with production management in SMEs.

Keywords: Maintenance management, production management, integration, SME, manufacturing.

1   Introduction

The importance of maintenance in manufacturing has been increasing in the recent years [1] considering its effect on the long-term improvement of equipment availability, product quality and production costs [2] and the growing concern that profit and productivity can be improved when maintenance potential is exploited [3]. Nonetheless, maintenance is not yet developed in many industries: according to [4], reporting a survey on 118 companies in Sweden, 55 % from the mechanical industry, relevant weaknesses emerge; we achieved similar evidences in Italy through a survey on 128 manufacturing companies [5]. Nonetheless, it is worth remarking a positive issue with regard to the use of TPM (Total Productive Maintenance), as a good share of companies in the mechanical industry declares TPM as standard practice. Since TPM is an opportunity space for better integration of maintenance with production [6], the aim of this paper is to study the relationship between production and maintenance function within mechanical plants. This is discussed in a wide number of publications; even so, literature is still lacking attention on the integration of maintenance and production within SMEs. Thus the paper aims at providing the results of an exploratory research carried out in 10 SMEs in the wire drawing industry, a sector of the mechanical industry. This industry operates downstream from the steel-making industry and, according to the *Comité Européen de la Tréfilerie*, in Europe it is composed of nearly 500 active companies, with about 50,000 employees.

B. Grabot et al. (Eds.): APMS 2014, Part I, IFIP AICT 438, pp. 507–514, 2014.

The study starts with the design of the exploratory research (section 2), its implementation is then described (section 3) and the results are discussed (section 4) before concluding with limits and next steps for future work (section 5).

2   Design of the Exploratory Research

2.1   Scope and Framework

Figure 1 summarizes research scope and conceptual framework used to drive the next step of research implementation.

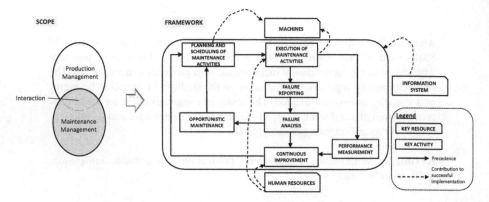

Fig. 1. Reseach scope and conceptual framework

The framework is based on maintenance management with special regard to TPM practices [6, 7]; further on, due to the scarcity of SMEs-related literature, interviews to 2 SMEs as pilot cases have been carried on, to identify the most important matters perceived in regard to the integration between production and maintenance. As first result of the pilots, the framework includes the information system as key resource to support information and procedures required for the maintenance tasks and the interaction with the production function. Further on, it is worth remarking the logic for continuous improvement as a perceived need in SMEs: in this regard, the machines installed in the company are the entities driving the interaction between production and maintenance function; the human resources are the key resources to contribute to its successful implementation. Other relevant activities were identified in the pilots: i) failure reporting and analysis, enabling the integration by capturing information and knowledge from maintenance and production through simple "tools" (e.g. Ishikawa diagram as suggested by TPM); ii) opportunistic maintenance, whenever the failure creates a repair "opportunity" leading to consider the possibility to anticipate some preventive repairs; iii) maintenance planning and scheduling, that should be driven by the machines' criticality; iii) execution of maintenance activities, requiring training of operators, even production ones for autonomous maintenance; iii) performance measurement, to assess the achievement of production targets through Key Performance Indicators (KPIs).

2.2   Target Process Area

The conceptual framework was re-organized by defining 6 maintenance process areas as reference model for the implementation step (table 1).

Table 1. Process areas and matters of interest for integration within each area

Process area	Matters of interest for integration
Maintenance Planning and Scheduling	Production and maintenance function should share common objectives and coordinate accordingly plans and schedules of machines' usage, considering all machines and a prioritization approach to plan and schedule maintenance activities. Furthermore, it is opportune to consider the availability of production operators, with the purpose to develop autonomous maintenance plans.
Coordination for Maintenance Execution and Reporting	Production operators need the necessary knowledge to manage a failure in a standardized way, to solve problems by means of an autonomous maintenance execution, or to identify the right person to restore the machines to the normal condition. Reporting is also required for the necessary recordings of activities, to suit further needs of failure analysis; reporting starts with the request issued by production operators.
Failure Analysis and Opportunistic Maintenance	When a failure happens, it is possible to allocate unscheduled preventive maintenance as repair "opportunity"; this requires a short-term coordination between production and maintenance function.
Failure Analysis and Continuous Improvement	Failure analysis could bring to new procedures that, inside maintenance and production function, promote continuous improvement.
Human Resources Management	Human resources are a lever for effective integration: production operators should be trained on basic functions of the machines they work in, and their failure modes to autonomously make some activities, and to further collaborate with maintenance by sharing ideas for continuous improvement.
Performance Measurement	Performance measurement is needed to check the effectiveness of improvements: KPIs are an important "tool", shared between production and maintenance function, to control the adequacy of improvements.

3   Implementation of the Exploratory Research

3.1   The Questionnaire

The process areas were used to guide the generation of a questionnaire for the case study analysis: the questionnaire was structured with sets of questions, one for each area, while the pilots were helpful for transforming knowledge available from literature in questions understandable in practice. The questionnaire was then used to lead a discussion with target employees in each case study, allowing to gather open answers. Table 2 provides a sample of questions for the 'Failure Analysis and Continuous Improvement' process area. Accordingly to the related tasks expected within an organization, the questions are classified by indicating the responsibilities, either only within the maintenance function (M) or within the interaction with production function (M-P). The questions are also classified considering the capabilities of the maintenance function that the practices contribute to: the definition of capabilities – managerial, organizational and technological (MAN, ORG and TEC) – is based on previous works of the authors, as better explained in the next section 3.2.

Table 2. Sample of questions taken out from the questionnaire and their classification

Question	FUNCTION		CAPABILITY		
	M	M-P	ORG	TEC	MAN
If failure analysis is done in your tasks, do you analyze the trends and statistical properties of past failures?	√			√	
When you decide some improvement, who is consulted to finally assess the decision?		√			√
Who is in charge to check performances to monitor the improvements after implementing new procedures?		√	√		

3.2   Maturity Assessment Method

The quality of a business process can be evaluated through the concept of maturity. Indeed, maturity has been proposed to assess how business processes are carried on; correspondingly, maturity assessment methods have been developed with the purpose to assess the state of practices of such processes [8]. Maturity models lead to the provision of a normative description of the good / best practices [9], which helps to develop a rank of practices in the target processes. In particular, making a rank of practices is possible through the identification of a given maturity or capability level [10]: a company, subject to a quality audit, is assigned a maturity / capability level based on the observation of its practices in the target processes. Using terms originally developed for maturity assessment methods, a Maturity Level (ML) can be assigned to a process, or to a set of processes, so called Process Area (PA); several models have been used for the definition of maturity, many of which are based on the Capability Maturity Model (CMM) and its later integrations [10]. As such, adopting the MLs can be considered a way to assess tangibly – by using a score – the state of practices in a business process / process area.

Some authors of this paper have already experienced the use of maturity assessment: a concept of maturity assessment for maintenance management was presented in [11] and tested in case studies from different industries [12, 13, 14]. More recently, the method is presented in its theory [8], inherited in the present paper in the main assumptions. Summarizing them, PAs are assessed in terms of their managerial, organizational and technological capabilities: when making a quality audit of business processes, one can analyze, at the most aggregated level, the MLs reached by a company in terms of such capabilities; afterwards, the MLs can be split to detect the criticalities through the maturity profiles, firstly, of the PAs and, after further decomposition, of their component processes. The difference of this paper, with respect to the original concept of [8], is due to the extended scope of analysis: the method is herein adopted with the purpose to study the interaction between maintenance and production management instead of only focusing on maintenance. Another difference is related to the intended use of the method: it is to support a rough analysis aimed at the identification of two MLs, high and low. This rank does not achieve a precise granularity, as it would be possible when more established approaches are adopted – e.g., those recommended by CMMI, with 5 to 6 levels. The limited use proposed for the present paper was sufficient for the purpose of the exploratory research: the maturity assessment helps making a rough rank of practices in the target processes; more precise granularity is required if the aim is to assist companies improving their practices.

The following procedure was then adopted for each case study: i) the case is initially analyzed through a narrative description of the interviews carried on (step 1: "written report of the interview"); the narrative description is the starting point to synthesize the state of practices in the target PAs and the emergent capabilities (step 2: "summary of the observed practices in the target PAs and subsequent capabilities"; the PAs are defined accordingly with previous Table 1); comparing all the cases, and considering the behavior resulting from the practices currently observed, the PAs are classified according to two MLs, i.e. high and low maturity; this enables to make evident their contribution to capabilities and, more in general, the quality of interaction between production and maintenance (step 3: "maturity assessment of target PAs and subsequent capabilities"). Table 3 provides the definition of managerial, organizational and technological capabilities as used in this research; Table 4 reports a sample of result for a case study, showing the outcome of step 2 and 3.

Table 3. Definition of managerial, organisational and technological capabilities

Capability	Definition
Managerial	Decision making capabilities within the planning and control cycle, considering also the responsibilities, either only within the maintenance function or involving the interaction with the production function.
Organizational	Definition of organisational roles and duties, organisational relationships between production and maintenance function, and mechanisms to support knowledge management, motivation and growth of human resources.
Technological	Support provided by ICT tools and techniques/methods for data analysis, with particular concern on their effective use in the company's practices (i.e. it is interesting how tools/techniques/methods are effectively adopted, not solely their availability).

Table 4. Sample of a case study result

Process area	Sample of evidences emergent for the company's capabilities	ML
Maintenance Planning and Scheduling	(MAN): the maintenance plan is updated every year but there are weaknesses in the planning process: the decisions do not result from any collaboration with production function, while the plan changes are based only on special, big events worthy of remark.	L
Coordination for Maintenance Execution and Reporting	(ORG): the company adopts a standardized reporting process, with the purpose to gather all inputs from the work request issue to the work order execution; organizational roles are identified with their task responsibilities along the process.	H
Failure Analysis and Continuous Improvement	(TEC): time series of past failures are not stored in electronic means; their trends and statistical properties cannot be analyzed.	L

4   Results of the Exploratory Research

The outcome of case study analysis is now presented focusing on main features to characterize each capability (Table 5): the features are synthesizing the most meaningful observation of practices emerged through the maturity assessment in different PAs; to comply with privacy issues, the SMEs are named by an anonymous number.

Table 5. Cross-analysis of main features emerging in the case studies

Features / ORG	1	2	3	4	5	6	7	8	9	10
Cross-functional communication	H	H	H	H	H	H	H	H	H	H
Task standardization along the reporting process	H	H	H	L	H	H	H	H	H	H
Production operator involvement in maintenance	L	L	L	H	L	L	L	L	H	L
Features / TEC	**1**	**2**	**3**	**4**	**5**	**6**	**7**	**8**	**9**	**10**
IT support to condition monitoring	L	H	L	L	H	L	H	H	L	H
IT support to opportunistic maintenance	L	L	L	L	L	L	H	H	L	L
IT support to failure analysis	L	L	L	L	L	L	H	L	L	H
Features / MAN	**1**	**2**	**3**	**4**	**5**	**6**	**7**	**8**	**9**	**10**
Alignment of maintenance planning with requirements	L	L	L	L	L	L	H	H	L	H
Decoupling of production and maintenance programs	H	H	H	H	H	H	H	H	H	H
Decision criteria for opportunistic maintenance	L	L	L	L	L	L	H	H	L	L
Standard KPIs driving performance management	L	L	L	L	L	L	H	H	H	H

A good maturity is evident for the organizational capability, especially in: i) the cross-functional communication, facilitated by the simple organizational structure; ii) the standardization of the reporting process, with task responsibilities of different functions along the process; this enables gathering all inputs required for work order management, from work request issue to order execution. Conversely, serious weaknesses regard the involvement of production operators in the execution of autonomous maintenance: in almost all the companies, production operators are forbidden to execute any maintenance activity on machines; further on, training only aims at guaranteeing skills to correctly use the machines and to identify particular symptoms that the failure has occurred or is close to occur; all in all, there is a clear separation between production and maintenance functions at the execution level.

A poor maturity is evident in most of the sampled companies for what concern the technological capability, due to a low maturity in: i) the scheduling of opportunistic maintenance, not relying on a tool that, based on the information of machines' expected workload and maintenance downtimes, could support the planner in more informed decisions; ii) the storage of failure reports, kept in paper forms in case of non-mature companies; this causes hard consultation and analysis of past events. On the other hand, the IT support to condition monitoring of machines is exploited in half of the sampled companies: this is a promising issue for mature practices.

Managerial capability did not result mature, except for maintenance scheduling. Maintenance scheduling is eased in all companies by cyclic programs in case of regular stoppages for frequent activities (every Saturday) or longer durations (once or twice a year): the maintenance function can manage the programs autonomously, and there is no real need for coordination with the production function, thanks to a decoupling mechanism defined through simple rules (e.g. Saturday is only dedicated to maintenance, and it is scheduled once every week, or every more weeks). On the other hand, many weaknesses arise, such as the followings: i) maintenance planning is carried on once a year, even if decisions concerning preventive maintenance frequencies are not aligned with the actual requirements, being not driven neither by an analysis of failure trends nor by the production needs arising from the demand forecast; ii) scheduling of opportunistic maintenance is not engineered in its decision criteria, because the analysis of maintenance downtimes is usually missing and, further on, scheduling is not based on a priority list of activities, which could guide opportunistic decisions; iii) performance management is not currently observed; in particular, management driven by performances such as OEE is missing; as positive remarks, it is however opportune to point out that some KPIs – i.e. production yield and productivity –, which can be related to the OEE components – i.e. quality, availability and performance –, are used in the most mature cases.

5   Conclusions

The exploratory research of this paper has provided first evidences on practices used in manufacturing SMEs to improve maintenance thanks to its integration with production: a wide number of weaknesses, concerning managerial and technological capabilities, are revealed, while organizational capabilities seem more robust. Future works will continue the research focusing in other districts and industries. The purpose will be to enlarge the sample and make a cross-analysis of different SMEs context. It will be relevant to identify the common weaknesses, then the correspondent gaps, to establish a further research phase aimed at technology transfer helpful to SMEs.

References

1. Cholasuke, C., Bhardwa, R., Antony, J.: The status of maintenance management in UK manufacturing organisations: results from a pilot survey. Journal of Quality in Maintenance Engineering 10(1), 5–15 (2004)
2. Swanson, L.: Linking maintenance strategies to performance. International Journal of Production Economics 70, 237–244 (2001)

3. Pinjala, S.K., Pintelon, L., Verecka, A.: An empirical investigation on therelationship between business and maintenance strategies. International Journal of Production Economics 104, 214–229 (2006)
4. Alsyouf, I.: Maintenance practices in Swedish industries: Survey results. International Journal of Production Economics 121, 212–223 (2009)
5. TeSeM: Offrire valore gestendo la manutenzione come un'impresa: utopia o sfida reale?, yearly report "Osservatorio Tecnologie e Servizi per la Manutenzione", Report TeSeM (2012), http://www.tesem.net/english-site (accessed May 15, 2012)
6. Cooke, F.L.: Implementing TPM in plant maintenance: some organisational barriers. International Journal of Quality & Reliability Management 17(9), 1003–1016 (2000)
7. Ahuja, I.P.S., Khamba, J.S.: Total productive maintenance: literature review and directions. International Journal of Quality & Reliability Management 25(7), 709–756 (2008)
8. Macchi, M., Fumagalli, L.: A maintenance maturity assessment method for the manufacturing industry. Journal of Quality in Maintenance Engineering 19(3), 295–315 (2013)
9. Volker, L., Van der Lei, T.E., Ligtvoet, A.: Developing a maturity model for infrastructural asset management systems. In: Beckers, T., Von Hirschhausen, C. (eds.) Proceedings of 10th Conference on Applied Infrastructure Research - Infraday 2011, Berlin. TU Berlin, October 7-8 (2011)
10. CMMI Product Team: CMMI –SVC, Version 1.3, Carnegie Mellon Univ., Pittsburgh (2010)
11. Garetti, M., Macchi, M., Terzi, S., Fumagalli, L.: Investigating the organizational business models of maintenance when adopting self diagnosing and self healing ICT systems in multi site contexts. In: Proceedings of the IFAC CEA (Conference on Cost Effective Automation in Networked Prod-uct Development and Manufacturing), Monterrey, Mexico (2007)
12. Fumagalli, L., Elefante, D., Macchi, M., Iung, B.: Evaluating the role ofmaintenance maturity in the adoption of new ICT in the process industry. In: Proceedings of 9th IFAC Workshop on IMS (Intelligent Manufacturing Systems), Szczecin, Poland (2008)
13. Gomez Fernandez, J.F., Fumagalli, L., Macchi, M., Crespo Marquez, A.: A scorecard approach to investigate the IT in the Maintenance Business Models. In: Proceedings of the Annual 10th International Conference on The Modern InformationTechnology in the Innovation Processes of the Industrial Enterprises, Prague, Czech Republic (2008)
14. Macchi, M., Fumagalli, L., Pizzolante, S., Crespo Marquez, A., Gomez Fernandez, J.F.: Towards e-Maintenance: maturity assessment of maintenance services for new ICT introduction. In: Proceedings of the APMS 2010 Conference, Como, Italy (2010)

A Multidisciplinary Framework for Robust Planning and Decision-Making in Dynamically Changing Engineering Construction Projects

Hajnalka Vaagen[1] and Bjørnar Aas[2]

[1] SINTEF Technology and Society, Department of Applied Economics,
S.P. Andersensvei 5, 7432 Trondheim, Norway
hajnalka.vaagen@sintef.no
[2] Molde University College, Britveien 2, 6411 Molde, Norway
bjornar.aas@vissim.no

Abstract. This paper proposes a multidisciplinary framework for robust planning and decision-making in dynamically changing engineering construction projects. The aim is to facilitate 'optimal' levels and 'trade-offs' between the major factors affecting decision-making throughout the project phases, to manage design changes and other disturbances, and to generate the maximum possible value. Offshore shipbuilding case analysis is applied to refine the model and to illustrate its value in decision-making.

Keywords: construction project, uncertainty, lean, decision-making, behavior.

1 Introduction and Motivation

One-of-a-kind specialized vessel construction is specific for European offshore shipbuilders. To achieve economic sustainability and compete with price-focused shipbuilders, combining quality with cost effective productivity *and* agility to meet customer changes throughout the construction process, is key. In this context, the minimization of the use of resources and the reliable adherence to a tight schedule is challenging. The dynamic dependencies, the production processes and the involved resources are complex. Frequent changes in design and legal regulations lead to continuous adjustments in planning, procurement and execution, and define the grade of uncertainty to be dealt with on a daily basis. Deviations in judgment that depart from the standards of logic and accuracy [12] may also worsen uncertainty and the process of decision-making. These characteristics trigger the need for competences, skills and tools to manage the disturbances and optimize the output.

Despite the growing number of issuant solutions, many of them ignore important characteristics of real systems; e.g. advanced design and engineering taking place concurrently with production [18]. As such, many solutions lack the flexibility necessary, and are therefore perceived to be difficult to apply in practice. Industrial state-of-the-practice shows to be largely disconnected from the theory, and is more-or-less based on intelligent rules-of-thumb [6]. And even when methods are known and do

B. Grabot et al. (Eds.): APMS 2014, Part I, IFIP AICT 438, pp. 515–522, 2014.

apply (e.g. LEAN), the success of implementation relies heavily on the human behavior [14]. Lack of trust between supply chain partners, incentive misalignment, natural risk aversion, human limitations in working memory [15] and social motivations [29] are just a few behavioral issues that can negatively impact operational success. Even the most sophisticated technology requires judgment on design and input variables. Finally, high performance teams often demonstrate unique solutions that are not visible within engineering solutions [7], and network based project organisations are not captured by existing project management literature [18]. These challenges motivate the connection of the *operational element* (planning & managing tasks and resources, utilizing control functions) and the *behavioral/social elements* within a single framework, to facilitate robustness in decision-making and planning. Although these two elements are intertwined, the traditions in the construction industry and academic literature are to treat them separately with different focus [7].

The remaining of the paper is organized as follows. Theories to connect and relevant literature is discussed in Section 2. The proposed conceptual model for robust decision-making is presented in Section 3. Case specific applications to prove the proposed model's usefulness and a list of research paths that serve to further validate the developed framework are given in Section 4, along with the conclusion.

2   Multidisciplinary Literature Study

This section highlights best practice and shortcomings in different research streams discussing *robust planning and decision-making in engineering construction projects*. This field is mainly steered under QMS or LEAN production principles. Most advances stop, however, at the connection of classical project management theories and techniques with lean production methodologies (originally established within the context of repetitive production), and the integration of these with innovations in information technology and ERP systems to improve information availability and quality. Despite the common understanding on 'uncertainty' and 'judgment' being major elements of construction projects, it is not clear how these are treated in existing project management literature [10]. Lean theory - as a fundamental management philosophy using whatever methods and tools that fit the purpose to deliver customer requirements with no waste [4] - attempts to treat variability on a conceptual level; as opposed to Earned Value Management, a second widely applied project planning approach [8]. It is, however, unclear how this is done operationally. Recent advances, suggesting improvements and the triangulation of different methodologies exist though; see for example [8] and [13]. Lack of a structured integration of 'uncertainty' and 'judgment' into the on-going discussions, however, potentially limits the success of existing approaches. For recent behavioral discussions in operations see [11] and [6]. Flyvbjerg in [9] addresses the bias of over-optimism and the planning fallacy in risk assessment in quality control in projects. Relevant project management and planning &control theories, their shortcomings and potential behavioral gaps - providing the motivation of this multidisciplinary approach to robust planning and decision-making in construction projects - are summarized by Table 1.

Table 1. Relevant theories, their shortcomings and potential behavioral gaps

Theory of project		Intentions	Shortcomings and possible behavioral gaps	Chosen references
Theory of Project Management	Lean PM	Generate the maximum possible amount of value	Lack of explicit discussion on 'uncertainty' and 'judgment'; Sequencing choice affected by individual prejudice; Concurrency in design, engineering and execution is not treated	[2], [4], [10], [18] [19, 20, 21] ,
	PM under uncertainty	To explicitly reflect the factual reality at all project phases	May underweight downside risk aversion;	[16],[22, 23], [26, 27]
Theory of project planning & control	Scheduling under uncertainty	Minimize expected lateness; Create flexible schedules	High complexity schedules, that are not followed due to bounded rationality;	[17], [24] [28],
	Last Planner System (LPS) and its derivatives, like Lean Project Planning (LPP)	Lean Construction's main tool for making design and construction processes predictable;	Fails to properly connect higher and lower level plans; Biased interpretation of the LPS assignment release rules; Samples are taken randomly, and humans are not good randomizer; Worker differences increase task variability	[3, 4, 5], [8], [13]
	Earned Value Management	Maximal earned value; Effective integration of key aspects of a project (budget control and schedule)	Assumed independence between activities and cost accounts (leading to subjective interpretation); Earned-value priority when releasing tasks - fails when time-to-market and flow are critical;	[8], [25], [30]

3   The Framework Proposed to Facilitate Robust Decision-Making in Dynamically Changing Construction Projects

The framework is generated by an initial case study research for scope definition and the multidisciplinary literature study presented in Section 2. It is built around the typically *critical factors* that affect robustness in construction project planning and execution, and the understanding on how the behavioral element is affecting these throughout the project phases. The following example from the case shipbuilder attempts to indicate the major aspects to be captured by a multidisciplinary framework: Extensive grade of tacit knowledge and collaboration networks "built on trust" impact strategic decisions on the design flexibility offered to the customers during the construction process. Flexibility in design is, then, affecting tactical level engineering& production planning decisions. Flexibility in project scheduling in offshore shipbuilding potentially means modeling hundreds of activities, complex dependency patterns and a large number of activities with uncertainty; schedules that are difficult to follow due to bounded rationality (even when we disregard the complexity of developing such plans). The state-of-practice is more like *judgmental adjustments* of deterministic solutions provided by some standard software. Such multilevel interactions, involving both automated and judgmental processes, trigger the connection between the engineering and human elements. Although the importance of the human element is recognized, neither judgmental decision-making nor the discussion on the tradeoff between automated and judgmental processes throughout the project phases has so far become an integrated part of how project planning is commonly done.

Having a starting point in [1], this paper assumes the major factors affecting decision-making to be *information availability* and *solving capability*. The authors in [1] define efficient management of logistics planning as efficient resource allocation across planning ability and information gathering. The authors state that if for instance a company enters into a supply chain collaboration which dramatically improves information availability, or if the company implements new optimization software, the production possibility curve (in a microeconomic point of view) will shift. The underlying motivation for such actions is to increase the overall productivity since a state of inefficiency arises when there is a mismatch between the level of information availability and solving capability: hence resource utilization and exploitation is not optimal. The major aim of the framework is to enable the development of robust solutions, by 'understanding' and consciously facilitating optimal levels and tradeoffs of information availability and solving capability at all project phases. Information availability (**IA**) is defined here as objective information, factual and observable for the decision maker; such as, legal regulations, market and customer data, supplier data, production times, guidelines from the owners on the grade of risk to be taken, etc. Objective information is the same for multiple reporters, close to the universal truth, and as such, helpful for decision-making. Interpretation and judgment transforms objective into *subjective information*. The authors in [1] did not focus on the human element, and hence lose the differentiation between objective and subjective information. While most decision-makers know that poor quality data fed into a computer results in poor output, few question the quality of judgments when the input information is good. This belief is opposed to recent research showing that there is substantial bias in judgments [15]. Solving Capability (**SC**) summarizes over analytical and critical thinking skills to evaluate problems and to make decisions, creativity and lateral thinking skills, experience, competence and tacit knowledge held by the individuals, 'language' as communication strategies, the ability to form high performance teams for generating innovative solutions, organisational traditions, and the decision methods and tools (design, engineering planning methods& tools, information technology, others).

Figure 1 illustrates the **conceptual multidisciplinary model** proposed, summarizing over the factors identified to affect robust planning and decision-making. To clarify, planning and decision-making are interrelated, and to some extent discussed interchangeably, but with some distinction. Decisions can be made without planning, but planning cannot be done without decision-making since it is an embedded feature of planning. In an ideal setting the aim is objectively rational decision-making (in fact the correct behavior for given objective information in a given situation). However, it cannot be assumed that humans are able to 'see and interpret' the full picture of a problem. Compared to the task complexity the human-centered information-processing capacity is limited, and humans are adaptive [15] and at best subjectively rational. The goal of modeling is to bring decisions as close as possible to subjective rationality; however, models also require human decisions on design and input variables. Their appropriateness in a given situation depends on the decision-maker's knowledge and aspiration level. In summary, the impact area of the human behaviour is substantial, as highlighted by the model on Figure 1. The objective information is subject to interpretation and prediction. The interpretations and predictions are also constrained by the sophistication level of the information technology.

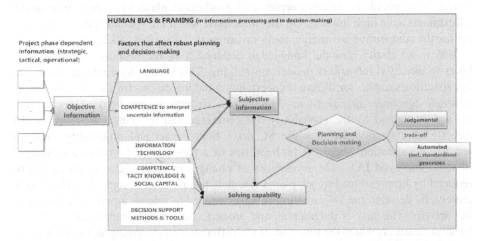

Fig. 1. Conceptual model for robust planning and decision-making

Concluding the section, developments of robust solutions can be summarized by improvements in either information availability or solving capabilities. In construction projects, decision-making & planning differ along the project phases; as also information availability and solving capabilities differ. It is generally known that information availability is low at the start of the project, while the impact of changes is relatively low. Towards the end of the project life-cycle uncertainty reveals, but the ability to influence/change is low. If the conditions for maneuverability (i.e. flexibility) are not created on a higher level, unexpected events and variation orders potentially lead to process disturbance with high adaptation costs. Some of the answers to the challenges to be solved have embedded options on different levels of the project life-cycle (from product architecture, to engineering, planning and execution). The in-depth understanding on *how* decisions, information and solving capability changes during the project life-cycle is, as such, crucial for the project's success; and a central message in this paper. To enable this understanding, the general framework provided by Figure1 is further developed to capture the project phase-specific aspects and the major connections across phases; not presented here due to space limitations. In the validation process, the offshore shipbuilding case allowed first to *refine* the model and, then, to *prove* the model by more-or-less known examples. A future step is to illustrate process improvements, by applying knowledge from the proposed model.

4   Model Discussion in Offshore Shipbuilding and Conclusion

On a general level, the proposed framework facilitates adequate levels and trade-offs between judgmental and automated decision-making to reflect strategic orientation and competitive advantage. For example, recognizing that social capital is a critical 'asset' in enabling the competitive advantage of the case shipbuilder (i.e. design flexibility throughout the construction processes), extended focus is to be given to improving **SC**; by mapping the social preconditions for operational excellence to design policies that enable further success, and by integrating judgment into the decision processes (particularly in engineering and production planning, where judgmental adjustments have high impact). On the other hand, when the social capital is not critical for the competitive advantage, focus on automated decision-making is crucial.

Below we clarify how the knowledge deduced from the proposed model contributes to increased robustness in decision-making. This is done by applying shipbuilding specific examples for different uncertainty handling cases - for ex. *late changes in strategic equipment specifications, like engines.* Uncertainty can be risk or opportunity, and is defined by the probability of occurrence and its impact if it occurs. **IA** directly affects probabilities, while **SC** drive both impact and probability. *Case 1* handles the situation where the probabilities of a particular uncertainty are changed (that is, improved **IA**). The probability of changes in engine specifications can be reduced by front-end loading supplier strategies, before basic design takes place; concretely, by defining the 'minimal information' needed to release a particular engineering activity. This task is judgmental, and prone to bias in data interpretation. *Case 2* handles situations where the outcome of the different states is changed, by implementing actions that affect **SC**. The negative impact of changes in engine specifications can potentially be reduced on many levels: On a strategic level, building the vessel differently to handle different engine types (e.g. platform based architecture); on a tactical level, planning the vessel differently to enable alternative sequencing in engineering and execution (planning with and without embedded uncertainty gives structurally different solutions); in execution phase, search for the social preconditions that enable maneuverability to handle variations. *Case 3* handles the situation where the decision process itself is changed, by affecting **SC**. Changed design and project management strategies, and explicit integration of the human element, are leading to changed decision processes. *Case 4* is a special situation of Case 3, and refers to increased decision frequency; affecting both **SC** and **IA**. An extreme situation of this case is when decisions are broken down to a level where the impact of taking the wrong decision is rather low compared to the overall wealth of the company; hence, the decision-maker can take a risk neutral attitude. Such cases assume that corrective actions can be taken for the next decision period. The Last Planner System in [3], implemented in the context of a shipbuilder, can be seen as a case utilizing this opportunity. The danger of maneuvering in the wrong direction (often systematically) still exists, however.

Concluding the paper, in-depth understanding of *how* information availability and solving capabilities change during the project life-cycle, what are the 'optimal' levels and trade-offs between these, and how the human and social elements affect these, is crucial for a project's success. The proposed framework facilitates the development of this understanding to enable robustness in decision-making. The following ongoing research activities, within the context of the case shipbuilder, aim to illustrate process improvements by applying the proposed model: (i)Uncertainty planning in Lean Construction; (ii)Organisational network and behavioral studies to identify how social capital and micro level behaviour (like motivation, trust, risk attitudes, cognitive overloading) influences solving capabilities and macro-level decision-making; and (iii)Cognitive bias in project planning; (iv)Front-end-loading supplier strategies.

Acknowledgements. This paper is part of the competence building research project NextShip, under Norwegian Research Council grant agreement 216418/O70. The authors thank Jan Emblemsvåg, Senior Vice President Innovation and Process Management VARD, for valuable discussions.

References

1. Aas, B., Wallace, S.W.: Management of Logistics Planning. International Journal of Information Systems and Supply Chain Management 3(3), 1–17 (2010)
2. Ballard, G., Howell, G.A.: Lean project management. Building Research & Information 31(2), 119–133 (2003)
3. Ballard, G., Howell, G.: Last Planner Update. In: Proceedings of the 12th Annual Conference on Lean Construction, Elsinore, Denmark (2004)
4. Ballard, G., Kim, Y.W., Jang, J.W., Liu, M.: Road Map for Lean Implementation at the Project Level, Research Report 234-11, Construction Industry Institute, The University of Texas at Austin, Texas, USA, 426 (2007)
5. Ballard, G., Hammond, J., Nickerson, R.: Production Control Principles. In: Proceedings of the 17th Annual Conference of the International Group for Lean Construction, Taipei, Taiwan, pp. 489–500 (2009)
6. Bendoly, E., Donohue, K., Schultz, K.L.: Behavior in operations management: Assessing recent findings and revisiting old assumptions. Journal of Operations Management 24(6), 737–752 (2006)
7. Chinowsky, P., Diekmann, J., Galotti, V.: Social network model of construction. Journal of Construction Engineering and Management 134(10), 804–812 (2008)
8. Emblemsvåg, J.: Lean Project Planning in Shipbuilding. Journal of Ship Production and Design 30(2), 79–88 (2014)
9. Flyvbjerg, B.: Quality control and due diligence in project management: Getting decisions right by taking the outside view. International Journal f Project Management 31, 760–774 (2013)
10. Freeman, C., Seppänen, O.: Social Aspects Related to LBMS Implementation – A Case Study. In: Proceedings of the 22th Annual Conference of the International Group for Lean Construction, Oslo, Norway, p. 677 (2014)
11. Gino, F., Pisano, G.: Toward a Theory of Behavioral Operations. Manufacturing & Service Operations Management 10(4), 676–691 (2008)
12. Haselton, M.G., Nettle, D., Andrews, P.W.: The evolution of cognitive bias. In: Buss, D.M. (ed.) The Handbook of Evolutionary Psychology: Hoboken, pp. 724–746. John Wiley & Sons Inc., NJ (2005)

13. Hamzeh, F.R., Ballard, G., Tommelein, I.D.: Rethinking Lookahead Planning to Optimize Construction Workflow. Lean Construction Journal, Paper 2, 15–34 (2012)
14. Halse, L., Kjersem, K., Emblemsvåg, J.: Lean Project Planning in shipbuilding: Theimplementation challenge. Paper read at 21st EurOMA Conference, Palermo, June 20-25 (2014)
15. Hogarth, R.: Judgment and Choice: The Psychology of Decision, 2nd edn. John Wiley & Sons, Ltd., Chichester (1991)
16. Husby, O., Kilde, S., Klakegg, O.J., Torp, O., Berntsen, S.R., Samset, K.: Styringavusikkerhetiprosjekter. Rapportnr: NTNU 99006. Produksjonog Lay-out Vestfjorden AS (1999)
17. King, A., Wallace, S.W.: Modelling using stochastic programming, 173 p. Springer, Berlin (2012) ISBN: 0387878165
18. Kjersem, K., Emblemsvåg, J.: Literature review on Planning Design and Engineering Activities in Shipbuilding. In: Proceedings of the 22th Annual Conference of the International Group for Lean Construction, Norway, Oslo, p. 677 (2014)
19. Koskela, L., Howell, G.: The Theory of project Management: Explanation to Novel Methods. In: Proceedings of the 10th Annual Conference of the International Group for Lean Construction, Gramado, Brazil, IGLC 10, vol. 6(8) (2002)
20. Koskela, L., Howell, G.: The Underlying Theory of Project Management is Obsolote. In: Proceedings of the PMI Research Conference, pp. 293-302 (2002)
21. Koskela, L., Howell, G., Ballard, G., Tommelein, I.: The Foundations of Lean Construction. Design and Construction: Building in Value. In: Best, R., de Valence, G. (eds.) Butterworth-Heinemann. Elsevier, Oxford (2002)
22. Pieters, D.A.: The Influence of framing on oil and gas decision making: An overlooked human bias in organizational decision making. Lionheart Publishing Inc., Marietta (2004)
23. Richards, C.W.: A Swift, Elusive Sword: What If Sun Tzu and John Boyd Did a National Defense Review, p. 88. Center for Defense Information, Washington, DC (2003)
24. Steinhauer, D., Heinemann, M.: Looking for Gold in the Virtual Shipyard Simulation as Basis for Production Development and Production Planning in Shipbuilding, Hansa, pp. 25–27 (2004)
25. Sumara, J., Goodpasture, J.: Earned Value - The Next Generation - A Practical Application for Commercial Projects. Project Management Institute 28th Annual Seminars & Symposium. Chicago, IL, Project Management Institute, pp. 13–17 (1997)
26. Traore, Y., Rymarava, Y.: The Human Bias in Shipbuilding Decision Making – Case study STX OSV Søviknes. MSc Thesis Molde University College, Molde, Norway (2011), http://www.nb.no/idtjeneste/URN:NBN:no-bibsys_brage_20299
27. Tøssebro, A.: Error and variation order handling in shipbuilding–case study in VARD. MSc Thesis. Molde University College, Molde, Norway (2013), http://www.nb.no/idtjeneste/URN:NBN:nobibsys_brage_46144
28. Vaagen, H., Wallace, S.W.: Modeling consumer directed substitution. International Journal of Production Economics 134(2), 388–397 (2011)
29. Urda, J., Loch, C.: Social preferences and emotions as regulators of behavior in processes. Operations Management 31(1-2), 6–23 (2013)
30. Yong-Woo, K., Ballard, H.G.: Is the Earned Value Method an Enemy of Work Flow? In: Proceedings of the 8th Annual Conference of the International Group of Lean Construction, Brighton, UK, p. 10 (2000)

Analysis of Factors for Implementing TPM: A Study in Welded Tube Manufacturers

Rodolfo Alves de Oliveira, Jorge Muniz Jr., and Fernando A.S. Marins

Universidade Estadual Paulista (UNESP), Guaratingueta, Brazil
{jorgemuniz,fmarins}@feg.unesp.br

Abstract. This study aims to identify and assess critical factors influencing on the implementation of continuous improvement projects, specifically the TPM. This research is a quali-quanti study and collects data with managers who lead TPM implementation in the shop floor. In this perspective, the present work can contribute to production managers with an assessment of the critical factors that will assist in decision-making processes for implementing improvement projects and troubleshooting methods, more specifically based on the TPM and Autonomous Maintenance.

Keywords: Total Productive Maintenance. Critical factors. Continuous improvement projects. Welded tube industries.

1   Introduction

Companies seek solutions to increase their profitability through eliminating losses, reducing time spent in models and tools exchange, setting standards of speed to productive machines and improving the final quality of products [3,4]. With a view of improving operational performance, continuous improvement programs have been run with control and production management tools.

It is discussed the influence of contextual factors as size, age of the plant, and the influence of the workmen union of the sector in successful TPM's implementation, and other good production practices [6,7].

This study aims to identify and assess critical factors influencing on the implementation of continuous improvement projects, specifically the TPM. This research is a quali-quanti study and collects data with managers who lead TPM implementation in the shop floor.

Autonomous maintenance aims to increase operational uptime of equipment through training and involvement of operational staff, but this goal can be hindered if there is an inadequate implementation of the program, blurring in planning, coupled with a lack of top management support and commitment of the staff.

Searching for better results, for the solution of recurring problems and due to fierce competition, the industrial sector has been striving to carry out improvement projects, targeting gains through the implementation of appropriate tools, among which the TPM stands out, but it is necessary to monitor, track and identify the critical success factors involving the entire staff.

B. Grabot et al. (Eds.): APMS 2014, Part I, IFIP AICT 438, pp. 523–530, 2014.

In this perspective, the present work can contribute to production managers with an assessment of the critical factors that will assist in decision-making processes for implementing improvement projects and troubleshooting methods, more specifically based on the TPM and Autonomous Maintenance.

The present work is structured into sections. Section 2 presents a theoretical exploratory review that discusses continuous improvement, TPM and Critical Success Factors. In Section 3, it is presented the used research method. Section 4 discusses the case study on the metallurgical industry and the Critical Success Factor for the improvement project are consolidated. Section 5 presents the final considerations, followed by references.

2   Theoretical Basis

Critical factors for a successful implementation of TPM are need for training, allocation of necessary resources, definition of workload and an autonomous working group focused on the TPM [4]. It was registered gains of 83% increase in productivity, and a reduction in the rate of 517 machine stops for 89 times [4].

The literature analysed indicates a methodology that uses computational resources through a system developed to compare the losses of different machines and equipment by the OEE and identify the hidden times that saddled the process [5]. There are applications of *Single Minute exchange of dies* (SMED) methodology added to *Method Time Measurements* (MTM) to preserve the best arrangement through standardization to be incorporated by the TPM [3].

It is also explores the use of the SMED and its relevance in studying tools exchange, particularly the reduced-time ones [2]. The present study did not use the SMED, but notes the importance of attention in quick exchanges. Next, it is going to be demonstrated significant gains revaluating and redefining operation routines, but the author goes further and emphasizes that it must be applied during the development and design of equipment. Table 1 presents the definitions for the Critical Success Factors adopted in this paper.

Table 1. Definition of the Identified Critical Success Factors

Critical Success Factor (CF)	Description
1. Top Management Commitment	Full support by Top managers of the company in following, participating and monitoring actions for the result.
2. Project Financing	Financial contribution that must be measured and invested in the program for fulfilling all steps necessary to achieve the expected results [4].
3. Responsibilities Definition	Definition of the ones who are directly responsible for the project, with autonomy and authority to assign responsibilities to the staff [4],[6].
4. Adopted Methodology and Scope	Tools and methods defined for the project implementation, the way in which it was sectioned a more comprehensive program in relation to the initially defined scope [4].
5. Steps Planning	Fulfillment of the previously established steps, respecting necessary time and sequence for the project success [4].

Table 1. (*continued*)

6. Leadership	The needed profile of the Leader for conducting teamwork, with influence and motivation to seek results, assumptions which are fundamental for the project success.
7. Training	Personnel training, knowledge dissemination, and information level equalization among all those involved [2,3,4].
8. Supporting areas	Support and assistance that should be given by the support areas that are not directly involved in the project.
9. Management Dedication	Attention that must be devoted by a part of the Managers in the actions defined by the group that are not associated to routine activities, giving them due importance and providing necessary resources [4].
10. Workload	Definition of the activities and an association of routine with the dedication needed by the whole staff in relation to the project [3].
11. Goals and Indicators	Definition of indicators that are aligned and have an interaction with business objectives. Bold targets, but compatible with projects underway [2,3,4,5].
12. Staff Motivation	Recognition of the achieved work and applicability of developed projects in order to contribute to the growth of the company and generate gains for the staff [4].
13. Staff Commitment	Commitment of each staff member with a continuous improvement [6].

3   Research Method

This study was developed in two metallurgical industries of São Paulo, the most industrialized State in Brazil, which are manufacturers of carbon steel products for the industrial, oil and gas sectors for the national and international markets (Table 2).

Table 2. Companies Description

	Company 1 (E1)	Company 2 (E2)
Employees	350	450
Annual Turnover	R$ 60 and 110 million / year	R$ 40 and 90 million / year
Productivity	110 thousand ton / year	70 thousand ton / year
Time in operation	Over 50 years	Over 50 years

The sectors defined for carrying out these projects were conformation and welding, involving a group of professionals of different levels and areas of expertise.

The open questionnaire was comprised of questions as follows. It sent by email to 5 leaders who held leadership positions in the company's structure.

a) In your opinion, what does it take for an implementation project of Autonomous Maintenance to succeed? Why?

b) Given the assessment made on question (a), answer: what was missing and/or undermined the implementation of Autonomous Maintenance and TPM in the unit? Why?

c) What do you expect from the TPM implementation in the unit? Which results? Why?

The respondents are Project Leaders of implementation. They are professionals with technical training dedicated to shop floor management, all with years of experience in the metallurgical industry. Open interview responses were obtained with professionals in the following profiles: 4 Improvement project Leaders in company 1 (E1) and 1 improvement project leader in company 2 (E2). The open interview was analyzed according to the method of Content Analysis defined [1].

A closed questionnaire was elaborated in order to obtain the opinion of each of the respondents on the order of importance of each of the 13 Critical Success Factors obtained in the open interview.

Respondents were asked to indicate the most important factor with the number 1, and so on until the number 13, the least important, in the column called "Rating" on the Survey Form of the Critical Success Factors. The closed questionnaire was conducted with 12 leaders with 83% return of responses.

Both companies launched their programs with embryonic projects. As mid-size companies, they invested in continuous and manufacturing processes improvement within possible. The need to establish a position on the market and modernize the plant significantly reduced investment aid in modern management tools that require more extensive programs. However, the quest for better results has led these companies to adopt some programs of continuous improvement in a fragmentary form. In this study, it was adopted the Autonomous Maintenance that represents only one of the pillars of the TPM.

Data management and ordering Critical Success Factors aims to highlight those that were considered of utmost importance. Table 3 presents the weightiness assigned to each of the 13 factors.

Table 3. Importance Indication and assigned weight for indication

Importance Indication	1	2	3	4	5	6 to 13
Assigned Weight	100	75	50	25	10	1

4   Results Analysis

Detailed data on respondents and companies can be found in the Appendix. According to Leaders of company E1, the CSF1 (Top Management Commitment) was appointed as being the most important factor, which was also appointed by Leaders of company E2. Another coincidence was the CSF11 (Indicators and Targets) were ranked as the fourth most important factor in both companies. However, other rated factors follow their own characteristics. CSF9 (Management Dedication) appears in second, CSF5 (Steps Planning) in third, and CSF3 (Definition of Responsibilities) was ranked as the fifth most important factor.

It is noted that the most important critical factors presented by Leaders of company E1 demonstrate its structural and sizing needs, i.e. it is not clear what resources are available and the adopted standardization through measurements and targets for achieving project success, pointing also to financial aid, staff motivation and leadership profile, basic factors that must be previously defined.

The result of the assessments made by Leaders of company E2 show needs for planning, organization and defining responsibilities for the project to succeed.

By comparing the results of assessments carried out by Leaders of companies E1 and E2, it is possible to observe that company E1 lacks basic structural definitions, while leaders of company E2 direct their actions towards activities organization and project participant assignments.

Note that in a joint evaluation of the results obtained between E1 and E2 companies, as shown in Figure 8, the ratings of Critical Success Factors changes again. Figure 1 presents the ratings of factors with a joint assessment. Top Management Commitment (CSF 1) is indicated as the most important factor to both companies. Some results of the TPM implementation were identified along the survey, as Table 4. In these projects, even though it has been an attempt of partial implementation and despite the flaws in program structure, it was found that the analyzed companies had significant gains.

The reduction in time of tool exchange generated gains of R$42,835.06/year to company E1 and R$10,162.60/year to company E2. The improvement work in productivity involved other actions focused on machines performance that go beyond the work conducted on non-detailed Machines Stops. However, reducing time span and considering the productivity achieved after the improvements indicated a potential annual savings of R$723,644.23 to company E1 and R$333,959.81 to company E2.

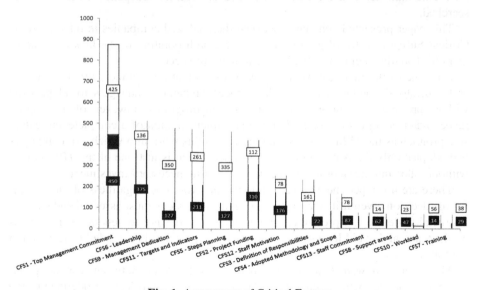

Fig. 1. Assessment of Critical Factors

Table 4. Gains (2007-2009)

Item	Before	After	Gain	Company
Tool Exchange [h/month]	43,08	28,54	33,75%	E1
	12,68	10,52	17,03%	E2
Machine Stops "minor events" [h/shift]	1,47	0,51	65,31%	E1
	2,51	1,27	49,49%	E2
Production Availability [h/ shift]	7,53	8,49	12,75%	E1
	6,49	7,73	19,09%	E2

5   Conclusion

This study aimed to identify the determining factors for the success of implementing the TPM from managers' perspective. Top Management Commitment, Leadership, Management Dedication, Indicators and Targets, and Steps Planning were identified and assessed.

Furthermore, this study is also proposed to present positive results, but warns that savings could have been greater if the program had been restructured, even if abiding by prior decision to be implemented just under the pillar of Autonomous Maintenance, being reoriented by factors herein indicated, though.

There is coherence among the results and the literature by presenting similar factors. This indicates that the factors analyzed are similar independent the sector researched.

This paper presented coherence between the analyzed companies in relation to the Critical Success Factor of greatest importance, both pointing to the lack of commitment by Top Management as being determinant for success.

It is noteworthy that positive and proven results that are routinely divulged in several specialized communication media induce companies' managers to adopt, even without preparation or pre-planned improvement programs, however, often by ignorance and/or being poorly advised, a partial implementation of a complete and extensive program as the TPM, as it was highlighted in this work into which two companies had adopted only the Autonomous Maintenance which is just one of the TPM pillars, without following the steps and adequately predicting necessary investments.

There are no impediments to adopting partial programs, regardless of the reasons for the decision, even if it were a strategic definition, steps must assessed and sized. It is crucial to define and present clear objectives in order not to generate expectations on the team, and avoid losses and disrepute if the program is extended or resumed in the future.

This work showed that the competitive differential between capital goods companies that act with commodities, which are goods with prices (pre)defined by the market, lies in continuous improvement, and that programs which are properly implemented with support from Top management could mean the survival of the business.

Staff participation and contact with the culture of continuous improvement, necessary to introduce the concepts of Autonomous Maintenance, brought changes in behaviour for all those involved in both companies, in the form of seeing and participating in results in a more active way, in the perception that it actually adds value to product, and even in their attitude towards safety.

As proposal for further work, it is suggested the use of decision making methods with multiple criteria, such as the Analytic Hierarchy Process (AHP) for assigning weights that were arbitrarily set, aiming to highlight the 5 most important critical factors, as shown in item Section 3 (Table 3). It is also recommended the use of statistical methods and software for evaluating results. The AHP can give more accuracy in the weights set for each factor.

It would be interesting to deepen in performance results, extending to sales lead and measuring profit, not only comprising savings that reflect in production costs, as presented in this study, but going beyond the definition of the Critical Factors and introducing boundary conditions and delimitations in order to effectively restructure the adopted program, and make a comparison between a complete program and a partially implemented one.

References

1. Bardin, L.: Content Analysis (Análise de Conteúdo), 5th ed., Edições 70, Lisboa, Portugal (2008) (Portuguese)
2. Cakmakci, M.: Process improvement: performance analysis of the setup time reduction-SMED in the automobile industry (2008)
3. Cakmakci, M., Karasu, M.K.: Set-up time reduction process and integrated predetermined time system MTM-UAS: A study of application in a large size company of automobile industry (2006)
4. Chan, F.T.S., Lau, H.C.W., Ip, R.W.L., Chan, H.K., Kong, S.: Implementation of total productive maintenance: A case study. Hong Kong: Int. J. Production Economics (2003)
5. Joeng, K.-Y., Phillips, D.T.: Operational efficiency and effectiveness measurement, USA (2001)
6. Shah, R., Ward, P.T.: Lean manufacturing: context, practice bundles, and performance. Journal of Operations Management 21, 129–149 (2003)
7. Muniz Jr., J., Batista, J.B., Batista Jr., E.D., Loureiro, G.: Lean Management Practice: Toyota Brazilian Plants Case. In: POMS - Production and Operations Management Society, Denver (2013)

Appendix: Data collected from TPM Implementation Leader

	CSF1		CSF2		CSF3		CSF4		CSF5		CSF6		CSF7		CSF8		CSF9		CSF10		CSF11		CSF12		CSF13		Interviewee / Company
	Indic	Weight	Indic	Weight	Indic	Weight	Indic	Weight	Indic	Weight	Indic	Weight	Indic	Weight	Indic	Weight	Indic	Weight	Indic	Weight	Indic	Weight	Indic	Weight	Indic	Weight	
	1	100	1	100	6	1	6	1	4	25	1	100	9	1	4	25	3	50	8	1	1	100	4	25	6	1	Leader 1 — E1
	2	75	2	75	5	10	9	1	2	75	2	75	4	25	9	1	4	25	7	1	2	75	3	50	5	10	Leader 2 — E1
	1	100	3	50	5	10	3	50	7	1	4	25	9	1	5	10	6	1	9	1	4	25	4	25	4	25	Leader 3 — E1
	2	75	5	10	3	50	5	10	8	1	2	75	6	1	7	1	3	50	5	10	5	10	2	75	8	1	Leader 4 — E1
	1	100	2	75	7	1	4	25	4	25	1	100	8	1	5	10	8	1	10	1	6	1	6	1	4	25	Leader 5 — E1
		450		310		72		87		127		375		29		47		127		14		211		176		62	
	6	100	1	1	5	10	6	1	1	100	3	50	5	10	8	1	2	75	6	1	2	75	4	25	12	1	Leader 6 — E2
	7	100	1	1	6	1	6	1	5	10	4	25	4	25	5	10	1	100	5	10	5	10	3	50	9	1	Leader 7 — E2
	5	50	5	10	9	75	9	1	3	50	7	1	7	1	5	10	4	25	5	10	6	1	7	1	5	10	Leader 8 — E2
	3	75	3	50	3	50	3	50	2	75	5	10	8	1	7	1	2	75	4	25	1	100	9	1	13	1	Leader 9 — E2
	1	100	3	50	4	25	4	25	1	100	3	50	6	1	9	1	2	75	5	10	2	75	9	1	8	1	Leader 10 — E2
		425		112		161		78		335		136		38		23		350		56		261		78		14	
		875		422		233		165		462		511		67		70		477		70		472		254		76	

CRITICAL SUCCESS FACTORS

A Distributed Production Scheduling Method for Highly-Distributed Manufacturing Systems

Eiji Morinaga, Yuki Sakaguchi, Hidefumi Wakamatsu, and Eiji Arai

Division of Materials and Manufacturing Science, Osaka University
{morinaga,yuki.sakaguchi,wakamatu,arai}@mapse.eng.osaka-u.ac.jp

Abstract. Recent development of computer network technologies is realizing highly-distributed manufacturing systems from the hardware point of view, where each facility is computerized and manages itself autonomously by communicating with other facilities. For this new type of manufacturing systems, a new discrete event simulation paradigm has been discussed, in which sorting of events is performed by exchanging messages about their occurrence times among the facilities. To make this paradigm beneficial enough, it is desirable that re-scheduling process performed after the simulation is carried out in a similar paradigm. We have developed some production scheduling methods for flexible flow-shop production of only one kind of products with just one stage. This paper presents an improved method which can be applied to flexible flow-shop of multiple kinds of products with multiple stages.

Keywords: production scheduling, distributed method, agile manufacturing.

1   Introduction

Production scheduling is one of the key issues for achieving sophisticated design, management and operation of manufacturing systems. Numerous works have been conducted for a long time and various approaches have been discussed such as mathematical programming [1], heuristic dispatching methods [2], and so on. For detailed evaluation of a production schedule, simulation needs to be performed. Simulation techniques for manufacturing has been also discussed and many methods has been proposed [3]. Most of those researches have been conducted with the centralized concept in which the whole manufacturing system is modeled and then the optimal schedule is generated or simulation is performed based on it.

These days, it has been desired to realize agile manufacturing, which can adapt to change of situation flexibly and quickly. The centralized concept should not meet this requirement, since it would be hard to re-model the whole system and find the optimal way of management and operation for each new situation. From this point of view, distributed manufacturing systems have been discussed, where each production area is managed by a computer and the whole system is controlled by communications among the computers. In the research field of production scheduling, distributed methods using auction mechanisms [4], active databases [5], etc. have been actively discussed. Also in the simulation area, high-level architecture was proposed and distributed methods based on it have been discussed [6].

B. Grabot et al. (Eds.): APMS 2014, Part I, IFIP AICT 438, pp. 531–538, 2014.

Recent development of computer and network technologies is achieving highly-distributed manufacturing systems (HDMSs) from the hardware point of view, where each facility is computerized and manages itself autonomously by communicating with other facilities. This point has been discussed in the field of manufacturing simulation, and a new discrete event simulation paradigm for HDMSs was proposed [7]. In this paradigm, events, each of which is simulated in one of the facilities, are sorted by their occurrence time and this sorting is performed by exchanging messages about the occurrence times among the facilities. To make this paradigm beneficial enough, it is desirable that re-scheduling process performed based on the simulation result is carried out in a similar paradigm. From this point of view, we have proposed a highly-distributed scheduling method [8-10] in which priority of each facility based on the shortest processing time (SPT) rule is dynamically updated with indirect decision making and information control performed by message exchanges. This method was applied to an example and its fundamental feasibility was proven. However, this method was developed only for a very simple flexible flow-shop production where only one kind of products that require only one process are produced, and should be enhanced so that the method can be utilized in real manufacturing. This paper presents an enhanced method which can be applied to flexible flow-shop production of multiple kinds of products which require multiple processes.

This paper is organized as follows: Section 2 provides a brief explanation about the key concept of the simulation method and the conventional scheduling method for HDMSs. Section 3 describes an enhanced scheduling method which can be applied to flexible flow-shop production of multiple kinds of products that require multiple processes. In Section 4, feasibility of the proposed method is shown through a case study, and Section 5 presents conclusions.

2   Concept of the Conventional Scheduling Method for HDMSs

In the new discrete event simulation paradigm for HDMSs [7], the following simple algorithm was proposed for sorting events to be simulated in each simulation model implemented on each facility. Let assume that there are N computerized facilities (agents) each of which has its own simulation model. Each model has its own event whose occurrence time and priority are T_i and O_i. Sorting of these events can be performed by the following three steps:

1. Values of O_i of all the events are set to 1, which means the highest priority.
2. Each agent (facility) broadcasts T_i as a message.
3. When an agent A_j, receives a message from another agent A_i, A_j compares its own value T_j with the received value T_i. Next, V_j is set to 1 if $T_j > T_i$, and to 0 otherwise. Then O_j is updated to $O_j + V_j$.

Figure 1 shows an example with four agents, and proves that the initial priority sequence ($O_i = 1$, $i=1,...,4$) can be updated to the correct one by the proposed algorithm. Since each model has several events and a new event is generated after the simulation

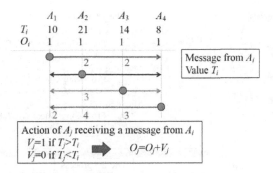

	A_1	A_2	A_3	A_4
T_i	10	21	14	8
O_i	1	1	1	1

Message from A_i
Value T_i

Action of A_j receiving a message from A_i
$V_j=1$ if $T_j>T_i$
$V_j=0$ if $T_j<T_i$ $\Rightarrow$ $O_j=O_j+V_j$

Fig. 1. Example of event sorting by the sorting algorithm proposed in [7]

for the prior event in the model, it is necessary to update the priority sequence. This dynamic determination can be also achieved by algorithms based on the same concept. Therefore the whole simulation can be performed just by message exchanges.

To make this simulation method beneficial enough, it is desirable that rescheduling process performed based on the simulation result is carried out in a similar way. A major approach for production scheduling is using heuristic dispatching rules. In this approach, a schedule is generated by determining the priority sequence of facilities by the given dispatching rule and then assign a material to the facility with the highest priority. This priority sequence determination is regarded as a sorting process of the facilities according to the rule. Therefore it is expected that a distributed method of production scheduling can be established by applying the above concept and sorting algorithm to this sorting process. We have developed some methods for simple flow-shop production of one kind of products which require only one process, and fundamental feasibility of those methods was proven [8-10]. In order to make those methods practical, it is necessary to develop them further so that they can be applied to real complex production. In the following sections, an enhanced method for flow-shop production of multiple kinds of products with several processes is discussed.

3   Enhanced Scheduling Method for Flow-Shop Production of Multiple Kinds of Products with Multiple Processes

In this paper, flexible flow-shop production of multiple stages shown in Fig. 2 is considered. Multiple kinds of materials are transported to the buffer (or automated storage/retrieval system) of the first area one-by-one at various time period. There are several same kind of machines in the area having different performance, and an arrived material is assigned to one of the machines by the shortest processing time (SPT) rule. The material whose first process has completed is transported to the second area and then assigned to one of the machines in the area in the same way.

Each assignment of materials to one of the machines by the SPT rule in each area can be achieved by sorting the machines according to the rule. Therefore, the assignment can be performed by message exchanges among the buffer and the machines by

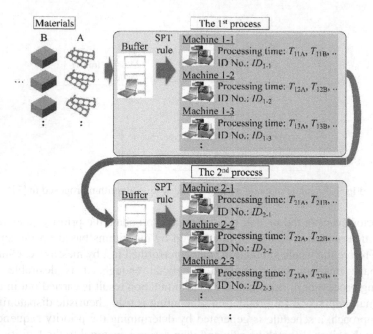

Fig. 2. Considered production scenario

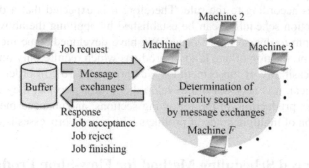

Fig. 3. Materials assignments by message exchanges

applying the algorithm described in Section 2 to this sorting process (Fig. 3). We have proposed scheduling methods based on this idea by defining procedures for message exchanges among the buffer and the machines and also for updating internal states of them [8-10]. It is possible to enhance the conventional methods so that they can be applied to the production scenario shown in Fig. 2 by improving those procedures.

The improved procedures for the buffer and each of the machines in each area are shown in Figs. 4 and 5, respectively. The parts described by red symbols and arrows are new components for applying this method to the production scenario in Fig. 2. Variables P and S were introduced so that each facility can distinguish received messages by the ID number of process and by the kind of materials, respectively. In addition, variables B_i and S_i, which specify static and dynamic priority value of a machine, are defined for each kind of materials. Enhancement for considering multiple processing areas can be easily achieved just by introducing message filters so that a facility execute its own processes only if the received message is for the production process which the facility is in charge. Enhancement for considering multiple kinds of materials can be also achieved easily just by adding the same processes for arranging priority values for each kind of the materials. (Unfortunately, detailed explanations have to be omitted due to page limitation. To understand the processing flows, we would like the readers to read also [8-10].)

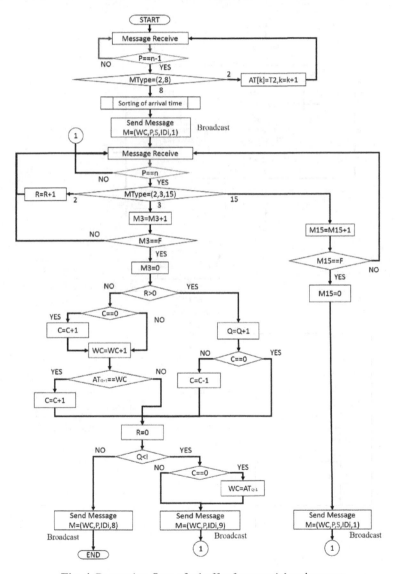

Fig. 4. Processing flow of a buffer for material assignment

536   E. Morinaga et al.

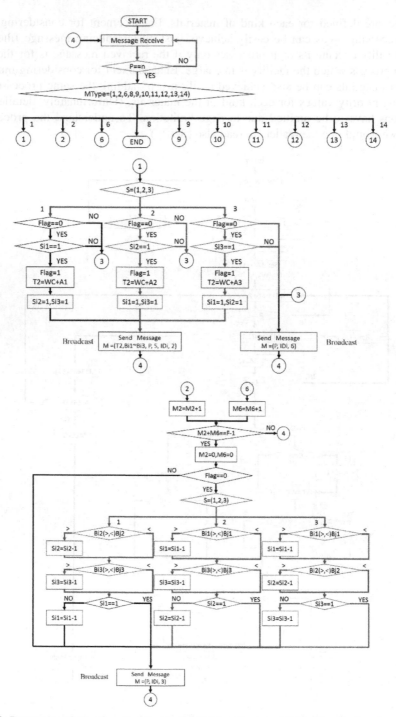

Fig. 5. Processing flow of a machine for material assignment (This flow is for the case the number of machines in the area is 3)

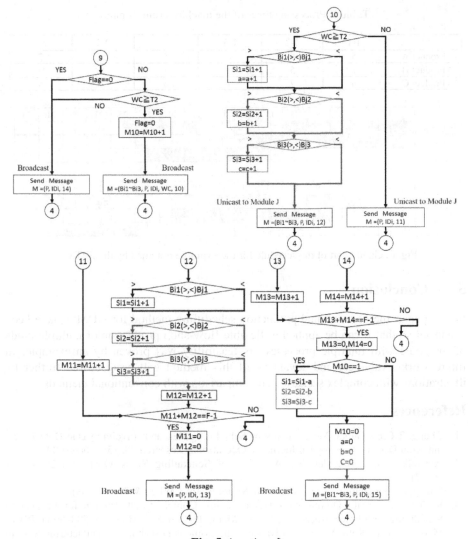

Fig. 5. (*continued*)

4   Case Study

The proposed method was applied to an example of flexible flow-shop production of three kinds of materials with two processes. There are three machines in each area and their performance are given as in Table 1. The number of materials is 3 for A, 4 for B, and 3 for C. These materials arrive at the buffer in the first area in each 2 minutes with the order of "AABCCBBBAC". Figure 6 shows the Gantt chart of the schedule obtained by the SPT rule. The method was implemented on one computer by coding in the C language and performed by using interprocess communication, due to equipment constraints. The same schedule as in Fig. 6 was successfully generated.

Table 1. Processing times of the machines (unit is min.)

	1-1	1-2	1-3	2-1	2-2	2-3
Product A	5	6	7	5	6	7
Product B	7	5	6	7	5	6
Product C	6	7	5	6	7	5

	1	3	5	7	9	11	13	15	17	19	21	23	25	27	29	31	33
1-1	1			4			7			10							
1-2	2				5				8								
1-3		3				6				9							

	1	3	5	7	9	11	13	15	17	19	21	23	25	27	29	31	33
2-1			1				4				7			10			
2-2					2				5				8				
2-3						3			6					9			

Fig. 6. Gantt chart of the schedule for the example obtained by the SPT rule

5   Conclusion

In this paper, the conventional production scheduling method for HDMSs have been enhanced so that it can be applied to flexible flow-shop production of multiple kinds of materials with multiple processes. Its feasibility was proven by an example. In future works, validness and advantage of this method will be discussed further by illustrations with complex scenario and comparison with conventional methods.

References

1. Cheng, T.C.E., Gupta, M.C.: Survey of Scheduling Research Involving Due Date Determination Decisions. European Journal of Operational Research 38, 156–166 (1989)
2. Panwalker, S.S., Iskander, W.: A Survey of Scheduling Rules. Oper. Res. 25, 45–61 (1977)
3. Carrie, A.: Simulation of Manufacturing Systems. John Wiley & Sons (1988)
4. Kaihara, T., et al.: Optimization Method using Combinatorial Auction for Production Scheduling with Batch Processing. J. Adv. Mech. Design, Sys. Manuf. 4, 588–596 (2010)
5. Matsumoto, T., Kato, Y., et al.: Advanced Autonomous Distributed Manufacturing System Using Active Database. Trans. the Japan Society of Mech. Eng. Ser. C 65, 837–843 (1999)
6. Inukai, T., Hibino, H., et al.: Enhanced distributed-simulation using orin and hla. In: Mechatronics for Safety, Security and Dependability in a New Era, pp. 261–264. Elsevier (2007)
7. Fujii, S., et al.: A Basic Study on A Highly Distributed Simulation of Manufacturing Systems Under The Ubiquitous Environment. Proc. Int. Symp. Flex. Auto., 7208 (2012)
8. Morinaga, E., Arai, E., Wakamatsu, H.: A Basic Study on Highly Distributed Production Scheduling. In: Emmanouilidis, C., Taisch, M., Kiritsis, D. (eds.) APMS 2012, Part II. IFIP AICT, vol. 398, pp. 638–645. Springer, Heidelberg (2013)
9. Morinaga, E., Takagi, A., et al.: A Basic Study on Production Scheduling for Highly-Distributed Manufacturing Systems. In: Proc. the 22nd Int. Conf. Production Res., vol. 417 (2013)
10. Morinaga, E., Takagi, A., et al.: Basic Study on Production Scheduling Method for Highly-Distributed Manufacturing Systems. J. Adv. Mech. Design, Sys. Manuf. (accepted)

A Multidimensional Multiple-Choice Knapsack Model for Resource Allocation in a Construction Equipment Manufacturer Setting Using an Evolutionary Algorithm

Alejandra Duenas[1], Christine Di Martinelly[2], and G. Yazgı Tütüncü[2,3]

[1] IESEG, School of Management (LEM-CNRS), Socle de la Grande Arche,
1 Parvis de la Défense, 92044 Paris, France
[2] IESEG School of Management (LEM-CNRS), 3 rue de la Digue, 59000 Lille, France
[3] İzmir University of Economics, Department of Mathematics, Sakarya cad.
No:156, Balçova, İzmir, Turkey
{a.duenas,c.dimartinelly,y.tutuncu}@ieseg.fr,
yazgi.tutuncu@ieu.edu.tr

Abstract. This paper presents an approach to production resource allocation. The approach is applied to a real-world problem within the construction equipment manufacturing industry. A multidimensional knapsack problem formulated; was the proposed model being based on an evolutionary algorithm using a three-dimensional binary-coded chromosome. Various tests were carried out to show the appropriateness of the solution. The experiment results suggest to be satisfactory from the manufacturing company perspective.

Keywords: Multidimensional multiple-choice knapsack problem, Evolutionary Algorithm, Combinatorial Optimization, Resource Allocation, Heuristics.

1 Introduction

This paper presents a real-world existing problem, which occurred in a construction equipment manufacturer. A variety of complex products is produced sequentially on the high-variety assembly line; the components are added as the semi-finished products move from station to station. Component specifications are dependent upon the products being assembled. Component assembly is made on-site on dedicated machines and requires specific manpower competencies. While the demand for components in number is stable, the workload of the component assembly department is subject to high variations; this causes dissatisfaction among the personnel, increased overtime work and delays on the main production line.

In the context described above, the optimization of the assignment of personnel to the different components, so as to level the workload and minimize operational disturbances on the main assembly lines, is addressed using an evolutionary algorithm.

The described assignment problem is known as the generalized assignment problem (GAP). The problem has been and is of acute interest for researchers as it has

B. Grabot et al. (Eds.): APMS 2014, Part I, IFIP AICT 438, pp. 539–546, 2014.

various applications in a wide range of areas from vehicle routing, to assigning jobs to computers in a network and it is known to be NP-hard [1, 2].

Researchers are thus interested in finding, in an efficient way, feasible and near optimal solutions. A wide range of techniques have been developed to solve the problem. Cattrysse et al. [3] provided a survey of branch-and-bound techniques and LP relaxation used to solve the GAP. However, the size of this combinatorial optimization problem makes it well suited for meta-heuristics solution methods. Various techniques have been applied such as meta-heuristics based on a single solution approach (tabu search [4], greedy heuristics [5]) or meta-heuristics based on a search within a population of solutions (genetic algorithms [6], bees algorithms [7]). Hybrid approaches combining exact and heuristics methods have also been developed to solve this combinatorial optimization problem [8].

Multiple variants of the GAP [9] exist, which differ from objective functions, constraints and dimensions (or indices). The efficiency of the pre-listed methods is dependent upon the characteristics of the problem.

In this paper, the problem described is characterized as a three-dimensional (3D) assignment problem [10, 11] to which we apply an evolutionary algorithm. Section 2 contains the definition of the (real-world) problem, based on the operators' allocation of jobs. The evolutionary algorithm proposed to solve the resource allocation problem is presented in Section 3. The results analysis is presented and discussed in Section 4. Finally, conclusions and directions for future work are outlined in Section 5.

2   Multidimensional Multiple-Choice Knapsack Problem

The objective of the proposed model, elaborated in collaboration with a construction equipment manufacturer, is to minimize the longest completion time.

A final product is composed of m/c types of components; the component assembly department is composed of m machines ($m = 1,..,M$); each machine is dedicated to the assembly of one type of component. Every day, the main assembly line produces E construction equipment (excavators). As a result, the demand for the component assembly department on the previous day is $E * M = C$ components. For instance, if 6 products are being produced on day d+1 on the main assembly line and the component assembly department is composed of 7 machines, the component assembly department must have assembled 6*7 components on day d. The number of components constitutes the items to schedule. The assembly time of component c of product e on machine m is denoted as $a_{c_e m}$; which can then be further simplified as the processing time of component c on machine m, a_{cm} (the component m of product e can only be produced on machine m).

The number of employees available in the component assembly department is fixed to O. Each operator o ($o = 1,..,O$) possesses different competencies on each machine, which depends on his level of training, k_{om}. The processing time of component c of product e on machine m (or component c) by operator o is denoted p_{ocm} and is equal to $k_{om} * a_{cm}$. Each operator o can be reallocated and transferred from machine to machine in order to fulfil assembly activities according to his competencies, as long as it does not exceed a maximum number of working hours, W_o.

The generalized assignment problem can be described using the terminology of knapsack problems [12]. It has therefore been decided to model this allocation problem as a multidimensional multiple-choice knapsack problem (MMKP). The MMKP is a variant of the 0-1knapsack problem which is an NP-Hard problem [13]. Table 1 presents the MMKP notation used in this model.

Table 1. MMKP Notation

Sets		Indices	
O	Set of operators in the component assembly department	o	A operator
M	Set of machines	m	A machine
C	Set of components	c	A component
Parameters			
a_{cm}	Assembly time of component c on machine m		
k_{om}	Competencies of operator o to work on machine m		
p_{ocm}	Processing time for component c being produced on machine m by operator o		
W_o	Maximum number of working hours of operator o		
Variable			
	$x_{ocm} \begin{cases} 1 & \text{if operator } o \text{ is selected to produce on machine } m \text{ componer} \\ 0 & \text{otherwise} \end{cases}$		

The mathematical formulation of the MMKP with the objective of minimizing the longest completion time is as follows:

$$min\ max_m \sum_{o=1}^{O} \sum_{c=1}^{C} p_{ocm} * x_{ocm} \tag{1}$$

Subject to

$$\sum_{m=1}^{M} \sum_{c=1}^{C} p_{ocm} * x_{ocm} \leq W_o, \forall o = 1,..,O \tag{2}$$

$$\sum_{o=1}^{O} \sum_{m=1}^{M} x_{ocm} = 1, \forall c = 1,..,C \tag{3}$$

$$x_{ocm} \in \{0,1\}$$

Where equation (2) represents the constraint that operators cannot work longer than W_o hours per day. Equation (3) represents the constraint that only one operator can be assigned to one machine at a time.

Figure 1 presents a schematic representation of the binary-coded chromosome, considering o different operators, m different machine and c different components. This representation is similar to the representation proposed in [14].

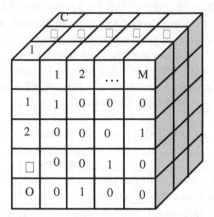

Fig. 1. Binary-coded chromosome for the MMKP

3   Evolutionary Algorithm

Evolutionary algorithms (EAs) are instances of algorithms that work with evolutionary principles. An EA is a search algorithm, inspired by natural selection and genetics that uses a population of possible solutions (candidate solutions) instead of a single solution. The candidate solutions are usually represented as strings (chromosomes) and they are evaluated by an objective (fitness) function. The search is iterative, where better solutions are generated in each iteration after applying certain genetic operators (selection, recombination, mutation etc.) [15].

Due to the problem formulation and especially due to constraint (3), it was decided to propose an EA where only a mutation operator is applied without using recombination in order to keep constraint violations to a minimum. As demonstrated by Hesser and Manner [16], the mutation operator can be considered as a search operator in itself. Hence, Figure 2 shows the EA's pseudocode with selection and mutation operators:

```
begin
        t ← 0
        initialise P(t)
        evaluate P(t)
        while (not termination-condition) do
        begin
                t ← t + 1
                select P(t) from P(t - 1)
                mutate P(t)
                evaluate P(t)
        end
end
```

Fig. 2. EA's pseudocode

   The EA's initial population is generated making sure that all individuals are feasible (i.e., meet constraints (2) and (3)).
   To determine the position of undergoing mutation a uniform random choice is
used, so each position has the same probability of mutation p_m; where, p_m is defined as
the probability of independently inverting the value assigned to operator o from 0 to 1
or from 1 to 0. Once the inversion is performed, a repair algorithm is applied to make
sure that only one operator is allocated a value of 1 as shown in Figure 3.
   In this way, the mutated offspring meets the constraint that only one operator can
be assigned to one machine at a time eq. (3) but might generate infeasible solutions
with respect to the constraint that operators cannot work longer than W_o hours per
day eq. (2).

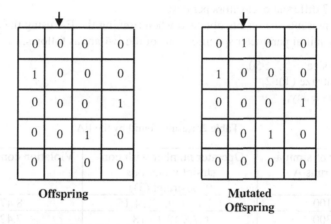

Offspring   **Mutated**
                                     Offspring

Fig. 3. Mutation operator for the MMKP

   In most applications of population-based search methods (such as EA) to constrain
optimization problems the penalty function approach of handling constraints is used.
In this way comparisons between two feasible solutions, one feasible and one
infeasible solution, and two infeasible solutions are possible. In this paper, it was
decided to use the constraint handling approach presented by Deb [17]. Therefore, a
tournament selection operator is used where two solutions (mutated offsprings) are
compared enforcing the following criteria: any feasible solution is preferred to any
infeasible solution; from two feasible solutions the one with the better objective function value is preferred; and from two infeasible solutions the one with the smaller
constraint violation is preferred. Consequently, in the comparison of two infeasible
solutions only the constraint violation is used without having to compute the objective
function value [17].

$$F(\bar{x}) = \begin{cases} f(\bar{x}) & \text{if } \bar{x} \text{ is feasible} \\ f_{max} + g(\bar{x}) & otherwise \end{cases} \qquad (4)$$

where $f(\bar{x})$ represents the objective function value given by eq. (1), f_{max} is the objective function value of the worst feasible solution in the population and $g(\bar{x})$ represents the constraint violation defined as follows:

$$g(\bar{x}) = \sum_{o=1}^{O}(W_o - \sum_{m=1}^{M}\sum_{c=1}^{C} P_{ocm} * x_{ocm}) \qquad (5)$$

4   Results Analysis

The problem under consideration is a real-world production resource allocation problem defined in collaboration with a construction equipment manufacturer. In this problem, 18 operators with different skills are to be allocated to 7 machines in order to produce 7 different excavators per day.

Table 2 presents the results obtained when running the EA using the approach presented. The initial parameter specifications of the EA are as follows:

Population size (. . . : 50,
Tournament size (T): 2,
W_o= 8 hours a day,

Table 2. Results found by the EA

Number of simulation runs A	Operator number with constraint violations (Constraint (3))	Violation constraint value
100	1,2,4,5,8,9,12,14,15	8.4714
300	6,7,8,12,13,18	7.4206
500	1,4,5,16,17,18	4.296
800	2,6,11,12	3.1923
1000	2,16,18	1.63205
1500	3,15,18	1.50405

From Table 2, it can be observed (as expected) that the violation constraint value decreases as the number of simulations increases. It is also shown that the number of operators which have a constraint violation may decrease, because the constraint violation is related to the fact that operators cannot work longer than W_o hours per day. This, in economic terms, means that the company has to pay overtime to those operators with a constraint violation, having a direct impact on the company's profit.

Furthermore, when comparing the algorithm run 300 and 500 simulations, it is possible to see that the number of operators with a constraint violation remains the same. However, the violation constraint value for 500 simulations is almost 50% lower than the value found for 300 simulations. This shows that the EA has not been defined to decrease the number of operators with a constraint violation but to decrease the violation constraint value. In future work, the minimization of number of operator with a constraint violation can be considered as a second objective resulting in a multiple objective optimization problem.

Finally, when comparing the violation constraint values between 1000 and 1500, it can be seen that the difference between them is not as big as in other instances. This suggests that it may not be advisable to run the EA for a bigger number of simulations since the results might not improve after a certain number of iterations.

5   Conclusions

In this paper, an approach to solve the MMKP is presented. The approach is applied to a real-world problem of a construction equipment manufacturer with the aim of allocating different operators to different components to be processed on different machines. The main characteristic of the problem is that the operators' different skills and competences need to be considered in the operators' processing times.

The MMKP is an NP-complete problem therefore an EA was developed to solve the problem. The MMKP coding considered is a 3D binary-coded chromosome which is then transformed to a 2D representation in order to apply 2D crossover and mutation operators. The EA's fitness function is represented by the sum of the objective function and a penalty term.   The proposed EA seems to have good performance.

Future work should include the variant where two or more operators can be allocated to the same component and the problem solution when more than one objective is simultaneously considered. Another aspect to analyze is the uncertainty related to the processing time definition since no historical data is available. The use of fuzzy sets for modeling this uncertainty could also be interesting for future research.

References

1. Ramanan, P., Deogun, J.S., Liu, C.L.: A personnel assignment problem. Journal of Algorithms 5(1), 132–144 (1984)
2. Fisher, M.L., Jaikumar, R., Wassenhove, L.N.V.: A Multiplier Adjustment Method for the Generalized Assignment Problem. Management Science 32(9), 1095–1103 (1986)
3. Cattrysse, D.G., Van Wassenhove, L.N.: A survey of algorithms for the generalized assignment problem. European Journal of Operational Research 60(3), 260–272 (1992)
4. Díaz, J.A., Fernández, E.: A Tabu search heuristic for the generalized assignment problem. European Journal of Operational Research 132(1), 22–38 (2001)
5. Romeijn, H.E., Morales, D.R.: A class of greedy algorithms for the generalized assignment problem. Discrete Applied Mathematics 103(1-3), 209–235 (2000)
6. Chu, P.C., Beasley, J.E.: A genetic algorithm for the generalised assignment problem. Computers & Operations Research 24(1), 17–23 (1997)
7. Özbakir, L., Baykasoğlu, A., Tapkan, P.: Bees algorithm for generalized assignment problem. Applied Mathematics and Computation 215(11), 3782–3795 (2010)
8. Woodcock, A.J., Wilson, J.M.: A hybrid tabu search/branch & bound approach to solving the generalized assignment problem. European Journal of Operational Research 207(2), 566–578 (2010)
9. Pentico, D.W.: Assignment problems: A golden anniversary survey. European Journal of Operational Research 176(2), 774–793 (2007)

10. Geetha, S., Vartak, M.N.: The three-dimensional bottleneck assignment problem with capacity constraints. European Journal of Operational Research 73(3), 562–568 (1994)
11. Gilbert, K.C., Hofstra, R.B.: multidimensional assignment problems. Decision Sciences 19(2), 306–321 (1988)
12. Martello, S., Toth, P.: Knapsack problems. Wiley, New York (1990)
13. Hifi, M., Michrafy, M., Sbihi, A.: Heuristic algorithms for the multiple-choice multidimensional knapsack problem. Journal of the Operational Research Society 55(12), 1323–1332 (2004)
14. Tavana, M., Khalili-Damghani, K., Abtahi, A.-R.: A fuzzy multidimensional multiple-choice knapsack model for project portfolio selection using an evolutionary algorithm. Annals of Operations Research 206(1), 449–483 (2013)
15. Bäck, T. (ed.): Introduction to evolutionary algorithms. In: Bäck, T., Fogel, D.B., Michalewicz, Z. (eds.) Evolutionary Computation. ch. 7, vol. 1. Institute of Physics Publishing (2000)
16. Ouranos, I., Stefaneas, P.: Towards an Optimal Mutation Probability for Genetic Algorithms. In: Schwefel, H.-P., Männer, R. (eds.) SERA 2013. LNCS, vol. 496, pp. 23–32. Springer, Heidelberg (1991)
17. Deb, K.: An efficient constraint handling method for genetic algorithms. Computer Methods in Applied Mechanics and Engineering 186(2-4), 311–338 (2000)

The Influence of Human Factors on Access and Scheduling of Primary Care Services

Jane Guinery[1,*], Susan Brown[1], Martina Berglund[2], and Kezia Scales[1]

[1] Nottingham University Business School, UK
{jane.guinery,s.brown,kezia.scales}@nottingham.ac.uk
[2] Linkoping University, Sweden
martina.berglund@liu.se

Abstract. This paper explores human and organisational factors (HOFs) related to access and scheduling (A&S) of Healthcare services. Here human factors relate to the 'processed' (patients) as well as the 'processors' (people working in the operation). A 'whole system perspective' is taken to investigate how these influence outcomes. The analysis differentiates acceptable demand on the service from failure demand [1], where *failure demand* represents unnecessary demand placed on acute care (such as Accident and Emergency in hospitals) as well as primary care services. For eight General Practices in the UK, approaches to practice organisation, including A&S, are analysed to establish HOFs that influence service delivery and performance. Findings highlight HOFs affecting outcomes and ways in which A&S arrangements can be modified to improve them. These should inform the choice and management of effective A&S in a range of Health service scenarios, as well as for General Practices in the UK.

Keywords: Human factors, Scheduling, Access, Primary care.

1 Challenges in Primary Care Services

With a major reorganisation in the National Health Service (NHS) in the UK, transferring the commissioning of healthcare services to Primary Care providers, the need to effectively manage Primary Care has come into sharp focus [2]. In particular there is currently much research on how to reduce levels of referral of patients to acute care in hospitals, where service costs are higher and represent a more serious intervention than in primary care. There have been dual and potentially conflicting responses to this, with multiple Primary care initiatives attempting to manage high levels of demand and shortfalls in health and social service provision through a combination of efficiency driven initiatives (*e.g.* integration of services; new technologies), and those that rejuvenate traditional practice such as extended opening hours and greater continuity of care (where GPs regularly sees specific patients).

---

* Corresponding author.

B. Grabot et al. (Eds.): APMS 2014, Part I, IFIP AICT 438, pp. 547–554, 2014.
© IFIP International Federation for Information Processing 2014

Tensions between a drive towards efficiency and quality of service need to be rationalised. In previous studies on Lean initiatives in healthcare [3], *throughput* was considered the most important focus for improvement, with a qualification that this should be tempered by an appreciation of Healthcare specific issues (including ensuring quality of care). However, this view has been challenged by Seddon et al. [1], who identify that for services (including healthcare), a focus on such measures lacks sufficient critique because not all service activity is value-adding. A 'system' that may appear to be utilising available resources efficiently may in fact be expending effort on activities that are non-value adding, handling failure demand rather than what is required. According to their studies unrecognised 'failure demand', due to an inability of a service to absorb the *variety* of customer demands, represents the biggest cost associated with services.

In primary care the handling of patient consultations can be operationalised in a variety of ways, and there has been considerable research on appointment systems, taking a 'scientific approach' to optimise performance based on measures that include waiting times and utilisation of clinicians [4]. Such studies make assumptions on 'system' performance that exclude human behaviours (of staff and patients), and do not recognise the varied demands and expectations placed on the service. Despite this shortfall, human and organisations factors (HOFs) have been extensively studied in the context of production planning and scheduling in manufacturing businesses and supply chains [5; 6]. Here the contribution made by humans in real world situations has been studied in detail and humans have been demonstrated to perform vital roles that enable flexible responses through making effective judgment in situations where information is limited, systems/procedures are in place but problem solving and negotiation is required, and/or where constraints need to be relaxed to support competing demands in complex situations. In such scenarios people can act as gatekeepers, assessing and routing customer requests for services [7]. Based on this, it is anticipated that HOFs will influence the service performance of primary care services as a whole and at an individual level, and HOFs should be influential in the selection of access and scheduling (A&S) approaches and how they are operationalised.

Further challenges in primary care relate to specific characteristics of the operation inherent to services [8]. In this context they are: simultaneity (the service is consumed as the demand is placed on it); intangibility (the service is experienced and as such the quality of service is difficult to measure); heterogeneity of demand (each customer has a unique combination of requirements and expectations and may need to be 'processed' in different ways); perishability, customers cannot be stored; and 'customers' take part in the service. Additionally the HOFs that need to be taken into account (that influence decision making and action, and ultimately the behaviour of the whole system) relate both to patients who experience the service and take part in it, and to the staff who deliver the service. This increases the complexity of A&S, as well as making service performance measurement more problematic.

The focus of this paper is on one aspect of an exploratory study investigating organisational aspects of General Practices (Practices) that influence levels of referral to acute care. The aspect of interest is the approach taken to A&S arrangements and the HOFs that influence their operation and performance.

2   Study Objectives, Scope and Methodology

The original objective of this study was to identify and explore the HOFs in primary care services that influence the level of referrals to acute care. The study collected and analysed qualitative data from interviews in eight General Practices (Practices) in the UK. Practices were purposively selected to be representative, having a variety of characteristics such as list size, resourcing level, location, demographics and approaches to care. In total 48 semi-structured interviews were conducted with Practice staff in a range of roles including General Practitioner (GP), receptionist and nurse. These were transcribed and NVivo used to undertake a thematic analysis [9].

In relation to referrals, A&S arrangements emerged as a significant theme. Here, 'access' and 'scheduling' are closely related in the way they are defined. Whereas access refers to how patients manage to communicate and obtain appointments with Practice staff including GPs and nurses, scheduling relates more specifically to the decisions made by staff, procedures or systems in relation to how to prioritise and allocate appointments to patients. It is the patients' needs, and in some cases perceived needs, that will place demand on Practice resources. This raises the issue of how Practices should manage the balance between urgent and routine booking of appointments; and in the case of urgent appointments, how the urgency of appointments should be established. Without an appropriate balance patients might be able to book routine appointments in advance but fail to access care in times of acute need; or they may be able to access same-day care but struggle to make appointments to manage their chronic or anticipated health needs. In either case this might lead to a need for hospital acute care due to service failure.

This paper explores this theme; its aim is to scrutinise the alternative A&S approaches that are employed taking a combined operations management and HOFs perspective. Additional themes complementary to the analysis included: roles (of receptionists, nurses and GPs); referrals to acute care and reasons for them; patient needs, expectations and behaviour; and patient-service interaction. Data on these emergent themes was then analysed to better understand: the role of A&S arrangements in managing demand; types of failure demand and reasons for their occurrence; the different A&S approaches that have been employed to meet demand, their objectives, how they are operationalised, and the extent to which they appear to be effective; the influence of HOFs on the choice of approach and outcomes.

3   The Study of HOFs and Access and Scheduling Arrangements

The following sections describe findings and examine their relevance and implications on a topic by topic basis. The topics address, in order: types of failure demand; alternative A&S arrangements and their relationship to failure demand; HOFs and how they might influence A&S choices and outcomes; and the receptionist (gatekeeper) role, and how it can be enhanced to support responsiveness.

3.1   Types of Failure Demand and Reasons for Their Occurrence

The analysis identified a number of types of failure demand. The most substantial, in relation to cost, was patient use of acute care hospital services. This occurred through patient self-referral (at Accident and Emergency or 'A&E') or GP referral (due to a health crisis). Clearly in many cases these referrals may be necessary, however, in relation to self-referrals many do not translate into treatment or admission and are viewed as 'inappropriate'. According to the qualitative data, Practice staff articulated the following reasons for 'inappropriate' self-referral: patients not being able to access an appointment (for example, lack of GP availability or the Practice being closed); patients calling 111 (an NHS medical hotline) and being told to self-refer to hospital as a precautionary measure; convenience where access to hospital was easier than to the Practice (whether in terms of distance, or patients perceptions that they would be seen more easily). GP referral occurred mainly due to clinical reasons, however in some cases this is a failure demand should the deterioration in a patient's condition be due to delayed access. Other reasons include inadequate support during illness from other health and social care providers. There was also evidence of concerns about limited time and flexibility for patient consultation, and lack of knowledge of a patient's specific conditions (medications and response to treatments, and circumstances) particularly where there was limited provision for continuity of care. These concerns are corroborated by findings from other studies [10].

In relation to failure demand on the Practice, lack of continuity of care is considered to be inefficient as GPs have to refer to notes and ask more questions in consultations and can miss signs of change in patients. This was particularly problematic for more elderly patients with multi-pathologies and medications. Other 'within Practice' forms of failure demand included: underutilisation of GPs and nurses due to patients missing appointments ('did not attend' - DNA); call back time of staff when they cannot respond to patients on first contact; additional consultation time due to patient deterioration; and patient waiting time (in the Practice and in telephone queues). Many of these should be addressed through effective A&S arrangements and practice.

3.2   Alternative Approaches to A&S and Their Effectiveness

Figure 1 shows how consultations can be booked through the receptionist via telephone or face-to-face, or through online booking. The types of GP consultation available were planned appointments, urgent same day appointments, 'sit and wait' sessions (where patients come at specific times to queue to see the GP), or home visits. An alternative that some Practices employ was for the GP to ring the patient back for a telephone consultation either at a predetermined time (when the GP has purposively reserved time for this), or on an *ad hoc* basis. Home visits were rarely provided, as they were inefficient due to the travel time involved. Appointments could similarly be made with nurses, who generally undertook more standardised healthcare activities, e.g. monitoring and support of chronic conditions; this provided more time for GPs to handle other priority demands that required their expertise. This and other variables, such as urgency, create a need to carefully channel appointments to both the appropriate person and form of consultation. Bar web based appointment booking (most applicable to routine appointments), receptionists act as gatekeepers, and it is this role that needs to be understood in relation to what actually occurs regarding A&S.

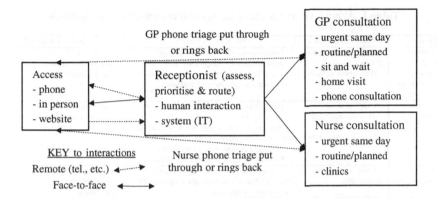

Fig. 1. Access and alternative forms of consultation

The authority for making decisions regarding the urgency of a request from patients is problematic. Clinical triage can be used to alleviate pressure on the receptionist to make clinical judgements. GP or nurse telephone triage was used to differing extents to assess urgency including as a specific access stage where GPs or nurses act as first responder to a patient. In half the Practices receptionists were seen to have some level of autonomy and flexibility in also making access decisions; in others processes were more standardised and the receptionists' authority more limited.

Table 1 shows the different access arrangements available and the associated demand failures. Trade-offs of different arrangements are evident from this, as choices made to improve efficiency may have a negative impact elsewhere. For example arrangements in relation to the mix of routine and urgent appointments vary (see 'A' in Table 1). One Practice saved 'a majority' of consultation slots to same day appointments, as a way to reduce DNAs. However, as a consequence, handling of priorities is complex as requests pour in at the start of each day. Although this approach may seem to improve the utilisation of GPs, it has specific disadvantages: patient time is lost when making appointments; planned appointments are limited disrupting continuity of care; and, prioritisation is difficult to manage. This can cause anxiety and delays for patients, or deterioration in condition, and may lead to self-referral or a later need for GPs to refer patients to acute care at a much higher cost. Similarly, whilst telephone consultation (see 'E' in Table 1) seems to be efficient, used in the wrong circumstances it can impact on the quality of consultation as it tends to focus on obvious symptoms rather than holistic care. Multiple forms of service provision in combination (*e.g.* 'sit and wait' clinics alongside doctor's triage and ring back consultations) were used to satisfy the specific requirements of different patient groups. For example elderly patients may be more able to access or prefer to use 'sit and wait' clinics; advice on medications may be managed effectively through telephone consultation. In these cases Practices can be responsive to non-standard demand or situations where standard access arrangements are not effective for all groups. However, not all Practices had these alternatives, and in some the same arrangements acted as an overspill when demand was high, compensating for system inadequacy or lack of capacity.

Table 1. Alternative access arrangements and associated failure demands

ACCESS	ADVANTAGES	DISADVANTAGES	FAILURE DEMAND
A – Limited planned appointments; more same day appointments	- Perceived reduction in DNAs - High service utilisation	- Patients queuing to make appointments - Implications of FCFS approach, particularly on specific patient groups, e.g. patient waits - Continuity of care more problematic	- Patient lost time - Reception's lost time - Patient frustration/anxiety
B – Pre-booked appointments	- Easily managed - Allows continuity of care - Less stressful for GPs	- High DNAs as patients forget or no-longer require appointments - Registrars (in training) often have to deal with urgent cases as experienced GPs are booked up! - May lengthen time to next consultation - Still need to slot in same day appointments	- Under-utilisation of service - Potential quality issues around inexperienced GPs on urgent cases
C – Web-booking system	- Reduces demand on receptionists	- Less accessible to non-computer literate (spaces filled by others), implications of FCFS *Triage not operational!*	- FCFS approach may lead to referrals of others due to poor prioritisation
D – Sit and wait	- Same day access for all patients with perceived urgent needs - High service utilisation	- Extra stress for doctors - Long patient waiting times - Potentially hasty consultations - Delays other activities, e.g. home visits - Continuity of care more problematic	- Quality of consultation may lead to need for acute care - Lost time for patients and inconvenience may lead to self-referral
E – Overspill triage ring back or consultation	- Supports urgent cases and improves access - Efficient on GP time	- Needs informed management & processes - Reduced thoroughness of consultation if not appropriate category	- Risk of ineffective consultation may lead to need for GP acute care referral
F – Home visits	- Patient confidence - Holistic view of needs - Enables very ill patients to receive care	- High level of resourcing; may be conducted by nurses to reduce this	- Lost time for GPs in travelling to patients' homes
G – Nurse appointments	- Holistic view of needs - Less costly resource	*- Only considered appropriate for those with more standard chronic conditions*	- No apparent failure demand associated with these

3.3   How HOFs Influence Access Arrangement Choices and Outcomes

The heterogeneity of the population impacts on the types of demand placed on primary care for different types of resource and interaction, the corresponding routes followed by patients, and their ability to access the service and make use of it. Looking at the needs of different patient groups it is evident that the 'first-come-first-served' (FCFS) approach to scheduling can be very problematic, particularly as opportunities for access are not equal for all patient groups. For example, where access is through websites and telephone systems, this requires particular competences and equipment. Similarly, some groups' attitudes and expectations may mean that they communicate their needs less or more effectively. Some patients will also require different lengths of consultation, or prefer continuity of care; physical access including transportation may also be more problematic. More standardised A&S arrangements may not be able to recognise or take this into account. There is, therefore, a need for more flexibility to adjust appointment lengths and reserve slots for specific categories of patient and types of demand on the service. Whilst some patients may overstate, others may understate or not appreciate the urgency of their need, and non-medical staff may feel unable to offer opinions. The type of consultation that should be offered will also vary and needs to be discerned; the patient might have a new episode requiring diagnosis, or require general advice on chronic disease management. In these cases the appropriateness of nurse appointments or telephone consultation needs to also be decided. The heterogeneity of demand and inability to customise means that some patients may inadvertently be restricted in their ability to access services, due to: limited use of technology (e.g. telephone redial), reluctance to 'bother the GP', poor communication skills, and a perceived need to see the same GP.

3.4   The Role of the Gatekeeper

Patient demands are assessed, prioritised and routed in different ways dependent on the nature of the demand and the individual requesting the service. It was the gatekeeper's role to perform this relatively complex task. Their role in some Practices was also to reassure patients, reducing their anxiety and enabling the patient to assess and potentially manage their own condition. Sensitive and timely interactions can build the trust of patients. In these areas the human contribution in the gatekeeping role is particularly important. To prevent failure demand it is important to distinguish between types of demand placed on a service that can be handled in a standard way and those requiring non-standard attention [1]. Receptionists can attempt to differentiate these, in some cases supporting patients as they make an access decision. In some Practices this level of engagement was discouraged, with Receptionists allocating appointments based solely on a patient's perception of urgency, and often without recourse to others. However, active assessment of patients' situations was encouraged in other Practices. In these cases receptionists worked in a more autonomous and flexible way, frequently calling for input from GPs or handling aspects of an enquiry based on their own knowledge and capability (e.g. where trained to differentiate urgent and non-urgent situations). It was apparent that their ability to support patients depended not just on this empowerment, but also on the availability of appointments and the choice, flexibility and responsiveness of the arrangements, e.g. in one Practice, GPs were provided with extra time for consultations (including via telephone) and to be more accessible to other staff in the Practice, including receptionists.

4   Conclusion

This empirical research has identified different forms of failure demand associated with A&S; where and how HOFs (related to patients and staff) impact on A&S; and, the implications of this on the approaches that can be taken to A&S. Although data is drawn solely from UK General Practices, it has identified important aspects of A&S that may also be relevant in other health service contexts. Findings demonstrate that it is both the heterogeneity and 'non-specific' nature of demand that makes A&S problematic, and the need to recognise this when considering alternative ways in which demand can be handled. Implications of not doing so are illustrated through the failure demand types associated with A&S alternatives. In relation to how A&S might be improved, different forms of service delivery in combination have been demonstrated to address the variety of patient demands placed on them. Also, the receptionist's gatekeeper role has been found to be central in effectively prioritising and routing patients. We can postulate that to deliver a customised response and support a variety of needs, distinct cohorts of patients may need to be identified and communicated with differently either on an *ad hoc* or systematic basis so that appointments can be prioritised and delivered in different ways. Receptionists, as gatekeepers to the service, need to provide a range of standardised and customised responses; and their capabilities and organisational arrangements that support or inhibit them are pivotal to effective service delivery. To be flexible enough to handle heterogeneous demand and reduce failure demand it is apparent that complementary A&S approaches, gatekeeper roles, forms of service delivery, and sufficient resources need to be in place.

The study findings question any over simplification and assumptions made that exclude HOFs in the evaluation and selection of A&S approaches. HOFs provide an additional dimension to understand A&S arrangements and their subsequent performance, and this dimension needs to be included when exploring system alternatives. Related failure demand explained by HOFs can be expensive and must be factored into any A&S assessment (including models and simulations) and in choices made by healthcare practitioners when selecting, managing and implementing A&S systems.

References

1. Seddon, J., O'Donovan, B.: Rethinking Lean Services. Process Excellence Net- work (2009), http://www.systemsthinking.co.uk/6-brendan-jul09.pdf (accessed May 14, 2014)
2. Goodwin, N., Dixon, A., Poole, T., Raleigh, V.: Improving the Quality of Care in General Practice. King's Fund Institute (2011)
3. Walley, P.: Designing Accident and Emergency Systems: Lessons from Manufacturing. Emergency Medical Journal 20, 126–130 (2003)
4. Gupta, D., Denton, B.: Appointment Scheduling in Healthcare: Challenges and Opportunities. IIE Transactions 40(9), 800–819 (2008)
5. MacCarthy, B.L., Wilson, J.R. (eds.): Human Performance in Planning and Scheduling. Taylor and Francis (2001)
6. Fransoo, J.C., Wafler, T., Wilson, J.R. (eds.): Behavioral Operations in Planning and Scheduling. Springer publications, Heidelberg (2011)
7. Berglund, M., Guinery, J., Karltun, J.: The unsung contribution of production planners and schedulers at production and sales interfaces. In: Fransoo, J.C., Wafler, T., Wilson, J.R. (eds.) Behavioral Operations in Planning and Scheduling, pp. 47–81. Springer, Heidelberg (2011)
8. Lovelock, C., Gummesson, E.: Whither services marketing: In search of a new-paradigm and fresh perspectives. Journal of Service Research 7(1), 20–41 (2004)
9. Guest, G., MacQueen, K.M., Namey, E.E.: Applied Thematic Analysis. Sage publications, Inc. (2012)
10. Wilson, A., Childs, S.: The relationship between consultation length, process and outcomes in general practice: A systematic review. British Journal of General Practice, 1012–1020 (December 2002)

Applicability of Planning and Control in a Port Environment

Peter Bjerg Olesen*, Cecilie Maria Damgaard,
Hans-Henrik Hvolby, and Iskra Dukovska-Popovska

Centre for Logistics, Department for Mechanical and Manufacturing Engineering,
Aalborg University, Denmark
{pbo,cmd,hhh,iskra}@celog.dk

Abstract. There is a lot of focus on intermodal transportation, maritime efficiency and port governance in the literature, but there is little regarding how to plan and coordinate activities in ports, especially in the context of small and medium sized ports. This paper will approach the planning tasks in port by using knowledge from the well-investigated field of planning and control in manufacturing and make use of the structure of strategic, tactical and operational planning, but relating this to the non-hierarchical setup found in most smaller ports. The paper finds that the general planning functions found in manufacturing planning and control can be applicable if approached as a way to align capacity and demand, and not focusing on the methods in the planning functions.

Keywords: Port, planning, coordination, non-hierarchical, maritime.

1   Introduction

Historically, ports in Denmark and Europe have been owned by the government and have primarily operated as landlord for other companies and as provider of dock and crane resources [1]. Because the port authorities have operated as landlords, they have had little focus on developing and streamlining the operations in the ports. Specifically there has been little focus on improving the competiveness of the logistic system, as they have not been taking part in this aspect, as stated by the port management of the case port. The lack of involvement in the logistic activities has meant there is no systematic coordination within the port system. In the manufacturing industry, planning and control (P&C) have been used for many years to aide companies with aligning capacity and demand as well as coping with uncertainties and inventory [2]. When identifying how smaller ports operate in Scandinavia, it is clear there is no tradition for using P&C methods. Most planning and execution is done ad-hoc, resulting in non-optimal utilisation of resources. In addition, a port is a service provider, and is required to have certain resources, so it is important to ensure that these are utilised optimally.

There is a large base of literature relating to the optimisation of larger ports, see review by Stahlbock & Voß [3], however, Danish ports are small and medium-sized

---

* Corresponding author.

B. Grabot et al. (Eds.): APMS 2014, Part I, IFIP AICT 438, pp. 555–562, 2014.

ports, which may make the use of large port literature difficult, as the complexity of the methods in the literature is often on high level.

Small and medium sized ports have not received much attention either in academia or in politics. One reason is that the focus in maritime transport research has been on globalisation. Especially the Europe/Asia container traffic have received a lot of attention, with ports as Rotterdam, Antwerp, Hong Kong and Shanghai being heavily represented in academia. The literature regarding these ports, have focussed on large-scale operations, with use of very advanced mathematical models and computer systems to control the container terminals [4], [5] and [6]. The problem is not the quality of these methods and models, but rather that smaller ports do not have the resources required to make use of these methods, and that introducing computer systems and mathematical models in ports that are not prepared for this can have negative consequences. Another case for discussion is how much the methods benefit the small ports in terms of monetary and competitive value. With a much lower volume, the total benefit for e.g. a 1% cost reduction from a mathematical model does not have the same effect as it does in a multimillion-dollar enterprise, in terms of payback.

Therefore, there is a need for developing the small ports both in terms of strategy, but also in terms of planning and coordination, inside the port and in the supply chain. Brooks et al. [7] defines collaboration and coordination as the two most important parameters in smaller ports, collaboration can be defined as the strategic frame for enabling tactical and operational coordination. However since a port is a non-hierarchical system, it might prove difficult to use traditional P&C methods directly.

This paper addresses the issue of using planning and control methods for aligning capacity and demand in smaller ports. This is done by defining and understanding characteristics the port environment and analysing the applicability of P&C functions. The characteristics of a small Danish port will be analysed to find the unique profile and thereby give the opportunity to define how the different production P&C tools and methods can be applied to a port system. Further, it will provide an understanding of the nature of a port system, which can provide the knowledge of how to optimise and reconfigure it.

2   Theoretical Background

Keeping the production data such as demand, supply, product, inventory, accounting, costing, lead-time, and routing in an integrated manner, these systems have become the central systems widely implemented in manufacturing environments.

Manufacturing Planning and Control (MPC) is an overall approach, which control everything from material management, scheduling of machine capacity, suppliers, and human resources to find the best solution. Besides the physical material flow, the flow of information also needs to be taken into consideration [2]. MPC Systems are generally described as being divided into three time horizons, these being strategic planning, tactical planning and operational planning [8], [9]. Generally, planning and control (P&C) aims for matching customer demand with supply of products and materials in terms of timing, volume, and quality [10]. Different P&C paradigms have been proposed in the literature. However, the hierarchical P&C paradigm has become an accepted P&C structure in many medium and large companies [11], by coordinating the material flow and capacity for optimal outputs levels. This paradigm is mainly implemented with the Manufacturing Resource Planning (MRPII) framework, which is the basic logic behind the Enterprise Resource Planning (ERP) systems. The majority of the modern manufacturing firms use MRP II/ ERP systems for production P&C activities [12]. The MRP II framework is a well-known model that consists of interconnected material and capacity P&C functions with hierarchical guidelines, in different time frames and aggregations [2]. As the purpose is to define a P&C system for smaller ports, this framework will be further analysed.

The MRP II system segments the P&C tasks in to three time frames; strategic (1-12 months), tactical (1 week - 3 months) and operational (1-5 days), [8]. The structure lies in both the length of the planning horizon as well as the level of data aggregation. The aggregation levels depends on the time horizon, and thereby the uncertainty. P&C is made for a hierarchical system setup, and since a port is not necessarily a hierarchical system, there might be some challenges in adapting this concept. However, in P&C the central tasks or functions are generic to any environment. These different planning tasks and functions are required to align a company's setup to the demand for products and handle different parts of the planning processes according to when and where it is required. E.g. aligning capacity of resources with the strategic demand, committing actual demand to different time fences in the production system's capacity and ensuring correct inventory levels at required time fences. Based on primarily Vollmann et. al [2]:

- The long term planning is necessary for planning the overall capacity. This include equipment, buildings, suppliers, and so forth. These decisions set the parameters for responding to current and future customer demand. In the long-term planning phase, Resource Planning, Demand Management, Sales and Operations Planning, and Master Production Scheduling (MPS) functions exists.
- The mid-term planning in MPC combines the detailed material planning and the detailed capacity planning in order to create a plan to satisfy customer demand. This means coordinating the supply and demand with the production capacity, levels of raw material and finished goods. Here the functions involves Detailed Material Planning, Detailed Capacity Planning, and Material and Capacity Plans. To ensure success, it is important to communicate with the customers and the suppliers about expected delivery times and quantities [2].
- In the short-term planning the scheduling of resources (time, people, material, equipment, and facilities) is done on detail, which is required in the production plan. Here the function of the Shop-Floor Systems and the Supplier Systems exists.

All functions have varying importance depending on the environment in which they are applied, and varying detail level. Any environment will therefore have a unique profile depending on its characteristics.

3   Case Description from a Port System

The port system is configured around handling cargo transformation between land and sea, and is made up of several companies handling different tasks. It is necessary to understand how the port system is organised, as this greatly influences how the different tasks are planned and executed, and how information can be propagated in the port system. The amount of autonomous companies present in the operations is one of the larger challenges in attempting to plan tasks in a port. Firstly, the companies mostly operate in a craftsman's type fashion where they go from job to job, without planning the activities. This gives some challenges when coordinating the actual move of goods, as there is no clear responsibility as to who have the overall planning responsibility. This is especially true in the situations where there are several actors involved in the port operations, which is most bulk and special cargo transport transformation operations. In the container terminal there is typically one actor, but the interfacing with mainly the landside and the arrival of trucks, presents some of the same coordination challenges, such as the timing of arriving trucks and the placement of containers in the container inventory. To illustrate the different planning functions in the port system, each actor and their involvement in the system are explained:

- **Shipping broker:** A shipping broker is an agency that provides transport solutions for customers, either by booking transport in the market or by providing some services themselves. In some cases, the shipping agent facilitates the booking of the transport activities and coordination of these activities to meet delivery deadlines etc. In other cases, the shipping agent is only hired to handle the cargo transformation, and the shipping line or other supply chain actor books the necessary transport solutions. Seen from the port system the shipping agent often have a coordinating role.
- **Terminal services:** This is cranes, dockworkers and other equipment required to services ships and trucks at the dockside. Different companies own these
- **Truck transport:** These operate within or in connection to the port, the owner of the goods or a shipping broker most often hires these. Currently they arrive when it fits their own plans combined with deadlines for cargo submission and withdrawal in the ports.
- **Shipping line:** The company that owns and operate the ship. Ships are as trucks often hired by the owner of the cargo or on their behalf hired by brokers. Some ships are however also operating on regular shipping routes. These routes are controlled by the shipping lines and are based on market demand.
- **Port authorities:** The port authority is the owner of the land and docks. They are also the authority, which control and manage the waters in and around the port, giving permission and overseeing the ships in these waters. Further, they are landlords for most companies operating in the port system.
- **Support services:** There are many different support services offered to both ships and companies in the port system. Ships can receive supplies, repair crews and other related services. Depending on the service, different companies handle this, and both the port authority and the shipping broker can facilitate contact for the ships.
- **Warehousing:** Is an essential service in port, as it provides a possibility for creating distribution functions or a temporary storage space when sending and receiving large quantities of goods, which is often the case in ports. Further it also possible to use warehousing as a consolidation function, batching smaller quantities of cargo with other small shipments, so the utilisation of ship and container space becomes higher and the cost lower.

Besides the description of the different resources involved in servicing a ship, Figure 1 gives a simple overview of the resources. The resources are handled by different companies, depending on the types of goods. Common for these resources are that they are very expensive, making resource utilisation an important factor. The resources all influence each other as they are used in all operations, which also means that the operations are dependent on each other, underlining the need for coordination.

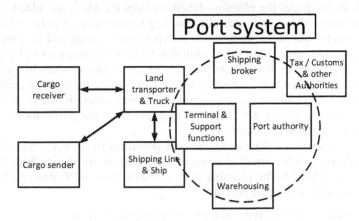

Fig. 1. The boxes are resources and companies, and the circle represents the port system

One major problem regarding the organisation of resources is the many different owners with different priorities, which means the planning and the coordination is segmented from the resources. Even though, some of the ports P&C system can be defined on a hieratical level, this is not entire the possible due to the structure of the port system. Furthermore, planning becomes even more challenging as most of the actors in the port system uses calendar based planning, where they put in ship arrivals and make loose plans regarding resources and personnel around these events. The information in the calendar is based on sales orders issued through the shipping agent, and the port authority's monitoring system for approaching ships. However, the information available in the monitoring system is not actively communicated to all parties in an organised way, which means it is not used to keep the existing plans updated. Further, the knowledge about how to handle the specific orders is based on silent knowledge accumulated within the operational staff in the port.

Olesen et al [13] proposes an implementation of a form of centralized platform for information sharing. This will improve the coordination that handles information about the flow of goods. In the current setting there are challenges with communicating this information to the workers early enough to plan other activities before committing resources to service an incoming ship. Also not all resources need to be present as soon as the ship docks. By centralising the information flow, it will be easier to make a feasible plan for the common resources, and thereby easier for companies at the port to plan based on ship arrival and crane and dock availability. However, to ensure the correct use of such an information-sharing tool, it is important to have an overview of the different functions needing information. Therefore, the following will give a structured overview of the planning activities in the port system.

4   Defining the Planning Environment in a Port System

The reason for utilising P&C is to be able to create a model that allows configuration of a planning environment in a port. A review of intermodal operations research have been done by Macharis & Bontekoning [14], where they also focus on the three time horizons of strategic, tactical and operational which align with the effort in this paper, however, in this paper the planning functions from the MPC are added to be able to relate operations with a planning task. Planning is necessary, as ports are very dynamic environments were a lot of different transport actors come and go every day. This builds in an uncertainty into the system that lacks a mechanism to plan and re-plan activities according to demand and delivery of goods and services in a close to real-time manner. Another issue regarding the lack of P&C in ports is the ability to measure, evaluate and compare operations in the port with other similar ports. By creating a structured environment with variables and functions, the performance control will also be structured and be comparable.

The port system and the cases have been described to show the need for planning and coordination in the small to medium sized port environment. With that in mind the cases are related to the planning functions mentioned in Vollmann [2]. The main challenges found in the case port are:

- Aligning port activity with incoming ships and trucks
- Pushing information about activities in the port to external partners
- Planning of shared resources and individual activities
- Coordination and sequencing

In reference to the case description, it is also evident that the planning functions are relevant in the port environment. However, the use of MRP as the engine is not relevant as there is no BOM and thereby material requirements calculations. Further, the MPC model also implies a hierarchical setup, which is not present in most ports. These factors means that MPC is not directly transferable to this context. However, since it is a system made up of resources, processes, products and demand it is comparable to the MPC when looking purely at the planning functions. The MPC functions are translated in Table 1 to a comparable function in a port setting. It is important to stress that it is only the concept of aligning capacity and demand in all planning faces, and this approach does not expect to make use of all methods and tools attributed to each planning function in a P&C environment.

The frame of the MPC model is very descriptive of what is relevant when planning in any type of environment, as it at simplest is a time fencing of activities segmented into resources, capacity and materials. In the port system, resources and capacity also apply and materials are the goods passing through the port.

The MPC framework is hierarchical, which the port system is not. Therefore, this cannot be applied directly on the port system. However, all planning activities are still relevant to all industries. Therefore, only the hierarchical perspective of the framework cannot be applied. Table 1 shows the function of the port system applied in a P&C contests, with especially focus on the MPC framework.

Relating the port system to the planning functions and the time frames, it becomes evident that one of the major challenges is to assign responsibility for the different planning functions. However, since the port system is fragmented, most of these functions in the strategic and tactical layer would have to be handled by the port authority and the shipping broker, as these have contact with all partners.

Table 1. An interpretation of the MPC system in a port context

Port Function	MPC Function	Purpose
Port System Planning	Sales and operations planning	The port strategy based on input from demand and resource planning (Strategic)
Resource Planning	Resource planning	The alignment of resources to port strategy and forecasted demand (Strategic)
Hinterland management	Demand management	Creating and finding demand in the port's hinterland (Strategic)
Port system capacity check	Master production scheduling	The aggregation of the strategic demand sorted into time fences with capacity check on the resources. (Tactical)
Port Data System	Detailed material planning	The commitment of resources to certain ship arrivals in a common data platform. (Tatical)
Port capacity planning	Detailed capacity planning	Booking of capacity in relations to production orders within time fences. (Tactical)
Arrival manifest	Material and capacity plans	List of ship arrivals, with details of cargo and actors, sorted into time fences. (Tactical)
Coordination/ sequencing	Shop floor systems	The order and timing of actions and the execution of these (Operational)
Port Data system	Vendor systems	Information sharing system between all actors related to specific jobs. (Operational)

5   Discussion and Conclusion

The paper discuss P&C as a method for coordinating activities in a port. The elements of the well-described MPC are used to illustrate the planning functions and the aggregations levels. Because of the expectation of a hierarchical system structure in the MPC model, it is not entirely applicable to the non-hierarchical port system. However, the general purpose of the planning functions is to align capacity and demand in different aggregations, and this is what the port system need. Therefore, the port system should make use of the overall approach of the MPC planning functions, placed in the port context as in Table 1. The motivation behind this approach is to utilise a well-known model to create a general approach for ports to align their activities. Some of the elements within the MPC model are not relevant in relation to a port service system, such as the MRP logic, but the method for aligning capacity and demand on the three different time scales, is highly relevant.

When the timing of a ship arrival changes the information has difficulty permeating through the port system. The reason for this is two-fold, firstly is the lack of information sharing amongst the partners. Secondly is the lack of methods to understand, plan and re-plan the activities based on the available information. This is why the ability to think in strategic, tactical and operational time frames are essential, as well as the ability to match capacity with demand and operational execution.

To utilise the P&C features, a method is created that will allow a structured approach to identify how to handle certain events within a P&C system. This is done by defining the tasks in a port, e.g. loading and unloading containers, stone or grain. The difference between these tasks is not large, but the demand and supply structures are different, and the need for equipment and resources are also different. Further, each type of goods going through the port have a unique requirement in terms of services and tools required to perform these services.

This paper presents a new way of looking at planning and coordination in a port and this method needs to be tested in a port system. Further, a framework based on these findings needs to be created, in order to present a planning and coordination model that applies fully to a port system, considering the non-hierarchical structure.

References

1. Beresford, A.K.C., Gardner, B.M., Pettit, S.J., et al.: The UNCTAD and WORKPORT mod-els of port development: evolution or revolution? Marit. Policy Manag. 31, 93–107 (2004), doi:10.1080/0308883042000205061
2. Vollmann, T.E., Berry, W.L., Whybark, D.C., Jacobs, F.R.: Manufacturing Planning And Control Systems For Supply Chain Management: The Definitive Guide for Professionals, 5th edn. McGraw-Hill Professional (2004)
3. Stahlbock, R., Voß, S.: Operations research at container terminals: A literature update. Spectr. 30, 1–52 (2007), doi:10.1007/s00291-007-0100-9
4. Kia, M., Shayan, E., Ghotb, F.: Investigation of port capacity under a new approach by computer simulation. Comput. Ind. Eng. 42, 533–540 (2002), doi:10.1016/S0360-8352(02)00051-7
5. Tahar, R.M., Hussain, K.: Simulation and analysis for the Kelang Container Terminal operations. Logist. Inf. Manag. 13, 14–20 (2000), doi:10.1108/09576050010306350
6. Ng, W.C., Mak, K.L.: Yard crane scheduling in port container terminals. Appl. Math. Model. 29, 263–276 (2005), doi:10.1016/j.apm.2004.09.009
7. Brooks, M.R., McCalla, R.J., Pallis, A.A., van der Lugt, L.M.: Coordination and Cooperation in Strategic Port Management: The Case of Atlantic Canada's Ports. Work 902, 494–1825 (2010)
8. Silver, E.A., Pyke, D.F., Peterson, R.: others Inventory management and production planning and scheduling. Wiley, New York (1998)
9. Koh, S.C.L., Gunasekaran, A.: A knowledge management approach for managing uncertainty in manufacturing. Ind. Manag. Data Syst. 106, 439–459 (2006), doi:10.1108/02635570610661561
10. Slack, N., Chambers, S., Johnston, R.: Operations Management. Pearson Education (2010)
11. McKay, K.N., Wiers, V.C.S.: Planning, scheduling and dispatching tasks in production control. Cogn. Technol. Work 5, 82–93 (2003), doi:10.1007/s10111-002-0117-4
12. Stevenson, M., Hendry, L.C., Kingsman, B.G.: A review of production planning and control: the applicability of key concepts to the make-to-order industry. Int. J. Prod. Res. 43, 869–898 (2005), doi:10.1080/0020754042000298520
13. Olesen, P.B.: Framework for Information sharing in a Small-to-medium Port System Supply Chain. Adv. Prod. Manag. Syst. Innov. Knowl.-Based Prod. Manag. Glob.-Local World (2014)
14. Macharis, C., Bontekoning, Y.M.: Opportunities for OR in intermodal freight transport research: A review. Eur. J. Oper. Res. 153, 400–416 (2004), doi:16/S0377-2217(03)00161-9

A Knowledge-Based Decision-Making Framework for the Design of Manufacturing Networks for Custom-Made Products

Dimitris Mourtzis and Michalis Doukas

Lab for Manufacturing Systems and Automation, University of Patras, Patras 26500, Greece

Abstract. Efficient design of manufacturing networks is paramount for a sustainable growth. The establishment of mass customization and the transition to personalization complicates design activities and leads to vast amounts of unexploited data. This research work aims to exploit existing knowledge for enhancing decision-making during the initial manufacturing networks design, which carry out custom orders of industrial equipment. A method developed into software is proposed, comprising a Genetic Algorithm with knowledge-enriched operators and an intelligent initialization algorithm that exploits existing planning knowledge. The validation of the method is performed using data from a high-precision mold-making manufacturer and its network of first-tier suppliers.

Keywords: Manufacturing Networks, Knowledge, Decision making.

1 Introduction

The establishment of mass customization and the gradual transition towards personalization affects manufacturing network design [1]. To achieve the desired variety, quick adaptation and re-configuration of production networks is necessary [2]. Also, vast amounts of planning-related data are generated daily, which however, remain unexploited. Reuse of past knowledge can improve decision-making, as design, planning, and operation activities of past and new projects, share numerous commonalities [3].

This research work presents a method for the initial design of manufacturing networks subject to unpredictable customer requirements for custom-made products. The suggested approach attempts to identify near optimum manufacturing network configurations for a specific custom product, while minimizing the total flowtime. It also allows the timely reconfiguration of the system to adhere to actual manufacturing capacity and availability. The method is validated with data from the mold-making industry.

2 State of the Art

Knowledge reuse in manufacturing has yet to reveal its full potential [5] after almost three decades of research [4]. Numerous approaches are available for knowledge reuse in product design [6], process planning [7] and part family representation [8].

B. Grabot et al. (Eds.): APMS 2014, Part I, IFIP AICT 438, pp. 563–571, 2014.
© IFIP International Federation for Information Processing 2014

Regarding the problem of design of manufacturing networks, the identification of optimum multi-stage, multi-product manufacturing network or system configurations, under hard pre- and post-condition constraints is strongly NP-Hard [9]. Enumerative methods are non-applicable for such problems; instead optimization methods are being applied, aiming at multi- or single-objective optimization. A GA was used in [10] for addressing to the job-shop scheduling problem. The method included random input turbulences, multiple criteria and multiple job routes. A scheduling approach was developed in [11] using a GA, to determine the efficient assignment of machines and workers in order to optimize performance criteria such as the mean flow time. The problem of scheduling of a Flexible Manufacturing System using a GA with knowledge based genetic operators is included in [12]. The way that these operators exploit past knowledge was unclear. The authors in [13] attempt to discover know-ledge patterns that are generated in each generation of a GA using Rough Set Theory. The combined utilization of knowledge-based methods directly incorporated in the metaheuristic optimization algorithm is missing from the literature to the best of the authors' knowledge.

The presented research work combines knowledge-based techniques with an opti-misation engine for supporting the initial design of manufacturing networks for cus-tom-made industrial equipment. Existing knowledge regarding past design and planning projects is embedded in evolutionary operators in the form of rules. In addi-tion, the formation of the initial GA population is pre-optimised, since similarity mea-surements against known planning cases are used. Based on successfully executed past planning projects, the search for optimum configurations for new problems becomes guided.

3   Knowledge-Based Manufacturing Network Design

The proposed method focuses on identifying near-optimum feasible selections of manufacturing nodes and suppliers, while minimising manufacturing flowtime for an engineer-to-order product. The structure of the manufacturing network is shown in Fig. 1.

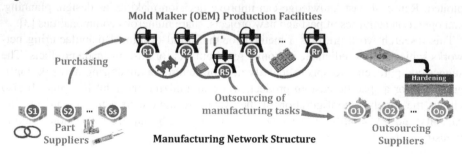

Fig. 1. The manufacturing network nodes

A number of processes are performed by the mold maker, while others, such as hardening of metallic components, are outsourced. Also, some components, such as guide columns, bolts, and sealant O-rings are purchased from 1st-tier suppliers.

The facilities of the suppliers, as well as the individual machines possessed by the OEM, are characterised by an availability index that models manufacturing capacity to meet market demand. Static capacity models are widely used by industry as cost-effective means for communicating capacity across the supply chain [17, 18]. The availability index values of OEM nodes and for suppliers are defined using historical observations.

3.1 Formulation of the Design Problem

Let the processing time for the task t to be performed by machine k be p_{tk} and a task selection p = {p1, p2,..., p_n}, where n tasks (j = 1, 2,..., n) will be processed by m machines (k = 1,2,..., m). Similarly, we define the setup times for machine k to perform task t as s_{tk}, and the waiting time of task t in the queue of machine k as w_{tk}. The sum of w_{tk}, p_{tk} and s_{tk} for all product components, represents the flowtime of the product. The Total Flowtime $FT_{tot(p)}$ of a design p can be computed by summing all flow times (1):

$$FT_{tot} = \sum_{t=1}^{\pi} FT(\pi_t) = \sum_{t=1}^{\pi} C(\pi_t, m) \tag{1}$$

3.2 Knowledge Enriched Genetic Algorithm

The problem is solved by a Genetic Algorithm (GA) [14], with knowledge enriched operators. In contrast to a regular GA, the proposed enriched GA includes an intelligent initialization process and rule-based selection of genetic operators (selection, crossover and mutation). The steps of the knowledge enriched GA are visualized in Fig. 2.

Each manufacturing process can be performed by both a machine tool family and by specialized suppliers. However, based on technological differences and availability, different flow times are associated with different machines or suppliers carrying out the same task. Thus, each chromosome is encoded to represent alternative selections of nodes to carry out the required tasks. The encoding uses integer values in a matrix structure. This encoding structure is beneficial since it reduces decoding complexity.

Initialization Procedure

Instead of generating the initial population of alternative designs in a totally random fashion, each newly investigated planning case is compared to previously executed cases through a pairwise comparison of their most important attributes, i.e. number of components, special works, machining features, volumetric data, etc. Thus, based on similar past design cases, an appropriate adaptation of the task sequence and their mapping to processing nodes is done to best fit the new case requirements. This leads

to a pre-optimised initial set of individuals to be fed to the GA. The similarity between numerical attributes is computed using the Euclidean distance (2).

$$D_n = \sum_{i=1}^{n} \sqrt{\left|1 - \left|1 - \frac{T_{pi}}{T_{ni}}\right| * w_i\right|} \tag{2}$$

where: n = no. of features, T_{ni}, T_{pi} = new and past case features, w_i = feature weight.

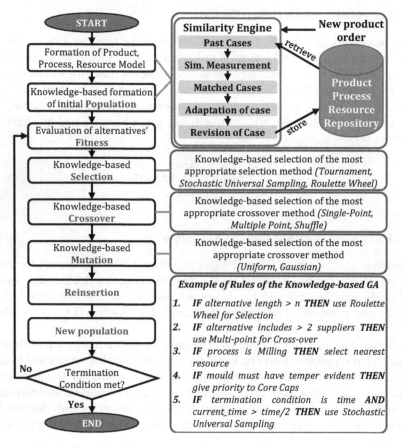

Fig. 2. The workflow of the knowledge enriched Genetic Algorithm

Selection Operators
Selection is used in GAs to identify individuals that will carry their genes to the next
generation. Here, the following widely used operators Roulette Wheel Selection
(RWS), Stochastic Universal Sampling (SUS) and Tournament Selection (TS) are
used [15]. To exploit previous knowledge coming from network and human planner,
and to imbue it in the algorithm, a set of IF THEN rules has been developed in cooperation with the industrial partner of the case study. An analysis involving semi-
structured questionnaires that were filled in by employees led to defining these rules.

Moreover, literature findings about the performance of different operators in specific situations are encapsulated [15]. A rule example for adapting the selection method is the following:

IF *current_CPU_time < termination_CPU_time/5*
    THEN *Selection_method = RWS*
ELSE IF *current_CPU_time > termination_CPU_time/2*
    THEN Selection_method = SUS
ELSE *Selection_method = TS*

RLW is known to drive to convergence and SUS forces an even faster convergence by the algorithm. In case the predetermined runtime is near exhaustion, then SUS is assigned for deriving a solution. Additional rules are similarly implemented.

Crossover Operators
Crossover, handles mating between chromosomes, by selecting two (or more) parents in order to produce off-springs. The crossover operators used are: Single, Multi-point and Uniform. A rule example follows:

IF *hardening_quality = very_good*

THEN *Crossover_Method = Single_Point_Crossover(n)*

Through a characterisation of hardening types (normal, good, very good) by experts, based on thickness quality (in μm), specific partners must be selected that can offer the required precision. Due to the fact that these partners are located in distant countries from the mold maker facilities, hardening may require disproportionately large lead times (up to 3 weeks). Thus, a single crossover point is set right before the gene assignment that represents the partner that carries out the hardening. This ensures a higher degree of exploration of alternative paths and possibly great reductions in flowtime.

Mutation Operators
Mutation is necessary for maintaining the genetic diversity in the population. Fine tuning of mutation operators can alter the behavior of the search from explorative (visit new areas of the search space by creating new individuals) to exploitative (local optimization by fine-tuning existing individuals). The mutation operators are: Uniform and Gaussian Mutation. A rule for selecting each one of these methods is the following:

IF *Best_of_Pop(n) < Best_of_Pop(n-1)* **FOR** *5 consecutive gens*
THEN *Mutation_Operator = Gaussian_Mutation*

In case the population stagnates to local optima and no improvement is observed in subsequent generations, then, a Gaussian mutation with reduced variance is selected, to ensure a higher probability of mutation compared to a purely stochastic sampler.

4   Industrial Pilot Case from the Mold Making Industry

Mold making is technology, knowledge and labor intensive [16]. Each new mold is a unique product, which yet shares a number of commonalities with previous cases on process plan and resource level. Thus, reusing knowledge from finished mold-making cases can reduce overhead times required for initial network planning, decrease ramp-up, improve response time to volatile market requirements and lead to cost savings.

The case study for the validation of the method was an already finished mold with documented process plans from a company that manufactures high precision injection molds. The dataset included alternative machines and also operations and processing, setup and waiting times for similar machines to perform identical processes (Fig. 3).

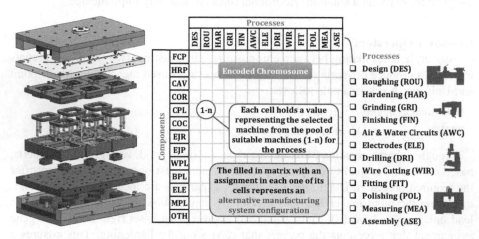

Fig. 3. The components of the mold and the integer encoding of the chromosome

The resource model of the pilot case includes the characteristics of the manufacturing nodes, and the required processing times of components in technologically similar resources, as well as the flowtimes required by suppliers for supplying the requested material or for performing a specialized process (e.g. hardening). Moreover, the availability of the resources and suppliers has been modelled based on historical data, as follows: 75% for part suppliers, 50% for outsourcing suppliers, and 35% for milling operations (roughing, finishing, air and water circuits cutting) performed in the manufacturing facilities of the OEM, 70% for wire cutting and die sinking, and 45% for manual tasks, such as fitting, polishing and assembly.

The product model includes: geometric characteristics of the components, number of cavities, tolerance specifications, cooling mechanisms, ejection methods and other process plan related information. The manufacturing processes required include: roughing, finishing, hardening, creation of air and water circuits, drilling, wire cutting, grinding, fitting, creation of electrodes for die sinking, polishing, measuring and assembly.

5   Experimentation: Results and Discussion

A set of experiments were carried out to investigate the performance of the developed GA. The total number of feasible alternative configurations for this problem is 156×10^{15}, as a combinatorial analysis indicates. The optimal set of tuneable parameters of the GA was identified through a Statistical Design of Experiments (SDoE) and was the following: Population Size = 50, No. of Generations = 50, Generation Gap = 0.9, Termination Time = 20 sec and Mutation Probability = 0.009. Moreover, a correction factor is applied on the obtained flowtimes in order to take into consideration machine breakdowns, shortage of materials and other unpredictable factors. The correction factor was adjusted through the deviation of actual times obtained by the mold maker and experimental values for different mold cases. The results of the execution of the GA are shown in Fig. 4. The algorithm converges after 28 generations to an optimum flowtime of 1,211 hours requiring a total runtime of 19.56 seconds. In comparison, a regular GA (again with optimised parameters based on a SDoE) yielded in the same number of generations a globally best solution of 1,450 hours, i.e. a 17.96% worse solution. Most importantly, this obtained value is significantly lower (38.26%) when compared to the actual flowtime for the specific order, which, as reported by the production engineer of the mold maker was 1,784 hours.

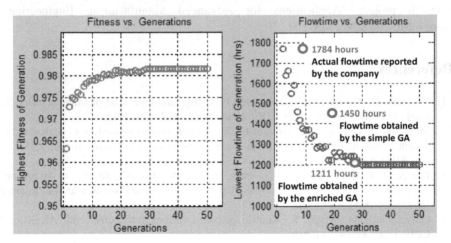

Fig. 4. Evolution of the fitness function (left) and improvement of total flowtime (FT) obtained by the enriched GA after 50 generations and comparison to historical data and a simple GA

6   Conclusions and Future Work

The presented research work investigated the initial design of a manufacturing network for custom-made products. The problem was tackled by a knowledge enriched Genetic Algorithm (GA) and its performance was tested in a real case study coming from the high precision mold making sector. The results depicted an improvement against both a regular GA and actual historical data. The encapsulation of knowledge into the genetic operators and the intelligent initialization process enhanced the robustness of the GA. The quality of the obtained solutions surpasses actual historical performance of the network, which was configured based on human experience and was therefore sub-optimal. Moreover, the small execution time of the algorithm facilitate the need for near real-time reconfiguration of the network for compensation to unforeseen disturbances. The proposed method and tool can be exploited by a planning manager in order to support the design and planning of efficient manufacturing networks and systems. The results obtained by the tool can be overridden by the manager in cases when the proposed solution is not satisfactory and the algorithm may be executed repeatedly until an accepted solution is found. The low computation requirements of the algorithm constitute it suitable for deployment on mobile devices and enables fast decisions on the go.

Future work will focus on extending the rule-base in order to cover additional historical observations and expert knowledge. Also, the method will be developed into an app for mobile devices. The GA will be executed into a company-owned private Cloud server and services will be exposed for distributing information to mobile devices.

Acknowledgements. This research work is partially supported by the EU funded research project "Applications for Advanced Manufacturing Engineering - Apps4aME" (GA No. 314156).

References

1. Mourtzis, D., Doukas, M., Psarommatis, F.: Design and Operation of Manufacturing Networks for Mass Customisation. CIRP Annals 63(1), 467–470 (2013)
2. Mourtzis, D., Doukas, M., Psarommatis, F.: A multi-criteria evaluation of centralized and decentralized production networks in a highly customer-driven environment. CIRP Annals 61(1), 427–430 (2012)
3. Baxter, D., James, G.X., Keith, C., Jenny, H., Bob, Y., Sean, C., Shilpa, D.: An engineering design knowledge reuse methodology using process modelling. Research in Engineering Design 18(1), 37–48 (2007)
4. Chryssolouris, G., Wright, K.: Knowledge-based systems in manufacturing. Annals of the CIRP 35(2), 437–440 (1986)
5. Chryssolouris, G.: Manufacturing Systems: Theory and Practice, 2nd edn. Springer, New York (2006)
6. Cochrane, S., Young, R., Case, K., Harding, J., Gao, J., Dani, S., Baxter, D.: Knowledge reuse in manufacturability analysis. Robotics & Computer-Integrated Manuf. 24(4), 508–513 (2008)
7. Züst, R., Taiber, J., Schultschik, R.: Knowledge-Based Process Planning System for Prismatic Workpieces in a CAD/CAM-Environment. CIRP Annals 39(1), 493–496 (1990)
8. Mäntylä, M., Sohlenius, G.: Representation of Process Planning Knowledge for Part Families. CIRP Annals - Manufacturing Technology 42(1), 561–564 (1993)
9. Garey, M., Johnson, D.: Computers and Intractability – A Guide to the Theory of NP-Completeness, 1st edn. W.H. Freeman & Co. Ltd., New York (1990)

10. Chryssolouris, G., Subramaniam, V.: Dynamic scheduling of manufacturing job shops using genetic algorithms. J. of Intelligent Manufacturing 12(3), 281–293 (2001)
11. ElMaraghy, H., Patel, V., Ben Abdallah, I.: A Genetic Algorithm Based Approach for Scheduling of Dual-Resource Constrained Manufacturing Systems. CIRP Annals - Manufacturing Technology 48(1), 369–372 (1999)
12. Prakash, A., Chan, F.T.S., Deshmukh, S.G.: FMS scheduling with knowledge based genetic algorithm approach. Expert Systems with Applications 38(4), 3161–3171 (2011)
13. Yan, G., Xie, G., Chen, Z., Xie, K.: Knowledge-Based Genetic Algorithms. In: Wang, G., Li, T., Grzymala-Busse, J.W., Miao, D., Skowron, A., Yao, Y. (eds.) RSKT 2008. LNCS (LNAI), vol. 5009, pp. 148–155. Springer, Heidelberg (2008)
14. Holland, J.: Adaptation in Natural and Artificial Systems. University of Michigan Press (1975)
15. Mitchell, M.: An Introduction to Genetic Algorithms. The MIT Press, Cambridge (1999)
16. Klocke, F., Bilsing, A., Wagner, C.: Perspectives for the German Die and Mold Manufacturing Industry. Werkstatt und Betrieb 133(5), 18–21 (2000)
17. Witte, J.D.: Using static capacity modeling techniques in semiconductor manufacturing. In: Proceedings of the IEEE/SEMI 1996 Advanced Semiconductor Manufacturing Conference and Workshop, ASMC 1996, pp. 31–35. IEEE (1996)
18. Ozturk, O., Coburn, M.B., Kitterman, S.: Conceptualization, design and implementation of a static capacity model. In: Proceedings of the 2003 Winter, vol. 2, pp. 1373–1376. IEEE (2003)

An Analogy between Bin Packing Problem and Permutation Problem: A New Encoding Scheme

Michel Gourgand, Nathalie Grangeon, and Nathalie Klement

LIMOS CNRS UMR 6158, Universit´e Blaise Pascal,
Complexe scientifique des C´ezeaux, 63173 Aubi`ere Cedex, France
{gourgand,grangeon,klement}@isima.fr

Abstract. The bin packing problem aims to pack a set of items in a minimum number of bins, with respect to the size of the items and capacity of the bins. This is an NP-hard problem. Several approach methods have been developed to solve this problem. In this paper, we propose a new encoding scheme which is used in a hybrid resolution: a metaheuristic is matched with a list algorithm (Next Fit, First Fit, Best Fit) to solve the bin packing problem. Any metaheuristic can be used but in this paper, our proposition is implemented on a single solution based metaheuristic (stochastic descent, simulated annealing, kangaroo algorithm). This hybrid method is tested on literature instances to ensure its good results.

1 Introduction

The bin packing problem has been introduced by [1]. It considers a set of N items, each item with a given size w_i, and several bins with a same capacity C. The aim of this problem is to pack all of the items in a minimum number of bins. The sum of the size of the items packed in a bin has to be smaller than the capacity of the bin. Each item has to be packed in one bin.

This problem can be met in industrial application or computer network design and memory allocation [2]. [3] makes a state-of-the-art review about the container loading problem: the bin packing problem can be used to pack a set of cargo into a minimum number of containers. It can also be used to solve assembly line balancing problems [4] or multiprocessor scheduling problems [5].

In [6] we use the bin packing problem to model the problem of activities planning and resources assignment, called the HCT problem. The problem considers a system composed of resources and of a set of activities to assign. Each activity needs a resource to be treated and a time slot, a period when it will be done. Each activity has a known process time. Each activity starts in one period and finishes in the same period. Resources have a planning defining their available time: the resource opentime. Each resource cannot treat all the activities, there is a list of incompatibilities between activities and resources.

The aim is to assign each activity to one resource and one period. Activities have to be done as soon as possible, so the assigned periods have to be the smallest possible. The aim of the HCT problem is not to make a precise schedule of the activities but to assign a period to each activity.

B. Grabot et al. (Eds.): APMS 2014, Part I, IFIP AICT 438, pp. 572–579, 2014.

The HCT problem has to respect some constraints: resources have to be able to process their assigned activities according to the incompatibilities; activities have to be assigned to a resource during the opentime of this resource; each activity has to be assigned to one resource and one period. Figure 1 gives an example of an assignment in such an application. A couple (resource, period) can be seen as a bin. Activities are assigned to resources during periods. All the resources have the same opentime.

Table 1 summarizes the analogies between the bin packing problem and this application. A new constraint in the HCT application is the incompatibility constraint between resources and activities. The HCT problem can be seen as an extension of the bin packing problem with incompatibility constraints.

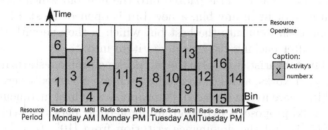

Fig. 1. Example of the HCT application

Table 1. Analogies between the bin packing problem and the HCT problem.

	Bin packing problem	Problem of activities planning and resources assignment
Data	Item	Activity
	Bin	Couple (resource, period)
	Size of an item	Process time of an activity
Objective	To assign items in bins	To assign activities to periods and resources
Constraints	Capacity of the bins	Resources opentime
	-	Incompatibility constraint
Criterion	To minimize the number of used bins	To minimize the number of used couples (resource, period)

In Section 2, a brief state of the art about approximate algorithms used to solve the bin packing problem is made. In this paper, we propose an encoding scheme, which is used in the hybridization between a metaheuristic and a list algorithm. The used method is described in Section 3, as its theoretical justification. The experimental results on literature instances are presented in Section 4. This paper is ended by a conclusion and some further works.

2   State of the Art

Given the size of the real problems that can be solved thanks to the bin packing problem, exact methods quickly reach their limit about computational time. Moreover, [7] shows that it is an NP-Complete decision problem. Approximate algorithms seem to be a good way to solve this problem.

The most popular list algorithms have been developed by [1]. Items are considered one by one according to a list. **Next Fit** (NF) is the most intuitive method for the bin packing problem. The maximum number of items is packed into the current bin. If the available space in the current bin is smaller than the size of the considered item, this bin is closed and a new bin is opened and becomes the new current bin. **First Fit** (FF) is different from NF in that none of the bins is closed. Each item is packed into the first bin which can contain it. Once an item cannot fit in any bin, a new bin is opened. **Best Fit** (BF) consists in packing each item into the best bin which is the one with the smallest available space after packing the considered item into it.

The use of metaheuristics to solve the bin packing problem starts in the 1990s. In most published works, a classical encoding scheme S is used where $S(i)$ is the index of the bin where item i is placed. [8] proposes a hybrid metaheuristic based on tabu search. [9] proposes a hybrid grouping genetic algorithm which uses the heuristic FFD [1] and the dominance criterion from [10]. To a better use of grouping genetic algorithm, it uses the classical encoding, augmented with a group part which defines the used bins. [11] applies a new approach method: the weight annealing. It uses the classical encoding scheme. [12] uses a hybrid ant colony optimization, inspired by Falkenauer's works. It does not individualize the items, they are designated by their size and not their index: $S = (w_i)_{i \in N}$ with w_i the size of item i. In these papers, the hybrid part consists in matching a known metaheuristic (like genetic algorithm, tabu search method, ant colony optimization) to an additional improvement method such a local search.

Another encoding scheme has been exploited. [13] uses a permutation coding to hybridize the genetic algorithm. [14] uses a permutation with separators representation: it is a list of n items and l separators of bins, integers from range $\{1, ..., n\}$ represent the item, integers $\{n + 1, ..., n + l\}$ represent the separators. A simplified version of the genetic algorithm is developed: a simple evolutionary based heuristic.

Most of the works on the bin packing problem uses population based metaheuristics.

3   Proposed Hybrid Method

The method proposed in this paper uses a hybridization between a metaheuristic and a list algorithm (Next Fit, First Fit, Best Fit). This method is performing in two search spaces: Ω where a solution represents a list of items and S where a solution represents the assignment of each item to a bin. The aim of this purpose is to reduce the size of the set of solutions where the metaheuristic is performing.

3.1   Encoding of the Set of Solutions

The used encoding is inspired by the one used in the permutation problems. A solution $(X_i)_{i \in N} \in \Omega$ is a list of items as in a permutation problem with X_i an item index. A list algorithm L, such as NF, FF or BF, is applied to the list of items X to determine the assignment of the items to the bins: $(Y_i)_{i \in N} \in S$ as the classical scheme, with Y_i the bin index assigned to item i. Then a cost function H is applied to the assignment Y. The general scheme of the encoding is the following:

$$X \in \Omega \xrightarrow[Heuristic\ L]{} L(X) = Y \in S \xrightarrow[Criteria\ H]{} H(Y)$$

Figure 2 summarizes the considered sets of solutions.

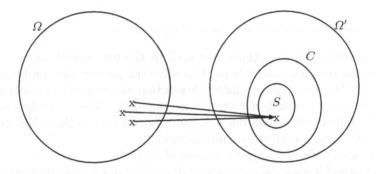

Fig. 2. Sets of solutions

- Ω is the set of all the lists of items. $\mathrm{card}(\Omega) = N!$
- Ω' is the set of all the possible assignment of items to bins, without checking the capacity constraint. $\mathrm{card}(\Omega') = N^N$
- C is the set of the admissible solutions: a solution is admissible if the capacity constraint is respected. $C \subseteq \Omega'$.
- S is the set of all the solutions built by the application of a list algorithm on a list of items. $S \subseteq \Omega'$ and $S \subseteq C$.

Proof that S contains the set of optimal solutions: Let be Y^* any optimal solution. $Y^* = (Y_1^*, ..., Y_N^*)$ with Y_i^* the bin index assigned to item i. A list of items assigned in each bin is deduced. By concatenation of these lists, an ordered list of all the items is determined: $X^* \in \Omega$. By applying the heuristic FF or NF to X^*, Y^* is found, so $Y^* \in S$. As a consequence the set of the optimal solutions written C^* is included in S.

The following example considers the assignment of eight items. Two different solutions in Ω give the same element in S. In total, $2 \times 4! \times 2 = 96$ elements in Ω give the same element in S.

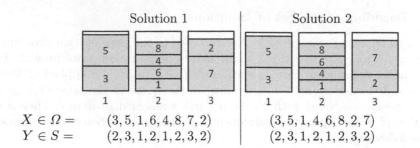

$$X \in \Omega = \qquad (3,5,1,6,4,8,7,2) \qquad (3,5,1,4,6,8,2,7)$$
$$Y \in S = \qquad (2,3,1,2,1,2,3,2) \qquad (2,3,1,2,1,2,3,2)$$

Let be S_B the set of solutions $\in \Omega'$ built by the heuristic BF, S_F the set built by FF and S_N the set built by NF. We have the following assumption: $C^* \subseteq S_B \subseteq S_F \subseteq S_N \subseteq C \subseteq \Omega'$. By exploiting this encoding scheme, the search space is reduced and it is assured that the optimal solution can be reached.

This proposition presents some advantages:

- Admissibility of the solutions is ensured by the list algorithms.
- Many metaheuristics already exist to solve the permutation problems, with their neighborhood systems for single solution based metaheuristics and their crossover operator and/or mutation for population based metaheuristics.
- The metaheuristic is performed on a smaller set S than the original one Ω'.
- The set S contains all the optimal solutions.
- S conforms with the property of accessibility.
- This method is a combination of simple existing methods easy to implement.

3.2   General Framework

The general framework can be used with any metaheuristic. Algorithm 1 shows the principle of hybridization between a local search and a list algorithm where $V : \Omega \longrightarrow \Omega$ denotes the neighborhood system and $H : S \longrightarrow \mathbb{N}$ the cost function.

Algorithm 1: Principle algorithm of the hybridization

---

1 Let be $X \in \Omega$ the initial solution
2 $Y = L(X)$: a list algorithm is applied to the list X
3 **while** *necessary* **do**
4 $\quad$ Choose uniformly and randomly $X' \in V(X)$
5 $\quad$ $Y' = L(X')$
6 $\quad$ **if** $H(Y') \leq H(Y)$ **then**
7 $\quad\quad$ $X = X'$
8 $\quad\quad$ $Y = Y'$

Neighborhood system $V(X)$: Several classical neighborhood systems for permutation problems can be used; $P_{i,j}$: the item at position i permutes with the one which is at position j. $|P_{i,j}| = \frac{N.(N-1)}{2}$; $I_{i,j}$: the item at position i is inserted at position j. $|I_{i,j}| = N.(N-1)$. In both cases, V satisfies the accessibility and reversibility properties.

Cost function $H(Y)$: The most intuitive cost function is the number of used bins. But many solutions have the same value of cost function. To avoid it, [15] proposes a new cost function H which characterizes the average bin utilization, defined by Equation (1).

$$H(Y) = -\frac{\sum_{j \in N}(F_j(Y)/C)^k}{M(Y)} \tag{1}$$

Where $F_j(Y) = \sum_{i=1}^{N} w_i . \delta_{j,Y_i}, \forall j \in \{1, N\}$ is the sum of the sizes of the items packed in bin j (we use the Dirac function δ, $\delta_{a,x} = 1$ if $a = x$, 0 otherwise), $M(Y)$ is the number of bins used by the solution Y, $k > 1$ is a constant which defines how much a solution with equally filled bins is preferred over one in which some bins are rather full and other rather empty. A good value is $k = 2$ [9].

4   Experimentation

Hybridization has been tested with both metaheuristics: simulated annealing or kangaroo algorithm (iterated local search).

Originally, the inhomogeneous simulated annealing was used by [16] to simulate the physical annealing in metallurgy. Unfavorable transitions are accepted with a probability $e^{-\frac{H(Y')-H(Y)}{T}}$. Simulated annealing converges in probability to the set of optimal solutions if neighborhood system V satisfies the accessibility and reversibility properties [17]. The initial temperature T_0 is chosen such as all the transitions are authorized at the beginning, i.e. $e^{-\frac{H(Y')-H(Y)}{T_0}} \simeq 1, \forall (Y, Y')$ according to the algorithm proposed by [17]. The decreasing factor α is computed by $\alpha = \sqrt[IterMax]{(\frac{T_a}{T_0})}$. T_a is the latest temperature close to 0.

Kangaroo algorithm is an iterated local search. This algorithm consists in a stochastic descent, but if there is no improvement of the current solution after a number of iterations $A \geq |V|.ln(2)$ [18], a jump is made. To make this jump, a solution is chosen in a neighborhood system W different from V. Kangaroo algorithm converges in probability to the set of optimal solutions if neighborhood system W satisfies the accessibility property. W consists in applying several times neighborhood system V, it satisfies the accessibility property.

We compared all the possible combinations: choice of the metaheuristic (kangaroo algorithm or simulated annealing), choice of the list algorithm (NF, FF or BF) and choice of the neighborhood system ($P_{i,j}$ or $I_{i,j}$).

All of the referenced papers in the state of the art used the same instances, except [13]. In the instances, the bin capacity is equal to 150 and sizes of items between 20 and 100. Four sizes of problems are used: 120 items, 250, 500 and 1000. For each size, twenty different instances have been created. "u120" to "u1000" define the size of the instance. The results are about the sum of the differences between the optimal solution and the solution found by the considered method for all the instances of the same size. For example, for the twenty instances of size "u120", [9] finds the optimal solutions + 2 bins in total.

Table 2 compares our two best methods SABFP (Simulated Annealing + Best Fit + $P_{i,j}$) and KABFP (Kangaroo Algorithm + Best Fit + $P_{i,j}$) to the bibliographic ones. SABFP and KABFP use the Best Fit heuristic and the neighborhood system $P_{i,j}$. At the opposite, our hybridization does not work very well with the list algorithm Next Fit or with the neighborhood system $I_{i,j}$ (which disturbs too much the current solution).

This method gives good results. Our strength is the easy implementation of our proposition. It can be easily used on a lot of applications (resource constrained scheduling, assembly line balancing, multiprocessor scheduling).

Table 2. Results of the different methods to solve the bin packing problem

Prob	[9]	[12]	[8]	[11]	SABFP	KABFP
u120	+2	0	0	0	0	0
u250	+3	+2	0	0	+1	+2
u500	0	0	0	0	+2	+2
u1000	0	0	0	0	+3	+4

5   Conclusion

In this paper, we propose a hybridization between a metaheuristic and a list algorithm to solve the bin packing problem. Some methods already exist to solve it and perform very well. The main advantage of our proposition is its intelligibility because it combines two simple well-known methods. This method allows us to work on two different search spaces. This eases the used method. Several reasons justify this encoding scheme: it is not useful to check the admissibility of the solutions, many methods already exist to solve permutation problems, the set used for the metaheuristic is reduced and contains all the optimal solutions.

This resolution method used on the bin packing problem is currently applied on real applications such a problem of activities planning and resources assignment. We can also solve more sophisticated models thanks to this encoding scheme. Indeed, more constraints can be added to the list algorithms: incompatibilities between items, between items and bins, precedence.

Hybridization between a metaheuristic and a list algorithm can be used with any metaheuristic. In further work, hybridization will be used with population

Hybridization between a metaheuristic and a list algorithm can be used with any metaheuristic. In further work, hybridization will be used with population based metaheuristic. The use of particle swarm optimization is the next step of our approach.

References

1. Johnson, D.S.: Near-optimalbin packing algorithms. PhD thesis, Massachusetts Instituteof Technology (1973)
2. Chandra, A., Hirschberg, D., Wong, C.: Bin packing with geometric constraintsin computer network design. Operations Research 26, 760–772 (1978)
3. Bortfeldt, A., Wäscher, G.: Container loading problems: Astate-of-the-artreview. Univ., Faculty of Economics and Management (2012)
4. Wee, T., Magazine, M.J.: Assembly line balancingas generalized bin packing. Operations Research Letters 1, 56–58 (1982)
5. Coffman Jr, E.G., Garey, M.R., Johnson, D.S.: An application of bin-packingto multiprocessor scheduling. SIAM Journal on Computing 7, 1–17 (1978)
6. Gourgand, M., Grangeon, N., Klement, N.: Activities planning and resource assignmenton multi-place hospital system: Exactand approach methods adapted from the bin packing problem. In: 7th International Conference on Health Informatics, Angers, France, pp. 117–124 (2014)
7. Garey, M.R., Johnson, D.S.: Computers and Intractability: A Guide to the Theory of NP-completeness. WH Freeman and Company, NewYork (1979)
8. Alvim, A.C., Ribeiro, C.C., Glover, F., Aloise, D.J.: A hybrid improvement heuris- tic for the one-dimensional bin packing problem. Journal of Heuristic 10, 205–229 (2004)
9. Falkenauer, E.: A hybrid grouping genetic algorithm for bin packing. Journal of Heuristic 2, 5–30 (1996)
10. Martello, S., Toth, P.: Lower bounds and reduction procedures for the bin packing problem. Discrete Applied Mathematics 28, 59–70 (1990)
11. Loh, K.H., Golden, B., Wasil, E.: Solving the one-dimensional bin packing problem with a weight annealing heuristic. Computers & Operations Research 35, 2283–2291 (2008)
12. Levine, J., Ducatelle, F.: Ant colony optimization and local search for bin packing and cutting stock problems. Journal of the Operational Research Society 55, 705–716 (2004)
13. Reeves, C.: Hybrid genetical gorithms for bin-packing and related problems. Annals of Operations Research 63, 371–396 (1996)
14. Stawowy, A.: Evolutionary based heuristic for bin packing problem. Computers & Industrial Engineering 55, 465–474 (2008)
15. Falkenauer, E., Delchambre, A.: A genetic algorithm for bin packing and line balancing. In: International Conference on Robotics and Automation, pp. 1186–1192. IEEE (1992)
16. Metropolis, N., Rosenbluth, A.W., Rosenbluth, M.N., Teller, A.H., Teller, E.: Equation of state calculations by fast computing machines. The Journal of Chemical Physics 21, 1087–1092 (1953)
17. Aarts, E.H., van Laarhoven, P.J.: Simulated Annealing: Theory and Applications. Kluwer Academic Publishers (1987)
18. Fleury, G.: Méthodes stochastiques etdéterministes pour les problémes NP- difficiles. Ph.D.thesis, Université Blaise Pascal, Clermont-FerrandII (1993)

Applicability of ERP for Production Network Planning: A Case Study

Taravatsadat Nehzati, Anita Romsdal, Heidi Carin Dreyer, and Jan Ola Strandhagen

Department of Production and Quality engineering, Faculty of Engineering Science and
Technology, Norwegian University of Science and Technology, 7491 Trondheim, Norway
{taravatsadat.nehzati,anita.romsdal,
heidi.c.dreyer,ola.strandhagen}@ntnu.no

Abstract. A production network enables a company to develop capabilities to
respond to diversity in national or regional demand, while at the same time integrate and coordinate their activities. Many companies have implemented enterprise resource planning (ERP) systems to overcome problems associated with
coordination and planning in an organization, in recent years. In addition, advanced planning and scheduling (APS) systems have emerged to address the
planning insufficiencies of ERP systems. However, due to complexity and
competence dependency of these systems, advantages of them are overlooked
by large organizations, and therefore ERP systems are still in use for planning.
ERP systems are used in production networks for coordination of various plans
and decisions across network partners. This paper aims to assess the fit and
alignment between ERP functions and production network requirement for supporting production planning processes. Using a case study approach, the paper
illustrates and discusses the applicability of ERP systems for planning in production networks. The case study showed that ERP systems have limited ability
in coordinating order allocation in the network, detailed short term production
planning and inter network distributions. It is concluded that use of ERP systems for network planning may in fact limit the network's ability to reap the full
benefits associated with planning across several facilities in a network.

Keywords: Production planning, Production network, Enterprise resource
planning, ERP system.

1   Introduction

Dynamic and unstable consumer markets require more agility in manufacturing companies [1]. Keeping proximity to customers to reduce response times to changes in
demand has been a motivation for companies to spread the production sites geographically or to find industrial partners to cooperate with. This motivates the formation of
production networks. Göttlich, Herty [2] defined production networks as "a set of
processes utilized to efficiently integrate suppliers, manufacturers, and customers so
that goods are produced and distributed in the right quantities, to the right location".
A production network enables a company to develop capabilities to respond to diversity in national or regional demand, while at the same time integrate and coordinate

B. Grabot et al. (Eds.): APMS 2014, Part I, IFIP AICT 438, pp. 580–588, 2014.

their activities to reduce costs and improve productivity. Parameters like speed, flexibility, productivity and cost are improved, but the need for integration and coordination of processes and information are increased drastically [3].

Many companies have implemented an Enterprise Resource Planning (ERP) system to support their internal processes. New requirements for collaboration across facility borders have led to increased demand for different functionalities in the enterprise software, such as high degree of adaptability to diverse conditions, a concise provision of comprehensive information, the capability to be applied across facilities in the network and good capabilities to support key planning processes. In order to fully exploit the advantages of the network setting, supportive information system should be capable of meeting the mentioned production network needs. ERP systems are designed to provide business benefits such as data visibility and task automation, particularly for large enterprises. ERP systems are therefore still the backbone of most companies' production planning processes. However, it has been argued that ERP systems are ill-equipped for planning in certain environments [4, 5]. The fact that ERP systems are applied to support planning in production networks motivated us to study in more detail the particular challenges and limitations these practices impose on production planning for production networks.

The paper is structured as follows: in section 2 we explain about methodology used in this paper, section 3 briefly presents the production network concept and production planning processes in a network perspective. Section 4 focuses on the case study, describing production network characteristics and discussing how production planning tasks are executed through the use of an ERP system. Section 5 analyzes data from case study before Section 6 presents some conclusion and suggestions for further research.

2   Methodology

A case study is used to provide a better understanding of the applicability of ERP to support production planning in production network and to understand the practical limitations and challenges. Case studies are known as a strong means for conducting descriptive research and help to gain insights into areas that have not been explored in the literature [6]. This study focuses on the production network of one company and studies the consequences of applying an ERP system for managing production planning processes. Data was collected through semi-formal interviews with central and local planners. *Explanation building* is used as analytic technique for analyzing the case study data [6]. Using this method of analysis we will explain the link between phenomena and reason(s) behind that, which may be complex and difficult to measure in precise manner. After analysis, the results were discussed with other researchers and verified with key resources in the case company's supply chain department.

3   Planning in Production Networks

A production network consists of manufacturing plants that cooperate and share resources with each other. To describe type of production network, different elements need to be considered. Rudberg and Olhager [7] classified types of production networks based on number of organizations in the network and number of sites in each organization. For example multiple organization in the network and single site per organization is defined as supply chain while single organization and multiple sites in that organization is described as intra-firm network. Thus, they define different types of network based on number of organization/sites involved in composition. Phillis, D'Angelo [8], on the other hand, had specific focus on configuration of the production network. They stated that plants in production network may connect to each other in series (sequential), in parallel, or in series-parallel, where in parallel networks, all stations/plants operate in the same level of value adding and can work independent to each other, while plants/works stations in serial (sequential) networks need to work at the same rate and each facility is proceeded or succeeded only by one facility [9]. Beside organizational characteristics, which may affect collaboration in production network, the applied control principle plays a significant role in planning for production network, as it to a large extent determines the flow of goods in the network. Wiendahl and Lutz (2002) have listed three control principles from literature, known as; centralized, decentralized and load-oriented control [9]. With having several plants in the production network, one of the key logistical challenges will be to coordinate deliveries and production plan accordingly. Therefore having an effective control principle for the network can be a challenge. In addition, Scholz-Reiter, Dashkowskiy [10] have listed scheduling of shop floor and planning [11] (Where to produce what?) of transport operations [12] (optimize intra network transportation), as other two planning problems in production network.

Information systems are used widely for supporting coordination in production networks. Sheu, Chae [13], focused on ERP application in multisite firms, and highlights the complexity of module integration among facilities. Jacobs and Whybark [14] and Markus, Tanis [15] believe that implementation of ERP system in production networks can end up in failure unless differences in production methods and customer demand could be reconciled.

Regardless of production network type, Wiendahl and Lutz [16] stated that intensified cooperation between manufacturing companies leads to modified tasks for production planning and control.

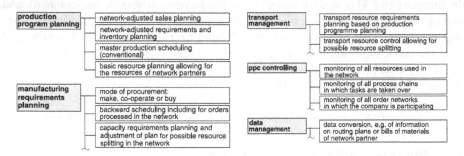

Fig. 1. Production planning and control functions in production network [adapted from 16]

Figure 1 shows how the core tasks of production planning and control (PPC) are oriented toward synchronization between network partners. Production program planning include synchronization between plants in the network, regarding sales, inventory and resource planning. Manufacturing requirements planning has to consider modified modes of planning for procurement, backward scheduling and capacity requirements. Thus, the collective functions of order coordination, inventory management and controlling will become more important for planning in networks than in conventional PPC environments, since every decision need to take to account complex interrelationships between processes. Control of plan in the network and planning for transportation plays significant role in the network planning. As it discussed by Kanyalkar and Adil [17] and Scholz-Reiter, Dashkowskiy [10] transport and distribution need to become an integral part of PPC processes in the network.

In general, PPC tasks in a production network are characterized by intensive communication between network partners and in broader perspective, with suppliers and customers. The goal is to get everyone in the production network into a common platform for logistics transactions and information systems [18]. This integration can result in significantly faster system responses to changes in marketplace events and patterns of demand. As a result, a highly organized network of complementary companies across the supply chain can rapidly build strategic effectiveness.

4   Case Study

This section firstly describes the case company and its key network planning processes, and secondly summarizes the key insights from the case study with regards to the applicability of ERP for network planning.

4.1   Introduction to the Case Company

The case company is food producer with over 40 production facilities. The plants produce three main categories of products and the case study focuses on one of these. The products in this category are produced in three facilities, totaling over 100 product variants with varying production volumes. Although the three plants produce the same category of products, the variants are partially distributed among them and each facility is partly specialized for producing a set of variants. However, some variants are produced in all three plants. The company has strategically positioned the three facilities in different geographical positions in order to keep proximity to both suppliers and customers. Based on definition given in section 3, the case company can be defined as intra-firm production network (one organization with multiple plants), with parallel structure.

The company uses a combination of centralized and decentralized PPC, and uses an ERP system for production planning. In addition, the company has recently started using specialized supply chain planning software for strategic planning and design of the production network.

584   T. Nehzati et al.

4.2   Production Planning

The company's main planning and control principle is make to stock (MTS) based on forecasts and inventory levels. The main argument for this is that in many cases the production lead time is longer than customer order lead time expectations. Therefore, not only the tactical production planning is based on forecasts, but also short term and tactical planning operations [19]. The planning and control process consists of both centralized and local planning performed by resources belonging to different functions. Below, the PPC processes are described using the framework in Figure 1.

Production Program Planning in ERP
Production planning (including demand management, master production schedule, and rough cut resource planning) [20] is the responsibility of the supply chain management department and is performed both centrally and at the individual facilities. As mentioned, planning and control is based on forecasts. The central forecasting department updates weekly sales forecasts continuously at the stock keeping unit (SKU) level with a horizon of 104 weeks. The central planner performs the weekly production planning for all three facilities. The ERP system suggests a production plan for each facility based on the forecasts, and this is then manually adjusted by the central planner for main two reasons. Firstly, more up-to-date information about orders and changes in the market place needs to be incorporated into the forecast, and secondly, the central planner uses the forecast for subsequent weeks to bring production forward in order to level the production for each plant over the next two weeks.

A key drawback of the company's ERP system is that it is not designed to automatically adjust the sale forecasts based on actual orders. In addition, since there is no possibility to have a view of all production plants at the same time, and due to high number of product types, it is difficult to analyze the effect of plan adjustments on performance criteria such as inventory level and capacity utilization.

Manufacturing Requirement Planning in ERP
Replenishment planning (including detailed material and capacity planning) is also the responsibility of the supply chain management department and performed at both the central and facility level with a planning horizon of one day up to four weeks. The company's ERP system uses closed loop MRP which includes capacity requirement planning (CPR) for evaluating the consequences of the material plan on capacity.

Since ERP systems used by case company was not using advanced planning and scheduling (APS) extension, the material and production plans need several adjustments before they can be executed. The reason is that the ERP system does not have an over view of all three plants before planning, and therefore leveling of capacity has to be done for every plant, individually, without taking to account the effect of changes in order allocation, and capacity load of other plants. The problem is amplified when the capacity of the production system has high correlation with the skills and availability of human resources since these are variable and have a direct effect on the feasibility of the production plans. Further, the lack of coordinating functionality to support planning in a network of parallel production plants complicates the use of the ERP system for requirement planning.

Transportation Planning in ERP

The company's distribution division is responsible for transport scheduling, which involves planning of transport between facilities on a weekly horizon. The transportation plan is not only meant to plan distribution of finished goods based on customer orders, but also transportation between plants. Since the production plan is mainly based on forecasts, inter network transportation is important when actual demand exceeds available inventory volumes at each facility. Therefor planning of transport requirements depends on both customer orders and the central planner's allocation of orders to the individual plants.

Production Planning Control in ERP

As it explained earlier case company uses combination of decentralized and centralized control principle, where in, detailed planning is done internally by individual network partners and the general planning (Production program planning) is performed at the network level. Using ERP system, the central planner have a good overview of resource used in the network, and can monitor production processes which are under process at each plant in the network, however any corrective action in the plan needs excessive communication between network partners and central planners.

Data Management

Since all plants in the production network are belong to one organization, ERP system gives good access to data for all members of the production network in the case company.

5   Analysis

The previous section described some of the key production planning tasks in the case company's production network, including production program planning, manufacturing requirement planning and transportation management. Based on interviews and observation of the current situation in the case company, a number of insights on the effect of using an ERP system for network planning were generated.

5.1   Production Program Planning

The ERP system in the case company is not capable of distributing orders between network facilities and therefore a number of manual adjustments are needed before volumes are allocated to each plant. As a result, the ERP system does not provide any support in the optimization of order allocation to plants in the network based on available capacity, inventory status, or proximity to the customer.

5.2   Manufacturing Requirement Planning

The ERP system's functionality is limited in terms of taking into consideration detailed planning parameters from each facility in the network such as:

-     Coordinating material plans between all facilities
-     Coordinating capacity plans between all facilities

This means that the local planners at the individual facilities must make decisions based on their own experience and rules of thumb, without support from the ERP system. This includes daily schedules and personnel planning. Since the ERP system used by case company did not have advanced planning and scheduling (APS) extension [5] details on local personnel availability is not considered in the plan, therefore the system provides little or no support for short term planning for production operations that are human resource dependent [21].

5.3   Transportation Planning

Although ERP system is used for distribution planning, however, internal transportation is not included in the planning phase as an option for resource splitting. That means, potentials of the network is not used in planning phase but considered in control of the plan as a potential for support in unscheduled events, reactively.

5.4   Production Planning Control

Although the control principle used by the case company gives a reasonable chance to all plants in the network to have a control over production processes, there is still strong arguments in the theory for applying fully centralized planning in production network [17, 22]. The applicability of ERP system in production networks under fully centralized control principle [15] need to be studied for the case company.

5.5   Data Management

Being part of one organization and producing the same family of product in all three plants, and as a consequence using the same resources gives a good motive for plants in the network to share relevant data and ERP system showed to be effective in that regards.

The production network context can provide advantages in terms of using network partners for controlling and reducing the effects of demand uncertainty. However, the ERP system does not support internal distribution decisions in the network and such decisions therefore have to be made manually and require considerable communications between the facilities. Moreover, the ERP system was found to have limited flexibility to cope with unforeseen events in short terms plans caused by for instance changes in demand and machine breakdowns that affect capacity.

6   Conclusion

This paper used a case study to investigate the applicability of ERP systems for production planning in production networks. The conclusion is that the ERP system provides limited support for the major planning activities in the production network and prevents the company from fully exploiting the network setting.

The results obtained from this study may not be generalizable as findings are verified in only one case. However, we believe that the case company is not unique and that many other companies are also attempting to use their ERP systems to support planning across network facilities. Therefore, the results from our study may provide valuable insights for managers and executives on how the use of ERP systems for network planning may in fact limit the network's ability to reap the full benefits associated with planning across several facilities in a network.

The paper contributes to theory by highlighting that although ERP systems are not designed for planning in the network context, and despite the availability of advanced planning systems, in practice, companies are still trying to use their ERP systems to support their main planning processes. This provides good motivation for future research to find solutions and tools that can be used together with ERP systems to meet production network requirements and reap more benefits of the network context.

Acknowledgment. The research in this paper was financed by the Norman project (see www.sfinorman.no) and the Research Council of Norway.

References

1. Thoben, K.D., Jagdev, H.S.: Typological issues in enterprise networks. Production Planning & Control 12(5), 421–436 (2001)
2. Göttlich, S., Herty, M., Ringhofer, C.: Optimal Order and Distribution Strategies in Production Networks. In: Armbruster, D., Kempf, K.G. (eds.) Decision Policies for Production Networks, pp. 265–287. Springer, London (2012)
3. Jagdev, H.S., Thoben, K.D.: Anatomy of enterprise collaborations. Production Planning & Control 12(5), 437–451 (2001)
4. Van Nieuwenhuyse, I., et al.: Advanced resource planning as a decision support module for ERP. Computers in Industry 62(1), 1–8 (2011)
5. Aslan, B., Stevenson, M., Hendry, L.C.: Enterprise Resource Planning systems: An assessment of applicability to Make-To-Order companies. Computers in Industry 63(7), 692–705 (2012)
6. Yin, R.K.: Case Study Research: Design and Methods. Sage Publications (2013)
7. Rudberg, M., Olhager, J.: Manufacturing networks and supply chains: An operations
8. Phillis, Y.A., D'Angelo, H., Saussy, G.C.: Analysis of Series-Parallel Production Networks without Buffers. IEEE Transactions on Reliability 35(2), 179–184 (1986)
9. Wiendahl, H.P.: Load-oriented Manufacturing Control. Springer (1995)
10. Scholz-Reiter, B., et al.: Autonomous Decision Policies for Networks of Production Systems. In: Armbruster, D., Kempf, K.G. (eds.) Decision Policies for Production Networks, pp. 235–263. Springer, London (2012)
11. Kopanos, G.M., Puigjaner, L.: Multi-Site Scheduling/Batching and Production Planning for Batch Process Industries. In: de Nascimento, C.A.O., de Brito Alves, R.M., Evaristo Chalbaud, B. (eds.) Computer Aided Chemical Engineering, pp. 2109–2114. Elsevier (2114)
12. Guinet, A.: Multi-site planning: A transshipment problem. International Journal of Production Economics 74(1-3), 21–32 (2001)

13. Sheu, C., Chae, B., Yang, C.-L.: National differences and ERP implementation: issues and challenges. Omega 32(5), 361–371 (2004)
14. Jacobs, F.R., Whybark, D.C.: Why ERP?: A primer on SAP implementation. Irwin/McGraw-Hill (2000)
15. Markus, M.L., Tanis, C., Fenema, P.C.V.: Enterprise resource planning: Multisite ERP implementations. Commun. ACM 43(4), 42–46 (2000)
16. Wiendahl, H.P., Lutz, S.: Production in Networks. CIRP Annals - Manufacturing Technology 51(2), 573–586 (2002)
17. Kanyalkar, A.P., Adil, G.K.: Aggregate and detailed production planning integrating procurement and distribution plans in a multi-site environment. International Journal of Production Research 45(22), 5329–5353 (2007)
18. Kuehnle, H.: A system of models contribution to production network (PN) theory. Journal of Intelligent Manufacturing 18(5), 543–551 (2007)
19. Romsdal, A.: Food Supply Chains; concept, frameworks and guidlines for differentiated production planning and control. N.U.O.S.A. Technology (ed.) (2013)
20. Vollmann, T.: Manufacturing Planning And Control Systems For Supply Chain Management: The Definitive Guide for Professionals. McGraw-Hill Education (2005)
21. Dreyer, H.C., et al.: Global supply chain control systems: A conceptual framework for the global control centre. Production Planning & Control 20(2), 147–157 (2009)
22. Scholz-Reiter, B., Meinecke, C., Rippel, D.: Network Collaboration. In: Intelligent Non-Hierarchical Manufacturing Networks, pp. 169–184. John Wiley & Sons, Inc. (2013)

Designing a Decision Support System for Production Scheduling Task in Complex and Uncertain Manufacturing Environments

Emrah Arica[1], Jan Ola Strandhagen[1], and Hans-Henrik Hvolby[2]

[1] Department of Production and Quality Engineering, NTNU, Norway
[2] Centre for Logistics, Aalborg University, Denmark
emrah.arica@ntnu.no

Abstract. The production planning and control process is performed within complex and dynamic organizations made up of equipment, people, information, IT systems, and influenced by a multitude of external factors. How to effectively schedule in uncertain and complex manufacturing environments, still remains a central question to academics and practitioners. In this paper, we propose a framework that can be utilized to design/enhance decision support systems for scheduling activities in complex and uncertain manufacturing environments. The framework is based on the analysis of the relevant literature that addressed human, organizational, and technological aspects of the production planning and scheduling.

Keywords: production scheduling and control, complex and uncertain manufacturing environments, decision support system.

1   Introduction

Today, a rich amount of scientific literature exists, addressing the planning and scheduling task in uncertain manufacturing environments by proposing advanced methods, techniques, and algorithms that can predict and/or react on unscheduled events [see for example the recent literature reviews provided by 1, 2-5]. Majority of the theoretical studies view this task from a technical perspective with well-defined, simplified and objective-driven analytical problems [6, 7], incorporating a limited number of events and their estimated or identified time impact on single schedules [1, 2, 5].

In stable and reliable environments, these analytical tools and computerized systems can yield expected performance results, especially for the high level material and capacity planning decisions [3]. However, shop types with high uncertainty and complexity where many factors affect the decision making process can be substantially challenging [8-12]. As such, very few of the advanced models and systems that address dynamic scheduling/ re-scheduling decisions have influenced and provided guidelines in the industrial practice [2, 13, 14]. This results in substantial efforts for customizing the scheduling systems to the actual needs of the production environment and decision makers [15].

B. Grabot et al. (Eds.): APMS 2014, Part I, IFIP AICT 438, pp. 589–596, 2014.

Thus, the basic reason behind this theory and practice gap can be attributed to the inconsistency between the theoretical definition of the dynamic scheduling process and the complexity of this process in practice. Several field-based studies investigated and captured the important characteristics of the scheduling and control practice in order to reduce this gap and improve the applicability and implementation of the decision support models and tools [e.g. 9, 16-22]. These practice-based studies showed that the scheduling activity is driven by unscheduled events in practice; involving a multitude of aspects (e.g. human, organizational, and technological - HTO) in the decision making process to identify and solve the problems effectively, besides the technical aspect. These upcoming insights might flesh out a holistic view on important requirements of designing decision support systems for effective scheduling/re-scheduling decisions. This view is not clear as these field-based reports and contributions addressed different elements of this process in isolation, based on different objectives, methodologies and methods (e.g. hierarchical task analysis, cognitive task analysis). Depending on the objective and the chosen methodology, they pointed out various characteristics and requirements of the decision making process.

The overall aim of this paper is to develop a framework for guiding the design/enhancement of a decision support system for dynamic scheduling decisions, utilizing the contributions and linkages in related literature. While the design of current scheduling systems are mainly focusing on generating the initial schedules with a top-down approach, this framework implies that the design/enhancement of decision support system should start with a bottom-up approach. More specifically, we focus on the dynamics of the event handling and rescheduling process and emerging HTO aspects around the information needs to make effective informed decisions. The impact of the characteristics of this process on the design of a decision support system is examined and reflected. As such, the applicability and practicality of the system can be enhanced, addressing the needs of the production control situation and decision makers.

2   Dealing with Unscheduled Events in a Typical IT Configuration

The majority of the modern manufacturing firms use Enterprise Resource Planning (ERP) systems for production planning and control activities [21]. The fundamental benefits of the ERP systems come from their abilities to process and record transactions efficiently, rather than their inherent planning and control capabilities [23]. When used for production planning and control, ERP systems deploy the Material Requirements Planning (MRP) logic [24]. The MRP translates the MPS into time-phased net material requirements and calculates the Planned Order Release (POR) for the detail scheduling and execution use on the manufacturing shop floor. At the shop-floor, the generated POR schedule is exposed to uncertainties that the system is not accountable for. This creates many problems for the production execution later on the shop-floor, such as varying workloads and changing bottlenecks [25].

Over the past two decades, APS systems have emerged to supplement the ERP systems and eliminate some of the major MRP assumptions [26]. APS has by far outperformed the planning and scheduling functionality of the ERP system by for example considering the limited resource capacities simultaneously with the material planning function. A strong feature in APS is the ability to simulate different planning scenarios before plan release [27], which leads to meeting the customer order deadlines with most efficient capacity planning solutions. By doing that, they prevent some of the shop floor uncertainties that ERP systems are bound to encounter on the shop floor. APS is recently standardized and presented as an advanced scheduling technology and how this technology can handle uncertainties is still an open research topic [12].

Manufacturing Execution Systems (MES) have been evolved to aid production execution, monitoring, and control activities on the shop floor, closing the drawbacks of the ERP systems in real-time detailed information exploitation from the shop floor. MES can be described as shop floor information and communication systems that provide feedback on a real-time basis [28]. The functionalities of MES cover the manufacturing execution and control tasks in an enterprise, making the shop floor data available and measuring the real time performance indicators (e.g. equipment utilization, inventory availability, quality status). This makes it a powerful tool to detect and identify the disturbances. However, MES especially lacks decision making capabilities, more specifically in evaluation and diagnosis of what re-planning and re-scheduling actions should be taken [29].

3   The Decision Making Process and Associated Systems

The results of number of field-based reports indicate that taking event-driven rescheduling decisions is an iterative problem identification and solution process, performed in a continuum of activities with information gathering and interactions between different parties in the organization [e.g. 7, 16, 17, 21]. The scope and dynamics (e.g. how to identify and solve the problem, what information is needed, who and what systems should be involved, what actions can be taken) of this decision making process depends on the situational factors (e.g. a machine breakdown happened on a bottleneck machine).

As such, the basic decision making process to handle unscheduled events is to detect, identify, evaluate, and response (see figure 1). Once the cause of the event is detected via automated systems or humans [30], the decision maker(s) should identify the significance of the problem(s) within given situation in order to classify what needs an immediate attention and who should be involved [9]. At the next stage, the alternative re-scheduling solutions are evaluated in order to find an appropriate one in the given situation and constraints. This evaluation stage also involves communication and information sharing efforts across the organization (e.g. operators, schedulers, planners, and even the sales department in some cases) in order to see what constraints can be relaxed, such as what jobs can be delayed [21]. Once the appropriate solution is chosen and actions are taken, schedulers then deal with the consequences. This post-analysis stage may also result in further planning adjustments (e.g. changes in executional priorities of jobs).

Hence, the decision making process involves multiple functional roles (e.g. PPC, maintenance, quality, sales) and IT systems in the problem identification and solving process. There can be many different configurations, applications, and functionality of ERP, APS, and MES systems, supporting different functional processes and roles in an organization in varying extents and contents. But, in an abstract level, possible support of these systems in the event handling and rescheduling process can be given based on the previous section where we discussed a typical setting. However, the realization of these benefits still suffers from the complexity of the re-scheduling process in practice for different reasons, in terms of an effective decision making process. Many of these challenges can be gathered around the paradigm of information needs which may encompass several issues explained in the following framework. The framework also indicates the HTO aspects involved to acquire the required information in the decision making process.

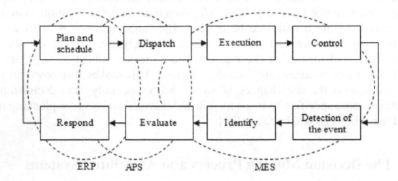

Fig. 1. Decision-making loop for responding unscheduled events and major support areas of the systems

4   Framework

As mentioned above, we have formulated the requirements of the decision support systems around the information needs that emerge when unscheduled events occur. Many of the HTO aspects are involved in the problem identification and solution process because of the efforts to incorporate the right information into the decisions.

4.1   Information Representation/Modelling

This issue relates to the information introduced and represented in the modelled version of scheduling/re-scheduling task in the APS system. With varying degrees, mathematical models make assumptions and define the problem space with lesser complexity than actually it is [10]. This results in part of the internal or external constraint information to be left out of the model, which leads to a perceived problem space. When changes are detected, the adjustments are still done in the perceived problem space which leads to a new perceived problem. However, depending on the type of event and the situation, these changes causes some of the "un-represented" constraints (i.e. internal or external) to be considered in the decision making process. As such, new information is needed to identify the problem and solve in given situation. Let's consider a simple fictional example of machine breakdown that disturbs a local schedule. To take a re-allocation action, the decision maker need to get additional information about the situation such as status of the alternative machines that can run the disturbed jobs, status of the required additional resources to run the new operation (e.g. operator, tools, other consumables), internal and external status of other jobs sharing the alternative machine (e.g. their schedule, inventory levels, and priority status). This example can be widened with much more situational information to identify the problem (constraints) and find an appropriate solution.

This issue brings up different interrelated HTO aspects in the problem identification and solution process. The human schedulers deal with this ill-defined situation by experience, knowledge, and communication and feedback efforts to reach at informed decisions [19, 21, 31]. Furthermore, during this communication and feedback process, they acquire part of the required information from the existing IT systems [20]. A related aspect is the division of the decision making autonomy. This aspect can be considered in two dimensions; (i) division of autonomy between shop floor personnel and schedulers [11] (ii) division of autonomy between humans and tools [32]. It is very difficult to implement the advanced scheduling rules and systems, if there is no agreement on the division of autonomy, namely who should decide what [11]. The multiple case study of Ivert [12] also confirms the importance of this issue for successful implementation of the APS in the type of shop floors where uncertainty is high and many options exist to deal with them.

4.2 Information Availability

This issue relates to the availability of the required information in the IT systems to identify and solve the problem. As the occurrence of the event entails a need for additional information to solve the episode in a given context effectively, the availability of the information becomes a salient characteristic of this process [33]. Most of the information might be available in the systems, however, in this respect, the use of IT systems may be challenged with the availability of the information in an updated form. In a periodic control decision, this prerequisite wouldn't be a problem to put in place as the aggregated information (e.g. inventory levels at the end of the week) is captured and used. However, the event-driven decision making is a demanding process in terms of the need for detailed updated information about both the primary (e.g. the current inventory levels of the disturbed jobs with the machine breakdown) as well as the secondary constraints (e.g. the current inventory levels of the other jobs sharing the alternative machine) of the problem. Jonsson and Mattson [34] argue that accurate lead times and safety stocks are two of the most critical parameters for achieving high planning and control performance. Furthermore, poor data quality is one of the main causes of the use of specific tools and spreadsheets to complement the scheduling tools [33].

4.3 Information Accessibility

This issue relates to the integration of the other systems with the scheduling/rescheduling system in order to retrieve and exploit the required information in the decision making process. A key factor to implement such an event-driven control mechanism is providing the information at the time of perceived information need

[35]. In many cases the information may be available in different systems and formats, which makes it difficult to access it when needed [36]. In this respect, some of the authors proposed automated solutions that utilizes the real time information from other systems and technologies [e.g. 14]. Authors that follow the practice-based research stream mainly favored the human-computer interactive solutions [e.g. 32]. Whether it will be processed by the algorithm or visualized as a supportive function, the integration of the information sources to the scheduling system becomes a relevant issue. In this context, Framinan and Ruiz [33] emphasize that integration of systems may become too complex and impossible and suggests simple and modular approaches such as using data exchange protocols for information exchange.

4.4   Information Structuring and Visualization

This issue relates to how information is presented to the decision maker. The studies show that most of the IT systems have drawbacks to take into consideration of the cognitive skills of the people. As this is an information-driven process, the effectiveness of the decisions also relies on how quick the decision maker can make the sense of the situation from the available information. Today a great deal of real time information is available with recent technological advancements [30]. However, besides the advantage of improved possibility for decision making with more available and accurate information, a challenge of dealing with the increased data in a practical way arises. Hence, visualization also plays an important role in the successful implementation of systems. The use of planning support computer programs is device dependent with psychological relevance but yet event independent [37]. In general, the person who needs to interact with the program and the real time information are disregarded. Having a better perception of the planning system for the scheduler needs a better availability and visibility of the required information, based on the cognitive analysis of the human scheduler [38]. The limits of human decision making skills should be well understood when designing the display content.

5   Conclusions

This study provided indications to the design of the decision support systems for production scheduling task in complex and uncertain manufacturing environments. The motivation behind this study was to build a framework that can facilitate operationalization of the important HTO aspects derived from field-based studies addressing the gap between scheduling theory and practice. There is need for a further study to explicitly reflect the outlined requirements on the design and architecture of a scheduling system and test it in a real life case study for a validity check.

Acknowledgements. This study was financed by the research center called The Norwegian Manufacturing Future (SFI NORMAN).

References

1. Vieira, G.E., Herrmann, J.W., Lin, E.: Rescheduling manufacturing systems: A framework of strategies, policies, and methods. Journal of Scheduling 6(1), 39–62 (2003)
2. Aytug, H., et al.: Executing production schedules in the face of uncertainties: A review and some future directions. European Journal of Operational Research 161(1), 86–110 (2005)
3. Mula, J., et al.: Models for production planning under uncertainty: A review. International Journal of Production Economics 103, 271–285 (2006)
4. Ouelhadj, D., Petrovic, S.: A survey of dynamic scheduling in manufacturing systems. Journal of Scheduling 12(4), 417–431 (2009)
5. Hozak, K., Hill, J.A.: Issues and opportunities regarding replanning and rescheduling frequencies. International Journal of Production Research 47(18), 4955–4970 (2009)
6. Higgins, P.G.: Interaction in hybrid intelligent scheduling. International Journal of Human Factors in Manufacturing 6(3), 185–203 (1996)
7. Crawford, S., et al.: Investigating the work of industrial schedulers through field study. Cognition, Technology & Work 1(2), 63–77 (1999)
8. Wiers, V.C.S., Van Der Schaaf, T.W.: A framework for decision support in production scheduling tasks. Production Planning & Control 8(6), 533–544 (1997)
9. McKay, K.N., Buzacott, J.A.: The application of computerized production control systems in job shop environments. Computers in Industry 42(2), 79–97 (2000)
10. McKay, K.N., Wiers, V.C.S.: Integrated decision support for planning, scheduling, and dispatching tasks in a focused factory. Computers in Industry 50(1), 5–14 (2003)
11. Wiers, V.C.: The relationship between shop floor autonomy and APS implementation success: evidence from two cases. Production Planning and Control 20(7), 576–585 (2009)
12. Ivert, L.K.: Shop floor characteristics influencing the use of advanced planning and scheduling systems. Production Planning & Control 23(6), 452–467 (2012)
13. Kreipl, S., Pinedo, M.: Planning and scheduling in supply chains: An overview of issues in practice. Production and Operations Management 13(1), 77–92 (2004)
14. Georgiadis, P., Michaloudis, C.: Real-time production planning and control system for job-shop manufacturing: A system dynamics analysis. European Journal of Operational Research 216(1), 94–104 (2012)
15. Pinedo, M.L.: Planning and Scheduling in Manufacturing and Services, 3rd edn. Springer, Berlin (2007)
16. Jackson, S., Wilson, J.R., MacCarthy, B.L.: A new model of scheduling in manufacturing: Tasks, roles, and monitoring. Human Factors: The Journal of the Human Factors and Ergonomics Society 46(3), 533–550 (2004)
17. McKay, K.N., Wiers, V.C.S.: Planning, scheduling and dispatching tasks in production control. Cognition, Technology & Work 5(2), 82–93 (2003)
18. Berglund, M., Karltun, J.: Human, technological and organizational aspects influencing the production scheduling process. International Journal of Production Economics 110(1), 160–174 (2007)
19. Cegarra, J.: A cognitive typology of scheduling situations: A contribution to laboratory and field studies. Theoretical Issues in Ergonomics Science 9(3), 201–222 (2008)
20. Karltun, J., Berglund, M.: Contextual conditions influencing the scheduler's work at a sawmill. Production Planning and Control 21(4), 359–374 (2010)
21. de Snoo, C., et al.: Coordination activities of human planners during rescheduling: Case analysis and event handling procedure. International Journal of Production Research 49(7), 2101–2122 (2011)

22. Webster, S.: A case study of scheduling practice at a machine tool manufacturer. In: Mac-Carthy, B.L., Wilson, J.R. (eds.) Human Performance in Planning and Scheduling, pp. 67–81. Taylor & Francis, London (2001)

23. Powell, D., Riezebos, J., Strandhagen, J.O.: Lean production and ERP systems in small- and medium-sized enterprises: ERP support for pull production. International Journal of Production Research 51(2), 395–409 (2013)

24. Koh, S., Saad, S.: A holistic approach to diagnose uncertainty in ERP-controlled manufacturing shop floor. Production Planning & Control 14(3), 273–289 (2003)

25. Chen, K., Ji, P.: A mixed integer programming model for advanced planning and scheduling (APS). European Journal of Operational Research 181(1), 515–522 (2007)

26. Steger-Jensen, K., et al.: Advanced planning and scheduling technology. Production Planning & Control 22(8), 800–808 (2011)

27. Hvolby, H.-H., Steger-Jensen, K.: Technical and industrial issues of Advanced Planning and Scheduling (APS) systems. Computers in Industry 61(9), 845–851 (2010)

28. Manetti, J.: How technology is transforming manufacturing. Production and Inventory Management Journal 42(1), 54–64 (2001)

29. De Ugarte, B.S., Artiba, A., Pellerin, R.: Manufacturing execution system–a literature review. Production Planning and Control 20(6), 525–539 (2009)

30. Cowling, P., Johansson, M.: Using real time information for effective dynamic scheduling. European Journal of Operational Research 139(2), 230–244 (2002)

31. McKay, K.N., Wiers, V.C.S.: The human factor in planning and scheduling. In: Herrmann, J.W. (ed.) Handbook of Production Scheduling, pp. 23–57. Springer Science+Business Media, Inc., New York (2006)

32. Van Wezel, W., Hoc, J.M., Cegarra, J.: Allocating Functions to Human and Algorithm in Scheduling. In: Fransoo, J.C., Waefler, T., Wilson, J.R. (eds.) Behavioral Operations in Planning and Scheduling, pp. 339–370. Springer, Berlin (2011)

33. Framinan, J.M., Ruiz, R.: Guidelines for the deployment and implementation of manufacturing scheduling systems. International Journal of Production Research 50(7), 1799–1812 (2012)

34. Jonsson, P., Mattsson, S.-A.: Inventory management practices and their implications on perceived planning performance. International Journal of Production Research 46(7), 1787–1812 (2008)

35. Tang, O., Naim, M.: The impact of information transparency on the dynamic behaviour of a hybrid manufacturing/remanufacturing system. International Journal of Production Research 42(19), 4135–4152 (2004)

36. Leung, Y., Choy, K., Kwong, C.: A real-time hybrid information-sharing and decision support system for the mould industry. The Journal of High Technology Management Research 21(1), 64–77 (2010)

37. Wezel, W., Cegarra, J., Hoc, J.M.: Allocating Functions to Human and Algorithm in Scheduling. In: Behavioral Operations in Planning and Scheduling, pp. 339–370 (2011)

38. Riezebos, J., van Wezel, W.: Planner-oriented design of algorithms for train shunting scheduling. Planning in Intelligent Systems: Aspects, Motivations, and Method, 477–496 (2006)

Dynamic Rebalancing of an Assembly Line with a Reachability Analysis of Communicating Automata

Manceaux Antoine[1,2,3], Bril El-Haouzi Hind[1,2],
Thomas André[1,2], and Pétin Jean-François[1,2]

[1] Université de Lorraine, CRAN, UMR 7039, Campus Sciences, B.P. 70239,
Vandœuvre-lès-Nancy Cedex 54506, France
{antoine.manceaux,hind.el-haouzi,
andre.thomas,jean-francois.petin}@univ-lorraine.fr
[2] CNRS, CRAN, UMR 7039, France
[3] TRANE SAS, rue des Amériques, 88190 Golbey, France
Antoine_Manceaux@trane.com

Abstract. This article proposes a method for dynamically rebalance an assembly line when disturbances occur, by reassigning the tasks to the line's workstations. The method is based on reachability analysis of an automata network that represents the tasks and workstations to be performed. The execution trace leading to the desired state provides one feasible solution to rebalance the assembly line. The method is illustrated by an industrial case study.

Keywords: Assembly Line Balancing, Dynamic, Reconfiguration, Automata, Discrete Event Systems, Reachability analysis.

1 Context

Assembly lines are flow-oriented production systems. They are still typical in industrial production systems of high quantity standardized products. In this kind of systems, the problem of properly assigning operations to workstations is called assembly line balancing problem (ALBP). The ALBP is older than 1960 and has been tackled by Operational Research over several decades as can be seen in surveys [1, 2]. Furthermore, several classifications were proposed for this kind of problem, [3, 4] contributing to fill the gap between real problem and academic ones [5].

Scholl, in 1999, [6] gives three levels in line balancing problems that correspond to long and medium-term decisions in case of yet-to-be-built assembly line for a 2 - 5 years horizon, line re-engineering for 6 months - 2 years horizon (for example in [7, 8]), and rebalancing engineering due to a market dimension change for a 1 month - 1 year horizon. This classification does not deal with short planning horizon balancing. Indeed, for this horizon (less than 1 month) the decision is mainly made on scheduling or sequencing decisions (master scheduling or daily sequencing) rather than a line rebalancing. For example, the 2005 ROADEF's Challenge aim was to find a solving algorithm car sequencing which better fits the existing line balancing for a daily production objective [9].

B. Grabot et al. (Eds.): APMS 2014, Part I, IFIP AICT 438, pp. 597–604, 2014.
© IFIP International Federation for Information Processing 2014

Our objective here is to introduce dynamic rebalancing for short time horizon when disturbances occur, such as shortage, shutdown or when the theoretic production durations differ from the realized ones. We assume that the manual assembly line is initially balanced (computed by a predictive balancing process) and the sequencing is fixed. To face the disturbances, a modification of the tasks' assignment will be proposed in such a way that the line is kept balanced. The aim is to quickly react to disturbing events with an on-line algorithm even if the new obtained balancing is not optimal. To initiate this kind of on-line dynamic rebalancing, real-time information about the work in progress must be available, leading to put this study in the intelligent manufacturing systems context (IMS) where resources and products can share and update their own data.

This paper explores the use of communicating automata to deal with dynamic rebalancing of a manual assembly line. In section 2 a formal description of the problem is presented. Following, the reachability analysis to resolve an ALBP is presented and explained in section 3. An industrial application from Trane Company and its results are discussed in section 4. Finally, section 5 concludes and displays some future works.

2   Problem Formalization

A well-balanced assembly line is one where all the workstation loads are smoothed with a working time very close to the takt time. It is defined by the available time divided by the number of products to do. This takt time leads to define a moving frequency and synchronization events where products move from a workstation to the next one. The following section provides some notations for the balancing problem that is addressed by the paper.

2.1   Data

- $T = \{t_i, i \leq \text{Tmax} \in \mathbb{N}\}$ is the set of tasks (t_i is the task identifier and Tmax the number of tasks).
- $Dt = \{dt_i \in \mathbb{N}, i \leq \text{Tmax} \in \mathbb{N}\}$ is the set of task durations.
- $W = \{w_i, i \leq \text{Wmax} \in \mathbb{N}\}$ the set of workstations (w_i is the workstation identifier and Wmax the number of workstations).
- $Dw = \{Dw_i, \in \mathbb{N}, i \leq \text{Wmax} \in \mathbb{N}\}$ is the set of workstation durations, that is defined by the sum of task durations that are assigned to this workstation.
- $E = \{e_i, i \leq \text{Emax} \in \mathbb{N}\}$ is the set of synchronization events, *i.e.* the instants when the products change of workstations (e_i is the event identifier and Emax the number of events in the studied period).

2.2   Constraints and Objective

Assignment is given by a surjective function A: $T \rightarrow W$ that defines for each task $t_i \in T$, the workstation $w_k \in W$ t_i where is assigned: $A(t_i) = w_k$ (one task must be assigned on one and only one workstation, a workstation can host several tasks). Two kinds of constraints must be fulfilled for a proper line rebalancing:

- **Takt Time (C1):** The assignment of the task t_i to the workstation w_k is possible only if the remaining available capacity of w_k (takt time minus the sum of assigned task durations dw_k) is upper or equal to the task duration dt_i.
- **Precedence (C2):** this constraint is given by the precedence matrix P where P_{ij} equals "1" if t_i must precede t_j, 0 otherwise, for a couple of tasks $(t_i, t_j) \in T^2$.

The reconfiguration (rebalancing of the assembly line) consists in finding one feasible solution (a new task assignment "A_w") that respects the previous constraints and with a short computing time compliant with the workshop time scale.

2.3   Related Works

Dynamic rebalancing problem can be addressed by traditional constraint solving methods using scheduling and operational research theories. Due to its complexity, most of the addressed solving approaches are based on metaheuristics ([7, 8]). Even if these approaches are efficient in engineering steps, their computing time is often not compliant with production time scale when applied for purely reactive solutions.

Faced to these classical approaches, methods based on Discrete Event Systems (DES) theory are emerging to model and solve scheduling problems. More particularly, the efficiency of Timed Automata (TA) and reachability analysis techniques have been demonstrated by [10] and [11]. The basic underlying idea is to use reachability analysis and model-checking tools [12] in order to find a possible path for reaching an expected state (*i.e.* the state where all the tasks has been reassigned in such a way the line is kept balanced). The trace from initial state to the expected state provides one admissible balancing solution. Main benefits of DES approaches rely on the modular and parametric way of modeling, and finally, the ability to find feasible solutions with a computing time that is compliant with on-line constraints.

3   Using Reachability Analysis for Rebalancing

Our approach is based on two models using a set of communicating automata:

- The task model TM defines the tasks that have to be assigned,
- The workstation model WM defines the ability of a workstation to accept an assignment, taking into account the constraints C1 and C2.
- The synchronization between task and machine models is supported by a competing request/answer mechanism [13].

3.1   Used Formalism

Communicating Automata are a subclass of the Timed Automata formalism defined by Alur and Dill in 1994 [14] that share variables and are synchronized by transition labels. A communicating automaton A is an N-tuple A = (D, X, L, T, Q_m, q_0, v_0), where:

- Q is a finite set of locations;
- X is a finite set of integer variables;
- L is a set of synchronization labels, decomposed into three separated sets: reception labels (noted *label?*), emission labels (noted *label!*) and local labels;
- T is a set of transitions (q, l, g, m, q') $\in$ Q $\times$ L $\times$ G $\times$ M $\times$ Q where G is the set of guards (conditions on the variables of X) and M is the set of updates of the valuations of variables; l, g and m are optional but a transition must contain at least a label or a guard;
- $Q_m \subseteq Q$ is the set of marked locations;
- $q_0 \square \in Q$ is the initial location;
- $v_0: X \leftarrow \mathbb{N}$ is the initial valuation of the variables.

A network NA = A_1 ‖ A_2 ‖ ... ‖ A_n of n (n $\in \mathbb{N}^*$) is defined as the synchronous product of all the A_i automata. A state of the network is defined by a couple (q; v) where q $\in$ Q and v $\in$ X. Two kinds of evolution of the automata network NA(q, v) $\overset{t}{\rightarrow}$ (q', v0) may occur:

- only one transition is fired in one automaton, if this transition contains only local label or if its guard is satisfied;
- two transitions t_k^γ, t_m^β of a pair of automata (A_γ, A_β) with t_k^γ containing the emission label $l_k^\gamma \in L^\gamma$ (noted l_k^γ !) and t_k^β containing the emission label $l_m^\beta \in L^\beta$ (noted l_m^β ?) such that $l_k^\gamma = l_m^\beta$ are fired simultaneously, providing that the guards of these transitions are satisfied.

Note that simultaneous firing of transitions is possible only when two transitions of two different automata are considered; no broadcast mechanism that implies more than two automata is possible. Notation conventions are as follows: initial locations are indicated by a source arc, location names are in bold, label names are in italics and followed by the symbol "!" (resp. "?") for emission (resp. reception) labels, variables updates are underlined, and guards are denoted by brackets.

Task Generic Model

The generic task model TM (Figure 1.a) defines a task t_i which has to be assigned and is composed by three locations.

In the initial location, the task t_i is waiting for an assignment on a workstation w_k. The transition that can be fired corresponds to the emission of an assignment request on the workstation w_k.

Once this request has been emitted, the model is waiting in the *"waiting for a workstation answer"* location for an answer from a workstation model that can be:

- a refusal: in this case, the task comes back in its initial location, ready for another possible question;

- an acceptance: in this case, the template attains the last location;

The last location *"task assigned"* represents an assigned task which could not make another request (uniqueness of the assignment).

Workstation Generic Model

The generic workstation model WM (Figure 1.b) is composed by two locations. It defines a workstation w_k which accepts or refuses task assignments according to defined constraints (C1 and C2). In the initial location, the workstation w_k is waiting for an assignment request. Once a request is received from a task model TM, the location called *"Computing answer"* is reached. From this location *"Computing answer"*, there is two transitions with exclusive guards containing the two constraints depending from the current workstation capacity:

- if C1 and C2 are false, the workstation rejects the assignment by sending a refusal to the task t and returns to its initial location.
- if C1 and C2 are true, the workstation accepts the assignment by sending an acceptation message.

If the request is accepted, the assignment parameters are recorded as the list of already assigned with $A(t_i) = w_k$.

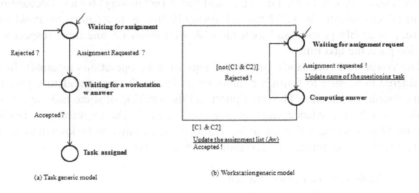

(a) Task generic model   (b) Workstation generic model

Fig. 1. Generic models of tasks (a) and workstations (b)

The Assembly Line Generic Model and the Initialization of the Model

The complete model is a network of communicating automata that is composed of (Tmax − m) instances of the task model (where m represents the number of tasks that are already finished when the rebalancing is done), and Wmax instances of the workstation model. The initial capacity of workstations is set according to the already finished tasks.

The correct synchronization is ensured by sending and receiving message (*"Assignment Requested"*, *"Rejected"*, *"Accepted"*). To avoid inconstancies (the sender task must be the same that the one who receive the workstation answer), the request/answer mechanism must be designed as a critical section protected by a semaphore represented by logical variable *Lock* involved in the guards.

Obtaining a Solution

An acceptable solution is obtained if a trace reaches a state where all tasks are in their final location "task assigned" exists. If such a trace exists, the recorded assignment parameters constitute the searched solution. Model-checking is a formal technique that explores the state space of a DES model to identify some properties, expressed using temporal logics, is enforced (or not) in the whole or partial state space. This technique can easily be used for reachability issue with a depth-first strategy to avoid explosion. The property can be expressed using CTL expression (Computation Tree Logic) [12] as: *EF("All tasks are assigned")* where E is the exist path quantifier, F the eventually temporal quantifier. This property means: there exists a path where "all the tasks are assigned" will be true one day.

4   Case Study: Trane's Application

4.1   Case Study Description

This approach is evaluated using an industrial case study given by Trane Company. Trane is a firm selling cooling and heating air conditioning products and services. This firm's particularity is that the production is organized in manual assembly mixed model lines according to the DFT (Demand Flow Technology) basics. Because of the products' dimensions, a well-balanced assembly line is mandatory to avoid stocks between assembly process and its feeders. A well-balanced line must respect a production pace, the takt time.

The considered case study first three steps of a 14 operations assembly line are considered to be sure to finish a product's part before the test mandatory performed on the fourth workstation. The description and the duration of some tasks are given in Table 1 and the precedence graph is given on Figure 2. The targeted takt time is 67 minutes (4020 seconds). The initial line balancing is assumed to be known as depicted on the Figure 3 (maximum takt deviation = 228 seconds).

Table 1. Some Tasks desciption

Name	Description	Duration (minutes)	Duration (seconds)
1	Prépa & pose Base	3,3	198
2	Pose Evaporateur	6,4	384
15	Pose compresseurs C1	22,55	1353
16	Pose compresseurs C2	2255	1353
17	Brasage ligne Compresseur C1	16,2	972

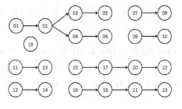

Fig. 2. Precedence Graph

4.2   Results

Example 1

For the first example, the delay is detected during the task t_3 on the first workstation (this task is longer than planned, but it can't be moved, because it is already started).

The two first tasks assigned to the first workstation are already finished. As a consequence, the remaining available capacity is reduced.

With a delay of 60 seconds a new assignment is found: the task t_9 could be moved from the first to the second workstation leading to the following balancing (Figure 4) (maximum takt deviation = 280 seconds, Fig.4).

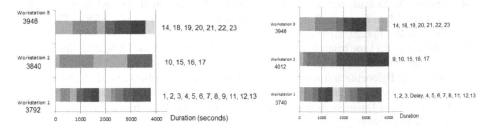

Fig. 3. Initial Line balancing

Fig. 4. First disturbance, 60s delay, corrected line balancing

Example 2

For the second example, the delay (120 seconds) is detected during the task t_{15} on the second workstation. The 15 first tasks assigned to the two first workstations are already finished. According to these constraints no new better solution could be found (maximum takt deviation = 280 seconds). With a delay superior to 165 seconds, there is no acceptable solution agreeing with precedence constraints and the takt time constraint. (In this case, we must raise the takt time constraint value to obtain a solution.)

5   Conclusions, Future Works and Perspectives

In this article, we have shown how the reachability analysis could be used for an assembly line rebalancing. This algorithm is inserted in a predictive/reactive process in an intelligent manufacturing system context. It quickly gives an acceptable solution to adapt locally the predictive optimal balancing.

But sometimes, if there is no free space left, delays could not be absorbed by a simple reassignment of tasks. That is why our future works would deal with the parallelization of tasks. Furthermore, the cost of the reconfiguration would be included in the model. In fact, sometimes moving a task is more expensive than just dealing with the delay. Of course, this new approach will be compared with other methods concerning its ease of initialization, and the execution speed.

References

1. Becker, C., Scholl, A.: A survey on problems and methods in generalized assembly line balancing. European Journal of Operational Research 168, 694–715 (2006), doi:10.1016/j.ejor.2004.07.023

2. Boysen, N., Fliedner, M., Scholl, A.: Assembly line balancing: Which model to use when? International Journal of Production Economics 111, 509–528 (2008), doi:10.1016/j.ijpe.2007.02.026
3. Boysen, N., Fliedner, M., Scholl, A.: A classification of assembly line balancing problems. European Journal of Operational Research 183, 674–693 (2007), doi:10.1016/j.ejor.2006.10.010
4. Battaïa, O., Dolgui, A.: A taxonomy of line balancing problems and their solutionapproaches. International Journal of Production Economics 142, 259–277 (2013), doi:10.1016/j.ijpe.2012.10.020
5. Falkenauer, E.: Line balancing in the real world. Presented at the PLM 2005: International Conference on Product life Cycle Management, pp. 360–370 (2005)
6. Scholl, A.: Balancing and sequencing of assembly lines (Publications of Darmstadt Technical University, Institute for Business Studies (BWL)). Darmstadt Technical University, Department of Business Administration, Economics and Law, Institute for Business Studies (BWL) (1999)
7. Grangeon, N., Leclaire, P., Norre, S.: Heuristics for the re-balancing of a vehicle assembly line. International Journal of Production Research 49, 6609–6628 (2011), doi:10.1080/00207543.2010.539025
8. Makssoud, F., Battaïa, O., Dolgui, A.: Reconfiguration of Machining Transfer Lines. In: Borangiu, T., Thomas, A., Trentesaux, D. (eds.) Service Orientation in Holonic and Multi Agent. SCI, vol. 472, pp. 339–353. Springer, Heidelberg (2013)
9. Estellon, B., Gardi, F., Nouioua, K.: Two local search approaches for solving real-life car sequencing problems. European Journal of Operational Research 191, 928–944 (2008), doi:10.1016/j.ejor.2007.04.043
10. Behrmann, G., Brinksma, E., Hendriks, M., Mader, A.: Production scheduling by reachability analysis-a case study. In: Proceedings of the 19th IEEE International on Parallel and Distributed Processing Symposium, pp. 140a. IEEE (April 2005)
11. Subbiah, S., Engell, S.: Short-Term Scheduling of Multi-Product Batch Plants with Sequence-Dependent Changeovers Using Timed Automata Models. In: Pierucci, S., Buzzi Ferraris, G. (eds.) Computer Aided Chemical Engineering, pp. 1201–1206. Elsevier (2010)
12. Clarke, E.M., Emerson, E.A.: Design and synthesis of synchronization skeletons using branching time temporal logic. In: Kozen, D. (ed.) Logics of Programs. LNCS, vol. 131, pp. 52–71. Springer, Heidelberg (1982)
13. Lemattre, T.: Allocation de fonctions de commande de systèmes critiques par recherche d'atteignabilité dans un réseau d'automates communicants. École normale supérieure de Cachan - ENS Cachan. In: Behrmann, G., Brinksma, E., Hendriks, M., Mader, A. (eds.) Production Scheduling by Reachability Analysis - A Case Study,19th IEEE International Parallel and Distributed Processing Symposium, p. 140a (2013), doi:10.1109/IPDPS.2005.363
14. Alur, R., Dill, D.L.: A theory of timed automata. Theoretical Computer Science 126, 183–235 (1994), doi:10.1016/0304-3975(94)90010-8

Author Index

Printed in the United States
By Bookmasters